A HISTORY OF THE
MENNONITE BRETHREN CHURCH

PILGRIMS AND PIONEERS

A HISTORY OF THE
MENNONITE BRETHREN CHURCH

PILGRIMS AND PIONEERS

BY JOHN A. TOEWS

Edited by A. J. Klassen

Board of Christian Literature
General Conference of Mennonite Brethren Churches
Fresno, California

To the "Company of the Committed" in our brother-hood, who with faith and courage under the guidance of the Holy Spirit endeavor to translate the Anabaptist Vision of Christian discipleship and community into the work, witness, and life-style of the church in the contemporary world.

Introduction

The Mennonite Brethren Church had its origin in the great awakening that came to the Russian Mennonite community in the middle of the nineteenth century. Some twenty years later, the early brethren assigned to P. M. Friesen, the leading Russian Mennonite historian, the task of researching and recording that beginning as a twenty-fifth anniversary tribute. However, it was not until 1910 that he finally completed his monumental account of the background and development of that movement in *Die Alt-Evangelische Mennonitische Bruederschaft in Russland* (The Old Evangelical Mennonite Brother-hood in Russia).

In many ways, J. A. Toews' *A History of the Mennonite Brethren Church: Pilgrims and Pioneers*, is a fitting sequel to P. M. Friesen's work. The intervening years have witnessed many changes in the life of the church that he described. It is the purpose of this book to complete the story of the Mennonite Brethren to the present day.

The need for an up-to-date history was born in the crisis of the search for identity that has become so apparent in the life of the church during the last decade or two. When the Board of Christian Literature received the mandate of the conference for the realization of this project in 1969, J. A. Toews was the unanimous choice for the difficult task. His training in the historical disciplines have led him to understand that the roots of the present are deep in the past. His many years of teaching and conference-wide ministry have involved him in the three main theaters of the Mennonite Brethren Church life which he describes: Russia, U.S.A. and Canada.

We are greatly indebted to the author for the careful work he has done in recounting the Mennonite Brethren story with sensitivity and courage. His conclusions are based on a lifetime of careful research in Anabaptist-Mennonite history and theology as well as personal involvement in the life and ministry of the people he describes. The book is suffused with a love that is as warm as it is deep. Each chapter is a careful blending of the general with the particular, and the abstract with the concrete, to keep the history alive and moving.

Mennonite Brethren will see themselves mirrored as they actually have been in the past and are in the present. The author is aware that the heart and life of the church are to be found in the local congregations. He has therefore chosen to tell their inner spiritual history in large measure through the institutions they have created to serve an increasingly productive role in the work of the denomination. However, throughout the story he shows a strong awareness of the political, social and cultural forces that have influenced the life and witness of the church. He has maintained a delicate balance between historical objectivity and personal conviction. A thorough knowledge and careful analysis of the primary sources are evident throughout the book.

The general scheme of organization is chronological and thematic. Part I surveys the origins and development of the Anabaptist-Mennonite Brethren Church in the European setting and recounts the courage of those pilgrims and pioneers who were transplanted to North America through several migrations that began one hundred years ago. Part II portrays Mennonite Brethren beginnings and development in the U.S.A. and Canada, as well as the Krimmer Mennonite Brethren story. Conference organization, Christian education in the local church, music, institutional education in the conference, publications, ministry, cultural change, church-state relations, theology, inter-church relations and the worldwide brotherhood (missions) are described as facets of Mennonite Brethren church life.

No attempt has been made at completeness in detail. Representative illustrations have been interspersed in the text. The appendixes are designed to supply additional information and summation in handy reference form. The indexes were prepared particularly for the student who needs to locate specific information. The casual reader will find them a ready guide to information of particular interest.

As editor appointed by the Board of Christian Literature I have been involved in every stage of the development of this volume. It has been a privilege to work with the author during this time. I am convinced that *A History of the Mennonite Brethren Church* will become a standard guide to the understanding of the Mennonite Brethren and will be used for decades to come by those who want to be informed about their life and witness. Not everyone will agree with every interpretation in this book. However, every reader will be enlightened and inspired.

A History of the Mennonite Brethren Church represents a new stage in the writing of the Mennonite Brethren. It is the first full-length history to appear in the English language. It is therefore fitting that it be published during the centennial celebration of the coming of the first Mennonite Brethren to North America in 1874. It also marks a first in the literary endeavors of the Mennonite Brethren Church through the provision of a stipend that allowed the author to concentrate nearly full-time on the writing of the basic manuscript over the period of a year.

The General Conference is to be commended for making this possible. The author is to be congratulated upon the successful completion of a long and arduous task. May he be rewarded by a wide reading of this book in the families of the church constituency, the institutions which they support, and across the entire Mennonite brotherhood.

A. J. Klassen, Editor

Preface

The vision for an up-to-date, interpretive account of the history of the Mennonite Brethren was born in the Board of Reference and Counsel of the General Conference a number of years ago. In 1969 the Board of Christian Literature was given the responsibility of realizing this vision. In 1971 the writer accepted the assignment — not, however, without some serious apprehensions in view of the delicate and difficult nature of the task.

Searching the records and describing the origin and pilgrimage of these spiritual heirs of the early Anabaptists has been an interesting and rewarding experience.

In the initial planning of this history several consultations were held with members of the Executive of the Board of Christian Literature and others interested in the project. It was agreed that the book should be well documented and adapted for use in colleges and Bible institutes. The history was also to be written with the wider reading constituency in mind — including people who are not acquainted with the cultural and ethnic background of European Mennonitism. It was also thought that the scope and purpose of the book would not permit a treatment of developments on a local church level. Congregational histories are found in some of the earlier books.[1] Developments in local churches have been described if these were considered to be significant for understanding general trends in the brotherhood.

It is not easy for an active participant in the work of the church to attain and maintain the perspectives of historical objectivity. It has been my earnest endeavor to give an accurate and balanced account of developments in the M.B. Church. I have sought to honestly portray not only its vision, faith and achievements, but also its limitations, weaknesses and failures. To bring a history up-to-date is always a hazardous undertaking, since it involves the treatment of men and movements, churches and institutions, policies and programs which are in "the process of becoming," and which will have to await a more objective appraisal by future historians. Hence the opinions expressed about contemporary trends and developments must of necessity be regarded as provisional in nature. One thing I gladly admit, however: I

xi

have written this history as one who has a loving concern for the brotherhood and a deep appreciation for its spiritual heritage. For any error of fact or judgment I accept full responsibility.

In the preparation of the manuscript I have greatly profited from the work of those men who have blazed the trail of Mennonite Bethren historiography before me. Others have labored, and we have entered into their labors. The following sources have been most valuable in my research in early M.B. history: P. M. Friesen, *Die Alt-Evangelische Mennonitische Bruederschaft*; Franz Isaac, *Die Molotschnaer Mennoniten*; and Jacob Becker's *Memoirs (Tagebuch)*. For information on recent history I have relied heavily on conference yearbooks, reports, periodicals, historical monographs, and unpublished theses.

I am grateful to the administration of the Mennonite Brethren Biblical Seminary in Fresno, California, for providing adequate facilities for the research and writing assignment. The stimulating fellowship with teachers and students in the seminary community provided many opportunites for testing hypotheses and verifying factual information. I am especially indebted to the brethren Elmer Martens and A. J. Klassen for their sustained interest and constant encouragement which have made the completion of the assignment possible. Brother Klassen, with his special training in Anabaptist historiography and his wide teaching experience in this field, has not only served as a competent consultant through all stages of preparing the manuscript, but in his capacity as editorial assistant has also rendered invaluable services in the revision of the text. Both in content and in form the book has profited from his insights and scholarship. He has also assumed the responsibility for such items as the glossary, illustrations, bibliography, appendixes, and index.

To Mrs. Betty Klassen I am grateful for her painstaking effort in typing the manuscript in its several stages of preparation. A special word of thanks and recognition is extended to Paul W. Wohlgemuth who prepared the chapter on music in the M.B. Church with assistance from Herbert C. Richert and Mrs. Esther Horch. A "Committee of Readers," appointed by the Executive of the BCL, has read the entire manuscript and offered many helpful suggestions. The following brethren served on this committee: Harold Jantz and Abram Dueck, Winnipeg: A. E. Janzen, Orlando Harms, Clarence Hiebert and Wesley Prieb, Hillsboro; and Peter Klassen and Delbert Wiens, Fresno. C. F. Plett, former chairman of the KMB Conference, has read the chapter on the Krimmer Mennonite Brethren. The librarian of Pacific College, Adonijah Pauls, deserves recognition for his constant readiness to assist in locating documents, pamphlets and books in the Archives. The librarians of Tabor College and of the Mennonite Brethren Bible

College have also been most helpful during my brief stay in these schools.

The contribution of my wife Nettie is hard to assess properly. She not only made personal sacrifices, but also read the entire manuscript. Her intuitive judgments were most helpful in dealing with contemporary issues and personalities. Above all I am grateful to God who in His gracious providence gave the necessary strength to complete the task.

Summer, 1973   J. A. Toews

Glossary of Terms and Abbreviations

Afrika Missionsverein — Africa Mission Society

AMVL — *Allrussischer Mennonitischer Landwirtschaftlicher Verein* (All-Russian Mennonite Agricultural Union)

Allianz Gemeinde, Allianz Bewegung — Alliance Church, Alliance movement

ASW — Alternative Service Work

AMR — American Mennonite Relief

ARA — American Relief Administration

Armenschule — School for the poor

BCL — Board of Christian Literature

Bibelbesprechung — Bible conference

Bibelstunden — Bible study hours

BOMAS — Mennonite Brethren Board of Missions and Services

Brotbrecher — Breadbreakers

Bruedergemeinde — literally "Brethren Congregation," a term commonly used to identify the Mennonite Brethren

Bruderschule — Brotherhood School

Bundeskonferenz — General Conference

CIM — Congo Inland Mission

COMBS — Council of Mission Board Secretaries, a consultative group from North American Mennonite and Brethren in Christ churches

CO — Conscientious Objector

CPS — Civilian Public Service

CS — Christian Service

Dirigentenkurse — choir conductors' workshops

Empfaengnisstaette — place of inception

EFC — Evangelical Fellowship of Canada

EFMA — Evangelical Foreign Missions Association

ETTA — Evangelical Teacher Training Association

Forsteidienst — forestry service

Froehliche Richtung — the joyous or exuberant movement

Fuersorgekomitee — Supervisory Commission

Gebietsamt — colony administrative office

GC — General Conference Mennonite

Immigrantenkomitees — immigrant committees

Initiativniki — initiators or dissenters

Jugendverein — Christian Endeavor

Kanaedier — Canadians

Kernlieder — congregational songs unique to the MB spiritual heritage

Kirchenkonvent — council of elders

Kirchenvorstand — church council

Kirchenordnung — church organization

Kleine Gemeinde, Grosse Gemeinde — small church/congregation, large church/congregation

Kolchos — collective farm

KfK — *Kommission fuer Kirchenangelegenheiten* (Commission for church affairs)

KMB — Krimmer Mennonite Brethren

Kulturkampf — internal religio-cultural conflict between progressives and conservatives

Kunst — art, or the arts

Kurseleiter — workshop director

Landwirtschaftlicher Verein — Agricultural Improvement Society

Leseverein — Christian Literature Society

Licht den Indianern — Light to the Indians

MB — Mennonite Brethren

MCC — Mennonite Central Committee

MWC — Mennonite World Conference

Missionsstunden — mission meetings

NAE — National Association of Evangelicals

Oberschulze — colony adminstrator

OM — (Old) Mennonite

Prediger-Wirt-Schulz Komplex — preacher-landowner-colony administrator complex

Russlaender — Russian countrymen

Saengerfest — song festival

Saengerkurse — choir workshops

Sanitaetsdienst — noncombatant medical corps

Schulze — village mayor

Schulzenaemter — village offices

Selbstschutz — self defense corps

Singstunden — evening singing schools

STP — Service Training Program for lay church workers

Studienkommission — study commission

Suchdienst — tracing service for missing persons

VBHH — *Verband Buerger Hollaendischer Herkunft* (Association of Citizens of Dutch Extraction)

VMSR — *Verband der Mennoniten Sued-Russlands* (Union of Mennonites in South Russia)

Vereinsschule — school of the association

VS — Voluntary Service

Vorsaenger — lead singer

Waisenheim — orphanage

Ziffern — a system of music notation by number or cipher

List of Illustrations

List of Tables

List of Maps

Credits

Contents

PART I — MENNONITE BRETHREN: EUROPEAN BACKGROUND AND DEVELOPMENT

PART II — THE MENNONITE BRETHREN CHURCH IN NORTH AMERICA

PART I

MENNONITE BRETHREN: EUROPEAN BACKGROUND AND DEVELOPMENT

Chapter 1

Spiritual Heirs
of the Early Anabaptists

"All attempts to interpret the past are indirect attempts to understand the present and its future."[1] The study of the origin and development of the Mennonite Brethren Church is also to serve this purpose — to understand more fully the spiritual dynamic in the origin of the church, to see more clearly the gracious providence of God in the history of the brotherhood, and to discern more adequately the present and future missionary role of the Mennonite Brethren in today's world.

Church renewal and new life movements cannot be explained simply in terms of an historical framework of cause and effect. An understanding of events in redemptive and religious history requires more than an analysis and evaluation of social, cultural or economic conditions in the context of which these events occurred. A proper interpretation and appreciation of events as well as developments in religious history demands the dimension of faith — a faith that acknowledges the gracious sovereignty of God, who guides, intervenes and overrules in the affairs of men and nations, and also in the history of His people. Such faith is a confession that Jesus Christ is the Lord of history, also of the history of the Mennonite Brethren Church.

The name, "Mennonite Brethren," which the founding fathers gave to the new church, was not the result of practical expediency, nor a matter of ecclesiastical diplomacy. It was a conscious and deliberate identification of the early Brethren with the historic theological position of the Anabaptist-Mennonite movement. In the Document of Secession (Jan. 6, 1860) they make four specific references to the teachings of Menno Simons, with which they identify, and then conclude their declaration with the significant statement: "In all other articles of our confession we are also in accord with Menno Simons."[2] The early Brethren regarded their withdrawal from the existing Mennonite

3

churches not as a retreat from true Mennonitism, but as a return to it.[3]
Although strongly influenced in their early history by Lutheran Pietists
and German Baptists, they were careful to maintain their spiritual
identity as an Anabaptist-Mennonite body.

P. M. Friesen, the father of Mennonite Brethren historiography,
also expressed the indebtedness of the new church to Menno Simons
when he referred to the two "reformers" of the M.B. Church: Menno and
Wuest. However, he considered Menno the builder of the spiritual home
and Wuest as the servant whom God used to refurnish the impoverished
structure.[4] This historical connection and theological identification of
the Mennonite Brethren with Menno Simons and the early Anabaptists
calls for a brief review of the sixteenth century Anabaptist movement as
well as the nature of the Anabaptist Vision.

ANABAPTISM AND THE REFORMATION

The Protestant Reformation of the sixteenth century constitutes
one of the greatest religious upheavals in the history of the Western
World. The long-smoldering fires of discontent and disillusionment
with the moral and spiritual corruption in the Medieval Church were
fanned into a blazing conflagration by Martin Luther's posting of his
ninety-five theses in Wittenberg on October 31, 1517. In many ways,
this historic event marks the end of the Middle Ages and the beginning
of the Modern Era in church history. The Anabaptist movement is
related directly to the reform movements initiated by Luther in
Germany and by Zwingli in Switzerland. The Anabaptists agreed with
the Reformers on the cardinal doctrines of salvation. They were
thoroughly orthodox in their views concerning the atonement even
though they rejected Luther's one-sided interpretation — commonly
known as the "Satisfaction Theory." They agreed with the Reformers on
justification by faith through grace. Although they rejoiced at the work
Luther had done, they were deeply disappointed when he did not
proceed to establish a "believers' church" after the New Testament
pattern. Because they demanded more radical changes in the faith and
practice of the church, the Anabaptists have often been described by
church historians as the "Left-Wing" of the Reformation.[5] George H.
Williams treats them as part of "the Radical Reformation."[6]

Anabaptism originated and developed independently in several
areas of South-Central and Northern Europe. This largely accounts for
differences and peculiarities in its manifestation. The "Rebaptizers" or
"Anabaptists" (*Wiedertaeufer*) as they were derisively called were
found in four principal areas: Switzerland, Moravia, South Germany
and the Netherlands.

It should be pointed out that many radical reform groups of the sixteenth century were labeled "Anabaptist" by their opponents, even though these groups had little in common except their rejection of magisterial Protestantism and Roman Catholicism. It does not fall within the scope and purpose of this chapter to trace the origin and development of such "Anabaptist types" as the Spiritualists, the Mystics, the Anti-Trinitarians and others. Moreover, most of these groups have become extinct in the course of time. The present study will thus be restricted to two groups of "mainline" Anabaptists who are the spiritual progenitors of most Mennonites in Europe and North America.[7]

Even among the latter there was no homogeneous, organizationally-united Anabaptist-Mennonite Church in the sixteenth century, and it would be historically correct to say that in some respects the various branches of the Mennonite family in the twentieth century show a greater spirit of mutual recognition and practical cooperation than their forefathers. Although the religious and ethnic heritage of the Mennonite Brethren must largely be traced back to Dutch Anabaptism, a brief reference to the "Swiss Brethren," the pioneers of the free-church movement, is in place.

Swiss Anabaptism[8]

When Ulrich Zwingli (1484-1531) came to the *Grossmuenster* in Zurich in 1519, he was already deeply committed to the task of reform. His exposure to humanism as a student, and his personal studies of the New Testament while a priest at Glarus and Einsiedeln, had prepared him for his mission. At Grossmuenster he startled his listeners by preaching expository messages based on Scripture. Through his study of Scripture, he became increasingly critical of the traditional practices of Roman Catholicism.

By 1522 the Reformation in Zurich had quickened its pace. Although Zwingli resigned as priest of the Roman Catholic Church, he was immediately reinstated by the city council of Zurich. Among his most ardent supporters and devoted followers at this time were two brilliant, university-trained young radicals, Conrad Grebel and Felix Manz. Several reform-minded priests, such as Wilhelm Reublin, the fiery preacher of Wytikon, also joined the group. They appreciated Zwingli's preaching against tithes and rents, church fasts, and the mercenary system, which had attracted many Swiss youth to the papal armies. However, when Zwingli proceeded to abolish the mass, he met stiff resistance from the city council. Under these circumstances he took the course of expediency and compromise, and delayed action. A "disputation" on this issue was arranged in October, 1523. On this occasion a basic schism began to develop between Zwingli and the Radicals. The record of the debate states:

Conrad Grebel rose and thought that the priests should be given instructions, since they were all present, as to what should be done about the Mass; [the disputation] would be in vain, if something were not done about the Mass. . . .

Zwingli: My Lords [the Council] will decide how to proceed henceforth with the Mass.

Simon Stumpf: Master Ulrich. You have no authority to place the decision in the hands of My Lords, for the decision is already made: the Spirit of God decides.[9]

This kind of unreserved commitment to the guidance of the Holy Spirit through the Word of God led the Radicals inevitably to a new concept of the church as a voluntary association of true believers and to a new concept of the Christian life as *Nachfolge Christi*, or discipleship. By the end of 1524 the question of baptism had become the chief issue, and it was on infant baptism that the conflict centered. Zwingli saw clearly that if infant baptism were surrendered, he would also have to surrender the whole idea of *Corpus Christianum*, or the territorial concept of the church.

Because of the gravity of the situation, the city council of Zurich called for a public meeting in which this question was to be settled. The outcome of this pseudodisputation on January 17, 1525, was never in doubt. The Radicals who preferred to be known as "Brethren" now had the choice between compliance and exile. On the evening of January 21 they met in the home of Felix Manz to consider what they ought to do. What happened on that memorable evening is reported in a moving account in the Hutterian *Geschichtsbuch* and given in English translation by Bender as follows:

And it came to pass as they were together anxiety came upon them, yes, pressed upon their hearts. Therefore they began to bow their knees before Almighty God in heaven and to call upon Him as the one who knows the heart; and they prayed that He would grant them to do His divine will, and that He would reveal His mercy unto them. Flesh and blood or human wisdom had not brought them to this point, because they well knew what they would have to suffer on account of it. After prayer George of the House of Jakob [Cajacob-Blaurock] arose and entreated Conrad Grebel for God's sake to baptize him with the right Christian baptism upon the confession of his faith. And as he kneeled down with this request and desire, Conrad baptized him, since at that time there was no ordained minister to perform such work. . . .[10]

After his baptism at the hands of Grebel, Blaurock baptized all the others present. The newly baptized then pledged themselves, as true disciples of Christ, to live lives separated from the world and its evil works, and to spread the Gospel and keep the faith.

This, according to Estep, "was the most revolutionary act of the Reformation."[11] Here, for the first time in the course of the Reformation, a group of Christians dared to form a church after what they conceived to be the New Testament pattern. All free churches of the present day — including the Mennonite Brethren — are indebted to them.

DUTCH ANABAPTISM

The early decades of the sixteenth century constituted a period of great social and religious ferment in the Low Countries. The Brethren of the Common Life, the Humanists (e.g., Erasmus) and the Sacramentarians all contributed to this ferment and prepared the way for the reform and renewal of the church. The Sacramentarians offered growing opposition to the Roman Catholic view of the Eucharist by rejecting the doctrine of the physical presence of Christ in the bread and the wine of the Communion. Here, as in Switzerland, there was general dissatisfaction with the state of the Medieval Church. The yearnings and frustrations of these people found new hope of fulfillment in 1530 with the arrival in the Netherlands of Melchior Hoffman. Earlier in his spiritual pilgrimage this gifted but uneducated man had moved from Catholicism to Lutheranism. For several years he was the stormy apostle of this new faith in the Scandinavian countries and Northern Germany. Later he moved closer to the views of Zwingli and Carlstadt, both of whom differed from Luther in their understanding of the Lord's Supper. In Strassburg he first met the Anabaptists and accepted many of their views, but he also added ideas of his own. He was especially attracted to the prophecies of the Bible as they appeared in the books of Daniel and Revelation, "those most dangerous of all books in the hands of unlettered enthusiasts."[12]

Hoffman returned to Emden, East Friesland, shortly after he had become an Anabaptist. Here his message found a ready response and about three hundred were baptized. Two Hoffmannite apostles visited Leeuwarden in West Friesland later that year (1530) and succeeded in winning and baptizing Obbe and Dirk Philips, two brothers who became important leaders in the movement. Under the severe persecution which set in almost immediately, the chiliastic seeds of Hoffman's gospel produced an evil harvest. According to Hoffman's prediction, the new age would be ushered in in 1533 (the Great Tribulation having begun in 1526) with Strassburg as the New Jerusalem. After Hoffman's imprisonment in Strassburg, Jan Matthijs, a follower of Hoffman, used a new prophecy to change the location to Muenster in northwest Germany.

The resort to violence and the practice of polygamy in the "Muenster Kingdom" must be viewed as a tragic aberration and a complete denial of the basic views of mainstream evangelical Anabaptists. Unfortunately, most church historians of the established churches have magnified this incident and put the Muenster stigma on the whole Anabaptist movement until recent times.

Under the sane leadership of Obbe and Dirk Philips a large segment of the Dutch Anabaptists repudiated the revolutionary Muensterites. In this crucial period of reorientation Menno Simons joined the movement. He was destined, under God, to become the most important leader of the persecuted and scattered flock.

MENNO SIMONS (1496—1561)

Menno Simons was born in Witmarsum, a small village in the northern Dutch province of Friesland. He studied for the priesthood and was ordained in 1524, receiving his first assignment in Pingjum. His emancipation from Roman Catholicism and his conversion to an evangelical faith was a gradual process. Already in 1525 he had serious doubts about the Catholic doctrine of transubstantiation when he handled the bread and wine in the Mass. At first he regarded these doubts as temptations from the devil, who wanted to separate him from his faith. "Finally," Menno writes, "I got the idea to examine the New Testament diligently. I had not gone very far when I discovered that we were deceived. . . ."[13] This discovery had a profound effect on Menno; he became a diligent student of the Scriptures and a genuine biblicist in his theology. Several years later, when Menno heard of the beheading of Sicke Freriks at Leeuwarden because of rebaptism, he was deeply troubled. Thus far he had never doubted the validity of infant baptism. Again he turned to the New Testment for light, but he found no justification for this practice. Since Luther's writings had been a help to him in accepting the *Sola Scriptura* principle, he consulted Luther on this question, and somewhat later also Bucer and Bullinger.[14] Menno found that these reformers not only differed from one another in their justification of the doctrine of infant baptism, but also deviated from the plain teaching of the New Testament.

Although he was convinced that his church was in error on two important teachings of Scripture, Menno still hesitated to break with Rome. On the one hand stood his promotion to a more honorable and lucrative position in Witmarsum. On the other hand, there was the odium of Muenster which had brought the Anabaptists into general disrepute. In all probability, these were the main reasons for his vacillation and delay. For several years Menno fought on two theological fronts: he exposed the errors of Rome and also repudiated the violence of Muenster. The tragic death of his brother Peter probably provided the final impulse to take a firm stand for his scriptural convictions. Peter became involved with a fanatical group of Anabaptists at Bolsward who had taken to the sword in self-defense.

In a public statement on January 30, 1536, Menno expressed his new commitment to the cause of Christ, and then went into hiding with the help of the peaceful Anabaptists with whom he was in basic agreement. Like the Apostle Paul, who withdrew to Arabia after his

1. Anabaptist Martyrs

2. Menno Simons

conversion, Menno felt the need for prayer, meditation, Scripture study and a reorientation in his conception of the nature of the church. At the end of this year of preparation he was visited by a delegation of seven or eight men who asked him to become leader and pastor of their people. In his "Reply to Gellius Faber," Menno gives a moving account of his inward struggle in accepting this call.[15] After counting the cost of leading an outlawed persecuted group, he finally consented to serve and was ordained by Obbe Philips, who had baptized him earlier.

Until the end of his life twenty-five years later, Menno remained true to his vision and calling. He preached the gospel, instructed new converts, organized believers' churches, defended the faith against attacks from without and dangers from within, and guided the entire brotherhood to a deeper understanding of "costly grace" and true Christian discipleship. Judged by the personal sacrifice he made and by the principles which he practiced in establishing churches according to the apostolic pattern, Menno must be regarded as one of the noblest and most heroic Christians of his age — and perhaps any age. He and his associate ministers were trailblazers and pioneers in insisting on freedom of conscience, separation of church and state, and the renunciation of war and violence.

Speaking from the present vantage point, it appears extremely unfortunate that the Swiss Brethren and the Dutch Anabaptists did not enter into a closer association and dialogue during the sixteenth century. The two movements could have complemented and enriched each other, and thus given expression to a fuller and more balanced form of New Testament Christianity. The Dutch Mennonites with their strict and sober biblicism and a tendency toward legalism, would have profited from a more intimate fellowship with the Swiss Brethren with their broader sympathies and warmer evangelical piety. Perhaps the subsequent history of the Dutch, Prussian, and Russian Mennonites would have taken a different course as a result of such influence.

Already during Menno's lifetime the Mennonites (as peaceful Anabaptists came to be known after 1544) established congregations in Northern Germany and the Vistula Delta. The movement spread to those areas largely as a result of the continued severe persecution in the Netherlands. In the Schleswig-Holstein area Mennonites were able to settle on the estates of sympathetic noblemen who welcomed these refugees because of their knowledge about dikes and the recovery of marshy land for farming. Congregations were founded near Hamburg and Luebeck, and eventually in Altona, near Hamburg.

Menno moved into this area for the last years of his life. He lived in Wismar (on the Baltic Sea) until he had to flee after a theological debate with Micron in 1554. He then settled on an estate of the Baron von

Ahlefeldt located between Luebeck and Hamburg. Here, in the village of Wuestenfelde, he built a printshop and was active in writing. He died on January 31, 1561, and was buried in his own garden.

The movement, however, to which he had given such outstanding and heroic leadership for twenty-five years, did not die but continued to grow and expand. Mennonite congregations were established in the Vistula Delta and also in the free city of Danzig, where government authorities exercised greater religious tolerance. Close ties were maintained with the churches in the Netherlands, as the many old letters preserved in the files of the Amsterdam congregation show.[16] Menno Simons visited the congregations in the Danzig area in 1549, and Dirk Philips actually lived in Schottland, a suburb of Danzig, from approximately 1561 to shortly before his death in 1568. The emergence of a particular life-style among Mennonites in Prussia, and the developments in their congregational life will receive further consideration in chapter two.

The crises and controversies among the Mennonites of South Russia in the 1850's and 60's must be analyzed and interpreted against the background of the original Anabaptist Vision. The early Mennonite Brethren considered their views on the nature of the church to be in harmony with those of their "beloved Menno." This claim of the Mennonite Brethren calls for a closer examination of the church concept of Menno Simons.

In his "Reply to Gellius Faber" Menno differentiates between the Church of Christ and the Church of Antichrist. Both may be identified by certain "signs." What characterizes the true church? According to Menno, the true signs by which the Church of Christ may be known are the following (given in brief summary):[17]

1. An unadulterated, pure doctrine. Deuteronomy 4:6; 5:12; Isaiah 8:20; Matthew 28:20; Mark 16:15; John 8:52; Galatians 1. This pure doctrine, according to Menno, includes the clear presentation of the grace of God for man's salvation (Gal. 1), and the responsibility to share this good news with others as demanded by the Great Commission (Mt. 28, Mk. 16).

2. A Scriptural use of the sacramental signs. Matthew 28:19; Mark 16; Romans 6:4; Colossians 2:12; 1 Corinthians 12:13; Mark 14:22; Luke 22:19; 1 Corinthians 11:22,23. Menno insists that only those are to be baptized who "by faith are born of God, who sincerely repent, who bury their sins in Christ's death, and arise with Him in newness of life." The Lord's Supper is to be received by those who have experienced forgiveness through the blood of Christ, and "who walk with their brethren in love, peace, and unity . . . and who prove by their fruits that they are the church and people of Christ."[18]

3. Obedience to the Word. Matthew 7; Luke 11:28; John 7:18; 15:10; James 1:22. In the discussion of this "sign" Menno stresses a life of holiness and conformity to the life of Christ.

4. Unfeigned, brotherly love. John 13:34; Romans 13:8; 1 Corinthians 13:1; 1 John 3:8; 4:7, 8. According to Menno, "wherever sincere brotherly love is found . . . with its fruits, there we find the Church of Christ."[19]

5. A bold confession of God and Christ. Matthew 10:32; Mark 8:29; Romans 10:9; 1 Timothy 6:13. Menno finds no such sign among papists or Lutherans. A faithful confession of Christ, especially in the face of "all cruelty, tyranny, tumult, fire, sword, and violence of the world,"[20] is an incontrovertible proof of membership in the Church of Christ.

6. Oppression and tribulation for the sake of the Lord's Word. Matthew 3:10; 10:39; 16:24; 24:9; Luke 6:28; John 15:20; 2 Timothy 2:9; 3:12; 1 Peter 1:6; 3:14; 4:13; 5:10. The "pressing cross of Christ" was for Menno an unmistakable sign of membership in the true church.

The concept of the true church occupies a central place in Menno's theology. Voluntary church membership based upon true conversion and involving commitment to holy living and discipleship is the heart of this concept. This vision, according to H. S. Bender, "stands in sharp contrast to the church concept of the Reformers who retained the medieval idea of a mass church with membership of the entire population from birth to the grave compulsory by law and force."[21]

Closely related to the church concept of Menno was his understanding that the essence of the Christian life finds expression in discipleship (Nachfolge Christi). The Anabaptists believed that the believer's entire life should be fashioned after the teachings and example of Christ. For Menno and the other Anabaptists a major element in the life of discipleship was the ethic of love and nonresistance as applied to all human relationships.

The subsequent history of the Mennonite Church must be examined against this New Testament ideal as found in the writings of Menno and other Anabaptist leaders. How the vision and zeal of the "incendiary fellowship" of the early Mennonites was gradually lost constitutes the story of the next chapter.

Chapter 2

From Believers' Church
to Parish Church

By the mid-nineteenth century the Mennonite churches of the Ukraine had moved far from their origins in the Netherlands and the Vistula Delta, not only in terms of geography and culture, but also in terms of Christian faith and practice. Church history is replete with illustrations that religious movements tend to decline and deteriorate spiritually. That which was begun in the Spirit, may end in the flesh.

INFLUENCES IN PRUSSIA

The distinctive life-style of the Mennonites in South Russia prior to 1850 had been largely conditioned and shaped by their 250-year (1540-1790) sojourn in the Vistula Delta settlements, which were at first under Polish jurisdiction, but in 1772 came under Prussian rule. The Mennonites had arrived in the Vistula area as refugees from the Netherlands where severe persecution continued until the end of the sixteenth century. Later other smaller groups from Moravia, Bohemia and Austria joined them. They were welcomed on the large estates of the Polish nobles because of their experience in land-drainage and their general competence as farmers. Even so they were restricted in the exercise of their faith as well as in their acquisition of land, and often suffered harassment from local authorities and unfriendly neighbors.

Moreover, the Mennonites continued to suffer from their earlier division into Frisian and Flemish factions, who usually organized separate congregations. Originally coming from different cultural backgrounds, the two groups differed from one another in the mode of baptism (Frisians baptized by sprinkling, the Flemish by pouring), in the administration of communion, and in other minor matters.

These divisions were perpetuated in the Mennonite colonies of South Russia. Although the Mennonites were congregational in church polity, authority was concentrated largely in the hands of the elders.

13

Church membership in many instances was expressed only through church attendance and obedience to church tradition. To be sure, there were always notable exceptions, but in general, spiritual life was at a low ebb. Religious and cultural isolation and the lack of missionary vision and involvement eventually produced a conventicle-type of Christianity, so that Mennonites became known primarily as *die Stillen im Lande* (the quiet in the land).

In Prussia their conservatism and resistance to change are also seen in the fact that the Dutch language was retained in the worship services for over 200 years in their new environment. After 1750 the congregations gradually shifted from the use of Dutch to German in their public meetings.[1] Had the Mennonites emigrated to Russia some fifty years earlier, they would in all probability have continued to speak the Dutch. It would have been well if later generations in Russia (and even in Canada and the United States) would have reminded themselves that the change from Dutch to German was a mere historical coincidence, and that the German language was not an integral part of the Anabaptist heritage. The constant identification of true Mennonitism with German language and culture created serious problems for the faith and mission of the church.

The growing pressure of Prussian militarism under Frederick the Great made it increasingly difficult for the non-resistant Mennonites to remain loyal to their convictions. Moreover, because of the Mennonites' refusal to pay taxes in support of the state church and the military establishment (both based on land ownership), a regulation was passed by the state ministry in 1774 prohibiting the purchase of land except with the consent of the king. In 1789 Frederick's successor issued an edict which categorically denied further acquisition of land to the Mennonites. It is not surprising, therefore, that the far-sighted land settlement policy of Catherine II of "all the Russias" (as expressed in the Manifesto of 1763) was interpreted by many Mennonites as a special manifestation of divine providence.

A New Environment

The special charter of privileges granted to the Mennonites in 1788 (and reaffirmed by Tsar Paul I in 1800) did not vary significantly from the privileges granted to other immigrants. Russian colonial policy at that time was designed to separate all foreigners from the native population.[2] This pattern appealed to the Mennonites, who cherished the right to control their own religious, educational and civic affairs. Among the chief provisions of the *Privilegium* was the guarantee of complete religious freedom and exemption from military service for "all eternity."

In connection with this "charter of privileges" a popular misconception should be pointed out. The Mennonites of Russia have often been accused of having promised not to evangelize among the Russian people. "Such a promise," Gerhard Lohrenz claims, "was never made."[3] It is true that the Manifesto of 1763 (issued 25 years before the Mennonites came to Russia) contained a provision forbidding all proselytizing among members of any "Christian" denomination. To persuade a member of the Russian Orthodox Church to leave the establishment was considered a criminal offense.[4] It is doubtful, however, whether the Mennonites coming into Russia were even aware of this restriction and hence it seems unfair to state that "they had to suppress the missionary imperative of the Gospel."[5] Since the Mennonite settlements in the Ukraine were surrounded almost exclusively by non-Russians (primarily Tartars who were adherents of the Muslim faith) the issue was not a particularly relevant concern in the early period of Russian Mennonite history.

In response to the "Open Door Policy" of the Russian Tsars, two Mennonite colonies — Chortitza and Molotschna — were founded on the steppes of the Ukraine. The Chortitza Colony, founded in 1789, was named after a small tributary of the Dnieper River, and became known in later years as the "Old Colony" because it was the first settlement.[6] The Molotschna Colony (founded in 1804) was also named after a small river (Molotschnaya, meaning "milky") and was located approximately seventy-five miles southeast of the Chortitza settlement. By the turn of the century, the Chortitza Colony consisted of some fifteen villages in which 400 families had become established. Between 1803 and 1806 approximately 365 families arrived in the Molotschna Colony. By 1835 the stream of new settlers had slowed to a mere trickle. Altogether some 1,200 families had made their homes in the Molotschna Colony by that time, settling in fifty-eight villages with an acreage of 324,000, thus making it the largest Mennonite settlement ever established in Russia.[7] The Mennonite Brethren Church originated almost simultaneously in these two colonies in the early 1860's.

In order to understand the developments in church and society in this new environment, one needs to understand the economic and political factors that conditioned or influenced these developments. The Mennonite colonies, with few qualifications, constituted almost a state within the state. The Russian government granted them a large measure of self-government. The only direct link with the government in Petersburg up to 1870 was a Supervisory Commission (*Fuersorge-komitee*) appointed by the Tsar. This commission, located in the city of Odessa, performed primarily administrative functions. Thus, for the first time in their history, the Mennonites had to assume civic

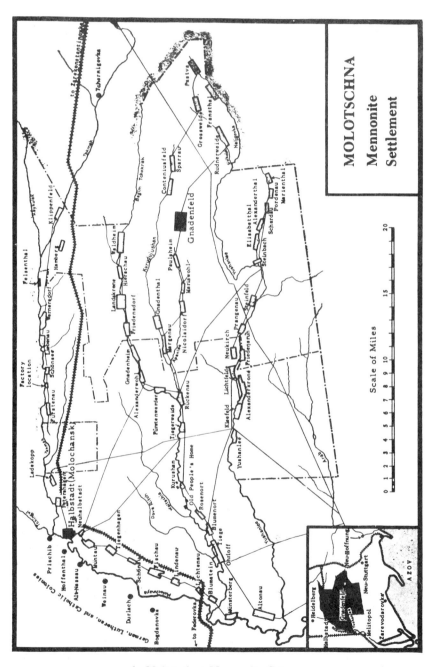

1. Molotschna Mennonite Colony

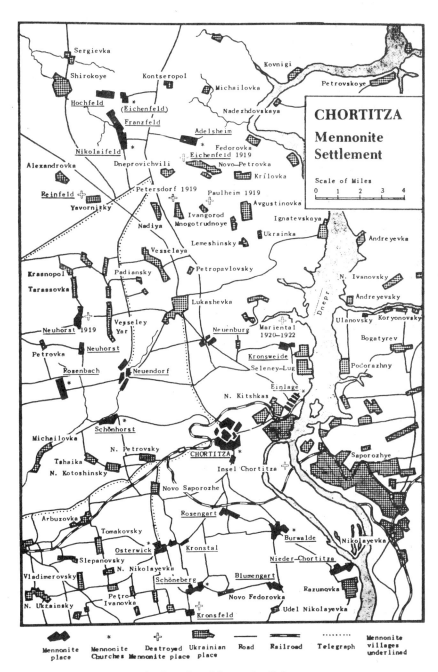

2. **Chortitza Mennonite Colony**

responsibilities and reconcile these new functions with their historic Anabaptist principle of the separation of church and state.

Economic conditions also played a decisive role in shaping the social and religious life of the colonies. The Mennonites established large, closed settlements in keeping with government colonial policy. This isolation made them independent of the "world" around them, but interdependent in their social and economic life. Moreover, they had been invited to Russia as model farmers, and a model farm supposedly contained 175 acres. The government regulation stipulated that the original estates were not to be subdivided by the colonies. Soon the rapid increase in population resulted in a serious shortage of available land. The situation became most acute in the Molotschna Colony with a ratio of 2,356 landless workers to 1,384 landed farmers in 1865.[8] This division of the population into landowners and landless workers resulted in a social stratification approaching a caste system. The landless families usually lived on the outskirts of the village, and for that reason were known as *Anwohner*. The landless lacked voting rights in village meetings, and intermarriage between these groups was frowned upon by the wealthy class.

These socio-economic problems were compounded by the absence of competent and far-sighted leadership. In an earlier period Johann Cornies (1789-1848) had given such leadership. From the time he was appointed permanent chairman of the Agricultural Improvement Society in 1817 until his premature death in 1848, Cornies was the ardent champion and promoter of improved agricultural practices and better schools. Under his auspices the first secondary school was founded in Ohrloff in 1820. He laid the groundwork for an excellent school system by his insistence on teacher training and curriculum reform. He personally wrote a major pedagogical treatise entitled "General Rules Concerning Instruction and Treatment of Children." However, these efforts came to fruition too late to prevent the crises in the 50's and 60's. After 1865 a temporary solution was found in the distribution of crown lands (which the landowners had previously rented for minimal fees). Somewhat later the two oldest colonies, with a vision they had not shown before, launched a long-range program of establishing "daughter colonies" for the landless and their young people. In the course of the next fifty years approximately forty new settlements were established in the Ukraine, Crimea, Caucasus, South-central Asia and in Siberia.

RELIGIOUS AND MORAL CONDITIONS

Given these geographical, political, economic and social conditions, it is not surprising that religious life and ethical practices gradually declined. Mennonite historians are generally agreed that the spiritual life in the colonies was at a low ebb in the first half of the nineteenth century. Robert Kreider observes that "the Mennonite Church in the Russian Mennonite environment moved in the direction and exhibited many of the characteristics of the *Volkskirche* or what the English call the 'parish pattern of the Church.' "[9] Gerhard Lohrenz describes the problems of the pioneer era similarly:

> Under these circumstances a slow stagnation crept into the intellectual and spiritual life of the group. When missionary David Schlatter visited the colonies in 1835 he reported that the church had "lost its salt." But the spiritual life was to sink even lower during the next two decades.[10]

The late C.H. Smith, prominent Mennonite scholar and historian, confirms these impressions when he writes: "The spiritual life of the colonists through the first two generations was not of a high order."[11] This low level of morals and spirituality cannot simply be explained in terms of the socio-economic conditions described earlier. Other, more basic causes must be considered.

CAUSES OF SPIRITUAL DECLINE

Lack of Spiritual Leadership

A river cannot rise higher than its source. But for the grace of God, a people can rise no higher than their heritage and their leadership. It appears almost incomprehensible that among the 228 families who comprised the first contingent of immigrants who settled in Chortitza there was not a single minister! They arrived at their new home religiously unorganized and spiritually shepherdless. This situation can partly be explained by the customary election of ministers at that time. Ministers were chosen from the laity and were expected to serve without pay. It was natural, therefore to choose them from the well-to-do class, who could afford to serve. The wealthier members among the Danzig Mennonites were originally denied passports, and hence no preacher or elder accompanied the pioneer group. Although this problem was solved through ordination of some men by proxy, the churches in Chortitza continued to suffer from poor leadership. In the Molotschna the situation was somewhat better because several groups had come as organized congregations with their elders and ministers (e.g., Alexanderwohl, Gnadenfeld). Unfortunately, no provision was made by the churches for the education and training of their ministers, and hence their biblical knowledge was derived mainly from the religious instruction received in the elementary schools. This, coupled with almost complete cultural isolation, inevitably produced an intellectual stagnation and a leadership with very limited mental horizons.

The chief problem of church leadership of that day, however, appears to be a lack of a vital Christian experience and a living, dynamic faith. J. F. Harms makes the sweeping statement: "Converted preachers or elders were rare exceptions."[12] Bernhard Harder, a gifted evangelist and preacher of the Ohrloff-Halbstadt Mennonite Church, was one of these "rare exceptions." He was one of the "weeping prophets" who remained in the "old" church and diligently worked for reform from within. In a letter to the *Mennonitische Blaetter* (a periodical of the German Mennonites), dated July 22, 1862, Harder severely criticizes the ministry in his own church.

"What is lacking among us?" he asks.

In the first place, there is something wrong with us — the witnesses and watchmen. A large number among us lack the very first and all-important capital "A" of Christianity: "Wake up, o man, from your sleep of sin" . . . What can be expected from complacent and self-satisfied preachers who are reluctant to do anything but read an occasional sermon which for a half century has been a part of the family heritage, without consideration whether it is relevant to the times or not . . . all that we have left is a dry formalism, a shell without a kernel, a church without living members. [13]

This severe indictment of the clergy basically agrees with the chief criticism of the early "Brethren" — that the ministers (*Lehrer*) are not taking a firm stand against the increasing decay and corruption of the church.[14] On the other hand it may be observed that the critics lacked a deeper historical perspective in their analysis, not realizing that the ministers themselves were the product of a socio-economic and ecclesiastical system, and thus could not be charged with total responsibility for existing conditions.

Loss of the Biblical Church Concept

For the early Anabaptists the church was a voluntary fellowship of regenerated believers, a Christian brotherhood, a community of the redeemed. Menno insisted that only those who "are born of Christ's Word by means of faith by his Spirit" are to be members of the church.[15] Baptism is an ordinance which has significance only for believers. "The holy apostles have taught and used no other baptism," Menno wrote, "than baptism upon confession of faith."[16] This concept of a believers' church was obscured and almost lost in the Russian Mennonite environment. "Appraised from the perspective of the Anabaptist conception of the church," Kreider claims, "the Mennonites in Russia forfeited at the outset the possibility of being a brotherhood-type of church . . . they accepted a system of privileges which were bound to qualifications, not of faith, but of blood."[17] One had to be an ethnic Mennonite to enjoy the privileges offered to the colonists. Because the surrounding Russian culture was so different in its socio-economic character, it was obviously disadvantageous for anyone to separate himself from the Mennonite colonies. Hence the stage was set for a Mennonite spiritual and cultural exclusivism, and for the development of a territorial church (*Landeskirche*) in which church men.bership and citizenship were coextensive. Although the elders and ministers continued to be orthodox in their views of salvation and the nature of the church, in practice they began to surrender or compromise basic biblical principles. A serious "credibility gap" developed between formal confession and actual practice. In many instances baptism seemed to be more a civil than a religious rite, since it enabled young people to get married.[18] It is true, all candidates for baptism were required to become members of the preparatory class for church membership in which the *Catechism* and *Confession of Faith* were studied. All too often, however, the elder was satisfied with the memorized answers of the candidate, and did not insist on a personal commitment to Jesus Christ as a condition for baptism. "Believer's baptism" had become mere "adult baptism" in many instances. Communion also took on certain characteristics of the "sacrament" as practiced in the state churches.

Church history teaches that a wrong church concept vitiates a proper concept of salvation sometimes in the second, and inevitably in the third generation. This phenomenon can also be observed in Mennonite history.

Closely related to the loss of the brotherhood-concept of the church was the development of a power structure, an ecclesiastical hierarchy, among the Mennonites in Russia. In Prussia the elders had enjoyed growing prestige and power, but their authority had been restricted largely to the internal life of their congregations. In Russia, the Supervisory Commission in Odessa, and the District Office (*Gebietsamt*) of the colonies found it convenient to consult the elders in the solution of difficult questions. In order to present a more unified position to the civil authorities, the elders and ministers met periodically for discussion of mutual concerns. (One of these concerns, for instance, was the question of public education, which for many years was under their jurisdiction.) In 1850 the elders declared themselves "the highest ecclesiastical authority of the churches" under the designation of *Kirchenkonvent* (Council of Elders).[19]

The development of such a hierarchy was contrary to the historic understanding of the early Anabaptists and Mennonites with regard to the nature of the New Testament church. Moreover, it did not originate as a conscious and deliberate policy on the part of the congregations. The latter had gradually abdicated their responsibilities in actively shaping church policy, thus giving the elders an almost monarchical position. To speak against an elder was considered a grave misdemeanor.[20] At church business meetings the recommendations of the elders were usually accepted without discussion or debate. The crises in the Mennonite fraternity in the 1850's and 60's were in part precipitated by the natu.. .nd composition of the Council of Elders (*Kirchenkonvent*).

MANIFESTATIONS OF SPIRITUAL DECLINE

Certain conditions called for reform and renewal of the church.

1. *Lack of Church Nurture and Discipline*

With the possible exception of the Gnadenfeld and Ohrloff congregations, church services were usually neither stimulating nor edifying. In many instances sermons were read from old manuscripts and thus were not "geared to the times" nor to the particular needs of the membership. Singing was poor and monotonous. Religious instruction of children was neglected by the church, although they did receive some religious instruction as part of their public school training.

Church discipline was exercised in the form of excommunication or the "ban," but only in connection with grave public moral offenses such as adultery or physical assault. Preventive church discipline in the form of pastoral counseling and mutual watch-care was virtually unknown. Jacob Martens, a minister of the church at Tiegenhagen, Molotschna, expresses his concern over this lack of pastoral care in a letter to the *Mennonitische Blaetter* in these words: "Concerning our dear young people, I find that children, young men and young women are permitted to go their own ways as sheep without a shepherd, indulging in sins and vices of all kinds. . . ."[21]

2. *Serious Tensions and Tragic Schisms*

In early years the old rivalry between the Frisians and the Flemish consumed a great deal of spiritual energy. By 1820 these traditional differences were largely forgotten and a new alignment of churches took place. The Frisian Church of Rudnerweide, for instance, cooperated with the Flemish Church of Ohrloff in the organization of a branch of the Bible Society of St. Petersburg. Bernhard Fast, the progressive elder of the Ohrloff Church, introduced a number of innovations in his religious practices which aroused the bitter opposition of the majority of his conservative membership. Three-fourths of his congregation (some four hundred families) withdrew and organized a congregation of their own which, because it embraced the larger part of the membership, became known as the "Grosse Gemeinde."[22] Thus a theologically progressive minority emerged in Ohrloff, in contrast to a conservative majority centered in Lichtenau.

The involvement of the Mennonites in the civil administration of the colonies also resulted in some bitter controversies and serious conflicts between the representatives of church (elders) and state (village mayors and colony administrators, known as *Schulzen* and

Oberschulzen). The membership was also divided on the issue of using force against fellow-Mennonites when the latter had violated village or colony regulations. Many felt that corporal punishment or imprisonment of a fellow church member was inconsistent with the historic faith and practice of the church. The secession of a small, culturally conservative group in the years after 1812 under the leadership of Claas Reimer was primarily over this issue. Between 1820 and 1850 the Mennonites of South Russia went through a kind of *Kulturkampf* of their own. The progressive measures of Johann Cornies for the improvement of the colonies were authorized and enforced by the District Office (*Gebietsamt*) and the Supervisory Commission of Odessa. Jacob Warkentin, elder of the Lichtenau Church (*Grosse Gemeinde*) for seventeen years, was deposed from his office in 1841 because of his opposition to certain regulations of the Agricultural Improvement Society. The large church, to which about three-fourths of all Mennonites in the Molotschna belonged, was divided into three parishes by the District Office and the Supervisory Commission in order to weaken its opposition to civil authorities.[23]

In 1847 Heinrich Wiens was deposed from office as elder of the Margenau-Schoensee Church and exiled for similar reasons.[24] Before his banishment from the Molotschna, Elder Wiens prepared a moving farewell address which was read to the congregation by one of his associate ministers. This message provides a significant glimpse into the life of the church at that time. As reasons for his exile Wiens mentions hatred, the spirit of revenge, false accusations and slander. Then he appeals to his parishioners with these words:

Members and brethren living in enmity and strife, be ye reconciled! And you, who have to this day indulged in excessive drinking, and have not renounced the pleasures and the pride of life, I plead with you, for God's sake and the salvation of your souls, leave all this and come in true repentance so that there may be rejoicing before God and his holy angels.[25]

Perhaps the moral and spiritual decline among the Mennonites is manifested most vividly in the controversies that centered around the "land-question." The socio-economic aspects of this problem were accompanied by moral and spiritual implications. In describing the decline of the spiritual life in the colonies, J. H. Lohrenz observes that: "The long period of strife between the landowners and the tenants largely destroyed the brotherly relationship between the two classes."[26]

The fact that the ministers and elders belonged almost exclusively to the wealthier class of the landed farmers, added a tragic dimension to this problem. The church leaders sided with the landowners and became defenders of the status quo. In their sad plight the landless appealed not only to the district officials and the Supervisory Commission, but also presented moving petitions to the Council of Elders (*Kirchenkonvent*).

In a petition of 1865 they made their appeal on the basis of scriptural teaching.

We beg the honorable members of the *Kirchenkonvent*, as stewards, to provide for our needs since we are members of one body (1 Cor. 12:26) and members of God's household (1 Tim. 5:8), and that they act as true believers who according to James 2:16 not only say, "be warmed and filled," but as our spiritual fathers become actively and helpfully involved in our plight. . . . [27]

This appeal to the Council of Elders went unanswered. In order to discredit the movement, a large group of landowners even sought to smear the landless as revolutionaries, dangerous to the peace and welfare of the settlement.[28] In studying this dark blot on the pages of Mennonite history one cannot help but agree with Kreider in the following evaluation: "No problem in the Mennonite colonies created such misunderstanding and class hatred as the land problem . . . this conflict demonstrates how class and property interests soil the church as an 'ethical community of brotherly love.' "[29] Spiritual and moral decline were seen also in the realm of personal and social ethics.

3. *A Loss of Christian Virtues*

Christ has given a practical criterion of the appraisal of any religious movement or professing Christian group: "You will know them by their fruits" (Mt. 7:20). The Christian graces will come to proper fruition and expression only when rooted in an evangelical theology and a vital Christian experience. Eventually any code of Christian ethics will disintegrate when not sustained by a living faith. Contemporary observers and later historians are agreed that moral standards had reached a new low before the "great awakening" of the late 1850's. In 1856 the Agricultural Improvement Society, which had administered the school system of the Molotschna colony since 1843, asked each teacher to comment on the moral condition of the people. The unanimous response was that the moral life of the people was in a degenerate state.[30]

In his memoirs, Jacob P. Becker, one of the signers of the Document of Secession, reports widespread drunkenness. Almost all villages had their taverns (*Branntwein Schenken*). Becker writes,

This resulted in a number of alcoholics who at times lay drunk and almost naked in the streets. . . . The preachers knew of these drunkards, yet the offenders were allowed to remain members of the church and were permitted to partake of the Communion. As long as a man had not openly whored, stolen, or brawled he could remain a member of the church."[31]

Becker goes on to describe various social events (e.g. weddings, community fairs, etc.) which often were the occasion for drunken orgies. In a treatise entitled, "Faith and Reason," written in 1833, Heinrich Balzer also gives a critical description of the contemporary Mennonite Church. He finds that these members of the Christian church are not morally superior to their pagan neighbors, the Nogaians, indulging in "pride, ostentation, vanity, greed for money and lust for wealth, avarice, drunkenness, luxury, vicious life, masquerades, obscene songs, gambling, and above all the miserable smoking of tobacco."[32] Later historians[33] generally confirm this dismal moral picture of many Russian Mennonites in the mid-nineteenth century. Such conditions called for spiritual renewal and moral reform. God, in His gracious providence, raised up men and movements to usher in a new day.

Chapter 3

Renewal and Reorientation

The "Great Awakening in Russian Mennonitism"[1] must be studied in the context and against the background of earlier "new life" movements. Even during the darkest decades of spiritual decline God always had His faithful remnant who had not "bowed their knees to Baal" — whether that Baal be a dead orthodoxy or a spirit of secularism and worldliness. There were always those who were concerned about a deeper experience in their personal life and about the spiritual renewal in the church as a whole. Several such channels of renewal shall be considered briefly.

EARLIER RENEWAL MOVEMENTS

1. The Kleine Gemeinde[2]

Between 1812 and 1819 a group of dissatisfied members of the Flemish church began to meet for worship in private homes under the leadership of Claas Reimer, an ordained minister of the church. According to Lohrenz, the religious awakening which led to the formation of the Kleine Gemeinde was the result of small prayer circles.[3] These groups also became known for their diligent study of the Bible, the works of Menno Simons and Dirk Philips, and of the Martyrs' Mirror.[4] Their reform efforts and criticism of contemporary Mennonite society must be interpreted as attempts to return to early Anabaptist principles and practices — even though inadequately understood. The members of this group faulted the laxity of church discipline and the formality of worship services in the Mennonite Church. They especially objected to the use of force in punishing evildoers in the Mennonite community. Although threatened by the elders of both colonies, Molotschna and Chortitza, Reimer with eighteen others seceded from the main body and organized a church of their own. The Mennonite elders put up a strong protest against the move, but the group eventually secured government recognition as a separate ecclesiastical organization. Through the intervention of Johann Cornies the elders were compelled by the civil authorities to recognize the *Kleine Gemeinde* and validate the functions of its unordained elder by a decree of the Supervisory Commission on January 28, 1843. Twenty years later, history had to repeat itself, because neither civil nor ecclesiastical authorities had learned from the earlier experience.

Historians have been inclined to magnify the narrow conservatism and *Kultur-Feindlichkeit* (opposition to culture) of this movement, thereby overlooking its emphasis on personal experience and piety. The treatise by Heinrich Balzer of the *Kleine Gemeinde* on "Faith and Reason"[5] reflects an intimate and personal relationship to Jesus Christ. His "testimony" would have found a warm response among the early Mennonite Brethren:

> When in a reborn heart the Holy Spirit exclaims, "Abba, our Father," divine gifts effuse into the believer and enter his understanding. They fill him with a new wisdom and a knowledge of Jesus Christ. The more and the freer the heart of man is opened to the Spirit, the more knowledge will he gain, the greater riches of divine gifts will he receive, and the more will his heart be prepared as an abode of the Triune God.[6]

The present Mennonite Brethren Conference has a historic connection with this movement through the former Krimmer Mennonite Brethren who formed a part of the *Kleine Gemeinde* prior to their separate organization in 1869.

2. *Fellowship Center at Ohrloff*

After the withdrawal of the large body of ultra-conservative members from the Ohrloff Mennonite Church, Ohrloff became a center of new light and new life under the progressive leadership of elder Bernhard Fast. If Gnadenfeld can be considered as the center of the pietistic revival movement, Ohrloff may be designated as the center of an "intellectual Renaissance" among the Molotschna Mennonites. The origin and early history of the Mennonite Brethren cannot be fully understood apart from the fellowship center at Ohrloff. Of great significance for the religious developments in the colony was the establishment of a *Vereinsschule* in 1820 under the auspices of an educational society headed by Johann Cornies, the great Mennonite organizer and colonizer.[7] The first teacher was Tobias Voth, whom Cornies invited to come from Prussia. Several years prior to his coming to Russia in 1822, he reported in his diary that he and his wife had been converted through Jung Stilling's writings, and then had fellowship with other Pietists.

Voth was not only a gifted educator but also a spiritual leader who was deeply concerned about the religious welfare of the community. According to P. M. Friesen, Voth organized prayer meetings, in which "free prayers" (not memorized or read) were the rule.[8] He also

sponsored mission meetings (*Missionsstunden*) and organized a
Christian Literature Society (*Leseverein*) for the express purpose of
distributing Christian books and writings. Heinrich Huebert, first elder
of the Mennonite Brethren Church, as well as many other students of
Tobias Voth, attribute to him their first indelible impressions of the
Christian faith, as well as their appreciation for higher education and
culture.[9] Voth's interest in the distribution of good Christian literature
became the special concern of one of his former students, Jacob
Martens, a deeply pious minister of Tiegenhagen. Martens was actively
involved in a "Christian Literature Crusade" until his death around
1870.

The significance of Tobias Voth for the Mennonite colonies in
general, and for the Mennonite Brethren Church in particular, is
succinctly stated by Friesen as follows:

> Among us here in Russia Tobias Voth has given expression for the first time
> to something which we call 'brotherhood' (*Brudertum*) or intimate Christian
> fellowship; which today is found in the Mennonite Brethren Church as well as
> among all groups of true believers in the 'old' or 'churchly' congregations. [10]

3. *The Fellowship Center at Gnadenfeld*

In the forties and fifties the center of the "Brotherhood" movement
shifted from Ohrloff to Gnadenfeld (Field of Grace). This congregation
had a unique history dating back to approximately 1540, when a group
of Dutch Anabaptists fled their homeland and eventually found a new
home in the state of Brandenburg, Prussia. Here, a relatively large
number of Lutheran Pietists joined them in the early years of the
nineteeneth century.[11] Because of continuing pressure from the
Prussian government, mainly due to Mennonite opposition to military
service, the congregation under elder Wilhelm Lange migrated to the
southern Ukraine in 1835 and founded the village of Gnadenfeld in the
Molotschna. From the very beginning Gnadenfeld became an important
center of spiritual life. Their church calendar included two Sunday
services, a midweek meeting, mission study hours and festivals, as well
as meetings in private homes consisting of *Bibelstunden* (Bible study
discussion hours) and prayer. The Gnadenfeld Church also championed
the cause of temperance in the colony. In his memoirs Jacob Becker
reports as follows:

> The Gnadenfeld Church Council ordered tracts that pointed out the evil and
> condemned the drinking of liquor, organized a union and gathered signatures of
> those who renounced drinking. Since they distributed many tracts and organized
> a Temperance Union, they came to be derisively called the Temperates
> (*Maessigen*). [12]

The contribution of the Gnadenfeld congregation to the larger
Mennonite brotherhood during its first quarter century in the Russian
environment was significant and lasting.[13] The Mennonite Brethren

3. Bernhard Harder   4. Eduard Wuest   5. August Lenzmann

Church is indebted to Gnadenfeld in a special way. Most of the early leaders among the "Brethren"[14] were either members or adherents of this church.[15] P. M. Friesen calls Gnadenfeld the "place of inception" (*Empfaengnisstaette*) of the Mennonite Brethren Church of 1860, and claims that the history of our church is "unthinkable without the history of the Gnadenfeld congregation."[16] Even after the moral lapse and deposition of its elder Friedrich Lange (1849), and the death of Pfarrer Eduard Wuest (1859) Gnadenfeld continued to be a center of fellowship for the "Brethren." August Lenzmann, ordained as elder in 1854, although cautious and conservative by nature, was considered to be a friend of the "Brethren" up to 1860. The "Brethren" cooperated wholeheartedly with Elder Lenzmann in the founding of a *Bruderschule* (Brotherhood-school) which finally opened its doors in 1857. Johann Claassen, a member of the Gnadenfeld Church and of the educational society, made two trips to Petersburg in the interests of this new venture. After the secession of the "Brethren" in 1860, and the withdrawal of the "Jerusalem Friends" or "Templers" in 1863,[17] Gnadenfeld ceased to be the center of the new life movement in the Molotschna.

4. *"Pfarrer" Eduard Wuest (1818-1859)*
   (The Influence of Pietism)
      One of the greatest influences contributing to the religious awakening among the Mennonites in Russia was the ministry of Eduard Hugo Otto Wuest, pastor of the Separatist Lutheran (Pietist) Church of Neuhoffnung, a village near the city of Berdjansk. All early Brethren express their admiration for Wuest. As mentioned earlier, Friesen regards him as the "second reformer" of the M.B. Church.
      Wuest had had an unusual spiritual pilgrimage before coming to South Russia. He was born in Murrhardt, Wuerttemberg, Germany, on February 23, 1818, the son of an innkeeper. During his student days in

the Gymnasium in Stuttgart (1832-35) and the University of Tuebigen (1835-41) he was torn between the desire to study and pray, and the desire to please his sinful companions. Although preparing for the ministry, he prayed for the first time (according to his personal testimony) after six years of theological study at Tuebingen, just before his final examinations.[18]

A great change took place in his life when he became assistant pastor at Neuenkirchen in 1841. He devoted his time to serious study and the preparation of sermons. Two years later, at Murrhardt, he began to associate with the Wuerttemberg Pietists. By 1844 he had come to a genuine experience of forgiveness of sins and a joyous assurance of salvation. This experience affected his message — he developed into a powerful preacher of true repentance and God's free grace. His pietistic zeal, in tension with certain practices of the church, made it impossible for him to continue his service. After his dismissal, he occasionally served pietistic circles in the vicinity. He also came in contact with a Methodist minister from the United States, and for a while seriously considered emigrating to America. But in God's providence he was directed to go to Russia. In 1845 he was invited by the Neuhoffnung congregation to become their pastor. Wuest accepted the call with the inner assurance that it was from God.

Wuest was an outstanding preacher: tall, good physique, endowed with a powerful, melodious voice, and well trained in the art of communication. He had an attractive, winsome personality, but also strong Christian convictions, and people who had contact with him either loved him or hated him — depending on their attitude toward Christ.[19]

From his inaugural sermon at Neuhoffnung (in close proximity to the Molotschna) on September 28, 1845, one senses the spirit of his message and ministry. After presenting "Jesus Christ, the Crucified" as the central theme of his preaching, he calls for personal commitment to the truth:

> Beloved, it's either-or- This I want to make clear to you in my first sermon. Either believing — or unbelieving, either converted — or unconverted, either a natural man — or a regenerate man. . . . This choice I will present to you. I will not leave believers and unbelievers side by side; but you shall be separated according to Paul's teaching in 2 Corinthians 6:14 ff. [20]

The church was packed on this occasion, and among the many attentive listeners were a number of Mennonites. The scriptural and authoritative preaching of Wuest deeply impressed them, and initiated a fruitful relationship with this servant of God in the years to follow.

Pfarrer Wuest exerted a profound influence on the Mennonites in several ways. Already in 1846 he was invited to speak at a missions festival in Gnadenfeld. In subsequent years he often served as guest speaker on such occasions. These missionary meetings were eagerly attended not only by members of the Gnadenfeld Church, but also by concerned individuals from all the churches of the Molotschna. In a more direct way he influenced the Brethren by attending their monthly meetings on Saturday afternoon. Jacob Reimer, a prominent leader in the early M. B. Church and a regular attendant of these gatherings, explains the purpose of these meetings in his memoirs:

> The purpose was to strengthen one another in our common faith, and to exhort each other to walk and work worthy of our position as members of the body of Christ who have their treasures in heaven and not on earth, and to come to a deeper knowledge of our (moral) corruption and of Christ's infinite love. [21]

Jacob Becker, another participant in these fellowship meetings, reports that many people came to hear Wuest out of curiosity, especially at the missions festivals, but "they left with a different impression than when they came" and often asked the question: What must I do to be saved? [22]

Wuest's popularity soon aroused the envy of his fellow-pastors in Lutheran churches as well as among the ministers and elders of the Mennonite churches. As a result, he was barred from preaching in the pulpits of these churches. He continued to attend the devotional meetings of the Brethren, however, where he would not "preach," but responded to questions addressed to him.

Wuest's emphasis on the "full and free and present grace of God" was exploited by some members of his own congregation at Neuhoffnung. A group of these emotional enthusiasts withdrew from Wuest's congregation in 1858, under the leadership of a teacher named Kappes. This movement also influenced the Brethren in the Molotschna and Chortitza colonies and almost wrecked the early M.B. Church (cf. Chapter 5). Wuest himself was deeply grieved by these developments in the last years of his ministry. His premature death on July 13, 1859, was interpreted by his opponents as a judgment of God, but by his friends as a deliverance from tribulation.

All early Brethren are agreed in their deep appreciation for his contribution to the new life movement in South Russia. And yet it was perhaps providential that the man to whom so many Brethren were emotionally attached had to leave the scene at that particular time. Wuest was a "Moses" who led many people out of the bondage of a lifeless tradition and dead orthodoxy to a joyous assurance of a personal faith. But by training and experience he was not equipped to be the "Joshua" to lead these redeemed people into the promised land of a believers' church. In his own congregation believers and unbelievers remained "side by side" (cf. his inaugural sermon). He did not introduce "believers' baptism" and remained a pedo-baptist to the end of his ministry. Like Luther, he found it impossible to bring his original vision into actual realization.

After Wuest's death, the orphaned Brethren were compelled to find their orientation with regard to the nature of the church in their historic Anabaptist tradition and in the study of the New Testament. The statement that the Mennonite Brethren Church was "born of Anabaptism and Pietism"[23] must hence be accepted with some reservations. Pietism revitalized the fellowship-concept, but did not provide a New Testament church-concept for the Brethren. In this respect they were probably more indebted to the German Baptists than to the Pietists.

MOVING TOWARD SEPARATION

The new life emanating from Neuhoffnung, Gnadenfeld and Ohrloff had resulted in numerous conversions in many villages. The Brethren continued to meet in several centers for Bible study and prayer. In a very real sense these *Bibelstunden*, held in private homes, became the cradle for the birth of the M. B. Church. Two major developments led to the ultimate break with the old church.

1. *Observance of Separate Communion*

According to an early tradition, the Gnadenfeld Mennonite Church practiced "open communion" for some time, in which Lutheran Separatists and Mennonites participated. Although P. M. Friesen is inclined to accept this view, he has not been able to find any documentary evidence for such practice.[24] The growing estrangement of the Brethren from the existing churches, and the cultivation of an intimate fellowship in their Bible study groups created a spiritual atmosphere in which the desire for separate communion was to be expected.

That the Brethren did not act rashly or thoughtlessly in this matter can be seen in their request to Elder Lenzmann to administer this ordinance in their group. Here is Jacob Reimer's account:

> As our fellowship based itself more and more upon the Word of God, there arose among us the desire to observe the Lord's Supper more frequently and so we asked our Elder Lenzmann to break the bread more often for us — also in our private homes, according to Acts 2:46, 47.[25]

This request shows that Lenzmann was regarded by them as a true shepherd and brother, and that the Brethren were reluctant to secede from their mother church. Unfortunately, although understandably, the request was denied. Some years later Lenzmann mentioned several reasons why he had taken the stand he did: private communion was without historical precedent, it would foster spiritual pride, and it would cause disunity in the church.

Having failed in their attempt to enlist the services of an elder for a separate communion, a small group of believers met in late November, 1859, in the home of Kornelius Wiens, Elizabethtal, to observe this ordinance. Abraham Cornelsen, a schoolteacher and member of the Rudnerweide (Frisian) Church was in charge of communion which was observed in all simplicity according to Paul's teaching in 1 Corinthians 11. Present at the service were several members from the Flemish Church and six members from the Gnadenfeld Church, but not Johann Claassen and Jacob Reimer.

The news of this event spread rapidly among the churches and caused consternation and displeasure, especially among the elders. Those members of the group who belonged to the Flemish Church were immediately put under the ban, which in some instances meant social ostracism and economic ruin. The Gnadenfeld Church was more moderate and sympathetic in its treatment of the "offenders." The six members who had participated in communion had to appear before the ministers of the church, who reproved them for their conduct and elicited from them the promise that "they would submit to all things not contrary to the Word of God and their conscience."[26]

There the matter would have rested if it had not been for a highly critical and very vocal element in the church. At two church meetings held on December 19 and 27, 1859, not only the small group, but the whole new movement came under attack. Especially Claassen and Reimer were singled out. At the last stormy session some members shouted, "Away with them, they are no better than the others."[27] Slowly Jacob Reimer made his way to the front and asked Elder Lenzmann for permission to leave. Reluctantly the latter consented. When it appeared that only Reimer and Claassen would leave the meeting, Heinrich Franz, who had been in conflict with the Brethren regarding the *Bruderschule*, challenged Claassen with these words: "You are otherwise such a courageous man; why don't you call on your associates to follow you?" Claassen then turned around and said: "Well brethren, whoever is like-minded, come along."[28] About ten brethren arose and left the church. In all, Gnadenfeld lost approximately twenty-five baptized members. But because of this rift, many visitors and "adherents" from other churches also ceased to attend the services there. Gnadenfeld had ceased to be center of the new life movement. The stage was now set for the final dramatic step in the development of a separate church organization. After consultation with several brethren, Claassen called on Abraham Cornelsen, schoolteacher in Elizabethtal, and the two agreed, "that Cornelsen would write the letter of secession and Claassen would call a Brotherhood meeting for Epiphany, on January 6, 1860, in Elizabethtal...."[29]

2. *The "Founders' Meeting"*

A meeting of the "charter members" of the Mennonite Brethren Church took place in the home of Isaak Koop on January 6, 1860. The letter of secession prepared by Cornelsen was carefully examined and the brethren agreed to accept this document as a basis for their action. Deeply conscious of the serious implications of this step, "the entire afternoon until evening was spent in ardent prayer."[30] Then the document was presented for voluntary signatures. Eighteen heads of families signed it on that day. On January 18, nine other brethren added their signatures. The documents, submitted to the Council of Elders, reads as follows:

To the total body of church elders of the Molotschna Mennonite Church!

a) We, the undersigned, have by the grace of God, recognized the decadent condition of the Mennonite Brotherhood and can, for God's and conscience' sake no longer continue therein; for we fear the inevitable judgment of God, since the openly godless living and their wickedness cries to God in heaven. We also fear the loss of the rights and privileges granted us by our benevolent government because the transgressions and disobedience against it increase continually. It is tragic to behold (O Jesus, have mercy, and open the eyes of the spiritually blind!), when in the market places (*Jahrmaerkten*), before the very eyes of their neighbors, our Mennonite brethren live satanic lives; and even the teachers (preachers) go about and see it, yea even in the restaurants, sit quietly by, see and hear how people serve the devil. Of such persons the Scripture says (Ps. 109:17-18): He clothed himself with cursing, like as with his garment; as he loved cursing, so let it come unto him. The teachers do not stand in the gap as of old. Hosea 13:5. Ezekiel 22:30.

b) Therefore, we herewith completely dissociate ourselves from these decadent churches, though we pray for our brethren, that they shall be saved. We want to be innocent of the souls of the erring. But Thou, O Jesus, equip faithful living witnesses, who will direct Thy children and the work of Thy hands to Thee! Amen.

c) We speak here of the entire Mennonite Brotherhood, because the supreme government authorities consider it one true brotherhood.

d) In the articles, we are, according to our convictions from the Holy Scripture, in agreement with our dear Menno.

e) We confess a baptism on faith, as a seal of faith; not on a memorized faith, as is the practice but on a genuine, living faith effected by the Spirit of God. For without faith, it is impossible to please God. Hebrews 11:6. And he that hath not the Spirit of Christ. is none of his. (Romans 8:9). And again our dear Saviour says to Nicodemus, John 3:3: Except a man be born again, he cannot see the kingdom of God. Baptism is not the new birth, as some of the unconverted maintain, but serves as a sign for the baptismal candidate, that he is really born again.

f) Regarding holy communion we confess that it serves to strengthen the faith of true believers, for they remind themselves of their mighty salvation through the death of the Lord Jesus. Yes, it is a sign that they stand in very intimate (*ganz genauer*) union (*Verbindung*) with Jesus, their Saviour. 1 Corinthians 10:16. Furthermore, it serves as a sign of the covenant and fellowship of believers v. 17, and not as a sign of the fellowship of believers and unbelievers with one another, as it is presently practiced. This is likewise stated in Menno Simons' *Grundfundament* (basic doctrines), Vol. I, pp. 115-121. Page 121 reads: If someone errs in doctrine and faith, and walks in the flesh, he can in no case be permitted to fellowship with the godfearing and repentant. . . ." In 1 Corinthians 5:11 the apostle Paul states: If any man that is called a brother be a fornicator, or covetous, or an idolater, or a railer, or a drunkard, or an extortioner; with such an one no not to eat. How much less partake of holy communion with him? Unfortunately, there are many covetous, drunkards and blasphemers with whom one shares the Lord's Supper, for not only those are drunkards who are almost continually under the influence of liquor, but also those who occasionally gorge themselves with food and drink at markets and taverns. 1 Corinthians 10:20-21 says "that the things which the Gentiles sacrifice, they sacrifice to devils." Likewise also, those who walk in the flesh cannot glorify God in the communion, because they do not know him, but as usual they serve the devil herewith, for no man can serve two masters. Matthew 6:24. Now the apostle did not want the believers to have fellowship with the devil and the idolater who serves the devil, and thus become one body. For as there is one bread, so also those who partake are one body. 1 Corinthians 10:17. In Revelation 18:4 the Saviour says, "Come out of her, my people, that ye be not partakers of her sins, and that ye receive not of her plagues." 2 Corinthians 6 states that believers shall have no fellowship with unbelievers, but shall come out from among them, and be separate.

g) Regarding footwashing, we confess that the Lord Jesus instituted it, John 13; to be practiced among one another, for the blessing is in the deed, not in knowledge.

h) Teachers (preachers) may be called in two Scriptural ways: Some are chosen by God alone, without human assistance, and sent out by His Spirit, as were the prophets and apostles, and also the house of Stephanas was self-appointed to the ministry of the saints. 1 Corinthians 26:15. Such are also mentioned by Paul in 1 Timothy 3. Others are called through the instrumentality of true believers, as recorded in Acts 1. Menno recognized this, as he clearly proves in his *Grundfundament* (basic doctrine), Vol. I, p. 148.

i) Regarding the ban, we confess that all carnal and reprobate sinners must be banned from the fellowship of believers, as Paul states in 2 Thessalonians 3:14-15. In the event that someone falls into a carnal sin (God save us from it), and the Spirit of Christ, who alone can work true repentance, convicts him of his sin, so that he confesses and repents; in that case, the church has no authority to ban such a repentant sinner, because the forgiveness of sin is not obtained in or through the ban, but by the merit of Jesus Christ. This was also Menno's conviction, as recorded in Vol. III, p. 334 and 335. However, an unrepentant sinner may not be accepted into the fellowship of believers, until he be genuinely converted to Christ.

k) In all other articles of our confession, we are in full agreement with Menno Simons.

Elizabethal, January 6, 1860.
Abraham Cornelssen. Corn. Wiens. Isaak Koop. Franz Klaassen. Abr. Wiens. Martin Klaassen. Abr. Wiens. Daniel Hoppe. August Strauss. Jakob Boecker. Isaak Regehr. Andr. Voth. Jakob Wall. Joh. Claassen. Heinrich Huebert. Peter Stobbe. Abr. Peters. Diedrich Claassen. [31]

The brethren added a footnote to this document, informing the elders that if they desired to communicate with the fellowship in this matter, the brethren Cornelsen, Koop and Claassen had been appointed as their representatives.

A brief evaluation of this "Document of Secession" is in order. In the first place, it must not be regarded as a Confession of Faith, since it was composed too hurriedly and too much under the pressures of the immediate circumstance. It is, however, a statement that reveals the causes for the formation of the Mennonite Brethren Church, and the doctrinal position of the Brethren on some of the crucial and controversial issues of that day.

In the second place it may be noted, that the main charges brought against the "decadent church" were never publicly refuted by the elders. On the contrary, the elder of the Ohrloff Church generally agreed with the views of the Brethren regarding the moral and spiritual conditions within the churches, even though he disapproved of their proposed remedy.

On the other hand it should be pointed out that the charges brought against the church and its ministers (*Lehrer*) were far too sweeping and too severe in character. There were still some devoted and deeply concerned leaders in the pulpit, and many fine Christians in the pews. Men such as Bernhard Fast, Johann Harder (both elders of the Ohrloff Church), Bernhard Harder, the great evangelist and teacher, and even August Lenzmann, elder of Gnadenfeld — all actively opposed corruption and worked earnestly for the spiritual renewal of the church. It would appear that in the heat of battle, the brethren had temporarily forgotten the spiritual nurture they had received in the "mother churches."

Lastly, this document clearly and emphatically expresses the desire of the Brethren to remain true to the historic Anabaptist-Mennonite confession. They consciously saw themselves related to sixteenth century evangelical Anabaptism. "They did not want to be Pietistic, nor Baptist, but rather Mennonite. They wanted to be and remain historical consistent Mennonitism, a pure Mennonitism that was based not upon birth, but upon rebirth."[32]

3. *Beginnings in Chortitza*

A similar and yet somewhat distinctive new life movement originated almost simultaneously, yet independently, in the Chortitza colony. Religious and moral conditions here were even more deplorable than in the Molotschna. In 1853, however, a spiritual awakening took place in the village of Kronsweide. A young man, Johann Loewen, came to a saving knowledge of Christ through the reading of Hofacker's sermons.[33] Through his fervent testimony, some fifty persons, mostly young people, had a similar experience. As a result of both a lack of teaching and also false teaching the group was misled into a false freedom. After the moral lapses of several members the whole group was put under the church ban and the movement was discredited.

Fortunately, a new fellowship center in Chortitza developed in the village of Einlage under the sane leadership of such brethren as Abraham Unger, Heinrich Neufeld and Cornelius Unger. In the years 1859 and 1860 the group here became well established through devotional Bible study (*Bibelstunden*) and the reading of Christian literature. Some of this literature was obtained from the German Baptists. Abraham Unger, in his search for spiritual enlightenment. began to correspond with J. G. Oncken, a Baptist preacher in Hamburg. This initial contact led to increasing Baptist influence in the Chortitza groups. This influence became a major controversial issue in the early M. B. Church as will be shown later.

In 1861, the Einlage Brethren established contact with the Molotschna group and discovered that the latter had begun to baptize and in some instances rebaptize those who had experienced God's forgiveness and grace. In the spring of 1862, Abraham Unger, Heinrich Neufeld and a third brother visited the Molotschna Brethren and there, on March 4, these three received baptism on the confession of their faith.[34] One week later these Brethren baptized eighteen others in the Dnieper River near Einlage. Hence March 11, 1862, is generally accepted as the "Founders' Day" of the Einlage M. B. Church. Contrary to the early policy of the Molotschna Brethren, the church here made baptism by immersion the prerequisite for membership and a requirement for participation in communion from the very beginning.

The Brethren here were subjected to the same kind of repressive measures as their fellow-believers in the Molotschna. The account of this struggle for survival and recognition is the story of the next chapter.

Chapter 4

Through Storm and Stress

The late German Chancellor, Conrad Adenauer, once defined history as "the sum total of things that could have been avoided." The early history of the Mennonite Brethren Church contains many things that could have been avoided by more tolerance and discernment on the part of ecclesiastical and civil authorities, and by a little more discretion and moderation on the part of some early Brethren. However, Mennonite historians in recent years have been generally agreed that the major responsibility for the harassment and ill-treatment of the dissenting group must be placed upon the church leadership of that day.[1]

The submission of the Document of Secession to the *Kirchenkonvent* set off a chain reaction, the magnitude of which in all probability had not been foreseen by the Brethren. Although the Mennonites had always held to the doctrine of the separation of church and state in principle, their historical experience in Russia had produced a system which Adolf Ehrt has described as the "Preacher-Landowner-Colony Administrator-Complex" (*Prediger-Wirt-Schulz Komplex*).[2] In many instances church and civil officials collaborated to use coercion to advance what they considered to be the best interests of church and colony. This blending of interests is evident in the reactions to the secession of the Brethren.

OPPOSITION TO SECESSION
Opposition to secession came from several sources.

Reaction of the Elders

The first reaction came from the *Kirchenkonvent*. As soon as the elders had received copies of the Document of Secession, they called a meeting for January 18 at Alexanderwohl to discuss the matter. Strangely enough, the Colony Administrator, sometimes referred to as District Elder,[3] had also been invited to this meeting. According to

Jacob Becker, five of the six elders present "insisted that the seceding members be turned over to the District Court for prosecution."[4] There appears to be strong circumstantial evidence that David Friesen, the Colony Administrator, had a decisive influence on the formulation of the elders' response. Against the protest of elder Bernhard Fast and the Ohrloff-Halbstadt Church Council, (who had insisted on reform of church life on the basis of Scripture), the five elders signed a letter addressed to the Colony Administrative Office in which they state that the organization of an independent church cannot be tolerated and that the Colony Administrative Office should do its part in dissuading these people from their erroneous endeavor. The statement is signed by the church elders Heinrich Toews, Benjamin Ratzlaff, Peter Wedel, Dirk Warkentin, August Lenzmann.[5]

In a later explanation the five elders claimed to have exhausted all means at their disposal to persuade the erring members, with all "love and earnestness" to forsake their erroneous views, but without success.[6] This claim is not supported by any evidence. It is inconceivable that they had exhausted "all means at their disposal" in the short time of less than twelve days. Communications in midwinter were slow. By the time the document reached the last elder, several days must have passed. Not even an attempt to contact them "in love and earnestness" was made during this period.[7] Pastor Dobbert of the Lutheran settlement of Prischib calls this statement of the elders "a testimony of poverty."[8] They apparently lacked the spiritual resources to meet this crisis and hence resorted to "worldly weapons" in this conflict.

Reaction of District Officials

As might be expected, the second reaction to the secession of the Brethren came from the Colony Administrative Office (*Gebietsamt*). David Friesen, the powerful executive in the Colony Administrative Office, had no sympathy for the dissenters and "disturbers of public peace." He immediately contacted the three appointed representatives of the Brethren and demanded an explanation. In a clear, concise statement the Brethren explained "that all of us would have preferred to stay in our own congregations; but since the teachers — as explained in our document of January 6, do not act in accordance with God's Word, we can not do this for conscience' sake, and (hence) desire to form our own church as Mennonites."[9]

Obviously this explanation fell on deaf ears, because four days later, on January 27, 1860, a letter went out to all village offices (*Schulzenaemter*) prohibiting all religious gatherings on the basis of Article 362 of the Russian Penal Code. The article in question, issued in 1857, dealt with members of secret societies, and was intended primarily to curb the activities of political agitators and counter-revolutionaries.

According to this article, members of such societies were to be arrested and upon conviction, punished by imprisonment from one to three weeks; leaders of such groups were to be subject to a prison term from six months to one year. The village mayors were given strict orders to enforce this statute and report any violation immediately to the Colony Administrative Office. In their response to this unreasonable accusation the Brethren declared that they had no intention of forming secret societies; their only desire was to lead souls to Christ and organize a church in a peaceful way.

Reaction of Colonial Inspector

When Friesen realized that he could not frighten the Brethren into submission by his tactics, he ordered the three deputies to appear before Inspector Andrea, a member of the Supervisory Commission. The Inspector used subtle diplomacy to achieve his end. He expressed sympathy with the intentions of the Brethren to organize their own church. According to Becker, he assured them that religious freedom existed for all organized churches in Russia. However, a new fellowship would need to secure permission to organize before it could receive government sanction and approval.[10] The Inspector expressed his willingness to assist them in procuring the necessary documents, on the condition that they would promise to refrain from any further steps in organizing a new church until they had received express permission from the higher authorities. The Brethren Claassen, Cornelsen and Koop signed the prepared statement on February 10, 1860. Claassen later recalled, that before he reached home it dawned on him that this had been a foolish move, for the government would never grant such permission.[11] He resolved never again to ask for permission to organize, but only to request recognition of, and rights for an existing church.

In discussing this matter with the group at home, the Brethren came to the conclusion that the pledge made by them could not be binding for the whole fellowship, since it did not as yet constitute an organized church. The members of the little flock, nevertheless, were deeply grieved by this incident, since it barred the three Brethren, who had signed the pledge, from taking an active part in the organization and leadership of the group. It was during these crucial days, according to Harms, that many other brethren renounced their membership in the "old" church and joined the new movement, for "they would rather suffer tribulation with the seceders, than to participate in the persecution of God's children."[12]

INTERPRETATION OF SECESSION

It is interesting, though somewhat ironical, that after the summary indictment by church and state officials, the process of gathering more information about the new movement began. At the special request of Inspector Andrea, David Friesen, the Colony Administrator, sent a questionnaire to all elders on March 5, 1860. It contained the following questions:

1. What is the essential nature of this new religious movement?

2. What harmful effects could it have for the Mennonite Brotherhood?

3. What measures must be taken for the dissolution of this group?[13]

The Majority Report

All elders were asked to appear in person in the Colony Administrative Office on March 11 to present their answers. On the designated day the aforementioned five elders responded in a written statement, a summary of which follows.

1. *The Nature of their erroneous views:*

a) A one-sided interpretation of Scripture, coupled with the claim that their understanding and application of Scripture passages is the only true interpretation — hence they are not open to instruction.

b) A disrespect for church order and organization, as seen, for instance, in their observance of communion in private homes.

c) A presumptuous attitude, considering themselves to be the only true Christians.

2. *The Consequences for the Mennonite Brotherhood:*

a) The nature of their secession shows that a peaceful coexistence with them would be impossible.

b) The permission to organize a new church would result in disorder, and promote fanaticism (*Schwaermerei*).

c) The intermarriage of our members with theirs would lead to lamentable rifts in family relationships.

d) The agitation of the seceding members would draw other "innocent and well-meaning" people into the movement.

3. *The Means to be taken against the movement:*

We cannot give our permission for the formation of a new church. Since we have done our best to dissuade them from the error of their way, though without success, we have submitted this matter to the Colony Administrative Office. We do not think it is within our jurisdiction to recommend to "worldly authorities" the nature of their further treatment or punishment, but request that "moderate measures be used to bring these erring ones to a knowledge of their guilt — before ultimate steps are taken."[14]

The statement was signed on behalf of all (*saemtlichen*) church elders, even though Bernhard Fast (Ohrloff) could not attend for reasons

of health, and Johann Friesen (*Kleine Gemeinde*) was also absent. When
Elder Fast received the statement for his signature, he refused to sign
because of insufficient information about the movement. In his
preliminary reply to the Colony Administrative Office he also insisted
that elder Johann Friesen of the *Kleine Gemeinde* be contacted, since
the Inspector (Andrea) desired an explanation from all church elders.
"From now on Ohrloff became the protector of the Brethren until their
ultimate triumph."[15]

The Minority Report

Fortunate for the cause of the Brethren, the elders of Ohrloff and
Neukirch (*Kleine Gemeinde*) did not concur with the majority report of
the five elders.

The elder of the *Kleine Gemeinde*, Johann Friesen, no doubt
conscious of the severe struggle for recognition of his own group some
thirty years earlier, responded to the request with extreme caution. In a
letter dated March 24, 1860, he asked that no political means be
employed against the movement, but if necessary, church discipline be
practiced according to Paul's teaching in 2 Thessalonians 3:14.[16]

Of much greater significance in this encounter with the authorities
was the response of the tolerant elders of the Ohrloff Church. The ailing
elder Bernhard Fast resigned from his office and ordained Johann
Harder as his successor on March 17, 1860. The new elder was a man of
moral integrity and of deep concern for the spiritual renewal of the
church. He shared the conviction of his predecessor, that more firsthand
information on the new movement was necessary before any verdict
could be reached. To obtain this information, four brethren (the three
deputies and Heinrich Huebert) were invited by the Church Council
(*Kirchenvorstand*) of Ohrloff for discussion and consultation. (It should
be mentioned that Huebert had been a highly respected member of the
Ohrloff Church.) This was the first direct official contact of any leaders
of the "old" church with representatives of the Brethren. The Brethren
were shown a copy of the report of the five elders, and were asked to
prepare a written response.

In this document, to which thirty-three signatures are attached, the
Brethren refute the charges of the five elders. In their introduction they
point out that they have not renounced the Mennonite Brotherhood, but
only the corrupt churches. More specifically, they refute several
accusations as follows (given in brief):

First, a) Our exposition of Scripture is not one-sided. If this were so,
why have they (the elders) not responded to our plea to prove from
Scripture that we are wrong.

b) We respect church organization (*Kirchenordnung*), as can be seen from our statement of January 6.

c) We do not consider ourselves the only true Christians, and are ready to concede at any time that there can be other true Christians, known only to the Lord.

Second, We do not intend to form a new religious society, but to live as Mennonites according to the confession of our Fathers, in peaceful co-existence with others.

Third, We have not severed our relationship with the Mennonite Brotherhood, as stated above. With joy we would even now (at this late hour!) return to our churches and assist them in building and planting, if the ministers (*Lehrer*) would earnestly oppose corruption according to the Word of God.[17]

This explanation, received directly from the Brethren, served as the basis of Elder Harder's further communications with the administrative officials. In his first letter, dated March 25, 1860, Harder states that the Brethren are open to instruction and correction, and that they have even expressed a desire to return to their churches. To achieve such a reconciliation, however, he recommends "another way," the way of genuine reform on the basis of Scripture.[18] This "other way" was not acceptable to the five elders, nor to the administrative officials in Halbstadt. Elder Harder received another curt letter from the Colony Administrative Office in which he was advised to give clear and definite answers to the three specific questions submitted. Harder's second reply must have brought even greater dismay and disappointment to the hierarchy than his first response. Here is the body of his letter:

> *First*, the aspiration of these people finds expression in the desire to establish their own church on the foundation and confession of all other Mennonite Churches, and in keeping with our highly esteemed religious freedom, live according to their faith in the midst of the other churches in the hope that thus they will be able to establish a better church order. If they will pursue this goal, then *secondly*, the consequences need not be detrimental to the whole, and the single deviation in the manner they observed holy communion should be forgiven them. This, everyone that has learned to appreciate the mercy of God, and the benevolent toleration that we enjoy in this land, will be prepared to do wholeheartedly. *Thirdly*, the means to be used to dissuade these people from their intention to establish a church of their own, is, that we all begin in real earnest to act according to the Word of God, that the level of our church order (*Gemeindeordnung*) be raised, and the church be positively changed, for which God in his grace may grant us the power to will and to do. . . .[19]

Although this "minority report" was not accepted by the administrative officials, it served a very useful purpose: it prevented the authorities from taking any drastic action against the Brethren.[20] But complete freedom in the exercise of their faith was still several years away, and the pathway to that goal was often blocked by almost insurmountable barriers.

RECOGNITION OF SECESSION

1. *Recognition from the State*

By divine providence, Johann Claassen (1820-1876) became the trailblazer in the prolonged struggle for the civil and religious liberties of the Brethren. By nature, disposition and experience he was uniquely endowed for this special mission. Claassen was a Christian with a childlike faith in God, a fervent love for Christ, a deep concern for the brotherhood, and a man of indomitable moral courage. P. M. Friesen rates him with Johann Cornies and Bernhard Harder as one of the greatest contributors to the cause of Mennonitism in Russia.[21] His small business, as well as his active involvement with the *Bruderschule* in Gnadenfeld, had widened his horizons and given him a practical, experiential knowledge of men and their affairs. In the cause of Christian education Claassen made two trips to Petersburg (1854 and 1857) and through the Supervisory Commission in Odessa, secured recognition of the school as a teacher-training institution for Mennonites. This experience was an invaluable preparation for the difficult assignment a few years later.

Claassen's First Trip to Petersburg

When in March, 1860, the threats of local authorities became increasingly menacing against the cause of the Brethren, Claassen resolved that the time for decisive action had come. After brief consultations with his wife, his brother-in-law Cornelius Reimer, and his close friend Heinrich Huebert, he suddenly disappeared on the night of March 29. Claassen was on his way to Petersburg to seek help from the Russian government. He made his way to Charkow on horseback. From Charkow to Moscow he traveled by mail-coach. He had left none too soon — the following morning representatives of the Colony Administrative Office appeared at his home to arrest him.

Claassen's first mission to Petersburg was not very successful. He accomplished "little enough" and realized that "the matter is very difficult."[22] In his contacts in Petersburg he learned one thing, however: the Brethren would have to organize as a church in order to make effective representation of their cause possible. He returned to the Molotschna on May 23, 1860, in order to encourage the Brethren to do just that. A week after Claassen's return, on May 30, Heinrich Huebert and Jacob Becker were elected as minister and associate minister, respectively. With the ordination of these men on June 5, the basic organizational pattern was completed.

This election of ministers did not ease tensions between the Brethren and local authorities. Several days after their ordination Huebert and Becker were summoned to appear at the Colony

6. Johann Claassen   7. Heinrich Huebert

Administrative Office to explain their action, in the same manner as
Claassen had been asked immediately after his return from Petersburg.
According to Lohrenz, the two ministers were asked to make a promise
not to baptize, which they refused to do.[23] Throughout the summer
months the Brethren were subjected to intimidations and threats. The
gathering storm finally broke after the first public baptism in
mid-September, 1860.[24] Becker, who had performed this baptism, was
summoned to appear before the administrative officials. During this
hearing Becker remained calm and unruffled, and fearlessly defended
the position of the Brethren. After giving him strict orders not to
perform any religious acts, he was released. After another baptism
somewhat later, the Colony Administrative Office issued a summons to
all thirty-three Brethren who had signed the statement that was
presented to the Church Council of Ohrloff, to appear in Halbstadt on
October 11. Here they were interviewed not only by the administrative
officials, but also by the five elders and five other ministers. According
to Becker, this was a final attempt to bring the members who had
seceded back into the old church. When these efforts failed, David
Friesen, Colony Administrator, addressed the Brethren as follows: "We
give you one month to think it over. If within that time you do not
return to the church, measures will be taken in earnest to execute church
verdicts against you to disfranchise you as colonists and to banish you
from our midst."[25]

When a month had passed and the Brethren had not returned to their churches, some of them were put under the ban by the elders. For some families this meant economic ruin and incredible hardships. Abraham Cornelsen, the schoolteacher from Elizabethtal, for instance, was dismissed from his position and banished from the village with his large family. He found a temporary shelter in an abandoned village of the Nogaians (a nomadic tribe). Through the intervention of a prominent member of the Gnadenfeld Church, the family was permitted to return to the colony.[26] Another member of the group, Jacob Wall, was sentenced to imprisonment and hard labor. Some years later, in 1865, Heinrich Huebert was imprisoned for ten months on a false charge of having baptized a Russian girl.[27] This experience seriously affected his health in later years. Others who desired to leave the colony were denied passports. Thus the plight of the Brethren became more and more critical.

Claassen's Second Trip to Petersburg

After the October "ultimatum"[28] from the Colony Administrator, Claassen realized that unless some higher authorities intervened, the days of the young Mennonite Brethren Church in the Molotschna colony might be numbered. That Claassen was a man of quick decision and decisive action can be seen from the fact that he left for Petersburg the day after the second major encounter of the Brethren with the officials at Halbstadt. On October 31, accompanied by his Lutheran-Pietist friend Otto Forchhammer, Claassen started out on his prolonged and difficult mission which eventually was crowned with success. Traveling by mail coach to Moscow, the trip in itself proved to be a real ordeal, especially since they experienced several serious mishaps. The long drawn-out negotiations in Petersburg (until June, 1862) constituted severe tests of faith, patience and courage for Claassen.[29]

The purpose of Claassen's mission in Petersburg was twofold: first, to obtain recognition and protection from the government for the Mennonite Brethren Church in the Molotschna; and second, to secure permission for resettlement in another part of the country. (After some preliminary discussions, in which even the *Amur* area in Eastern Siberia was under consideration, Claassen and the Brethren decided on the *Kuban* area in the Caucasus.)[30]

While Claassen was engaged in these negotiations, the Brethren in Chortitza experienced even more severe oppression than their fellow-believers in the Molotschna. Even before the church was officially organized, strong measures were taken to prevent all private religious gatherings. Wilhelm Janzen, one of their members who attended the prayer meetings, was given ten lashes and jailed in an unheated room because he refused to promise not to attend these meetings anymore.[31] The situation of the Brethren in Chortitza reached a critical stage in

March, 1862, shortly after the first baptism. On March 29, twenty-seven Brethren were summoned to appear before the Colony Administrative Office where they were asked to discontinue their services. To this they could not consent. Then they were asked to sign a document declaring their willingness to leave the colony. This they likewise refused to do. (It may be injected here, that in Chortitza, contrary to the situation in the Molotschna, the elders apparently took no official part in dealing with the dissenting group, but left the entire matter in the hands of civic officials.) The matter of procuring some measure of relief and recognition reached a state of such urgency that the Chortitza Brethren sent one of their members, Gerhard Wieler, an exiled schoolteacher from the Molotschna, to Petersburg to work together with Claassen in the common cause.

Claassen's numerous connections with high government officials and with prominent "evangelicals" in the aristocracy of Petersburg were a major factor in the eventual success of his venture. In a private letter to his wife he lists the people with whom he associated during his stay in the capital; the list reads like a "Who's Who" among the elite of Petersburg.[32] When Claassen applied to the Molotschna Colony Administrative Office for a renewal of his passport, his request was denied. He went for counsel to his gracious friend, Senator von Hahn, who informed him that a citizen who had paid his taxes could not be denied a passport. He permitted Claassen to use his name in the communications with the Colony Administrative Office. After some delay, the petition for renewal was granted. Claassen's "connections" were a matter of curiosity among the villagers and a matter of extreme displeasure among ecclesiastical and civil authorities in the Molotschna.

Claassen's mission culminated in a special petition presented to the Russian Tsar on May 21, 1862. In the preamble of this document an account is given of the circumstances under which the Mennonite Brethren Church originated. The petition emphasizes the fact that the Brethren intend to form a church in the spirit of strict and true disciples of the Gospel and of their first teacher, Menno Simons.[33] The Brethren find historical precedent for their venture in the establishment of the *Kleine Gemeinde* and the *Grosse Gemeinde*, both of which have been fully recognized as Mennonite churches. The petition closes with a special appeal for protection and the request for basic freedoms:

a) Freedom of worship — without molestation and persecution from local authorities.

b) Freedom to exercise their religious and civil rights under legal protection.[34]

A similar petition was presented on June 4, 1862 by Gerhard Wieler, the deputy of the Chortitza Mennonite Brethren Church.[35]

Although the two representatives received assurances from high
government officials that their petitions would be given a favorable
hearing and response, it was only on May 30, 1866, that Claassen
received official confirmation of full religious and civil privileges for
Mennonite Brethren. The wheels of the official bureaucracy moved very
slowly in Russia. Two years earlier, on March 4, 1864, "Heinrich
Huebert and Associates" had received permission to establish a
settlement on the Kuban. This permission was given by the Land Office
upon the presentation of a written petition on December 30, 1863. The
granting of these petitions paved the way for recognition and
resettlement of the Mennonite Brethren in the two oldest Mennonite
Colonies. When numerous "daughter colonies" were established in the
last quarter of the nineteenth century, Mennonite Brethren who settled
there were given all the rights and privileges of the other colonists.

RECOGNITION FROM THE CHURCHES

Claassen's return inspired the Brethren with new confidence, but it
also aroused new opposition on the part of local authorities. In a special
letter on October 11, 1862, David Friesen, Colony Administrator in the
Molotschna, asked all elders to choose between two options for the new
group: expulsion from the colony, or recognition of their rights. In all
probability he hoped to achieve the former objective by this drastic
proposal.

A break in this tense situation came with the response of the
Ohrloff Church through its elder Johann Harder. In a letter of
November 12, 1862, he wrote:

Following the general conference held on the 11th of October, 1862, in the
colony administration building, in which the administrator proposed that the
Mennonites who had left the corrupt churches be either banished from the colony
or recognized as congregations with equal rights, our congregation, having the
matter presented to them, declared that since the former is not scriptural, it is
willing to accept the latter on the condition that their confession of faith, should
they be asked for the same, be in accordance, essentially, with ours.

As a result of our request the seceders have declared in writing that the
*Confession of Faith of the So-Called United Flemish, Frisian, and High German
Anabaptist Mennonite Church*, published by the congregation of Rudnerweide,
South Russia, was their own. Consequently, nothing hinders the Ohrloff-Halbstadt congregation from recognizing the Mennonites in question as an
independent congregation of which I now, according to our verbal agreement,
wish to inform the colony administration. [36]

This formal recognition of the Mennonite Brethren Church by the
elder of the mother church (*Stammgemeinde*) in the Molotschna marked
the turning point in the troubled history of the early Brethren. It fore-
stalled any attempt on the part of the Colony Administrative Office
(*Gebietsamt*) to send the group into Siberian exile. Senator von Hahn
was no doubt accurate in his appraisal of the situation when he said to

Claassen: "For your deliverance you are indebted to Elder Harder."[37] A year later Elder Harder also sent a personal letter to Heinrich Huebert, the leader of the Mennonite Brethren Church, in which he confirmed the formal recognition given earlier.

Much later, and with great reluctance, the other five elders submitted the proposal of the Colony Administrative Office (*Gebietsamt*) to their churches. It would appear that this was the first opportunity — three years after the secession of the Brethren — at which the members of the churches could express themselves on an issue of crucial importance to the entire Mennonite community. Although the churches could not agree on extending full recognition to the Mennonite Brethren Church, a majority of the members were also against exile from the colony. This decision prepared the way for an attitude of tolerance, if not acceptance, on the part of the larger Mennonite bodies. The *Kleine Gemeinde*, as always, maintained an attitude of benevolent neutrality.

Recognition did not mean complete cessation of hostile acts by individuals and local authorities. As a result of Claassen's efforts in Petersburg, the Colony Administration could no longer deny passports or impose a civil ban. Sporadic attempts to discredit and destroy the young church, however, continued for some time. One such attempt was made by the administration of the colony later in 1863, by ordering village officials not to recognize marriages performed by the Brethren. The children of such marriages were to be recorded in the mother's maiden name as in the case of illegitimate births. The employment of such shameful tactics roused the Brethren to send a petition to the Russian government's Department of the Interior in which they explain that "marriages are performed in the Lord according to the Word of God and in keeping with the Confession of Faith of the Anabaptist-Mennonite congregations."[38] The petition was answered on March 5, 1864, with the coveted government recognition that they were still considered Mennonites, and that all restrictions on their marriages were to be lifted. Moreover, they were also granted official permission to resettle in the Caucasus. The attack upon their marriages was related to this question, since the Brethren were required to register as families for the purpose of resettlement. Although formal litigation came to an end, the "marriage question" in the Molotschna was not satisfactorily solved until the retirement of David Friesen from the office of chief administrator of the colony in 1865.

The controversies, misrepresentations and mistreatments engendered much bitterness which poisoned the relationship between the two groups for many years. Gradually some things were forgotten, others were rectified and leaders as well as members began to cooperate in matters of common concern. This process of reconciliation reached a historic milestone at the Centennial Conference of the Mennonite Brethren Churches held in 1960 in Reedley, California, when the President of the General Conference Mennonite Church, Erland Waltner, presented the "Centennial Study Conference Statement to Mennonite Brethren." Because of its historic significance it is given here in full as a fitting and pleasant conclusion to an unpleasant chapter of Mennonite Brethren history.

Greetings to the Mennonite Brethren in the observance of their centennial year.

We, the delegates of the General Conference Mennonite Church, assembled in our Centennial Study Conference at Donnellson, Iowa from June 20-23 to discuss the theme "Christian Unity in Faith and Witness" wish to convey brotherly concerns and greetings in the spirit of Ephesians 4:13, "Till we all come in the unity of the faith, and of the knowledge of the Son of God, unto a perfect man, unto the measure of the stature of the fullness of Christ."

During these days of fellowship and prayer and serious study of the Scriptures we are reminded of our common unbroken heritage of 335 years, from 1525 to 1860. We regret, however, that circumstances and events developed so that a rupture in the brotherhood occurred a century ago.

We, of this generation, do not really know the details of the events that led to separation. We are, however, sorry for all feelings, words and deeds expressed by our fathers in an unbrotherly way and in a manner contrary to the spirit of Christ. We are sorry that these events resulted in such an intense break within the Anabaptist-Mennonite brotherhood, that for a full century two parallel lines of explanation have been advanced as to the historical facts and that these parallel explanations are still perpetuated today.

We recognize the need for spiritual renewal that existed within the Mennonite brotherhood in Russia a century ago and we now feel constrained by our Lord to seek for more discussion as to what did happen in Russia, and thus understand that which now prevents us as a new generation of the church from having a closer fellowship.

It is our prayer that for the sake of the Gospel of Jesus Christ, the sake of our children, and in behalf of a more united Mennonite witness within the Christian brotherhood, efforts be made in the spirit of humility to explore ways in which we could develop a closer fellowship in such areas where we live and work side by side.

In spite of human weaknesses, we thank God for the way He has used both conferences to proclaim the Gospel, and for those common experiences of service such as MCC and in the Congo which have enriched our respective fellowships.[39]

Had the spirit and sentiment of this statement been predominant in the Mennonite brotherhood in 1860, the schism would probably have been avoided.

Chapter 5

Faith in Ferment

The early history of the Mennonite Brethren Church is not only characterized by controversy and conflict in its relations to church and state, but also by internal tension and turbulence among its members. As in the beginning of many other new life movements, faith was in a state of ferment, and church order in a state of flux. The search for a new expression of worship and witness, and the attempt to restore a New Testament believers' church in both pattern and polity, was not always guided by an enlightened understanding of Scripture, even though the motivation was unquestionably sincere. It is important, however, to see this religious ferment in its social, historical and theological context in order to understand it properly.

Before we enter upon a discussion of the underlying causes and expressions of this ferment it might be well to examine the theory that the religious agitation and protest of the early Brethren was merely an extension of their economic problem. On the assumption that most of them belonged to the landless proletariat, such an explanation appears natural and logical. The following analysis is typical of this approach:

> As was the case of the Anabaptist movement in Reformation times, the *Bruedergemeinde*-movement found its adherents chiefly in the lower strata of society. This can be clearly proved by the fact that the *Bruedergemeinde* was much stronger in the newer colonies, which were composed chiefly of the former landless groups, than it was in the two old mother colonies. [1]

Too much significance has been attached to this "economic theory" in explaining the origin of the Mennonite Brethren. Although economic motivation can not be ruled out, this interpretation does not take all the facts into account.

The early Brethren were found chiefly in the eastern part of the Molotschna colony, in the villages that had been established more recently, and where the landless problem was not as acute as in the older (western) part of the settlement. The fact that the Mennonite Brethren

51

were stronger in some of the daughter colonies cannot simply be explained in terms of economic motivation. Religious oppression and even persecution in the Molotschna Colony, played a major role in the establishment of the Kuban settlement in late 1863.

The records also show that many members of the new group did not come from the "lower strata of society." Johann Claassen was owner of a flourishing retail business in Liebenau.[2] He was a strong promoter and generous supporter of the *Bruderschule* in Gnadenfeld. He apparently paid his expense accounts in Petersburg largely out of his own pocket. As has already been mentioned, he associated freely with the "upper strata" of society in Petersburg. Jacob Reimer of Felsental was owner and proprietor of a large and attractive estate.[3] He was also one of the founders of the *Bruderschule*, and later of the *Armenschule* (school for the poor). Abraham Unger of Einlage, Chortitza, owned a large wagon factory in which he employed up to sixteen men.[4] Isaak Matthies was one of the wealthier businessmen of the Molotschna colony before his economic ruin caused by the religious and civil ban.[5] At least four of the early leaders belonged to the teaching profession: Abraham Cornelsen, Daniel Fast, Gerhard Wieler and Johann Wieler. The father of Abraham Friesen, first missionary of the Mennonite Brethren to India, was a wealthy manufacturer.[6] That the Mennonite Brethren did not chiefly belong to the landless group can be seen from a resolution of the church which stipulated that members should abstain from any involvement on either side of the landless-landowner conflict.[7] Thus it would appear that although economic conditions may have contributed to the religious restlessness of that period, their primary significance cannot be established.

The spiritual ferment in the early Mennonite Brethren movement is closely connected with several questions related to the organization and practice of the church.

1. *The Problem of Church Leadership*

Historians of this period tend to agree that the early Mennonite Brethren Church suffered, especially in the Molotschna, from lack of proper leadership. In the election of ministers on May 30, 1860, two potential candidates for the leadership, Claassen and Cornelsen, were not considered because of their pledge given to Colonial Inspector Andrea a few months earlier. That tragic mistake had serious consequences for the growth and inner stability of the young church. There would be reasons to agree with Friesen who thinks that the whole development of the M. B. church would have been more wholesome if Cornelsen had been elected as leader (or elder) and Claassen and Huebert as his "associate elders."[8] Cornelsen, the author of the Document of Secession, in whose personality keen discernment, moral courage and a cool, even temper were happily blended, would have been the ideal "elder" to guide the group through its early period of storm and stress. Claassen, with his tremendous drive and energy, and with his experience and knowledge in public affairs, would have provided the needed initiative in blazing new trails. Huebert, the quiet thinker and perhaps only "theologian" of the group, could have conserved his strength for teaching and pastoral ministries in the growing congregation. Because of his ordination as leading minister, and later as elder, Huebert had to bear the brunt of the opposition from without, and also became the chief target of the unruly elements from within.

With Cornelsen excluded from active participation, and with Claassen absent from the church for almost two years (because of his mission in Petersburg), the movement lacked strong, positive leadership, and thus became very vulnerable to false teaching and to the influence of immature, self-appointed leaders. True, this weakness was rectified later by the emergence of a new leadership, and by Claassen's return and active involvement in the solution of the crucial problems the church faced at the time, but the costs in terms of lost spiritual vitality and of a positive witness in the Mennonite community, can hardly be over-estimated. Friesen reminds us that even the slightest deviation from God's perfect will, whether it is against better knowledge or because of willful ignorance on the part of church leaders, always has resulted in serious consequences for God's people, especially for a young religious movement.[9]

In Chortitza the early Mennonite Brethren Church also experienced serious leadership difficulties. Already before the official organization of the church, in 1859-1861, Abraham Unger, the recognized leader of the group, was corresponding with J. G. Oncken, the Baptist preacher in Hamburg and was seriously considering inviting the Baptists to assist the Brethren in the formation of a new church. Gerhard Wieler convinced him that this would not be in the best interests of the group.[10]

Unger's Baptist leanings had the effect of polarizing the group theologically. Moreover, his associate minister took sides against him during the period of excessive emotionalism, which Unger tried to combat. The unruly elements made Unger's leadership so difficult that he finally resigned. Eight brethren then united to send a request for help to Hamburg. In the spring of 1866, August Liebig, an ordained Baptist minister, came to serve the Brethren with his counsel and teaching.

Liebig's ministry was highly beneficial and greatly appreciated. He brought the unruly brethren to order by serving as chairman at their meetings! Liebig realized that much of the confusion and controversy within the congregation could be attributed to the fact that the brethren kept no "minutes" of their deliberations. This absence of any records

8. Johann Harder   9. Abraham Unger

made it easy for self-willed individuals to resort to arbitrary procedures and change or modify previous resolutions accepted by the group. Liebig's suggestions on how to keep minutes were readily accepted. Moreover, he taught them the elementary aspects of parliamentary procedure; e.g., that the speaker must rise before he addresses the congregation, that he must speak to the church and not become personal, and that he must not speak more than three times on any question under discussion "in order that the mind of the church be revealed." When these simple rules were not observed, he would call the meeting to order by saying: "God is a God of order!"[11] Those members who had monopolized the discussions in the past were not too happy with these innovations; but the majority accepted these practical suggestions with deep appreciation.

Liebig's ministry lasted only two weeks. Local Mennonite authorities had him arrested and deported. His ministry, however, marks the beginning of a new period of constructive development in the Chortitza Mennonite Brethren Church.

An analysis of the problems of the Mennonite Brethren Church during this early period leads to the conclusion that the divinely ordained role of the leadership for congregational life was not sufficiently recognized and appreciated by most members. The negative reaction against the arbitrary and oppressive leadership of the established church influenced the Brethren (no doubt unknowingly) to develop a negative attitude toward a properly constituted, scriptural authority of the ministry. At times, equality and fraternity were emphasized at the expense of proper authority.

2. *The Mode of Baptism*

Contrary to popular opinion, the question of the mode of baptism was not an issue for the first group of Brethren. In the Document of Secession they simply stress the importance of believer's baptism: "Concerning baptism we confess it to be upon faith, as a seal of faith, but not upon a memorized belief as it is now being practiced. . . . "[12] In 1837, Jacob Reimer, one of the early leaders, had already begun to question whether sprinkling or pouring were biblical modes. As an eighteen-year-old, before his baptism, he had read the biography of Anne Judson and had expressed the desire to be baptized by immersion. When he asked his father whether there were still people who baptized by immersion, the latter answered that he had learned to know such people in Prussia in 1835. (The German Baptist Church originated in 1834.)

The first baptism by immersion, according to early records, was performed on September 23, 1860. The *Origin of the Mennonite Brethren Church* by Jacob Becker throws some light on the development that led to the introduction of the practice of immersion in the Mennonite Brethren Church. He writes:

> At that time (June 1860) we knew nothing about immersion. . . . After three months, however, two sisters who had not as yet been baptized by sprinkling in the church, desired to be baptized by us. Their testimony before the congregation was satisfactory, and I was to perform the baptism. Then he who had been in Petersburg (Claassen) took me aside and asked: If you are going to baptize how are you going to do it; are you going to sprinkle and pour? This to me was a strange language, and I didn't know how to answer.[13]

Subsequently the mode of baptism became a central issue for study and discussion and added to the religious ferment in the new church. Claassen had cited several New Testament illustrations and had given Becker a pamphlet on baptism. Becker studied it carefully with his friend Heinrich Bartel. They both came to the conviction that they had not been baptized on true faith, nor by the proper mode, and that they themselves would need to be baptized before they could baptize others. Fearful lest the elders and government officials might interpret this as proof that they were indeed organizing a new religious fellowship, Becker began to read the works of Menno Simons to see whether he confessed baptism in water. To his consolation he found a reference in which Menno states "that baptism has changed many times since the time of the Apostles but the Apostolic baptism was no other than in uninhibited water."[14]

Although Becker and Bartel now were convinced they had scriptural as well as historical proofs for immersion, they did not proceed independently, but presented the matter to the church for consideration and approval. At the church meeting they discovered that other members had become familiar with baptism by immersion through the reading of religious books and periodicals. The majority of the Brethren agreed with Becker and it was decided that he should baptize the sisters who had applied for baptism, by immersion. He himself, however, felt that he would first need to be immersed. This is how he describes the historic event: "Soon thereafter . . . in the month of September, 1860, a wagon loaded with members drove to the water where we first knelt for prayer. Then we stepped into the water. Jacob Becker baptized Bartel, and then Bartel baptized Becker. The latter then baptized three others."[15]

During Claassen's absence in the winter of 1860-61, there were no baptisms, but communion was observed frequently. According to Becker, a number of the members of the seceded group "were not yet sufficiently rooted and grounded for baptism by immersion."[16] After further study and orientation during the winter months, baptisms were resumed during the Easter season of 1861.

The early Brethren did not make immersion obligatory for those who had been baptized by sprinkling or pouring in the Mennonite Church. Many had been baptized after a genuine conversion experience in the old church,[17] and did not consider the mode of baptism important enough to warrant "rebaptism." Heinrich Huebert, the first minister and elder of the Mennonite Brethren Church, was baptized in May, 1861, a year after his election as a minister. Johann Claassen highly esteemed among the Brethren, was not baptized until after June 30, 1862. As late as September, 1863, it was possible for non-immersed members to partake of communion, although by that time this may have been an exception.[18]

Throughout the first two years of Mennonite Brethren history this question repeatedly came up for discussion and was also the subject of an animated correspondence with Baptist and Mennonite leaders. By 1862, immersion had been established as the general practice in both colonies. It should be noted that developments in Chortitza differed from those in the Molotschna. Abraham Unger who had been under the influence of the German Baptists from Hamburg, considered baptism by immersion a prerequisite for church membership. Thus organized church life began in Chortitza only after the leaders and members had submitted to baptism by immersion in the spring of 1862. The strict view of the Chortitza Brethren finally prevailed in all Mennonite Brethren churches. As a result, a number of members in the Molotschna withdrew from the church, among them four brethren who had signed the Document of Secession. P. M. Friesen, a life-long advocate of "open communion" laments this move toward a "closed communion," with participation by immersed members only.[19] As will be shown later, the question of an "open communion" came up for discussion again and again in later years, and by the time of the Mennonite Brethren Centennial in 1960 it had become an accepted practice in most local churches. On the issue of the mode of baptism, so closely related to the question of "open communion," the General Conference of Mennonite Brethren in 1963 accepted a resolution which reflects the attitude of the Brethren "as it was in the beginning." Part of the resolution reads: "As a brotherhood we permit local churches to accept into fellowship believers who have been baptized upon an experiential and confessed faith with a mode of baptism other than immersion."[20]

3. The Manner of Public Worship

The fervor and ferment of faith also found expression in the meetings of the early Brethren. In his description of the new movement Krahn states that "the new emphasis upon a strong personal experience of the Grace of God with its accompanying assurance of salvation produced a very sturdy and active type of Christian." He is impressed with the great zeal in their Christian witness, and the "intensely active participation of the members in the meetings of the church."[21]

The meetings of the early Brethren were characterized by informality and spontaneity. The fact that they had to meet in private homes for many years promoted such an informal atmosphere. Moreover, the use of the vernacular Low German dialect for preaching and discussion encouraged a wider participation. We are indebted to the Ohrloff Church Council for several reports on the nature of the worship services as conducted by the early Brethren. In order to form a more enlightened opinion on the new movement, the Ohrloff Mennonite Church sent special delegations to attend the services of the Brethren on three different Sundays.

Here is an account of a service held in the home of Johann Claassen, Liebenau, on July 23, 1861, during his absence on a mission in Petersburg.[22] The service was opened by singing: "Son of God, Lord of Glory." The words of this hymn, as well as of subsequent songs, were first read, since members had no song books. After singing two songs, Jacob Becker, the minister of the group, arose and offered a "long prayer." The prayer was an expression of praise and a petition for true enlightenment. Then followed more singing. With the exception of the opening and closing hymns, which were sung according to the melodies in the traditional hymnal, the songs were of a more lively nature, accompanied occasionally with handclapping and other manifestations of joy. Singing was followed by a brief exhortation of Becker, based on 1 Corinthians 2, in which he stressed Christian simplicity. He also made reference to the minstry in the Mennonite Church, stating that it is not sufficient to preach the Word of God from the pulpit — it must also be taken into the homes. The exhortation, given in the Low German language, was interrupted from time to time by comments from others, to confirm and complement what had been said. A worship season followed, in which singing and prayer alternated. The prayers reflected a sense of missionary obligation to the whole world.

Benjamin Becker, a brother of the leading minister, spoke briefly on the importance of a present and personal assurance of salvation. Before closing the service, another brother spoke briefly on Psalm 87 on the basis of which he justified the special manifestations of joy. The representatives from Ohrloff (three ministers and six members) conclude their report with these words: "On the whole, they do conduct themselves more freely than is customary in our services, but, with the exception of the unusual expressions of joy, we observed nothing that was offensive."[23] The other two reports recorded by Becker describe a similar pattern in their worship services. The "unusual expressions of joy," however, degenerated into some very unwholesome and unscriptural tendencies that almost wrecked the young church. These tendencies crystallized in the views and practices of the *Froehliche Richtung* (the joyous or exuberant movement)[24] which constitutes a painful episode in the early history of the Mennonite Brethren Church.

4. *The Danger of Excessive Emotionalism*

In every great revival movement there is the danger of "strange fire." The "great awakening" among the Russian Mennonites is no exception — it manifested all the "positive and at the same time dangerous features" of a radical renewal movement.[25] Since the *Froehliche Richtung* bears some resemblance to the modern charismatic movement, it is of particular interest to the student of church history of our day.

EARLY BEGINNINGS[26]

1. *In the Molotschna*

A general misconception needs to be dispelled at the outset. Contrary to popular opinion, the *Froehliche Richtung* did not begin *with* nor *in* the Mennonite Brethren Church — neither in the Molotschna nor in Chortitza. The movement originated in the congregation of the Evangelical Separatists at Neuhoffnung several years before the founding of the Mennonite Brethren Church. As a result of Pfarrer Eduard Wuest's preaching, a genuine revival had taken place in that church. This revival provided the occasion for the origin of the movement. Some members misinterpreted Wuest's "joyous justification-doctrine" (*Froehliche Rechtfertigungslehre*) and began to express their new joy and freedom in an unbecoming manner. When Wuest took a firm stand against the noisy and disorderly behavior of these enthusiasts, they accused him of being a pharisee and denying his own gospel. Leader of the group was a schoolteacher by the name of Kappes. According to Friesen, he was "richly endowed with a keen memory, eloquent speech, imagination and wit, and a good singer."[27] At a missions festival in 1858, Kappes and his followers left the church meeting singing and shouting in an open protest to Wuest's more moderate position. Strongly influenced by Kappes was Wilhelm Bartel, a member of the Gnadenfeld Church at the time.[28] It was through Bartel that the views and practices of the "happy brethren" were propagated among the Molotschna Brethren. Even such well-balanced and sober-minded brethren as Johann Claassen and Jacob Reimer were at first slightly influenced by this movement. Claassen's initial tolerance of these "enthusiasts" can be partly explained by his prolonged absences from the colony, and his reluctance to part company with brethren with whom he had enjoyed intimate fellowship. It must be said to their credit, that as soon as they discerned its dangerous and unscriptural features, Claassen and Reimer became the sharpest critics and most outspoken opponents of the movement.

2. *In Chortitza*

As pointed out earlier (in chapter three), a revival movement took place in the village of Kronsweide in 1853. The young converts in this group, however, were led astray by an expelled minister of the Mennonite Church. A wrong interpretation of Scripture led to Antinomian tendencies and excessive emotionalism among its members — tendencies which later characterized the *Froehliche Richtung*. This movement, which was suppressed in 1855 by a ban on all participating members, preceded a similar movement in the early Mennonite Brethren Church by some seven years.

The ideas of the *Froehliche Richtung* were brought into the Chortitza Mennonite Brethren Church by Gerhard Wieler and Benjamin Becker. Wieler, a "charismatic leader," succeeded in winning H. Neufeld, the assistant minister in Einlage, to his position. Together they indoctrinated the majority of the members with their extreme teachings, at least temporarily. After all his efforts to combat this false movement had failed, Abraham Unger resigned as leader and withdrew with a smaller group in late 1864. A closer analysis of the nature and manifestations of this movement seems necessary at this point.

SPECIAL MANIFESTATIONS

In discussing an earlier episode in Anabaptist history Smith makes the observation that the "union of intense enthusiasm with ignorance is almost sure to bear evil fruit. . . . Even knowledge of the Bible, if not backed up by a sane and well-balanced world view may not be a safeguard against religious fanaticism and spiritual anarchy."[30] This observation is also applicable, with some qualifications, to the leaders of the *Froehliche Richtung.* Their one-sided interpretation and literal application of certain passages of Scripture gave rise to practices that were unbecoming to Christians and offensive to the community.

The movement was marked by an *excessive emotionalism.* Such passages as Jeremiah 31:4, "and shall go forth in the dance of the merrymakers," and Psalm 47:1, "Clap your hands, all peoples! Shout to God with loud songs of joy!" were taken quite literally. Musical instruments played an important part in making a "joyful noise unto the Lord." The tambourin (a kind of drum) was used extensively at these meetings. The earlier emphasis on Bible study and prayer disappeared, and meetings became primarily occasions for sharing experiences and for "entertainment."[30] Unfortunately for the young church in the Molotschna, Heinrich Huebert, the leading minister, withdrew largely from his pastoral responsibilities during this crucial period (1861-1862) because of personal infirmities and the serious illness of his wife. Although opposed to the movement, he did not have the strength or courage to take an active stand, whereas Jacob Becker, his assistant, gave the "loud Brethren" wholehearted support for a while.[31] Those who participated in this noisy merrymaking considered themselves as "the sound and strong," whereas the others, who did not go along, were described as "the weak and sick." Such leading brethren as Jacob Reimer, Abraham Cornelsen, and others were put on the "sicklist" by W. Bartel in a letter to Claassen in November, 1861.[32] It is obvious from the description of their meetings that these brethren lacked the spirit of discernment and could not differentiate between true Christian joy, which is the fruit of the Spirit, and an emotional ecstasy which is psychological or sensual in nature.

The *Froehliche Richtung* also expressed itself in a *false freedom.* This "freedom-doctrine" originated in a group of five prominent brethren who were known as the "strong" and the "free." These brethren taught that in Christ all distinctions cease, for in Christ, "there is neither Jew nor Greek, there is neither slave nor free, there is neither male nor female."[33] This meant that sexual differences did not really exist in the community of believers. Moreover, the proponents of this "freedom doctrine" declared that according to Scripture, brothers and sisters in the congregation should greet one another with the "holy kiss." The so-called "sister kiss" gave rise to some serious controversies, but was categorically rejected by the majority of the church members in the Molotschna. Among the Schwabish-speaking congregations on the Volga the "sister-kiss" remained an issue for a number of years.[34] The five brethren who propagated the pernicious false freedom doctrine considered all members not in agreement with them as being carnal and still in bondage. Even when one of their group fell into grievous moral sin, they were not willing to admit that the moral lapse of this brother (as well as of two sisters) was the direct result of their false teaching. They banned the fallen brother with a self-righteous indignation, not realizing that they were involved in his guilt. The brother who had suffered this moral lapse went through great spiritual agonies; through genuine repentance he was restored to fellowship and later became a useful member of the church in America. The false freedom aspect of the movement was completely overcome by the end of 1862.[35]

The movement finally culminated in an incredible *spiritual despotism*, personified primarily in three leading brethren: Gerhard Wieler, Bernhard Penner, and Benjamin Becker. The religious fanaticism of these "apostles" (as they called themselves) found expression in the imposition of arbitrary rules and restrictions upon the members. All friendly associations with those who disagreed with their views were strictly prohibited, even the friendly greeting of blood-relatives, since this was "fellowship with the world." Religious books, such as Hofacker's sermons and Arndt's *Wahres Christentum* (*True Christianity*), which had been deeply appreciated earlier, were now proscribed and burned. That a false literalism in Scripture interpretation played an important part in this "regime of tyranny" can be gathered from the fact that even photography was condemned on the basis of the Second Commandment.[36] The spiritual egotism of the three leaders reached its most frightening expression, however, in the arbitrary use of the "ban." Members who did not participate in the noisy and hyper-emotional meetings were excommunicated and "delivered unto Satan." In Chortitza Abraham Unger and his followers were banned because of their opposition to this movement. In the Molotschna Jacob Reimer, his wife and daughter, as well as elder Heinrich Huebert were excommunicated for similar reasons.

Huebert was deposed from office because he was not considered "blameless" since he had to appear before local authorities, and was subsequently imprisoned for ten months. The fact that Huebert's trial and imprisonment resulted from false charges, and that consequently he had suffered as a Christian, apparently did not enter into their judgment. Wieler even banned his own protesting father and twenty other brethren with the "raised fist" — the severest form of the ban. Perhaps providentially for the young Mennonite Brethren Church, Wieler was removed from the scene by imprisonment for "perverting"

Orthodox church members. Furthermore, other men with sane scriptural views joined the Mennonite Brethren and contributed greatly to the ultimate defeat of the *Froehliche Richtung.*

PROTEST AND REFORMATION

1. *Single Voices of Protest*

Almost from the beginning of this "false movement" (as H. Huebert called it) there were single voices of protest against it. Jacob Reimer was probably the first to express his deep concern in a letter to Johann Claassen in June, 1861. About the same time Mrs. Claassen wrote her husband about the emotional outbursts of the movement and commented: "To me it appears sinful." Abraham Unger, a firm opponent of the movement from the beginning, wrote to the Brethren in the Molotschna and challenged them to become spiritually sober and not to be misguided by a one-sided interpretation of Scripture. Heinrich Huebert, although he did not wish to be judgmental, warned the brethren by reminding them of the early experiences in the *Kleine Gemeinde* and in the revival movement at Kronsweide. As soon as Claassen was adequately informed about the excesses of the *Froehliche Richtung,* he made his position clear, although he continued to work for reconciliation of the two groups.[37] However, Claassen's extensive work towards the move of the church to the Kuban area, which he began in the late summer of 1862, delayed the complete conquest of the movement by almost three years.

2. *First Formal Protest*

In God's gracious providence several men with outstanding leadership ability joined the Mennonite Brethren Church during this crucial period. They were the men of the hour, called for an important ministry in the church "for such a time as this." The Lord found these "chosen instruments" in the ranks of the Ohrloff Mennonite Church — the church that had played such an important role in the struggle for recognition and survival of the Mennonite Brethren. The following five young men, among others, joined the Mennonite Brethren Church in 1864: Daniel Fast, a schoolteacher from Blumenort who later became an elder in the church and had a long and fruitful ministry in the Kuban settlement; Johann Fast, a nephew of Daniel Fast, who became an associate elder and "father of pastoral care" in the Mennonite Brethren Church — also widely known as an itinerant minister; Jacob Jantz, who later became the elder of the congregation at Friedensfeld, and a "pillar of the Mennonite Brethren church to his end;"[38] Abraham Schellenberg, later a successor to Huebert as elder of the Molotschna Mennonite Brethren Church, and after 1879 an outstanding leader in the United States; and Philipp Isaak, who became known as "governor"

10. Philipp Isaak   11. Jacob Jantz

(*Regierer*) in his work as administrator and treasurer. He was the right-hand man of the ailing Elder Huebert in all administrative matters. His wise leadership proved to be a blessing to the larger brotherhood for many years. These five brethren together with Johann Claassen and Christian Schmidt formed the "team" that emerged victorious in the struggle with the unruly elements of the church.

It was the unfair treatment and unscriptural deposition of Huebert that prompted these brethren to take united action. Daniel Fast prepared a statement on behalf of the group in which he refuted the errors of the *Froehliche Richtung*, and more specifically the views of the "ruling brethren." The declaration, dated April 1, 1865, contains the following points, given here in brief summary.[39]

(a) *Concerning the deposition of ministers.* In their demands for blamelessness of character for ministers the "ruling brethren" go beyond the demands of Scripture. The passage in 2 John 7 cannot be applied to the brethren that have been banned, since none of them has denied the deity of Christ.

(b) *Concerning the use of the ban.* The ban is not exercised according to Scripture. 1 Timothy 5:20 and 1 Corinthians 5:4 do not give a few brethren the right to excommunicate those who are not in agreement with them. Excommunication is the prerogative and responsibility of the whole church.

(c) *Concerning the respect of persons.* Respect of persons is manifested in that only those members are accepted by the "ruling brethren" who zealously defend their views; others, who serve the Lord in meekness and love, are declared to be evildoers.

(d) *Concerning the nature of the godly life.* True godliness does not find expression in dancing, leaping, and shouting as some teach on the basis of certain Old Testament passages. According to the New Testament, the mark of a true faith is not an outward happiness, but a genuine love.

The statement concludes with a plea for acceptance of the above principles, since otherwise there will be no possibility of further cooperation with brethren who are "not of the same mind with us."[40] This statement paved the way for Claassen to lead the Mennonite Brethren Church to final triumph over the entire *Froeliche Richtung.*

3. *Church Restoration Through June Reform*

In response to an urgent request of the Molotschna Brethren, Claassen left his responsibilities in the young Kuban settlement and spent two and one half months (from May 4 to July 20, 1865) in the congregations of Chortitza and Molotschna to assist the brethren in the reestablishment of a scriptural church order. At this time Claassen was perhaps the only leader who enjoyed a certain amount of prestige and confidence among all groups within the Mennonite Brethren Church. (During the entire two and a half months Claassen had to stay in hiding because local authorities wanted to arrest him on charges of having violated certain state laws!) After numerous private contacts and discussions, Claassen called several brotherhood meetings (*Bruder-beratungen*). Since these meetings were held at intervals throughout the month of June, they are often referred to as the "June Reform."[41]

Some of the more important issues that were resolved by the June Reform are the following:[42]

No leading minister may act independently of the church as a whole in any important church matter, such as, for instance, excommunication. The church governs itself through its elected ministers, who, if they teach and act according to God's Word, are worthy of double honor.

The reinstatement of Heinrich Huebert in his office as first minister (elder) was a matter of serious and prayerful concern. After fasting and prayer the lot was cast in a very solemn ceremony. The lot confirmed Brother Huebert's call to the ministry, to which he had been ordained earlier.

The unscriptural and unconstitutional bans were declared null and void. Jacob Reimer and others who had been excommunicated without a hearing before the church, should now be readmitted, if personal differences would be forgiven and resolved in love.

The "wild manifestations of joy," such as dancing, were

unanimously condemned as "not pleasing unto the Savior." The tambourin, a musical instrument which had caused a great deal of negative reaction and criticism, was not to be used any more in worship services. Loud and exciting music was to be avoided, and that which was lovely and pleasant was to be cultivated. The joy of the Lord was not ruled out, but was to be expressed becomingly.

The friendly greeting of non-members was regarded as pleasing to the Lord, whereas a contrary behavior was on the level of publicans and sinners.

Church discipline was to be practiced according to the Word of God, but marit-' avoidance was not to be imposed.

In conclusion the document made reference to the complete eradication of the false freedom doctrine three years earlier. It also gratefully acknowledged that former adherents of this movement had confessed their error and had been forgiven.

These "resolutions" were presented publicly to the entire congregation in Gnadenheim (Molotschna) on August 4, 1865, and later shared with the Mennonite Brethren Churches in Chortitza and in the Kuban settlement, who fully approved of the measures taken by the Brethren in the June Reform. Not all the erring brethren, however, were willing to mend their ways and return to the "Reformed" Mennonite Brethren Church. Wilhelm Bartel, who introduced the *Froehliche Richtung* in the Molotschna, although disillusioned by the movement, separated from the church permanently. Gerhard Wieler, the chief advocate and defender of the *Froehliche Richtung*, tried unsuccessfully to revive the movement after 1865. Later he withdrew and joined the Chortitza Mennonite Church. It is significant to note here, that none of the leaders of this "charismatic movement" had any influence on the growth and development of the Mennonite Brethren Church in later years. P. M. Friesen, who joined the church through baptism in the summer of 1866, states that he has never detected even a slight trace of the movement in the Mennonite Brethren Church.[43]

There is an interesting postscript to the chapter on the June Reform. In September, 1865, the church appointed two gifted young ministers, Jacob Jantz and Christian Schmidt, to prepare a "Confession" (*Selbstbekenntnis*) which was to be submitted to the administrative adviser of the Minister of the Interior, *Staatsrat* Brun. The latter had been commissioned by the Russian government to investigate the whole secession movement among the Mennonites. In this "Confession" Jantz and Schmidt attempt to give an account of developments (still somewhat narrowly interpreted) but they also admit the shortcomings and failings of the group. The statement concludes with a plea for continued government benevolence and help, and with the request for the release of imprisoned members, especially Elder Huebert.[44]

These same two ministers were also commissioned to go on a general itinerary (*Rundreise*) through the villages of the Molotschna colony to share with members of both the "old" and "new" congregations "the present mind of the church," as well as its regrets over past failings. In their "diary" Jantz and Schmidt express their delight at the open doors and the friendly reception in the homes of such prominent leaders of the Ohrloff Mennonite Church as Bernhard Harder (Halbstadt), Hermann Janzen (Tiege), Jacob Martens (Tiegenhagen), and elder Johann Harder (Blumstein).[45] This was the first important step on the part of the young Mennonite Brethren Church to establish a more cordial and fraternal relationship with leading "brethren" in the Mennonite Church.

Some Lessons from History

It might be well at this point to pause briefly and ask the question whether this period of religious ferment in M.B. history has taught the brotherhood some lessons that are also of importance to the present generation. What the Apostle Paul writes to the Corinthians concerning the experiences of Israel is also applicable to the experiences of the church in history: "Now these things happened to them as a warning, but they were written down for our instruction, upon whom the end of the ages is come."[46] The late A. H. Unruh, Mennonite Brethren historian and theologian, and a keen observer of trends and developments in the brotherhood, points out a number of important lessons in his history of the Mennonite Brethren Church.[47] We present these here in an abridged form and in free translation.

1. *The need for systematic Bible teaching*

The great joy that was manifested by practically all members of the early Mennonite Brethren Church was a natural result of their discovery and experience of the free grace of God in the forgiveness of sins and the assurance of salvation. It can also partly be explained psychologically as a reaction to the cold and lifeless services in the old church. Strong emotions, however, that are not controlled by a proper knowledge of Scripture, can be very dangerous. That Christ's Great Commission was a teaching commission, in which new converts were also to be taught to obey the commandments of Christ, was overlooked by the early Brethren. Pfarrer Wuest had instructed them in the doctrine of justification by faith, but not in the doctrine of the sanctification of the believer. Any new life movement without sound and systematic Bible teaching is bound to end in a disintegrating emotionalism. Zeal without knowledge is destructive.

2. *The need for the discernment of spirits*

During times of religious ferment and excitement, there is the danger that men who are powerful emotionally but shallow intellectually may gain control of a movement. The more mature men who could provide stability and direction are often pushed into the background. Emotional leaders have a tendency to emphasize personal experience at the expense of Bible study in devotional meetings. The brethren learned through harsh experience, that the church must also exercise the gift of discernment, and must not be deceived by a mere verbalization of the Christian faith. Emotion is a good servant, but a poor master.

3. *The need for sane church leadership*

The brethren soon realized that Heinrich Huebert in his quiet way could do more for the nurture of the congregation than Jacob Becker with his more sensational manner. Because the church had learned this lesson, it entrusted the leadership to men of integrity and spiritual balance who were able to overcome the *Froehliche Richtung*. "Since that time the Mennonite Brethren Church has given preference to calm and soberminded men. To the more emotional (men) they gave the position of evangelist, but were less inclined to be guided by them in the congregation."[48]

4. *The need for congregational church polity*

The church learned to suspect and reject dictatorship in any form. Since the arbitrary and willful decisions of G. Wieler and B. Becker had created such havoc in the early church, the Mennonite Brethren have insisted on congregational participation and action. Only that is binding for the congregation, which the majority agreed to do. This does not exclude the right of the ministering brethren to give guidance on the basis of Scripture, but no minister or leader can act independently of the church.

5. *The need for a strong ethical emphasis*

In the early years Christian doctrine was divorced from Christian ethics. The doctrine of "joyous justification" was separated from the teaching on holiness and Christian discipleship. "Separation" was interpreted primarily in terms of isolation from the world around us, rather than in terms of death to sin within us, as Paul teaches in Romans 6:4. The Brethren also realized that happiness can easily be divorced from holiness and thus lead to a false freedom. The Brethren learned that faith without works is dead, and that doctrine and ethics, faith and practice, must be kept in proper balance.

6. *The need for meaningful church worship*

Mennonite Brethren have learned that lukewarmness and coldness in the life of a congregation may open the door to a hyperemotional movement. If worship services do not provide for meaningful participation of members, they will look for greener pastures elsewhere. Loud complaints and protests, as well as church resolutions, will not prevent members from attending other meetings which they consider to be more attractive. The whole schism in the Mennonite Brotherhood could have been avoided by a radical renewal in the large churches.

Such lessons from history ought to be carefully heeded when movements similar to the *Froehliche Richtung* appear within church circles in the present day.

Chapter 6

Consolidation and Expansion (1865-1885)

The two decades following the period of storm and stress (1860-65) were marked, on the one hand, by increased stabilization and maturity in the inner life and organizational structure of the Mennonite Brethren Church, and on the other by rapid growth and expansion into new geographical areas. This is the period in which the "landless problem" was finally solved by the division of crown lands and the purchase of large tracts of land for daughter colonies. It is also the period in which the Russian government abrogated some of the cherished privileges originally granted to the Mennonites. The anomalous situation, in which Mennonites enjoyed rights and privileges far beyond those of their Russian neighbors, could not last forever. The Imperial Decree of 1870 contained provisions which implied radical changes: the Supervisory Commission in Odessa was to be abolished; Russian was to be the official language in the local Colony Administrative Office (*Gebietsamt*), as well as a subject of study in all the schools; and worst of all for the Mennonites, military exemption was to be terminated. Emigration of a larger group to America and of a smaller group to Central Asia were the direct consequences of the new government policy. These and many other factors affected the growth and development of the Mennonite Brethren Church during this period. Some of the more significant aspects of these developments will be treated briefly.

GENERAL DEVELOPMENTS AFTER THE JUNE REFORM

The three areas in which the Mennonite Brethren Church became firmly established during the first decade of this period are Molotschna, Chortitza, and Kuban.

1. *Developments in the Molotschna*

Numerical growth during this period was steady but not spectacular. Somewhat hard to explain is the fact that the rate of growth from 1860 to 1866 — the period of oppression and harassment — was more rapid than in the period of relative peace that followed. Whereas the increase through baptism during the first six years averaged fifty per year, the average increase during the next seven years was only twenty-two. The socioeconomic tensions in the Molotschna colony, as well as the struggle for the inner stability in the Mennonite Brethren Church, may have influenced and retarded the rate of growth during this latter period.[1] Although approximately 465 members had been accepted into the Mennonite Brethren Church in the Molotschna from 1860 to 1872, the church had a membership of only about 200 by the time of the first General Conference (*Bundeskonferenz*). There are several reasons for this anomaly. During 1865-66, a group of about twenty members withdrew from the Mennonite Brethren Church under the leadership of a man by the name of Hermann Peters. This group belonged to the faction of the *Froehliche Richtung* and would not accept the guidelines set forth in the June Reform. This group, which came to be known as the "Hermann Peters Congregation" developed various idiosyncrasies based on a hyper-literalism of Scripture interpretation. For instance, they believed that the bread for communion should not be cut, but only broken, and hence they were popularly nicknamed the "Breadbreakers" (*Brotbrecher*). The pilgrim path of this group led first to the Crimea, around the turn of the century to Western Siberia, and from there prior to World War I to Oklahoma, U.S.A.[2]

Another more important reason for the small membership in the Mennonite Brethren Church in 1872 was the relatively heavy migration of Mennonite Brethren families to the new settlements of the Kuban, Friedensfeld, Crimea, and other areas.[3]

The worship services of the Mennonite Brethren underwent a marked change during this period. The earlier pietistic emphasis on informal sharing and devotional talks gave way to an emphasis on more systematic teaching and preaching. The members of the congregations seemed to be "hungry for order! order! and for lectures!"[4] This change was accompanied by a change in language (although not without struggle) from the Low German dialect to High German in the public worship service. In the midweek Bible study hours (*Bibelstunden*) and smaller fellowship meetings, the Low German remained the preferred medium of communication. One of the most popular and powerful preachers of this new era was Christian Schmidt, whom the Brethren affectionately called "our Wuest" or "our Spurgeon." The development of church music in Mennonite Brethren circles will be treated later.

In their church polity the Brethren moved closer to the organizational structure of the "old" church — at least in one area: the office of "elder." Although Heinrich Huebert had been ordained as "first minister" in June, 1861, and had often been referred to as "elder," he was not officially designated as such until after his second ordination seven years later. In late summer, 1868, the "associate elder," Johann Fast, in a solemn ceremony, at the home of C. Neufeld, Neukirch, ordained Huebert as the first elder of the Mennonite Brethren Church. Later Huebert ordained Abraham Schellenberg as his successor in the Molotschna (1876), and Daniel Fast as elder of the Kuban Mennonite Brethren Church (1877). This office was abandoned in later years, both in Russia and America, for reasons that will be considered later.

The interest in missions was revived during this period. As mentioned previously, the early Brethren were attracted to the missions festivals which were held regularly in the Gnadenfeld Mennonite Church. The inspiring messages of Pfarrer Wuest and others produced a widespread interest in missions. This interest, however, was dampened and pushed into the background by the struggle for recognition and survival that followed the secession. In the spring of 1867 a new day for missions dawned for the Mennonite Brethren with the observance of their first missions festival in the spacious warehouse of Johann Fast, who operated a large lumber business in Neuhalbstadt. The guest speaker on this occasion was Abraham Unger of the Einlage Mennonite Brethren Church (Chortitza) whose message on missions was deeply appreciated by church members and visitors. From this day on the missionary vision of the Brethren expanded and deepened until it found practical expression in the commissioning of their first missionaries to India during the last decade of the nineteenth century.

Another progressive step in the growth of the Molotschna Mennonite Brethren Church was the acquisition of a "meeting house"[5] in the village of Rueckenau. Rueckenau was chosen for its central location after a costly venture in the village of Ladekopp had failed. To the great relief of the pious village mayor, the Mennonite Brethren purchased the village saloon (*Schenke*) and transformed it into a church in 1874. Since this building was used primarily for the monthly assemblies of the entire church, as well as for inter-church Bible Conferences (*Bibelbesprechungen*) it soon proved to be too small. In 1883 a fine new church edifice (84'x42') was erected. An ingenious method of financing this project was accepted: since most of the members were farmers, they agreed to donate the proceeds of either one, two or three acres (depending on their landholdings) to the common church building fund. Professional people made cash contributions according to their income. This method of fund-raising proved so popular that it was retained even after the church was paid for in order to finance the erection of church buildings in new settlements.[6] Since Rueckenau became the center of Mennonite Brethren activities and meetings, the Molotschna Church came to be known as the Rueckenau Mennonite Brethren Church.

2. *Developments in Chortitza*

The Mennonite Brethren Church in Chortitza experienced rapid growth, right from its inception, and in early years was even larger than the church in the Molotschna.[7] The main center was in the village of Einlage, with affiliated groups at Andreasfeld and Tehornoglas. The troubles of the Einlage Mennonite Brethren Church (as it came to be known) were not ended by Wieler's removal and Neufeld's withdrawal from the settlement. The Baptist-Mennonite polarization, caused by Abraham Unger's pro-Baptist leanings, continued to create problems within the fellowship and in the relationship of the church to the civil authorities, who made repeated attempts to classify the Brethren as "Baptists" and to deprive them of their privileges as Mennonites.

Reference has been made to August Liebig's profitable, though short-lived, ministry in 1866. It so happened that in 1868 a German Baptist deacon, Karl Benzien, moved into the area for business reasons. Benzien, an educated and gifted Christian, soon ingratiated himself by his sympathetic attitude and wise counsel. Like Liebig before him, Benzien chaired their church business meetings and assisted the Brethren in establishing a more functional church polity. At a brotherhood meeting in May, 1868, Abraham Unger was elected as elder and Aron Lepp as minister. Since Lepp was not in agreement with Unger on the question of Mennonite-Baptist relations, the tensions were not resolved.[8]

In the fall of 1869 J. G. Oncken, the founder and leader of the German Baptist Church, came to the Southern Ukraine to visit some scattered Baptist congregations. Upon invitation, he also ministered to the Mennonite Brethren in Chortitza.[9] On October 18, 1869, Oncken ordained Abraham Unger as elder, Aron Lepp as minister, and Cornelius Unger and Benjamin Nickel as deacons. Oncken's itinerary, which also included a ministry in the Molotschna, was cut short because of the approaching Russian winter, and hence his visit to the latter colony did not materialize. In view of the consequences of Oncken's ministry for the brotherhood, some brethren then and later have considered this change in his travel plans as "providential."[10]

The official involvement of a Baptist minister in a Mennonite Brethren ordination service raised a number of questions and provided a great deal of fuel for the fires of controversy. Since Oncken was a Baptist, some brethren felt that those ordained by him were also Baptists now. Another matter which came up for discussion was the question of nonresistance. Since Baptists were not opposed to military service,

12. Aron Lepp   13. August Liebig

would fellowship with them jeopardize the Mennonite exemptions from such service? Was it right to observe communion with them? A practical ethical issue came up in connection with Oncken's visit. The latter was addicted to the use of tobacco, and his example influenced some members of the church to imitate him. After considerable discussion, the Brethren resolved that members of the Mennonite Brethren Church should abstain completely from its use. This stand of the church resulted in the excommunication of twelve brethren, who were not willing to renounce this habit. After one hundred years, in 1969, the General Conference of Mennonite Brethren Churches reaffirmed its stand on this issue.[11]

In order to restore the inner peace in the Einlage Mennonite Brethren Church, Aron Lepp recommended to the membership that Baptists (mostly of non-Mennonite ethnic background) and Mennonite Brethren should form separate congregations, but maintain a cordial relationship and fellowship, including communion. This proposal was accepted by the majority of members, but not by elder Abraham Unger, who was reluctant to sever his Baptist connections and also considered the disciplinary measures against the "smoking brethren" too harsh.[12]

Tensions continued until another Baptist, August Liebig, by his "benevolent neutrality" reconciled the two factions. Liebig, who graciously accepted this second call for assistance, arrived in the Chortitza Colony, this time accompanied by his wife and daughter, in

June, 1871. He took up residence in the village of Andreasfeld (where Lepp also lived) and stayed for a whole year. His impartial judgment and personal counseling earned the compliment: "He has done much good among us" from one of the Brethren. Among the good things that Liebig introduced were the Sunday school and the public prayer meeting as part of the Sunday morning worship service. The church business meetings, as mentioned earlier, were now conducted according to guidelines suggested by Liebig.[13]

Under his guidance, a committee for itinerant preaching (*Reisepredigt*) was established. The relationship of the various Mennonite Brethren congregations was also regulated through the organization of the annual congregational, district and general church-wide conferences. In addition he assisted in regulating the financial aspects of conference activities, especially with respect to the method of soliciting support and supervising the conference treasury. An annual monthly training course, designed for preachers and candidates for the ministry, was also introduced by him. For these and other positive contributions Liebig's memory will always be cherished in the Mennonite Brethren Church.

Although internal tensions with respect to Mennonite-Baptist relations were largely resolved by 1872, this issue continued to plague the church in its relation to the Mennonite Church and to civil authorities. Early in 1873, an official of the Russian government was commissioned to investigate various problems pertaining to the Mennonites and the impending draft law. In his discussions he raised the question of the relationship of the Mennonite Brethren to the newly organized Baptist groups. The leaders of the Einlage Mennonite Brethren Church went to great lengths to describe the differences between the Baptists, the "old" Mennonite Church, and themselves.[14] A report explaining these differences was drafted and carefully studied by the entire congregation. This report was then sent to the government, together with a confession of faith chosen for this purpose. This confession was published at Basel in 1876, together with the "Explanations" (*Erklaerungen*). According to Ehrt, this confession was an exact reproduction of Oncken's Baptist *Confession of Faith* published in Hamburg in 1849, to which the publisher, elder Abraham Unger of Einlage, added the distinctively Mennonite norms of nonresistance, rejection of the oath, and footwashing.[15] According to P. M. Friesen, this confession was an adaptation of the Hamburg confession to Mennonite teachings.[16]

The arrival of the printed confession coincided with a concerted effort on the part of the larger brotherhood to sever all relations with the Baptists. The reference to fellowship with the Baptists, as given in the

"Explanations," was therefore somewhat embarrassing. Thus it is not surprising that this confession was never formally adopted by the older congregation in the Molotschna. Certain statements describing the relationship to the "old" Mennonite Church also evoked considerable criticism from the very beginning.

When the Baptists in Russia received official recognition as a branch of Protestantism in 1879, a government survey was made with respect to their number and place of residence. The Chortitza Colony Administrative Office in its report classified all seceded brethren with the Baptists. Unger and Lepp were commissioned by the Einlage Mennonite Brethren Church to negotiate with the government concerning this issue. The latter demanded a confession of faith in German and Russian. Two leading educators in the Molotschna, Johann Wieler and P. M. Friesen, were asked to assist in the translation of the confession and the revision of the "Explanations" which dealt with Mennonite-Baptist relations. In response to these documents the Department of the Interior issued a special statement on March 6, 1880, confirming the rights of the Brethren as Mennonites. Elder Abraham Unger died six days later, and it is doubtful whether he became aware of this happy ending of the prolonged struggle before his passing. In spite of certain limitations and weaknesses, Abraham Unger must be considered, next to Johann Claassen, as one of the greatest men in the early history of the M.B. Church. Greatness must be defined, according to P. M. Friesen, in terms of loyalty to one's conviction, and self-sacrifice for the ideals which one considers scriptural.[17]

3. *Developments in the Kuban*

The Kuban settlement, located on the Kuban river in the Northern Caucasus, was the only daughter colony established under the auspices of the Mennonite Brethren. Partly because of the oppressive religious and economic conditions in the Molotschna and Chortitza colonies, the Brethren through Johann Claassen petitioned the government in 1862 for an additional tract of land. This was granted and the villages of Wohldemfuerst and Alexanderfeld were established in 1863 and 1866, respectively. Although land had been reserved for one hundred families, only sixty-seven had settled by 1866. Several reasons may be given for the slow growth of the settlement in the first two decades. The economic difficulties were unusually severe during the pioneer period. Moreover the recognition of the Mennonite Brethren Church in the Molotschna removed one of the main incentives for resettlement. And finally, the emigration of a large contingent of Mennonites to America in the 1870's made more land available in the older colonies.

In subsequent years the settlement began to prosper economically and culturally under the leadership of Johann Claassen, the "Johann

Cornies" of the Kuban. Claassen, who was elected chief administrator of the colony (*Oberschulze*) in 1869, received special recognition from the Tsar for his services. At a reception of Alexander II in 1872 he received the silver medal and two years later the gold medal. Besides these he received from the government a gold watch with an inscription recognizing his services as a colonizer and administrator. By 1904 the settlement reached its peak population of about 2,000, with the Mennonite Brethren constituting the largest group.[18]

In their church life the Brethren here experienced some of the same difficulties that had plagued their fellow-believers in the older settlements. In addition to the unruly elements of the *Froehliche Richtung* that had found their way here, the Jerusalem Friends (or Templers)[19] exerted strong influence in the Kuban area for a time. Under the sane leadership of Christian Schmidt and Johann Claassen the church triumphed over these difficulties and achieved inner stability and healthy progress. In 1873, after waiting for ten years, Heinrich Huebert also moved to the Kuban, where he was immediately reconfirmed as elder. Because of failing health, however, he had to retire from public duties after three years. In May 1877 he ordained Daniel Fast as his successor. In 1895, at the age of 85, he died. Claassen (who died at 56 in 1876) and Huebert will always be remembered by Mennonite Brethren for their sincere faith and moral fortitude during the period of storm and stress in the early history of the Mennonite Brethren Church.

4. *The First General Conference* (*Bundeskonferenz*)

From the very beginning the Mennonite Brethren have shown a remarkable propensity, if not genius, for conference organization and conference work. Already in 1872, twelve years after the founding of the church, and eleven years before the Mennonite Churches organized into a conference (1883), the Mennonite Brethren met for their first conference in Andreasfeld. At this convention, held from May 14-16, 1872, delegates from the three congregations (Kuban, Molotschna and Chortitza) with their affiliated groups, representing a total membership of over six hundred, met for inspirational meetings and business sessions. August Liebig, the Baptist minister residing in the Chortitza colony, was asked to preside at the meetings.

It is significant, and perhaps prophetic, that the major item of business at this conference was the establishment of an itinerant ministry for evangelism and church extension. A committee of seven brethren was elected to supervise and regulate this work. Five brethren were appointed to this ministry: Eduard Leppke, Christian Schmidt, Johann Wieler, Aron Lepp and Daniel Fast. The first two consented to serve full-time with an annual salary of four hundred rubles. The other three, because of vocational responsibilities, were willing to devote half-time to this work with an annual allowance of two hundred rubles. An annual budget of one thousand rubles was no mean achievement for the young church. It was also decided that the itinerant ministers (*Reiseprediger*) should keep a diary, and report quarterly to the conference secretary. These reports were to be circulated among the congregations to promote interest in evangelism.[20]

A brief note concerning two of these "traveling evangelists" might be added here. Eduard Leppke had been a Baptist before he came to South Russia where he joined the Mennonite Brethren and, according to P. M. Friesen, became a "hyper-Mennonite." In his teaching he went so far as to claim "that only nonresistant Christians could be saved."[21] His severe criticism of the Baptists gradually limited his usefulness as evangelist and led to an estrangement from the Mennonite Brethren Conference. Later he migrated to America where he eventually joined the Seventh Day Adventists.

Johann Wieler (1839-1889), a high school teacher at Halbstadt, was perhaps the only one among the five appointed ministers who had a good command of the Russian language. He had a burden for the conversion of the Russian people, and preached occasionally among them. In 1883, he proposed to the Mennonite Brethren Conference that it engage in evangelism among these people, even though this was strictly prohibited by the Russian government. When the conference rejected his proposal, he launched out on his own and carried on an effective ministry among the Russians in the Odessa area. Soon the Russian police suspected him of "subversive activities," and after baptizing a Russian woman he was sentenced to exile in Siberia. But Wieler went into hiding for six months, after which he escaped to Germany, where he was granted temporary asylum of eight months. Since he could not return to Russia, he found a place of service in Rumania, where he ministered to Russian Baptists. Wieler, who died in exile, must be considered the first Mennonite missionary among the Russian people.[22]

EXPANSION ACROSS LAND AND SEA

The expansion of the Mennonite Brethren during the second decade of their history into new geographical areas was as much due to the migration of a people as it was to the propagation of a faith. By 1925 almost 40 percent of the population in the daughter colonies belonged to the Mennonite Brethren, whereas only 15.5 percent belonged to them in the mother settlements of the Ukraine. This makes it clear that the greatest increase in Mennonite Brethren, which was due primarily to winning converts from the Mennonite Church, was found in the daughter colonies. "It could also indicate that the Mennonite Brethren of the mother settlements were more active in the establishment of daughter settlements."[23] Before we consider Mennonite Brethren emigration to America, let us briefly sketch the beginning of Mennonite Brethren churches in the daughter colonies.

1. *Expansion in European Russia*

(1) *Friedensfeld.* Three Mennonite Brethren families from the Molotschna settled here in 1867 with a number of families from the *Kleine Gemeinde.* This settlement consisted at first of one village and was located about thirty miles north of Nikopol, near the Dnieper River. The faithful ministry of Jacob Jantz resulted in conversions and increased membership. Since the *Kleine Gemeinde* congregation here was in the process of dissolution, "all the remaining inhabitants of the village joined the Mennonite Brethren."[24] Friedensfeld was at first a subsidiary of the Molotschna Mennonite Brethren Church, but in 1875 it was organized as a separate congregation with forty-five members. At the same time Jacob Jantz was ordained as elder and Christian Schmidt as "associate elder" by the elders Abraham Unger (Einlage) and Abraham Schellenberg (Rueckenau). By 1885 the church had a membership of one hundred, and approximately 150 adherents. It also had an effective outreach in the surrounding areas and had general supervision of the small Baptist church at Michailowka.

(2) *Zagradowka.* This settlement, established in 1872, was situated on the Inguletz River about sixty miles north/northeast of the city of Kherson. By 1883, sixteen villages had been established here on excellent farm land. After surviving early pioneer hardships, the colony became one of the most prosperous of all the newer settlements. Here too, there was a nucleus of three Mennonite Brethren families among the first contingent of settlers. Through the itinerant ministry of such men as Jacob Jantz and Eduard Leppke the small group was strengthened and increased in numbers. By 1885 the congregation had a membership of one hundred, with an additional one hundred and fifty adherents. The earlier meeting place had been in the village of Altonau, but in 1888 a new church was built in the more centrally located village of Tiege, so that the church came to be known as the Tiege-Zagradowka Mennonite Brethren Church.[25]

(3) *On the Don.* Along the Don River, in the land of the Cossacks, a relatively large number of German Lutherans and some German Catholics established settlements in the middle of the nineteenth century. Through the ministry of Pfarrer Wuest, a large-scale revival took place. Through contact with the Molotschna Brethren the question of believer's baptism became a live issue and after some time, resulted in a schism. Those who were baptized formed a separate congregation and elected Abraham Cornelsen, the author of the Document of Secession, as

their presiding minister and elder. After Cornelsen's emigration to America in 1879, the group that did not want to become "Baptist" followed him to the new world; the others joined the Baptist Union in 1887. Because of their ethnic and religious background they were not permitted to become "Mennonite" in their church affiliation.[26]

It should be noted that in addition to these semi-independent centers of Mennonite Brethren church life, the older congregations all had affiliated groups (*Filialen*) or stations which were under their general supervision. The Molotschna Mennonite Brethren Church during this time counted among its affiliated "stations" Puchtin and Herzenberg, which were both located in another province (Ekaterinoslav). The fellowship at Spat in the Crimea was also for many years a division (*Abteilung*) of the Molotschna Mennonite Brethren Church.[27] Moreover, in the Molotschna itself, with its more than fifty villages, there was only one Mennonite Brethren Church with Rueckenau as its center. To be sure, there were a number of meeting places where members gathered for worship on "ordinary" Sundays, but organizationally these groups considered themselves one body. The same can be said of the Chortitza (Einlage) Mennonite Brethren Church which had subsidiaries or stations during this period at Andreasfeld, Wiesenfeld, Jasykowo, Sergejewka-Alexandertal, Burwalde and Nepljujewo.[28] Through the ministry of itinerant preachers and the regular visits of elders these groups maintained the unity of the spirit. From this description of the organizational pattern it seems obvious that the early Brethren did not stress the "autonomy" of the local church. In this respect they followed the earlier Anabaptist (and we might add, the New Testament) pattern of congregational interdependence. The emphasis on the "absolute autonomy" of the local congregation in some Mennonite Brethren churches in later years was the result of exposure to Baptist influence. This influence tends to weaken the concept of the church as a brotherhood independent of geographical location or distance.

2. *Expansion to the American Continent*

The emigration of approximately eighteen thousand Mennonites from Russia to the United States and Canada between 1874 and 1880 constitutes the most outstanding event of this period. The Imperial Decree of 1870, to which reference has been made at the beginning of this chapter, clearly reflected the spirit of the "Slavophiles" who were convinced that "the day of Russianizing all Russia had come."[29] The introduction of universal military training was a part of this new policy. In anticipation of this conscription law (which was passed in 1874) the Mennonites sent five delegations to Petersburg to plead for the preservation of their privileges. Eventually the Mennonites were promised an acceptable form of alternative service, instead of military training, but even this was more than some would tolerate. The delegates acknowledged that they recognized the necessity of government, and also their readiness to submit in all matters not contrary to their conscience, but they could not accept any form of military service.

This experience of the Mennonites in Russia was not without historical precedent; their fathers had faced a similar situation in Prussia a hundred years earlier. At that time emigration had been the solution for all those who desired to preserve their nonresistance without compromise. Again Mennonite leaders began to investigate seriously this possibility. Various prospects were considered — Russian Turkestan and even the distant Amur region, because in these recently acquired territories the military law was not to be applied. There were two leaders, however, both living in the city of Berdjansk, who favored a Mennonite emigration to America. Elder Leonhard Sudermann and Cornelius Jansen, a grain merchant, both tried to educate the general public and also endeavored to establish preliminary contacts to initiate such a migration.[30]

In 1873 a twelve-man delegation left for America to spy out the promised land. The delegation visited what was then the frontier line in America of cheap land — Kansas, Nebraska, Dakota, Minnesota, and up the Red River into Canada. They also inquired about political conditions and military regulations. The more liberal inducements granted by the "Dominion of Canada" to prospective settlers were offset, perhaps, by the less hospitable climate in that country. The generally favorable report of the delegates upon their return resulted in one of the greatest migrations of Mennonites in their history. Entire congregations (e.g. Alexanderwohl) and whole villages prepared for the "great trek." The Russian government became alarmed and sent a special envoy, General von Totleben, to stem the tide, but with little success. Approximately ten thousand of these immigrants eventually found their new home in the United States; the other eight thousand, belonging to the more conservative groups, settled in the Red River Valley of the newly established Canadian province of Manitoba.

The Mennonite Brethren formed an integral part of this whole movement. This would indicate that they were equally concerned about the preservation of their scriptural and historical heritage, especially the principle of nonresistance. According to elder Abraham Schellenberg, about one-third of the Mennonite Brethren Church emigrated to America between 1874 and 1880.[31] For those remaining, the fact that a number of leading ministers were also leaving was probably even more disturbing than the sharp decrease in membership. Especially painful for the Molotschna Mennonite Brethren was the decision of their highly respected elder, Abraham Schellenberg, to leave his congregation and emigrate to America. Schellenberg justified his action on the basis of a personal conviction that he had finished his task in the church in Russia, and that the Lord had a new assignment for him in the new world. Privately he also expressed the concern that freedom of religion for "alien groups" in Russia might soon come to an end.[32]

Before Schellenberg left, he endeavored to provide for proper leadership after his departure. In a special brotherhood meeting on December 28, 1878, Johann Fast was appointed as "substitute elder" (*Aeltestenvertreter*) and Jacob Dirksen as his assistant. Franz Nickel and David Schellenberg had been ordained to the ministry earlier that year.

A formal farewell was arranged for May 6, 1879, in the church at Rueckenau. Representatives of both groups participated in this special service. Jacob Dirksen and Klaas Enns spoke on John 16:32,33 and Matthew 26:54 respectively, and addressed themselves primarily to the parting group; Elder Schellenberg and Johann Poettker based their messages on John 14:19 and Revelation 2:10, respectively, and addressed themselves mainly to the group that remained. This moving service reached its climax when representatives of the remaining body asked those who planned to leave whether they would make a public pledge of their continuing loyalty to Christ. The group responded by rising. Elder Schellenberg then addressed the same question to those who remained. This group also made a solemn pledge by responding in the same manner.[33] Thus the continuing witness of the Mennonite Brethren on two continents was reaffirmed in this historic moment by a mutual covenant before God.

Several groups of Mennonites from the "Trakt" settlement on the Volga River chose to migrate east rather than west in order to find a place of refuge for the free exercise of their faith. Under the direction of Claass Epp these groups left in 1880 for Central Asia (Turkestan). These pilgrims were joined by a group of more than fifty families from the Molotschna under the leadership of elder Abraham Peters. Both groups were inspired by the chiliastic ideas of Jung Stilling. After suffering incredible hardships for many years, the fanatical faction under Epp's leadership disintegrated. The more liberal element of Epp's following joined the party of Elder Peters and established a settlement at Aulie Ata, about one hundred and fifty miles northeast of the city of Taschkent. This settlement is of interest to Mennonite Brethren for at least two reasons: in the first place, approximately one half of its total Mennonite population of one thousand before World War I belonged to the Mennonite Brethren Church; and secondly, this area has had the greatest concentration of Mennonite Brethren in the Soviet Union after World War II.

All the Mennonites, including the Mennonite Brethren, who remained in Russia proper accepted an alternative service in the forestry division in lieu of military training. This form of civilian public service will receive further consideration in the next chapter.

3. *Expansion of Spiritual Horizons*

The decade of the seventies is not only known for changing political and social conditions in Russia which resulted in emigration and acceptance of alternative service on the part of the Mennonites, but also for significant spiritual trends within the larger Mennonite brotherhood. The desire for greater spiritual unity in different "camps" led to the convening of an inter-Mennonite Faith Conference in the fall of 1875. The initiative in this matter was taken by the Mennonite Brethren under the leadership of elder Abraham Schellenberg.[34]

That there was a keen interest in such a "dialogue" can be seen by the fact that "brethren" from various churches of the Molotschna and even from Chortitza filled the Mennonite Brethren Church in Rueckenau to capacity on that occasion. Discussion centered on such subjects as silent or audible prayer, the form of prayer, the prayer of sisters in public services, and baptism. On this latter issue, which had been so controversial and divisive in the past, the brethren from both sides endeavored to speak the truth in love. After a lengthy discussion, Bernhard Harder, teacher and evangelist of the Mennonite Church, arose and addressed his "churchly brethren" with these words: "What do you think, my brethren, if the Lord should desire of us that we should be baptized in running water (*Fluss*) should we then not be ready to do it? For my part, I am willing."[35] The representatives of the various churches found the fellowship so enlightening and profitable, that they agreed to have another conference in November of that same year. More important, perhaps, than the subjects discussed, was the spiritual atmosphere in which the deliberations were carried on. Abraham Unger (Einlage) who had also been a participant, commented later: "I do not see any danger in such fellowship for our church, since truth will conquer on the way of love, and God's Word is truth."[36] In 1876, the year following these Faith Conferences, eighty persons joined the Mennonite Brethren Church through baptism, among them were those who had attended the meeting where baptism had been discussed.

For the first time in some twenty years the question of "open communion" was taken up again in the Mennonite Brethren Church. The two men who submitted the question for consideration, P. M. Friesen and Johann Wieler, had wide contacts with believers also among non-Mennonites, especially among the Russian people. The

14. David Duerksen   15. P. M. Friesen

Rueckenau Mennonite Brethren Church, where the question first came up in 1882, referred the matter to the General Conference that was to convene the following year. At this conference Friesen and Wieler told the brotherhood that they could no longer be bound by the regulations of the church in this matter. Although the conference could not give its approval to "open communion" at this time, it did not take any action to curb the freedom of these brethren, who were highly respected in both church and community.[37'] Around the turn of the century this question again assumed major significance in General Conference discussions.

In the years 1884-85 the Mennonite Brethren Church experienced "seasons of refreshing" through large scale revivals in both the Molotschna and the Crimea. In 1884, eighty-four members joined the church and in 1885 one hundred and seventy-one were baptized, the largest addition in any one year since the founding of the church. Among these new members were several men with outstanding leadership ability who helped to expand the spiritual horizons of the Mennonite Brethren: David Duerksen, schoolteacher and minister of the Margenau Mennonite Church, who became the "prince among preachers" in the Mennonite Brethren Church; Jacob W. Reimer, teacher and evangelist of the Ohrloff Mennonite Church; and Peter Bergmann, a candidate for the ministry in the same church. All three brethren continued their preaching ministry in the Mennonite Brethren Church. It was also at this time (1884) that P. M. Friesen, principal of the teacher training school in Halbstadt, was called into the ministry. It may be noted, in passing, that a relatively large number of men from the teaching profession were drawn into the ministry of the Mennonite Brethren Church. It is largely due to the high spiritual and intellectual caliber of these brethren that the church continued to grow and find favor with God and with men.

Directly and indirectly the Mennonite Brethren contributed to the reformation within the "old" Mennonite Church. "Catholicism," it has been suggested, "is never so exemplary as when and where it is confronted with a vigorous Protestant competition." According to Kreider, the "struggle with basic spiritual issues gave new vitality to a dormant church."[38] Men like Bernhard Harder were encouraged in their labors for the renewal of the church by this contact with the Brethren. In the course of time the older congregations appropriated many ideas and practices which they considered to be right and scriptural in the new church.[39] Krahn states the most important contribution of the Mennonite Brethren as follows: "What it gave the Russian Mennonites was a rebirth of personal piety, a living piety in which the individual believer receives assurance of the forgiveness of his sins, and orders his life definitely according to the teachings of Christ, particularly the Sermon on the Mount." After enumerating other blessings which the new religious movement brought to the Mennonites, he concludes with these words: "So we see that the new religious life that came into Russian Mennonitism through the *Brueder-Gemeinde* movement exerted a powerful influence both upon the religious life and the social attitudes of the group."[40]

The observance of the twenty-fifth anniversary of the Mennonite Brethren Church on January 6, 1885, in Rueckenau, Molotschna, constitutes a significant milestone in the growth and progress of the brotherhood. This festive event, attended by approximately one thousand people, was marked by a spirit of praise and thanksgiving. A brief history of the church, prepared by Johann Wieler and Johann Fast, was read on this occasion. The church statistics compiled for this anniversary contain the following: six main congregations — Molotschna, Einlage, Kuban, Friedensfeld-Zagradowka, the Don Settlement, and the Volga Settlement; groups affiliated with the main churches — seventeen; houses of worship — seven; ordained elders — four; other ministers — thirty-five; total church membership — eighteen hundred. (In addition, there were approximately twelve hundred members in America at this time.)

The highlight of this celebration was a public acknowledgement of indebtedness and gratitude to the Ohrloff Mennonite Church for its benevolent attitude toward the early Brethren and its courageous intervention on their behalf. The entire audience expressed their appreciation first by rising to their feet, and later by prayers of thanksgiving on bended knee.[41]

By this time the Brethren had developed a certain "historical consciousness" which found practical expression in a conference resolution to ask P. M. Friesen to write a definitive history of the Mennonite Brethren Church. One prominent member of the church (a former administrator of the colony) commented: "This is a nice work for Friesen, and he will make good money on this assignment, for he will complete it in two weeks."[42] It may be of interest that P. M. Friesen worked on this *magnum opus* with some interruptions for twenty-five years (1886-1911)! While he was engaged in this difficult task of research and writing, the Mennonite Brethren Church enjoyed an unprecedented period of prosperity and progress. The developments of these three decades before the "gathering storm" constitute the next chapter.

Chapter 7

Era of Prosperity and Progress (1885-1914)

The three decades prior to World War I could well be described as the "golden age" of the Mennonites in general, and of the Mennonite Brethren Church in particular. The Mennonites, including the Mennonite Brethren, had unparalleled opportunities for establishing and maintaining communities on the basis of their understanding of biblical truth and their heritage. "The course of this unhampered development," Smith observes, "also suggests the direction Mennonitism may sometimes take when it is free to apply its principles, economic and religious, to every day living."[1]

This is also the period in which the earlier isolation of the Mennonite Brethren from the rest of the Mennonites, as well as their withdrawal from public affairs, comes to an end. Increasingly Mennonite Brethren become involved, often in positions of leadership, in the socioeconomic and cultural life of the larger Mennonite community.

In the spiritual realm this period is marked by continued increase in membership and by founding of churches in new areas. A growing missionary vision finds expression in the commissioning of workers for ministries in the "regions beyond." In the internal life of the church the tensions between the conservative and progressive elements lead to serious confrontations on such issues as "open communion." The theological self-consciousness and maturity of the Mennonite Brethren Church finds expression in the formulation of a new *Confession of Faith* (1902).

These developments are presented here only in broad outline.

1. *New Frontiers in Colonization*

Throughout the second half of the nineteenth century Imperial Russia pursued a vigorous expansionist policy. It secured its borders to the South, especially in the Caucasus, and pressed on relentlessly in Asia — first into Central Asia (Turkestan) in the sixties and seventies, and then into Far Eastern Asia (Eastern Siberia) in the eighties and nineties.[2] Mennonite settlements, in many instances, were established along the frontier in these newly acquired territories. Some colonies were established near the original ones, as in the Crimea and in the Caucasus, but others were as far away as Siberia and Turkestan.

TABLE I
Major Mennonite Settlements over 10 Villages
in Russia in 1918[3]

No.	Settlement	Date of Founding	Location	Number of Villages
1.	Molotschna	1804	Ukraine	58
2.	Chortitza	1789	Ukraine	18
3.	Memrik	1884	Ukraine	10
4.	Zagradovka	1871	Ukraine	17
5.	Jasykovo	1868	Ukraine	10
6.	Terek	1901	Caucasus	17
7.	Old Samara	1861	Middle Volga	10
8.	New Samara	1891	Middle Volga	14
9.	Trakt	1851	Middle Volga	10
10.	Orenburg	1893	Middle Volga (West of Urals)	21
11.	Crimea	1860	Crimean Peninsula	35
12.	Omsk	1900	Siberia	58
13.	Slavgorod and Barnaul	1907	Siberia	51
14.	Pavlodar	1907	Siberia	16

(For map of Mennonite Settlements in European Russia see Appendix 3)

We shall briefly sketch the founding and development of Mennonite Brethren churches in a number of daughter colonies.

(1) *Crimea*[4] (Spat-Schoental). The Mennonites began to settle here soon after the Crimean War (1854-56). In all probability they had become acquainted with this area in the course of their transportation duties for the government during the war. In the next four decades some twenty-five villages were established in this "Florida" of Russia, with most of the settlers coming from the Molotschna Colony. In 1869 a group of believers seceded from the *Kleine Gemeinde* and organized the Krimmer Mennonite Brethren Church, as reported earlier. This church emigrated to the United States as a body in 1874, under the leadership of their elder Jacob A. Wiebe.

The Mennonite Brethren Church in the Crimea was born in the

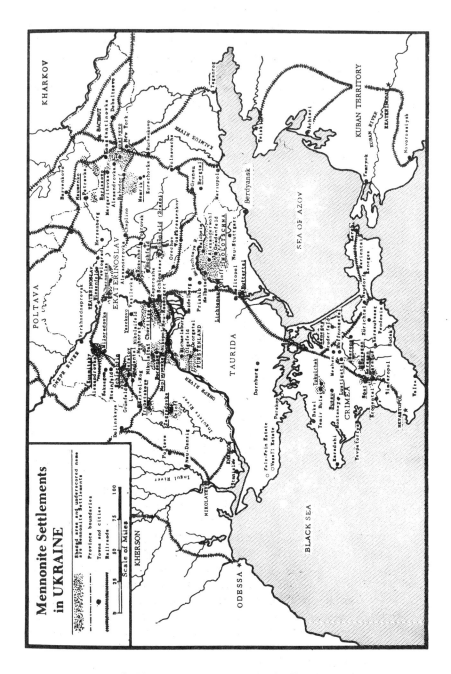

3. **Mennonite settlements in the Ukraine**

revivals of 1883-84, which may be considered as an extension of the great awakening in the Molotschna during the same time. Itinerant evangelists from the Molotschna visited the Crimean settlements and revivals occurred in Spat, Tokultschack, Timir Bulat (A. H. Unruh's birthplace) and in other villages. Some Mennonite Brethren families who had moved to this area gave leadership in arranging Bible studies and prayer meetings for the new converts. Upon the request of the group, David Schellenberg, elder of the Rueckenau M.B. Church, and several other brethren came to the village of Spat in the spring of 1885 to assist the believers here in organizing a church. On April 28, 1885, Schellenberg baptized twenty-one people and organized the group as a branch-church (*Filiale*) of the Rueckenau M.B. Church. A little more than a year later, in the fall of 1886, David Schellenberg ordained Hermann Konrad as elder of the Spat-Schoental congregation in the presence of Abraham Schellenberg, who had come from the United States for an extensive visit to the Mennonite Brethren churches of Russia. The congregation prospered under the multiple ministry of dedicated preachers. In 1895 Abraham Kroeker returned from Rumania where he had served a Baptist congregation for more than two years, and two years later his cousin Jakob Kroeker came back from Hamburg after completing his theological studies there.[5] In 1897 the Spat-Schoental congregation extended a call to David Duerksen, an evangelist of the Molotschna M.B. Church, to assume leadership responsibility for the rapidly growing constituency. In 1899 David Duerksen was ordained as elder by elders Aron Lepp (Chortitza) and David Schellenberg (Molotschna). At the same time the Spat-Schoental congregation became independent in its organizational structure. Spacious church buildings were erected at Spat (1887) and at Schoental (1905). In 1902 the church membership stood at three hundred and thirty, with an additional five hundred adherents.

David Gerhard Duerksen (1850-1910) must be regarded as one of the "chosen instruments" of God in building the Mennonite Brethren Church. The following description of Duerksen appeared in the *Mennonitisches Lexikon* shortly after his death:

> He was one of the greatest channels of blessing to Russian Mennonitism during the last fifty years preceding World War I. For those who knew him, either as educator, preacher, elder or author, his life and service were an ideal, or a pattern to emulate. During more than two decades, he was one of the strongest influences for the awakening, nurturing, and influencing of the spiritual life in the Mennonite Churches. [6]

Through another family of the Spat-Schoental congregation great blessings have come to the larger brotherhood on three continents — the Unruhs. Heinrich and Cornelius, both trained in the Baptist Seminary in Hamburg, went as missionaries to India with their families around the turn of the century; Abraham and Benjamin both became outstanding educators, first in Russia, and later in Canada and Germany respectively, and Gerhard served faithfully as a preacher in the Mennonite Brethren Church in Russia as well as in Canada. Because of the high spiritual and intellectual caliber of its leaders, the Spat-Schoental church became one of the most influential Mennonite Brethren congregations in South Russia.

The Mennonite Brethren here became actively involved in the promotion of better education. David Duerksen and Jakob Kroeker served as members on the commission which supervised the teaching of religion and German in the schools. The whole church actively supported the establishment of Christian private high schools — in 1905 in Karassan, and in 1906 in Spat. The first Bible school among the Mennonites of Russia, built by Mennonite Brethren in the Crimea in 1918, will receive special consideration in the next chapter.

(2) *Memrik* (Kotljarewka). The Memrik Mennonite settlement was established as a "daughter colony" of the Molotschna in 1885 in the so-called Don basin of the Ekaterinoslav province. The necessary qualifications of a settler were that "the head of the landless family conduct a quiet and moral life, be industrious and in possession of a wagon, plow, harrow, two horses, two cows, and the necessary means to establish a home."[7] A total of 221 families settled here in ten villages. Among these settlers were also twenty-eight members of the Mennonite Brethren Church, who had an elected minister, Isaak Fast, and a deacon in their midst. The group functioned as a subsidiary of the Molotschna M.B. Church until 1900, when it became independent and the center for other "branch churches." In 1902 the congregation had a membership of three hundred and fifty, with a total of six hundred and seventy worshipers. Here as in some other new settlements, local government authorities occasionally identified the Brethren with the Baptists and consequently they suffered from various types of harassment. The Mennonite Brethren meetinghouse, for instance, was temporarily closed by the police in the winter of 1896-97. The wider horizons of the Brethren here are shown in that two brethren of this congregation studied theology in St. Crischona, Switzerland, around the turn of the century.[8]

(3) *Barwenkowo*. Barwenkowo, a city of about fourteen thousand inhabitants (1914) became the center of Mennonite settlement in the province of Charkov. Mennonites from the Chortitza and Molotschna colonies settled here and in Naumenko and Somoilowka after 1889. This "settlement" differed from the other daughter colonies in that Mennonites moved to Barwenkowo to engage in trade and industry. A number of flour mills, a factory for agricultural implements, and various machine shops were owned by Mennonites, including one of the founders

of the Mennonite Brethren Church in Barwenkowo, Gerhard Froese. In 1903 the Brethren of this area extended a call to a young teacher, A. H. Unruh, to come and help them in their school program and church work. Unruh, who was twenty-five at the time, had been teaching for eight years in the Crimea, but had a desire to enter a wider spiritual ministry. After six years of teaching in the elementary school, Unruh was asked to become a member of the faculty of the "Commerce School" (*Kommerzschule*) which was established in 1909, supported by both Russians and Mennonites. During these years in Barwenkowo, Unruh developed the expository preaching method which made his ministry so effective.[9] In 1904 Unruh was ordained to the ministry by elder D. Schellenberg. In this congregation he served faithfully as leading minister, with a temporary interruption during World War I, until after the Russian Revolution in 1918. The Barwenkowo congregation was actively involved in a ministry to the Russian people. In connection with this mission A. H. Unruh and G. P. Froese were arrested by government officials and imprisoned for thirty days.[10] During the Civil War (1918-20) the congregation here dissolved.

(4) *Ignatjewo.* Another prosperous agricultural settlement in the province of Ekaterinoslav was established by Chortitza Mennonites at Ignatjewo in 1888. The village of Nikolajewka became the center of the Mennonite Brethren Church in this settlement. A large secondary school built here by the Brethren, was used for worship services on Sunday. Hermann Neufeld, who had moved here from Chortitza, became the leading minister of this congregation. In 1895 he was ordained and the church ceased to be a subsidiary of the Mennonite Brethren Church of Chortitza. Already in 1892 Neufeld had become an itinerant minister of the Mennonite Brethren Conference, and he continued this work for twenty-five years. His ministry took him on four extensive trips to the congregations in Siberia and Turkestan. He was ordained as elder in 1903 and became an outstanding leader of the Mennonite Brethren Church, serving as moderator of the conference and on various important committees. In 1923 he emigrated to Canada where he established his home in Winkler, Manitoba. Older ministers will remember his booklet, *Handbuch fuer Prediger* (Handbook for Preachers). During Neufeld's prolonged absences from the congregation in Ignatjewo other ministers carried on the work of the church.[11]

(5) *Terek.* A Mennonite settlement in the southeastern part of European Russia on the Terek river, which flows into the Caspian Sea in the Eastern Caucasus, was founded by the Molotschna Mennonites in 1901. Of the projected seventeen villages only fifteen had been established by 1904. Because of severe drought, which resulted in repeated crop failures, irrigation was introduced — a practice perhaps

unique in Mennonite settlements in Russia. With the Revolution of 1917 a new period started. The Tartar tribes who inhabited the surrounding mountainous terrain, swept down from their hideouts, pillaging and plundering Mennonite villages. In February, 1918, long caravans of settlers abandoned the Terek colony, leaving everything behind that they had built up in seventeen long years. The "Terek" chapter constitutes one of the most tragic episodes in Mennonite colonization experiments.

A Mennonite Brethren Church was established here during the first year of settlement. Jacob Doerksen, elder, and Christian Schmidt were two of its early leaders. The congregation became independent in 1910, and two years later erected a church building in the village of Talma. During the Civil War the Terek refugees found a temporary home among their brethren in the Kuban and Molotschna colonies.[12]

(6) *On the Volga.* In the nineties Mennonite settlements were extended toward the Northeast into the region of the middle and upper Volga. Two colonies had been established here earlier, with immigrants coming directly from Prussia: Trakt (1853), and Alexandertal (Alt-Samara) 1861. In the latter colony an M.B. church was organized in the late sixties. Very little is known of the history of this church which had its center at Hahnsau. Of greater significance were the congregations in the newer settlements of Neu-Samara (1891), Orenburg (1893), and Ufa (1894). In Neu-Samara the Mennonite Brethren Church had its center at Lugowsk, where it erected a fine church building in 1901, the year it ceased to be a subsidiary. Some prominent Christian laymen have their spiritual roots in this congregation, among them C. F. Klassen (1894-1954), outstanding leader and administrator in Mennonite relief and colonization work in Russia, Canada, and Europe, and from 1945 to his death, director of the refugee and resettlement program of the MCC in behalf of the Russian and Danzig refugees. Among the early ministers of this congregation, Abraham Martens, church leader and ordained elder, and Cornelius Klaassen, preacher, who also served as itinerant minister in Orenburg and Siberia, should be mentioned. In the Orenburg settlement the M. B. Church began in 1894 at Kamenka and in the Ufa settlement at Gortschakowo in the same year. By 1900 both colonies had growing and self-sustaining M. B. congregations.[13]

(7) *In Siberia.* Among the Mennonites of Russia, the first decade of the twentieth century is characterized by *"Drang nach Osten"* (compulsion to move east). The rate and scope of expansion exceed those of any earlier period. By 1914, one hundred and twenty-five villages had been established: in Omsk (58), Slavgorod-Barnaul (51), and Pavlodar (16) in Western Siberia.[14] Although the total Mennonite population in

Siberia before World War I was only about fifteen thousand, they owned more than one million acres of land, about one-third of all the land occupied by the Russian Mennonites. Siberia has been described as a "dark chapter in Mennonite research" because the settlements originated just before World War I and were far removed from the cultural centers of the Mennonites in the Ukraine.[15] The first Mennonite Brethren Church was established in the Omsk region in the village of Tschunayevka shortly after 1900. Elder Jacob Wiens served as leader for many years, not only of this congregation, but also of other churches in Western Siberia. In the Barnaul settlement the Mennonite Brethren Church was divided (like the Mennonite Church) into five districts, with meetinghouses in six villages. Elder Jacob Wiens of Omsk assisted the congregations here as well as in Pavlodar in their organization and establishment during the difficult pioneer period. Statistics concerning membership during this period are either unavailable or unreliable. According to one elder, Mennonite Brethren in Siberia may have numbered about 1640 in 1926.[16]

In closing this section on geographical expansion reference should be made to the establishment of the Mennonite Brethren Church at Deutsch-Wymyschle in Russian Poland about 1884. The repeated visits of elder Jacob Jantz (Friedensfeld) were a significant factor in the development of this congregation. Peter Ratzlaff gave effective leadership to this congregation for many years.[17]

As one reflects on the expansion of the Mennonite Brethren during this period, a certain pattern emerges. The establishment of congregations in new settlements usually began with a nucleus of M. B. families. Their work and witness were reinforced by itinerant ministers, who played a key role in this process. At first the young congregation functioned as a subsidiary of the "mother church," sometimes for a number of years. As soon as it became self-sustaining and self-governing, the new church itself functioned as a center of outreach and established branch-churches in the surrounding area. The itinerant ministry and congregational interdependence were the two basic factors in the successful church-extension of the Mennonite Brethren in Russia. and congregational interdependence were the two basic factors in the successful church-extension of the Mennonite Brethren in Russia.

2. *New Frontiers in Cooperation*

In the areas of general education and public health and welfare the Mennonite Brethren continued to cooperate with the other Mennonite bodies after the secession. In the early sixties, it is true, a number of brethren lost their teaching positions when they joined the M. B. Church (e.g. A. Cornelsen, G. Wieler, D. Fast and others). In the seventies and eighties the situation gradually changed, however, and it would appear that a relatively large number of Mennonite Brethren were engaged in the teaching profession — both on an elementary and secondary level. On a secondary level (*Zentralschule*) the Mennonite Brethren in Ignatjewo founded their own school, but this was probably an exception.[18]

Educational growth paralleled the economic prosperity especially after 1870. By 1914 the Russian Mennonite settlements had four hundred elementary schools, thirteen secondary or high schools, four girls' schools, two teachers colleges, two four-year trade schools, and one eight-year business college (both trade and business schools required three languages, Russian, German and French or English), one school for the deaf and dumb and one deaconess institution.[19] Many of the teachers were graduates of universities in Russia, Switzerland or Germany. About two hundred and fifty Mennonite students, moreover, were attending higher Russian institutions and fifty were in seminaries and universities abroad. Aron A. Toews, the author's father, who taught for nineteen years in the Molotschna colony, has expressed the view that practically all teachers in Mennonite schools at the turn of the century were committed Christians. Since "religion" was an integral part of the curriculum, such teachers were in a strategic position to exert a powerful moral and spiritual influence in the community.

In the area of health and general welfare the Mennonite Brethren not only cooperated with the other groups, but often gave outstanding leadership. The founder of the orphanage in Grossweide (1906), Abraham Harder, for instance, was a member of the M. B. Church. The various Mennonite groups also cooperated in the establishment and support of homes for the aged and hospitals, including a mental hospital known as "Bethania."

A new frontier for cooperation between the Mennonite Brethren and the Mennonite Church was provided by the Forestry Service (*Forstei Dienst*) initiated in 1880. Even before the universal conscription law of 1874 was passed, Mennonites endeavored to secure some form of alternative service. The threat of emigration in the event that this request would be denied, forced the Russian government to make liberal concessions. It then proposed a system of release from military service by service in (1) the shops of the Navy Department, (2) the Fire Department of a city, or (3) the Forestry Department. The Mennonites accepted the third option, because this service would enable them to keep their young men together in larger units, and thus make pastoral care possible.

In the course of a few years, eight "barracks" were built in different areas to accommodate the young men from all parts of the Mennonite constituency.[20] Each company had an "economist-preacher" (*Oekonom-Prediger*) who was in charge of pastoral care as well as material supervisions. This combination of duties was not always conducive for creating a wholesome spiritual atmosphere. Nevertheless, many young men who spent four years (the regular term of service) in these forestry camps have testified to the fact that this experience widened their intellectual horizons and also led to a deeper Christian commitment. In 1913 the total number of young Mennonites in alternative government service numbered about one thousand, at an expense to the churches of three hundred and fifty thousand rubles. This was the price, in terms of money, that the Mennonites of Russia, including the Mennonite Brethren, were willing to pay for the preservation of their biblical and historic position of peace and nonresistance.

This cooperation and involvement in the forestry service, according to one observer, "led to a reuniting of all Mennonite groups for one purpose. Such a union . . . within the Mennonite fraternity created a 'consciousness of kind,' and opened the way for united efforts in various directions for the good of Mennonitism as a whole."[21]

3. *New Frontiers in Publication*

In the realm of production and distribution of Christian literature Russian Mennonite history in the nineteenth century is marked by an almost incredible sterility. By 1845 only one item had been printed, a polemical tract on the *Kleine Gemeinde*.[22] In the next few decades a few minor works of a pedagogical and historical nature were published. A refreshing oasis in this literary desert was the poetry of Bernhard Harder, teacher and evangelist of the Ohrloff Mennonite Church. Over one thousand of his poems and hymns have been published.

Among the Mennonite Brethren interest in publication manifested itself relatively early in their history, and they became trailblazers in several areas. This is certainly true in historical writing. P. M. Friesen's monumental work, *Die Alt-Evangelische Mennonitische Bruederschaft in Russland, 1789-1910*, begun in 1886, describes not only the history of the Mennonite Brethren, but constitutes the best collection of source materials on Russian Mennonite history in general. Mennonite Brethren were also pioneers in providing Christian periodicals for the general public. It is almost incomprehensible that for about one hundred years the Mennonites of Russia managed to carry on without a religious periodical of their own. During the last quarter of the nineteenth century two Mennonite papers from America found their way into many Mennonite homes, the *Mennonitische Rundschau* (after 1880) and the *Zionsbote* (after 1885). During the first seventy-five years of their history, the religious diet of Russian Mennonites consisted almost

16. Abraham Kroeker   17. Abraham and Maria Friesen

exclusively of the reading materials drawn from Pietist and Baptist sources in Germany.

The "father" of Mennonite Brethren publication in Russia was Abraham J. Kroeker (1863-1944) a minister and writer. Kroeker entered publication work in 1897, when, in cooperation with his cousin Jakob Kroeker, he began to publish the *Christlicher Familienkalender*, a Mennonite almanac. As it was the only almanac published by the Mennonites in Russia, it was read by nearly every Mennonite family and reached an annual circulation of 15,000. In 1899 the *Christlicher Abreisskalender*, also published by A. Kroeker, made its appearance. This daily devotional booklet, in the form of a wall calendar consisting of detachable sheets, was not particularly Mennonite in character, but was designed to serve an interdenominational public. Before World War I over one half of the twenty-five thousand copies sold were purchased by non-Mennonites.[23]

Equally important for the constituency was Kroeker's venture of faith in publishing the first Mennonite periodical in Russia in 1903.[24] The semi-weekly *Friedensstimme* was printed for the first three years in Berlin, but in 1906 permission was granted to publish it (under censorship!) in Halbstadt. Here a Mennonite publishing company had been organized in 1904 under the name of *Raduga* ("Rainbow") of which A. Kroeker was a partner. Although privately owned and published, the *Friedensstimme* became the semi-official organ of the Mennonite Brethren Church, and the *Botschafter* served in the same manner as voice of the Mennonite Church. In March, 1913, the subscription of the

Friedensstimme had reached its highest point, five thousand eight hundred. Shortly after the outbreak of World War I it was discontinued.

Jakob Kroeker (1872-1948) who assisted A. Kroeker in his publication efforts, must be ranked as the leading theologian and writer of the Mennonite Brethren in Europe. He traveled widely as evangelist and Bible conference speaker, and had contacts with leading evangelicals in Russia, the Baltic States and Germany. After he moved to Wernigerode am Harz, Germany, in 1910, he began to publish his classic Old Testament studies, entitled *Das Lebendige Wort* (the Living Word) which appeared in eight volumes. A number of other smaller devotional and doctrinal books were published by this gifted man, who according to Christian Neff, was "recognized as a theologian by leaders of the German, Swiss, and Dutch, Lutheran and Reformed Churches."[25] A missionary paper *Dein Reich Komme!* (Thy kingdom come) was also published by Jakob Kroeker for a number of years.

In 1876 Abraham Unger of Einlage had published the "Baptist" *Confession of Faith* which was regarded with a considerable amount of uneasiness by the brotherhood as a whole. This growing uneasiness finally resulted in the appointment of a study commission in 1898,

to compare the Einlage confession with the first official Mennonite Brethren confession, commonly known as the 1853 Rudnerweide confession and all subsequent doctrinal statements, and then make appropriate recommendations in the light of the present (1898) understanding and need. [26]

After attempts at revision proved unsatisfactory, a new draft was written in 1900. This *Confession of Faith*, accepted and published in 1902, became the normative confession of the Mennonite Brethren on both sides of the Atlantic and will receive further consideration in connection with the study of theological developments in the Mennonite Brethren Church.

Although getting off to a late start, Mennonite Brethren publication efforts were expanding rapidly just prior to World War I. The anti-German attitudes in Russia at the outbreak of war, however, made German language papers especially vulnerable to attack from the propaganda of Slavophiles, and hence all were forced to terminate publication eventually.

4. *New Frontiers in Missions*

As we have noted earlier, the Mennonite Brethren Church was born in an atmosphere of missions which prevailed in the Gnadenfeld Church. This emphasis on evangelism and missions has molded the faith and life of the church from its inception, and constitutes a basic ingredient in its understanding of the nature of the church. "Whereas the old church had lost most of its zeal," Gerhard Lohrenz writes, "and contented itself with peaceful coexistence, the new church soon found ways of

implementing the Great Commission."[27] Although at first the Brethren
shared their faith primarily with their Mennonite neighbors, they soon
began their witness to Russians who lived in villages adjacent to the
Mennonite colonies. This certainly was a new and a dangerous frontier
since the law provided that "for the seduction of a member of the
Orthodox Church to any other confession the guilty party will be
condemned to the loss of all personal property as well as of his rights
and privileges. He will be exiled to Siberia or else condemned to serve in
corrective penal institutions."[28] The risks of imprisonment or exile, however, did not stop the Brethren from moving again and again into this
vast and "whitened" harvest field. G. W. Peters records several instances of such outreach in his survey of this period.[29]

As indicated earlier, Johann Wieler, evangelist and itinerant
minister, considered the evangelization of the Russians the most
important mission of the Mennonite Brethren Church. Personally he
became deeply involved in work with the Baptists. In 1884 he called a
conference of Russian Baptists at Novovasilewka to organize the
"Union of the Russian Baptists." In 1886 Wieler was elected first
chairman, a position he held until his flight to Rumania. The impact and
influence of the Mennonite Brethren on the origin and development of
Russian Stundism[30] and the Baptist movement is generally admitted.
C. D. Bondar states that "in common with the German Baptists the new
Mennonites have played a prominent role in the development of the
South Russian Baptism. . . ."[31] The late A. V. Karev prominent leader
and historian of the Russian Baptists after World War II, strongly
emphasizes the significance of the Mennonite Brethren in the origin of
the Baptist movement in Russia.[32]

In 1906 the Mennonite Brethren Conference formed a committee for
evangelism among the Russian people. By 1908 nine brethren were
supported by them — most of them Russians. New Testaments and
tracts were distributed, often by owners of factories and flour mills to
their workers and customers. Despite several imprisonments of
Mennonite organizers, the work continued to grow, but it reached its
greatest scope and effectiveness only after the Revolution of 1917.

The missionary efforts of the Brethren, however, did not lead to the
establishment of Mennonite Brethren churches among the Russians.
This would have been an infringement of the law which prohibited
Russians from becoming Mennonites, and would in all probability have
endangered the privileges the Mennonite Brethren enjoyed with the
other Mennonites. "Thus the new converts of non-Mennonite
background were advised to join the Baptist Church."[33]

The missionary concern of the Brethren during the last decades of
the nineteenth century was not restricted to the field of home missions.

Through the reading of missionary literature their interest in the "regions beyond" was kindled and found expression in regular contributions to various mission societies, primarily German Baptist. Involvement in missions through financial support, however, did not completely satisfy the Brethren. With increased frequency they expressed the desire to send out a missionary of their own.[34]

This aspiration was fulfilled in 1885, when a young couple, Abraham and Maria Friesen, volunteered for foreign missionary service. With the blessing of the church they enrolled in the German Baptist Seminary in Hamburg to prepare for a ministry abroad.[35] During his last year of studies there, Friesen corresponded with the church leadership at home with regard to the choice of a mission field. Since he had become acquainted with the work of the American Baptist Missionary Union in India, he felt inwardly constrained to go to that needy field. The Friesens were accepted by the Union and commissioned by their home church for a ministry in India, the Mennonite Brethren assuming full responsibility for financial support. After travel and language study, the Friesens arrived on the Nalgonda field in October, 1890, to begin a fruitful missionary career.

The arrangement with the Baptist Missionary Union of Boston was such that the Mennonite Brethren were virtually independent in the administration and operation of the mission among the Telegus of this area. The growing missionary interest and strong financial support of the M. B. churches in Russia encouraged the Baptist Union to accept two more couples, the Abraham Hueberts and the Heinrich Unruhs, as missionaries to India in 1898. Eventually six couples and six single missionaries went out to India, and two men left for Africa — all supported by the Mennonite Brethren of Russia. When the Friesens were forced to terminate their ministry in 1904 because of ill health, they left behind four indigenous churches with a total baptized membership of over one thousand.[36]

The First World War severed all connections between the Nalgonda field and its home base in the M. B. churches of Russia. Consequently, the once flourishing work of the Mennonite Brethren became an integral part of the American Baptist Mission Board and is now completely supported and supervised by that society.[37] Even before this time, however, American Mennonite Brethren had begun to contribute financially to this work and had also commissioned their own workers for mission service in India. Thus the mission of the Mennonite Brethren in India can be considered a direct outgrowth of the missionary spirit developed in the Mennonite Brethren Church of South Russia.[38]

5. *New Frontiers in Inter-Mennonite Relations*

From the annals of Mennonite history it would appear that it is easier for various Mennonite groups to work together than to worship together. Although the Mennonite Brethren cooperated with the "churchly" Mennonites in public education, general welfare, and alternative service, it was not until the beginning of the twentieth century that new frontiers for fellowship in various areas were explored and won. No doubt the constant contact in practical working relationships through the years broke down many barriers of suspicion and prejudice and prepared the way for more intimate spiritual fellowship between the "new" and the "old" churches.

Many of the early Brethren were "alliance men" at heart. In a letter to Abraham Unger in January, 1865, Jacob W. Reimer wrote,

I am wholeheartedly for the alliance, because the true body of Christ consists of all true believers from all confessions and nations who will come from east and west and north and south and sit with Abraham, Isaac and Jacob in the kingdom of God, and you and I with them through God's grace and the merits of Jesus Christ. [39]

After 1865, according to P. M. Friesen, a new element came into the Mennonite Brethren Church, largely from the conservative Flemish Mennonite Church, which showed the same narrowness and intolerance that had been characteristic of their attitude in the old church.[40] Old sins have a tendency to appear in new clothes. The same kind of mentality that had earlier produced the hyper-emotional movement by insisting on literalism in Scripture interpretation, now manifested itself in a rigid legalism in church practices. The leaders of the ultra-conservatives, according to Friesen, were men who lacked any historical perspective, and seldom, if ever, read a serious theological book.[41] Gradually, however, the progressive element gained the upper hand and built bridges of mutual recognition and fellowship with the "separated brethren." Several new frontiers in inter-Mennonite relationships will now be considered briefly.

(1) *Open Communion.* As has been pointed out in chapter five, the early Brethren in the Molotschna practiced open communion until the fall of 1863. After 1865 the strict view of the Chortitza Brethren prevailed, and no "brother" from the Mennonite Church was admitted to the communion table in the Mennonite Brethren Church. Communion with the Baptists became a highly controversial issue in the seventies, because the latter "confessed the sword" and endangered the privileges of the Mennonite Brethren. Attempts to exclude them from communion failed, however, because many of the strict brethren had pro-Baptist leanings.

At the turn of the century an increasing number of Mennonite Brethren, including several leading ministers, desired a wider communion fellowship with other confessions, but especially with the believers of the "churchly Mennonites."[42] At the annual conference in 1883, P. M. Friesen and Johann Wieler declared their intention to practice open communion, as was mentioned in chapter 6, but the matter was not taken up for discussion.

The question of open communion came to a head in 1899, when the conference evangelist, Jacob W. Reimer, conducted such a service at Steinbach.[43] When after a baptismal service the Brethren gathered for communion, Reimer, at the prompting of a visiting brother, announced that all followers of Christ, regardless of church affiliation, would be welcome at the Lord's table.

This deviation from regular practice created a storm in the Rueckenau M. B. Church, of which Reimer was a member. One brother even called for his expulsion. Since Reimer was conference worker, the Missions Committee, composed of the elders and several representatives of the churches, considered the matter. The committee released Reimer from his position as itinerant minister of the M. B. Conference and suggested that he should perhaps withdraw from the church with which he disagreed in practice. The elder of the Rueckenau Church, David Schellenberg, was inclined to go along with the recommendation of the Missions Committee. At the brotherhood meeting where this matter came up, Reimer addressed his fellow-members as follows: "Brethren, should I leave you whom I love and with whom I am one in spirit? I can understand the separation of light from darkness, but not the separation of light from light. I will not leave you voluntarily; you will have to excommunicate me."[44]

Missionary Abraham Friesen, who was home on furlough from India at the time, then moved that even though the church did not agree with Reimer and his associates on all points, it was grateful to God for these brethren and under no circumstances would ask them to leave. This motion was accepted by a large majority of the members, and with this action the recommendation of the Executive of the General Conference (*Bundeskonferenz*) was rejected. Since Jacob W. Reimer, Peter Koehn and others who took the same stand were subsequently not engaged by the M. B. General Conference for an itinerant ministry, the Rueckenau congregation and other friends provided the financial support for these brethren. At the annual convention of Mennonite Brethren in Waldheim (Molotschna) in 1903 it was discovered that approximately one fourth of all delegates shared the views of the "open brethren." The conference then agreed that in the matter of open communion the whole brotherhood should exercise mutual forbearance and love.

(2) *Intermarriage.* It will be recalled that the *Kirchenkonvent* feared the disruptive effects of intermarriage between members of their

congregations with members of the new movement (see chapter four).
The marriage regulations of the early Brethren, however, left no room
for these apprehensions. Right from the beginning a prospective
member had to promise not to marry outside of the church. During the
early period of withdrawal and isolation from the rest of the Mennonite
community this regulation created no problems. With the establishment
of more cordial fraternal relationships in the seventies and eighties, the
Mennonite Brethren Church became divided on the issue. At the annual
conference in 1895 the delegates agreed to drop this rule, and to exercise
discernment and discretion in each individual case.[46] In North America
marriage to believers who were not members of the M. B. Church was
still a controversial issue forty years later.[47]

It should be added here, that the Mennonite Brethren differed from
the Mennonite Church in their attitude toward the marriage of
unbaptized young people. In the latter church only baptized persons
could enter "holy matrimony" with the approval of the church. Since
there was no provision for civil marriage in the Mennonite colonies
young people, even though unconverted, submitted to baptism in order
to be married. The Mennonite Brethren felt that this "ordinance of the
elders" set aside the commandment of Christ concerning baptism,
which is to be administered only to those who believe. They taught that
marriage belongs to the "creation order" and not the "church order." A
church wedding, however, could be meaningful even for non-Christians
in showing them the way for establishing a Christian home. P. M.
Friesen felt strongly that the linking of marriage and baptism in the old
congregations was one of the greatest obstacles to the renewal of the
Mennonite Church.[48]

(3) *Inter-church Conferences.* The previous chapter described the
so-called "Bible Conferences" (*Bibelbesprechungen*) which were begun
in 1875 under the auspices of the Rueckenau M. B. Church, and in which
members of various Mennonite churches participated. In later years,
"Faith Conferences" (*Glaubenskonferenzen*) were held from time to time
to which speakers from Germany were also invited.[49] No formal
affiliation between the two bodies (Mennonite and Mennonite Brethren)
was realized, however, until the first decade of the twentieth century.
P. M. Friesen finds fault primarily with the Mennonite Brethren who
were reluctant to respond to invitations for a more fraternal relationship.[50]

The winds of change that affected all social and political structures
in the Russian empire after the abortive revolution of 1905, also
influenced inter-Mennonite relationships, although indirectly. When the
law against sectarianism was passed, representatives of the "old"
Mennonites asked the Mennonite Brethren to clarify their mutual

relationships. The latter responded by officially adopting a resolution to extend communion fellowship to all true believers, regardless of denominational affiliation.[51] A special incentive for more formal inter-Mennonite relations was the question of military service. It was felt that in this matter all Mennonites should speak to the government with a united voice. An inter-Mennonite Conference dealing primarily with this issue was convened in 1908. The first official All-Mennonite Conference was held on October 26 and 27, 1910, in the Mennonite Church of Schoensee, Molotschna. At this conference about one third of all delegates were Mennonite Brethren representing practically all congregations located in the Ukraine. A three-member "Faith Commission" (*Glaubenkommission*) was elected at this convention, with Heinrich Braun representing the Mennonite Brethren. Two years later the name of the commission was changed to *Kommission fuer Kirchenangelegenheiten* (KfK).[52] The *KfK*, or commission for church affairs, became the executive committee of the united Mennonite conference to carry out its decisions insofar as they did not conflict with the local autonomy of the congregation, and also to represent the collective Mennonite body to the government. [53] During the time of the Revolution and the confusion following it, all activities of this commision were temporarily ended.

(4) *The Alliance Church (Allianz Gemeinde)*.[54] The progressive "Left wing" of the Mennonite Brethren Church in the Molotschna, which had been advocating open communion and fellowship with all believers, regardless of church affiliation, finally gave rise to the founding of a new fellowship, "The Evangelical Mennonite Brotherhood," also known as "Evangelical Mennonite Brethren Church,"[55] in 1905. It was popularly known as *Allianz Gemeinde* because it symbolized the attempt to bring together all true believers who had been separated by the polarization in doctrine and organization of the two main bodies: the Mennonite Church and the Mennonite Brethren Church.

The founders of this inter-church movement in the Molotschna were ministers and elders from both groups. Peter M. Friesen, a lifelong advocate of such an "alliance" was not among them and hence cannot be considered as "the founder of the Evangelical Mennonite Brethren" as claimed by one historian.[56] Important leaders of the new church were Peter Schmidt (1860-1910), well-known Mennonite philanthropist, and Abraham Nachtigal (1876-1950), its leading minister for nineteen years.

In their church polity the "Lichtfelder"[57] Evangelical Mennonite Brethren differed from the other two Mennonite bodies in that they rejected the "one elder system" and replaced it by a council of elders. Of special interest is the fact that at the time of the "founders' meeting," the new church elected three Mennonite Brethren ministers, Jacob W.

18. Jacob W. Reimer   **19. Heinrich Braun**

Reimer, Peter Unruh and Jakob Kroeker, as "associate elders" of this council, although these brethren did not officially join the group.[58] Their strong emphasis on "the unity of all true children of God" found concrete expression in their practice of open communion, and the acceptance of believers who had been baptized by a mode other than immersion.[59] As a result of this development P. M. Friesen concludes, "the Mennonite Brethren Church (justly) lost its monopoly in the realm of being a 'church of believers.' "[60]

Two years later, in 1907, a similar church was founded in Altonau, Zagradowka, which differed, however, in its historical background and motivation from the *Allianz Gemeinde* in the Molotschna. In 1903 the whole church council (*Kirchenvorstand*) of the Nikolaifelder Mennonite Church under its evangelical elder Franz Martens agreed to practice believers baptism, believers communion and scriptural church discipline. This new policy led to serious tensions and to severe criticism of the council on the part of many members. By 1907 Elder Martens and his supporters experienced so much opposition that they withdrew from the church and organized the Evangelical Mennonite Church.[61] Later this church, because of its similarity in faith and practice, established fraternal relations with the Evangelical Mennonite Brethren in the Molotschna. The relationship of both groups with the Mennonite Brethren was cordial and warm.

In Canada some "Alliance Churches" continued their separate existence for a number of years, but then joined the Mennonite Brethren.[62] In Paraguay, on the contrary, they have continued as a separate group, whereas in Brazil they have joined the General Conference Mennonite Church.

The "Alliance movement" (*Allianz-Bewegung*) rapidly gained ground among the Mennonites of South Russia before World War I, and it is conceivable that a new organizational pattern would have emerged in due time had not the Communist Regime, especially under Stalin, put an end to all organized church life in the 1930's. What hapened to the Mennonite Brethren and all Mennonites in Russia in the period between 1914 and 1945 can best be described as "a story of blood and tears."

Chapter 8

In the Shadow of Death

On June 28, 1914, an event occurred in an obscure city of Bosnia, a dependency of the Austro-Hungarian Empire, which shook the whole world and resulted in revolutionary changes throughout Europe. The assassination of the Austrian Archduke Francis Ferdinand and his wife in Sarajevo on that day triggered off a series of events: war, revolution, terror, famine, emigration, deportation, and suffering unprecedented in modern history. These events also shook the religious and economic foundations of Mennonite life in the Russian Empire. The century of peace and prosperity was followed by a succession of tragedies that led to a complete termination of all organized religious life in the Mennonite colonies.

The Imperial Decree of 1870, with its partial abrogation of privileges, and the Revolution of 1905, had been ominous precursors of more radical social and political changes in the reactionary Russian autocracy. But neither the Russian state officials, nor the Mennonites for that matter, were able to discern the "handwritng on the wall." P. M. Friesen, who died in 1914, believed to the end that the Mennonites would continue to enjoy their privileges under the benevolent protection of the Tsars, and that those who had left Russia in the 1870's had perhaps committed an historical error. Events after 1914, however, confirmed the earlier concerns of elder Abraham Schellenberg, which he had expressed to Friesen on a visit from America in 1886-1887.[1] The Mennonite Brethren were deeply involved in the events of this period, not only in the privations and sufferings, but also in the relief and rescue operations that followed. Only a brief survey of these eventful decades can be given here.

THE WORLD WAR AND THE BOLSHEVIK REVOLUTION

Soon after the outbreak of war a hate campaign against the German colonists was initiated by the super-patriots of Russia. The Mennonites,

106

because of their language and cultural contacts with Germany, were also labeled as "agents of an enemy." A decree published on November 3, 1914, prohibited the use of the German language in either public assembly or press. The following year a second official action included property liquidation laws, which however, affected very few Mennonites, since most of the Prussian and Swiss Mennonites, who had made their home in Volhynia after 1800, had migrated to America in the 1870's.[2]

Because of hostile public opinion the Mennonites soon realized that they would have to undertake some form of service beyond forestry work. A delegation was sent to Petersburg and an agreement was effected by which Mennonites would also be able to serve in a noncombatant medical corps (Sanitaetsdienst). All able-bodied men up to the age of forty-five were eventually inducted into state service; approximately six thousand served in hospitals, in the ambulance corps, and on hospital trains behind the battle front, and an equal number in the forestry service. The churches and colonies underwrote the complete cost of the program, which ran as high as three million rubles in 1917.[3] Leading Mennonite Brethren ministers served in the noncombatant medical corps.[4] This medical service must not be equated or identified with the noncombatant medical corps in the Canadian or United States armies during World War II or after. In an article, "Noncombatant Service Then and Now," F. C. Peters clearly shows the difference in administration between the Russian and American noncombatant medical services. In Russia, the medical corps (Sanitaetsdienst) was under the jurisdiction of the Zemstvo Union, a civilian organization that cooperated with the Red Cross and hence it was not part of the military.[5] In spite of the excellent services rendered by the men in the medical corps, the anti-German propaganda continued, and close police supervision, even in Mennonite worship services, was often in evidence.[6] The overthrow of the Tsarist regime in February, 1917, and the setting up of a liberal-minded interim government gave temporary relief to the hard-pressed Mennonites.

The rapidly changing political situation called for reorientation and adjustment on the part of the Mennonite colonists in many areas of their endeavors, and so an "All-Mennonite Congress" was called in the summer of 1917. The first and only "Congress" convened in Ohrloff, Molotschna, August 14-18, and was attended by 198 delegates. B. H. Unruh, a member of the M. B. Church, served as its first chairman. The matter of education, the men in alternative service, and the relationship of the Mennonites to the new Kerensky government were some of the major concerns of the "Congress." It was unable to carry out its plans,

however, because of the overthrow of the provisional government a few
months later.[7]

The triumph of the Bolsheviks in the "October Revolution"
(November 7, 1917, according to the Gregorian calendar) ushered in a
new era. Mennonite men in the forestry and medical service returned
home after the Bolsheviks had signed the peace-treaty of Brest-Litovsk
in March, 1918. By the terms of this treaty Lenin's government lost the
Ukraine. German troops, assisted by Don-Cossack regiments, moved
into the area. Between November, 1917, and April, 1918, when the
Germans arrived in the Ukraine, the Mennonites were subjected to a
reign of terror. The "workers' soviets" replaced the administrative
officials in the Colony Administrative Offices. As the "dictatorship of
the proletariat," they exploited the revolutionary situation. Thus the
German occupation forces were welcomed by the Mennonites, since their
presence promised some respite from the prevailing terror.
Unfortunately the presence of German troops in the Ukrainian
Mennonite settlements fostered a spirit of militarism among Mennonite
youth which found embodiment in the organization of a Self-Defense
Corps (Selbstschutz).[8] The spirit of militarism progressively infecting
the Mennonites, especially in the Molotschna colony, did not go
unchallenged. Pleas for moderation and repentance were heard from
Mennonite pulpits and in Mennonite periodicals. These warnings,
however, were not heeded.

To avert a catastrophe church leaders convoked an All-Mennonite
Conference in Lichtenau, Molotschna, between June 30 and July 2, 1918.
At this historic meeting, a paper by B. H. Unruh reiterated the
traditional Mennonite position on nonresistance. B. B. Janz, another
representative of the Mennonite Brethren, also made a strong plea for
abiding by the teaching of Christ and the confession of faith. These
views were not shared by all delegates, including some prominent
Mennonite Brethren ministers. A plea for tolerance and compromise was
made on the ground that the matter involved two biblically sanctioned
principles — nonresistance and Christian subservience to the state.[9] In
the end, two resolutions emerged. The first advocated the right of
private interpretation concerning nonresistance. The second reaffirmed
the conference's belief in nonresistance as the highest Christian ideal.
Paradoxically enough, both proposals were accepted by a large majority. Leaving the matter of nonresistance to private interpretation, however, opened the way for a radical minority to take up arms in an emergency and thereby placed the survival of the majority in jeopardy.[10]
Mennonite church conferences in later years condemned the Self-Defense Corps (Selbstschutz) not only as a tactical blunder, but also as a

gross violation of historic biblical nonresistance. It must always be regarded as a dark blot on the pages of Mennonite history.

The withdrawal of German troops left a "power-vacuum" in the Ukraine. It must be remembered that the Bolsheviks initially controlled only the areas around Moscow and Petersburg and were resisted on all sides by remnants of the Tsarist (white) armies. The period between November, 1918 and the fall of 1920 is therefore best described by the term "anarchy." The most notorious leader of the partisan, anarchistic forces in the Ukraine was Nestor Makhno, whose cruelty and brutality became proverbial. In his youth he had been a cattle herder on the estates of wealthy Mennonite landowners. Perhaps this experience caused him to make the Mennonite colonies the special targets of his depredations.

When roving bandits of Makhno approached the Molotschna colony from the north, a number of Self-Defense units joined similar forces from the adjacent Lutheran and Catholic colonies to stop the invaders. After putting up an heroic defense for three months, the Self-Defense Corps (*Selbstschutz*) had to yield to superior numbers. By this time the Bolsheviks had joined forces with Makhno and when the Mennonites discovered this, they laid down their arms because they had resolved from the beginning not to fight against government troops. On condition that they could reign in the province of Taurida, the followers of Makhno placed themselves under the command of the Bolsheviks. The year 1919 proved to be a year of horror for the Mennonites, especially in the Molotschna. Faced with possible annihilation, many now resorted to spiritual weapons. Under the leadership of a church elder in Elizabethtal, prayer meetings were organized in many villages. Nevertheless the Mennonites paid dearly for their attempt at self-defense and their secret collaboration with the White Army.

In the Molotschna, the village of Blumenort was hardest hit. Here is a description of what happened:

On November 10 fourteen men were sent into the basement of a home. After shooting at them for a while, the Makhno bandits threw hand grenades and finally slaughtered with their swords those still living. Six others were killed outside. The women and girls were raped. Wives in the advanced stages of pregnancy were not spared. The village was burned to the ground. [11]

In the Zagradowka and Chortitza colonies similar atrocities were committed. In Eichenfeld (Yazykovo) eighty-one men and four women were murdered in one night. Only two men above sixteen years were left. The village and six others were burned to the ground. Many of these victims of terror gave eloquent testimony to their faith in Christ before they were shot or hacked to pieces with sabers. [12]

After the reign of terror came to an end, the colonies continued to suffer from the ravages of the Civil War. The Molotschna lay in the direct path of the "Red" and "White" armies. For weeks the line of battle seesawed back and forth over the region, some villages changing hands as many as twenty times.[13] It is estimated that between 1914 and 1921 more than two thousand two hundred Mennonites met death by violence or disease.[14] The loss of property ran into millions of rubles. By the end of 1920, the Bolsheviks had gained control of all the Ukraine and peace came finally to the devastated Mennonite colonies, where blood and tears had saturated the soil for more than three years.

The Great Famine and American Relief

As in the apocalyptic judgments described in Revelation chapter six, so also in the experience of the Mennonites of Russia the red horse of war was followed by the black horse of famine and the pale horse of pestilence and death. The unsanitary conditions produced by the armed forces and the robber bands quartered in Mennonite homes for protracted periods, led to the spread of disease on a frightening scale. Such dreaded diseases as spotted typhus, cholera, syphilis, and even malaria made their appearance everywhere. The typhus epidemic claimed more lives than either war or anarchy. In the Old Colony, which was hardest hit by this plague, three hundred Mennonites had perished from typhus in the villages of Chortitza and Rosenthal alone by June 1, 1920.[15] At least one hundred women and girls who had suffered violence at the hands of the anarchists were under treatment for venereal disease. The combination of malnutrition and disease resulted in a heavy loss of life. The population of the Chortitza colony declined from eighteen thousand in the fall of 1917, to approximately thirteen thousand in the fall of 1920. Statistics from the Molotschna and Zagradowka settlements tell a similar story. Under such distressing conditions it is understandable that economic activities and social functions were reduced to a minimum, and all organized religious life was nearly paralyzed.

As if the terrors of civil war, the ravages of the Makhno bandits, and the devastations caused by disease epidemics were not enough for any people to bear at one time, a famine of unprecedented proportions followed hard on the heels of these calamities. The famine was caused by a combination of factors. All reserves of wheat and other grains had been confiscated by the robber bands or requisitioned by the Red Army. The lack of draft horses and seed grain excluded any sizeable seeding operation in the spring of 1921. More important, however, was the severe drought that affected the entire Ukraine, the "bread basket of Europe" for two successive years, resulting in total crop failures. It seemed as though divine providence had closed the heavens in judgment over a nation that had been engaged in a bloody fratricidal war for several years. Except for the timely arrival of American food supplies, many, if not most of the Mennonites in the Ukraine would have died of starvation. In the book, *Feeding the Hungry* (Russia Famine, 1919-1925), P. C. Hiebert and others have given graphic descriptions of the abject poverty and widespread famine which relief workers witnessed upon their arrival in South Russia.[16]

The contact with the European and American Mennonite constituencies had been established in 1920 by the Study Commission (*Studienkommission*) of which A. A. Friesen and B. H. Unruh were leading members. It was through the reports of these men that Mennonites in Holland, Germany, Switzerland, and somewhat later in America, became aware of the tragic plight of their brethren in Russia. In America the Russian famine became the occasion for organizing a new Mennonite relief agency. In response to the reports and requests from four members of the Study Commission, who were at that time visiting the United States and Canada, a special meeting of representatives of all existing Mennonite relief organizations assembled in Elkhart, Indiana, on July 27, 1920. The delegates agreed to form a united relief agency, the Mennonite Central Committee (MCC) whose first task involved the planning of the Russian relief program. P. C. Hiebert, who represented the Mennonite Brethren, was elected chairman — a position which he held for thirty-three years.

The first relief unit, composed of three young men from Pennsylvania: Arthur Slagel, Clayton Kratz and Orie O. Miller, endeavored to launch their relief efforts in the Ukraine via Constantinople and Sevastopol (Crimea) in October, 1920. This effort failed because of the disastrous defeat and retreat of the White Army. Clayton Kratz fell into the hands of the Bolsheviks at Halbstadt and was never heard from again.

A new approach was sought and negotiated by Alvin J. Miller, director of American Mennonite Relief (AMR), and B. B. Janz, chairman of the *Verband der Mennoniten im Sueden Russlands* (VMSR = Union of Mennonites in South Russia) through the central government in Moscow. Officials of ARA (American Relief Administration) and members of the Friends Service Committee were of great help to Miller in gaining entrance into Russia. After innumerable delays and disappointments because of bureaucratic bigotry and inefficiency, relief supplies finally reached the Mennonite colonies, where conditions had become desperate during the winter of 1921-22. Actual feeding operations, started first in the Volga area, were not begun in the Ukraine until March, 1922. For some this help came too late, but thousands were saved from death by starvation.[17] Following the example of the ARA, with whom the American and Dutch Mennonites had become affiliated, the AMR established feeding kitchens in the Mennonite villages. By May these kitchens were feeding twenty-five thousand persons every day. The peak was reached in August when forty thousand rations were issued daily. (It should be injected here, that all the hungry of a given area had access to these kitchens, regardless of nationality, race or creed.) This work was continued for three years, although the need gradually declined after 1922. In addition to these feeding kitchens, centers for distribution of clothing were set up. Among the present-day Mennonite Brethren in Canada there are hundreds of families who owe their survival to the sacrifical giving and selfless service of their "American Brethren" in those dark days of the post-revolutionary period.

It was in the crucible of suffering that the Mennonites of Russia once again learned the deeper meaning of Christ's words: "Man shall not live by bread alone, but by every word that proceeds from the mouth of God."[18] They had learned through bitter experience that "a man's life does not consist in the abundance of his possessions."[19] Many leaders as well as members in Mennonite and Mennonite Brethren churches were inclined to interpret the calamities that had befallen them as a judgment of God upon a complacent church. A deep hunger for the things of the Spirit resulted in genuine spiritual renewal and a new sense of mission throughout the Mennonite brotherhood.

Spiritual Revival and Missionary Outreach

The "October Revolution" of 1917 resulted in several changes of government policy which were welcomed by the Mennonites. The restrictions placed on the use of the German language in churches and schools were lifted because the new regime prided itself of being "international" in character. Moreover, the old law which forbade proselytizing among members of the Russian Orthodox Church was no longer enforced. It almost appeared as if the Communists favored "sectarian" activity to weaken the Orthodox Church, the great bulwark of Russian autocracy. Although a few members of the M.B. Church responded almost immediately to these new opportunities, the harshness of "War Communism" during the Civil War period (1918-21) made any organized evangelistic effort virtually impossible.

With the introduction of the New Economic Policy (NEP) in 1921, however, a new day seemed to dawn for the Russian people in general, and for Mennonites in particular.[20] Confiscation and collectivization of land was halted. To stimulate an economy that had come to a complete standstill, private trading and commerce were again encouraged. It seemed for a while that Mennonites might even recover a measure of their former religious freedom. It was in this post-war period that the

20. J. G. Wiens

21. Adolph Reimer

Mennonites of Russia experienced a widespread revival which might justly be termed their "second awakening." Mennonite Brethren played a leading role in this renewal movement, consisting of several phases.

1. *A Bible School in the Crimea.*[21]

The first Bible school of the Mennonite Brethren in Russia was not started in the pre-war era of cultural progress and material prosperity, but in 1918, the year of anarchy and civil war. A missionary on furlough from India, Johann G. Wiens, who was prevented by circumstances from returning to the mission field, was the man God used to respond to a vision and a need. The Missions Committee of the M.B. Church favored the idea and promised support. When the *Friedensstimme* brought this prospective venture to the attention of the general public, it was discovered that not only missionary candidates were interested in such preparation, but many other Christian workers as well. To meet this need the M.B. Conference accepted the Bible School as a conference institution in the fall of 1918 and appointed Heinrich Braun, the secretary-treasurer of the conference, as a second teacher. Tschongraw, a village in the Crimea where missionary Wiens had taken up residence, was chosen as the location for the new school. Because of the great differences in the educational background of the thirty students that had enrolled for such training, Wiens divided the group into two classes — those with more advanced training taking upper level courses. The curriculum was patterned somewhat after that of the German Baptist

Seminary in Hamburg, which Wiens had attended. From Tschongraw this pattern was transplanted to Winkler, Manitoba, Canada, where it became one of the "models" for Bible school curricula. A. H. Unruh joined the teaching staff in Tschongraw in 1920.

For six years (1918-1924) the school operated under the evident blessing of God, although not without opposition. When the Bolsheviks regained control of the Crimea in the fall of 1920, all teachers and students were arrested and committed for trial. At the hearing it was established that the charges brought against the school were false and so teachers and students were released. In March, 1924, however, the local authorities decreed that the school had to be closed.[22] Petitions to the central government in Moscow as well as to the government of the Crimea for permission to reopen the school were unsuccessful. In God's providence three of its teachers — Unruh, Wiens, and Reimer — were able to emigrate to Canada where they founded the Winkler Bible School a year later, in 1925, under the leadership of A. H. Unruh.

Another Bible school was organized in 1925 in Orenburg by Peter Koehn, a minister of the Mennonite Brethren Church who had studied theology at St. Crischona (near Basel) in Switzerland for two years.[23] After the school was closed by the government, Koehn and others organized a *Wandernde Bibelschule* (a "traveling" Bible school) which offered short-term courses for ministers and Christian workers, shifting its base of operation every three or four weeks. The revivals of 1924-25 are related to these renewed efforts to study the Word of God and constitute the next important phase of this "second awakening."

2. *Cooperative Evangelism in Mennonite Colonies*

The suffering and persecution which had been the common lot of ministers and members of all churches had lowered denominational barriers sufficiently for joint endeavors in building God's kingdom. Bible conferences (*Bibelbesprechungen*) on an inter-church basis prepared the way for united efforts in evangelism. The fraternal spirit among ministers is reflected in the following report:

> Thus we spent the week together under the blessings (of God); the spirit of unity and brotherliness prevailed in our meetings, and love, the bond of perfection, united the brethren. How and through whom the various churches (*Richtungen*) were represented could only be ascertained from the statistical records. We had gathered under the motto of "Jesus only". . . . and we left with the consciousness "and Jesus was also there." [24]

The personnel for this cooperative venture in evangelism was made available in a strange way by divine providence. In 1923 all ministers and "teachers of religion" were barred from teaching in public schools by the Communist government.[25] It so happened that a relatively large number of Mennonite Brethren were engaged in the teaching profession.

This was also true of the ministers in the *Allianz Gemeinde* and perhaps to a lesser extent, of the ministers in the Mennonite Church. With partial financial support from the congregations these men were now commissioned for evangelism. They were usually sent out "two by two" representing different churches. Aron A. Dueck, minister of the Margenau Mennonite Church and J. A. Toews, minister of the Alexandertal M.B. Church (both from the Molotschna) conducted a series of successful evangelistic campaigns together.[26] These meetings were often held in public schools or halls, since not nearly all villages had a church building. (In the Molotschna there were twenty-three church buildings in a colony of fifty-eight villages in 1925). Beginning in the Molotschna colony, the revival spread to Chortitza, Zagradowka and other settlements in the Ukraine. Evangelistic teams also visited the churches in Siberia and kindled revival fires on this "eastern frontier" of Mennonitism. The ministers of the *Allianz Gemeinde*, because their church maintained cordial relations with both older Mennonite conferences, played a key role in this revival movement. Hundreds made public commitments to Christ in these meetings, but an even greater number, perhaps, experienced God's forgiveness and grace as the result of personal evangelism.[27]

The revivals of 1924-25 are significant from a historical perspective since they coincided with the mass emigration to Canada (1923-26). The immigrants who came to the new world had few earthly possessions, but they brought with them an enriched Christian experience and a new spiritual concern born in the harsh school of human suffering and in the warm atmosphere of religious revival. The Mennonite Brethren from this background who came to Canada had a decisive influence on the future development of their denomination in this country.

The "second awakening" among the Mennonites of Russia is also characterized by an increased concern for the evangelization of their neighbors: the Russian people.

3. *New Efforts of Evangelism Among Russians*

Prior to the Revolution of 1917, evangelistic work among the native Russian population could be carried on only under stringent government regulations and often in the face of severe opposition. Nevertheless, as Saloff-Astakhoff has pointed out, "they (the Mennonites) had a very strong spiritual influence upon the Russian population surrounding them, and eventually helped to spread the Evangelical Protestant movement in that country."[26] Both before and after the Revolution, the Mennonite Brethren were in the vanguard of this movement to bring the gospel to the Russian people. One Mennonite historian, who admits that the old Mennonite church had practically no part in this outreach, explains that as a result:

many of the old church joined the new Mennonite movement because they shared
the rising vision in evangelism together with a longing for deeper spiritual
life. . . . Thus, while the Mennonite Brethren Church comprised only 4.3 percent
of the total Mennonite population in Russia in 1888, they had grown to include
22.5 percent by 1925. [29]

Among the outstanding leaders in this new era of evangelism, Adolf
A. Reimer (1881-1921) deserves special consideration. As a young teacher in the village of Tiege (Molotschna) he began to preach to Russian
servants, who eagerly responded to the gospel. Burdened for these
people, and encouraged by this response, Reimer resigned from his
teaching position to devote himself completely to the task of
evangelism.[30] For years he traveled the length and breadth of European
Russia assisting the Russian Baptists and Evangelical Christians in
their evangelistic outreach. But he often also preached in theatres of
cities where as yet there were no believers.

Reimer's golden opportunity came during the days of the Civil War,
when he resided in the village of Alexandertal, Molotschna. During the
White Army offensive in 1919 and again in 1920, when the front line of
battle was temporarily just north of the Molotschna colony, every
village was occupied by troops. On one occasion the White Army
general, who was favorably disposed toward Reimer, called together a
whole regiment on the street of Mariental (a neighboring village) and the
evangelist had a unique opportunity to preach to this multitude as a
dying man to dying men. On another occasion he was permitted to
address a cavalry regiment (on horseback) for fifteen minutes just
before they rode on into bloody battle.

There was no abatement in Reimer's zeal and compassion when the
Bolsheviks regained control in November, 1920. When the church
council of the M.B. Church in Alexandertal met during this time, Adolf
Reimer pled with his co-laborers: "Brethren, the Reds also have a soul
that needs to be saved, and we have to preach the gospel to them."[31]
Against the advice of his friends, he preached to the soldiers of the Red
Army, and God protected His servant.

During the time of the great famine he labored for four months in
the city of Kiev and the surrounding area. Here he contracted the
dreadful spotted-typhus disease; he died four days after he returned
home. His last words, which he repeated three times, left an indelible
impression on the members of his family: "Lord Jesus, how is your
gospel so simple, and your grace so marvelous."[32] Heinrich Enns, a
personal friend, and Daniel Reimer, his son, continued the fruitful
ministry begun by Adolf Reimer, the former dying a martyr's death.[33]

Another pioneer missionary among the Russians in the immediate
post-war period was Jacob J. Dyck (1890-1919), the leader of the
tent-mission (*Zeltmission*). Dyck's vision for this mission was born

during the war, when he served as a conscientious objector in the medical corps (*Sanitaetsdienst*) in Moscow. A group of young men, including Dyck, organized a society for the distribution of Gospels, New Testaments, and tracts among the Russian soldiers. Dyck hailed the March Revolution (1917) as the dawn of a new day of religious freedom and of new missionary opportunities.[34]

After the armistice, many Russian army units disbanded and soldiers returned to their villages. Dyck and his faithful associates decided to follow them into the villages and hamlets with the gospel. But in most Russian villages there were no halls or facilities to conduct public meetings. When the brethren were able to obtain five tents from the Russian Red Cross without charge, they accepted them as a special gift of Providence to meet their need. Immediately a number of teams, usually composed of five members, were sent out.[35] Among the members of the tent-mission there were Mennonites, Jews, Latvians, and Russians.

The Mennonite Brethren in the Molotschna manifested a special interest in this mission. When a new call for volunteers went out in the early summer of 1919, twenty-four young people responded — twelve men and twelve women. In a special dedication service in the Rueckenau M.B. Church, they were commissioned for the work of evangelism among the Russian people. Anarchy and Civil War soon led to the termination of this unique ministry. Dyck and several of his coworkers were executed in a brutal manner by the roving bandits after an evangelistic service in the village of Eichenfeld.[36]

In the early twenties there was such a proliferation of evangelistic efforts among the Russian people, that an exhaustive survey seems impossible. *Unser Blatt*, the all-Mennonite periodical from 1925 to 1928, published reports frequently about such work in almost all parts of Russia. Of special interest is a missionary report by Johann Peters, about the work among the pagan Ostjakes and Tunguse in Northern Siberia.[37] Upon graduating from the Berlin Bible School shortly before World War I, Peters and his wife returned to Russia. Beginning in 1918, they launched their mission among these semi-nomadic tribes, accompanied by Peters' sister Helen and a relative by the name of Johann Kehler. By boat, train and other means, they traveled into the region three hundred miles north of the city of Tomsk. From here to the Arctic, especially along the Ob river and its tributaries, these stalwart pioneers found their field of labor for many years. The hardships endured are indescribable, and so also the moral conditions of the people. The task of evangelizing these tribes was staggering in its magnitude.

Peters was deeply disturbed by the fact that so few responded to the call of missions. In a report in 1926 he wrote: "Have we and our fathers been faithful in seeking the lost? Brethren, for nine years now we have religious freedom in this country. Why are so many leaving for America and so few workers come to this vast northern mission field, where we can preach the gospel free and without restriction?"[38] Many of the brethren who left for America, however, were deeply convinced that religious freedom in Russia would soon come to an end, and that God would open new doors of service for them in Canada. Their premonition was confirmed by political developments under Stalin shortly afterwards. The emigration of Mennonites from the Soviet Union in the 1920s constitutes one of the greatest mass-movements of a religious group which left its homeland for conscience' sake.

CONTINUED OPPRESION AND MASS EXODUS

The desire to emigrate had its beginnings in the days of anarchy and famine, but it came to fruition and practical realization only in 1923. The Study Commission (*Studienkommission*), which left for North America in 1920, had been instructed not only to report on conditions among Russian Mennonites but also to investigate immigration and settlement possibilities. As reported earlier in this chapter, the visit of the Study Commission was the occasion for the organization of the Mennonite Central Committee in Elkhart, Indiana in July, 1920. In Canada the members of the commission also urged the various Mennonite groups to consolidate their relief efforts. After prolonged and often difficult negotiations, the Canadian Mennonite Board of Colonization came into being on May 17, 1922.[39] This board, under the able leadership of elder David Toews, was to assume the central role in the immigration and colonization of the Russian Mennonites.

The two organizations served distinct though related purposes in the overall program of meeting the needs of the Russian Mennonites: The MCC concentrated on relief and reconstruction, whereas the Canadian Mennonite Board of Colonization concentrated on immigration and resettlement. With the organization of this latter board the Canadian situation seemed to be prepared for mass-immigration from Russia, except for one major obstacle — the Order-in-Council passed by the Canadian government in 1919 which barred Mennonites and other conscientious objectors from entry. After several delegations to Ottawa by Mennonite representatives, the Order-in-Council was repealed on June 2, 1922, thus opening the door for the Mennonites to enter Canada.[40] However, grave and almost insurmountable obstacles had to be removed for the would-be immigrants on the other side of the Atlantic.

Among the Mennonites of Russia two organizations also emerged to cope with the post-war problems of the colonists — the *VMSR* (Union of South Russian Mennonites) and the *AMLV* (All-Russian Mennonite Agricultural Union). As a result of the disruption caused by the Revolution and the Civil War, two separate organizations became necessary to serve Mennonites in different geographical areas: the *VMSR* came to represent primarily the interests of some sixty-five thousand Mennonites in the Ukraine, whereas the *AMLV* represented the forty-five thousand Mennonites in northern Russia and in Siberia. Although both associations were organized primarily for agricultural and industrial reconstruction, they became increasingly involved in the problems of emigration. The name of the organization representing the Mennonites in the Ukraine was later changed from *VMSR* to *VBHH* or *Verband Buerger Hollaendischer Herkunft* (Association of Citizens of Dutch Extraction) in order to obtain a charter.[41]

In God's gracious providence the *VBHH* became the chief agency in preparing the way for the mass-emigration of Mennonites from Russia. Its distinguished chairman from the beginning and throughout this period was a Mennonite Brethren minister and teacher, B. B. Janz from the Molotschna village of Tiege. Janz has sometimes been called the "Moses" of the Russian Mennonites, who led his people out of Soviet bondage. At the Alexanderwohl convention (February 19, 1921) where Janz was elected chairman, this relatively unknown man had impressed the delegation by his quiet dignity, and his ability to analyze complex issues. The following character profile, given by someone who knew B.B. Janz rather well, portrays his outstanding leadership abilities.

His friends knew him as a man of broad sympathies and great courage. He possessed a keenly analytical mind and a persistence bordering on stubbornness. Deeply committed to the faith of his fathers, he seemed to personify the corporate ideals of Russian Mennonitism. Janz was capable of astute diplomacy. He frequently displayed a rare quality which allowed him to press his advantage in an encounter until he arrived just a shade short of the breaking point. [42]

B. B. Janz was the man of the hour whom God gave to the Mennonite brotherhood for a crucial period in their history. Janz was ably assisted by the vice-chairman of VBHH, Philipp Cornies, also a man with outstanding leadership qualities. In the executive of the AMLV in Moscow a young man from the Mennonite Brethren Church in Neu-Samara, C. F. Klassen, was the right hand man of chairman Peter Froese. In October, 1922, the *VBHH* and the *AMLV* joined hands in order to speak with a united voice to the central government in Moscow.[43] With tireless energy and selfless dedication these men assisted the thousands of applicants to obtain passports and other credentials for emigration.

. It is somewhat difficult to make an accurate analysis of the motivation behind this mass-movement. Not only was there a great complexity and diversity in motivation, it also changed considerably as time went on. Whereas in 1922 human suffering was perhaps a primary motive to seek relief and refuge in another country, this pressure gradually declined during the years of the New Economic Policy. By 1926, the year of heaviest emigration, "this consideration was minimal and had been supplanted by long-range ideological and social considerations."[44] An enlightened leadership, however, perceived the long-range effects of communism on the Christian faith and on organized church life as early as 1922. In a reply to the *Studienkommission* the representatives of the *VBHH*, Philipp Cornies and B. B. Janz, summarized the reasons for the decision to emigrate.

After stating several economic factors, which had strongly influenced many settlers in their decision to emigrate, the document concluded with the following significant observation:

> In addition to the motives already cited here there are chiefly the ethical, moral and religious motives for consideration. There are persons with deeper and clearer vision from all classes and all places of our society, especially in the original colonies, who are unable to make any compromise, or begin any rebuilding because they have recognized that not only the economic, but also the social and moral foundations for such building are missing, which alone can be the determining factor for us. For the system of communistic influence, which is at present being carried out largely and with disregard for our principles of freedom and religion, goes contrary to our ideals and can therefore not be accepted by us. Therefore it is impossible for us to stay here. [45]

As in the great migrations of earlier times, religious concerns were the overruling motives in the mass exodus in the twenties. To substantiate this claim one only needs to point out the fact that in spite of great improved economic conditions by 1926, the movement still increased in scope and would have continued to do so if the government had not imposed severe restrictions on emigration, making it virtually impossible for applicants to obtain passports. Between 1923 and 1927 over eighteen thousand were able to make the "trek to Canada." Although records of church affiliation of these emigrants are not available, it can be assumed that the Mennonite Brethren comprised close to twenty-five percent of the above figure. The story of the almost endless difficulties of these emigrants in trying to obtain passports, pass medical examinations, sell their property and arrange for transportation on credit, is ably told in the book *Lost Fatherland*. The account of their arrival and settlement in Canada will be given in chapter eleven. But what happened to those who remained in Russia?

| 22. B. B. Janz | 23. C. F. Klassen | 24. Johann J. Toews |

THE END OF AN ERA

With the initiation of the first five-year plan on October 1, 1928, began the forced collectivization of farms and the systematic "liquidation" of the "kulaks."[46] Those who refused to cooperate with the new order lost all civil rights and in many instances were exiled to concentration camps in northern Russia or Siberia. Since Mennonites as a class were regarded as "kulaks," they were the special target of punitive policies.

The anti-Christian character of Communism manifested itself now in all its severity. Churches were closed and religious instruction forbidden since religion was considered "an opiate of the people." Ministers and church officials who protested against this ruthless liquidation of church property and religious freedom were arbitrarily arrested as counter-revolutionaries. Many Mennonite Brethren ministers suffered the fate of the latter. Typical perhaps is the experience of Johann J. Toews, outstanding teacher, leader and minister of the M.B. Church. During the time of mass emigration (1923-26) he felt duty-bound to stay with the flock. At the last All-Mennonite Conference (Ukraine) in the city of Melitopol in 1926, he delivered an eloquent address on spiritual renewal and improvement of congregational life.[47] When doors began to close, Toews made several attempts to emigrate (in 1927 and again in 1929) but these attempts failed. While waiting near Moscow for exit visas, Toews was forcibly separated from his family and sentenced to eight months imprisonment. Here he was literally tortured for his faith in Christ. Repeatedly he was offered freedom if he would deny his faith. But he remained faithful. After imprisonment followed exile in northern Russia, where he died as a true hero of faith in 1933.[48]

Besides ministers and Christian workers, another group bore the brunt of the Stalinist attacks: the young Mennonites who were conscientious objectors to military service. Although the so-called People's Courts (who examined conscientious objectors) granted exemption from military service during the NEP period, this policy changed in the late twenties. Even in the earlier post-revolutionary period the legal provisions for conscientious objectors were not universally carried out, and it is estimated that more than two hundred men were shot because of their refusal to bear arms. The Stalin Constitution of 1936 made no provision for conscientious objectors. Article 133 stated, "The defense of the Fatherland is the sacred duty of every citizen of the U.S.S.R."[49] When World War II broke out, exemption from military service had ceased. The number of martyrs for their faith in this area of discipleship will probably never become known.

By 1929 the Mennonites who remained in Russia realized the implications of the first five-year plan for their economic and religious survival. The prospects were indeed bleak. When rumors began to circulate in the Mennonite colonies that a few families had been able to secure legal passports in Moscow, a mass flight to the capital began. In a desperate attempt to escape, some fourteen thousand Mennonites made their way to Moscow in the fall and winter of 1929. The dramatic story of this flight and its consequences is told in the book *At the Gates of Moscow*.[50] Fewer than six thousand managed to get to Germany from where they left for Canada and South America. More might have been able to leave if Germany and Canada had been quicker to grant visas, but these nations were entering a period of economic depression and had serious unemployment problems. The fate of the eight thousand Mennonites who were unable to leave was indescribably tragic. They attempted to return home, but many never arrived; they were sent to prison or exile with hard labor in the forests of the North.

The period from 1930 to 1940 is characterized by the dissolution of congregations and the cessation of all organized religious activity. By 1935 most churches were being used as clubhouses, theatres or granaries. Anti-religious propaganda and a lack of religious leadership led to a serious decline not only in membership, but also in Christian faith and ethics. In the purges of 1937-38 many of the remaining Mennonite leaders and ministers were sent into exile. The invasion of the Soviet Union by Hitler's armies in 1941 brought further suffering to the Mennonites, especially in South Russia. Many were evacuated and deported to Siberia or Central Asia.

For those who were able to remain in the Mennonite colonies, or return to them, the German occupation from 1941 to 1943 provided a brief interlude of relative religious freedom. "While Russians suffered miserably at the hands of the Nazis, German-speaking peoples enjoyed numerous privileges: churches were opened and religious instruction introduced into the schools."[51]

This freedom was short-lived, however. With the retreat of the German armies in 1943, some thirty-five thousand Mennonites were evacuated. The retreat turned into a disorganized flight under the constant attack of Russian guerrilla bands and armed forces. Hundreds of refugees died on this long trek from the steppes of the Ukraine to the Vistula area of occupied Poland (Wartegau). Scores of families were separated. In the closing days of the war and its aftermath, thousands were forcibly repatriated into Russia, and only some twelve thousand escaped into the Western zones of Germany. Most of them subsequently migrated to Canada and South America. In God's inscrutable but gracious providence, however, a new day was to dawn even for the people who had remained under the shadow of death for several decades longer. The survival and renewal of the Mennonite Brethren Church in the Soviet Union will constitute a brief epilogue to their history in Russia.

Chapter 9

The Powers of Death
Have Not Prevailed

Although the Soviet Union had formed an alliance with the Western Powers against the Axis Powers (Germany, Italy, and Japan) during World War II, the so-called "Iron Curtain" descended shortly after the end of the war, separating the East from the West and causing an almost complete blackout of information on the life of the church in the U.S.S.R. The "cold war" continued wthout abatement until the death of Stalin in 1953, when a gradual relaxation of restrictions found expression in amnesties to inmates of labor camps, to which many Mennonites had been sentenced.

The first direct contact in the post-war period with the Mennonite and Mennonite Brethren Churches in Russia was established in October, 1956, by a delegation from North America consisting of H. S. Bender and D. B. Wiens.[1] Although they were not permitted to visit Mennonite settlements, these brethren were able to meet a number of Mennonite leaders in Alma Ata and in Moscow. From these contacts Bender and Wiens learned that all Mennonite colonies in the Ukraine, Crimea, Alt-Samara, and Caucasus had been completely eliminated, and their population resettled mostly in the republics of Central Asia and in southwest Siberia. Subsequent delegations in 1958, 1966, and in 1970 have confirmed this information.[2]

In response to the Bender-Wiens report, the MCC established an East-West office in Frankfurt, West Germany, in 1957, to facilitate the "tracing service" (*Suchdienst*) for missing persons, and to gather as much information on the Mennonites of the Soviet Union as possible. Peter J. Dyck, prominent leader in the rescue and resettlement of Mennonites in the post-war period, was appointed director of this office. In October, 1959, Dyck reported that the East-West card-index at Frankfurt embraced twelve thousand alphabetically-listed names of the one hundred thousand Mennonites estimated to be in Russia.[3]

The tracing service established not only the location of Mennonites in Russia, but it also brought forth information about the religious, cultural, and economic life of the scattered groups. In some places Mennonites worshiped alone, in some together with the Baptists, in others with the Lutherans. Meetings were held in private homes, and in a few churches. The degree of freedom for religious assembly depended to some extent on the attitude of local authorities.[4]

MENNONITES IN SOVIET PERSPECTIVE

It might be of interest to view the activities and contemporary developments among the Mennonites of Russia through the eyes of Soviet writers. Until recently, mention of the Mennonites in the U.S.S.R. occurred only rarely in the Soviet anti-religious press. These references were usually of a negative character, dealing largely with Mennonite preachers who were reported to have been brought to trial for their "anti-Soviet propaganda." The impression created by these references was that the former large Mennonite communities had been dispersed and their remnants absorbed by the Protestant body nearest to them in matters of faith — namely the Evangelical Christian Baptists.[5] In 1965, however, a book by F. Fedorenko entitled *The Sects: Their Faith and Their Affairs*, devoted a few pages to the Mennonites in the U.S.S.R., remarking that they had experienced a revival in the years since 1957.[6] In 1967 V. F. Krestyaninov published a booklet on the Mennonites in the series of popular anti-religious publications entitled "Contemporary Religions," in which he describes their faith and life from a Marxist perspective.[7]

Discussing the relative numerical strength of the various groups, Krestyaninov expresses the view that today the New Mennonites (name for Mennonite Brethren) are in the majority: in the Omsk Oblast, for example, they constitute two-thirds of the total.[8] Krestyaninov is especially disturbed by the remarkable activity of the traveling preachers among them. Mennonite preachers pay special attention to young people. They have considerable experience as educators, and are able to arouse the interest of young people in religious questions by organizing activities such as performance in choirs and orchestras, Bible classes (at which prizes are offered for knowledge of Scripture), dressmaking and embroidery courses.

Krestyaninov is impressed with the ethics and industry of the Mennonites, but he questions their motives. The following summary of his views is given by Teodorovich:

> The Mennonites do not drink or smoke, and pay particular attention to bodily cleanliness as a symbol of spiritual purity. Their life tends to be concentrated upon the family, and their cultivation of reading, handicrafts, singing and other music serves as a protection against the distraction of political

and anitreligious club activities outside the home. The language spoken at home is usually Low German, and embroidered religious texts are a prominent feature in every Mennonite home. The Mennonites are noted for their industry and their conscientious attitude to the work entrusted to them at Soviet enterprises, collective and state farms. . . . For a long time, these qualities concealed from the Communist "activists" the fact that these people belonged to a religious community, for the Communists, true to the teachings of Marx, Lenin, and Krupskaya, considered that socialist labor was in itself a sufficient guarantee against religious "obscuratism."[9]

Although the Mennonites attempt to reconcile their Christian convictions concerning work with the socialist view about the purpose of labor, Krestyaninov is unconvinced. He reports a conversation with a Mennonite Brethren minister, J. J. Klassen, from the village of Shumanovka, Rayon Slavgorod, in the district of Altay, whom he quotes as follows: "Our faith does not teach men to do evil, to drink, to behave disorderly, or to steal. The believers work well in the *Kolchos* (collective farm), and that is the important thing in the up-building of Communism."[10] Klassen then proceeds to draw an analogy between Paul's admonition that "if any would not work, neither should he eat" (2 Thess. 3:10) and the socialist principle, "he who does not work, also does not eat." Krestyaninov maintains that the main emphasis in Mennonite teaching is the concern for salvation, and their labor is related primarily to this concern.

According to Krestyaninov, a study of Mennonite communities revealed, contrary to popular opinion, that most of their members are not representatives of the older generation, but of the middle and younger generation, the older people on the average amounting to no more than thirty percent. A similar situation was noticed among Mennonite communities in the city of Karaganda, where a good half of their members were no older than fifty.[11]

Although the Marxist historian is impressed with the ability of the Mennonites to retain the loyalty of their young people, it must be stated here, that this is only partly true. A relatively large number of young people have accepted the materialistic and atheistic ideology of Marxism to which they have been subjected in the elementary and secondary schools. Only a few have become members of the Communist party, but many have accepted the world-view of the larger society. It is encouraging to note that during the last few years, especially since 1965, a spiritual awakening has occurred among Mennonite young people in many areas.[12]

One distinctive principle of Anabaptism and of the Mennonite Brethren confession of faith, namely nonresistance, appears to have been given up almost completely. Krestyaninov makes the somewhat startling claim, however, that Mennonite ministers are making special efforts to maintain and instill in their young people the idea of nonresistance. The author also cites numerous cases of Mennonite young men who objected to service in the Red Army during World War II.[13] What happened to those who refused to serve in the army is not revealed. According to the Baptist delegation that visited Canada in June, 1969, all young men in the Soviet Union serve in the Red Army unless they are exempted for medical reasons.

MENNONITE BRETHREN AND BAPTISTS

In the Soviet Union every local religious community has to be registered with the Council for the Affairs of Religious Cults. Religious meetings as such are not permitted even in private homes. The registration of a congregation for worship purposes depends on meeting very exacting conditons. Certain persons and a minister must be approved to function as a nucleus for a congregation. In addition, a number of members must support the petition. Even if these conditions are met registration may be refused or delayed.[14]

The Mennonites who became uprooted during World War II lost these privileges because of their transfer to other areas and their German background. Since their rehabilitation as full-fledged Soviet citizens in 1955, great changes have taken place as far as their religious status is concerned.[15]

Because most Baptists enjoyed the status and rights of registered churches, the Mennonite Brethren began to worship with them as early as 1959 in Kazakhstan, Kirgizia, and West Siberia. In 1963 the Council of the Evangelical Christians-Baptists decided to accept the Mennonites into the Baptist Union. This decision affected primarily the Mennonite Brethren because of the similarity of views and practices, including the mode of baptism. However, Zhidkov, the chairman of the Baptist Union, is reported to have stated in September, 1964, that the plan was "to work out the necessary arrangements for a strengthening of the ties with both Mennonite groups."[16] This plan, it appears, never materialized.

It is estimated that there are approximately twenty-two thousand members of the Mennonite Brethren Church in Russia today. Of these about eighteen thousand are registered with the Baptist Union. The others belong to separatist groups usually referred to as *Initiativniki* (initiators or dissenters). A number of Baptist congregations also belong to this movement which is sometimes, although falsely, called the "underground church."[17] Attempts are being made at present to reconcile the two factions of Baptists. The difference between the registered and unregistered groups is primarily one of the degree of submission to state regulations with regard to the work and witness of the church. In recent years it has become possible to register independently of the Baptist Union, and Mennonite as well as Mennonite Brethren congregations are now considering this option.

It has been estimated that there are some two hundred and forty places in the Soviet Union where Mennonite Brethren and Baptists worship together, but not nearly all of these are registered with the government. Their public worship services in northern Kazakhstan are described by Krestyaninov as follows:

> On Sunday they meet in the afternoon for worship purposes followed by musical presentations by the youth. The evening service is closed with a prayer meeting. On Tuesdays and Wednesdays there is special instruction of youth and their relatives who intend to be baptized. On Thursday evening choir and orchestral practices take place. On Saturday evening musical performances are given followed by prayer meetings.[18]

From the above description it is obvious, that Mennonite Brethren in Russia carry on a church program that is spiritually enriching and meaningful. Visitors, however, have expressed concern over the somewhat "narrow pietism" of the Mennonite Brethren in the Soviet Union. The lack of a trained ministry, the restriction of the expression of their Christian faith to the home and the worship services in the church, the absence of theological books and periodicals — all these have contributed to this type of "otherworldly" pietism. The promotion of an itinerant ministry, and the introduction of correspondence courses for ministerial candidates and Christian workers in the last few years, are perhaps the first steps to correct this situation.

Although severely restricted in the expression of its faith there is a living and growing Mennonite Brethren Church in the U.S.S.R. today. A survey of its history during the past fifty years provides a vivid demonstration of the truth of Christ's great prophetic utterance which we often heard from the lips of our brethren in Russia: "I will build my church, and the powers of death shall not prevail against it" (Mt. 16:18). A definitive history of this last period in the Soviet Union is contingent on future developments in that country.

PART II

THE
MENNONITE BRETHREN
CHURCH
IN NORTH AMERICA

Introductory Note: In order to facilitate a greater "in depth" study of the various aspects in the faith and life of the M.B. Church in North America, a different methodology in the organization of historical materials will be employed than in Part One. After a brief survey of the initial settlement and subsequent geographical expansion of Mennonite Brethren and Krimmer Mennonite Brethren in the United States and Canada in the first several chapters, an attempt will be made to present the concerns and activities of the brotherhood in topical form, showing growth and development as well as changing conditions and needs throughout this entire period.

Chapter 10

Mennonite Brethren Come
to the United States

Almost two hundred years before the first Mennonite Brethren set foot on American soil, other heirs of the early Anabaptists had found a home in the New World — a haven of rest from the religious and economic oppression in Western Europe. Although the first Mennonite immigrants who founded Germantown (now a suburb of Philadelphia, Pa.) in 1683 were of Dutch ethnic origin from the city of Krefeld in Northwest Germany, the larger groups that settled in Pennsylvania and Virginia at the beginning of the eighteenth century were of Swiss-German background, coming to America from the Palatinate in Germany and from Switzerland. By the 1870's these original settlements had expanded westward to the states of Ohio, Indiana, Illinois, and Iowa. It is highly improbable that the migration of eighteen thousand Mennonites from Russia to the United States and Canada in the 1870's would have been practically possible if there had not been concerned Mennonite churches on this side of the Atlantic.

Earlier (in chapter six), it has been pointed out that Cornelius Jansen, who championed the cause of emigration to America in Russia, established contacts with British and United States officials and Mennonite leaders in preparation for the mass exodus of Mennonites from the Ukraine. Two men with whom Jansen corresponded and who gave outstanding leadership throughout the period of immigration and resettlement were John F. Funk (1835-1930) of Elkhart, Indiana, and Christian Krehbiel (1832-1909) of Summerfield, Illinois.[1] As editor of *Der Herold der Wahrheit* and its English counterpart, *The Herald of Truth*, Funk was in an especially favorable position to disseminate information about the plight of the Mennonites in Russia during the 1870's and to aid the immigrants upon their arrival in the United States. In a November, 1872, issue of *The Herald of Truth*, Funk appeals to the

129

members of the (Old) Mennonite Church to demonstrate the spirit of a true Christian brotherhood: "Our church," he writes, ". . . ought to think seriously over this matter, the new relations into which it will bring us; the liberality and generosity it will require of us . . . a helping hand, information, and a kind of fraternal feeling towards them . . . our sympathies and our prayers. Let the Church not be behind in good works and good words, and a friendly welcome, with willing hearts if need be."[2]

Krehbiel was an active leader in the Western District Conference (General Conference Mennonite Church) and promoted the cause of the Russian brethren in his constituency. Representatives of the two major Mennonite bodies met on December 2, 1873, to form the "Board of Guardians," anticipating the organization of the MCC fifty years later.[3] Once organized the committee decided to negotiate with the railroads to obtain the most favorable terms, speed up the collection of gifts and loans, and to assist the immigrants in the selection of suitable settlement sites. The ultimate success of the whole venture must be attributed, next to God's gracious, overruling providence, to the wise and dedicated leadership of these men.

It should be remembered that for the Mennonites a primary motive for leaving Russia was the desire to preserve the principle of nonresistance which was threatened by the Imperial Decree of 1870. Could they expect complete exemption from military service in America? The Mennonites who decided to emigrate to Canada received such assurances from Ottawa. The response from Washington was not as unequivocal. The 1870's constitute the "Era of Reconstruction" in U.S. history. Ulysses S. Grant was in his second term of office, when the Mennonites filed their petition in 1873. Influenced, no doubt, by the pressure from the large railroad companies (who had contributed to his election funds) Grant was favorably disposed toward the request of the Mennonites.

The debate in Congress, however, revealed a negative attitude on the part of many government leaders. There was protest and opposition to the closed nature of Mennonite communities, to their refusal to defend the country, and to the granting of special concessions in the purchase of large tracts of land.[4] The so-called "Mennonite Bill" (Senate Bill No. 655) failed to come to a vote. This did not stop the Mennonites from coming into the country, however, since they had public and private assurances from various government officials that they would be exempt from "militia service," a matter which was under the jurisdiction of the state legislatures. Eventually all states where Mennonites desired to settle provided such exemption, and for forty years the Mennonite Brethren, together with the other Mennonite groups, enjoyed complete freedom — not only from military service, but also from alternative service, to which their brethren in Russia were subject.

On the basis of their attitude toward government service the Mennonites of Russia in the 1870's might be divided into three main groups, according to C. Krahn. The more progressive culturally, approximately two-thirds of the total number, remained in Russia. The most conservative Mennonites, who had lived in the Old Colony and its daughter-colonies, migrated to Canada because they were promised complete exemption from all compulsory military service by the Canadian government. Ther third, a moderately conservative group, came from the Molotschna Colony and settled in the United States. The Mennonite Brethren who came to North America all belonged to the latter group. They were a part of the larger movement of approximately ten thousand Mennonites who exchanged the Russian steppes for the American plains in the decade following 1873. The founding and the expansion of Mennonite Brethren churches in the states of the Midwest and the expansion of these original congregations to the North, South, and Far West, constitutes the main story of this chapter.

TABLE II

Mennonite Immigration to the United States [6]

1. Lower Rhine to Germantown (1683-1702)	200
2. Swiss and Palatine Mennonites to Eastern Pa. (1707-56)	4,000
3. Swiss and Palatine Amish to Eastern Pa. (1738-56)	200
4. Alsace-Lorraine, Hessian and Bavarian Amish to Western Pa., Ohio, Illinois, Iowa (1815-60)	2,700
5. Swiss Mennonites to Ohio and Indiana (1817-60)	500
6. Palatine Mennonites to Ohio, Illinois, and Iowa (1825-60)	200
7. Prussian Mennonites to Nebraska and Kansas (1874-80)	300
8. Russian Mennonites to the prairie states (1874-80)	10,000
9. Russian Mennonites to Reedley, California (1930)	256
10. Scattered individuals (second half of the 19th century) from Germany, Switzerland, France, and Russia to states west of the Mississippi	200
Total immigrants	**18,556**

I. MENNONITE BRETHREN — PIONEERS ON THE AMERICAN PLAINS

The original Mennonite settlements in the 1870's were all established in prairie states which at that time were located on the "Western Frontier": Kansas, Nebraska, Dakota and Minnesota. A keen rivalry developed among these states in advertising the economic advantages and opportunities of their respective territories. The railroads had a vested interest in securing thrifty and experienced settlers to become established in areas served by them. The Northern Pacific Railroad endeavored to interest them in northern Minnesota and the Dakotas; the Chicago, Burlington and Quincy Railroad tried to recruit settlers for Nebraska; and the Atchison, Topeka and Santa Fe Railroad, through its enthusiastic agent C. B. Schmidt, sought to win them for Kansas. Although none of the official delegates had favored Kansas for settlement, this state finally received the largest number of immigrants.[7] The majority of the Mennonite Brethren also settled here.

1. *Mennonite Brethren in Kansas*

It would appear from the records that relatively few Mennonite Brethren families arrived with the first groups of immigrants. The majority came after 1876 and settled mainly in Marion, Harvey, Reno and McPherson counties. They experienced the usual hardships of pioneer life — primitive homes (sod houses), crop failures due to drought and grasshoppers, lack of markets for their produce, and limited educational opportunities. Although they originally attempted village settlements patterned after the Russian Mennonite colonies, they soon found this arrangement impractical and moved on to their own land to establish their farms. The most important economic contribution of the Mennonites was the introduction of hard winter wheat which they had brought with them from the Ukraine. After some experimentation it was discovered that the red Turkey winter wheat was best suited to the soil and the climatic conditions of Kansas. The Mennonite Brethren helped to make the "Sunflower State" the "breadbasket of America." It was relatively easy for Mennonite Brethren living in these agricultural communities to keep the traditional marriage between the Bible and the plow (*Bibel und Pflug*) intact.

There appears to have been little organized religious life among the early Brethren in Kansas. Whereas other groups had come into this state as organized congregations (e.g. the Alexanderwohl Mennonite Church, and the K.M.B. Church), the Mennonite Brethren prior to 1879 seem to have suffered from a lack of strong leadership. Wherever members of the M.B. Church settled, however, they met in homes for prayer and fellowship. As soon as schoolhouses were erected, these served as meetingplaces for the small groups of believers.

The early period (1874-79) is characterized by religious ferment and inner tensions. The Mennonite Brethren coming from the Molotschna and Chortitza colonies could not come to terms with the Volga group. The latter still insisted on the "sister kiss" and held other views not acceptable to the former. The Krimmer Mennonite Brethren Church which had established itself at Gnadenau near Hillsboro, under the leadership of elder Jacob A. Wiebe, had much in common with the

Brethren from the Molotschna, but the difference in the mode of baptism was an obstacle to a complete merger of the two groups.[8] Moreover, a Mennonite Church under the leadership of Bernhard Buhler was also established in the Hillsboro area. This church emphasized newness of life and made the mode of baptism optional. Although Buhler himself had not been baptized by immersion, he administerd this mode of baptism upon request. The centrifugal forces operating in this ferment finally prevailed, and no "alliance" was achieved among the various groups even though several attempts were made.

The history of the founding, growth, and development of all M.B. congregations in North America transcends the purpose of this book.[9] The following representative local congregations reflect economic, social, cultural and religious trends or problems of earlier and later periods in Mennonite Brethren history.

An analysis of the pattern of church establishment in Kansas as well as in other states reveals that all churches were initially located in rural areas. Some of these were later relocated in nearby towns; others became extinct; and still others have managed to survive but have had difficulty in maintaining their membership level as well as essential services. Kansas provides illustrations for all these categories.

The Ebenfeld Mennonite Brethren Church

The Ebenfeld Mennonite Brethren Church claims the distinction of being the first organized M.B. congregation on the North American continent. It began in 1874 when a number of M.B. families settled in this community a few miles southeast of Hillsboro in Marion County. In 1876 an additional seventy-five families arrived. The church grew rapidly and in 1888 had a membership of two hundred and fifty-three. In 1971, almost ninety years later, its membership stood at two hundred and thirty-five, illustrating the problems that a rural congregation (in this case with strong leadership) faces in a changing economy and culture.

The Ebenfeld congregation had its "storm and stress" period in the early years. The majority of the group that arrived in 1876 were from the Volga settlement; others came from the Kuban and Chortitza colonies. Elder Peter Eckert, the first presiding minister and a tolerant and open-minded man, attempted amalgamation with the K.M.B. group established in nearby Gnadenau in 1874. The latter preferred to remain separate, however, and the attempt failed. Elder Eckert found it difficult to control and unite the diverse elements in his own local group, especially the Volga brethren who still insisted on the "sister kiss" and other practices which the group could not accept, and hence resigned from leadership. Abraham Cornelsen, the author of the 1860 Document of Secession, who had arrived with a group from the Don

Settlement in 1879, succeeded Eckert as leader and served the congregation as elder until his death in 1884.[10]

Other problems in the Ebenfeld M.B. Church were created with the arrival of Eduard Leppke, an ex-Baptist who had become a "hyper-Mennonite" in South Russia.[11] After failing to win members for his views and a separatist group, Leppke united with the Krimmer Mennonite Brethren, but soon left them as well and joined the Seventh Day Adventists.

The Mennonites and the Mennonite Brethren congregations then (and now!) have been considered fertile fields for proselytizing, or "sheep stealing" by various other denominations. A traveling Baptist minister named Janicka came to Ebenfeld. He succeeded in winning a number of members of the Volga group and founded a Baptist church in Hillsboro.[12] Eventually, it appears, most of the Volga brethren moved to other localities and many joined the Baptists.

Under the leadership of Johann Foth, who was ordained as elder by Abraham Schellenberg in 1885 and served the congregation in this capacity for thirty years, the Ebenfeld Church became one of the pillars in the M.B. Conference.[13] The *Steinreich* * Mennonite Brethren Church, ten miles to the east, was founded by Ebenfeld in 1905, and remained affiliated with the mother church until 1946, when it became the *Marion* M.B. Church.

The Ebenezer-Buhler Mennonite Brethren Church

The Ebenezer Mennonite Brethren Church, located four miles east of Buhler in Reno County, began in 1878 when a number of M.B. families from Russia settled in this community with Franz Ediger and Peter Wall as leaders. In 1921 this congregation amalgamated with its "daughter-congregation" at Buhler. The latter had been started in 1901 as a Sunday school and established as an independent church under the ministry of elder Heinrich Adrian. The Ebenzer M.B. Church was destined to play a leading role in the early history of the Mennonite Brethren in America. It also became the mother church of several congregations in Reno, McPherson and Harvey counties.

The man whom the Lord used as a "chosen instrument" in organizing and establishing the Ebenezer Church as well as scattered groups of believers throughout the Midwest was elder Abraham Schellenberg (1845-1920) who arrived in Kansas on July 7, 1879. At the age of thirty he had been elected elder of the Rueckenau, Molotschna, M.B. Church in Russia, and served effectively as local leader and itinerant minister until his emigration in 1879. Upon his arrival in Kansas the Ebenezer M.B. Church immediately elected him as elder and he served in this capacity for thirty years. J. H. Lohrenz gives the following summary of the many significant involvements of Schellenberg in the work of the brotherhood:

> He at once began to minister to other M.B. Churches and was helpful to them in organization, guidance, discipline, exhortation, and nurture in the Word. He filled a very important role in the M.B. Conference. He served as moderator eighteen times between the years 1880 and 1900. The Conference assigned to him evangelistic and itinerating work for sixteen years. He strongly urged the M.B. Conference to begin its own Foreign Mission, and when this was begun he was chosen chairman of the Committee and served for many years. He was among the first to advocate the publishing of a church paper and later continued to be a hearty supporter of the publishing efforts of the Conference. He understood the importance and need of advance in education in the M.B. Church, and the Conference began the German Department School in McPherson . . . largely because of his influence. He encouraged the founding of Tabor College and continued to be a faithful supporter of the school. . . .[14]

The Ebenezer M.B. Church prospered under Schellenberg's leadership. When a sanctuary was built in 1880, the mother church in the Molotschna contributed two hundred rubles. It was perhaps inevitable that Schellenberg's strong personality, which in so many ways overshadowed that of his coworkers, would create tensions in the leadership of the congregation. In 1893 the associate ministers Franz Ediger, Peter Wall and Gerhard Franz with a number of members withdrew from the congregation and formed a separate fellowship. Although the Ebenezer schism was discussed on the conference floor on several occasions,[15] the conference was reluctant to intervene in the affairs of a local congregation especially since it involved the conference chairman. Fortunately for church and conference, the schism was healed by 1899.[16]

In 1921, a year after Elder Schellenberg's death, the entire Ebenezer congregation transferred to Buhler, greatly strengthening the ministry of the "daughter church." In 1926 the *Inman* M.B. Church also joined the congregation in the town of Buhler. During the last two decades, however, even the small town congregations have experienced difficulties in maintaining their membership levels because of the steady movement of Mennonite Brethren to the larger metropolitan centers. Whereas the membership of the Buhler M.B. Church stood at five hundred and twelve in 1951, it had dropped to four hundred and fifteen by 1971.

The Hillsboro Mennonite Brethren Church

This congregation, which was destined to become one of the largest and most influential churches in the M.B. Conference, began in a revival movement among the newly arrived Mennonite settlers in the "French Creek" area north of Hillsboro around 1880. After several baptisms the group here was organized by Elder Schellenberg on April 25, 1881, as the "Johannestal Church of French Creek."[17] The congregation met in rural homes until 1882, when a school building was purchased in Hillsboro. After beginning with thirty-four charter members, the church experienced steady growth so that the present (1971) membership of eight hundred and fifty-five makes it the second largest congregation in the M.B. Conference.

Several factors have contributed to the growth and development of this congregation through the years. Aside from able leadership, the establishment of conference institutions in the town of Hillsboro has been of major significance in this respect. Tabor College, the first institution of higher learning in the brotherhood, was established here in 1908. The chronicler of the local history of the church describes the influence of Tabor as follows:

> The natural result was an increased attendance as well as membership. . . . The very presence of students and faculty members exerted considerable influence in the thinking of the congregation, and their participation in the Sunday school, the young people's work, the choir and congregational singing as well as in the preaching became a powerful influence.[18]

The congregation profited from the ministry of such outstanding leaders and teachers as H. W. Lohrenz, P. C. Hiebert, H. F. Toews and others, whom Peter E. Nickel, church leader for twenty-three years, was able to draw into the work. In the words of the local historian,

> It seemed proper in the eyes of Brother Nickel to put the burden of the public preaching ministry very largely into the hands of these three ministering brethren. This practice gave him more time . . . to devote to the direct shepherding of the believers and looking after the many church interests.[19]

The relocation of the conference publishing house from McPherson to Hillsboro between 1909 and 1913 also strengthened the work and witness of the local congregation. Such brethren as A. L. Schellenberg, P. H. Berg, and others engaged in the work of publication, made their contribution to the ministry in the church. The General Conference Offices — Board of Foreign Missions, Board of General Welfare and Public Relations, and Board of Trustees — located in Hillsboro in later years similarly benefited the local congregation. Pastors J. W. Vogt (1936-1948), Waldo Hiebert (1949-1959) and Marvin Hein (1959 to the present) have given effective leadership to this large congregation.

Congregations Rise and Fall

Not all the M.B. churches that were established in the early decades have survived. Several examples will show how congregations may rise and flourish, and then decline and become extinct or be absorbed by others. The *Goessel* M.B. Church, earlier known as the Alexanderwohl M.B. Church, was begun in 1880 and for some time was an influential congregation in the conference. Although the church had a membership of seventy in 1896, it decreased steadily until the congregation was dissolved in 1926.[20] The *Woodson County* M.B. Church, about one hundred miles east of Marion County, was established in 1877 by a number of families coming from the Chortitza Colony. In the fall of 1878 Bernard Pauls and David Dyck were elected as ministers. This congregation became known in the conference for its strong support of missions. Here the example of the leading ministers seems to have influenced the church members. Dyck moved to Lehigh in 1884 as did Pauls a year later. Although the congregation still had a membership of fifty-two in 1888, by 1892 most of them had moved to other localities and the church was dissolved.

The *Lehigh* M.B. Church was organized in 1884 under the leadership of David Dyck, who had moved here from Woodson County. The membership of this congregation fluctuated greatly through the years: one hundred in 1890, twenty-three in 1892, one hundred in 1928, and fifty-two in 1953. In 1955 the Lehigh congregation was amalgamated with the Gnadenau (now *Parkview*) M.B. Church.[21]

The *Dorrance* Mennonite Brethren Church in Russell County was organized in 1913 with thirty members under the leadership of the elders Johann Foth and M. M. Just. Through the years it was also known for its interest in missions. Membership remained small however, and by 1960 the church was extinct.

The *Ingalls* Mennonite Brethren Church in Gray County, Western Kansas, was an outgrowth of an original mission church founded in 1923. Among its early ministers were D. W. Siemens and B. C. Willems. In the late 1950's the church relocated to *Cimarron* and is known under that name at present. Other M. B. churches in Western Kansas have been established at *Ulysses* and *Garden City*. The *Olathe* Church has been established in Eastern Kansas near Kansas City.

In Kansas the move to the cities began during World War II. In *Wichita* the *First* Mennonite Brethren Church was organized in 1943 with Estil Schale as its first minister. In the 1950's a second congregation, the *Open Bible* M.B. Church, was established. Also about the same time, the *Fairlawn* M.B. Church was organized in Topeka, and the *Koerner Heights* M.B. Church in Newton.[22]

2. *Mennonite Brethren in Nebraska*

Among the prairie states Nebraska attracted the second largest number (after Kansas) of the incoming settlers in the 1870's. One of the objections to Nebraska often emphasized by those interested in other states was the fact that water could be secured only from deep wells.[23] Most Mennonites, including Mennonite Brethren, who came to Nebraska settled in the fertile agricultural region in the southeastern half of the state.

The Henderson Mennonite Brethren Church

This congregation had its beginning in 1876 when seven M. B. families settled in York and Hamilton counties. Peter Regier, who served as its first minister, was succeeded in 1882 by his brother, Johann J. Regier, the first elder of the church and active conference worker for many years. The congregation experienced a constant growth through conversions and baptisms as well as through new M.B. families arriving from Russia. By 1888 membership had increased to two hundred and twenty-six — a figure only slightly below its present membership (1971). The congregation worshiped in a meetinghouse three miles northwest of Henderson until 1926, when it moved into a new church in town. In the early years, according to H. E. Wiens, "the church endured severe testings through strange teaching on divine healing, sanctification, and Seventh-Day Adventism, but weathered them through the wise counsel and guidance of Elder Regier."[24]

Several "branch-churches" were started by the Henderson congregation; these, however, did not survive. One such daughter congregation was established in *Boone County*, eighty-five miles north of Henderson, when Elder Regier and other members settled there in 1879. After Elder Regier moved to Henderson in 1882 Isaac Wall succeeded him as leader. When the latter moved to Jansen in 1899, most families left for Henderson or Jansen shortly after. The fear of intermarriage with Roman Catholics, who settled among the Mennonites, is also mentioned as one of the reasons for the dissolution of the church.[25] Another congregation emerged at *Sutton*, sixteen miles south of Henderson, as the result of extension work among the Volga Germans. During the 1890's it was a flourishing congregation with its own meetinghouse. During the first two decades of the twentieth century its membership decreased and in 1924 the church was dissolved.

In 1879 a congregation was also established in the southwestern part of the state, at *Culbertson*, among the so-called "Volga Brethren." For some time it prospered and increased to a membership of sixty. Later a large part of the congregation joined the Seventh-Day Adventists and by 1960 it had ceased to exist as an independent church.[26]

The First Inter-State Meeting

The Henderson congregation has the distinction not only of being the host church of the first three General Conferences of the Mennonite Brethren Church (1879-1881) but also of initiating the ideas that led to the formation of a larger working fellowship. In 1878 Peter Regier invited the brethren from Kansas, Dakota, and Minnesota to a meeting in York County, Nebraska. Four brethren from Kansas responded to the invitation and joined seven representatives from Nebraska on September 28, 1878 for a discussion of common concerns. This meeting was not recognized in later years as a *de jure* conference because of a lack of proper representation of the churches, and also because several resolutions passed were not considered to be in agreement with Mennonite Brethren principles.[27] It was, however, a first step in the direction of conference organization, and the agenda may be of interest.[28]

All representatives favored the uniting of the congregations into a conference. Resolutions were passed on the following issues. (1) *Excommunication*: The practice of "avoidance" is not to be applied to the marriage relationship. (2) *Baptism*: A single immersion (backward) is to be the mode of baptism. The mode of the K. M. B. Church (forward immersion) is also recognized as valid. (3) *Marriage*: Ministers may officiate at the marriage of the unsaved children of church members, but should refrain from any official function when the groom and bride belong to other confessions. (4) *The Sister-kiss*: Although this form of greeting is rejected between brothers and sisters in the congregation, it is agreed that the leading minister may also accept sisters into church membership with this form of greeting.[29] (5) *Headcovering for Women*: With some opposition a resolution is passed requiring headcovering for sisters not only in the church, but also in the home. (6) *Positions in government*: Brethren are not to serve in any government offices. (7) *Relations to Baptists*: Union, and even communion, with the Baptists is declared to be unacceptable.

The above resolutions reflect the problems of young churches in a new environment. They are closely related to the desire to "walk according to the same rule" in the various groups and congregations. The "hard line" against fellowship with the Baptists was strongly advocated by the ex-Baptist Eduard Leppke, one of the representatives from Kansas. Later this position was modified to conform with the general policy of the Mennonite Brethren in Russia.

3. *Mennonite Brethren in Minnesota*

The state of Minnesota, known as "the land of ten thousand lakes," is not only attractive to vacationists in our day; it was also attractive to many Mennonite settlers in the 1870's. By 1880 three hundred and fifty families had arrived at Mountain Lake, a small railway town in Cottonwood County in the southern part of the state.

Among those who immigrated in 1875 and 1876 were six M. B. families who organized as a church on June 11, 1877, the day of their first baptism.[30] Among those baptized was a young schoolteacher from the Molotschna, Heinrich Voth and his wife who had made a deep Christian experience prior to their coming to the United States. The

25. Abraham Schellenberg   **26. Heinrich Voth**

small group at nearby Bingham Lake elected Voth as leader in 1878 and in 1885 he was also ordained as elder by Abraham Schellenberg from Kansas.

The first meetinghouse was constructed in 1885 about three miles north of *Bingham Lake*. Because members living in and south of the town of Mountain Lake could not attend regularly, another meetinghouse was built about five miles south of *Mountain Lake*. Elder Voth served as pastor of both churches until 1918, when he moved to Canada, where he died on November 26 of that year at Vanderhoof, British Columbia.[31]

The "North Church" and the "South Church" functioned as one congregation for many years. A commendable innovation of this church, begun in 1887, was the observance of the "Fourth of July" as a missions festival. In this way the church offered its young people and the community something better than the usual celebrations held in surrounding towns. From the very beginning the Minnesota congregations manifested a great interest in missions, and hence it is not surprising that from 1896 to 1950 they commissioned twenty-seven missionaries for foreign and city mission work.[32]

Later both churches found it expedient to relocate in nearby towns, following the general pattern observed in other areas. The "South Church" (now Mountain Lake Mennonite Brethren Church) moved its building to its present location in 1901. The new church building, constructed in 1931, was enlarged in 1948 and replaced by a new structure in 1972. The Bingham Lake M.B. Church (now *Carson* M.B. Church) moved into a new edifice in the town of Delft (township of Carson) in 1949.

The Minnesota congregations must be regarded as the "mother churches" of the early Canadian congregations. In addition, the South Side Mission founded in Minneapolis in 1910, and the New Hope M. B. Church established in the same city after World War II, may also be regarded, at least in part, as the result of the extension efforts of the churches in Cottonwood County.

4. *Mennonite Brethren in South Dakota*

Mennonites began to arrive in southern Dakota sixteen years before the territory was admitted into the Union in 1889. The great bulk of the immigrants arriving from Russia in the 1870's and early 1880's settled in Turner and Hutchinson counties, some thirty miles north of Yankton.

Among the settlers that came to Turner County were several M. B. families who began to meet in homes for fellowship as early as 1876. The congregation was organized in 1878 with Heinrich Adrian as leading minister. Adrian, who was ordained as elder in 1881 by Abraham Schellenberg, guided the young and struggling congregation for more than twenty-five years until he moved to Kansas in 1904.

The congregations consisted of groups scattered over a wide area. *Bruderfeld*, near Parker, was the main station, but meetings were also held in Wittenberg, Rosenfeld, and at Emanuel's Creek. More than any other M.B. church, it appears, this congregation has suffered from the inroads of Seventh-Day Adventism. After a short period of growth and prosperity, thirty-one members left and joined the Adventists because of internal tensions. The church recuperated from this loss and experienced an increase in membership as a result of revivals. An even more severe blow to the church came in 1886, when more than half of its membership, seventy-nine in number, left and joined the Adventists.[33] The congregation also survived this crisis but its center shifted further west to *Silver Lake*. In 1891 a church was constructed near Silver Lake and about three miles southwest of Dolton.[34]

The Mennonite Brethren constituency in South Dakota was strengthened and enriched by the merger with the Krimmer Mennonite Brethren in 1960. Among the K.M.B. churches that joined the conference were the following: the *Salem* congregation at Bridgewater, the *Ebenezer* congregation at Doland, the *Bethesda* congregation at Huron, the *Emmanuel* congregation at Onida, and the *Bethel* congregation at Yale.

II. FROM ORIGINAL SETTLEMENTS TO NEW FRONTIERS

The period from 1890 to 1920 was marked by a rapid expansion of the M. B. Church into new areas. More attractive economic prospects on the constantly expanding "frontier" prompted many M. B. families to leave the older settlements and move out to the "growing edge" of the country. Since this migration and resettlement was in most instances not the result of a planned strategy, nor of an organized effort on the part of the larger Mennonite community, the story of this expansion is filled with accounts of frustrations and failures.[35] Small splinter groups scattered over wide areas, making organized congregational activity virtually impossible, especially under pioneer conditions. That so many of these groups survived is an eloquent testimony to the caliber and courage of the settlers. The following account of the expansion relates to Mennonite Brethren.

1. *Toward the Canadian Border*

With the admission of *North Dakota* into the Union in 1889, the settlement opportunities in this state became better known. The fact that land was available at reasonable prices seems to have been the special attraction. Mennonites, with several M. B. families among them, began to move into the state in the late 1890's from the older settlements in South Dakota, Nebraska, and Minnesota. The Mennonite Brethren organized congregations at *Munich* (1897), at *Harvey* (1898), in the *McClusky* area (ca. 1900) and at *Sawyer* (1909). After World War II churches were also established in the cities of *Minot* and *Bismarck*. Among the pioneer church leaders in North Dakota, Christian Reimche deserves special recognition. He not only served the Harvey congregation for about thirty years, but also assisted in the organization and nurture of other churches.[36] The elders H. Adrian (South Dakota) and H. Voth (Minnesota) were frequently invited to serve the young congregations at baptismal, ordination, and dedication services. Growth in membership has been slow during the past few decades. This phenomenon can be explained partly by the fact that the membership of the older congregations is composed largely of rural people; but it must also be seen in the light of a constant movement of families to the West Coast.[37]

Montana, which was admitted into the Union at the same time as North Dakota (1889), attracted Mennonite settlers to its wide open spaces at the beginning of the twentieth century. General Conference Mennonites and Mennonite Brethren settled along the Missouri River at Frazer and Wolf Point and north as far as Lustre and Larslan in Eastern Valley County during World War I (1915-16).

The Mennnonite Brethren organized a church at *Lustre* in 1917. A group at *Volt*, also organized in 1917, has remained affiliated with the Lustre group. The total membership of the Lustre congregation stood at one hundred and thirty-three in 1952, but had declined to one hundred and sixteen by 1971. A group at *Larslan* was organized in 1945, but membership has remained very small. Small groups of Mennonite Brethren existed for brief periods at Chinook, Whitefish, Hydro, and Poplar.[38]

A cluster of three Mennonite churches in Lustre (M. B., E. M. B. and G. C. M.), support the Lustre Bible Academy, established in 1928, illustrating the close cooperation of all Mennonites in the community.

2. *Toward the Rocky Mountains*

Several things attracted Mennonite settlers to the state known for its lofty mountain peaks. Colorado offered special agricultural resources. The wide arid plain on the eastern slope of the mountains was well adapted for cattle raising and the production of grain and feed crops, The favorable climate also attracted health seekers from the hot and humid plains.

The first Mennonite Brethren who settled at Kirk, Colorado, came from Nebraska in the late 1880's. A larger group arrived in 1892 from Marion and Woodson counties in Kansas.[39] Elder David Dyck, who had served the Lehigh congregation for some time, was called to give leadership to the group. The congregation experienced economic hardships and spiritual testings. Periodic droughts resulted in crop failures. Although the land was more suitable for stock-raising than grain-raising, Mennonites were somewhat reluctant to go into cattle-ranching because they did not want their sons to become "cowboys."[40] Elder Dyck left Colorado in 1895 to serve the newly established M.B. church at Winkler, Manitoba. Fluctuating economic conditions and lack of strong leadership produced discouragement among the Mennonite Brethren. Consequently ten families, under the leadership of H. Bergthold, trekked to Westfield, Texas, in fourteen covered wagons. But Texas also did not prove to be the "promised land." In less than two years all families had moved to Corn, Oklahoma, where they found bread and hospitality.[41]

The M. B. Church at *Kirk*, Colorado, however, survived economic depressions and religious upheavals. It is known today as the *Joes* Mennonite Brethren Church, since it is located near the town of Joes.

An M.B. church at *Loveland*, organized in 1906, became extinct by 1924, as are the groups that once existed at *Johnstown, Keenesburg* and *Brighton*. In the city of *Denver*, however, a church was established in the post-war period which has experienced a steady growth and today (1971) has a membership of two hundred and thirty-eight.

3. *Toward the Mexican Border*

Oklahoma

From the central midwestern states of Kansas and Nebraska Mennonites did not only move north and west, but also south as soon as the Oklahoma (Indian) territories were opened up for settlement. The involvement of Mennonites and Mennonite Brethren in the so-called "Oklahoma Runs" constitutes a fascinating chapter in colonization history. The first of these rushes occurred on April 22, 1889 into the region known as the "Oklahoma District."[42]

The first Mennonite Brethren congregation in Oklahoma was established near present-day Watonga in 1893 and came to be known as the *Cooper* M.B. Church (so named after the Cooper post office). Early-day religious activities, including a convention of all the Mennonite Brethren churches in Oklahoma Territory, were held in the large barn on the Cornelius Grunau farm. Church membership declined after 1896, when many left the area because of crop failures. In 1902 the settlement was disbanded.

The *Okeene* M.B. Church, founded in 1902 with sixty charter members, has not only managed to survive the hardships of pioneer life, but has experienced a slow but steady growth through the years.

The lands in the western part of the Cheyenne Arapahoe Territory were generally considered not very suitable for farming. But the optimistic appraisal of J. J. Kliewer, founder of the Shelly Mission near the present community of Corn, initiated an extensive Mennonite movement into what are now Washita and Custer counties.

The *Corn* Mennonite Brethren Church, which was destined to become one of the largest and most influential congregations in the Southern District Conference, was founded in Washita County in 1893.[43] The town virtually grew up around the Mennonite Brethren Church built in 1894. In many ways the Corn congregation functioned as a "mother-church" to other emerging churches in the area. In 1907 the *Bessie* M.B. Church was established for the convenience of members on the western fringe of the settlement. Later, in the period following World War II, congregations were also organized in the larger towns of *Weatherford* and *Clinton*, and the Bessie Church was relocated to *Cordell*.[44]

The Corn congregation has the distinction of establishing the first denominational Bible school in 1902. In 1920 the curriculum was expanded and by 1934 it had become a fully accredited high school. Many early church leaders received their inspiration and training for service in the Kingdom of God in the "Corn Bible Academy."

During the same time that settlers were moving into the western parts of Oklahoma Territory, Mennonite Brethren were in the process of establishing a mission among the Comanche Indians in the southwestern part of the present state. The pioneers of this first missionary effort among the Comanche Indians were Henry Kohfeld and A. J.

Becker, who established the *Post Oak* Mission not far from where Indiahoma now stands.

The land known as "Cherokee Outlet" was opened to settlement by the greatest of all "Runs" on September 16, 1893. It has been estimated that more than one hundred thousand people joined in the race to claim the rich prairies of northwestern Oklahoma Territory. Mennonites were in the front ranks of the homesteaders who surged into this area. According to Marvin Kroeker, "they had a definite part in the founding and early development of the communities in Meno, Deer Creek, Orienta, Fairview, Lahoma, Jet, Lucien, Manchester, Kremlin, Medford, North Enid and Enid."[4]

By the end of the territorial period (1907) the following Mennonite Brethren churches had been established in the so-called "Cherokee Strip": *Fairview* (1894), meeting in two churches after 1895 (Nord-Hoffnungsfeld and Sued-Hoffnungsfeld); *North Enid* (1897);[46] and *Medford* (1899). The first pastor of the Medford M. B. Church, J. F. Harms, in addition to preaching and farming was editor and printer of the *Zionsbote*, the official periodical of the M. B. Conference. It was printed on Harms' farm at first, but later the press was moved to Medford. A church at *Lahoma*, also established during this period as an affiliate of the Sued-Hoffnungsfeld congregation had become extinct by 1923.

The last part of the Oklahoma District to be opened up for settlement in the first decade of the twentieth century was the so-called "panhandle." Mennonite Brethren established congregations at *Balko* (1906), south of Turpin, and *Hooker* (1905), in present Texas County.

In eastern Oklahoma two Mennonite Brethren Churches were established shortly before the first World War. The congregation at *Inola* organized in 1911, is now extinct. The congregation at *Collinsville* was established in 1913 and prospered for some time, reaching a membership of over 100 in 1924. In the thirties and forties membership declined so that in 1950 it stood at seventy-six. In recent years the church has experienced a remarkable growth so that its present membership is 151. Waldo Wiebe, who served as conference evangelist for many years, is the present (1971) pastor.

Texas

It was perhaps in the "logic of history" that Mennonite Brethren would also move still farther south and settle in the largest state of the Union — Texas. At *Littlefield* the brethren organized a congregation and dedicated an attractive church building in 1916.[47] The congregation flourished for a number of years, reaching a membership of about one hundred. The loss of leadership when A. L. Schellenberg returned to the Publishing House in Hillsboro (1922), contributed to the disintegration of the church at Littlefield.

Somewhat later, in 1927, Mennonite Brethren organized a congregation in the *Premont* area, about fifty miles southwest of Corpus Christi. This church has survived to the present (1972) but the membership is small.

Of special historical interest in this state is the emergence of the Latin American M.B. Conference — a result of conference missionary activities in which the Harry Neufelds have played a prominent part. Between Laredo and Brownsville a chain of seven mission churches has been established: Donna M.B. at Donna; Lull M.B. at Edinburg, La Casita M.B. at Garciasville; La Grulla M.B. at La Grulla; La Joya M.B. at La Joya; Mission M.B. at Mission; and Open Bible M.B. at Pharr.[48] Spanish is the main language in the worship services in all these Mexican-American congregations.

4. *Toward the Far West*

Although a number of Mennonite and a few scattered families of Mennonite Brethren had moved to Oregon and California in the last decade of the nineteenth century, a mass-movement from the prairies of Kansas and Nebraska to the San Joaquin Valley and other areas of the Pacific Coast took place in the first two decades of the twentieth century. Oregon seems to have attracted the first M. B. families moving westward,[49] but California soon became the "promised land" for most Mennonite Brethren, and here also the first permanent congregations on the west coast were located. The strong concentration of Mennonite Brethren in the "Pacific District"[50] and especially in the state of California, has been of great significance in the development of conference organization and activities.

California

The Mennonite Brethren, who presently constitute the largest Mennonite group in California both in terms of total membership (over 5,800) as well as in number of active congregations (thirty-three)[51] first settled in Fresno County in the fertile San Joaquin Valley around 1904. The first church to be organized was the *Reedley* congregation in 1905. This church, beginning with fourteen charter members, has grown to be not only the largest Mennonite congregation in California, but also the largest church in the North American Mennonite Brethren Conference. Present (1971) baptized membership stands at one thousand three hundred and thirty-five. Serious tensions over questions of church policy and discipline led to a withdrawal of one hundred and fifty-five members in 1925.[52] This group organized as the South-Reedley M.B. Church under the leadership of J. H. Richert. The congregation met in a hall south of Reedley for a number of years but relocated to *Dinuba* in 1937 where a large church was built in 1939. This congregation has a membership (1971) of four hundred ninety.[53] The majority of the members in both the Reedley and Dinuba congregations are engaged in farming or related occupations. Coming largely from the "wheat belt" of the Midwest, they had to adjust to a new climate and environment. The land, which had to be irrigated, was not suitable for raising wheat and corn, but was ideal for growing grapes and fruits of many varieties. The raisin industry of this area has become world-famous and Reedley is sometimes referred to as the "raisin capital" of the world.

Very early in their history the churches of this area, concerned for the spiritual welfare of their young people, arranged Bible classes for those of high school age. Eventually these efforts resulted in the establishment of Immanuel Academy — a Christian high school.[54]

A number of churches were also established in Southern California during this early period. In 1904 Mennonite Brethren families arrived in *Escondido*, near San Diego, and formed a congregation in 1905. Due to a lack of leadership and economic difficulties, this church was dissolved after 1921. Most members left for places farther north and settled in Kern County in the southern part of the San Joaquin Valley. In this area the *Rosedale* M. B. Church was organized in 1909, *Bakersfield* in 1910 and *Shafter* in 1918.

North of Fresno churches were established at *Lodi* (1912), Fairmead, now *Madera* (1919), *Winton*, now extinct (1922) and in *Orland* (1923). The Krimmer Mennonite Brethren established only one church in California, organized in 1917 near Dinuba as the *Zion* K. M. B. Church. This congregation joined the Mennonite Brethren Conference in 1960 at the time of the merger.

During the post-war period there has been a definite trend in California toward establishing city churches, reflecting on the one hand the shift of the M.B. population from rural to urban areas, and on the other a growing vision and concern in the brotherhood to reach the unchurched and unevangelized masses of metropolitan areas. The first city church was organized in *Los Angeles* in 1924. Contrary to the experience in most other cities where Mennonite Brethren have established congregations, the church here did not grow as rapidly as could have been expected. One reason has been a sizeable transient membership, with no large permanent M. B. residential group in Los Angeles.[55] This congregation on South Hoover Street has become extinct, but a mission church (*City Terrace*) established among Jews and Catholics in East Los Angeles in 1926, has manifested a healthy growth as an inter-racial fellowship.

Other city churches were established in central California. The *San Jose* M. B. Church was organized with twenty charter members in 1940. Although the church had to relocate several times, it has grown to a membership of four hundred at present (1971). The largest number of urban congregations, however, have been established in the city of Fresno. Beginning with the Bethany M.B. Church in 1942, there has been a continual growth of the M.B. population in the city so that at present there are six organized congregations: *Bethany, Butler, Clovis* (a suburb), *Faith, North Fresno,* and *West Park.* One of these (Faith) is a Spanish-speaking congregation, largely composed of Mexican-Americans. The location of two conference schools, Pacific College and the Mennonite Brethren Biblical Seminary, within the city of Fresno, no doubt is an important factor in this heavy concentration of Mennonite Brethren here. More recently churches have also have been founded in *Visalia, Kingsburg, Santa Clara, Santa Cruz,* and *Sacramento,* the state capital.

Another group of Mennonites, which included a fairly large number of Mennoite Brethren, came to California in 1930 — not from the Midwest, but from the Far East. Many of these "displaced persons" from various parts of Russia had been at the "Gates of Moscow" in 1929, when the door of escape to the West was suddenly closed. They eventually made their way to the Amur settlement in eastern Siberia. From here they fled across the Amur River during the winter of 1929-30 to Harbin, China. Through the mediation of P. C. Hiebert, chairman of MCC, 256 of these refugees were able to come to the United States. Here most of them eventually settled near Reedley.[56]

The rapid expansion and material progress of M. B. congregations, and their exposure to all the religious crosscurrents for which California has become known, pose special problems for the stability and spiritual identity of Mennonite Brethren in this state. Denominational training centers, therefore, are of special significance in meeting these needs and in providing the theological leadership which such a situation demands. The churches of California have through the years shown a great interest in missions, and many workers have been commissioned for various fields in the "regions beyond."

Oregon

Some of the first M.B. families moving to the Pacific Coast settled near *Dallas* in the beautiful Willamette Valley in central Oregon. Already in 1891 a small group was organized as a congregation with the assistance of Elder Voth from Minnesota. The church existed only a few years, partly because some families moved away and others joined the local Baptist church. According to J. F. Harms, the Mennonite Brethren never felt quite "at home" among the Baptists.[57] Thus in 1905 twelve families resolved to unite and again establish an M.B. church. They organized themselves as the North-Dallas M.B. Church. The brethren P. C. Hiebert and H. S. Voth were instrumental in the expansion and growth of this congregation. With the shift of population from the rural area north of Dallas to the town itself, the congregation rented a hall in Dallas which served as a meeting place of the group that resided there. By 1919 this group organized as the Dallas M. B. Church, and just four years later, in 1923, the remaining members of the mother church were received into the daughter church — thereby dissolving the former congregation.[58] The *Kingwood* Bible Church, established in Salem in 1940, can be regarded as a daughter congregation of Dallas. An M.B. Church established in *Portland* in the 1890's has become extinct, but in the 1960's a new urban fellowship emerged in the city of *Eugene*.

Washington

In the 1930's members from M.B. churches in Oklahoma, Kansas, Montana and California began to settle in Washington, a state in the northwest corner of the United States. In 1937 a congregation of twenty-three members was organized at *Blaine*, within eight miles of the Canadian border and only one mile from the Pacific Ocean. Although it might be classified as a rural congregation, the church has experienced steady growth and has a membership of one hundred and sixty-nine at present (1971). The church, removed geographically from other congregations of the Pacific District Conference, profits from mutual visits with Canadian churches in the nearby Fraser Valley. The *Shoreline* M.B. Church in the large metropolitan center of Seattle was established between 1963 and 1965 and has a present membership of ninety.

This brief survey of church planting and church growth in the United States reflects both the movement of a people and the propagation of a faith. The organization for united action, the work and witness of the brotherhood through its congregations and institutions, will constitute the story of subsequent chapters.

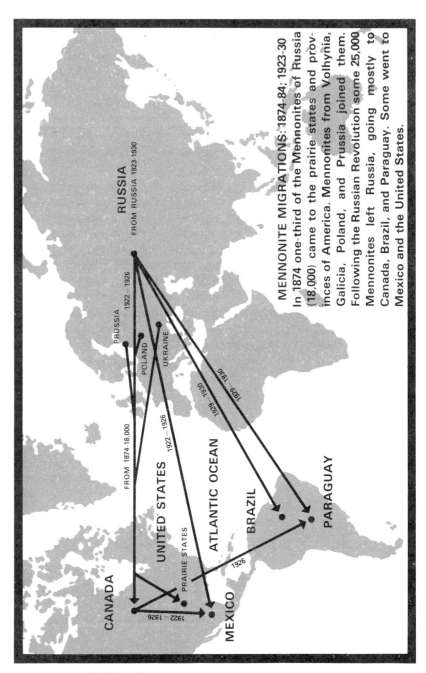

5. Major Mennonite Migrations: 1874-84; 1923-30

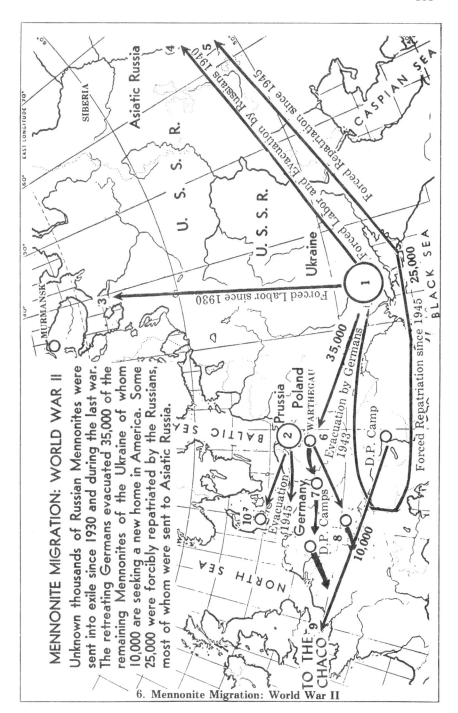

MENNONITE MIGRATION: WORLD WAR II

Unknown thousands of Russian Mennonites were sent into exile since 1930 and during the last war. The retreating Germans evacuated 35,000 of the remaining Mennonites of the Ukraine of whom 10,000 are seeking a new home in America. Some 25,000 were forcibly repatriated by the Russians, most of whom were sent to Asiatic Russia.

6. Mennonite Migration: World War II

Chapter 11

Mennonite Brethren
Come to Canada

During the last one hundred years probably no other country in the world has received the Mennonites as graciously and treated them as generously as Canada. It is not surprising, therefore, that during the twentieth century more Mennonites who were seeking relief from the religious and economic oppression of Europe chose Canada rather than any other country as their "home and native land." For many of these pilgrims who had gone through the wilderness experience of war, revolution, famine, confiscation of property and the restriction of religious freedom, Canada appeared to be in a very literal sense the "promised land," and so they affectionately called it "Canaan."[1]

The "open door policy" of the Canadian government[2] was largely determined by economic considerations. The country covers the whole of the North American continent north of the United States (excepting Alaska) and constitutes an area larger in size than the whole of Europe. What Canada desperately needed was settlers of the right kind, especially after the opening up of the "Great West" shortly after Confederation. Hence the Mennonites, and other religious pacifist groups as well, were admitted into Canada because of their desirability as farmers for a pioneer country. A statutory provision for exemption from military service dating as far back as 1808, and subsequently confirmed by a special Order-in-Council in 1873, gave Mennonites the assurance that their religious convictions regarding war and military service would be respected.[3]

Mennonites have come into Canada in a number of successive "waves," and it might be well to briefly identify these at the outset.

The *first* group came from eastern Pennsylvania to the Niagara Peninsula in 1786 to settle in Welland and Lincoln counties of what later became the province of Ontario. In the years immediately following,

152

others came, locating principally in three centers: Waterloo County, the Markham district, and the Niagara district. They were among the pioneers of Canada and by their favorable reputation in community and province they paved the way for other Mennonites to enter the country later.

A *second* large influx of Mennonites took place between the years 1874-80, when some eight thousand of them left the steppes of the Ukraine to settle in the newly established province of Manitoba on the so-called "East Reserve" and "West Reserve."[4] Jacob Y. Shantz, a Mennonite layman of Waterloo County, played a significant role in establishing these settlements. As mentioned in the previous chapter, the Mennonites who migrated to Canada belonged to the more conservative groups, coming largely from the Chortitza, Bergthal and Fuerstenland colonies, and from the *Kleine Gemeinde* of the Molotschna. According to all available records, no Mennonite Brethren settled in Canada at this time.

The *third* and largest wave of Mennonite immigrants to Canada (also from Russia) came in the years 1923-30. This movement brought well over twenty thousand Mennonites into Canada, the majority of whom settled on farms in the prairie provinces. This contingent included a large number of Mennonite Brethren.

The *fourth* and last wave of immigration came after World War II, when approximately seven thousand Mennonites entered the country between 1947 and 1952. Because of their experience under the Stalinist regime, many of these had no official church connection prior to their coming out of the Soviet Union. During their prolonged stay in German "refugee camps" many experienced a spiritual renewal and publicly identified themselves with one or the other Mennonite church before coming to Canada.

To trace the growth and development of the Mennonite Brethren Church from its beginning as a tiny mission church of sixteen members in southern Manitoba, to a Canada-wide brotherhood, with some one hundred and twenty-five congregations scattered literally "from sea to shining sea" is a somewhat difficult, yet very interesting task. Since logically and chronologically this expansion is related to distinct geographical areas, a geographic pattern has been adopted in the organization of materials for this chapter.

I. Early Congregations in Manitoba
The Winkler Mennonite Brethren Church

The first Mennonite Brethren church in Canada came into existence as the result of church extension efforts by Mennonite Brethren in the United States. The first reference to Canada as a possible "mission field" appears in the conference minutes of 1882 in connection with the

projection of itinerant ministries for the coming year.[5] Although there
was widespread interest in such a venture, plans were postponed
because of inadequate information about the religious situation in
Manitoba, and also because of insufficient funds.

At the conference held in Hamilton County, Nebraska, the
following year, the brethren Heinrich Voth (Minnesota) and David Dyck
(Kansas) were commissioned to visit the Mennonite communities in
Manitoba. In the spring of 1884 these two ministers visited southern
Manitoba (West Reserve) in order to familiarize themselves with the
field. Apparently missionaries of other denominations and cults were
making inroads into the Mennonite settlements of Manitoba at this
time.[6] Since David Dyck had relatives in the area, it was possible for the
brethren to establish a number of important contacts during this first
visit.

Encouraged by the reports of the two deputies, the October, 1884,
conference meeting in Kansas asked Heinrich Voth to devote his whole
time to a spiritual ministry in Minnesota and Manitoba for an annual
salary of four hundred dollars.[7] (David Dyck was not available for a
further ministry, because he had accepted pastoral responsibilities at
Lehigh, Kansas.) Voth was thus left alone to carry on the work in
Manitoba, and for the next five years he visited this area once or twice a
year.

Voth's actual ministry began on December 4, 1884, in the village of
Hoffnungsfeld, one mile southwest of the present town of Winkler. That
his ministry was not without opposition and tests of faith is illustrated
by the following incident. On one occasion, while he was conducting
meetings in the schoolhouse at Hoffnungsfeld, three men entered after
the service had begun. Since there were no vacant seats in the room,
Voth asked them to come forward and occupy the chairs behind the
speaker. After the service, the following conversation took place
between these men as they made their exit: "Why did you not take
him?" asked one. The other replied: "If what he says is the truth, then
we are lost." Later this man accepted Christ and disclosed that they had
planned to seize the evangelist, take him to the Canadian-United States
border, and send him home to Minnesota.[8]

Throughout the settlement (West Reserve) there were individuals
and families who had experienced God's forgiveness, but lacked
instruction and nurture. Through the ministry of Elder Voth these were
strengthened in their faith, and others were won to Christ. These efforts
came to visible fruition on May 30, 1886, at Burwalde, when two couples
were baptized in the Dead Horse Creek. Two weeks later, four additional converts were baptized. This group formed the nucleus of the first
Canadian M. B. church two years later. At the conference in Turner

County (South) Dakota in November, 1886, Elder Voth's report of the first baptism in Manitoba was received with joy and gratitude. Realizing the special needs of this area, the conference asked Voth to visit Manitoba three times the following year with a remuneration of four hundred dollars plus traveling expenses. The faithful preaching and pastoral ministry of Elder Voth laid the foundations for the establishment of a church in 1888.

Deeply conscious of the fact that periodic visits were inadequate to meet the spiritual needs of the group of believers in the West Reserve, Voth had invited Gerhard Wiebe, an ordained minister of the M. B. Church in Russia, to come to Manitoba and take charge of the work. When Wiebe arrived in April, 1888, the group at Burwalde was organized as a congregation with sixteen members.[9]

Although Wiebe served the local congregation well, there still was an urgent need for a "minister-at-large" to meet the challenge of open doors for evangelism and teaching. Elder David Dyck, whom the conference had asked repeatedly to assume this responsibility, finally consented to move to Canada. The long trek from Colorado to southern Manitoba was made on a "prairie schooner." When the Dyck family arrived at Burwalde on July 17, 1895, the young church consisted of eighty-four members. For eleven years Dyck gave effective leadership to the congregation and also engaged in an extensive itinerant ministry. In 1906 he moved to Borden, Saskatchewan, however, to claim a free homestead in that newly established province. Johann Warkentin, a former schoolteacher in the village of Hoffnungsfeld, assumed the responsibility of leadership and gave effective guidance through the next twenty-five years of the church's growth and expansion.

One year after the organization of the church, a meetinghouse was erected at Burwalde. As membership increased it was felt that the building was too small and not centrally located. At a church meeting on October 30, 1897, it was decided to move the building to a site on the northwest corner of the town of Winkler. An interesting little episode is reported in connection with this move, illustrating the philosophy of some early brethren that "urbanization" would have a corrupting influence on the life of the congregation. Some of the members thought that the new location for the church should be at least a mile out of town. Subsequently, "when the church was moved it was left standing a mile out of town for a few days because of the reluctance of some members to have their church located right in town."[10] But reason prevailed over prejudice and the church was moved to the edge of town to the delight of the members residing in Winkler.

The building proved inadequate for the needs of the congregation in Winkler from the beginning. Since the Mennonite Brethren Conference of North America had been invited to Winkler for 1898, the brethren decided to erect a new and larger structure on the same site. This building was remodeled and enlarged for the third time in 1930. The third stage in the process of "acculturation" was reached in 1947, when a new church building, with a seating capacity of one thousand, was erected on a new site in the heart of the town of Winkler.[11]

The Winkler M. B. Church played a leading role in establishing several new churches in the area during the pioneer period. The *Grossweide* M.B. Church, located near the town of Horndean, was organized as an affiliate of the Winkler church in 1896. The membership was composed largely of former members of the Sommerfeld and Old Colony Mennonite churches.[12] The church became independent in 1925 and experienced steady growth, so that by 1953 it had a membership of one hundred and seventy-four. In the decades following it suffered the fate of many rural churches in the conference. In spite of relocation to the town of Horndean, it declined in membership so that today (1971) it has only fifty-nine members.

The *Kronsgart* M. B. Church is also the result of church extension efforts of the mother church at Winkler. A number of Mennonite Brethren families settled in the area some eight to twelve miles north of Winkler. Meetings were held in public schools of the area for many years, but in 1920 a church building was erected near the station of Kronsgart. The membership of this rural congregation has remained small.

Beginnings in Winnipeg

In Winnipeg, the capital of Manitoba and "gateway to the West," the Mennonite Brethren Church had an inconspicuous beginning as a small city mission.[13] Winnipeg is perhaps unique among cities in Canada, in that Mennonite Brethren began to reside here long before the general "urbanization process" took place after World War II.

Already in 1907 a number of families were meeting in private homes for prayer and fellowship. Feeling their need for a spiritual ministry, the group extended a "Macedonian Call" to the M. B. church in Winkler.[14] The brethren who responded to the call and began to visit the group regularly were Peter H. Neufeld and Johann Warkentin, the leader of the church. Warkentin manifested a deep concern for the welfare of the small flock: he purchased an empty lot on the corner of Burrows and Andrews streets, bought a small chapel, and moved it onto the lot. The "little chapel on the corner" attracted many visitors from the surrounding area.

The numerous opportunities for evangelism among the German-speaking people of the city called for the appointment of full-time city missionaries. God's chosen instruments for this task were Mr. and Mrs.

Wm. J. Bestvater of Mountain Lake, Minnesota. At the fourth Northern District (Canadian) Conference held in Dalmeny, Saskatchewan in 1913, the Bestvaters were appointed for this work. During the eight years (1913-1921) of his ministry in Winnipeg, Bestvater performed a wide range of services. Many transient families received material and spiritual help. Visitation work in the community as well as in hospitals required time and effort. During the war years (1914-1918) Bestvater served as spiritual counselor to many young Mennonite men and assisted them in obtaining exemption from military service.

The expanding ministry demanded additional workers and Miss Anna Thiessen, who had just graduated from the Herbert Bible School, joined the staff in the fall of 1915. For almost forty years Miss Thiessen served faithfully in the city mission work of Winnipeg. As matron of the "Mary-Martha Home" for twenty-two years (1925-1947), she became a mother to many girls working away from home.[15]

Bestvater, who had received theological training at the Moody Bible Institute in Chicago, was very much appreciated for his preaching and systematic Bible teaching. When a new and larger chapel was erected on the same site in 1917, more people could be accommodated in the regular Sunday worship services and in the many meetings during the week.

In 1921 the Bestvaters accepted the responsibility of leadership in the Herbert Bible School. The Erdman Nikkels, of Laird, Saskatchewan, stepped into the gap and served the church and mission for several years. With the appointment of the C.N. Hieberts in 1925 a new epoch began for the expansion of the Mennonite Brethren Church in Winnipeg. This phase will be discussed in connection with the coming of the Mennonite Brethren from Russia. The total membership in the M.B. Church in Manitoba stood at three hundred and eighty in 1924.[16]

II. EARLY CONGREGATIONS IN SASKATCHEWAN

The name Saskatchewan is an Indian name meaning "rapidly flowing river." In fact, two rivers bearing this name — the North Saskatchewan and the South Saskatchewan — flow through the province, meet just east of the city of Prince Albert and from there continue as one to Lake Winnipeg. This vast territory in Central Canada, which was to become Canada's greatest wheat-producing area, entered Confederation as a province in 1905. Even before that date, Mennonite farmers were attracted to this area because of the availability of free homesteads and cheaper land. Mennonite Brethren, together with many other Mennonites, settled in two main areas which became known as the *Rosthern Kreis* (in North Saskatchewan) and the *Herbert Kreis* (in South Saskatchewan). Since the Mennonite Brethren of this province were organized for many years as North Saskatchewan and South

Saskatchewan District Conferences, this division will be observed in describing the founding of churches in these respective areas.[17]

North Saskatchewan (Rosthern Kreis)

According to J. F. Harms, the first M. B. families to come into the province, mostly from Manitoba, settled around the town of *Laird*.[18] The Laird congregation was organized in 1898 with approximately sixty members under the leadership of Jacob B. Wiens. Laird has the distinction of being the first organized M. B. church in Saskatchewan. This church, as well as other congregations that were established later, endured the hardships of pioneer life. Periodic droughts, long and severe winters and a widely scattered membership combined to test the faith and perseverance of the early settlers. One pioneer wrote in 1899 "that they could only go the nineteen miles to church every other Sunday as the horses were so thin and poor. . . ."[19] The church was located originally four and one half miles east of town in the Ebenfeld school district. For this reason the church was also known as the Ebenfeld M.B. Church until 1911, when it was relocated in the town of Laird.[20]

During the first two decades of the twentieth century a minor "wave" of immigration from the United States led to a rapid expansion of Mennonite Brethren settlements and congregational activities. Most of these Mennonite Brethren families came from Minnesota and Nebraska, but there were also a few from South Dakota and Kansas. In addition, small groups came directly from Russia just prior to World War I.

According to available records[21] congregations were established in the *Rosthern Kreis* as follows, (with number of charter members in parenthesis): *Bruderfeld*, six miles west of Waldheim, in 1901 (25); *Ebenezer* (now Dalmeny) in 1901 (39); *Hoffnungsfeld* (now Borden) in 1904 (72); *Aberdeen* (now extinct) in 1906 (22); *Hepburn* in 1910 (115); and *Waldheim* in 1918 (65).[22]

A man who gave strong leadership to the young congregations in this area was elder David Dyck who settled in the Borden area in 1906. In 1910 he purchased a farm four miles west of Waldheim and served both the Bruderfeld and Waldheim congregations as elder for many years. He also traveled extensively and preached frequently to Russian congregations. He served as moderator of the Northern District (Canadian) Conference on thirteen occasions, and also represented the brotherhood on the Board of Foreign Missions. Another man, who became a pillar in his own congregation and a progressive leader in the *Rosthern Kreis* was Jacob Lepp of Dalmeny. Coming to North Saskatchewan from Minnesota, as a young man, he was elected as minister in 1902, and installed as church leader in 1907. He served the church in this capacity until his retirement in 1941.[23]

27. H. S. Voth   28. Jacob Lepp

The pattern of church services in the pioneer era differed from that adopted later in most M. B. churches. In the "horse and buggy" days, one trip to church on Sunday was generally considered sufficient. Families met for worship in the morning and stayed together at the church for a fellowship meal, after which Sunday school classes were conducted. Evening services were held only on special occasions, usually in connection with the visit of an itinerant minister or evangelist. During this entire period, 1900-1925, services were conducted exclusively in German. District conferences provided wonderful opportunities for a wider spiritual and social fellowship, and were always considered highlights in the life of the brotherhood. Since church buildings were generally far too small to accommodate delegates and guests (who often attended with their families) large tents were usually erected for such occasions. The festive spirit of these conferences helped to lift church members to "higher ground" and provided pleasant breaks in the routine and drudgery of pioneer life.

South Saskatchewan (Herbert Kreis)

Mennonite and Mennonite Brethren settlements were established on both sides of the main line of the Canadian Pacific Railway, and south of the South Saskatchewan River in the first two decades of the twentieth century — somewhat later than in North Saskatchewan. Unlike the North Saskatchewan area, the prairies west of the city of Moose Jaw were bald and treeless, and this may have been a reason for late settlement. Whereas most M. B. pioneers in the *Rosthern Kreis* had come from Minnesota and Nebraska, a considerable number of the settlers here came from Manitoba and North Dakota, with a sprinkling of immigrants from other states and from Russia.

The following congregations were organized in the *Herbert Kreis* during the pioneer period: *Main Centre* in 1904 under the leadership of elder Benjamin Janz; *Herbert* in 1905, with J. J. Martens as first leader; *Gnadenau* (near Flowing Well, now extinct) in 1907 with John F. Harms as first leader; *Elim* (near Kelstern) in 1907 with Peter Penner (an ordained minister from Russia) as presiding minister; *Woodrow* in 1909 with G. Reimche as first leader; *Greenfarm* (now extinct) in 1912 with J.W. Thiessen as first leader; *Bethania* (now extinct) in 1913, in the Turnhill school district, with Johann W. Neufeld, an ordained minister from Russia, as first leader; *Fox Valley* (now extinct) some forty miles north of Maple Creek, in 1914, under the direction of elder Benjamin Janz.[24]

In Fox Valley as well as in several other congregations there were many members who had come from North Dakota. With their Volga-German (and in some instances Lutheran) background, they lacked a knowledge of Mennonite Brethren principles and practices. As a result, misunderstandings and tensions would often arise, and brethren from the more established congregations of Main Centre and Herbert would then be called in to assist in resolving these tensions.[25]

Besides Benjamin Janz, the Herbert District profited greatly from the rich spiritual ministry of several other prominent leaders. Heinrich A. Neufeld (1865-1933) who moved to the Herbert area in 1911, traveled extensively as evangelist and Bible expositor. C. N. Hiebert, with his unique gifts in evangelism, was used of God in many churches to call sinners to repentance and encourage believers.[26]

Of special significance for the whole *Herbert Kreis* was the establishment of a Bible school in the town of Herbert in 1913. This institution, the first of its kind in Canada, was largely the fruit of the vision, courage and labor of John F. Harms. Harms had been engaged in educational efforts in Kansas some years earlier. When he settled on a farm at Flowing Well south of Herbert in 1908, he began to teach Bible classes during the winter months. In 1913 the hopes of the Northern District Conference became a reality when eighteen students enrolled for studies under Harms. When Harms moved back to the United States in 1918, the school had to be closed because of financial difficulties. In 1921 it was reopened under the capable leadership of William J. Bestvater. Teachers and students of the Bible school helped to promote a greater interest in Christian service and missions in the entire constituency.[27]

III. Expansion and Growth Through Immigration

The year 1924 marked the beginning of a rapid expansion of the M.B. Church throughout Canada. This increase in membership and in the number of congregations was not so much the result of the propagation of the gospel as it was of large scale immigration of Mennonite Brethren from the Soviet Union as pointed out at the beginning of this chapter.

In his book, *Mennonite Exodus*, Frank H. Epp has given an excellent account of the rescue and resettlement of the Russian Mennonites since the Communist Revolution. In chapter eight we have also summarized this story, as well as the involvement of Mennonite Brethren in this movement. Rather than treating the economic and social problems of the immigrants, the primary emphasis will be on the contribution of the newly arrived *Russlaender* (Russian countrymen) to the growth and expansion of the M. B. Church earlier established by the *Kanaedier* (Canadians).[28]

Manitoba

Mennonite Brethren who came to Manitoba in the 1920's received hospitality and material assistance from the Mennonites who had come to Canada fifty years earlier and established themselves in the East Reserve and West Reserve. Others stayed in the city of Winnipeg and were assisted by C. N. Hiebert, city missionary, in finding housing and employment. To many immigrants it appeared providential that numerous farms (*Wirtschaften*) were available in the villages of southern Manitoba as a result of the mass exodus of Old Colony and Sommerfelder Mennonites to Mexico in the early twenties.

The Winkler M. B. Church and its affiliates were strengthened by the addition of many new members. "Not only did the congregations increase in membership . . ." writes Lohrenz, "but they also received from among them many gifted and devoted ministers, leaders, teachers and men qualified in practical affairs."[29] Former staff members of the Tschongraw Bible School in the Crimea, A. H. Unruh, J. G. Wiens and G. Reimer took up residence in Winkler and founded a Bible school in 1925 under Unruh's leadership. The preaching and teaching ministry of these brethren enriched and strengthened not only the local congregation, but also that of other M. B. churches that sprang up throughout the province. The East Reserve and West Reserve could not absorb the large number of newcomers, however, and consequently a number of new settlements originated in central and western Manitoba.

The number of organized M. B. churches in Manitoba jumped from two to fourteen between 1924 and 1930.[30] East of the Red River, congregations were established at *Arnaud* (1925), *Steinbach* (1927), and

Niverville (1933).[31] Except for a few members in Steinbach, the membership of these churches was composed exclusively of immigrants. In the West Reserve congregations were organized at *Gnadental* (1925) and at *Morden* (1930).

West of Morden churches were established at *Manitou* (1927), *Lena-Holmfield,* now located at Killarney (1928), and at *Boissevain* (1928). Also belonging to the "Western District" were the churches established at *Griswold* (1926) now located at Alexander, and at *Justice* (1930), both in the Brandon area.

Southwest of Winnipeg congregations were organized at *Newton Siding* (1928), *Elm Creek* (1929) and *Domain,* formerly Lasalle, (1926). Some years later an M.B. church was also founded at *Springstein* (1938) which is now extinct. Some forty miles west of Winnipeg a church was also organized at *Marquette* (1925), but because of its small size this group has become an affiliate of the North-End (now Elmwood) M. B. Church in Winnipeg.

The urbanization process of Mennonites in Manitoba during the last few decades has been phenomenal and Winnipeg today has the distinction of having the heaviest concentration of Mennonites of any city on the North American continent. The Mennonite Brethren have been in the vanguard of this process. Beginning with a small city mission church of twenty-two members in 1913, the Mennonite Brethren today (1971) worship in eight local churches with a baptized membership of two and one half thousand.[32] During the late twenties the entire congregation continued to worship in one place — the mission chapel at the corner of Andrews and Burrows. Because a large group settled in the suburb of North Kildonan, and another large group had taken up residence on the "Southside" (south of the Canadian Pacific Railway tracks) the M. B. church divided into three local congregations: *North End* (now Elmwood), a direct outgrowth of the city mission; *North Kildonan* (1929), composed of immigrants from Russia; and *South End* (1936), also composed of immigrants.

Partly the result of the division of larger churches, but also partly the result of church extension work in the city, five other congregations were established in Greater Winnipeg in the 1960's: *River East* M. B. Church in East Kildonan; *Portage Ave.* M. B. Church in West Winnipeg; *Salem* M. B. Church in the "inner city;" *Fort Garry* M. B. Church in South Winnipeg, close to the university campus; and *Brooklands* M. B. Church in the suburb of Brooklands. Initially the language in the worship services was German, but through the years this has changed; today the "mother churches" (Elmwood, North Kildonan, Portage Avenue and Central) still conduct bilingual services, but the "younger churches" have used only English in their meetings from the very beginning.

The establishment of the Mennonite Brethren Bible College in 1944, and of the M. B. Collegiate Institute in 1945, helped to make Winnipeg a strategic center not only for the Manitoba Conference, but also for the larger Canadian brotherhood. The Christian Press, established in Winnipeg in 1923 and later acquired by the Canadian Conference, also promoted this development.

In the post-war period churches were also planted in other cities of Manitoba — first in *Brandon* and later in *Portage la Prairie* and *Carman*. In Manitoba, as elsewhere, the shift from rural communities to urban centers is very much in evidence. The contributions of prominent leaders to the work of the brotherhood will be considered in connection with institutional and other activities of the conference.

Saskatchewan

In Saskatchewan more Mennonite Brethren immigrants who came from Russia in the 1920's settled in areas where churches had been established earlier; thus fewer new congregations were organized than in Manitoba. The amalgamation of the *Kanaedier* and *Russlaender* in a local church was not always easy, and as Lohrenz points out, "was sometimes fraught with friction and misunderstanding."[33] But the common faith in Christ and the love for the brethren helped to bridge cultural differences and united the two groups in the common cause of building God's kingdom.

New congregations composed almost exclusively of *Russlaender* were organized in North Saskatchewan at *Glenbush* (1928), *Mullingar* (1928) now extinct, and at *Watrous* (1927). The Watrous congregation, composed largely of members who in Russia had belonged to the *Allianz Gemeinde*, organized as an Evangelical Mennonite Brethren Church initially, but after five years joined the M. B. Conference.

In South Saskatchewan most of the *Russlaender* joined existing M.B. churches. Two smaller congregations established by immigrants, *Reinfeld* (1927) and *Blumenort* (1926), are now extinct. A considerable number of smaller mission churches have been founded in both North and South as the result of extensive home mission efforts.

Even in the wheat-growing province, where Mennonite life could aptly be expressed by the symbolism of the "Bible and the Plow" for many years, urbanization has overtaken the Mennonite Brethren. This is due in part to the general shift of population from rural to urban areas, but it is also the result of strategic planning for church extension.

The first Mennonite Brethren church (now *Central* M. B. Church) in Saskatoon began in 1927 when members gathered for worship under the leadership of Peter Funk. In 1932 a congregation was organized. Under H. S. Rempel, who began a long and fruitful ministry here in 1935, the city mission and the congregation were closely related. After World War

II, two other M. B. churches were established in Saskatoon: *Nutana* (1963) on the east side, and *West Portal* (1957) on the west side. In *Swift Current* an M. B. church was organized as early as 1933, and in *Regina*, the capital of Saskatchewan, in 1941. In recent years mission churches have also been established in *North Battleford* and in *Moose Jaw*.[34]

During the Depression in the 1930's the Mennonite Brethren churches of Saskatchewan suffered severely, along with the rest of the population. Drought, dust storms, low prices, and bleak economic prospects generally, prompted many families to look for greener pastures elsewhere. From South Saskatchewan a goodly number moved into the Abbotsford area of British Columbia; from North Saskatchewan a relatively large group moved eastward and settled in the Virgil area of southern Ontario. This "drainage" of members to British Columbia and Ontario retarded the growth of congregations in Saskatchewan.

Expansion through immigration presented a sociological problem: tensions between the *Kanaedier* and the *Russlaender* groups. Despite a common origin and a common faith, adjustment of the *Russlaender* immigrants to the *Kanaedier* group was in many ways as difficult as adjustment to society at large. In the words of E. K. Francis:

> The two Mennonite groups were divided by cultural and class differences. In the eyes of the native Mennonites the newcomers appeared worldly, overbearing, and unwilling to do manual labor. The *Russlaender* people, on the other hand, found their benefactors, on whose good will they were dependent . . . backward . . . and uneducated. [35]

Although these views must be modified somewhat in the context of the Mennonite Brethren community, they reflect some popular attitudes which prevailed in the twenties and thirties. Since education, and especially theological education, appears to have been a focal issue in these tensions, it is understandable that some of the more obvious differences came to the fore in the Hepburn and Winkler areas, where Bible schools were founded which originally were staffed largely by the *Russlaender* brethren. As time progressed, however, the dialogue between the two groups proved to be mutually beneficial: The *Russlaender* were stimulated by the *Kanaedier* to become more concerned about evangelism and missions; and the latter were stimulated by the former to become more interested in education and culture.

The coming of the Russian Mennonites marks a new chapter in the expansion of the Mennonite Brethren Church in the Canadian West. Until 1925 there was not a single M. B. church in the two western provinces.[36] Ten years later, thirteen churches had been established in these provinces by the immigrants from Russia.[37] The westward movement of Mennonites, and particularly of the Mennonite Brethren, which began in the twenties and thirties has continued to the present day, though at a greatly reduced pace.

IV. MENNONITE BRETHREN COME TO ALBERTA[38]

The Mennonite Brethren were not the first to arrive in "sunny Alberta." Between 1890 and 1920 Mennonite settlers belonging to the (Old) Mennonite Church established congregations at High River, Carstairs, Olds, Tofield and Duchess. The Mennonite Brethren in Christ (now United Missionary Church) also coming from Ontario after 1893, established churches at Didsbury and other places in central Alberta. Members of the Bergthal Mennonite Church from the West Reserve in Manitoba also settled in the Didsbury area after 1901, as did a Church of God in Christ, Mennonite (Holdeman) group at Linden in 1902.

Most of the Mennonite Brethren who first arrived in Alberta in the mid-twenties did not establish themselves in or near the older Mennonite settlements in the central part of the province. The Canada Colonization Association, a subsidiary of the Department of Immigration and Colonization of the Canadian Pacific Railway Company, played a vital part in directing many Mennonites to settle on "C.P.R. land" in southern Alberta.[39] In this area the railway company had recently completed an extensive irrigation system and was now concerned to get larger returns on its heavy investments. Irrigation and "truck farming" meant much back-breaking work, but Mennonites were willing to pay the price in return for a more regular income and the prospect of larger and more compact community settlements. Four major Mennonite settlements were established exclusively on irrigation lands at Coaldale, Gem, Vauxhall, and Rosemary. In the first three the Mennonite Brethren organized flourishing congregations.

The Coaldale Mennonite Brethren Church

The first M. B. church in Alberta, and the one destined to become the largest and most prominent was the one at Coaldale, ten miles east of the city of Lethbridge. For more than three decades, (from 1927 to 1957) this congregation overshadowed all other churches in the province since somewhat more than half of all conference members belonged to the Coaldale M.B. Church.

The pioneer of the church and community here was a minister, Klaas Enns. Peter Bargen graphically describes the beginning: "The Mennonite settlement at Coaldale . . . began when one man and his family decided to clean sugar beets for a local farmer."[40] This was in the fall of 1925. The enthusiasm of Enns, who envisioned the possibility of building a Mennonite settlement after the pattern of the "Molotschna" in South Russia, was contagious. Beginning in 1926, a steady stream of homeseekers found their way to Coaldale, the place where "milk and honey" quite literally flowed. Already in the spring of 1926 the brethren organized themselves as a congregation under the leadership of Klaas Enns. The church continued to grow through the years and reached its peak membership of over six hundred in 1955. The first church building, erected in 1928, had to be enlarged in 1929 and again in 1932. In 1939 a large new structure, with a seating capacity of one thousand, was erected.

Several factors contributed to make Coaldale a strategic center for the Mennonite Brethren in the second quarter of this century. The congregation was blessed with an outstanding leadership, among whom B. B. Janz deserves special mention. With his wide experience in church and community affairs, Janz gave wise leadership to the congregation through the "storm and stress" of pioneer life, the depression of the thirties, and the turbulent days of World War II. Coaldale also became the educational center of the province when the brethren established a Bible school here in 1929 and a private high school in 1946. Many leading brethren in the conference have received their initial inspiration and training for Christian service in the Coaldale M. B. Church and in the Coaldale Bible School.

Other (Rural) Mennonite Brethren Churches

The *Grassy Lake* M.B. Church, some sixty miles east of Coaldale, was organized in 1927. The *Gem* M. B. Church was organized in 1929 and accepted into the provincial conference the same year. In the Peace River area of northern Alberta, the *La Glace* church was organized in 1928, the same year that the church at *Lindbrook* (now *Tofield*), forty miles east of Edmonton, was established. The *Namaka* M. B. Church (now extinct) was organized as an Evangelical Mennonite Brethren Church in 1927 under the leadership of A. A. Toews, who had been the leading minister of the *Allianz Gemeinde* in Lichtfelde, Molotschna, prior to his coming to Canada in 1926. The Namaka congregation, with affiliated groups at Crowfoot, Gem, and Munson, joined the M. B. Conference in 1942.[41] The *Linden* M. B. Church, founded in 1930 and also affiliated with the Evangelical Mennonite Brethren Conference, joined the Canadian M. B. Conference in 1948. At *Vauxhall* a congregation was organized in 1933, and at *Pincher Creek* in 1946. A church at *Crowfoot*, organized in 1928, was dissolved around 1940, when most settlers moved north to the Tofield area because of repeated crop failures in southeastern Alberta.

Mennonite Brethren Move to Cities

The Mennonite Brethren had no city churches in Alberta until 1956, when the first congregation was organized in Calgary under the leadership of city missionary Jacob F. Froese. A few years later, in 1962, an M. B. church was also organized in Edmonton, the provincial capital.

Here also, city-mission work had paved the way for the establishment of the *Lendrum* M. B. Church. In 1965 the *Lakeview* M. B. Church in Lethbridge appeared on the scene, and finally, in 1968, the *Crestwood* Mission Church of Medicine Hat was accepted into the conference. Thus the Mennonite Brethren of Alberta have established a strong witness in the four major cities of the province in the short period of twelve years. All city congregations report a steady increase in membership.

V. MENNONITE BRETHREN COME TO BRITISH COLUMBIA

British Columbia has been called the "California" of Canada. The expansion and growth of Mennonite Brethren churches in Canada's third largest province has been phenomenal. Beginning with one congregation in the Fraser Valley in 1929, the B. C. Conference has grown to a fellowship of forty churches (including mission stations) in 1972, with more than one third of all Mennonite Brethren in Canada now residing in this province. This westward movement in Canada parallels somewhat the movement of Mennonite Brethren in the United States to California several decades earlier.

In the Fraser Valley

The first Mennonite settlers came to the Fraser Valley in 1928 and built homes in what is now the town of *Yarrow*, about forty miles inland from Vancouver. They had been attracted to this area by advertisements in the *Free Press Prairie Farmer* and the *Mennonitische Rundschau*, which described the fertility of the recently reclaimed land from Sumas Lake in glowing terms.[42] One pioneer of Yarrow gives the following reasons for Mennonite "resettlement" in the Fraser Valley:

The bleak economic prospects on the prairies; the mild climate of British Columbia; greater earning opportunities; and above all, the possibility of more compact settlements for the purpose of spiritual fellowship and the unified training of children in the spirit of the Scriptures.[43]

The Yarrow settlement grew rapidly, for only one year after the arrival of the first families a Mennonite Brethren church was organized with ninety-six members. Through admission of new members from the prairies as well as through baptism the congregation increased so that by 1948 it had become the largest M.B. church in Canada, with over nine hundred members.

The Yarrow community went through a difficult pioneer period. The main cash income was derived from earnings in the "hopyards" located some five or six miles away.[44] Here pickers worked for fifteen cents an hour. Later most settlers became prosperous raspberry farmers, so that in non-Mennonite circles Yarrow was described as the community of two "R's" — religion and raspberries.

The economic recession that set in after 1948 (which especially affected the berry market) prompted many families to look for employment elsewhere — especially in the city of Vancouver. As a result, membership gradually declined so that at present (1971) it stands at four hundred and thirty. Two flourishing private schools, a Bible school founded in 1930, and a high school started in 1945, eventually had to close their doors as a result of the recession.

The church and community benefited greatly from the services of dedicated leaders. J. A. Harder, who was leader of the M. B. church here for eighteen years (until 1949) did much to unify and stabilize the diverse membership during this early period. C. C. Peters, P. D. Loewen, Gerhard Sukkau, and others provided leadership in Christian education. Gerhard Derksen, a prominent layman, gave leadership in civic affairs and functioned as a kind of colony administrator (*Oberschulz*).

Other churches were organized in the eastern part of the Fraser Valley shortly after the establishment of Yarrow. The *Greendale* (Sardis) M. B. Church was founded in 1931. During a disastrous flood in 1948 the members of this church were especially hard hit. J. W. Reimer, the well-known Bible expositor, spent his last years in this congregation. A church established at *Agassiz*, also in 1931, is now extinct. A congregation organized at *Arnold* in 1934 with seventy-two members has not experienced any substantial growth through the years — largely because of changing economic conditions. In the Chilliwack area two prosperous congregations were established immediately after World War II: the *East Chilliwack* M. B. Church was organized in 1945, and the *Chilliwack* (city) M. B. Church in 1947. For a number of years the East Chilliwack congregation maintained a small Bible school, which proved a great blessing to the young people of the community.

Farther west, a new Mennonite center emerged in the Abbotsford area, where a cluster of M.B. churches was established — each in rapid succession. The *South Abbotsford* M.B. Church, organized in 1932, must be recognized as the "mother church" of this area.[45] The Abbotsford and Aldergrove districts had been deforested some years earlier leaving a wasteland of giant stumps and ugly charred snags. Hard work, indomitable courage, and perseverance transformed this wasteland into profitable strawberry plantations as well as poultry and dairy farms. By 1935 the settlement had extended northward, and members left the mother church to organize the *North Abbotsford* (now Clearbrook) M.B. Church. This church, located right in the heart of what is now the town of Clearbrook, has experienced a steady growth until today (1971) it is the largest M.B. congregation in Canada with approximately seven hundred members. A large number of these members are retired farmers or businessmen from the prairies. The location in this town of two large Christian schools — the Mennonite Educational Institute and the Columbia Bible Institute — has been a major factor in shifting the center of Mennonite Brethren activity in this province from Yarrow to Clearbrook.

As congregations grew larger, they divided and established daughter churches in the area. In 1945, A.D. Rempel, the leader of the South Abbotsford church from its inception, led a group of members (with the blessing of the church) in the formation of the *Matsqui* M.B. Church. As a result of continued growth and expansion the mother church experienced a third division in 1950, when the *Abbotsford* (now Central Heights) congregation was organized with one hundred and eighty-two members under the leadership of H.H. Nickel.[46]

The Clearbrook M.B. Church also went through several divisions as a result of continued expansion and growth. In 1947 the *East Aldergrove* M.B. Church was organized by a group of thirty-four families, because the North Abbotsford church, to which they belonged, was overcrowded. The second division came in 1965, with the organization of the *Bakerview* M.B. Church, also located in Clearbrook. Members from South Abbotsford also joined Bakerview because they preferred all-English services. A third division occurred in the late sixties when those who preferred to have their worship services exclusively in the German language (mostly recent immigrants from Europe and Paraguay) left the Clearbrook church and organized the *King Road* M.B. Church, about one mile south of town. This congregation so far (1972) has not joined the conference.

In the Interior

After World War II Mennonite Brethren began to move into the interior of this vast province. Attracted by the sunshine and fruit-orchards of the Okanagan Valley, a number of M.B. families settled here and established a church at *Kelowna* in 1947. A small congregation at *Oliver*, seventy miles south of Kelowna, was a subsidiary of the Kelowna M.B. Church for a number of years.

The other churches in the interior of the province are largely the result of an intensive outreach program on the part of the Home Missions Committee (formerly the "West Coast Children's Mission of B.C.") of the provincial conference.[47] In many instances a number of M.B. families who found professional employment in the larger towns and cities of the interior would form the nucleus of a Mennonite Brethren fellowship and witness. An M.B. church was organized in the city of Prince George (*Peden Hill*) in 1961. In the same year mission churches were established at *Ocean Falls* and *Kitimat*. In the northwest small subsidized churches were established in 1962 at *Port Edward* and *Hazelton*. In the following year groups were organized at *Fort St. John, Dawson Creek* and *Terrace*. The *Cariboo Bethel* Church at Williams Lake, established in 1966, show promise of growth and stability. In 1971 the newly organized congregation at Kamloops (*Valleyview* Bible

Church) was accepted into the Canadian M.B. Conference. A number of mission churches have also been established in the lower mainland during the fifties and sixties — Mountain View Gospel Chapel, Harrison Gospel Chapel, County Line Gospel Chapel, Brookswood M.B. Church, Lake Errock M.B. Church, and South Otter M.B. Church. Practically all of these began as church extension projects of the older congregations in the Fraser Valley.[48] The large influx of more than two thousand Mennonites coming from Russia after World War II has also led to an increase in membership in many M.B. churches of this area.

In the Greater Vancouver Area

The general movement from the country to the city was accentuated in British Columbia by the economic depression of the 1930's. Vancouver, a large seaport city, offered employment opportunities not available in the Fraser Valley. Here, as elsewhere, Mennonites were reluctant to take up residence in a city because their children and young people would be exposed to the temptations and "worldliness" of a large metropolis.

By 1937, however, the number of M.B. families in Vancouver had grown to a sizeable group. Leading brethren from the Valley (Gerhard Derksen and Petrus Martens, Yarrow, and C. C. Peters, Agassiz) were invited to assist in the organization of a church. Thus, the first M.B. church in the Vancouver area was established in 1937 with thirty-seven charter members.[49] The following year, Jacob G. Thiessen, a minister with wide experience in Russia and Saskatchewan, moved here and together with a number of other brethren provided spirtual nurture for the rapidly increasing membership.

After renting a hall for several years, the congregation was able to build a church basement in 1944 at the corner of Forty-third and Prince Edward. War restrictions on building materials delayed completion of construction until 1946. All other churches in the metropolitan area have their historic roots in this congregation.

During the war a number of M.B. families moved back to the Fraser Valley; others moved to North Surrey. Here an M.B. church was organized at *Strawberry Hill* (now Kennedy Heights) in 1944. By 1952 the Vancouver M. B. Church was overcrowded, so the group decided to erect another church building at the corner of Fifty-ninth and Culloden, in South Vancouver. Here the *Fraserview* M.B. Church was organized as an independent congregation in 1955. By 1960 both these churches again needed more room, so two new churches were organized in 1961. The Vancouver M.B. Church assisted in the establishment of the *Willingdon* M.B. Church in Burnaby, and the Fraserview congregation assisted in the establishment of the *Killarney Park* M.B. Church in southeast Vancouver. In 1968 the mother church once more faced the problem of inadequate space for a congregation of over six hundred members. This time aproximately four-fifths of the membership separated from the Vancouver M.B. Church to establish the *Culloden* M.B. Church. D.B. Wiens, pastor of the mother church for eleven years, continued to serve in this capacity in the new congregation.

In 1971 a congregation was also organized in Richmond, just across the Fraser river on Lulu Island, where members of the various Vancouver churches had taken up residence. Herbert Brandt, who had led the Killarney Park congregation for nine years, became the pastor of the *Richmond Bethel* M.B. Church.

In addition to these seven larger congregations in the Vancouver area, two mission churches have also been established here: *Queensboro*, near New Westminster (1960), and *Pacific Grace Mission* (1965). The latter had been in operation as a city mission of the provincial conference since 1951.

Beyond the Straits of Georgia lies beautiful Vancouver Island. During the Depression Mennonites moved to the Island to find employment in the large logging industry there. In 1935 a Mennonite Brethren church was established at *Black Creek*, in the northeastern part of the Island. In the late sixties a church extension project was also begun in *Saanich*, a suburb of Victoria, in the south. The Island became well known throughout the Mennonite Brethren constituency in Canada during World War II, when most conscientious objectors were employed here in Alternative Service Forestry Camps.

In the two oldest provinces of Canada, Mennonite Brethren have congregations that do not only worship God in English or German but also in French, which is unique on the North American continent. Separated geographically from the congregations in the West by more than 1,200 miles, they have nevertheless become an integral part of the brotherhood in the two decades following World War II. Again only a brief survey of beginnings and subsequent expansion is possible here.

VI. MENNONITE BRETHREN COME TO ONTARIO[50]

Although the Ontario Conference of Mennonite Brethren joined the Canadian Conference (Northern District) only in 1946,[51] the beginnings of church life and activity coincide with the arrival of the third large wave of Mennonite immigrants twenty years earlier. As mentioned in the beginning of this chapter, the first Mennonites to settle in Ontario came from Pennsylvania after the Revolutionary War. These so-called "Old" Mennonites living in Waterloo and Lincoln counties in southern Ontario not only manifested the spirit of fine Christian hospitality toward these newcomers, but in many instances also provided employment for them.

A relatively large number of M.B. families in this early period found employment in the Kitchener-Waterloo area. Here the first congregation was organized in Kitchener in 1925 with Jacob P. Friesen as leader. This congregation, named the *Molotschna Mennoniten Bruedergemeinde*, must be acknowledged as the mother church of the Mennonite Brethren churches in Ontario, since all congregations in the province were affiliated with Kitchener until 1932.[52] In church practice it differed from M.B. churches in the other provinces (as well as from those in the United States) in admitting non-immersed believers and practicing open communion. This was partly due to the fact that some of the founders of the church had belonged to the Evangelical Mennonite Brethren Church in the Molotschna. Under the Bible-centered preaching of such able ministers as J. W. Reimer, J. P. Wiens, and H. H. Janzen, the Kitchener congregation and its affiliated groups experienced a wholesome growth and development.

In 1927 the scattered members living around *New Hamburg* (twelve miles west of Kitchener) organized as a branch church of Kitchener. The membership dwindled through the years, however, and in 1952 those remaining joined Kitchener. In *Hespeler*, a large town nine miles southeast of Kitchener, a group affiliated with Kitchener since 1926 became an independent congregation in 1932. The history of this congregation runs somewhat parallel to that of New Hamburg, and in 1953 the church was dissolved with the remaining families joining Kitchener.[53]

The Mennonite immigrants coming from Russia to Ontario in the twenties settled in two areas that were somewhat isolated and removed from the older settlements. One of these was at *Port Rowan* on the north shore of Lake Erie, where a congregation was organized in 1927. It is one of the few rural churches in Ontario where most members are engaged in farming. J.A. Penner was presiding minister for many years during the early period. Another group of the *Russlaender* Mennonites went to Essex County where they found work in the tobacco and tomato plantations as well as in factories at Windsor and other cities. From 1925 to 1932 the scattered M.B. families and members of the United Mennonite Church had joint-services in several towns of the county — Kingsville, Ruthven, Leamington and Wheatley. In 1932 Mennonite Brethren organized the *Leamington* M.B. Church. A small group also settled on Pelee island, eight miles south of Leamington on Lake Erie, but these families all moved back to the mainland after several years.

The Leamington congregation experienced a painful schism in the thirties, when a number of families withdrew from the fellowship and organized their own M.B. church under the leadership of Heinrich Wiebe, a deacon. This group was opposed to open communion and the admission of non-immersed believers — a practice accepted by the Ontario Conference. When the Ontario Conference joined the General

Conference of Mennonite Brethren in 1939, the schism was healed and the group united with the church.[54]

According to A.A. Huebert, a minister of the Leamington congregation for many years, the "tobacco-question" became a "conscience-question" for many church members. Although all members had abstained from smoking tobacco, many had, especially during the early years, been involved in raising tobacco. In 1948 the church accepted a resolution which contained a confession of past failings and a pledge to adhere to the position of the Canadian M.B. Conference in this matter.[55]

The strongest concentration of Mennonite Brethren in Ontario is found in the attractive fruit-growing belt of the Niagara Peninsula. Here in the historical settlement of the "Twenty,"[56] the *Vineland* Mennonite Brethren Church was organized in 1932. Until 1934 the congregation had joint-services with the United Mennonite Church. After that separate meetings were held, first in a rented hall in Beamsville until 1937, and then in a remodeled building in Vineland. An active minister of this congregation for many years, Heinrich P. Wiebe, also founded a mental hospital in 1937, after having treated mental patients in his home for five years. Later, in 1947, Bethesda Mental Hospital became an institution of the Canadian Conference.

In 1937 about one half of the ministers and members of the Vineland congregation moved closer to Niagara-on-the-Lake and there organized the *Virgil* M.B. Church under the leadership of John F. Dyck. Beginning with a small membership, the congregation grew rapidly as a result of a strong influx of M.B. families from Western Canada, especially North Saskatchewan. Here the establishment of a Bible school in 1938, and a private high school (Eden Christian College) in 1945, played an important part in the growth of the Mennonite Brethren community.

Through evangelism and church extension work a daughter church was established in the late fifties at Niagara-on-the-Lake, known as *Niagara* Christian Fellowship Chapel. In 1971 a group separated from the Virgil congregation to form the *Orchard Park* Bible Church.

During the Second World War many M.B. families took up residence in the "Garden City" of Canada, *St. Catharines*. A congregation was organized here in 1943 under the leadership of Gerhard J. Epp. The church, located on Scott Street, has experienced a steady growth, partly as a result of immigration from Paraguay, so that today (1971), it is the largest M.B. congregation in Ontario.[57] Henry Penner, who became the pastor of the church in 1953, has provided able leadership through the years and still serves the congregation today (1972). This probably constitutes a record for length of term of service in the present era.

Because of rapid and continued growth, a second congregation was organized in this city in 1964, know as the *Fairview* M.B. Church. Harvey C. Gossen has been the leader of this church almost from the time of its inception. More city churches were organized in the sixties in the Kitchener-Waterloo area: the *Zion* M.B. Church in 1964, and the *Waterloo* M.B. Church in 1967. A few years earlier, in 1961, a Mennonite Brethren church had also been established in the large metropolitan city of Toronto, the capital of the province.

In 1945 the Home Missions Committee of Ontario began an intensive outreach program in several areas of the province. In 1951 a work was begun at Coldwater in an Anglo-Saxon district with Mr. and Mrs. H.H. Dick as pioneer workers. The *Hampshire* (formerly Coldwater) M.B. Church was received into the Canadian Conference in 1961. During the same year also the *Stoney Creek* M.B. Church (near Hamilton) was admitted into the conference after six years of mission work in that area.[58]

VII. MENNONITE BRETHREN COME TO QUEBEC

The story of the expansion of the M. B. Church in Canada would be incomplete without a brief survey of the origins of the French-speaking congregations in Quebec, Canada's oldest and largest province. The Canadian Conference became more aware of the great spiritual needs of the French-Catholics in Quebec through Mennonite Brethren missionaries to the Congo (now Zaire) who spent some time in language study there between 1949 and 1959.

When in the summer of 1960 all missionaries had to be withdrawn from the Congo, the Canada Inland Mission Committee of the M. B. Conference asked the Ernest Dycks to begin a ministry of evangelism and church planting in Quebec. The Dycks consented and thus became the Mennonite Brethren pioneers in Quebec.

In consultation with Henry Warkentin, the chairman of the Canada Inland Mission Committee, St. Jerome was selected as the first field of labor. The Dycks took up residence in St. Jerome in August, 1961. After three years of faithful "planting and watering," the harvest came in 1964. In June of that year the first baptismal services were held, and in October the first M. B. church was organized with sixteen charter members from *St. Jerome* and *Ste. Therese*. In 1968 the believers in these two places decided to form separate congregations.

Other workers from the conference as well as from Quebec joined the Dycks in an expanding witness. In September, 1967, a work was begun in *St. Laurent* (a suburb of Montreal) and three years later a church was organized there. The three churches today have a combined membership of seventy-one as well as a number of adherents. Two congregations are served at present by French-Canadian pastors.[59]

During the past few years Mennonite Brethren have extended their witness still further east. Between 1969 and 1971 the Walter Epps, Christian Service workers sponsored by the Board of Missions and Services, have assisted in the establishment of the *Mt. Edward* Bible Fellowship Church in Dartmouth, Nova Scotia.[60] Thus the Canadian M.B. Conference spans a territory of more than four thousand miles — from Dartmouth (a twin city of Halifax), Nova Scotia, to Black Creek, Vancouver Island, British Columbia.

Before considering the organization and function of the North American brotherhood in building God's kingdom, it is necessary to become acquainted with another Anabaptist fellowship that since 1960 has become completely identified with the Mennonite Brethren — the Krimmer Mennonite Brethren Church.

Chapter 12

The Krimmer Mennonite Brethren Come to North America

In previous chapters several brief references have been made to the origin and migration of the Krimmer Mennonite Brethren. The story of this evangelical Anabaptist fellowship, so closely related in faith and practice to the Mennonite Brethren Church, needs to be told more fully now. The ninety-one years (1869-1960) of separate historical experience and development of this body bear eloquent testimony to the depth of Christian commitment to Christ and His kingdom among the Krimmer Mennonite Brethren. This interesting chapter of church history now forms an integral part of the spiritual heritage of the Mennonite Brethren.

I. Historical Origin in the Crimea

The Krimmer Mennonite Brethren Church had its origin in the village of Annenfeld near Simferopol, Crimea, Russia, on September 21, 1869 — almost ten years after the M. B. Church was founded in the Molotschna. The birth of the Krimmer Mennonite Brethren Church is inseparably linked with the spiritual "rebirth," and practical initiative of its founder and leader of many years, Jacob A. Wiebe (1836-1921).

Elder Wiebe grew up in the village of Ohrloff in the Molotschna Colony. Through private study he acquired a fair education for his day. In his youth he was employed as driver for the colony administrator, whose daughter Justina he married in 1857.[1] A year prior to his marriage, as was customary in those days, Wiebe was baptized and received into the Lichtenau-Petershagen Mennonite Church. In 1861 the Wiebe family moved to the Crimea, where a group of Mennonite families had bought a Mohammedan village the previous year which they named Ànnenfeld. Through a spontaneous religious revival most of the people of this village experienced a genuine conversion and a radical change of life, Wiebe and his wife among them.[2]

Although these new converts were like "sheep without a shepherd"

176

in the beginning, Wiebe soon emerged as the leader of the group. Since Wiebe had learned to know the *Kleine Gemeinde* (the first "separatist group" among the Mennonites of South Russia) when he was a hired hand of a member of that church in the Molotschna, the group established contacts with the Crimean *Kleine Gemeinde*. In 1864 elder Johann Friesen from the Molotschna, upon invitation, visited the Annenfeld group.

When Elder Friesen offered to organize them as a *Kleine Gemeinde* congregation, Wiebe explained that first they all wished to be baptized on their faith. This, Friesen said, he could not do since it was against the rules of the *Kleine Gemeinde* to rebaptize.[3] Continued discussions did not resolve this problem, but in 1867 the group was nevertheless organized as a *Kleine Gemeinde* church. In the same year also Jacob A. Wiebe and Peter Berg were elected as ministers and in 1869 Wiebe was elected and ordained as elder. All this time, however, Wiebe and his group had serious reservations about their new church affiliation. They felt they should have been baptized upon the confession of their faith. They also found that they differed widely with the *Kleine Gemeinde* on the question of assurance of salvation (*Heilsgewissheit*). These convictions eventually led to a second "secession" of the group.

According to Elder Wiebe, the new movement was launched "after much prayer and searching of God's Word as well as in Menno Simons' writings."[4] On September 21, 1869, Wiebe, who first was rebaptized by Kornelius Enns, a senior member of the group, baptized eighteen others, including Enns. The mode of baptism on this occasion was not immersion, although that mode was adopted shortly after.[5] Forward immersion, with the candidate kneeling, became the general practice of the new church. The group chose the name *Bruedergemeinde* , but soon was called *Krimmer Mennoniten Bruedergemeinde*, to distinguish it from the Mennonite Brethren Church of the Molotschna.[6]

In effect, the act of rebaptism constituted a withdrawal of the Wiebe group from the *Kleine Gemeinde*, with which it had been affiliated for only a few years. However, as Bender correctly observes, "much of the ultra-conservative spirit of the *Kleine Gemeinde* was transmitted into the K.M.B. group, in combination with the new K.M.B. emphasis on conversion, assurance, and experience."[7] There was little further connection between the Krimmer Mennonite Brethren and the *Kleine Gemeinde*, but in the United States a preacher of the latter church, Abraham Klassen, who had been ordained in Russia in 1869, joined the K.M.B. Church in Kansas about 1879.

The new church emphasized conversion, baptism by immersion, strict observance of nonconformity, church discipline, nonresistance, feet-washing and refusal of the oath. The group chose as its motto: "By

29. Elder Jacob Wiebe   30. D. M. Hofer

this shall all men know that ye are my disciples, if ye have love one to another." A generally-observed practice with them was the New Testament injunction: "Salute one another with an holy kiss" — but only men with men, and women with women.[8]

Speaking at the fiftieth "jubilee-celebration" held at Bridgewater, South Dakota in 1919, Elder Jacob A. Wiebe stated the five basic principles of faith of the K.M.B. Church as follows:

1. The acceptance of the Bible as God's Word, written by men of God who were moved by the Holy Spirit.
2. Submission to Christ's teaching in Matthew 5, and to accept the beatitudes through faith in Jesus. This implies the practice of peacefulness, brotherly reconciliation, the sacredness of marriage, abstention from oath or revenge, and the practice of nonresistance and love of enemies as followers of Jesus. To such Jesus had granted the right of sonship. . . .
3. Observance of the teaching concerning baptism (Matt. 3:13-17), concerning the Lord's Supper (Lk. 22 and 1 Cor. 11), and concerning footwashing (Jn. 13).
4. Support of home and foreign missions according to ability, in order to save lost men for eternal life.
5. Practice of church discipline according to Matthew 18.[9]

During the five years of their "sojourn" in the Crimea (1869-74), the newly organized church made slow but steady progress and numbered about forty families by the time of emigration.[10] Johann Harder, a schoolteacher who became Wiebe's assistant, contributed much to the spiritual growth and the articulation of doctrine among the early Krimmer Brethren.[11]

Contrary to the experience of the Molotschna Mennonite Brethren, the Krimmer Brethren did not suffer any religious oppression or restriction of their civil rights. The recognition of the M. B. Church in the Molotschna and Chortitza colonies some years earlier may have been partly responsible for the tolerant attitude on the part of the church and state officials toward this new movement.

After experiencing great economic difficulties during their first few years the new church group began to prosper materially as they became adjusted to the new farming methods, new crops and weather conditions in the Crimea. Their hopes for peaceful progress were suddenly shattered, however, by the Imperial decree of 1870, which abrogated the Mennonite privileges, including exemption from military service. The Krimmer Mennonite Brethren were among the first to decide to emigrate to the United States. The story of their "exodus" constitutes a part of the larger movement that brought 18,000 Mennonites from Russia to America between 1874-80.

2. A New Beginning in Kansas

The group that left the Crimea on May 30, 1874, under the leadership of elder Jacob A. Wiebe, consisted of about thirty-five families.[12] After their disembarkation in New York, the group boarded a train for Elkhart, Indiana, where they expected to receive further direction and help from John F. Funk, whom they had learned to know and love as the editor of *Herold der Wahrheit*. When the immigrants arrived in Elkhart on the morning of July 20, 1874, it was a most inopportune time for Funk. The night before his daughter had died, the group had arrived without advance notice, and it was Sunday morning. Funk's spiritual stature is set forth in bold relief against this background. He not only welcomed these weary travelers and provided temporary housing for the large group, but invited Elder Wiebe to preach to a mixed audience of immigrants and Elkhart people that same morning.[13]

The group stayed at Elkhart for about a month. During this time Elder Wiebe, accompanied by Franz R. Janzen, went west to scout for a suitable place of settlement. After looking at land in Dakota and Nebraska, they came to Kansas, where C. B. Schmidt, the German-speaking Santa Fe agent, showed them his lands. Finally they decided to purchase a tract of land in Marion County, located ten miles west of "Marion Center," and fourteen miles northwest of Peabody, the nearest town on the newly constructed Santa Fe Railroad. At this station Wiebe and Janzen met the contingent of Krimmer Mennonite Brethren on August 16, 1874, upon their arrival from Elkhart.[14]

The immigration and settlement of the Krimmer group is unique for several reasons: Almost the entire church had come as a unit; it was the first church body (during the 1870's) to arrive in America, and "this group, more than any other, planned their villages, Gnadenau and Hoffnungstal, their schools, and their farming operations on the Russian village pattern."[15]

Gnadenau

The village of *Gnadenau* (which literally translated means "grace meadow") became the center of church and community life for the Krimmer Mennonite Brethren. The village never had a post office, however, and when a branch of the Santa Fe Railroad went through the north edge of the settlement in 1879 and Hillsboro was built on the line two miles north of the village, Gnadenau lost its future. After a few years the village form of settlement was found to be impractical, and the population became dispersed. The name "Gnadenau" was retained, nevertheless, for the local school, and especially for the church.

Almost immediately after their arrival, these pioneers erected a church of adobe walls and thatched roof. When it weathered badly a frame building was erected in 1877, the first such structure built by the 1874 immigrants in America. A novel feature of the church was a four foot high partition between the men's side and the women's side.[16]

Elder Jacob A. Wiebe continued to provide effective leadership for the Krimmer Brethren until his resignation in 1900. In 1877 the congregation was incorporated as the "Gnadenau Mennonite Church," but in 1899 the name in the charter was changed to "Crimean Mennonite Brethren Church." Popularly, however, they remained the "Krimmer Mennonite Brethren." The Gnadenau congregation grew and spread out to other areas and thus may be regarded as the "mother church" among the K.M.B. congregations in America.

The year 1954 was eventful for the Gnadenau church. The Lehigh Mennonite Brethren Church, which had never been very large, amalgamated with Gnadenau. In October the pastor of the Gnadenau congregation, D. V. Wiebe, reported to the K.M.B. Conference as follows:

We believe that a union of the spiritual and material resources of our groups will strengthen our fellowship and be a more effective witness for Christ in our community. It is the desire of the groups to function as a local Mennonite Brethren Church of the Southern District.[17]

Although the merger question had been "in the air" for some years, the above statement caused considerable uneasiness and concern among the delegates, especially since it came from Gnadenau, the "mother church" of the conference. With this withdrawal Gnadenau accelerated the pace of the merger-movement which was consummated six years later.

The combined membership of the united church stood at 155 in 1955. When fire destroyed the old church building on Christmas morning in 1956, plans were made immediately to erect a new building. Since the center of church membership had shifted to the north, it was decided to erect the new church in Hillsboro. The congregation, now known as the "Parkview Mennonite Brethren Church," has doubled its membership in the last fifteen years, and appears to have profited from both — the merger and the relocation.

3. EXPANSION INTO OTHER AREAS

In Gnadenau, as elsewhere in Mennonite settlements, rapid population growth led to the migration of younger families to new areas on the vast frontier, stretching from the plains of Kansas to the prairies of Saskatchewan. The expansion of the church cannot be simply explained, however, merely in terms of population growth. Right from the beginning the Krimmer Mennonite Brethren manifested a great zeal in evangelism, winning people for Christ and organizing local congregations. The concer of the early brethren found expression in a definite strategy. At a brotherhood meeting in January, 1883, the following two resolutions were passed:

(1) For sending forth (*Aussending*) the gospel in McPherson County and as far as Rice County, the church commissions Brother Johann Harder, to be accompained by Peter Wiebe and Johann Klaassen.

(2) For sending forth (the gospel) to Council Grove the brethren Abraham Klaassen and Abraham Harms are commissioned.[18]

Kansas

The second K.M.B. congregation in Kansas was organized in 1879 near Inman as a result of the westward expansion of the original settlement. Here Mr. and Mrs. Gerhard Kornelsen were instrumental in organizing a group of twenty-four members. Like almost all new congregations established by the Krimmer Mennonite Brethren, this group also chose a biblical name as part of its official designation — in this case it was *Zoar*. Although Zoar is a rural congregation, it has shown a remarkable stability and strength in church membership through the years and relocated in the town of Inman in 1969. The vision and concern of the church for its young people found expression in the founding of the Zoar Academy and Bible School in 1915. For thirty years the school operated under the direction and support of the Zoar church and community. In 1948 an inter-Mennonite corporation was organized which established the Central Christian High School in Hutchinson — a direct successor of the Zoar Academy.[19]

Another congregation closely related to the Gnadenau church is the *Springfield* K.M.B. Church, located five miles southwest of Lehigh. The Springfield community was settled in the 1870's by a dozen members of the Gnadenau church. In 1878 they began to meet for worship services in the homes. Although a church building was constructed in 1894 the group was organized as a congregation only in 1902. Like the Mennonite Brethren of that day, the Krimmer Mennonite Brethren also ordained elders as church leaders. In 1904 elder Jacob A. Wiebe of Gnadenau ordained David P. Schroeder as elder of the Springfield congregation.[20]

Two other early congregations in Rice and Butler counties (Kansas) and one founded in western Kansas some years later have not survived. The *Emmanuel* congregation, established twenty miles east of Garden City, came into being when members from various churches, especially from Jansen, Nebraska, settled here in 1918 with elder J. K. Ens as leader. In 1926 the membership had reached eighty, and the Sunday school enrollment 110. During the drought and Depression of the thirties the majority of the members moved to other localities, and the church was disbanded in 1936.[21] The last K.M.B. church to be established before the K.M.B.—M.B. merger was *Orchard Park* in Hutchinson, Kansas, in 1954.

The only K.M.B. congregation in Nebraska was established near Jansen in 1881. The *Salem* congregation (one of three by that name in the K.M.B. Conference) always remained small and was dissolved in 1930 after almost fifty years of continuous existence.[22]

South Dakota

A second center of K.M.B. church life and activity developed in the east-central part of South Dakota with the establishment of the *Salem* congregation (ten miles southwest of Bridgewater) in 1886. It is evident from the conference records of that period that this church was at least in part the fruit of the church-extension efforts of the Gnadenau church in Kansas. At a brotherhood meeting in October, 1885, it was decided to "ordain the two brethren in Dakota as ministers as soon as possible."[23] The names in this new congregation also indicate a different ethnic background. Whereas the more common names in Gnadenau were Wiebe, Klaassen, and Friesen, at Bridgewater, the more common names were Hofer, Tschetter, and Mendel.[24] Although the membership of the Salem congregation has declined slightly during the last decade, it continues to be a strong rural church.

Another K.M.B. church which dates back to the early period was established near Yale, in the northeastern part of the state. The membership of the *Bethel* congregation has declined somewhat in recent years, reflecting the general trend observed in rural churches elsewhere. Immediately after World War I the Krimmer Brethren established two additional churches in South Dakota. In 1919 the *Ebenezer* congregation (twelve miles from Doland) was organized by seven families under the leadership of Jacob J. Hofer. A year later, in 1920, the *Emmanuel* congregation was organized in Sully County, six miles east

of Onida under the leadership of Jacob S. Mendel. Both congregations
have maintained an active church life to the present.

Still another congregation, also located in the same general area of
the state, was founded in Huron in 1947. This church, bearing the
biblical name of *Bethesda*, doubled membership between 1953 and 1971.
The only K.M.B. church in North Dakota, the *Emmanuel* congregation
organized near Chasely in 1921, is now extinct. D. M. Hofer (city
missionary in Chicago) served the church with special meetings, at
baptisms, and in its organization. The church dissolved in 1932.[25]

Saskatchewan

The Krimmer Mennonite Brethren also established several
churches in Canada, although none of the K.M.B. immigrants of the
1870's settled there. In 1899 eight members of the church from Bon
Homme and Turner counties, S.D., settled in the municipality of Laird,
west of Waldheim. Here they organized the *Salem* K.M.B. church that
same year. The Henry M. Epp family, who spent a number of years in
missionary work in China, has its spiritual roots in this congregation.[26]
This church did not go along with the decision of the K.M.B. Conference
to merge with the Mennonite Brethren. After functioning as an
independent congregation for some time, the Salem congregation joined
the Evangelical Mennonite Brethren Conference.

Another congregation — *Emmanuel* — was organized by immigrants from South Dakota southeast of Langham in 1901. This church,
never very large, today (1971) has a membership of only sixteen.
The only K.M.B. church in Alberta, established in 1918 near *Clairmont*,
became extinct after a brief existence.

California

About the same time that Mennonite Brethren found their way to
the San Joaquin Valley of central California, some Krimmer Mennonite
Brethren from South Dakota also made the trek to the Pacific coast. In
1910 nine families arrived and settled on the so-called "Clark and
Kennedy Ranch" near Dinuba.[27] John Z. Kleinsasser, the leader of the
group, donated a plot of land for the construction of a church building.
On February 26, 1911, the new church was dedicated and a few weeks
later the *Zion* K.M.B. Church was organized under the guidance of Peter
A. Wiebe from Kansas. John Z. Kleinsasser served as pastor for the first
eight years. A K.M.B. Conference was held at the Zion church for the
first time in 1920. Through the years this congregation has produced a
number of effective Christian workers for service at home and abroad.[28]

Two congregations established in Oklahoma around the turn of the
century have both become extinct. The *Bethel* K.M.B. Church was
organized with twenty members under the guidance of Heinrich and

Peter A. Wiebe in November, 1897, near Weatherford. The church, never very large, became extinct in 1937 when the remaining members joined the Corn M.B. Church. Another *Bethel* congregation was established in the Oklahoma panhandle at Hooker in 1907. A year later it numbered sixty-four members. The congregation dissolved early in 1919, "scattered by war clouds and depressing experiences as a result of war."[29]

A brief study of its life and work follows this survey of the geographical expansion of the K.M.B. Church.

4. CONSERVATISM IN CHRISTIAN LIFE-STYLE

Historical observers of the Krimmer Mennonite Brethren have been impressed with its strong emphasis on a life-style that would conform as closely as possible to the teachings of Scripture. Thus H. S. Bender writes: "Always deeply religious in nature and emphasizing a deep inner experience, regeneration, assurance of salvation, and holy living, the K.M.B. group has stood for an intensely serious and strict manner of life."[30]

This conservatism manifested itself in the nature of their worship services. Men and women of the congregation were segregated in the services. Some children sat with their mother, others with their father, but families did not sit together. The service generally consisted of preaching, praying and the singing of hymns. Part singing was long forbidden, however, and musical instruments were introduced beginning in 1917-18.[31] Sunday schools were held in the afternoons so as to minimize the possibility of desecrating the Day of Rest by any less worthy activities.

The conservatism of the Krimmer Mennonite Brethren also expressed itself in church regulations governing the ethical and social practices of members. In 1896 the conference accepted resolutions forbidding the use of tobacco or strong drink. (The latter could be used for medicinal purposes.) The same conference also took action against worldliness in dress (*Kleiderputz*) and participation in political meetings and elections.[32]

The well-known Mennonite historian, C. H. Smith, makes the following observations with regard to the life-style of the Krimmer Brethren:

> They were strict disciplinarians of both the conduct and appearance of their members. The sale of tobacco and liquor was prohibited in their village at a time when a free use of both was not regarded as a major sin by most of the other Russian Mennonite groups. Young people were carefully chaperoned by their elders in all their gatherings both social and religious. . . . Dress regulations were like-wise strict. Like other groups, they discouraged worldliness in superfluous dress, excessive buying of land, attendance at theatres and circuses, carrying guns, hail insurance, and voting.[33]

An examination of early conference records and church regulations of the Mennonite Brethren reveals a great similarity to the ethical emphases mentioned above. Both groups affirmed that the inner experience of renewal must find expression in a "newness of life." The Krimmer Brethren were perhaps a little more reluctant to accept cultural change than the Mennonite Brethren. Thus David V. Wiebe writes: "The early church members were reluctant to accept anything 'new'. Shiny buggies were looked upon as vain and in some instances repainted a dull gray."[34] Even such things as bicycles, ties and photographs were permitted only after careful deliberations.

In their desire to be scriptural in all their practices, the Krimmer Mennonite Brethren developed a hyper-literalism which went beyond that of the early Mennonite Brethren. They had scruples about photographs because the Ten Commandments forbade the making of "any likeness of anything" (Ex. 20:4). They objected to musical instruments because Christians are to make melody in their heart to the Lord (Eph. 5:19 A.V.). Dresses were to be plain and jewelry was forbidden in keeping with the teaching of the Apostle Peter in 1 Peter 3:3.[35]

In retrospect it would appear that a certain "cultural narrowness," although sincerely motivated, may have been one of the factors that retarded the expansion of the group through the years. Paradoxically enough, this ethical conservatism was combined with an exemplary zeal in evangelism and missions which found expression in the founding of charitable institutions and in the commissioning of workers to many areas of the world.

5. INVOLVEMENT IN HOME MISSIONS

From its inception the K.M.B. Church has endeavored to integrate social concern and evangelism as inseparable aspects of an effective Christian witness. As early as 1890 the conference obtained a charter for the "Industrial School and Hygienic Home for Friendless Persons." This home for orphans was built just north of the original Gnadenau village site in 1894. In early conference minutes the *Waisenheim* (orphan's home) is referred to again and again and appears to have generated a great deal of enthusiasm as well as practical support.

It was operated for about twenty years, then converted into the Salem Home for the Aged and Helpless. In 1918 the Krimmer Mennonite Brethren, assisted by the Mennonite Brethren, established the Salem Hospital in Hillsboro. The ministry to the sick was inspired by Christ's example. In his report to the conference in 1919, D. E. Harder, the chairman of the board, stated: "The Lord Jesus chose to minister (to people) and alongside of the preaching of the gospel he gave primary attention to the ministry among the sick."[36]

But the concern of the K.M.B. Church was not limited to the poor and needy in the immediate area of their local congregations. The Lord used the vision, faith and training of two couples from the Salem church at Bridgewater, S.D., to start two new ministries in the K.M.B. Conference: city missions and publication work. The story of these "trailblazers" deserves special consideration.

David M. Hofer (1869-1944) and his wife Barbara (1876-1958) spent their first thirty years on the farm in South Dakota. For eleven of these years Hofer taught in elementary schools. After leaving the farm, Hofer became a successful businessman (banking and grain trade) for twelve years, until the Lord called him into the ministry. He sold out and moved to Chicago to study at Moody Bible Institute.

Joseph W. Tschetter (1876-1955) and his wife Katherine (1880-1957) also grew up in the K.M.B. community at Bridgewater. After their marriage in 1901, although serving in the local church, they continued to farm and thought of "buying more land and raising more grain and livestock."[37] But in 1910 the Tschetters responded to God's call and accepted the responsibility for mission work in North Carolina. Here Brother Tschetter served as Superintendent of the Salem Mission from 1911 to 1915. Then he also went to Moody Bible Institute in Chicago.

It should be mentioned that both Hofer and Tschetter had college education in addition to their training at Moody. While in Chicago, these brethren joined their spiritual, intellectual and material resources for a local ministry in Chicago and for a conference-wide ministry through the publication of Christian literature. In 1915, they organized the "Lincoln Avenue Gospel Mission" and founded the conference periodical, *Der Wahrheitsfreund*.[38]

The city mission, located at 2812 Lincoln Avenue, Chicago, was opened officially in October, 1915 with Hofer as superintendent and Tschetter as associate superintendent. Several Mennonite missions had been established before this time by other Mennonite conferences. The first meetinghouse, a two-story brick structure with a seating capacity of about 125, has provided the necessary facilities through the years for both rescue mission efforts as well as Sunday school work.[39] The present *Lakeview* M.B. Church in Chicago has grown out of these earlier mission activities. In the years following World War II a city mission (*Fontenelle Chapel*) was also established in Omaha, Nebraska.

The publication efforts of the K.M.B. Conference date back to 1914 when a committee was elected and authorized to proceed with the publication of a conference paper and, if possible, establish a publishing house owned and operated by the conference. Hofer and Tschetter provided the necessary funds for the purchase of the building at 2812

Lincoln Ave., Chicago, and the needed printing equipment, on the condition that a city mission could be conducted in a part of the building housing the publishing activities.

The *Wahrheitsfreund* (friend of truth), the German organ of the K.M.B. Church appeared weekly (except for ten months in 1934) from 1915 to 1947. In 1933 the Publishing Committee of the conference became the actual publisher of the paper, with the office of publication at Hillsboro for one year, and thereafter at Inman, Kansas. As a result of a declining readership, the *Wahrheitsfreund* was discontinued in 1947 and replaced by the *Christian Witness* as the official conference paper. After the K.M.B.— M.B. merger in 1960, the *Christian Witness* was amalgamated with the *Christian Leader*.[40]

Through the publication of the *Wahrheitsfreund* Hofer and Tschetter reached far beyond the K.M.B. constituency. In 1919 they reported a circulation of 5500 copies — at least three times the number of families in K.M.B. churches. In addition to the conference paper, they also published Yearbooks, Articles of Faith, the Constitution, and Sunday school quarterlies.[41] The printed page no doubt constituted an important medium in uniting a widely scattered brotherhood, and in promoting the missionary interests of the conference.

A very prominent feature of the church extension work of the Krimmer Mennonite Brethren through the years has been an itinerant ministry of elders, preachers and evangelists. In the earlier period these were always sent out two by two. In later years evangelists were appointed for full-time service, and the "team effort" was abandoned. After World War II, home mission efforts were expanded. By 1954 the work at Orchard Park Chapel in Hutchinson (Kansas) had developed into an organized church.

An area which received special consideration during this period was the Ozark region of Arkansas. Primarily through vacation Bible schools, an initial witness was established at Compton, Elkhorn, and Kingston.[42] Through Sunday schools, Bible classes, and special evangelistic efforts the work developed and resulted in the establishment of small fellowship groups.

6. INVOLVEMENT IN FOREIGN MISSIONS

In 1886 the Krimmer Mennonite Brethren opened a mission work in the black community of Elk Park, North Carolina. According to Bender this is "the first Mennonite Negro work."[43] In the conference reports the work at Elk Park is always listed under "foreign missions," even though it was a mission located within the borders of the United States. This classification of North Carolina as a "foreign mission" field in all probability stems from the fact that the concept of missions among the

Krimmer Brethren (as well as among most Mennonite groups) in times past has been determined not only by geographical distance, but also by the color of the skin. The K.M.B. churches of Kansas and South Dakota were, of course, also far removed geographically from the people living at Elk Park, North Carolina.

Through the faithful ministry of Mr. and Mrs. Heinrich Wiebe (1900-1908), Mr. and Mrs. Jacob M. Tschetter (1903-1912); Mr. and Mrs. Joseph W. Tschetter (1911-1916), and Mr. and Mrs. Peter H. Siemens (1925-1956), the work was established and extended over a radius of sixty miles, from the eastern tip of Tennessee into the heart of the Blue Ridge mountains. During Brother Siemens' ministry the work had grown to include eleven small congregations. Siemens served as superintendent of the churches and endeavored to visit each group once a month.[44]

The congregations of this area have been organized as the North Carolina Conference which today constitutes a district of the United States M.B. Conference. For a number of years Rondo Horton and his wife Ruth, a local black couple, have rendered effective pastoral services in the North Carolina district. At present (1972) the conference consists of six churches: one located at Boone, two at Ferguson, two at Lenoir, and one at Newland. Although somewhat removed from the rest of the M.B. constituency, contacts are maintained through fraternal visits and special ministries.

The K.M.B. Conference has supported its foreign missionaries at work under other boards. A "Foreign Missions Committee" has represented the mission interest of the conference through the years. The commitment of this small brotherhood (less than 2,000 in 1954) to world evangelism can be seen from the scope of its missionary activities. In 1954 the committee reported that a K.M.B. testimony was being heard in North Carolina, Mexico, Peru, Venezuela, Northwest Indies, Nigeria, Ethiopia, Belgian Congo, Southern Rhodesia, India, Japan and Germany. The financial receipts for foreign missions that year amounted to $47,743.80.[45]

China, where the Krimmer Mennonite Brethren supported their first overseas missionaries, is not listed above because that country was closed to missionaries by 1954. Mr. and Mrs. Henry C. Bartel established the first Mennonite mission in China in 1901. As the work expanded it was largely staffed and supported by the K.M.B. Church until 1949, when all work by foreign missionaries had to be terminated. Other missionaries who served in China are Mr. and Mrs. H. M. Epp (mentioned earlier), Mr. and Mrs. Frank V. Wiebe, Mr. and Mrs. John Wieneke, Mr. and Mrs. A. K. Wiens, Mr. and Mrs. George Willms, Miss

Sarah Balzer, Miss Mary Schmidt, Miss Anna Klassen, Miss Elizabeth Hofer, Miss Sarah Heinrichs and Mrs. Helen Duerksen.[46]

During the eighty years of K.M.B. conference activity in North America (1880-1960) fifty-two missionaries have been sent out to the "regions beyond." (This does not include mission workers in North Carolina or in the Ozarks.)

Since 1960 the missionary activities of the K.M.B. Conference have been integrated with the missions program of the Mennonite Brethren Conference. Support for some programs carried on under interdenominational missions has been gradually phased out. Other fields, such as Peru, for instance, have been accepted by the Board of Missions and Services as a responsibility of the M.B. Conference. The way was prepared for an eventual merger of the missions programs as early as 1946, when a "collaboration plan" was adopted by the mission boards of the two conferences.[47]

7. INVOLVEMENT IN CHRISTIAN EDUCATION

As in most pioneer Mennonite settlements the Krimmer Mennonite Brethren who settled in Marion County, Kansas established their own private elementary schools.[48] In later years (1915) a secondary school was established by the Zoar congregation as reported earlier. In higher education the K.M.B. Conference cooperated (although on an unofficial basis) with the Mennonite Brethren and with other Mennonite groups.

Already at the 1913 K.M.B. Conference D. E. Harder presented a report on Tabor College, and the conference expressed its goodwill toward the new school.[49] In 1916 the conference went on record to support the "Tabor College Corporation."[50] In later years annual reports from Tabor College appear on the conference agenda. In 1940 the K.M.B. Conference officially joined in the support of Tabor College by appointing a member to the college board. When the educational institutions of the Mennonite Brethren in the United States were coordinated and unified in 1955, the K.M.B. Conference also participated in the unified educational program.

At the 1957 convention C. F. Plett, the chairman of the Education Committee of the conference summarized the educational involvement of the Krimmer Mennonite Brethren as follows:

We recognize two groups of schools where our students and church members participate: First, schools of higher learning and Christian training; among these are the following: Pacific Bible Institute and Junior College, Mennonite Brethren Biblical Seminary, all of Fresno, California, and Tabor College, Hillsboro, Kansas. These are all schools of the M.B. and K.M.B. Unified Educational Program. Grace Bible Institute, Omaha, Nebraska, is also in this group, a recognized inter-Mennonite and interdenominational Bible Institute.

Second, schools on the local or regional level; among them may be mentioned Freeman Junior College and High School, Freeman, S.D.; Immanuel

Christian High School and Academy, Reedley, Calif.; Central Christian High School, Hutchinson, Kansas; and James Valley Christian High School near Huron, S.D., at Camp Byron, opened its doors for the first time September, 1957.[51]

Several outstanding educators have served in the schools listed above. David E. Harder (1872-1930) served on the faculty of Tabor College from 1909 to 1922, of Bethel College from 1922 to 1927, and of Freeman College from 1927 until his death in 1930. He also served as conference moderator for the K.M.B. Church for thirteen years in succession (1913-1926). Another teacher who served on the faculty of Tabor College for several years was C.F. Plett. He also served as conference chairman and in many other capacities in his brotherhood.

Another gifted educator was Joseph W. Schmidt, who served on the faculty of Grace Bible Institute from 1950 to 1960 (the time of his death), the last four years as president. He was also much in demand as a speaker at Bible and missionary conferences, not only in the K.M.B. constituency, but also in Mennonite Brethren churches.

8. MOVING TOWARD MERGER

In discussing the merger-question David V. Wiebe makes the observation that "it is much easier to divide than to unite."[52] The long history of intermittent "courtships" between the K.M.B. and M.B. groups certainly confirms that statement.

Contacts with the Mennonite Brethren date back to the early history of the K.M.B. Church in the Crimea. Unfortunately the only M.B. group with whom they established contact at that time was the Hermann Peters' group which had separated from the Molotschna Mennonite Brethren and moved to the Crimea. This group still defended the *Froehliche Richtung* and insisted on noisy demonstrations to express their "joy in the Lord." This aspect did not at all appeal to the Wiebe group and thus a closer fellowship was ruled out.

Shortly after the K.M.B. group settled in Marion County, Kansas, in 1874, Mennonite Brethren began to arrive and settled in the same general area. In 1876 a large group of Mennonite Brethren with a Volga-German background arrived, led by elder Peter Eckert. Both Wiebe and Eckert believed that it would be well if the two groups, who shared a common faith, would unite. On the question of the mode of baptism they were close to an agreement, but the Volga brethren still justified the "sister kiss." Moreover, they held strongly to certain millennial teachings which the K.M.B. group found unscriptural. Perhaps the most crucial question was the question of leadership. Neither group was quite prepared to submit to the leadership of the other party.[53] Hence, no union was achieved.

A historic consultation was held on January 28, 1895, in the

Springfield (Kansas) K.M.B. Church, where both groups met for a united conference. Elder J. A. Wiebe was elected chairman and John F. Harms, secretary. This session "resulted in fully recognizing each other and expressing willingness to work together 'shoulder to shoulder.' Elder Abraham Schellenberg made the close. All indicated by standing that they were in love and peace with each other."[54] Again, the discussions did not lead to a merger, but cordial fraternal relationships were strengthened.

As a result of close inter-church fellowship and a cooperative working relationship in several areas, differences in faith and practice between the two groups gradually vanished. By the time of World War II former lines of demarcation were hardly recognizable, especially in communities like Gnadenau. It was therefore perhaps logical that the Gnadenau church again spearheaded the merger-movement in 1945 by voting in favor of uniting with the Mennonite Brethren Conference.

On the conference level, however, there were some serious obstacles to union, especially in connection with the missions program of the Krimmer Mennonite Brethren. As noted earlier, this program was carried on under the auspices of a number of other mission boards. How could such a program be integrated with that of the Mennonite Brethren Conference? Through patience, persistence and continued negotiations these problems were all solved eventually.

In 1949 the Committee of Reference and Counsel of the Mennonite Brethren Conference took the initiative to reactivate negotiations and implement the merger by making concrete overtures to the K.M.B. Conference in session at Yale, South Dakota, in October of that year. This proposal was followed in 1951 by an invitation of the General Conference of the M.B. Church of North America to the K.M.B. Conference "to consider jointly the possibility of uniting their spiritual forces into one general conference for the sake of advancing the cause of Christ and for our mutual strengthening in the Lord."[55]

The initial response of the K.M.B. Conference to these overtures was negative. In 1952 and again in 1953 the merger proposal was not acceptable to the majority of the delegates attending these conferences.[56] The withdrawal of the Gnadenau church in 1954 (mentioned earlier) added a new dimension of urgency to the merger-question. In 1956 important agreements were reached by the K.M.B. Merger Committee and the Board of Reference and Counsel of the Mennonite Brethren Conference.

On October 8, 1957, the churches of the K.M.B. Conference voted by a two-thirds majority to merge with the General Conference of the Mennonite Brethren Church.[57] The official response of the K.M.B. Conference was submitted to the Mennonite Brethren Conference

31. Centennial Conference in 1960 at which MB-KMB Merger took place.

meeting for its triennial convention in Yarrow, British Columbia, October 20 to 23, that same year.

Steps toward merger were approved in 1958 and 1959, and in 1960 definite plans of merger on General Conference level and district level were ratified by the K.M.B. delegates. One local congregation in Kansas could not see its way clear to go along with the merger-movement, but in the last minute (before the official merger ceremony in Reedley) it approved the merger-plan as accepted by the K.M.B. Conference.

The official merger service took place on November 14, 1960, in connection with the Centennial Conference held in Reedley, California. In the introduction to the official ceremony C. F. Plett, the last chairman of the K.M.B. Conference, once more stated the reasons for the merger:

We are deleting the geographical designation of origin, the "Krimmer," not because we are bankrupt, discouraged, or too small to carry on a program, nor because we have lost vision. We are prepared to become one in body, one in program, and one in purpose because we believe it would honor the Lord. [58]

After the reading of two historic documents relating to the merger by Rueben Dirks and Henry Dick, secretaries of the K.M.B. and M.B.

conferences respectively, several leading brethren from both groups were called to the platform to join in extending the hand of fellowship in order to symbolize the new unity. Words of welcome and response were also exchanged by the brethren.

The service reached its impressive and beautiful climax when the chairmen of the two conferences, Dan E. Friesen (M.B.) and C. F. Plett (K.M.B.) clasped hands and led in a prayer of supplication for divine guidance and of dedication to faithful service as a united body of believers. The conference delegates expressed their feelings of mutual acceptance and love by singing, "Blest Be the Tie That Binds." The long-anticipated union had finally become a reality, and since 1960 the two conferences have functioned as one body. Because most of the former K.M.B. congregations are located in the Midwest, the Central and Southern District conferences are especially benefiting from this enlarged fellowship of faith and service.

Chapter 13

Organization for United Action

The well-known saying, "united we stand, divided we fall" is not only applicable to a nation, but also to a Christian brotherhood. Although the unity of believers is primarily a spiritual unity, it also includes organizational unity. The statement that "the church is an organism, not an organization" is not an adequate reflection of New Testament teaching on the nature and function of the church. The organism must organize its members for effective action. Early in their history the Mennonite Brethren realized the need as well as the importance of uniting their forces and pooling their resources for an effective witness at home and abroad.

As pointed out in chapter six, the Mennonite Brethren in Russia met for their first conference in 1872, twelve years after the founding of the church. It is significant that the early Brethren (both in Russia and in North America) always referred to this gathering of the larger brotherhood as the *Bundeskonferenz*, implying a covenant relationship among the member congregations. In contradistinction to the somewhat complex conference structure developed in later years in North America, the conference organization in Russia remained relatively simple and centralized. A unique feature in the organizational pattern of the conference in that country developed during the first decade of the twentieth century when the Mennonite Brethren began to have joint business sessions with the representatives of the Mennonite Church.[1]

Among the widely scattered congregations in the American Midwest a concern for a wider fellowship was manifested early in their history. The initiative in this matter was taken by the ministers of the larger congregations, who visited smaller groups and conducted services there. The lack of proper means of communication and transportation, as well as the struggle for survival during the pioneer years, made a gathering of brethren from the several states where Mennonite Brethren had settled virtually impossible.[2] Considering these problems, it is remarkable that several leaders met for their first interstate conference only four years after the first Mennonite Brethren had set foot on American soil.

For convenience, we shall divide the organizational development and the expansion of the activities of the Mennonite Brethren Conference in North America into several periods. It will be noted that historical, cultural, and occasionally even national developments have influenced the shape of the conference-structure from the 1870's to the 1970's.

I. CONFERENCE BEGINNINGS AND CENTRALIZATION
(1879—1909)

In chapter ten, the first attempt at conference organization in 1878 has been described. The reasons why it was not recognized by the brotherhood in later years have also been considered. Nevertheless, this first interstate church-meeting was a step that prepared the way for the organization of a Mennonite Brethren Conference in North America. The brethren from York and Hamilton Counties, Nebraska, and especially Peter Regier, must be given recognition for initiating this venture of united work and witness.

The first duly constituted M.B. Conference convened in October 1879, again in Nebraska. It was begun with a love feast and a missions festival on Sunday, followed by two days of business sessions. The congregations of Kansas, Nebraska and Minnesota were represented by twenty-two delegates.[3] This combination of devotional and inspirational meetings with business sessions established a pattern that has served as a model for Mennonite Brethren conferences through the years. A brief survey of the major concerns which came up for discussion on the conference floor during the first three decades (1879-1909) indicates a growing spiritual vision in the brotherhood.

Home Missions

From 1878 to 1888 the brethren regulated the home missions endeavor on the conference floor each year. The deliberations centered around the following issues: the promotion of evangelism in all M.B. churches; the approval of brethren for such a ministry; the assignment of time schedules to the various churches; the gathering of funds for the conference treasury to support this work; and the hearing of reports presented by those who had been involved in an itinerant ministry.[4]

By 1889 the work of evangelism required more planning and supervision and the conference appointed a committee which was asked to prepare a plan of procedure in home missions. This committee recommended that the work be divided into two phases: evangelism and spiritual care (*Seelenpflege*). With regard to evangelism the committee recommended the appointment of two evangelists for the whole conference, if means permitted. These could, with guidance from the churches, conduct revival services wherever there were open doors, whether within the constituency or outside of M.B. churches. Additional brethren could be engaged by the month if there were any funds left.

With regard to spiritual care the committee recommended financial support for elders who devoted much of their time to spiritual watch-care. An annual remuneration of one hundred to two hundred dollars is suggested for such a ministry. Funds for this purpose are to be remitted to the conference treasury for disposition.[5] These recommendations were accepted by the conference.

This arrangement for the promotion of home missions (*Innere Mission*) proved to be very beneficial to the young and scattered congregations. The ministry of itinerant elders and evangelists not only strengthened and stabilized the life of existing churches — it was also a direct means of planting churches in new areas. We have already observed how through the ministry of elder Heinrich Voth and others the first M.B. church in Canada was established in 1888. Through the well-educated and gifted Peter H. Wedel effective evangelistic campaigns were conducted in M.B. churches in Kansas, Nebraska, South Dakota, and Minnesota from 1888-95. His fervent preaching "led to sweeping revivals and the conversion of many."[6]

This pattern of organization and financial support enabled other leading brethren of the conference to devote a part of their time to itinerant preaching and teaching. It enabled Elder Schellenberg to assist young churches with organizational problems and at ordination services. N. N. Hiebert, returned missionary from India, was sponsored by the Home Missions Committee as "traveling missionary" for the whole conference.[7] John F. Harms was commissioned to work among the Russian people in North Dakota and Saskatchewan.[8] Others who served for shorter or longer periods under the Home Missions Committee were David Dyck, H. S. Voth, P. C. Hiebert, and J. J. Regier.

The crucial role of this itinerant ministry for the early M.B. Church in America cannot be overemphasized. It promoted unity in faith and practice, and was the most important avenue for church extension. In 1909 the whole area of home missions was delegated to the district conferences.[9]

Foreign Missions

As mentioned earlier, the Mennonite Brethren Church was born in a missionary atmosphere in 1860. When fourteen years later the Mennonite Brethren came to the United States, they brought with them a missionary vision and concern. Although many spiritual needs of the local church and community were pressing during the pioneer era, an understanding developed in the brotherhood that missions is incomplete unless it reaches people in darkness at the ends of the earth. As early as 1879 this conviction was voiced on the conference floor.[10] Through almost one hundred years of General Conference life and activity in North America no other issue has aroused as much popular interest and received as much sustained moral and financial support as foreign missions (*Aeussere Mission*). It is this major concern that has welded together a brotherhood that is quite diverse in social, educational, economic and cultural interests and backgrounds.

Before the Mennonite Brethren had a mission field of their own, their interest found expression in missionary giving. In 1881 action was taken to apply one-half of the conference love-offering ($26.36) to foreign missions. A year later the conference decided to send the foreign mission offering ($56.13) to the Baptist Mission in India.[11] In 1885 a "foreign missions" committee was elected — not to supervise a mission field, which the conference did not have, but to administer mission funds. In 1889 funds were designated not only for India, but also for Africa. In 1893 a larger amount was allotted for mission work in the Cameroon field, since P. H. Wedel had volunteered for service in that country.

The conference was not quite satisfied, however, with an arrangement which called for investment without supervision and control. The committee on missions began to look for a field in 1893, and discovered that there were also "heathen" closer to home who were in spiritual darkness. In 1894 a work was started among the Comanche Indians of Oklahoma, to which the Henry Kohfelds felt called.

Although the support of missionaries on Baptist mission fields met with general approval, "it was not considered the answer to the American Mennonite Brethren missionary responsibility, dynamic, and potential."[12] To meet this challenge the conference passed a resolution of principle in 1898 that neither our mission nor our missionaries should be subject to or controlled by other mission societies or boards, and that other societies accepting our young people for mission service should be responsible for their financial support.[13] The same year the N. N. Hieberts were accepted for mission work in India. In 1901 Brother and Sister J. H. Pankratz and Brother and Sister D. F. Bergthold followed the Hieberts to expand the work begun among the Telegus in the state of Hyderabad in southern India. The first and only foreign mission field

of the conference for twenty years (1899-1919), India has continued to
remain a major part of the total missionary program of the Mennonite
Brethren Church.

A Church Paper

In the far-flung constituency of the Mennonite Brethren in North
America it would have been impossible to "maintain the unity of the
spirit in the bond of peace" without a church periodical. As early as
1884, at the sixth annual conference held in Kansas, several leading
brethren emphasized the need for such a denominational paper in order
to keep the constituency informed and united. A committee consisting
of Abraham Schellenberg, Dietrich Claassen, and John F. Harms was
elected to promote publication interests, including the writing of a
history of the M.B. Church. During the course of the next year "there
originated within the publication committee the concept and the
implementation of publishing an M.B. periodical and naming it
Zionsbote."[14] John F. Harms, the conference secretary, was asked to
serve as editor of this new "messenger" to M.B. families.

Here again, as in home and foreign missions, organization and
united action made such an important ministry through the printed
page possible.

City Missions

City missions constitute the fourth general area of conference
concern during this early period. Although Mennonite Brethren did not
live in cities, they had occasion to become acquainted, especially
through reports of evangelists, with the physical, moral, and spiritual
needs of the "inner city" in several areas, especially in Hurley,
Wisconsin, and in Minneapolis, Minnesota. As in most conference
enterprises, only a few brethren initially felt a spiritual burden for city
mission work. Among these were N. N. Hiebert (Minnesota) and J. J.
Kliewer (Nebraska) who shared their concern with the brotherhood at
the conference in 1907.

The conference took immediate action in electing a committee of
three brethren. In keeping with what seems to be a Mennonite tradition,
the brethren who had expressed their convictions were elected to this
committee. In addition, Jacob C. Dick was elected to serve as treasurer.
Although Mr. and Mrs. B. F. Wiens, together with Miss Katharina
Klassen, had started to work in Hurley and Gile, Wisconsin, in 1908,
and Mr. and Mrs. A. A. Smith had begun to work in Minneapolis the
same year, the conference was not ready until a year later to accept full
administrative responsibility for city mission work. In 1909 the
conference adopted the Minneapolis City Mission (South Side) as a work
of the M.B. Church with the Smiths as conference city missionaries.
Financial responsibility was limited "to the extent the treasury
permits."[15]

City missions were eventually delegated to district and provincial conferences. A survey of early city mission efforts would lead to the conclusion that the "target group" for such a ministry were primarily the social outcasts, the people living "on the wrong side of the tracks." This policy of city missions, concentrating on rescue efforts among the down-and-out, has made the transition from "mission" to "church" very difficult, if not impossible in most instances.

Higher Education

Generally speaking, higher education did not receive the general and wholehearted support of the conference during this period, although eloquent pleas were made by individual brethren (especially J. F. Harms) to accept greater responsibility in this field. The financial support of the German Department at McPherson College (1899) was a partial response to meet growing needs in the constituency. The reaction of the conference in 1908 to the newly established "Tabor College School Association" is somewhat characteristic of Mennonite Brethren attitudes toward new ventures — especially in higher education. After a report and a request for moral and financial support by P. C. Hiebert, "the Conference delegation by a show of hands voted to wish the brethren of the Tabor College School Association the Lord's blessing in their endeavor, and assured them of the confidence of the churches."[16]

Christian Ethics

Even a cursory survey of early conference records impresses the reader with the fact that the brethren were deeply concerned about maintaining high standards of Christian life and discipleship. They were also concerned that churches might walk "according to the same rule" and thus strengthen the united witness of the brotherhood. Ethical issues and questions of church discipline were brought up again and again on the conference floor. From the perspective of the 1970's some of the issues may appear peripheral, but that does not minimize their relevance for the churches of that day.

The marriage question often appeared on the agenda. In 1889 a resolution was passed that only baptized believers should enter into holy matrimony and be married by the church.[17] In 1898 permission was given to marry outside the church only if the respective person qualified to be received into (M.B.) membership. This concession was coupled with serious warnings against marrying outside of the fellowship.[18] In 1899 the conference went on record that it was "unanimously opposed to performing of a wedding ceremony of a believer with an unbeliever."[19]

The question of political involvement is one with which the brotherhood has wrestled from the beginning. In 1890 the delegates resolved "that members of the church refrain from participation and involvement in the contentions of political parties, but are permitted to vote quietly at elections, and may also vote for prohibition."[20]

The regulation concerning the number of holidays to be observed at Christian festivals, or the oppposition to any form of life insurance, must be interpreted against the cultural background of the late nineteenth century. All in all, the motivation to maintain a "pure church" is certainly praiseworthy.

Although the Mennonite Brethren were congregational in their church polity, and endeavored to observe "democratic" parliamentary procedures at their annual conventions, it was perhaps inevitable that power would eventually concentrate in the hands of a few leading elders. They were often called upon to regulate matters in local congregations, they ordained all ministers and deacons in the brotherhood, and they were deeply involved in every activity of the conference. Elder Schellenberg, for instance, served as moderator of the conference eighteen times between 1880-1900. He also served as chairman of the Foreign Missions Board as well as of the Publications Committee for many years. At the turn of the century his strong personality seemed to overshadow that of his fellow-elders and occasionally serious tensions arose.[21] The decentralization of the conference effected in 1909 may thus have been a blessing in disguise.

In commenting on this "decentralization" which led to the organization of district conferences, P. M. Friesen writes as follows:

The centralization idea had become so strong, that one party desired a central bishop, "a Paul" (as some described him) whom they wanted to elect in the person of elder Abraham Schellenberg. It was hoped that through such complete unification and central leadership more spiritual life and greater unity of spirit could be achieved. The Mennonite spirit of autonomy triumphed in the moderate, and in our opinion, apostolic spirit through the act of the "expansion of the conference" as a *Bundeskonferenz* under one constitution with three district conferences. [22]

II. CONTINUED EXPANSION AND DECENTRALIZATION
(1909-1924)

Conference Reorganization

The division of the conference into several districts in 1909 was the culmination of years of discussions and planning. As early as 1902 the "brethren from the North" expressed their concerns at the conference which convened in Washita County, Oklahoma, in November. The brethren felt that the time of the annual conference (in late fall) as well as the great distance to the congregations in the South constituted real difficulties in participation.[23]

In 1903, a special committee was appointed to prepare a plan (*Vorlage*) for the expansion of the conference. The committee recommeded that since our church is expanding into Saskatchewan and possibly into the northwestern territory beyond, the need for enlarging into a northern and southern conference has become evident, to make possible a more active participation and thus help promote the extension of the kingdom of God. [24]

Detailed proposals for implementation of this recommendation were also presented.

However, no action was taken on these proposals. In 1904 the matter was again tabled for another year. In 1905 a new committee was appointed which recommended that the conference be divided into five districts: (1) Oklahoma, (2) Kansas, (3) Nebraska and Colorado, (4) Minnesota, South Dakota, and North Dakota, and (5) Canada. The churches in Oregon and California could join the district of their choice. Although the recommendation was accepted, no steps were taken for immediate implementation.

A major reason for postponing implementation appears to have been the concern of many leading brethren that decentralization might lead to disunity in the brotherhood and to disintegration of conference efforts in missions, publication and education. To safeguard against such dangers, the conference meeting in 1906 agreed to make proper provisions "so that upon the basis of a constitution the Conference be expanded without impairing the overall brotherhood unity."[25] A constitution was drafted in which the conference organization and activities were defined, and provision was made for their implementation and execution. According to this constitution the name of the organization was to be: "Conference of the Mennonite Brethren Church of North America."[26]

At the 1907 convention the brethren Heinrich Voth and N. N. Hiebert, who had been elected to serve on the "constitution committee," submitted the first draft of this document to the conference. It was published in the *Zionsbote* in the following year and after some revisions adopted by the conference in 1908. This constitution provided guidelines for conference work until 1936, and according to J. H. Lohrenz, "served a useful purpose, since work in the business sessions was now done more rapidly and efficiently."[27]

The conference of 1909 marks the end of an era, since it was the last annual convention in which the entire brotherhood participated. At this convention the General Conference interim was raised to three years. (The first triennial conference met in 1912.) Moreover, the following recommendation was accepted for the division of the conference into districts:

(a) That the Conference expand into three district conferences as follows: The Southern District Conference — Oklahoma, Kansas, and Escondido,

California. The other California churches may join either the Southern or the Central district. The Central District Conference — Nebraska, Colorado, North Dakota, South Dakota, Minnesota, Michigan, Oregon. The Northern District Conference — Canada and Rosehill, North Dakota. Manitoba and Rosehill, North Dakota, may join either the Northern or the Central district.

(b) That the district conferences are to deal with home missions and other local matters, and the General M.B. Conference with (foreign missions, publication, education, and) all endeavors of the General Conference. [28]

The brethren did not anticipate at the time that during the next few years there would be a major shift of the Mennonite Brethren population from the Midwest to the Pacific Coast and a realignment of churches in the North. In 1913 the congregations on the West Coast organized as the Pacific District Conference, and Manitoba, which had earlier joined the Central District, asked for admission into the Northern District Conference the same year. [29]

After several years of experimentation and adjustment, the four district conferences were organized as follows: The *Southern District* was composed of the churches in Kansas, Oklahoma, Colorado, and Texas. The *Central District* included churches in North Dakota, South Dakota, Minnesota, Nebraska, Michigan, and Montana. The *Pacific District* was composed of the congregations in California, Oregon, and Washington. The *Northern District* (later named the Canadian Conference) included all churches in Canada. Since there were three district conferences in the United States, and only one in Canada, it was natural that representation on General Conference boards was often on a three to one ratio. This ratio was maintained (more the result of tradition than deliberate policy, to be sure) even after the Northern District membership equalled that of the other three districts combined. [30]

Conference Activities

The period from 1909 to 1924 is marked by a continued expansion of activities on the part of the General Conference as well as that of the several district conferences. The General Conference, meeting every three years, experienced an increase in representation from the churches. Whereas at the 1909 convention thirty-seven churches had been represented by 115 delegates, there were 162 delegates present in 1912, representing forty-five churches. Since the conference now convened only once in three years, more responsibility had to be delegated to boards and committees. Administrative details no longer came up for discussion on the conference floor, but were decided at board level. The relationship between the General Conference and the district conferences appears to have been cordial and without any serious friction.

This period is also marked by the emergence of a new leadership. The "old stalwarts," who had served the conference faithfully for many years, were gradually passing from the scene. Several men were called home to their reward: Heinrich Voth in 1918, Martin M. Just in 1919, and Abraham Schellenberg in 1920. Others, such as Johann Foth and Heinrich Adrian, because of advancing age, withdrew from active involvement in conference work. The new leadership was composed mostly of brethren who were bilingual and college educated. Among these were the teachers at Tabor College: H. W. Lohrenz, P. C. Hiebert and H. F. Toews. Other brethren who rendered valuable service in the conference were H. H. Flaming, H. S. Voth and John Berg. In the Northern District Conference two older men continued to give good leadership: David Dyck (North Saskatchewan) and Johann Warkentin (Manitoba).

Missions

Throughout this period the work of foreign missions remained the most important phase of General Conference activity. At the triennial conferences "Festival Sunday" was usually "Missions Sunday," and during the business sessions a large part of the time was devoted to missions. The mission among the Telegus of southern India continued to be the major mission project of the conference. In 1923 the conference supported six married couples and four single missionaries on this field.[31]

A milestone was reached in the missionary history of the conference with the acceptance of the "South China" mission in 1919. Brother and sister F. J. Wiens had begun their work among the Hakkas in Fukien province in 1911. Although the conference had authorized the Mission Board to begin an M. B. mission work in China as early as 1909, this decision could not be fully implemented until ten years later. In the meantime Mr. and Mrs. Wiens had established a successful mission at Shanghang. In the immediate post-war period the mission in China was expanded and by 1924 three missionary couples and five sisters were supported by the conference.[32]

The South Side City Mission, established in Minneapolis in 1910, was continued throughout this period. A two story building, erected at 2120 Minnehaha Avenue in 1917, provided not only a residence for the mission workers but also a spacious chapel and classrooms on the main floor as well as a kitchen and recreational rooms in the basement. South Side Mission provided a haven of refuge for people with physical, emotional and spiritual needs. After the Northern District Conference had begun its own city mission work in Winnipeg in 1913, the question of continued support of the South Side Mission was raised by the Canadian delegation on the conference floor in 1915. The conference was not prepared, however, to assume administrative and financial responsibilities for any additional city missions in other areas, since "home missions" had been delegated to district conferences in 1909. After some study of the matter, the conference agreed to continue its support of the Minneapolis mission. "Aside from that," the resolution reads, "the Conference takes a sympathetic position toward the city mission efforts of the Northern Conference in Winnipeg and the Pacific Conference at Bakersfield, and wishes them God's blessings in their endeavor, and does not wish in any way to hinder these causes."[33]

Relief and General Welfare

From their earliest years Mennonite Brethren have emphasized not only the need for a ministry of evangelism, but also the need for a ministry of compassion. As early as 1884 the matter of relief was brought to the conference floor. It was a concern for impoverished immigrants in Russia who desired to migrate to America that prompted that discussion. The conference decided, however, to leave this matter to the individual churches for consideration and action.

Beginning with 1900, regular relief offerings for "oppressed children of God"[34] were gathered on Thanksgiving Day. Also in 1900, the conference approved the distribution of relief funds (from private gifts and special offerings) as follows: "for famine in India $3,150.50; Armenia, $127.78; miscellaneous needs, $16.00; for oppressed Christians, $392.44."[35]

From 1910 to 1920, the conference administered contributions for relief as part of the assignment of the Board of Missions. The Thanksgiving offerings were continued, but were directed more toward home missions in the cities, and toward distribution of Christian literature, especially among the Russian people.

A new epoch for ministries of compassion began in the immediate post-war period. As reported in chapter eight, the Study Commission that arrived in America in 1920 informed the Mennonite constituency of the tragic plight of their brethren in Russia. Because those in need had many relatives and acquaintances in America, their desperate situation was of special concern to Mennonite and Mennonite Brethren churches. Already in 1920 "this resulted in a decision by the Southern District Conference to provide $2,000 per month for relief for the Russian brethren."[36] That same year also P. C. Hiebert, a Mennonite Brethren educator and leader became chairman of MCC, an international relief and service agency, through which Mennonite Brethren channeled most of their relief funds henceforth.[37]

In 1924 the conference gave expression to its conviction that relief and social concern are an integral part of its mission by electing a seven-member relief committee. This was the birth of the Board of General Welfare and Public Relations which took its legitimate place alongside the Board of Foreign Missions and other boards of the Mennonite Brethren Conference.[38]

World War I was not only the occasion for a renewal of social concerns and relief efforts in the Mennonite Brethren Conference, it also challenged the brotherhood to rethink its position on peace and nonresistance. During the first forty years (1874-1914) of their church life in America the brethren did not have to face the question of the draft or military service. Although the conference in 1902 had accepted the *Confession of Faith* of the M. B. Church in Russia, which contains the sentence, "We also do not consider ourselves to have the right to wield the sword," the matter did not come up for discussion on the floor of the General Conference until 1919. At that time a committee on nonresistance was created, and a formal statement was accepted by the conference which forbade participation in military service on scriptural grounds.[39]

III. A Changing Constituency and Polarization
(1924-1954)

By 1924 Hillsboro (Kansas) had become the undisputed center of General Conference activity among the Mennonite Brethren. The conference publishing house and Tabor College, the only institution of higher education in the brotherhood, were located here. The Southern District, moreover, at that time included the area of heaviest concentration of Mennonite Brethren on the North American continent.

During the course of the next thirty years the distribution of Mennonite Brethren membership changed considerably. As a result of immigration on a large scale, the Northern District Conference grew rapidly and by 1951 its membership exceeded that of the other three district conferences combined. A similar shift in the distribution of membership occurred within the United States itself. By 1953 the membership in the Pacific District had surpassed that of the Southern District.[40] These new "realities" were perhaps not sufficiently recognized in conference representation, organization, and policy, and hence certain tensions developed between North and South and also between the Midwest and the Pacific Coast. Or, to state it another way, the leadership in the Canadian M. B. Conference began to feel that existing General Conference agencies and institutions were not adequately meeting the need of the large and growing constituency in the North. In the Pacific District Conference similar sentiments began to be voiced, although somewhat later perhaps than in Canada. It was also during this period, that the Ontario Conference of Mennonite Brethren Churches joined the General Conference, adding another dimension to the pattern of development of conference structures and activities. These changes in the constituency and their implications for the brotherhood as a whole shall now be considered briefly.

1. *Developments in Canada*

The geographical expansion and numerical growth of the Canadian Conference during this period had parallel developments in the founding of institutions and in increasing activities. The nature and scope of these activities were strongly influenced in earlier years by economic factors. A large number of the *Russlaender* Mennonite Brethren had incurred a heavy debt for transportation (*Reiseschuld*) which they endeavored to pay off as soon as possible to the Canadian Pacific Railway Company, which had extended this "credit" to them. The economic problems were accentuated by the general poverty of the settlers and the Depression which overtook them before the transportation debts were paid off. The Depression of the thirties did not only affect the new settlements, but also the older and more established Mennonite Brethren congregations who had extended a helping hand to the brethren from Russia upon their arrival.

This economic situation gave rise to a new effort in city missions. Since many girls found employment in cities like Winnipeg, Saskatoon, Calgary, and Vancouver, "Girls Homes" (*Maedchenheime*) were established in these centers. In some cities "homes" were operated on an inter-Mennonite basis, in others the Mennonite Brethren established their own. Perhaps the best known among the latter is the Mary-Martha Home established in Winnipeg in 1925, in which Sister Anna Thiessen served as matron for twenty-two years.[41] Although these "homes" were not accepted as Canadian Conference projects, they received partial financial support from the conference.[42]

The Mennonite Brethren who came to Canada in the 1920's gave new impetus to Bible school education. In a few years the Herbert Bible School, which had been established earlier, had a number of sister institutions. Mennonite Brethren founded Bible schools at Winkler (1925), Hepburn (1927), Coaldale (1929), Yarrow (1930), Gem (1933) and Virgil (1938). These schools, although not administered by the Canadian Conference, enjoyed the moral support of the brotherhood and submitted reports to the annual conferences.

The desire for Christian training found expression also in the founding of private high schools. During the thirties these aspirations could not be realized because of the stronger financial base required for such ventures. With improved economic conditions at the end of World War II, Mennonite Brethren high schools were established in Clearbrook, in 1944, in Yarrow, Winnipeg and Virgil in 1945, and in Coaldale in 1946. Here again the conference did not assume financial or administrative responsibility for these institutions, but gave its moral support to these schools.

Of greater significance for inter-conference relations was the founding of the Mennonite Brethren Brethren Bible College in Winnipeg in 1944 as an institution for higher theological training of the Canadian Conference. Although a few brethren had through the years gone to Tabor College for such training, it was felt that the Canadian Conference needed its own school to prepare teachers for Bible schools and Christian high schools as well as for the training of workers in expanding home missions programs. Perhaps it is significant that in that same year the conference also publicly expressed some concerns about student conduct in Tabor College.[43]

This gradual polarization in educational efforts, and especially in theological training, was reinforced by the language problem. Whereas the transition from German to English was almost ended in the Mennonite Brethren churches in the United States by 1940, the transition in Canada came more than twenty years later, largely as the result of large-scale immigration from Europe and South America. Most Canadian M. B. churches during this period demanded that their ministers, Sunday school teachers, and other church workers be able to communicate in German as well as English. Thus the Bible College in Winnipeg emphasized bilingualism in its teaching program during the first ten years of its existence.

That the preservation of the German language was considered of vital importance for the spiritual life of the brotherhood is evidenced by the fact that in 1950 the Committee of Reference and Counsel of the Canadian Conference recommended the creation of a committee for the nurture (*Pflege*) of the German language in the churches.[44] This cultural and language difference between North and South had a tendency, for a while at least, to become an obstacle in closer cooperation between the Canadian Conference and the General Conference, the latter largely being identified with institutions and concerns of the brotherhood in the United States.

Even in foreign missions a tendency toward an independent effort manifested itself in the organization of the Africa Mission Society (*Afrika Missionsverein*). The members of this society were Mennonite Brethren and the financial support for the work of the society came largely from Canadian M. B. churches. In 1932 Brother and Sister Henry G. Bartsch were commissioned by the society to go to the Belgian Congo (Zaire). Here they established a work among the Dengese people at Bololo, in the northern Congo. The society, through its Board of Directors, presented several petitions (in November, 1936; October, 1938; and March 1943) to the Board of Foreign Missions to accept the

Bololo field as a work of the General Conference of Mennonite Brethren. This desire was realized at the General Conference sessions in Buhler in May, 1943.[45] This helped to unite North and South more fully in the cause of missions, and provided new service opportunities for an ever-increasing number of missionary candidates, especially from Canada.

With the acquisition of the Christian Press, and the establishment of its own publishing house in Winnipeg, the Candian Conference had taken a further step in the direction of decentralization of conference activities. In response to a report by P. H. Berg, (manager of the M.B. Publishing House), at the Canadian Conference in 1944, A. H. Unruh raised the question of a Canadian publishing center.[46] At the conference in 1946 B. B. Janz reported that a number of brethren, with the approval of the Committee of Reference and Counsel, had purchased the Christian Press, and asked whether the conference could sanction this action. The conference showed its approval by becoming a shareholder in this venture.[47] A lack of news coverage of institutions and concerns of special interest to Canadian M.B. churches by the *Zionsbote* and the *Christian Leader* was often given as a reason for establishing publication on a Canadian Conference level.

In 1946 the Ontario Conference of Mennonite Brethren was received into the Northern District (Canadian) Conference. This was an important and historic event in the expansion of the Canadian Conference and greatly strengthened its program in evangelism, home missions and education.

2. *Developments in the United States*

The Mennonite Brethren in the United States were much more homogeneous in cultural background and in historical experience during this period (1924-54) than their Canadian brethren. The majority of the church members here were the descendants of the immigrants of the 1870's and their gradual acculturation had not been disturbed by the influx of several "waves" of newcomers as had been the case in Canada. Hence there was also a greater unity in supporting General Conference projects. The three district conferences all carried on an increasingly effective home missions program,[48] but cooperated fully with the General Conference in foreign missions, publication and higher education. On the level of secondary training, local churches and occasionally a group of congregations would establish a private Christian high school or "Bible Academy." Such academies were established in Corn (1902), and in Reedley (1912). In Lustre, Montana, Mennonite Brethren cooperated with other Mennonite groups to establish the Lustre Bible Academy (formerly the Lustre Bible School) in 1928. The Mountain Lake Bible School had earlier been established on the same basis.

On the post-high school level Tabor College continued to meet the needs of the entire United States constituency until World War II. The rapid growth of the Pacific District (both in terms of the number of congregations as well as total membership) during the forties and fifties, however, precipitated new developments in education on the West Coast. As early as 1940, the Pacific District Conference appointed a committee, which among other things, was assigned to study the possibility of establishing a district conference Bible school. In 1942 the proposal to establish a Bible institute in the city of Fresno was introduced by the Committee of Religious Education at the conference sessions held in Shafter, and was accepted with the provision of "not being too hasty in carrying out the recommendations."[49] This note of caution was added because of heavy financial commitments in support of the Civilian Public Service (CPS) Camps for conscientious objectors and of Tabor College.

The institute at Fresno, which opened its doors for the first time in the fall of 1944, experienced rapid growth, especially after G. W. Peters assumed the presidency in 1947. The new school soon looked for recognition on the General Conference level. Already at the 1945 General Conference sessions in Dinuba the Pacific District Conference presented the following petition:

We desire and herewith petition that the Pacific Bible Institute be recognized by the General Conference of the Mennonite Brethren Church of North America. However, the administration and management remains under the jurisdiction of the Pacific District Conference. [50]

This petition was made in order to be eligible for a share of the revenue from the educational endowment fund. With the acceptance of this petition the conference delegates implicitly recognized two educational centers in the United States, Hillsboro and Fresno.

The question of coordinating the programs of higher theological training came up for discussion on the conference floor in Mountain Lake in 1948 and again in Winkler in 1951. The report of the Seminary Commission presented to the Winkler convention, was referred to the Coordination Committee for further investigation.[51] This was no easy task. In speaking to the Pacific District Conference in the fall of the same year, G. W. Peters, president of Pacific Bible Institute, analyzed the problem correctly by pointing out that the difficulties of coordination were "not due to any one individual, but rather to the complexity of the situation which arises out of the geographical distribution of our churches, the ideals of our conferences, and the needs of our young people."[52] In his further elaboration of the question,

Peters expressed the view that coordination would not be achieved as long as one school was a General Conference project, and the other schools were administered by district conferences.

The question of unification and coordination of the educational institutions of the conference came to a head at the General Conference held in Hillsboro in October, 1954. With the Canadian delegation abstaining from discussion and voting, the conference accepted a recommendation of the Board of Education of Tabor College to "establish a unified educational program by which one board shall operate the schools of the General Conference (in the U.S. area) from one treasury. . . ."[53] The implementation of this decision finally resulted in the establishment of a Seminary and a Junior College in connection with Pacific Bible Institute at Fresno, and the continuation of the four-year liberal arts program with a strong Bible department at Hillsboro. The Krimmer Mennonite Brethren fully participated in the deliberations and decisions with regard to the unified educational program.

The General Conference of 1954 marks the beginning of a new pattern in conference organization — it marks the emergence of the concept of "area conferences." In 1953 the Canadian M.B. Conference had voted that certain activities be made "area" conference responsibilities, and designated the following: higher education, church schools (including Sunday schools), youth work, and home missions. Anticipating that the General Conference delegation of 1954 might accept the "area" proposition, the Committee on Constitution prepared "Draft No. 2." It eliminated the above four from General Conference jurisdiction, made them area conference responsibilities, and merely provided for "consultative committees" for these activities. This "Draft No. 2" was adopted by the 1954 conference as a provisional basis for its work in the ensuing interim.[54]

3. General Conference Expansion

The period between 1924 and 1954 is significant for its expanding organizational borders and its widening missionary horizons and activities.

Expansion in Organization

Two district conferences were admitted into the General Conference during this period. The Ontario Conference of Mennonite Brethren Churches, which had been organized in 1932 (as described in chapter eleven) was accepted as a district conference by the General Conference in 1939. It will be recalled that the Ontario Conference differed in its church policy from the General Conference in admitting non-immersed believers and practicing open communion.[55] H. H. Janzen, the chairman of the Ontario Conference from 1932 to 1945 and a well-known preacher and Bible expositor in the larger Mennonite Brethren constituency, led the brethren of that province in seeking closer fellowship and affiliation with the General Conference of Mennonite Brethren. The first attempt at affiliation, made in 1936, resulted in the provision of a working fellowship with rather severe limitations.[56]

In 1939 the General Conference, upon the recommendation of its Committee of Reference and Counsel, admitted the Ontario Conference with the following stipulations:

> The General Conference . . . extends full fellowship to the churches of the Ontario Conference that are of the same faith with the General Conference, that are willing to abide by our resolutions and to share in all undertakings. This covers the members of the churches who are baptized by immersion upon the confession of faith, provided that they submit to all provisions and obligations of our constitution. It will then be registered and officially recognized as the Ontario Conference. This agreement to be in force when the Ontario Conference has accepted the conditions and has published the decision in the *Zionsbote*. [57]

The Ontario Conference accepted these conditions and became a district conference of the General Conference. The conditions of conference affiliation also implied that non-immersed ministers and deacons were not members of the conference. Consequently, some of these requested rebaptism by immersion, others withdrew from the public ministry. Seven years later, in 1946, the Ontario Conference joined the Canadian Conference as a provincial conference, thereby giving up its status as a district in the General Conference.

The second district conference to join the General Conference during this period was located on another continent and in another hemisphere. The Mennonite Brethren churches in Brazil and Paraguay, established by immigrants from Russia who had settled there in 1930, met in 1948 and organized as a Mennonite Brethren Conference. That same year they also took steps to affiliate with the Mennonite Brethren Conference of North America. Two leading brethren, Kornelius Voth (Paraguay) and Gerhard H. Rosenfeld (Brazil), were sent as representatives to attend the General Conference sessions in Mountain Lake, Minnesota. The conference responded positively to the request of the South American brotherhood (through its Committee of Reference and Counsel) as follows:

> (1) We recommend that on the basis of Brother (B. B.) Janz's report concerning the reorientated church [58] . . . and the constitution of the churches of South America we accept the churches of South America as a District Conference of the Conference of the Mennonite Brethren Church of North America.
> (2) That we extend the hand of fellowship to the Brethren Gerhard H. Rosenfeld and Kornelius Voth, who are present at this Conference representing the churches of South America. [59]

The relationship of the General Conference to this district conference in South America is unique and differs markedly from that to all other district conferences. The South American Conference has no representatives on any conference boards or committees. Geographical distance makes practical participation in the work of the General Conference impossible. There has been cooperation, however, in the work of missions, especially among the Indians of the Paraguayan Chaco. In recent years this "district conference" has developed into a kind of "general conference" for South America, with its own district conferences in Brazil, Paraguay and Uruguay. Visits by fraternal delegates to the brotherhood in North America (and vice versa) have strengthened the bonds of a common faith and a common mission in both North and South.

Expansion in Missionary Activity

The enlargement of the "missionary borders" of the Mennonite Brethren Church from its original large field in India to include China (1919) and the Belgian Congo (1943) has already been noted. During the years of World War II (1939-45) it had become very apparent that the doors to mission fields can be closed overnight. This consciousness of the brevity of time for the task of world evangelism, coupled with a widening missionary horizon in the brotherhood, gave a sense of urgency to missionary activity in the post-war period. A. E. Janzen, the administrator of the Mennonite Brethren missions program at that time, described this new attitude in the brotherhood as follows:

Thus from 1945 forward, the constituency was ready, and this was a refreshing movement by the Spirit of God, to launch out to new countries and peoples and fields, to respond favorably to the many applications by young people both in Canada and in the United States who felt the call to missionary service and to respond commensurately with financial support. [60]

In response to such an attitude of faith and commitment, the Board of Missions moved aggressively forward. Beginning in 1945 and continuing through the next fifteen years, the Mennonite Brethren reached out to new fields on the average of one every two years. The conference accepted a number of fields in rapid succession. In 1945 the Daniel Wirsches entered Colombia. A mission project (orphanage) was launched in Brazil at the same time, with the Jacob D. Unruhs as the first workers. The mission work among the Lengua Indians in Paraguay, begun by Gerhard B. Giesbrecht in 1935, was endorsed by the conference in 1945. In the same year also, the West China mission of H. C. Bartel was underwritten by the Board of Missions. Japan was accepted in 1948, and the work in Mexico became conference responsibility in 1950. Just a year later a church planting program was begun in Germany and Austria, and two years after that, in 1953, the German Department of HCJB (radio) became a new avenue for Mennonite Brethren to spread the good news to Latin America and to

Europe. In retrospect one cannot help but exclaim: What hath God wrought!

The supply was equal to the demand in terms of personnel and funds. With the backing of a missionary-minded constituency, the board accepted and dispatched sixty-four missionaries from 1945 to 1948.[61] During the fifteen-year period (1945-60) 206 new missionaries were commissioned for service. Contributions to support the expanding program kept abreast of financial needs, increasing from $197,786.00 in 1945 to $638,483.00 in 1960.[62]

A parallel expansion can also be observed in service and sacrifice in the ministries under the Board of General Welfare and Public Relations. Over the years, a large part of the budget for relief and services has been channeled through MCC to the hungry and needy around the world "in the Name of Christ." The Board of Welfare, in addition to administering relief, has given both spiritual and material assistance to the Mennonite Brethren churches in South America, whose struggle for survival during the pioneer period was extremely harsh and difficult, especially in Paraguay.

Thus conference organization for an effective and sustained witness in word and deed remained strong, throughout this period in "missions and services," even though certain ministries had become the responsibility of district and/or provincial conferences. During the last decade, however, some new trends in conference activities are becoming evident.

IV. RENEWED COOPERATION AND PARTNERSHIP
(1954—1972)

The "constitutional crisis" of 1954 which resulted in a reorganization of the General Conference can be described in terms of the "growing pains" of a brotherhood that is expanding and maturing. Instead of being composed of four "districts," the General Conference now comprised two large "area" conferences. Although the transition from the traditional pattern of conference organization and activity to the new conference "model" was not without some problems and pains, it appears that the long-range effects of reorganization are more positive than negative. In recent years, moreover, a new spirit of cooperation and partnership between the Canadian and United States conferences seems to be in evidence.

The "consultative committees," created by the new constitution, have not only submitted reports to the triennial conventions, but have also entered into active cooperation in several instances. The Committee on Evangelism, for example, established in 1954 and composed of representatives of the participating districts or provinces, has promoted

32. Delegates at a conference session.

evangelism and arranged for exchange of evangelists between the area
conferences. The Church Schools Committee has been actively involved
in the production of needed materials for churches and Sunday schools.
Among other things this committee has published a *Handbook* for the
"Service Training Program," which is finding increasing acceptance
throughout the M.B. Conference. This committee is also responsible for
publishing the *Calendar of Activities* which ministers and church
workers have found extremely useful. The Church Schools Committee
also produces the *Mennonite Brethren Sunday School Standard*, as well
as the *Adult Sunday School Quarterly*.

To maintain the unity of faith within a brotherhood requires not
only common study materials for young and old, but also common
hymnals for worship and praise. After 1945 both the Canadian and the
United States Conferences felt the need for a new church hymnal.
Because of different needs, however, the Canadian Conference published
the *Gesangbuch* in German, and the General Conference (with token
Canadian participation) the *Church Hymnal* in English.

In 1963 the first steps were taken to produce a church hymnal
which would be suitable for all congregations of the General Conference.
At the convention in Winnipeg that year a joint-committee reported:

It has become the express purpose of the U.S. Mennonite Brethren Conference Board of Church Music and the Canadian Mennonite Brethren Conference Hymnbook Committee to combine efforts in the publication of a new church hymnal. Such a project would not have been possible 15 years ago when the language problem existed. At present such an undertaking seems advisable and could help strengthen the bond of unity between the two conferences. [63]

A little more than seven years later, the new and attractive *Worship Hymnal* appeared in the churches of the M.B. Conference. A church that sings the same great hymns of the faith should find it easier to witness and work together.

The trend to unify and strengthen the General Conference of Mennonite Brethren is also evidenced by creating a new board, "The Board of Christian Literature." The establishment of this board in 1966 (for which provision had been made in the 1963 constitution) was the response of the conference to a widely felt need to coordinate, promote and unify conference publication efforts. The devotional booklet, *Worship Together*, which has been published by this board for a number of years, also helps to unite the brotherhood in worship and intercessory prayer.

An event of great historic significance (as mentioned in the last chapter) for the General Conference occurred in 1960, when after prolonged negotiations the Krimmer Mennonite Brethren and the Mennonite Brethren extended to each other the hand of fellowship in order to form one body of believers. This merger of the two conferences coincided with the Centennial Conference of the Mennonite Brethren Church and constituted a fitting climax of the first "century of grace and witness" under God's gracious providence.

Chapter 14

Teaching Them to Observe: Christian Education in the Local Church

The early Brethren strongly emphasized a vital Christian experience. In the Document of Secession they state that baptism is to be upon a genuine, living faith, "not on a memorized faith as is (now) the practice." (Cf. chapter three) The expression "memorized faith" (*auswendig gelernten Glauben*) is an obvious reference to the instruction in the catechism classes which always preceded baptism in the Mennonite Church. In many instances the only preparation of the catechumen for baptism consisted of memorizing the prescribed answers given in the catechism.

The early Brethren reacted against this lifeless orthodoxy. They would have subscribed to the maxim that "the Christian faith is caught and not taught." However, they did not realize sufficiently the close connection between Christian experience and Christian teaching, and that the latter provides the framework for the former. This neglect of sound teaching resulted in the emergence of the *Froehliche Richtung* in the early M.B. Church, as described earlier. It was during that period of religious ferment and theological confusion that the brethren rediscovered the great significance of biblical teaching for the proper development of the church. As P. M. Friesen describes this new attitude, the brethren seemed to be "hungry for order! order! and for lectures."[1]

Through the years the Mennonite Brethren Church has endeavored to maintain a balanced emphasis on teaching and experience in its church program. This chapter will describe the educational agencies that have been most active on a congregational level to promote spiritual growth and development of all members of the church family.[2] Special consideration will be given to the Sunday school (including the midweek program), to youth work and, in a limited way, to Christian camping.

1. THE SUNDAY SCHOOL IN THE MENNONITE BRETHREN CHURCH

The Sunday school is not an "indigenous institution" of the Mennonite Brethren Church. As noted earlier, it was one of the innovations brought into the M. B. Church by August Liebig, the German Baptist minister. As time went on, the Sunday school became an integral part of the total educational and outreach program in Mennonite Brethren churches.

The early Sunday schools in Russia differed in several respects from those that later developed in North America. As a rule, they were not a part of the Sunday morning service, but were held in the afternoons. Since the public school provided systematic religious instruction, the emphasis in Sunday school was not so much on the transmission of a factual knowledge of Scripture, as on the appropriation and application of biblical truth.[3] The Sunday school, moreover, was also regarded primarily as an institution for children, not adults. This is one of the reasons, A. H. Unruh observes, why the Mennonite Brethren who immigrated into Canada in the 1920's found it so difficult to participate in adult Sunday school classes which had become an accepted part of the church program in American M. B. churches.[4]

There are no records of lesson materials especially adapted for Sunday schools. The Bible or the Bible story book (*Biblische Geschichte*) served as text for instruction and discussion. In later years a Baptist minister, Witte, from Poland, introduced some new forms of organization and methods of instruction into Mennonite Brethren Sunday schools. In general, however, instruction was carried on according to the traditional pattern, without a division of the children according to age groups.[5] There is also no record of Sunday school conventions designed to improve teaching and to set forth certain specific goals. According to I. W. Redekopp, the "philosophy of the early brethren seems to have been to assign learning to the public schools, and to look upon the Sunday schools as a supplement to evangelize, rather than to train children."[6]

Although the Sunday school in the M. B. churches in Russia never attained the status it later received in the United States and Canada, it nevertheless was one of the distinctives of Mennonite Brethren work and worship. It appears also, that the Mennonite Brethren were the pioneers among the Russian Mennonites to incorporate the Sunday school into their philosophy and program of Christian education.[7]

1. *Developments in the United States*

The Sunday school of the M. B. Church in the United States is the product of a European heritage molded by the educational and theological environment of the new world. The beginnings were small and insignificant. The Mennonite Brethren who came to the American Midwest in the 1870's initially followed the pattern which they had accepted in Russia some ten years earlier. Betweem 1874 and 1888 the Sunday school became a regular institution in all Mennonite Brethren congregations. At the conference sessions in 1883 a deep concern for the spiritual welfare of children as a primary mission work found expression in a statement by Elder Schellenberg. He exhorted delegates "to see to it that the little ones learn to read in Sunday school, and that all members of the church in all states be made responsible to send their children to Sunday school for the furtherance of their soul's salvation and knowledge of the Word of God."[8] The conference accepted this statement as a recommendation to the churches.

The first reference to a Sunday school convention appears in the conference minutes of 1889. The general sentiment of conference delegates was in favor of improving the Sunday school through a convention organized for that specific purpose. It is interesting to note that the responsibility for the arrangements of this convention was delegated to the Publication Committee. These Sunday school conventions, held at regular intervals, were a primary source of information and inspiration for teachers who had very few helps to aid them in their important ministry. By 1898 the Sunday school convention had become an established institution of the conference. Prior to the convention held on May 23, 1898, a complete program, listing topics and speakers, was published in three consecutive issues of the *Zionsbote*.[9]

Questions of greater uniformity and instructional aids in Sunday school work were early concerns of the brotherhood. Since the conference had no Sunday school manuals, either for teachers or pupils, the *Zionsbote* was used as a medium of instruction. During the summer months of 1898, editor J. F. Harms prepared and published twenty lessons on Bible study for youth, adapted to Sunday school use. The following year, P. F. Duerksen, an early promoter of the Sunday school, published an article in the same paper on Sunday school methods and hints for teachers.[10]

In 1900 the first M. B. periodical on the Sunday school and Sunday school lessons appeared as a private enterprise. Published monthly by P. F. Duerksen, *Der Sonntagschulbote* (The Sunday School Messenger) was made available at a small price to all churches who subscribed to it in various quantities. According to A. E. Janzen, this Sunday school magazine contained the S.S. lessons for each Sunday of the month: listing the subject of the lesson (following the "International" outline), giving the text from the Bible, an introduction, the golden text verse, an exposition of the lesson, questions adapted to children and practical suggestions for the Christian life. In addition, the *Sonntagschulbote* also carried articles and reports on M.B. missions, on the church, on the Sunday school, etc. [11]

Moreover, Duerksen also began to publish Sunday school lessons and a *Kinderblatt* (Children's Paper). At the conference in 1902 Duerksen reported that subscriptions to the Sunday school papers and lesson materials were adequate to cover all costs, and hence there was no need for a conference subsidy. The conference expressed its approval of Duerksen's ministry, and encouraged all churches to make use of the Sunday school material.[12]

Concern for a sound doctrinal content of the lesson materials found expression in the appointment of "editors" who adapted the "International S. S. Lessons" for use in Mennonite Brethren churches. During the early period (1900 to 1907) J. F. Duerksen, D. D. Bartel, and H. W. Lohrenz rendered valuable services in this area of conference work. Beginning in 1907, N. N. Hiebert served as "editor-in-chief" of Sunday school lessons for twelve years until 1919, and again from 1927 to 1936. Hiebert also served as associate member on the International Council of Religious Education.[13]

The concern for proper Sunday school materials gave rise to a serious discussion on the conference floor at the 1924 convention. Many churches favored the creation of more scripturally oriented lesson material, written by brethren of the conference. However, since the selection of the "International" lessons for the succeeding two years was considered more satisfactory than heretofore, the conference decided to elect a Sunday School Committee which was to oversee the selection of lessons, and when the latter were considered to be inadequate, to provide its own lesson materials.[14]

In the 1930's the transition from German to English made rapid progress and the younger generation found it increasingly difficult, if not impossible to use German lesson materials. At the 1939 convention the conference accepted a recommendation of the Publications Committee

to publish a sixty-four page Sunday School Quarterly in the English language for the younger classes, containing only one introduction, one text, based on the graded treatment of the International Lessons, but three expositions for pupils of the primary, intermediate and senior departments (respectively). The "explanations" (*Erklaerungen*) are to be written by three different persons in order to achieve a greater balance. We recognize this as an urgent need for achieving a greater unity in our Sunday school work. [15]

Three decades later hardly any adult classes in U.S. M.B. churches still used German Sunday school materials.[16] In Canada, as will be shown presently, the process of language change is still far from over, especially in the adult department of the Sunday school. With the change in language Mennonite Brethren also began to participate more actively in evangelical Sunday school conventions on a county or state level.

In the forties and fifties questions of the Sunday school curriculum and of suitable lesson materials were constantly on the agenda of the Sunday School Committee, and often came up for discussion on the conference floor. Leading brethren in the conference felt that denominational distinctives did not receive adequate consideration. At the General Conference held in Winkler (Manitoba) in 1951 the delegates accepted the following recommendation prepared by the Resolutions Committee:

> The Conference urges the Sunday school teachers and expositors of our Sunday school lessons to continue the nonresistance principle in the interpretation of the lessons when the war idea occurs in the Old Testament lessons, and have at least two lessons per year with special emphasis on nonresistance.[17]

This apprehension about the lack of New Testament teaching on Christian discipleship and nonresistance comes as no surprise, considering the lack of denominational Sunday school materials in Mennonite Brethren churches at that time. A survey in the 1950's disclosed that M.B. Sunday schools purchased their lesson material (except that for adults which was supplied by the M. B. Publishing House) from no fewer than fifteen different publishing houses. According to I. W. Redekopp, a member of the General Conference Sunday School Committee for many years, some of these would have seemed questionable to the fathers and founders of the M. B. Church.[18]

When the Sunday school was made an area conference matter in 1954, the question of curriculum continued to be a major concern in both Canada and the United States. In 1958 the Board for Sunday Schools and Related Activities of the United States M. B. Conference initiated a joint meeting with the Canadian Sunday School Committee to explore the advantages of the unified curriculum of the General Conference Mennonites and (Old) Mennonites. The Canadian Committee recommended these materials to its churches for the following reasons:

> a. The material places a more adequate emphasis upon certain truths of Anabaptist theology (discipleship).
> b. This is material which we can rightly call our own since it bears our imprint and the approval of our editors.
> c. This material bears the stamp of theological thoroughness and educational competence.[19]

The following year the conference accepted a recommendation to accept these "Mennonite Brethren" Sunday school materials for the primary, junior and intermediate departments "as they become available." This recommendation was reiterated at the conference held in Shafter (California) in 1960.[20] A significant change in the attitude and strategy of the Board of Sunday Schools and Related Activities, however, is evident from the recommendation presented to the conference in 1961. The recommendation reads: "We recommend that Scripture Press Sunday school materials be used in all departments of the Sunday school where M. B. Graded Sunday School Series or M. B. Adult Quarterly is not used."[21]

Whether the growing indifference toward an Anabaptist-oriented Sunday school curriculum was the result of lack of promotional activity or whether it was due to a new theological orientation cannot be ascertained from available records. By 1963 only fourteen churches were using the M. B. Imprint (Mennonite) material in the primary through intermediate departments. Eleven others were using it in one or two of these departments. In Canada the story was similar, but the decline of interest in the "Mennonite Brethren" Sunday school material was more gradual. Whether boards and conferences acted in the best interests of the churches on this important issue must be left to the verdict of history.

In other areas significant progress was made in the post-war era to improve the work of the Sunday school. In 1959 the United States Conference accepted the "Guideline for Church Schools"[22] as its minimal standard for the Christian education program on the congregational level. The following provisions indicate the desire for "quality education" in the field of religious instruction.

Leadership

1. Teacher training. A minimum course of six fifty-minute periods.
2. Teachers and officers meetings. A minimum of six meetings during the year other than teacher training.

Organization

3. A department Sunday school. A minimum of two departments for schools less than 100; three for schools of 100-200; four for schools of 200-300; and six for schools over 300.
4. A Graded Vacation Bible School. A minimum course of one week.
5. A Graded Wednesday Night Bible School.
6. Graded materials in all church schools.
7. Private classrooms. A minimum of 70 percent of the church school classes in classrooms with permanent or semi-permanent walls.

Outreach

8. Attendance Records. An individual attendance record for each enrollee in church school.
9. Attendance Followup. A contact program of all absentees.
10. Church Members Attendance. A minimum of 90 percent of the resident church members attending Sunday school. [23]

In keeping with the above guidelines the committee also recommended the introduction of the ETTA (Evangelical Teacher Training Association) course and the Gospel Light Record System for record keeping. Special teacher training institutes were also sponsored at

Tabor College and Pacific College in cooperation with the committees of the respective district conferences.

With the appointment of Elmo Warkentin as Executive Secretary for the Board of Church Schools in 1961 (from 1965 to 1969 Executive Secretary of the Board of Evangelism and Christian Education) a new emphasis on evangelism and missionary outreach was initiated. The program of the so-called "Decade of Enlargement" (1965-1975)[24] provided opportunities for self-study of existing programs and incentives for a more aggressive outreach in the community. From the records of Sunday school attendance it would appear that many of the objectives of the above program have been realized primarily in urban areas. This can be partly explained in terms of the general pattern of a constantly declining rural population and increasing movement to the cities.

In 1966 a new training program for Christian workers was launched. The Service Training Program (STP) is designed to provide leadership and service training for all church members. It offers approximately fifty individual courses of study. By 1968 the Christian Education Office had sent out 800 "Certificates of Credit" to people who had completed one or more courses in the Service Training Program. More and more Christian education, such as Sunday school curriculum, *Sunday School Standard* and athe Service Training Program, is done cooperatively with the brethren from Canada. Since 1969 Loyal Martin has provided strong leadership in Christian education. He also serves as field director for the students at the M. B. Biblical Seminary at Fresno.

2. Developments in Canada

The early Sunday schools in Mennonite Brethren churches in Canada developed along lines similar to those in the United States. The first Sunday school was organized in the M. B. Church at Winkler, Manitoba, in 1889, one year after the founding of the church. According to A. A. Kroeker, long-time chairman of the Canadian Sunday School Committee, growth and development of the Sunday school was very slow during the first twenty-five years. In Manitoba, for instance, there were only four Sunday schools by the end of that period.[25] Moreover, early Sunday schools lacked proper facilities as well as qualified teachers.

After 1925 the number of Sunday schools increased rapidly and great strides were made in improving teacher training. The numerical increase in the Sunday schools can in part be attributed to the large influx of Mennonite Brethren families who came to Canada from Russia at this time, but in part this growth was also the result of a better trained staff in most churches. Special recognition must be given here to the Bible schools who gave primary attention to the preparation and training of Sunday school workers. When the Evangelical Teacher

Training Association was formed in the United States in 1931, the Canadian Bible schools readily accepted the invitation to become members of that association. Through this affiliation a new and higher standard for Sunday schools, and especially for the training of Sunday school teachers, was established and in some measure enforced.

The first statistical report presented by J. F. Redekop to the Canadian M. B. Conference in 1943, affords certain insights into the nature and scope of Sunday school activities.[26] According to the report, there were Sunday schools in all sixty-six churches of the conference, and these were being served by 513 teachers and 217 assistants. Of these teachers, 295 had taken Sunday school courses, and an additonal 149 had received other special training. The total enrollment that year stood at 5,789 — about 2,000 less than the total church membership for the year.

With regard to Sunday school materials the statistician reported that thirty-two congregations used graded lessons, eighteen used Bible stories, and in three churches both were used. The International lesson outlines were used in most adult Bible classes. According to J. F. Redekop, a major problem was the language of instruction. In forty-three Sunday schools (67½) the German language was being used and in the others (33%) insruction was bilingual.

When the need for English lesson materials became more acute, the conference, guided by the S. S. Committee, decided that a way should be sought to retain unity in the curriculum in a bilingual constituency. This led to the arrangement with Scripture Press to adopt their outlines and translate them into German. The brethren A. H. Unruh, B. J. Braun, G. D. Huebert and others were made responsible for adapting these outlines to denominational needs. On the basis of the Scripture Press outlines the lessons were rewritten in the German language.

The Scripture Press materials were accepted with some reservations not only at the General Conference level, as noted earlier, but also in the Canadian Conference. In 1957 the latter adopted a recommendation by the Sunday School Committee to participate in the publication of graded lesson materials on an inter-Mennonite basis. A. P. Regier, who was appointed Mennonite Brethren editor for the new series, worked diligently to introduce these new materials in the Canadian Conference. At the 1957 convention he pointed out that the congregations were rapidly adopting the English language in their Sunday schools. "During this period of transition," Regier stated, "we are looking for English materials that we can heartily recommend, and which will also promote and preserve our unity. In this material (inter-Mennonite) we see how one can change from one language to another, and yet remain true to the faith of Scripture and of the fathers."[27]

In 1959 the new "Mennonite Brethren Graded Sunday School Series" were introduced in the primary departments in all congregations. In 1960 the new lesson material was also introduced in the junior and intermediate departments. More than 100 changes suggested from time to time by the Mennonite Brethren editors, A. P. Regier and Orlando Harms, had been accepted and incorporated in the preparation of these lessons.[28] In 1962 the chairman of the Sunday School Committee, I. W. Redekopp, reported to the conference that the new Sunday school materials were well received, with only a few exceptions. "The main difficulty," Redekopp claimed, "seemed to lie in the methods rather than in doctrine."[29] The members of the Committee of Reference and Counsel endorsed the material and encouraged the S. S. Committee in their endeavor.

By 1964, however, churches began to cancel their orders for the new material and the committee voiced its concern with regard to future participation in this inter-Mennonite endeavor. "We had hoped that some of our Anabaptist distinctives could be emphasized," H. R. Baerg reported, "without weakening our traditional stand on evangelism. . . . However, this appears to be most difficult, if not impossible."[30] Not all delegates shared the views of the committee, but by 1966 the "Mennonite Brethren Graded Sunday School Series" were on their way out in many churches. The main problems appear to have been methodological, rather than theological, since the new materials made greater demands with regard to the preparation of the teacher. As in the United States, so also in Canada, Mennonite Brethren churches turned to Scripture Press for their Sunday school curriculum. The decline of M.B. Sunday school material may be observed in the following table.

TABLE III
Mennonite Brethren Graded Sunday School Series Orders

	Oct. — Dec. 1962	Apr. — June 1963	Apr. — June 1964	Apr. — June 1965
Primary Pupil's Books	1881	1889	1478	1151
Junior Pupil's Books	1569	1542	1255	1021
Intermediate Pupil's Books	1343	1385	1092	887[31]

The Bible schools have played a major role in the training of Sunday school teachers. Special Sunday school teachers' courses conducted at the Mennonite Brethren Bible College also made a significant contribution. During the last decade Christian education conferences, which generally focus on the total church training program, have been conducted on a provincial as well as on a Canadian conference level. A Sunday school paper, the *M.B. Sunday School Instructor*, appeared in 1952. The *Instructor* served as a means to improve teaching

33. A. A. Schroeter   34. A. A. Kroeker   35. J. W. Vogt

methods, to promote new lesson materials, and to suggest ideas and helps for special occasions.

In 1964 the Canadian Sunday School (and Youth) Committee initiated a new ministry to promote the work of Christian education in the conference. George Konrad, a Bible school teacher engaged in post-graduate studies at Fort Worth, Texas, was appointed as executive secretary on a part-time basis. His job description included the writing of articles for the *Youth Worker*, preparing educational literature, corresponding with churches about educational needs, giving counsel and advice where required, and serving as speaker for Christian education conferences.[32] After the reorganization of the Canadian Conference in 1966, the interim Board of Christian Education assumed responsibility for the Sunday school, for youth work, and for church music. The new board appointed Wilmer Kornelson as executive secretary in 1967 with responsibilities related to the whole area of Christian education.

3. *General Observations*

A number of brethren deserve special recognition for many years of devoted service in the interests of better Sunday schools in the M. B. Conference. A. A. Schroeder of Reedley, California provided effective leadership as chairman of the Sunday School Committee of the General Conference. A. A. Kroeker served in the same capacity for many years in the Canadian Conference. In recent years, D. E. Redekop has given good leadership in this work. In addition to the executive secretaries and other workers mentioned earlier, a number of brethren have written lesson materials for the M. B. Quarterly for many years. Their services were recognized by the Christian Education Committee of the General Conference in 1969. Plaques were presented to D. Edmond Hiebert, J. B. Toews, G. W. Peters, G. D. Huebert, and

Orlando Harms in special ceremonies in Winnipeg, Hillsboro, and Fresno.

The following statistical report presents an overall picture of Christian education activities in the General Conference of Mennonite Brethren of North America for the year 1968, as reported at the 1969 conference.

TABLE IV
Church Educational Activities

	Canada	United States	Total
Sunday School Enrollment	19,986	16,293	36,279
Sunday School Teachers	1,982	1,719	3,701
Teacher Training Enrollment	543	722	1,265
Daily Vacation Bible School Enrollment	10,770	7,416	18,186
Midweek Services (No. of churches)	110	86	196
Women's Service Groups	113	123	236
Men's Fellowship Groups	4	35	39
Youth Clubs	132	146	

In recent years great emphasis has been placed on a meaningful midweek training program to supplement Sunday school instruction. The Christian Service Brigade (for boys) and the Pioneer Girls programs have gained widespread acceptance in M. B. churches during the last few years. That these programs were accepted with some reservations by leading brethren can be concluded from the recommendation of the Board of Christian Education to the Canadian Conference in 1969. In a "rider" attached to the recommendation the brethren caution against the "militaristic aspect" of the program, and emphasize the fact "that this program should be a part of the total church program and not an end in itself."[34] This program has in many instances been more successful in community outreach than the Sunday school, because of its combination of recreational activities and various handicrafts with Bible studies and devotional periods.

Other agencies of community outreach have been daily vacation Bible schools (see table) and mission Sunday schools. In 1951, thirty-eight M. B. churches in Canada reported that they sponsored such schools in their respective areas.[35] In the United States, where the transition from German to English had occurred earlier, children of the community were integrated more readily into the regular Sunday school program, with a possible exception being found in areas where Mexican-Americans still used the Spanish language.

The significance of the Sunday school for the growth (and even survival!) of the Mennonite Brethren Church can hardly be overestimated. The Sunday school of today is the basis for the church of tomorrow, since more than 80 percent of Mennonite Brethren church members come from the ranks of the Sunday school.[36] Since the separation of church and state in modern society has led to the elimination of all religious instruction in the public schools of America, we agree with Roger Babson, noted statistician and economist, that "there never was a time in the history of our nation, when the Sunday school was so much needed."[37]

II. Youth Work in the Mennonite Brethren Church

One of the greatest spiritual assets of the M. B. Church through the years has been a large, active youth group. Young people have often provided the vision and dynamic for blazing new trails in evangelism and Christian service. Denominational leaders from other churches have expressed their amazement (and sometimes envy) at the active participation of Mennonite Brethren young people in the work and worship of the church. This brief survey will be restricted to one particular aspect of "youth work," namely that ministry of the church which aims at building youth-constituted and youth-oriented fellowships within the context of the total church program.

1. *Early Developments in Russia*

The early Mennonite Brethren Church was a youthful church. According to a study made by Alan Peters, most of the first eighteen brethren were young married men with very small children.[38] This youthfulness of the adult members in the original church necessarily limited the number of young people in the Mennonite Brethren fellowship. It is not surprising, therefore, that one finds no record of any youth emphasis in the early church.

This lack of emphasis on youth, and on its special problems and needs, however, also persisted when conditions changed and relatively large numbers of young people became members of the M. B. Church. This tendency to neglect the young people in the church seems to have been historically conditioned. Mennonites in general, including the early Brethren, believed that the training of youth, even in matters of morality and religion, was the function of the school. Since the Mennonites were in full control of both elementary and secondary schools, provision was made for thorough instruction in biblical history, church history, and related subjects. From P. M. Friesen's comprehensive treatment of the "school-question" (*Schulwesen*)[39] one gathers the impression that he also shared this view.

The deeper spiritual needs of young people were not met, however, even by schools that provided religious instruction, in many instances under competent Christian teachers. As a result early youth activities and ministries arose spontaneously out of the spiritual concern of certain individuals for young people. How young people sometimes suffered because of a lack of spiritual nurture can be seen from the memoirs of G.P. Froese, who had become a member of the M.B. Church around 1885:

> The church had Bible study hours (*Bibelstunden*), Sunday school, and a church choir. But the young people were left too much to themselves. Bible schools did not exist at the time. . . . It may well be, that other congregations were farther ahead in making provisions for their young people. From the Molotschna M.B. Church it was reported that brethren had been appointed to work with young people. Our ministers were otherwise helpful in assisting (young people) to come to a true faith. But they were governed too much by the thought that after conversion we were safe. . . . I can only say that as a result I have suffered much. 40

In the first two decades of the twentieth century youth fellowship groups became generally accepted in the M. B. churches of Russia. It should be noted, however, that there was a separate organization for young men, the *Juenglingsverein* (young men's fellowship) and also for young women, the *Jungfrauenverein* (young women's fellowship). These fellowship meetings were not only attended by members of the church, but also by the unsaved relatives and friends of members. The purpose of these meetings was to promote the spiritual growth of believers, and to influence the unsaved to make a personal commitment to Christ.

According to A. H. Unruh, these "associations" were not so much a result of church policy, but rather a result of the vision of deeply concerned individuals who acted as "youth sponsors,"41 naturally with the approval and blessing of the church. After the large revivals in 1924-25, large youth festivals were also organized, but all such activities were terminated in the early years of the Stalin regime.

2. *Early Developments in America*

The North American situation differed widely from that in Russia. Here the principle of separation of church and state, as noted earlier, also implied that secular public schools were without any religious instruction. On the other hand, the churches had complete freedom to develop their educational and youth ministries as they pleased. At first, however, as Walter and Katie Wiebe remind us, "narrow viewpoints in regard to youth work had to be overcome."42

The first youth organizations among Mennonite Brethren of the United States were known as *Jugendvereine* (youth associations or youth fellowships).43 These *Jugendvereine* were begun in most of the churches in the early years and have provided opportunities for self-expression and the involvement of many young people. The *Jugendverein* was in several ways a unique institution. According to Walter and Katie Wiebe, it served an admirable purpose in providing a common experience of Christian fellowship and service for old and young Christians. In these services old and young joined in testimonies, Bible reading and song. . . . Christian Endeavor was an integrating factor in the spiritual life of our churches. There is nothing like it in many of our churches today. [44]

One thing seems clear from the available records of the early decades of church life in North America: Mennonite Brethren congregations did not experience any "generation gap" or "communication gap" between the older and younger members in those days.

In later years, especially in the 1920's the *Jugendverein* underwent a gradual transformation. The young people's societies were organized along constitutional lines with a specific membership.[45] There also appeared a shift in emphasis from mutual fellowship to public service. "In many churches," Alan Peters observes, "the *Jugendverein* developed into a periodic Sunday evening service for the benefit of the whole church, where youth in the church presented a program of general interest to the whole church. Thus, the *Jugendverein* was no longer a ministry *for* youth, but a ministry *by* youth."[46]

During the 1930's youth leaders and concerned pastors became increasingly aware of the inadequacies of the traditional pattern of youth work. Many young people as well felt the need for a program designed exclusively to meet the spiritual and social needs of youth. The "youth fellowships" (the English equivalent of the *Jugendvereine*) that came into existence in most churches prior to World War II were a direct response to a growing need throughout the brotherhood.

In 1945, J. W. Vogt, chairman of the Youth Committee of the General Conference, was able to report on this new phenomenon in the M. B. constituency.

The Christian Fellowship organizations are increasing slowly but steadily throughout our General Conference. We attribute this to the fact that they are filling a definite need for Bible study and spiritual fellowship of our young people everywhere. The support given to this organization by the local churches is greatly appreciated and we trust the C.F. will be a strengthening factor spiritually and morally of our whole conference constituency. Our committee has been assisting young people in organizing a Christian Fellowship upon their request as much as was possible to do through correspondence. [47]

From this report it is obvious that the conference had become actively involved in youth work. The first documentary evidence, however, for organizational involvement in youth work is found some twelve years earlier in the conference minutes of 1933. In that year, William J. Bestvater, secretary of the committee of a "Young People's Union" (*Jugendbund*) presented a recommendation to the conference which provided for the preparation and publication of quarterly leaflets of study helps for young people's organizations in the churches. P. R.

Lange, H. D. Wiebe and W. J. Bestvater were made responsible for the production of these study materials.[48]

The Youth Committee of the M. B. General Conference came into being at the Reedley convention in 1936. In 1937 this committee began to publish the *Christian Leader*, the first conference periodical in the English language dedicated to the interests of young people. P. H. Berg was appointed editor. It is rather interesting to note that this paper continued under the jurisdiction of the Youth Committee until 1951, when it became the official English organ of the conference.

The 1951 General Conference *Yearbook* contains the earliest statistics on youth work for all districts in North America. Of special significance is the fact that in Canada the *Jugendverein* was still the main youth organization, whereas in the United States the "Youth Fellowship" groups were showing substantial numerical increase.

TABLE V
Youth Organizations[49]

	Canadian District	Central District	Southern District	Pacific District	Total
No. of churches which have a *Jugendverein*	66	11	25	15	117
No. of churches which do not have a *Jugendverein*	10	2	3	3	18
No. of churches having an M. B. Youth Fellowship	0	7	13	12	32
No. of churches having no M. B. Fellowship	75	6	15	6	102
No. of churches with other youth organizations	66	3	2	4	75

Although youth work officially became an area conference responsibility only in 1954, youth organizations of the district conferences began to function more or less independently some ten to fifteen years earlier, and thus the youth activities of this later period are best described in terms of developments in the United States and Canada respectively.

3. *Youth Work in the United States*

The Youth Committee of the General Conference continued to play an important role in the promotion of youth work in the M. B. churches in the United States. The major concern of this committee in the late 1930's was the strengthening and promotion of the *Christian Leader* as an effective youth organ. The committee also encouraged the establishment of a "Christian Fellowship" for young people in every congregation.[50] Two booklets were published by the Youth Committee: *Your Church and You*, by F. C. Peters, and *What I Owe*, by C. E. Fast.

Most of the youth work was done, however, on a district conference level. The Central District Conference was the first to establish a district youth committee. This was in 1941. The Southern District followed shortly after, although a youth meeting for the whole district had been held as early as 1939 at the Ebenfeld M.B. Church (near Hillsboro). The Pacific District Conference was last to recognize youth work as a part of its responsibility. In 1948 the conference on the West Coast established a standing youth committee. This is not the earliest date, however, for organized young people's work in local congregations. The young people of the Bakersfield M.B. Church, for instance, had organized into a "Christian Youth Fellowship" as early as 1938.[51]

On the local church level youth work usually includes all or some of the following aspects, depending on the size and special needs of the group. A local Christian Fellowship organization conducts a regular program of services for young people at various age levels. In many churches these are held as an adjunct to the regular Sunday evening services. In midweek services there is usually a Bible study class for young people. All youth organizations sponsor a program of social and recreational activities adapted to the seasons. In addition, many youth groups are actively involved in a community-outreach program.

The district youth committees are primarily involved in the planning and supervising of the annual youth camps in their respective districts. This phase is perhaps developed most fully in the Pacific District Conference. In both the Southern and Central districts the youth committees have also sponsored youth rallies which are held in conjunction with the annual district conferences. These rallies were designed to integrate the young people's interests more fully with the work of the larger brotherhood, and thus played a significant role in making youth and its work an integral part of the conference.

When youth work became an "area" responsibility in 1954 the United States Conference at its second session in 1958 established a conference youth committee which in 1963 was renamed the Board of Youth Services. This board moved forward with vision and energy to implement the projections accepted two years earlier. First on the list was the hiring of a full-time executive secretary. This had been a major concern of the General Conference Youth Committee almost twenty years earlier.[52] In 1964 the Board of Youth Services was finally in a position to announce that Alan Peters had been appointed as the first Director of Youth Services. When Peters terminated his ministry at the end of 1965, the board was unable to find a replacement.

During the ensuing interim (1965-68) the board sponsored "youth caravans" which received widespread popular acceptance. The "youth caravan" consisted of a small group (four or five young people) deeply committed to Christ and the church, who would travel from church to church accompanied by a "youth sponsor." The purpose of the "caravan" was to communicate Christ — youth to youth. This ministry, carried on during the summer months, inspired youth groups in the churches to a life of Christian discipleship and service.

Since 1968 the Board of Youth Services has been merged with the Board of Evangelism and Christian Education. A special "youth commission" of this board is now in charge of coordinating and supervising youth work.

4. *Youth Work in Canada*

Youth work in the early Mennonite Brethren churches in Manitoba and Saskatchewan followed the pattern set by the congregations in the United States. This is understandable since the churches in Manitoba had been founded through the evangelistic outreach of the brethren from the south, and the first churches in Saskatchewan were established by immigrants from Minnesota, Nebraska, North Dakota, and several other states. By 1925 the *Jugendverein* was an established institution in these churches.

The large influx of Mennonite Brethren from Russia in the 1920's (described in chapter eleven) did not result in immediate changes in the pattern of youth work, although it appears that the *Jugendverein* in its traditional form did not become firmly established in many of these new congregations. Difficult economic conditions in the thirties and government service of many young men in the early forties, imposed serious limitations on the nature and scope of youth work during those years. The denominational Bible institutes rendered invaluable services to many Mennonite Brethren young people since they provided systematic Bible instruction not available in most congregations during that period.

The end of World War II marks a turning point in the history of youth work in the Canadian M.B. Conference. The experiences of the war had revealed serious weaknesses in the theological views of many young men who were called to give an account of their faith when they appeared before the Mobilization Board. Many were ignorant of scriptural teaching as well as of historical distinctives to which their church was committed.

In 1944 a joint meeting of several boards authorized H. S. Voth, the chairman of the Board of Directors of the Canada Inland Mission, to appoint a three-man committee. This committee was charged with the responsibility of preparing a "working plan" (*Arbeitsplan*) for youth work to be presented at the next conference.[53] H. F. Klassen, who had been leader of the youth work in Manitoba, was appointed chairman, and Reuben Baerg (Hepburn) and J. A. Toews, Jr. (Coaldale) as members.

In 1945 youth work appeared for the first time on the agenda of the Canadian M.B. Conference. In his report, Klassen called attention to the "shaking of the foundations," and the need for intensive youth work.

A new world order (or disorder) and new philosophies of life confront our young people. The latter, on the other hand, have more education and more contacts with the outside (non-Mennonite) world than the previous generation. If left to themselves, young people lack the spiritual discipline that could save them from unnecessary pitfalls. That so many young men went into the military, that so many young men and women come to the cities where they are reluctant to identify themselves as Mennonites we are compelled to admit as tragic facts. This calls for repentance for our past failures and the resolve to make better provisions for the future. — We must begin now to think of the possibility of another war and teach our children. Our Sunday school, youth fellowships, youth instruction, youth literature, etc., must all be governed by one sacred, overruling purpose: To lead our youth to Jesus Christ as the only Savior, to deepen their religious life, to assist them to perform better Christian service in their own churches, and to win them for the work of the kingdom of God in the whole world.[54]

The conference responded favorably to the report and the projections of the interim committee. A youth committee was elected composed of a central executive and representatives from the provinces. H. F. Klassen, Abram DeFehr, and David Reimer, all from Manitoba, were elected to serve as Youth Executive. F. C. Thiessen (British Columbia), J. A. Toews, Jr. (Alberta), and D. B. Wiens (Saskatchewan), were the provincial representatives.

The committee was charged by the conference with the responsibility of translating the booklet, *Fundamentals of Faith* (by H. F. Toews) into the German language, to be used in youth meetings as a basis for instruction in Bible doctrine.

The conference also accepted a recommendation of the Youth Committee to publish a youth paper in both German and English.[55] In 1945 the Youth Committee took over the publication of the *Konferenz-Jugendblatt*, formerly a publication of the Manitoba Youth Committee. This illustrated quarterly was published in Winnipeg until 1954 and edited by H. F. Klassen. Beginning in May, 1954, it was printed in Yarrow, B.C. and edited by H. H. Voth. During the last few years of its existence it was issued bi-monthly, and almost exclusively in English. This language change in the paper reflected the cultural and linguistic changes in the constituency.

Through its pictorial surveys of youth activities and its timely articles the *Konferenz-Jugendblatt* served as a strong unifying influence among the young people of the Canadian Conference during a difficult transition period. In 1957 this youth periodical was merged with the *Mennonite Observer*, published by the Christian Press.[56]

Other publications of the Canadian Conference Youth Committee include a pamphlet entitled, *Why I Should Be a Church Member* prepared jointly by F. C. Peters and A. H. Unruh and published in 1952. In the same year *The Youth Worker*, edited by Walter and Katie Wiebe, also appeared for the first time. This periodical, published at various intervals in its twenty-year history, has provided valuable suggestions and stimulating program materials for youth work on the local church level. In 1962 H. H. Dueck was appointed as editor of *The Youth Worker*, after the Wiebes resigned.

The Youth Committee through the years has sponsored various projects for financial support by youth groups throughout Canada. The projections for 1962-63 provide an insight into the nature and scope of this phase of youth work.

M.B. Bible College bursaries	$ 100.00
Radio ministry in Japan	1,000.00
Radio ministry in Quebec	1,500.00
Russian radio ministry in Saskatoon	1,000.00
Bethany Bible School, India	1,000.00
Youth work in South America	1,000.00
Undesignated project	500.00
Total	6,100.00 [57]

Beginning in 1960 the committee has also recommended the observance of the last week in January as "youth week." Youth workers' conferences have been sponsored from time to time by this committee.

Understandably, much of the youth work has been carried on by provincial youth committees. Manitoba took an early lead in this area by publishing its own youth paper and organizing annual youth rallies. These two-day rallies have emphasized missions, Christian service in the community, and a life of discipleship. In Saskatchewan, youth work has developed along a somewhat different pattern. In this province the Bible schools (located at Herbert, Dalmeny, and Hepburn) have provided leadership by sponsoring youth rallies and missionary conferences. The Western Children's Mission (later called the M.B. Mission of Saskatchewan) has provided service outlets in their extensive program of Daily Vacation Bible schools, camp work, and evangelism.[58]

In Alberta organized youth work began in the Coaldale M.B. Church as early as 1928. Sunday evening services were often devoted to the interests of young people. The provincial youth committee followed the same pattern as in the other provinces, sponsoring annual youth as well as youth workers' conferences.

In the Fraser Valley of British Columbia, with the heaviest

concentration of Mennonite Brethren young people in Canada, organized youth work was slow in beginning but once started, it moved ahead rapidly. In the last two decades the Youth Committee of the province has sponsored youth rallies, youth workers' conferences, the organization of the camp society, and various mission projects. In recent years Columbia Bible Institute (formerly Mennonite Brethren Bible Institute) at Clearbrook has served as a center for clinics and workshops in leadership training, both for Christian education (Sunday school) and youth work.

In Ontario annual youth rallies were sponsored for many years by the Sunday School Committee. In 1950 a youth committee was elected by the conference. This committee, in addition to organizing youth rallies and youth workers' conferences, sponsored the publication of *This Way* in 1958. This pamphlet, written by J. J. Toews, contains specific directives and words of counsel for young Christians. Two years earlier, a "Study Course Outline for Local Youth Groups" had been distributed in all the churches of the Ontario Conference. For a number of years, the Ontario M.B. churches sponsored six radio broadcasts in which many of the young people participated.[59] This involvement of young people in a radio ministry also occurred in several other provinces.

The Canada-wide youth rally held at the Banff School of Fine Arts on December 28 to 31, 1971, near Banff, Alberta, constitutes a milestone in the youth work of the Canadian M.B. Conference. Organized by the Board of Christian Education through its executive secretary, Wilmer Kornelson, this rally attracted young people from every province in which Mennonite Brethren live and work. From Nova Scotia in the east 3 had come, Quebec sent 1, Ontario 85, Manitoba 225, Saskatchewan 125, Alberta 65, and British Columbia 250. Seventeen came from the United States, including a small group of young people who were there to study the feasibility of a similar rally in their country and to consider the possibility of a North American rally of this kind some time in the future.

The mornings were devoted to study, interaction, and training sessions and the afternoons to recreation and various special events. The addresses on "Commitment" by F. C. Peters in the evening sessions were regarded by many participants as the highlights of the Banff rally. The response of hundreds of young people to the spiritual challenge of these meetings, according to one reporter, will make "Banff the most momentous spiritual event for our brotherhood in 1971."[60]

It should also be noted that some Mennonite Brethren young people in both Canada and the United States have been involved in such inter-denominational or non-denominational youth movements as Youth for Christ and Young Life. On university and college campuses M.B. students have often assumed a leading role in promoting Inter-Varsity Christian Fellowship (IVCF) and Campus Crusade.

III. Christian Camps in the Mennonite Brethren Constituency

The history of Christian camping in the Mennonite Brethren Conference (like that of the Sunday school) still waits to be written. The spiritual impact of Christian camps on the children and young people in Mennonite Brethren communities can hardly be overestimated. Quite often when congregations listen to the testimonies of baptismal candidates, they hear accounts from young people who experienced conversion or renewal of commitment to Christ while attending a Christian camp.

1. *Christian Camping in the United States*

In the United States the Pacific District has perhaps developed its camping program more fully than the other districts. The Hartland Christian Association was organized in 1945 by members of the M.B. and K.M.B. churches in the Reedley area. The association owns and operates the Hartland Bible Camp, located approximately ten miles east of Badger in Tulare County, providing a full range of camp activities for all age groups. A special "camping committee," elected by the Pacific District Conference, is responsible for the camping program with its spiritual ministry.

In the Southern District a camp program was begun in the early 1940's. At first attendance comprised only young people, but later the program was expanded to serve all age groups, including married couples. Camp facilities are usually leased from camping associations in the area. Since 1965 the Mennonite Brethren have become directly involved in the operation and financial support of the Deer Creek Christian Camp, Pine, Colorado, owned and operated by a group of Christian businessmen. In 1969 camp director Richard Heinrichs reported the following statistics to the Southern District Conference: "We have operated four Southern District camps (this year) with two at Deer Creek, Colorado, and two at Red Rock Canyon, Oklahoma. . . . Approximately 311 youth have enjoyed 1860 camper days in the Southern District planned camps."[61] In addition, the youth committee also encouraged and worked with regional camping programs.

The camp program of the Central District Conference has been in operation since 1949. Earlier camps were conducted at various places. In 1960 the camp was held at Lake Metigoshe, North Dakota. Since the early sixties Byron Bible Camp near Huron, South Dakota, has become the established camping center of the conference.[62]

2. *Christian Camping in Canada*

Several factors contributed to the widespread interest in Christian camping among Canadian Mennonite Brethren after World War II. Rapid urbanization, growing affluence, and a concern for the physical, social, and spiritual welfare of children and young people combined to give an impetus to the establishment of "summer camps" throughout the country. Perhaps because of the brief summer season, the Mennonite Brethren in the prairie provinces pioneered in this area.

In Manitoba the Mennonite Brethren established two camps. The Lake Winnipeg Mission Camp located near Arnes on the shores of Lake Winnipeg, was established in 1948 by a group of brethren from Winnipeg. Abram A. Kroeker and David Redekop spearheaded the movement. Through the years the brethren have emphasized the missionary character of the camp. Of the 252 children attending the three camps in 1954, for example, ninety-seven were "mission" children. Seventy-six decisions for Christ were recorded.[63] At present the camp offers facilities and services throughout the year under the supervision of a full-time camp director.

A similar camp project has been sponsored by Mennonite Brethren in the Winkler area. The Winkler Bible camp is located six miles northwest of the town of Winkler. Construction of buildings was begun in 1949-50. The camp can accommodate about eighty children at one time. The three children's camps sponsored in 1951 enrolled a total of 212.

John Boldt, director of this camp for a number of years, stated their objective as follows: "Our aim was to carry the ideals of the Christian life into all camp activities."[64]

In Saskatchewan camp work was begun even earlier than in Manitoba. The West Bank Bible Camp in South Saskatchewan was started by the Western Children's Mission around 1944. Under the energetic leadership of Rudolph Wirsche (Flowing Well) this camp was built up at a site three miles south of Seventeen Mile Bridge, northwest of Swift Current. Beginning with the 1948 camping season the work was enlarged to include youth camps. Total number of attendants for that year was 141.[65]

In North Saskatchewan the Redberry Bible Camp in the Blaine Lake area was officially opened in July, 1953. In previous years the M.B. Mission of Saskatchewan had operated the Sand Beach Camp, but since the latter campsite had been almost inaccessible during rainy weather, the brethren decided to move the camp buildings to the new location — a distance of sixty miles. Here a very intensive camp program has been developed for both children and young people. The first children's camp on the new grounds attracted 160 campers. Camping constitutes an integral part of the outreach program of the Saskatchewan M.B. churches.

Because the Alberta Mennonite Brethren congregations are scattered over a vast geographical area, it has been more difficult to organize activities of this nature on a conference level. Camps for young people were organized for a number of years and held on campgrounds leased from the Canadian Sunday School Mission in the Vauxhall area of Southern Alberta. In the 1960's the brethren were able to establish Camp Evergreen situated in the foothills of the Rocky Mountains.

In British Columbia the "camp idea" met considerable resistance in many of the Fraser Valley churches. During the winter of 1958-59 the Mennonite Brethren Camp Society was organized. The society purchased sixty acres of land overlooking Cultus Lake. Under the direction of Jack Block of the Fraserview M.B. Church (Vancouver), who was able to engage much voluntary labor, the society erected eleven cabins and a spacious dining hall by the summer of 1959. Here again the missionary character of the camp was evident from its very inception. In cooperation with the West Coast Children's Mission the society enrolled 168 children during the first summer. Over forty decisions for Christ were recorded, most of them children attending mission churches.[66] The Columbia Bible Camp presently offers year-round facilities and services to church and youth groups. The society has also employed a full-time camp director since 1970.

The Ontario Conference began to give serious attention to the question of a suitable site for a youth and children's camp in 1952. This need, as well as the need of Eden Christian College (a Mennonite Brethren high school near Virgil) was met by landscaping the Eden campus and completing a large auditorium in 1955. The first children's camp was held in the summer of 1953, when more than 100 children attended. In the afternoons children are bused to nearby Lake Ontario for recreational activities.

In 1971 the Camp Program Committee reported an enrollment of 169 campers for the four weeks in 1970, with approximately 75 percent coming from M.B. homes. A highly successful "teen camp" had also been organized with ninety-three young people in attendance. Both phases of work recorded decisions for Christ.[67]

In this cursory survey of the church agencies that are involved in teaching the children and training the young people of Mennonite Brethren in North America one cannot help but be impressed with the tremendous spiritual potential of the "church of tomorrow." One is equally impressed with the large number of dedicated teachers and workers who are faithfully responding to Christ's commission to teach them "to observe all that I have commanded you."

Chapter 15

Singing the New Song

Paul W. Wohlgemuth

Expression in music played a vital part in the birth of the
Mennonite Brethren Church. As is common to most renewal movements
a new type of song accompanied the revival spirit of this group of
believers. Many songs they had sung in the "old" church were good and
continued to be used. Nevertheless, their new life experience gave rise to
the use of a new type of song, namely the gospel song. Its subjective
texts, lively rhythms, and faster tempos blended well into this newer
style of religious worship. Furthermore, the use of musical instruments
became a part of this jubilant manifestation. Music, both new and old,
reflected the joyful liberating spirit which they felt as a result of their
new-found Christian experience.

In *Origin of the Mennonite Brethren Church* Jacob Becker relates
several incidents regarding the use of music during these revival days.
To many, these musical expressions were a part of the emotional
excesses of "ferment" (cf. chapter five) which seemed to put a cloud over
the movement. Becker quotes from the reports of visiting delegations
from the "old" church, who came to assess the nature of Mennonite
Brethren worship services, which included much music. Although the
opening and closing hymns were from the repertoire of the "old" church,
the many intervening songs "were sung to cheerful melodies
accompanied by the clapping of hands by some. Some displayed ecstasy
and made sounds which they called jubilations and groanings. . . ."[1]

Another new element introduced into the milieu of musical
experiences was the use of musical instruments. Undoubtedly their
musical experiences were enriched by the use of instruments as noted in
the description of a worship service in the home of A. Peters:

Their first song was accompanied by a harmonica and violin, but not in an unrestrained manner. The verses of the songs were first read (a line at a time — they had no song books) from the *Glaubensstimme*, Hiller's *Liederkaestlein*, and Gossner's *Schatzkaestlein* (in the possession of the leader) and then sung according to the tunes found in the *Glaubenstimme*. [2]

After attending a worship service, another visiting committee related that "while we were leaving and conversing outside the building with Bekker and others about one thing and another, several verses of a song were sung by the assembly accompanied by a flute." [3]

The use of musical instruments, however, brought considerable tensions to the brotherhood. An account is given concerning a drum maker, Herman Peters, who in a worship service, played his drum so loudly, accompanying the organs, flutes, violins, guitars and musical triangles, that the noise was heard over the entire village. When the mayor appeared and took away the drum, Peters simply made another. The fact that he later disassociated himself from the Mennonite Brethren movement [4] probably indicates that most members endorsed more subdued music for worship.

These accounts clearly indicate that a new song had entered the worship life of the Mennonite Brethren. By design they shortened their sermons, gave opportunity for personal testimony, and prayed and sang alternately in order to bring a more lively and joyful spirit into the worship service. Even though excesses were a part of the early movement, the main thrust was a genuine new spirit in worship supported by a new type of music.

The musical practices in Mennonite Brethren circles developed more as an outgrowth of its needs rather than by a prescribed pattern directed by personalities. Eventually music settled into serving the following general needs: (1) fostering a lively but meaningful spirit of worship, (2) lending reverence and spiritual feeling to the service, (3) undergirding the biblical emphasis in terms of doctrine, (4) assisting in the spiritual development of the believer, (5) giving expression to Christian fellowship and joy, (6) relating to all facets of the church and family life, and (7) promoting the missionary and evangelistic outreach of the church. [5]

From the very beginning Mennonite Brethren religious music was as vital in the home as it was in the church. Singing took place at mealtime with table graces, during family worship and at family visitation. Later, music lessons on violins, pianos, reed organs, etc., brought much music into the home. Although music-making has been an important activity in the past, its influence probably has diminished during the last two decades because of the introduction of radios, recordings, and televisions into the homes. However, in most homes one will find Bibles, one or more hymnbooks, and a piano.

Congregational Singing

Congregational singing probably has been at the heart of Mennonite Brethren music-making. Spirited congregational singing certainly was a hallmark of the early revival days, and is still greatly enjoyed. An interesting congregational singing practice was the use of the *Vorsaenger* (lead singer). He would set the pitch, recite the hymn line by line, and lead out in singing. The congregation would respond line by line with the melody, usually in unison. The *Vorsaenger*, a man who would sit at the front of the church, was expected to know all or most of the melodies. This developed into a very fine art and practice, followed partly because of the lack of hymnals.[6]

Some of the early hymnals in Russia were printed without notes. A common notation found in many other hymnals was numbers (*Ziffern*). The number notation was an aid in teaching note reading. An early collection designed for teaching singing in schools was the *Choralbuch* by Heinrich Franz. He issued both four-part (1860) and unison (1865) editions. The *Mennonite Encyclopedia* states that

Four-part singing in Mennonite congregations . . . started with the introduction of hand-copied collections of songs with notes and ciphers and the publication of the choralbooks. Four-part singing in congregations was gradually introduced through choirs, which were first school or community choirs and gradually found their place in the congregational worship.[7]

The popularity of the use of *Ziffern* is noted in that "J. Ewert transcribed the notes of the melodies to Gebhardt's *Frohe Botschaft* into ciphers, which were published in *Die Melodien der Frohen Botschaft* (Gnadenfeld, 1884)."[8]

The first German hymnal commonly accepted by Mennonite Brethren in Russia was T. Koebner's *Glaubensstimme*, a German Baptist publication. It came to North America with the migrations and was reprinted by the Mennonite Brethren Publishing House at Medford, Oklahoma, in 1905, edited by H. W. Grage, under the title *Zions Glaubensstimme*. Another popular collection was the *Heimatklaenge*. The *Mennonite Encyclopedia* states that it was

first published in Russia for the Mennonites by Isaak Born at Halbstadt, was taken over in 1903 by the Raduga Publishing House of Halbstadt. Seven editions appeared in Russia, after which A. Kroeker published the eighth revised edition in America. in the year 1924, which was followed by a second one (1939?) with notes.[9]

The extensively used hymnal, *Drei-Band*, was a collection of three songbooks, *Jubeltoene-Hosianna-Halleluja*. Another collection used widely among Mennonite Brethren included *Heimatklaenge-Glaubensstimme-Frohe Botschaft*. Both collections are of non-Mennonite Brethren origin.

After the migrations to North America had started, additional German hymnals were published by the Mennonite Brethren Publishing House at Hillsboro, Kansas. The two collections, *Zions-Klaenge* and *Neue Zions Lieder* are of interest since they were compiled by a Mennonite Brethren, J. J. Franz, and by D. B. Towner, Music Director at Moody Bible Institute. In addition to translating numerous texts, J. J. Franz wrote many of the tunes in these collections. A slightly different type of publication was the *Saenger-Bote*. It was a periodical published by the Mennonite Brethren Association of Singers (*Christlicher Saengerbund der Mennoniten Bruedergemeinde von Nord Amerika*) and edited by Aron G. Sawatzky, beginning in 1912. The *Lieder-Quelle* was a publication by Aron G. Sawatzky which appeared quarterly in 1929 and 1930. He wrote many of the songs in the latter two publications. These songbooks were basically of the gospel song type and were used extensively as inspirational literature for both worship services and Christian Endeavor (*Jugendverein*) meetings.

Probably the most popular of all German hymnals was *Evangeliums-Lieder 1 und 2* (1897) compiled by Walter Rauschenbusch and Ira D. Sankey. Because of its greater selections of gospel songs, this collection took the place of *Glaubensstimme* and *Glaubens-Harfe*.[10] It became the standard German hymnal used in the United States churches until their transition to the English language.

Evangeliums-Lieder was also in common usage in the Canadian Mennonite Brethren Conference until they published their own German hymnal, the *Gesangbuch* in 1952. In 1945, F. C. Thiessen, Dietrich Esau, and C. D. Toews were assigned the task of compiling the hymnal. After F. C. Thiessen died in 1950, the work was completed by the committee with the addition of the following members: Jacob Wedel, H. P. Neufeldt, Cornelius Klassen, Ben Horch, Peter Dick, and Dietrich Friesen.[11] The book was primarily intended as a tool to perpetuate the use of *Kernlieder* that had proved a spiritual inspiration to German-speaking Mennonite Brethren churches in Russia, Canada, United States and South America. The *Gesangbuch* went through several printings and was also used by some non-Mennonite Brethren congregations. It does reflect the influence of the *Evangeliums-Lieder* in that 30 percent of its hymns are from that source.

The Krimmer Mennonite Brethren published a German hymnal entitled *Die Geistreiche Lieder, Auswahl fuer Familien und Oeffentliche Erbauungen mit Sorgfalt gesammelt von der Krimmer Mennoniten-Brueder Gemeinde* (Elkhart, Ind., 1884). The K.M.B. evangelist-missionary, F. V. Wiebe, published a small German songbook in 1915 entitled *Erweckungs-Lieder* designed for use in his evangelistic meetings.

With the language transition beginning in the 1930's in the United States, and two decades later in Canada, it was inevitable that English hymnals would soon be introduced into the churches. The result was that a variety of hymnals appeared, again mostly of the gospel song type. *Tabernacle Hymns No. 3* seemed to be the most widely used.

The first mention of the possibility of the Mennonite Brethren Church compiling its own English hymnal came during the General Conference in 1945. The church membership felt that the English hymnals brought into churches from other sources were not adequately meeting their needs. There was also a growing awareness of the fact that the younger generation was on the verge of losing the heritage that was part of their culture.

The first official action taken on the compiling of a hymnal was the introduction of the following resolution:

> The Pacific District Conference has formulated the resolution that the General Conference investigate the possibility of publishing an all purpose hymnal which could be used in all departments of our churches; that this hymnal should include many of the gospel songs and hymns found in the hymn books used by our various churches, as well as some of the older choral numbers, which, although not used as frequently today, have genuine value and should be translated into the English language and preserved for this and future generations. [12]

Interest in this project was immediately evident. The General Conference accepted the recommendation of the Committee of Reference and Counsel "that we proceed energetically with the production of a song book with notes to satisfy the needs of our churches."[13] It also recommended that the hymnal should be produced both in the English and German languages. The following men were appointed to this committee: Ben Horch, Winnipeg; F. C. Thiessen, Abbotsford; Herbert C. Richert, Hillsboro; Cornelius Wall, Mountain Lake; and H. D. Wiebe, Bakersfield, with Richert serving as chairman.

Soon several problems began to emerge. One was that the Canadian Conference was in the process of publishing its own hymnal in the German language. The committee members felt that it would be an unnecessary duplication to publish a German and English hymnal along with the Canadian German hymnal. The 1948 General Conference decided to "recognize the German hymnal of Canada and proceed with arrangements of an English song book."[14] Herbert C. Richert was then authorized to appoint persons to assist him in publishing the hymnal. He chose P. C. Hiebert and L. J. Franz, the former serving as Aids to Worship Editor, while Richert served as Music Editor. Thus it became a United States project.

During the next three years the songbook committee compiled a list of seven hundred hymns and gospel songs which was published in the *Christian Leader*. As interested individuals and groups evaluated them, general trends and demands became apparent, resulting in the addition of many new hymns and gospel songs.

Several other groups, such as Richert's class in hymnology at Tabor College, along with other music teachers, helped in the selection of the hymns. On two different occasions ministers and church musicians gathered for all-day evaluating sessions where they listened to a mixed quartet sing through all the hymns and gospel songs on the list. The most critical work took place in what Richert called "The Hillsboro, Kansas, Meetings." During the fall and winter of 1951 a group of ministers and laymen met once a week, generally on Monday evenings from 7 to 10 p.m., for the expressed purpose of critically reading and examining every song. Resolutions authorizing the publication of the Mennonite Brethren hymnal and arranging for financial support were passed by the General Conference at Winkler, Manitoba, in 1951.[15]

Finally, after eight years of intensive work, the *Mennonite Brethren Church Hymnal* containing five hundred hymns came off the press in August, 1953. The demand for the hymnal was so great that the 7,500 copies of the first edition were immediately exhausted. It subsequently went through six printings with a total of 37,000 copies.

Its contents were largely from the gospel song tradition. Paul Wohlgemuth in his doctoral dissertation, "Mennonite Hymnals Published in the English Language," concludes "In comparison with earlier gospel song books used in Mennonite Brethren churches, the *Mennonite Brethren Church Hymnal* does present to its members a greater variety and better quality of hymn tunes."[16] B. J. Braun, chairman of the General Conference in 1953, evaluated the hymnal as "distinguished for its contents, its facilities for the ready use of its contents, and its broad scope of the evangelical message."[17]

Almost simultaneously with the publication of the Canadian German hymnal, *Gesangbuch der Mennoniten Bruedergemeinde* (1952), a new need began to appear in that country. With a gradual shifting from the use of German to the English language especially in Sunday schools, the need for an English hymnal was voiced. It was not until the 1955 Canadian Conference in Coaldale, Alberta, that the churches decided to publish an English translation of the *Gesangbuch*.

The task of compiling the hymnal was assigned to the Songbook Committee: Jacob Wedel, Cornelius Klassen, Henry Voth and Ben Horch. Many others assisted in this project, especially Mrs. Ben Horch. The Songbook Committee envisioned their objective in the light of the bilingual status of the church. Recognizing this they felt that this hymnal would:

First — afford the best opportunity for adopting into another language the spiritual heritage of congregational song epitomized for our forefathers by the term *Kernlieder* and

Second — assure the present time as most favorable for the retention of just such a bilingual position indefinitely and

Third — preserve the unifying concept of a "one hymnbook" congregation regardless of changing language problems. [18]

The problem of translating did not seem as much of a problem as did the concern of "recreating familiar spiritual concepts from one language origin into that of another. Musical considerations heightened the difficulties in terms of fixed melodies, fixed harmonies, and especially fixed rhythmic patterns."[19] It was discovered that many of the German *Kernlieder* were of better quality in their German translation than they had been in their original English. Consequently, some were retranslated into English.

Apparently the complete translation of the *Gesangbuch* was not an adequate solution to the changing language needs in the Canadian Mennonite Brethren churches for it went through only one printing. *The Hymn Book* (1960), nevertheless, was a step in the right direction for it did help keep alive the best of some of the traditional *Kernlieder*. Furthermore, it stands as a document of the hymn-singing practices and repertoire in the Canadian Mennonite Brethren churches during that period of history.

In view of the fact that *The Hymn Book* had received limited acceptance and the *Mennonite Brethren Church Hymnal* had been in use for a decade, a new interest arose in the publication of a new English hymnal by both the Canadian and United States conferences. The report of the Canadian Hymnbook Committee in 1963 states:

Our present English hymnbook, though satisfactory in many respects, nevertheless, has a number of serious weaknesses. Many fine hymns are not in it because they were not in the German *Gesangbuch*. Nor does the present book serve the more special needs of many of our new mission churches, so that they as well as many of our present churches, hesitate to purchase the present book and thus buy some other congregational hymnal. Many of the present translations are not too well received. Furthermore, many songs in the book are not really being used and could be replaced by better ones. There are insufficient hymns for children or young people.[20]

In the United States, pastors and church musicians indicated a need for more worship hymns and newer gospel songs which had become well known through meetings such as the Billy Graham Evangelistic campaigns and through the common use of the *Intervarsity Hymnal* among our young people. Sensing this need, the Canadian Hymnbook Committee and the United States Board of Church Music began preliminary discussions on the matter of publishing a new English hymnal.

During the area conferences in 1963, the respective music committees reported that both conferences were interested in publishing a common hymnal which would be a revision of the respective current hymnals of the two conferences. Work on this project was authorized by the area conferences (1963) in consultation with the respective Boards of Reference and Counsel, agreeing that it would become a General Conference project in 1966. A joint report[21] of the United States Board of Church Music and the Canadian Hymnbook Committee concerning this project was then given to the General Conference held in Winnipeg in 1963.

An inquiry was made into the possibility of joining the compiling of a new conjoint hymnal which had already been started by the "Old" Mennonites and the General Conference Mennonites. It was felt, however, that their work was too far along for effective influence by the Mennonite Brethren.

In January, 1965, two musicians selected from each area (total of four members) met in Winnipeg to discuss the organization and structure of the Hymnal Committee, selection of committee members, their duties and responsibilities, formulation of a survey for church music leaders and pastors regarding the Table of Contents and hymn selections, assignment of hymn studies in various areas, and the formulation of a tentative publishing schedule.

It was agreed that the Hymnal Committee should consist of two church musicians and one theologian from each of the area conferences. The area Boards of Reference and Counsel made the appointments of the theologians and the area Music Committees the musicians. Thus in June, 1965, the first meeting of the full Hymnal Committee was held in Fresno, California. The members were Paul Wohlgemuth (U.S.) — chairman, Eugene Gerbrandt (Can.), Peter Klassen (Can.), Dietrich Friesen (U.S.), Elmer Martens (U.S.), Victor Martens (Can.).

At this meeting a statement of the basic philosophy underlying the hymnal project was written and the Table of Contents revised. Most of the time, however, was given to evaluating each hymn in the Canadian and United States hymnals and selecting core material to be retained for the new hymnal. The project was officially undertaken by the General Conference at Corn, Oklahoma, in 1966, having previously been supported by the area conferences.[22]

The new hymnal of 678 hymns, entitled *Worship Hymnal,* finally came off the press in June, 1971. Because of the unexpectedly high prepublication sales, the first edition had to be increased from 15,000 to 25,000 copies. Within a year the first printing was exhausted and by 1973 the second printing of nearly 12,000 copies was made.

In its brief existence it seems to have proven itself as a worthy successor to the two Mennonite Brethren hymnals, *The Hymn Book* (Canadian, 1960) and the *Mennonite Brethren Church Hymnal* (United States, 1953). It retained its denominational tone through its selections of hymns and gospel songs as well as in the original contributions made by members of the Mennonite Brethren Church through translations, hymn texts, and musical settings. It also intended to be functional for any denomination of Christian believers of an evangelical persuasion. Subjects such as The Gospel Call, The Ministries of the Church (Christian Evangelism, Christian Missions, Christian Service, and Christian Nurture), Discipleship, and Social Concern were included to give expression to the evangelistic outreach of the Mennonite Brethren Conference. The addition of special sections for children and youth enhanced the hymnal's usefulness for all members. It was probably the first modern denominational hymnal to include contemporary folk hymns with chord indications for guitar accompaniment.

Marvin Hein, chairman of the General Conference commented thus on the project:

> Not to be overlooked is the fact that in this hymnal we have the first fruitful, cooperative effort in hymnal production between our Canadian and United States churches. As we come to appreciate hymns that are new to us but familiar to those who live above or below the border we will have reason to praise God that, in an age of increased polarization, we find it possible to have fellowship in worship, not only with God our Father and with His Son, Jesus Christ, but with one another. [23]

Of interest were the positive reviews which the *Worship Hymnal* received from outside Mennonite Brethren circles. *The Hymn*, the official journal of the Hymn Society of America, stated:

> Here is a well-organized, excellently printed and comprehensively-compiled hymnal "for everyone." Though it is produced by one of the smaller denominations on the American continent, it is a hymnal that can be used advantageously by practically any church. It has an excellent selection of both hymns and "worship aids" for every Christian. [24]

Choir Singing

Even though congregational singing has been at the heart of music-making among Mennonite Brethren, choirs and male choruses have served as significant outlets for musical expression. No matter how small the church, a choir would be formed to sing in worship services. The prestige of the church choir was such that even without promotion, most young people automatically became members. Another popular organization in most churches was the male chorus. To a more limited extent ladies choruses, children and youth choirs have also flourished. Unfortunately within recent years interests outside the church have begun to siphon off participation in church choirs.

In his *Die Geschichte der Mennoniten-Bruedergemeinde*,[25] A. H. Unruh states that during the earlier years in Russia the choir, in addition to its regular singing ministry, served to introduce to the church the newer gospel songs which eventually became a part of the congregation's repertoire. Choir singing became such an important activity that many hand-copied songbooks were made from imported publications, mostly into *Ziffern* notation.

The first official reference to choirs appeared in the record of the General Conference held in Mountain Lake, in 1919, indicating the existence of some 100 choirs in the various churches with approximately 2,000 singers.[26]

Choir singing was fostered in various ways. A meaningful tradition developed in which various church choirs would meet for a song festival (*Saengerfest*), a practice which had been established in Russia. Mrs. John P. Wall (Eva Janzen, b. 1885) writes in her "Story of My Life" (1970) about an event which took place sometime around 1900 in Russia:

> Since I stayed in (seamstress) training in Barwenkowo (Ukraine) for a number of months, and since I had my evenings free, I sang in the Mennonite Brethren Church choir. . . . Then, too, it afforded me quite some joy to go home when people from Barwenkowo went to Wasieljewka, my home village. It was on such an occasion that I was present at a song festival at which the Barwenkowo choir also sang, I was asked to be in their choir.[27]

In America these festivals developed into annual events of two to three-day duration, usually combined with Missions and Sunday school conventions, and generated tremendous enthusiasm and appreciation. Before the days of large auditoriums, huge tents had to be erected to accommodate the large audiences.[28] The spiritual fellowship of these occasions was anticipated each year. In participating choirs, these song festivals (*Saengerfeste*) instilled a valuable interest in choir singing. Within the brotherhood they created a feeling of community and cohesiveness. Although changing times have dissipated much of the interest in this valuable endeavor, song festivals are still being held in various parts of Canada and the United States. A recent innovation on a grand scale is the 500-voice Mennonite Men's Chorus Festival held annually in Kansas, with good participation by Mennonite Brethren men.

Another supportive factor for choir singing was the promotion of singing schools, conductors' workshops (*Dirigenten-Kurse*), and church music workshops. Before the time that reed organs and pianos were used in the sanctuary, learning how to read music was an absolute necessity. For this reason, evening singing schools (*Singstunden*) were arranged. They met in the local schoolhouse, home or church building. The specific objective was the learning of music notation in order to become self-reliant in reading parts without the aid of an instrument. In

America the *Ziffern* were gradually replaced by the sol-fa syllables, which proved to be of great value in learning new songs and in part singing.[29] The singing schools also taught correct conducting forms. Vocalization was primarily concerned with voice production and diction, while music theory was confined to the barest essentials for reading simple song literature with accuracy and good pitch. In the early years the men who guided this work were gifted lay musicians and often ordained ministers of the Gospel. Since the later 1950's the Mennonite Brethren colleges and Bible schools have offered many music workshops especially designed for choir directors. Specialists of national reputation were often brought in to conduct these sessions.

Another area of support came from publications and music committees. Isaak Born of Lichtfelde, Russia, published a monthly periodical for singers including songs with notes to be used in Mennonite churches and homes. At the General Conference sessions in 1893 he offered to edit his *Saenger-Zeitung* with notes for American readers and asked for an advance of $150.00. The conference did not accede to this request, but recommended that singers in America subscribe to this periodical.[30]

At the 1919 General Conference, J. P. Wiebe on behalf of the Canadian Mennonite Brethren "Association of Singers" asked the General Conference to take over the *Saenger-Bote*, a publication on church music which had a circulation of some 700-800. The conference suggested that individual churches consider the matter and deferred the decision until the next conference.[31] At the 1921 conference it was then decided together with the publication committee that a periodical be published to foster the ministry of music in the churches. This was the impetus for the formation of the first General Conference music committee with the following members: H. D. Wiebe, J. P. Wiebe, Aron Sawatzky, H. J. Pankratz, and J. J. Franz.[32]

Three years later (1924) this committee gave an oral report[33] emphasizing the need for (a) a music magazine, (b) diligent practice in hearty singing, and (c) a suitable church hymnal. The conference decided to affirm them as the songbook committee (*Komitee fuer Gesangessache*), with H. J. Pankratz as chairman. Their mandate was to recommend a hymnal suited for the churches' needs. Their report three years later (1927)[34] recommended the *Neue Glaubensharfe* (German Baptist publication) for use in Mennonite Brethren churches.

Thus, for a short period of time the conference responded to the on-going musical needs of the churches. However, for the next eighteen years the matter of church music received no attention on the General Conference level, nor was a special music committee provided for this purpose. In 1945 the conference again involved itself in church music activities with the resolution to begin the production of a Mennonite Brethren hymnal.[35]

The Songbook Committees in the Canadian Conference have continued to function to serve general church music concerns in addition to their production of the *Gesangbuch* and *The Hymn Book*. The United States Conference created a Music Committee in 1959.[36] It helped sponsor church music conferences, music scholarships, and published a few issues of a church music periodical. It was eventually merged with the Board of Christian Education. No General Conference music committee has been formed since the early efforts in the 1920's.

The Mennonite Brethren colleges, Bible schools, and academies have been important training grounds for choir directors and song leaders. Many continued their studies, received Master's and Doctor's degrees in music, and are recognized teachers, conductors, performers, and composers in Canada, United States, and abroad. In addition, thousands of young people received inspiration from singing in the school choirs and oratorio choruses, which then filtered into the churches.

Instrumental Music

Instrumental music was a part of the early renewal movement within the Mennonite Brethren Church. Various types of instruments served as an accompaniment for congregational singing in Russia, as was mentioned earlier. The reed organ was probably the first keyboard instrument to be introduced into the church sanctuary, with only a few in use by the turn of the century. At times considerable tension arose in congregations when the reed organ and later the piano were introduced, because of their strong secular associations. Some song leaders were of the opinion that the use of a keyboard instrument lessened the enthusiasm for full participation in congregational singing. Nevertheless, as reed organs and pianos were more commonly found in private homes, these instruments were eventually also accepted and appreciated as useful musical tools for worship services. The practical use of the piano was well adapted for the Sunday school. In the 1940's when electronic organs appeared on the market, they began to replace the reed organs in church sanctuaries, so that by the 1960's most churches had an electronic organ and a piano. Since no Mennonite Brethren college or Bible school had a pipe organ, limited awareness and interest in pipe organs developed. Only two have been installed in Mennonite Brethren churches, one in Canada and one in the United States. However, some new interest is being developed as more organists are trained on pipe organs outside of Mennonite Brethren circles.

The use of wind and stringed instruments has varied from church to church. Various churches did not allow the use of wind instruments but did permit the use of stringed instruments such as guitars, mandolins, and violins. The first third of the twentieth century saw string orchestras appear in some communities. In recent years the use of instruments of all kinds has been approved. Within the last decade percussion instruments such as drums and tambourines have been employed especially with youth music. There has also been a significant increase in the use of guitars with electric amplification.

Pioneers in Music

Much credit must be given to leaders who fostered the musical aspects of Mennonite Brethren worship. Many gifted, self-taught choir directors and song leaders served local churches through the years. The following are some of the pioneers who made significant contributions to the nurture and development of music in the Mennonite Brethren Church.

Canada[37]

John P. Wiebe (1868-1956) lived in Herbert, Saskatchewan. He conducted choir workshops (*Saengerkurse*) in the Mennonite Brethren Conference for many years. He may be credited with bringing an awareness of the worth of the congregational song form known as Mennonite Brethren *Kernlieder* — hymns whose melodies have qualities that are in a way unique to the Mennonite Brethren, and express a feeling of "hurt" but have a quality of hope which has served the Mennonite Brethren Church outreach in a powerful way.

Aron Sawatzky (1871-1935) resided in Aberdeen, Saskatchewan, and later in California. He was a well-known conductor of music workshops (*Kurseleiter*) prior to the Mennonite immigration (1923-1929), teaching gospel songs both in English and German. He was also a composer of gospel songs, and the compiler and editor of two song periodicals, *Der Saenger-Bote* and *Die Lieder-Quelle*. These books were published in the United States and were extensively used by Mennonite Brethren choirs in the United States and Canada.

Franz C. Thiessen (1881-1950) was one of the *Russlaender* who came to Manitoba in 1925. He was a highly qualified choral pedagog in the tradition of nineteenth-century Europe. His interests ranged beyond the restricted pragmatism of the Mennonite Brethren Church and included performances of complete oratorios, where possible with orchestral accompaniment. He may be credited with initiating the remarkable choral and instrumental music-making known today in Canadian Mennonite Brethren churches and schools. As an ordained minister his defense of the arts (*Kunst*), which up to this time had been somewhat suspect in the Mennonite Brethren tradition, began to be accepted.

K. H. Neufeld (1892-1957) was active as a conductor of music workshops (*Kurseleiter*) in both the Mennonite Brethren and General Conference Mennonite communities. He may be credited as having been the great "popularizer" of lay choir singing throughout the whole of Canadian Mennonitism. He embraced both the traditional Mennonite hymns as well as the classics. He wrote a handbook on conducting and was the compiler, arranger, and publisher of a collection for choirs, *Liedersammlung fuer Gemischte Choere.* The young people whom he motivated to study music was without parallel.

United States

J. J. Franz (1880-1947) is best known as the coeditor of *Neue Zions Lieder* and *Zions-Klaenge* together with D. B. Towner. He traveled as a singing evangelist for some time; taught at Corn Bible Academy, Corn, Oklahoma; and was voice instructor and choral director at Tabor College.

Henry W. Baerg (1890-1968) was an early Mennonite Brethren musical pioneer who taught at Tabor College for eleven years (1919-1930) and founded the Tabor College choir. He studied at Pomona College, University of Hawaii, University of California, University of Kansas, and Juilliard Conservatory of Music. He was particularly influential in setting a high standard for choral music and oratorio performances. Later he taught at Bob Jones University and Grace Bible Institute.

Herbert C. Richert (1900-   ), originally from Buhler, Kansas, emerged as the foremost leader of church music among United States Mennonite Brethren, having studied at Tabor College, Bible Institute of Los Angeles, University of Southern California, Sterling College, University of Colorado, Colorado College, and Kansas State Teachers College (Emporia). He achieved a high standard of excellence in choir performance as well as in solo singing. For twenty-five years (1935-1960) he served as chairman of the music department of Tabor College. His major conference activity came as Music Editor of the *Mennonite Brethren Church Hymnal* (1953). As composer, arranger, and publisher he produced many songs in addition to three publications: *Young People's Sacred Songs* (English, 1935), *Choral Compositions* (Male Chorus, German), and *Songs for Men* (English, 1960). Without doubt he has been the most important musical figure among the United States Mennonite Brethren.

Major contributions to music leadership in the contemporary M.B. Church have been made by brethren like Ben Horch, Dietrich Friesen, Peter Klassen, Victor Martens, Paul Wohlgemuth, and Larry Warkentin In addition a host of conductors, teachers, and performers could be listed.

Significance of Music

As a rural people, Mennonite Brethren did not have the opportunity to learn the more sophisticated music embodied in the cultural art of the western world, but they did appreciate and enjoy music at the level of folk art. The spontaneity of singing at Bible studies, prayer meetings, worship services, home visitations and mealtimes greatly aided in making these moments spiritually wholesome and meaningful. Fortunately, the simple, hard-surfaced walls of their church sanctuaries provided a natural, built-in, live acoustical aid for enjoyable, uninhibited congregational singing.

Since participation in "worldly amusements" was frowned upon, music served a vital social function along with its spiritual ministry. It seemed to act as an important catalyst for the experience of togetherness and fellowship. It was not uncommon for young people to gather in a home for an evening of singing. The place of music in Mennonite Brethren life has, however, changed somewhat during the last two decades. Many forces and activities have bid for the attention of the church. The excellent tradition of choir and congregational singing may be lost in future generations if the current trend continues. Another deterrent factor which in recent years has caused problems in singing has been the adverse acoustics in newly-built Mennonite Brethren churches. In many cases the extensive use of acoustical tile, rugs, and covered pews deadens the sound reverberation so that singing becomes a lifeless and unenjoyable experience for both the congregation and the choir. Attempts to use electronic amplification have been inadequate.

It was fortunate, however, that music infused itself so deeply into the fabric of the Mennonite Brethren, for it helped to bring together the spiritual power of their daily life with their worship life. It breathed life, vitality, and meaning into their spiritual pilgrimage.

Chapter 16

Training for Life and Service: Institutional Education in the Mennonite Brethren Church

Educational institutions have been established by the Mennonite Brethren Church to meet specific needs in the brotherhood. These needs were conceived of as being directly related to the primary task of the church. Among Mennonite Brethren in North America the basic motivation to establish and support Christian academies (high schools), Bible institutes, the Bible College, Christian liberal arts colleges, and the seminary, has been the conviction that "school and mission" are inseparably linked in the redemptive purposes of God.

At certain times and in certain institutions the desire for the preservation of cultural values may have overshadowed the primary objective of Christian education as stated above. This usually happened, however, when these cultural values were considered to be vitally related to the mission of the church.[1] In general, Mennonite Brethren have subscribed to the principle enunciated by George Konrad, Professor of Christian Education at the Mennonite Brethren Biblical Seminary: ". . . the Christian legitimacy of any educational institution (and agency or organization) must be determined by the degree in which it participates in the essential nature and mission of the church."[2]

The involvement of Mennonite Brethren in institutional education in the Mennonite colonies in Russia has been described earlier. It should be remembered that in Russia religious instruction formed an integral part of the curriculum in all primary and secondary schools. Thus all children and young people were introduced to an integrated Christian world view.

The one distinctively Mennonite Brethren institution in South Russia was the Tschongraw Bible School (Crimea) founded in 1918. Its program was related directly to the mission of the church in the immediate post-war era. When its doors were closed by government decree in 1924, institutional education for Mennonite Brethren in Russia came to an end.

Among Mennonite Brethren in America cultural forces and spiritual needs have given rise to several distinct types of institutional education. At the risk of oversimplification, the Christian schools of the Mennonite Brethren will be described under three broad categories: Bible schools and Bible academies, liberal arts and Bible colleges, and the seminary.

I. THE CONCERN FOR BIBLICAL INSTRUCTION: THE STORY
OF BIBLE SCHOOLS AND CHRISTIAN HIGH SCHOOLS

In reviewing the educational efforts of the early Mennonite Brethren, F. C. Peters, prominent M. B. educator and theologian, makes the following observation: "When viewed from the perspective of the American Mennonite educational scene, Mennonite Brethren have made a significant contribution in one area. . . . The growth of short term Bible schools has been largely a Mennonite Brethren phenomenon."[3]

This "Mennonite Brethren phenomenon" should be viewed, however, not in isolation but against the backdrop of the Bible institute movement in conservative Protestantism (Fundamentalism) with which it had some connections, and by which it was strongly influenced. The Bible institute movement in America is less than one hundred years old. It began with the two pioneer schools, Nyack Missionary College (1882) and Moody Bible Institute (1886). These were followed by numerous other Bible schools in the early decades of the twentieth century. According to S. A. Witmer, "the major development in number of schools took place from 1931 to 1960. In this thirty-year period, 73 percent of the existing Bible colleges and institutes were established."[4] It is significant that the Bible school movement among Mennonite Brethren also reached its peak during that period.

Institutional Christian education in the M. B. Church of America had an insignificant beginning. Two years after G. B. Simpson founded the Nyack missionary school in the state of New York, J. F. Harms began a small private school at *Canada, Kansas*. The school curriculum provided for elementary instruction in German, English, and Bible. After two years of operation in Canada, a School Association was formed which took over the school and relocated it in Lehigh (Kansas). Here Harms continued his teaching ministry for two more years (1886-1888). According to J H. Lohrenz, "this school . . . may be regarded as the first Mennonite Brethren school in America, and J. F. Harms as the pioneer educator of the M. B. Church."[5]

The School Association (*Schulverein*) also subsidized the training of young men for the teaching profession. P. H. Wedel was one of the most promising young scholars whom the association supported at the Baptist Seminary in Rochester. In 1890 Wedel accepted a call for evangelistic work in the conference. This decision was a great disappointment to the brethren in the School Association. Subsequently, according to one report, Harms asked Wedel: "Why have you done this to us?" The latter replied: "What can you expect? First you send me to a seminary, and make a preacher out of me, — small wonder, that I am no longer a teacher."[6] Shortly thereafter the Association was dissolved.

The Corn Bible Academy

The concern for biblical instruction led to the founding of a school some years later in the Corn community of Oklahoma. The Corn Bible Academy was established in 1902 as a Bible and language school, thanks largely to the efforts of Isaac Harms, the leading minister of the Corn M. B. Church. During the first four years of its existence the school operated a children's as well as a young people's department.[7] From 1906 to 1919 it was conducted only for young people with one instructor and three-year course.

In 1920 the curriculum was expanded and two teachers were employed until 1934, when it was fully accredited with the state of Oklahoma and more instructors were added to the staff. Since 1934 the Corn Bible Academy has combined biblical instruction with a four-year high school course. For a number of years the enrollment has been around 100, with students coming from the large local congregation and from M. B. churches in Oklahoma, Texas, and Kansas. Many early church leaders received their "Fundamentals of Faith" in this school under the able leadership of such men as J. F. Duerksen, H. D. Wiebe, J. J. Wiebe, H. R. Wiens and J. W. Vogt.

The Enid (Okla.) Bible School and Academy[8] (1921-1940)

Mennonite Brethren of the Enid community had made several attempts prior to 1921 to provide religious instruction for their young people. Peter F. Duerksen was engaged in the German Department of the North Enid school system for several years, until this program had to be discontinued.

The desire of many brethren for a school of their own culminated in the organizing of the Enid Bible School in 1921 with P. H. Berg (later manager of the M. B. Publishing House) as the first instructor. H. S. Friesen from Hillsboro (Kansas) was engaged for the 1922-23 school year. Interest in the school continued to grow so that in 1925 a suitable building was erected on a section of the church premises. From 1925 to 1927 P. E. Nikkel from Inman (Kansas) served as teacher. From 1929 to

1931 D. J. Dick was the main teacher who was followed by G. C. Wiens of Bessie (Oklahoma) who taught for another five years. When R. C. Seibel came to Enid in 1936, he set up a more standardized curriculum to meet associated state high school requirements. J. K. Siemens, who was engaged two years later, carried on the work with a dwindling number of students. Better educational facilities in the public high schools was one of the major factors in the decline of the student body which led to the closing of the school. The fact that R. C. Seibel, the pastor of the Enid Mennonite Brethren Church, was an instructor in the Kremlin High School nearby, in all probability also influenced parents to send their children to the public school. Some sixty students were graduated from the Enid Bible School and Academy during the twenty years of its operation.

Fairview (Okla.) Bible School (1926-1943)

The Fairview community felt the need for a Bible school to educate its young people. Responding to the initiative of several brethren, the Sued-Hoffnungsfeld church established a Bible school in 1926 and called J. E. Hildebrandt, a graduate of Tabor College, to serve as instructor. The regular course covered three years, with offerings in Bible and German. The school sought to prepare teachers for the Sunday school, to disseminate Bible knowledge among the young people and to prepare workers for the church.

After the outbreak of World War II, community opposition arose because of the school's use of the German language and its stand against participation in war.[9] By 1943 the student body had diminished considerably, and the school was closed. Among others, P. V. Balzer, missionary to India, and J. K. Siemens, well-known Bible teacher, have served as instructors of the school.

Hooker (Okla.) Bible School (1920-1931)

Intermittently from 1920 to 1931 the Hooker M. B. Church operated a small Bible school. Eighteen students enrolled for the first year with P. E. Nikkel as the teacher. Only eleven students attended the third year with A. G. Wall as instructor and the school was discontinued the following year. Several attempts were made to revive the school. When P. V. Balzer returned from India in 1931, he was engaged for two terms. However, with his leaving the work soon died out.[10]

Immanuel Academy

Immanuel Academy began in 1912 when the Reedley (California) M. B. Church felt the need of conducting daily Bible school classes for high school-age young people. By 1925 interest in the program had grown to the extent that the church erected a small school building, and named it Reedley Bible School. David V. Wiebe of Tabor College and his wife were the teachers. As first director of the school, Wiebe played an important role in its early development. By 1932 the school, which had never had a large enrollment, was closed down. However, it was continued by the Dinuba Mennonite Brethren Church until 1937 in the building now known as the Reedley hospital.[11]

In 1937-41 the Bible school met in the dining room of the Dinuba M.B. Church. In 1938 the Reedley M.B. Church reopened its Bible school in its own facilities and operated a parallel program to that in Dinuba. By 1941 the church-schism was healed sufficiently for the two schools to combine under the new name: Immanuel Bible School. J. P. Rogalsky (who died in 1960) had joined the staff of the Reedley school in 1926 and taught in it with great dedication for many years. He also served as principal during difficult times when the school was struggling for survival.[12]

In 1944 the four-year academy program was started and the name changed to Immanuel Academy. J. N. C. Hiebert, a missionary on furlough from India, served as first principal of the reorganized school. In 1946 another milestone was reached when the school relocated to its present campus overlooking the Kings River on the southwest corner of Reedley. The average attendance since 1950 has been around two hundred. A staff of ten to twelve teachers have given instruction in Bible and in courses required in a high school academic program. Other principals of Immanuel Academy were H. R. Wiens, Arthur J. Wiebe, Vernon Janzen, and Dan Neufeld.

In both schools, Corn Bible Academy and Immanuel Academy, one can observe a gradual transformation from a Bible school to a high school program. The change no doubt was caused by the increasing demand of young people for a high school education in preparation for vocational training or college. For the Mennonite Brethren churches of the Reedley area Immanuel Academy continues to make a vital contribution to the total Christian education program.[13]

The "genius" of Mennonite Brethren in establishing Bible schools found its full expression on the Canadian scene, especially in the prairie provinces.

The Herbert Bible School[14]

The Bible school movement among Mennonite Brethren in Canada was formally launched with the founding of the Herbert Bible School in 1913. In God's providence, J. F. Harms had come to the province of Saskatchewan five years earlier. Harms, who had imparted his vision for Christian education to the brotherhood in Kansas, now began to inspire the brethren in Canada by both his precept and practice. For a number of years Harms offered short one-month courses in the Saskatchewan churches during the winter months.

In 1911 the Northern District Conference appointed a committee to study the possibility of establishing a Bible school for the training of young people. The following year the conference accepted a recommendation to open such a school. J. F. Harms became its first principal and teacher in 1913, and continued to serve in this capacity until 1918 when he moved to Seattle, Washington.

The man who gave to the school its particular image was Wm. J. Bestvater, who was invited in 1921 to reopen the school which had been closed for two years due to financial difficulties. Training at the Moody Bible Institute,[15] and experience as teacher (1898-1908) and city missionary in Winnipeg (1913-1921), equipped Bestvater for his new task. Facilities were enlarged and improved, and the program strengthened. In the midst of a busy schedule as administrator, teacher and Bible conference speaker, Bestvater found time to write two much-needed textbooks: *Die Glaubenslehre* (Bible Doctrine) and *Die Bibelkunde* (Biblical Introduction). He also edited and published a modest monthly religious periodical entitled *Das Zeugnis der Schrift* (The Witness of Scripture).

The purpose of the Herbert Bible School as given in the following two statements reflects quite accurately the objectives of most M. B. Bible schools that were established later:

1. To establish and strengthen youth in the fundamental principles and doctrines of the Scriptures.
2. To provide sound Biblical training for definite Christian service in such work as Sunday School instruction, Daily Vacation Bible School, Young People's and choir work, as well as extended Mission work at home and abroad. [16]

Through the years, over 1000 students have attended the institution. A relatively large number of the graduates have gone into foreign mission work. Outstanding teachers of this school in the thirties and forties were H. Regehr, J. F. Redekop, H. Voth and others. From 1952 to 1957 C. Braun served as principal. As a result of decreasing enrollment, the Herbert Bible School was closed in 1957 and its program was amalgamated with that of the Bethany Bible Institute at Hepburn under the jurisdiction of the Saskatchewan M. B. Conference.

The Winkler Bible School

The second Mennonite Brethren Bible school in Canada was established in 1925. Among the newly arrived immigrants from Russia was A. H. Unruh, a former teacher of the Bible school in the Crimea. His vision and personal commitment led to the founding of the Pniel Bible School at Winkler, Manitoba .

Within two years, J. G. Wiens and J. G. Reimer, former associates of Unruh in the Crimea, likewise came to Canada and joined the staff of the new school. From the start the Winkler Bible School showed slow but steady progress. Attendance increased each successive year and even held its own during the trying depression years. Already in 1926 staff and students moved into their own school building. Since then the school has undergone a series of expansions to accommodate an increasing student body. Attendance reached its peak in 1951-52, with an enrollment of 138.[17]

A comparison between the Herbert and Winkler Bible schools reveals certain differences in perspective and emphasis. The curriculum in Winkler, especially during the early years, was patterned largely after that in Tschongraw which in turn was patterned after the curriculum of the German Baptist Seminary in Hamburg. This was inevitable given the educational and cultural background of its teachers. The emphasis on the training of ministers was a natural corollary of such a program. In Herbert, however, the pattern of the American Bible institutes found expression in curriculum and objectives. Here the emphasis was placed on missions and the preparation of Christian workers for a wider range of ministries. With the addition of the American-trained A. A. Kroeker to the staff of the Winkler Bible School, the program made greater provision for intensive training of Sunday school teachers. In later years, partly as a result of Bible school teachers' conferences, the curricula of the various Bible schools became more coordinated and uniform.

For a short period (1934-35), Unruh also published a theological periodical called *Die Antwort* (The Answer). It was intended to stimulate the study of ethical and theological questions and to promote inter-Bible school cooperation.[18]

In the thirties and forties the Winkler Bible School enjoyed considerable prestige and popularity throughout the Canadian M.B. constituency. The spiritual stature of such men as Unruh and Wiens, well-known throughout the brotherhood, attracted many students from other provinces as well and even from other denominations.

Unruh's transfer to the Mennonite Brethren Bible College in Winnipeg in 1944 was a great loss for the Winkler school. In that year the Manitoba M.B. Conference assumed responsibility for the operation of the Winkler Bible School. Under the leadership of such men as H. H. Redekop, G. D. Huebert, John Goossen, and H. R. Baerg the school has continued to serve its constituency well.

From 1929 to 1942 a *German Bible School* was conducted by the Mennonite Brethren in Winnipeg. It was largely an evening school to accommodate people who worked during the day. Abram Peters served as instructor for a number of years. The *Steinbach Bible Institute*, begun in 1932 by Mennonite Brethren, later developed into a community Bible school and is no longer under the auspices of the M.B. Church.

Bethany Bible Institute

The "migrant Bible school" conducted by J. F. Harms in 1911 and 1912 had created a desire among Mennonite Brethren in the Rosthern District for a completely Bible-centered school. For fifteen years (1912-1927) the Herbert Bible School attempted to meet this need in the North Saskatchewan constituency. However, geographic distance and other considerations called for the establishment of a second Bible school in the North. Thus Bethany Bible Institute at Hepburn came into existence in 1927, with D. P. Esau and G. Harms[19] as instructors.

Bethany Bible Institute has benefited through the years from the spiritual leadership of brethren well-known in the M.B. Conference. In 1933 J. B. Toews was called to the principalship of Bethany to strengthen the "spiritual life and gain even wider sympathies for the training of Christian young people."[20] He was succeeded in 1937 by G. W. Peters. During the five years of his leadership the Bethany Bible Institute developed a strong missionary emphasis. The Western Children's Mission was born in the missionary atmosphere of the school. For three years (1942-45) G. D. Huebert served as leader of the school.

During the long term of J. H. Epp as principal (1945-63) the school expanded its facilites and its services. It was during this time that the Herbert and Hepburn schools amalgamated. Since 1963 C. Braun, former principal of the Herbert Bible School, has given leadership to the expanding institution. In the late sixties the Alberta M.B. Conference officially joined the Saskatchewan Conference in its support of the Bethany Bible Institute. Its enrollment in recent years has been consistently high — with more than 150 students attending the school. Perhaps more than any other M.B. Bible school Bethany has inspired its students and graduates for mission work at home and abroad.

Several M.B. Bible schools in Saskatchewan have become defunct. The *Tabor Bible School* at Dalmeny, begun in 1928, was organized on an interdenominational basis. The strongest supporters and most of the teachers, however, came from the ranks of Mennonite Brethren. The following brethren served as principals of the school: J. Goertz, F. Wiens, J. H. Quiring, E. Epp, H. G. Rempel and O. Wiebe. The school's close proximity to the Bethany Bible Institute must be considered as a major factor in its gradual decline. In 1954 the school was closed permanently.

Another Bible school operated for a short period on a small scale at Glenbush, a new Mennonite settlement in northern Saskatchewan.[21]

Bible Schools in Alberta

In no other province (with the exception of B.C.) was there such a proliferation of effort in Bible school education as in Alberta. Mennonite

Brethren in widely scattered settlements, established five Bible schools within eight years (1929-1937). All of them had to close down, for various reasons, by 1965.

The Coaldale Bible School (1929-1965)

In 1929 the Coaldale Bible School (also known as "Morning Star") began operation with A. J Schierling[22] as its founder and first teacher. Schierling was joined the following year by J. A. Toews, Sr. For two decades the school experienced a steady growth in attendance, reaching its peak enrollment of 101 in 1948. A total of 784 persons attended the Coaldale Bible School during the first twenty-five years of its existence.[23]

Through its thirty-six-year history the school has been of great significance for the Coaldale M.B. Church and the larger Mennonite Brethren constituency. In addition to A. J. Schierling, the following brethren have served as principals for longer or shorter periods: B. W. Sawatzky, J. A. Toews, Jr., David Ewert, A. P. Regier, H. Derksen, and A. J. Konrad. A cultural transition (urbanization) plus other factors led to the eventual closing of the school after several years of heroic struggle for survival. The investment of spiritual and material resources in such a program is still bearing interest. According to John G. Doerksen, "Many of its former students are today occupying leading positions in church and community."[24]

The Bethesda Bible School (1933-1946)

In 1933 a small Bible school was opened at Gem, Alberta, a Mennonite settlement located approximately 100 miles east of Calgary. H. H. Siemens, a local M.B. minister, was instrumental in founding the school. Because the school drew its students from a very limited constituency, the enrollment remained small — with thirty-five students at its peak. G.D. Huebert, G. Thielmann, H. Unger, and B. Friesen have given leadership in the program at Gem. After the closing of the school, many young people attended the Coaldale Bible School.

La Glace Bible School (1933-1946)

The La Glace Bible School in the Peace River area of northern Alberta was founded in 1933 by G. Harder, a graduate of Calgary Prophetic Bible Institute. Other teachers who served the school and the constituency were I. Dyck, A. J. Schierling, J. Franz and D. Ewert. An exodus of M.B. families to British Columbia forced the school to close shortly after World War II came to an end.

In two other Mennonite Brethren communities there were short-lived efforts of Bible school training. In Vauxhall, a Bible school operated intermittently between 1937 and 1943, and in the small community of *Crowfoot* classes were conducted during the winters of 1935-36 and 1936-37 with Peter Goertz and George Martens as teachers.

Bible Schools in British Columbia[25]

The Mennonite Brethren who moved from the praire provinces to the Fraser Valley carried with them the vision of biblical instruction for their young people. Here too, Bible schools came into existence because there was a felt need, there were willing sponsors, and there were dedicated teachers to give leadership. Only one of the five schools founded has survived to the present.

The Yarrow (Elim) Bible School (1930-1950)

The Elim Bible School at Yarrow, (one of the most rapidly growing M.B. communities in Canada during the thirties and forties) was established in 1930. Instrumental in launching the Bible school movement here were P. D. Loewen, J. A. Harder, A. Nachtigall and G. H. Sukkau. In the early years attendance fluctuated between twenty and fifty. In 1937 C. C. Peters joined the staff and subsequently (1941) assumed the principalship of the school. In 1942 the Yarrow Bible School had its record enrollment of 155 students. G. H. Sukkau succeeded Peters as principal in 1947, and from 1952 to 1955 H. Warkentin served in this capacity. The presence of other Bible schools in the province and the trend toward secular education are cited as causes which led to the closing of the school in 1955.[26] Since then the students from Yarrow have generally attended the Bible institute at Clearbrook.

The Greendale Bible School (1938-1943)

The Bible school in Sardis (Greendale) was established in 1938 to meet local needs. H. G. Dueck and H. Lenzmann served as instructors. The school never progressed beyond its initial stages due, primarily, to the close proximity of the larger Bible schools at Yarrow and Clearbrook.

The Black Creek Bible School (1942-1945)

The Black Creek community on Vancouver Island has always felt its geographic isolation from the churches and schools in the Fraser Valley. When John Goertz, a former Bible school teacher from Dalmeny, Sask., moved there, the M.B. church launched out on its own Bible school program which had to be abandoned, however, after three years.

The East Chilliwack Bible School (1947-1959)

The last Bible school to be established in the Canadian M.B. constituency was located approximately five miles east of the city of Chilliwack. Founder and principal of the school from 1947 to 1956 was G. Thielmann, the leading minister of the local M.B. church. From 1956 to 1959 J. H. Friesen served as principal. Because of decreasing enrollment, the school closed its doors in 1959.

Since 1950 Canadian M.B. Bible schools have undergone a process of consolidation and amalgamation. Larger institutions have emerged, which make it possible to improve the quality of education, to expand services, and to operate more economically. The Bible institute at Clearbrook is an illustration of this consolidation process.

The Columbia Bible Institute

The Columbia Bible Institute (known as the Mennonite Brethren Bible Institute until 1970) had its insignificant beginnings in the Bible classes conducted by C. C. Peters at the South Abbotsford church during the late 1930's. In 1945 the South Abbotsford, Clearbrook, and Matsqui M.B. churches combined efforts to inaugurate a regular Bible school with F. C. Thiessen and W. Reimche as instructors. During the next decade the school experienced steady growth so that by 1954 it had an enrollment of eighty-four, and a teaching staff of five. Other churches of the Abbotsford area rallied to the support of the school, making relocation of the institution to its present beautiful campus near Clearbrook possible in 1955.

In 1960 the M.B. Conference of British Columbia assumed full responsibility for the operation of the school. Since the other M.B. Bible schools in the province had closed down one after the other, the conference now became united in its purpose to support one Bible institute. Since then the physical plant has been enlarged, and the enrollment (after some fluctuations) has increased. Among the many teachers who served the school through the years the following could be mentioned: J. F. Redekop, H. H. Nikkel, A. H. Wieler, J. B. Epp, H. T. Janzen, H. C. Born, A. J. Klassen, G. Konrad, and P. R. Toews, the present principal.

An event of great historic significance in the life of the school and for the Mennonite brotherhood in B.C. took place in 1970. In that year the two conferences — Mennonite Brethren and United Mennonite — decided to join forces in the operation of a single Bible school program. This event will receive further consideration in the chapter dealing with inter-church relations. Since the merger of the two schools (Mennonite Brethren Bible Institute and Bethel Bible Institute) the combined enrollment has exceeded 200.

Mennnonite Brethren Bible Institute of Ontario (1938-1963)

The Bible school training program in Ontario began when I. T. Ewert started to conduct evening classes in Virgil in 1938. The following year the Virgil-Vineland Bible School Society was formed and B. B. Boldt was engaged as instructor of the new day-school in Vineland. Due to the war, instruction was discontinued during 1941-42. Classes were resumed in Virgil in 1943 and as a result a new society was formed. Work continued under the auspices of the Virgil Bible School Society until 1948, when the Ontario conference assumed the administrative responsibility. High school classes had been added, beginning in 1944, so that two schools emerged on one campus.

The operation of two institutions on the same grounds created certain problems. Consequently the M.B. Conference of Ontario accepted a recommendation for relocation in 1953. In 1955 the Bible school relocated to Kitchener, where it was housed in the educational building of the Kitchener M.B. Church. However, relocation did not solve the problem of enrollment, which remained small. In 1963 the school was closed. In order to encourage young people to attend Mennonite Brethren Bible schools in Western Canada, the Ontario Conference subsidized each student who enrolled in a denominational Bible school.

A number of men have devoted years of service to the Bible school program in Ontario. Besides the brethren mentioned above, the following could be named: A. J. Block, H. Penner, F. Kroeker, P. J. Esau, and W. Kornelson, who served as the school's last principal.

Although only three Bible institutes have been in operation in recent years, the Bible school movement among Mennonite Brethren in Canada continues to be a vital spiritual force in the brotherhood. An upsurge in interest and enrollment during the past few years indicates that these schools continue to meet the needs of many young people in their preparation for life and Christian service.

Mennonite Brethren High Schools

Toward the end of World War II and in the immediate post-war period Mennonite Brethren in Canada established five private high schools. This accelerated effort to provide education on a secondary level was in part precipitated by the rapid rural-urban shift of the M.B. population; in part it was also the result of an increasing demand for such education in preparation for vocational training or university matriculation.

The basic motivation, however, in establishing Christian high schools has been an underlying philosophy of Christian education. The objectives of one of these institutions accurately reflects the goals of all M.B. high schools. Eden Christian College (high school) has stated the objectives as follows:

1. direct unsaved students to a conversion experience;
2. train the students in the nurture and admonition of the Lord;
3. lay the foundation for a fruitful life of service in the Kingdom of God;
4. seek to preserve the spiritual heritage with which God has blessed our church;
5. offer a course of studies in which scholarship and academic thoroughness are fostered in a truly Christian atmosphere. [27]

Only a brief historical sketch of these schools can be given here.

The Mennonite Educational Institute (MEI)

The MEI at Clearbrook, B.C., founded in 1944, has become the largest Mennonite high school in Canada. From an attendance of forty-three in 1944, the school's enrollment climbed to a record 505 in 1958. The doubling of enrollment during the early years of the school forced the construction of a $50,000 educational plant in 1946 on a new campus. In 1954 the construction of a junior high school added four classrooms and other facilities to the school. A spacious modern auditorium was built in 1970 which is also used for many conference and community functions.

The MEI is supported by six M.B. churches of the area and one United Mennonite church. Although enrollment has decreased somewhat during the last few years, the school continues to play a vital role in the education of Mennonite Brethren young people. I. J. Dyck and F. C. Thiessen were among the pioneer educators of the school.

Sharon Mennonite Collegiate (1945-1970)

A second private high school in B.C. was established in Yarrow, a Mennonite settlement booming because of high raspberry prices. A committee headed by J. A. Harder, leading minister of the local M.B. church, succeeded in making a 150-student high school a reality in 1945. A subsequent jump in enrollment led the Yarrow, Greendale and East Chilliwack Mennonite Brethren churches to construct a large educational plant with classroom space for more than 300 students. Yet in 1949 the school building had to be turned over to the public school board because an economic recession forced the abandonment of the ambitious venture.[28]

In 1951 another beginning was made by a new Society, actively supported by the Yarrow M.B. church. Beginning with sixty-four students in grades seven to ten, the school had expanded by 1960 to an enrollment of 114 in grades six to twelve with a staff of seven teachers. A gradual decrease in enrollment during the next decade forced the school to close its doors in 1970. Many of the Yarrow students now attend the MEI at Clearbrook.

The Alberta Mennonite High School (1946-1962)

In Coaldale, Alberta, Mennonite Brethren with a concern for Christian education formed the Mennonite Educational Society in the spring of 1946 under the leadership of B. B. Janz. That fall the Alberta Mennonite High School began operation with H. Thiessen as principal. Instruction was given in grades nine to twelve to a group of forty-two students. Enrollment fluctuated between a low of twenty-eight and a high of forty-nine during the first five years. When grades seven and eight were added in 1951 enrollment rose to ninety.

Although investment in buildings was moderate and teachers' salaries were low, the financial strains upon the society of a little more than 100 members was severe. Throughout its short and troubled history the school was plagued with financial problems. A closely related fact which hampered the development of the institution was an "intermittent rivalry between the Alberta Mennonite High School and the Coaldale Bible School."[29] The divided loyalty in the constituency was a factor in the eventual closing of both schools. Nevertheless, the Alberta Mennonite High School made a positive contribution in providing Christian training for the M.B. youth of the province.

Mennonite Brethren Collegiate Institute (M.B.C.I.)

By 1945 enough Mennonite Brethren residents in Winnipeg were interested in a private high school to found the M.B. Collegiate Institute. A supporting association was formed under the leadership of C. C. Warkentin. The school first held classes in the Mennonite Brethren Bible College, but in 1947 moved into its own premises next door on Talbot Avenue.

Several veteran educators — like H. Wall, G. H. Lohrenz, G. H. Peters and D. K. Duerksen — were associated with the school in its early history. Although the turn-over in the teaching staff was quite large (as in most private schools), the school continued to make slow but steady progress. By 1955, the year of its tenth anniversary, a total of 1042 students had attended the school; of these 197 had graduated. In 1959 the yearly attendance rose to over 200, and has remained well above that mark ever since. Instruction is offered in grades seven to twelve, with special emphasis on Bible and German language.

The school has continued to gain favor and support from an ever widening constituency. Of the 236 students enrolled during the 1962-63 year, more than thirty came from rural churches. In that same year approximately one third of the students came from a non-Mennonite Brethren background, an indication that the school is fulfilling a need not only in the M.B. churches, but also in the larger Winnipeg constituency. In the early sixties the M.B.C.I. was accepted by the Manitoba Conference alongside of the Winkler Bible School as a conference school.

Eden Christian College

As noted earlier a Mennonite Brethren high school was begun in 1945 in Ontario as a subsidiary of the Virgil Bible School. From its inception the Bible school accepted students for grades nine and ten. A separate high school building was constructed in 1947. In ten years the enrollment climbed to 183, 34 percent of whom had other than a Mennonite Brethren background.

In 1948 the Ontario M.B. Conference accepted the responsibility for the operation of the school. An auditorium and another classroom wing constructed in 1955 completed the campus. Eden Christian College continues to provide thorough academic instruction within the framework of a Christian philosophy of life. A recent upsurge in enrollment reflects a demand for such training in the constituency. Leadership to the program has been given by the following principals: H. Thiessen, D. Neumann, R. Bartel, and J. Wichert.[30]

In Saskatchewan Mennonite Brethren have not established any private high schools. In this province the Mennonite communities in many instances have jurisdiction over public high schools. These schools, largely staffed by Christian teachers, make private high schools virtually unnecessary.

In addition to their primary function, the Bible schools and Bible academies of Canada and the United States have fulfilled several secondary roles. With their strong emphasis on good music and Christian literature, the schools have served as cultural centers in the constituency. Moreover, these institutions have also been important "feeders" for the colleges and indirectly for the seminary of the conference.

II. THE DEMAND FOR HIGHER EDUCATION: THE STORY OF LIBERAL ARTS AND BIBLE COLLEGES

Tabor College

In the last decade of the nineteenth century the need of a college education for church leadership training became a serious concern among Mennonite Brethren — especially in Kansas. The opening of Bethel College in North Newton in 1893 by a corporation composed of members of the Mennonite Church probably intensified the desire of the Mennonite Brethren to establish a school of their own. Inadequate resources, however, seemed to make all such plans and aspirations look like an unattainable utopia.

In the meantime, some Mennonite Brethren in Kansas had established contact with the college of the Church of the Brethren (Dunkards) located at McPherson, in close proximity to major Mennonite settlements. According to J. F. Harms "the question came up in the M.B. Church, whether it would not be proper, in cooperation with the K.M.B. Church, to associate ourselves temporarily with the Dunkard College in McPherson and work hand in hand with that school."[31]

Elder Heinrich Wiebe (K.M.B.), and H. P. Ratzlaff, J. F. Duerksen and J. F. Harms (M.B.) entered into discussions with the faculty and administration of McPherson College. The college offered the M.B. and K.M.B. churches free use of a few classrooms and complete control of the German Department. A letter which spelled out the nature of the arrangement was presented to the M.B. Conference meeting in October, 1898, in Manitoba. The conference, however, was not prepared for such a move and tabled the matter.[32]

The promoters of higher education in Kansas, however, were not willing to abandon the project, and decided to move ahead without conference support. Again, according to Harms, "after Brother Schellenberg (Elder Abraham Schellenberg) had been won for the cause, it was comparatively easy that the offer of McPherson College was accepted and Brother J. F. Duerksen engaged for the German department."[33] Duerksen's salary was made up by voluntary contributions. Eleven students enrolled in the German Department during the first year.

Because the arrangement proved to be mutually satisfactory, the 1899 conference passed the following resolution: "That we receive free-will offerings in all of our churches to raise the $400.00 (per year) salary of the teacher J. F. Duerksen, instructing and in charge of the German department at McPherson College."[34] Under the arrangement Duerksen served as spiritual counselor to Mennonite Brethren students and the conference supported and supervised the department.

During the seven years (1898-1905) that the Mennonite Brethren were officially associated with McPherson College, there was a steady increase in enrollment. In all, 249 students from the M.B. constituency attended the college during that period. The future educational leadership of the M.B. and K.M.B. conferences received its stimulation under this provisional agreement with McPherson College. Difficulty in raising the annual budget (which had been increased to $525.00 per year) was a major factor in terminating the relationship with this school in 1905.[35]

The Founding of Tabor

After 1905 the school question remained dormant for about two years. Several former students of McPherson College, however, were beginning to dream about a conference school. Prominent among these were H.W. Lohrenz and P. C. Hiebert. In September, 1907, while Lohrenz was a senior at McPherson College, he invited J. K. Hiebert, minister of the Ebenfeld M.B. Church (near Hillsboro) for a consultation.[36] There these two friends of higher education took the initiative in the preparation of plans for the founding of a college. They must be credited with bringing the first Mennonite Brethren college into being.

J. K. Hiebert helped Lohrenz to promote the plan and bring the issue before the conference. The plan called for the establishment of a school association composed of M.B. and K.M.B. members who would make pledges of financial support for a period of five years. A special conference of Kansas Mennonite Brethren, meeting at the Ebenezer M.B. Church (Buhler) in 1907 approved the plan and thus opened the way for the active solicitation of financial support.

In March, 1908, the initial objective was reached and a meeting was called to organize the School Association. A Board of Directors was elected with J. K. Hiebert chairman, P. E. Nikkel vice-chairman, H. W. Lohrenz secretary, and H. J. Pankratz treasurer. Two things needed immediate attention: the school had no name, and its location had not been decided upon. Although several names were proposed, the board agreed on the name Tabor which had been suggested by P. P. Rempel, a minister of the Hillsboro M.B. Church.[37] Hillsboro was chosen over Aulne, Inman, and Lehigh as the site for the new school, when it offered $6533.00 in cash besides building lots, material and labor.

In the spring of 1908 the building was begun, but could not be completed in time for the opening of school in September. Instruction was begun on September 14 in the Hillsboro M.B. Church with three teachers — President H. W. Lohrenz, P. C. Hiebert, and P. P. Rempel — and thirty-nine students. Before the year was over the enrollment reached 102, and three more faculty members were added. A long-cherished dream of many Mennonite Brethren had become a wonderful reality.

Early History of Tabor

The early aims of the college as stated by H. W. Lohrenz, Tabor's first president, were to offer a liberal arts education in a Christian setting, to prepare young men and women for spiritual leadership in the church, and to provide a program of vocational training. According to Wesley Prieb, present Dean of Tabor College, it was "the special concern of the Association, of the Board, and of the teachers that the school be a seminary of real Christianity, where the spirit of prayer could prevail, and where souls could become better grounded in the spiritual life."[38]

The period from 1908 to 1918 was one of gradual expansion. The academy and the preparatory school dominated the early years of the program. The enrollment steadily increased until it reached 176 in 1920. It was only in 1926 that the college surpassed the academy in enrollment. By 1918 the faculty (for academy and college) had expanded to fifteen and the student body to 200. Influential faculty members during these first years (besides those mentioned above) were D. E. Harder (K.M.B.), B. E. Ebel, H. F. Toews, and A. A. Groening.

Proper leadership is of special significance for a small Christian

36. Tabor College administration building. Inset: H. W. Lohrenz, first president

college. A. E. Janzen gives the following character profile of Tabor's first president:

> From the very outset . . . the movement enjoyed the outstanding ability, educational preparation, sincere devotion, counsel, guidance and purposeful leadership of a qualified head. The election of H. W. Lohrenz to the first presidency of Tabor College was a formal acknowledgement and recognition on the part of the Board and the constituency that God in His providence had provided one who qualified to focus the educational interests and to harness sufficient support within the Brotherhood to bring into being the long looked-for school. . . . [39]

Testings and Trials

April 30, 1918, was a dark day in the history of Tabor College. On that day the school building and practically all of its contents were destroyed by fire. But it also was the day on which a new and larger college was born. "The ashes were still glowing," according to L. J. Franz, "when the student body, faculty, alumni, local merchants, and interested friends gathered to launch a drive to rebuild the college. By noon the next day they had subscribed 10,000 dollars."[40]

A new fire-proof three-story building and a dormitory known as the Mary J. Regier Ladies' Home were built.[41] Two years after the fire, Tabor was once more in its own home. In the meantime classes had been housed in temporary quarters throughout the city.

Following the dedication of the new building in 1920, Tabor enjoyed several years of prosperity and progress. In 1924 a gymnasium was built. Soon, however, the lack of full accreditation for the college division began to effect a decline in enrollment. Between 1927 and 1930 the college made concerted efforts toward state accreditation. This goal was achieved in 1930 with some reservations regarding the senior college division. In order to preserve this status, President Lohrenz made the proposal to the General Conference of 1930 that Tabor become a conference school. Although the conference agreed to provide a modest subsidy, it was not ready to accept the full responsibility for the operation of the college.

Economic insecurity continued to hamper the college program. The situation was further aggravated by the depression and its aftermath, a decline in student enrollment, the resignation of influential teachers, and hesitant support from conference. In 1932-33, with less than 100 students, and only six full-time teachers, the college lost its state accreditation. [42]

It was now apparent that only a larger supporting constituency could keep the college in operation. In 1933 the Tabor College Corporation made another official offer to the M.B. General Conference to accept Tabor College as a conference school. In the proposal the significance of the college for the brotherhood is pointed out. The following facts and figures from the 1930 report are cited:

In the past 22 years, 5212 persons have enrolled at Tabor College. Of these, 649 graduated from one or a number of courses. A good number, really several hundred, have made the decision to live and work for the Lord. . . . Directly engaged in mission or church work are 40 missionaries, 57 evangelists and preachers, 89 high school and Bible school teachers and many Sunday school workers. In addition there are (among the alumni) 19 doctors, 46 nurses, some 400 elementary school teachers, 160 business men, many farmers, etc. [43]

The conference accepted the proposal with the proviso that the matter be referred to the local congregations for ratification by a two-thirds majority vote.

Tabor — a Conference School

The churches ratified the plan as specified and Tabor College became a General Conference institution. After temporarily closing its doors in 1934-35 for reorganization, the school resumed operation in the fall of 1935. A. E. Janzen succeeded P. C. Hiebert (who had served from 1932 to 1934) as president of the college. Janzen, with his specialization in economics, was the right man to give leadership during this time of economic depression. He introduced the "Thousand Friends Plan" — each friend giving ten dollars annually — which, together with the church contributions, provided a more stable financial basis.

The years since 1935 have been marked by moderate but steady growth in physical facilities as well as in continuous improvements in the curriculum and in the quality of instruction. Already during the first year as a conference school Tabor was accredited again as a junior college. A new phase in the development of the school began in 1942 with the appointment of P. E. Schellenberg as president and the resumption of a four-year liberal arts program. The return of servicemen to the campus after World War II swelled enrollments to their highest point in the school's history, with 422 in 1946 (including academy and special students).

In 1947 a program was set up to meet state requirements for the Secondary Teacher's Certificate. The termination of the Academy Department two years later also marked an important milestone in the school's educational progress. After Schellenberg's resignation from the presidency in 1951, two men served in this capacity for short terms: J.N.C. Hiebert (returned missionary from India) from 1952 to 1954, and F. C. Peters from 1954 to 1956.

The College of Theology

When Tabor College was founded in 1908 the study of the Bible was regarded as the core of educational activity. The Bible Department from the first provided unity, direction and purpose for the entire college program. It was not until 1924, however, that a Collegiate Bible Course (which led to the degree of Bachelor of Theology) was introduced. After the reorganization of the school in 1934-35, the Bible Department was expanded. In 1938 the Bachelor of Religious Education (B.R.E.) was added, and four years later the Graduate of Theology (Th.G.) degree was introduced.

In 1944 the Bible Department was finally organized as a separate school of theology on a seminary level, offering the Bachelor of Divinity (B.D.) program. This program continued until the conference decided to move the seminary to Fresno in 1955. Since then Tabor has had a typical college Bible Department which is integrated with the liberal arts program.[44]

Students in the Bible Department have benefited greatly from the services of outstanding teachers. In earlier years men like H. W. Lohrenz, P. C. Hiebert, P. P. Rempel, D. E. Harder and H. F. Toews gave guidance and instruction to many students who have become pastors, teachers, and missionaries in the conference program. In more recent years P. R. Lange, A. H. Unruh, D. Edmond Hiebert, C. F. Plett, Lando Hiebert, Orlando Wiebe, and Clarence Hiebert have helped to promote biblical training at Tabor College. The spiritual impact of Tabor College and especially of its Bible Department, on the educational and missionary endeavors of the M.B. Conference can hardly be overestimated. It has been the chief training ground for church leadership for several generations.[45]

A New Era

In Chapter XIII the "constitutional crisis" of 1954 and the resultant conference reorganization has been briefly described. The reorganization affected especially the educational program. Under a unified board, the U.S. Area Conference was made responsible for operating Tabor College, Pacific Bible Institute, and the Mennonite Brethren Biblical Seminary. The board initiated the "Budgeted Giving Plan" which provided the economic basis for the expansion of the educational program. The full accreditation of Tabor College became a major objective.

Under the experienced leadership of L. J. Franz, who had succeeded F. C. Peters as president, the college moved forward in the expansion of its facilities and in the improvement of its program. The first project, a modern library, was completed in 1957. In 1959 accreditation by the Kansas State Department of Public Instruction and by the University of Kansas was achieved. In 1962 the new student center-gymnasium building appeared on the campus.

In that year also Roy Just succeeded L. J. Franz as president of Tabor College. Under his able administration the college has received further accreditation by the North Central Association of Colleges and Secondary Schools (1965).

One of the outstanding features of the college year at Tabor has been the annual Bible conference. It has brought to the campus prominent Bible teachers whose expository lectures and study of special topics have enriched the lives of all participants and made a significant contribution to the total college program. Through an annual missionary conference the college endeavors to promote a deepening interest in missions.

Pacific College (Pacific Bible Institute)

Pacific College, now located on a twenty-acre campus in the southeast corner of the city of Fresno, California, began its history as a Bible institute in a large residence at 1095 N. Van Ness in 1944. Pacific Bible Institute (as it was known until 1960) came into being in response to a longfelt need on the part of the Mennonite Brethren churches on the Pacific Coast "to have a Bible school where the young people might avail themselves of a sound Biblical training in an institution organically related to their own conference."[46]

The school had a modest beginning with twenty-seven students and four full-time and two part-time instructors. S. W. Goossen served as first principal of the institute. An increasing enrollment made new facilities mandatory. In 1945 the Board of Education of the Pacific District was able to purchase a former Y.W.C.A. building at a nominal price. The school moved into this three-story structure at 2149

Tuolumne in 1946. For the first few years the institute offered training primarily in Bible, Christian education and music. As the student body increased and the ministry of the school enlarged, the curriculum was expanded.

In 1947 G. W. Peters, a former principal of the Bethany Bible Institute at Hepburn, Sask., assumed responsibility as president of Pacific Bible Institute. Under his leadership the school expanded rapidly. The curriculum was organized into a Bible college program. For a number of years the institute offered four- and five-year programs granting the Bible college Bachelor of Arts and Bachelor of Theology degrees. In 1952-53 enrollment reached 134 day-students and fifteen evening students.[47]

With the reorganization of the educational program of the United States Conference in 1954, Pacific Bible Institute entered into a period of transition. The new unified Board of Education defined the nature and scope of each institution under its jurisdiction. The theological offerings of Pacific Bible Institute were curtailed in 1955 when the Mennonite Brethren Biblical Seminary was established in Fresno. The Th.B. course was transferred to the seminary and there expanded into the B.D. program. In keeping with the unification and coordination policy, the institute now offered a three-year course leading to a diploma in Bible and a two-year course (junior college) in liberal arts. R. M. Baerg served as acting president during the interim period (1953-1955). From 1955 to 1960 B. J. Braun served as president of both schools: Pacific Bible Institute and Mennonite Brethren Biblical Seminary.

By 1959 the classroom building on the new campus was ready for occupancy. A year later the name of the school was changed to Pacific College. That same year Arthur J. Wiebe became president of Pacific College and has given effective leadership to the growing institution since then. In 1961 Pacific College became the first church-related junior college in California to receive accreditation from the Western College Association. The new (Hiebert) library building, with special accommodations for the seminary, was constructed in 1962.

Because of a sharp decrease of enrollment in the Bible institute division, this program was phased out. An increasing number of students, however, have selected a B.A. course with a Bible major. By 1965 Pacific College had developed into a full four-year liberal arts college and was accredited as such by the Western Association of Schools and Colleges (WASC). Pacific College has experienced a steady growth in attendance; from 212 in 1964-65, the student body has increased to 447 in 1971. In 1972 the graduating class of the college numbered 104 students — the largest in its history.[48]

In its latest catalog the school is identified as an Anabaptist-Mennonite college which

seeks to recapture the faith and life of the early Christian church, placing central emphasis upon the Lordship of Jesus Christ for the totality of life, the authority of the Scriptures for all matters of faith and ethics, the Christian life as a life of discipleship, the Christian church as a fellowship of redeemed people, the voluntary nature of faith and the freedom of conscience, and the active application of love to the whole of life, including the promotion of peace and nonresistance, missions, relief, mutual aid and voluntary service. [49]

These lofty aspirations are worthy of emulation by any Christian school! — Much credit for the development of the unified program of higher education in the United States Conference must go to E. J. Peters, chairman of the Board of Education for seventeen years (1954-1971). His wise leadership has been of major significance in the unification and promotion of the entire program. Whether a small conference with a membership of less than 20,000 can support two senior liberal arts colleges over a longer period of time, is a question which only future history will be able to answer.

The Mennonite Brethren Bible College

The role of the Bible college in Christian higher education may be differentiated from that of the liberal arts college as well as from that of the theological seminary. S. A. Witmer defines a Bible college as "an educational institution whose principal purpose is to prepare students for church vocations or Christian ministries through a program of Biblical and practical education." [50] Its purpose is thus broader than that of a seminary, which prepares students primarily for the pastoral ministry; it is narrower than that of the liberal arts college, since it seeks to prepare students primarily for church-related ministries.

The need for such an institution was felt by many leading brethren in the Canadian M.B. Conference in the late thirties. Official expression of this need was given by the late J. A. Toews in his report on Christian education to the 1939 Canadian Conference meeting in Coaldale, Alberta. [51] Although the challenge presented by Toews found a favorable response in the brotherhood, no definite steps were undertaken unitl 1943 (largely due to war conditions) when a recommendation was accepted by the conference to found a Bible college in Canada, to be controlled and financed by the conference, and that such a college be centrally located.

The college board, which was elected by the conference, took immediate steps to open the school in Winnipeg in the fall of 1944. [52] A. H. Unruh, veteran Bible teacher and educator, was elected by the conference to serve as first president of the Mennonite Brethren Bible College. Thus in the same year when the Pacific Bible Institute was founded in Fresno, a similar school was established in Winnipeg. Among

37. M.B. Bible College administration building. A. H. Unruh, first president

the board members who rendered valuable services in the establishment of the college, C. A. DeFehr, H. P. Toews, and B. B. Janz deserve special recognition.

To relieve Unruh of administratve duties the conference extended a call in 1945 to J. B. Toews, a man with teaching, administrative and pastoral experience, to assume the responsibility as president of the college. Both Unruh and Toews deserve much credit for establishing the school on a sound theological and academic basis.

The educational program of the college has been determined in part by present-day educational standards, in part by the great variety of interests and needs of the young people in the church, and in part by the demands of a constantly expanding missionary and educational program of the conference. Through the years the college has offered the following courses : (1) the Theological Degree Course (Th. B.); (2) the Religious Education Course (B.R.E.); (3) the Sacred Music Course; and (4) Liberal Arts courses in several fields. The Music Department has been built up by Ben Horch, whose contributions in the area of church music have been appreciated throughout the constituency.

When J. B. Toews resigned from the presidency in 1948 in order to accept a call to the pastorate of the Reedley M.B. Church, H. H. Janzen, instructor in Practical Theology, became president of the college. Under Janzen's able administration, the college enjoyed steady progress. In 1950 the college was accredited in the college division by the Accrediting Association of Bible Institutes and Bible Colleges — the first Canadian school to receive this recognition.[53] A change in administration was necessitated by Janzen's resignation in 1956 when he accepted a mission assignment in Europe. He was succeeded by J. A. Toews, who had been on the staff of M.B.B.C. since 1947.

The growth of the college necessitated the erection of new buildings from time to time. Ebenezer Hall, a dormitory for married students and single girls, was built in 1946. A modern library building, containing an auditorium, several classrooms and offices, was completed in 1956. The "Unruh Memorial Hall" (providing additional library space as well as space for conference offices) and a large new dormitory were completed in 1964.

Under Toews' administration (1956-1963) the educational program of the school was expanded. F. C. Peters, who joined the faculty of M.B.B.C. in 1957 and became dean of the college in 1961, played a key role in this expansion. A Bachelor of Divinity program, authorized by the Canadian Conference as early as 1958, was begun in 1961. The offerings in the Liberal Arts Division were also expanded. From 1951 to 1961 the college had an agreement with Waterloo College for the transfer of credits. When Waterloo College became Waterloo Lutheran University, however, and received its separate charter in 1961, the "Mennonite Brethren College of Arts" became an affiliated college of the university by special action of the Canadian M.B. Conference.

From its inception to the mid-sixties the college experienced a steady increase in enrollment. Attendance rose from thirteen students in 1944-45 to 168 in 1964-65. The maturity of the students contributed much to the spiritual atmosphere of the school. The average age of students during the first two decades was around twenty-four years. Moreover, many had an educational or professional background which added another dimension to the image of the college. Of those enrolled in 1964-65, for instance, 63 had Bible school training, 62 had attended universtiy, 33 had been engaged in teaching, 11 in nursing, and 10 had served as ministers and mission workers.[54]

That the college received increasing moral and financial support throughout the Canadian M.B. contituency must in part, at least, be attributed to the calibre of its faculty. A number of the teachers were well-known in the conference as Bible school teachers, ministers, and conference leaders even before their appointment to the college faculty. John Doerksen comments: "A major reason for the success of the college experiment has been the calibre of its staff members."[55] Besides those already mentioned, D. Ewert (1953-1972) and J. H. Quiring (1945-1955, 1962-1966) have given many years of valuable service to the college. Equally valuable, although for a shorter period of time have been the contributions of I. W. Redekop, G. D. Huebert, C. Wall, P. Klassen,

V. Martens, H. Giesbrecht, H. R. Baerg, H. H. Voth, J. J. Toews, and others.

From 1963 to 1966 J. H. Quiring served as president. In 1967 V. Adrian assumed the responsibility of leadership. In recent years there has been a decrease in enrollment, partly due, it would appear, to the resignation of several teachers who had been with the college for a long time. The decline in attendance may also be the result of a reorientation in both school and conference with regard to the role of the college in the total educational program of the brotherhood.

The spiritual impact of the Mennonite Brethren Bible College on the growth and development of the M.B. Church can be seen, at least in part, from the following statistics with regard to the ministry of graduates and former students of the college as given in a report to the 1962 Mennonite World Conference: "in missionary service 106; in the preaching ministry 102; in the teaching ministry 241; in the ministry of music 51. In addition, hundreds of former students are active in church and Sunday school work."[56]

Practically all missionaries who have been commissioned by Canadian M.B. churches for service in foreign fields during the last twenty-five years have received a part or all of their training in the Bible College. Many teachers in M.B. Bible schools are also graduates of the college. In addition, the college has been a unifying factor in the scattered and far-flung Canadian M.B. constituency.

III. THE NEED FOR PASTORAL TRAINING: THE STORY OF THE MENNONITE BRETHREN BIBLICAL SEMINARY

With the change from the multiple lay ministry to the "pastoral system" in the thirties and forties, the brotherhood, especially in the United States, became seriously concerned about a denominational seminary for the training of pastors. The first official expression toward meeting this need was made in 1948 at the M.B. General Conference in Mountain Lake, Minnesota. At that convention the conference elected a Seminary Commission which was instructed "to consider and study the practical aspect of a seminary."[57]

The Seminary Commission reported its findings at the next General Conference which was held in 1951 in Winkler, Manitoba. The commission also outlined certain procedures for establishing a theological seminary.[58] The conference at this time submitted the seminary question to the Educational Coordination Committee, which was to study the question further together with the Board of Reference and Counsel of the General Conference. At the same time the conference suggested that the Bible and Theology Department of Tabor College strengthen its B.D. program.

At the General Conference sessions in Hillsboro, Kansas, in 1954 the whole educational program of the conference was reviewed with the result that far-reaching changes were effected. With the acceptance of Pacific Bible Institute as a General Conference school, the Board of Education proceeded to coordinate the educational program of the institute and Tabor College.[59] One result of this program of coordination was the establishment of the Mennonite Brethren Biblical Seminary in Fresno.

In the fall of 1955 the seminary opened its doors for instruction in the administration building of Pacific Bible Institute with five instructors, fifteen full-time and three part-time students, and G. W. Peters, former president of P.B.I., as first dean of the seminary. D. Edmond Hiebert and P. R. Lange of the Tabor College Bible Department joined the seminary staff at the beginning, as well as Arthur G. Willems. In addition several part-time teachers assisted in the program. From the beginning the B.D. and M.R.E. programs were offered on a graduate level.[60]

In 1956 the seminary relocated on a six-acre campus on the corner of Chestnut and Butler streets in southeast Fresno. The seminary building has adequate facilities to accommodate a student body of seventy-five. The close proximity of Pacific College to the seminary makes it possible to share institutional personnel and facilities for the mutual benefit of both schools.

In the late fifties and early sixties the seminary went through several administrative changes. In 1959 G. W. Peters resigned from the school and was succeeded as dean of the seminary by R. M. Baerg. When B. J. Braun resigned as president in 1962, Baerg also served as acting president for two years (1962-64). In 1964 J. B. Toews was called to the presidency of the school. Toews had joined the faculty a year earlier, after serving as General Secretary of the Board of Missions for ten years (1953-63). His experience as pastor, educator and administrator qualified him to give effective leadership to the seminary.

Under Toews' administration a reorientation with regard to the theological stance and the specific role of the seminary was initiated.[61] Facilities were improved and expanded. A prayer chapel was erected in 1966. The Mission Memorial Court of ten two-bedroom apartments was built to accommodate married students. Although the enrollment has not been large, there has been a substantial increase in recent years. Total enrollment, including part-time students for a recent three-year period has been as follows: 1968-69 — 60; 1969-70 — 55; 1970-71 — 64. Fifty-five students have graduated from the several courses offered by the seminary in the last six years.

Besides the teachers mentioned above, H. J. Harder and Waldo

Hiebert have taught in the seminary for a number of years. In more recent years, A. J. Klassen, George Konrad, and Elmer Martens have joined the teaching staff. Orlando Wiebe, who came to the seminary from Tabor College in 1968, was called home by the Lord in 1971. A milestone in the academic progress of the seminary was reached in the early spring of 1972, when the school received accreditation from WASC (Western Association of Schools and Colleges).

Although the Canadian M.B. Conference in 1954 had withdrawn from a unified seminary program, the issue of cooperation remained a serious concern on both sides of the border. In 1968 the Board of Reference and Counsel of the General Conference presented a proposal to the Canadian and United States conferences which called for the initiation of plans to establish a unified seminary in the Vancouver area. The responses from the area conferences were such that the following resolution was accepted by the 1969 General Conference in session in Vancouver. "In view of the responses (from the conferences) the Board of Reference and Counsel recommends that studies and/or negotiations for a unified approach to higher theological education be discontinued for the time being."[62]

Two years later, however, the Canadian Conference decided to phase out the B.D. program at the Bible College in Winnipeg. At the same convention in St. Catharines a study commission was appointed to explore possibilities of cooperation in higher theological education with other groups, including the U.S. M.B. Conference. The commission, composed of F. C. Peters, H. H. Voth and Wm. Wiebe reported its findings to the Council of Boards (Canadian Conference) meeting in Winnipeg in January, 1972. In view of the findings the council initiated steps of procedure which eventually may result in a unified seminary program with the Mennonite Brethren in the United States. It could be added that through the years a number of students from Canada have attended the seminary in Fresno.

The spirit of cooperation among the schools of the M.B. Conference has found expression in a joint-publication called *Direction*. This new theological periodical (which first appeared in January, 1972) is a successor to *The Voice*, published by the Mennonite Brethren Bible College since 1952, and the *Journal of Church and Society* published since 1965 by the Mennonite Brethren Biblical Seminary, Tabor College and Pacific College. *Direction* seeks to serve the constituency by dealing with theological and church-related concerns and issues.

Next to foreign missions, institutional education among Mennonite Brethren has been one of the major fields for investment of both spiritual and material resources. This investment can only be justified if these institutions in their purpose and program remain related to the mission of the church.

Many years ago P. M. Friesen warned against two deadly enemies of the Mennonite church: a dull, self-righteous *obscurantism* or hatred of education, and the shallow intellectual *rationalism* or deism, which places education above everything. Mennonite history is replete with developments that illustrate both dangers.

There is for us, according to Friesen, but one solution:

> To win education for Christ and to place it in his service like Moses and Daniel won the wisdom of the Egyptians and the Chaldeans for the service of Jehovah. May we inspire youth for education and the arts, but teach them to know Jesus as the "most glorious of all," and the "fullness that filleth all in all;" and witness that we have in Him all joy and power in life, as well as life and comfort in death, and that we have in Him the foundation of all that is worthwhile in our social, cultural, intellectual, and spiritual life. . . . For us only such a school has value. The "swamp" (obscurantism) and the "desert" (rationalism) are both abominable to us.[63]

Chapter 17

Publishing for the Brotherhood

Although the publication efforts of the Mennonite Brethren Church have never been epoch-making nor on a large scale, they have nevertheless played a major role in the promotion of conference interests and in the preservation of conference unity. Orlando Harms, editor of the *Christian Leader*, assesses this phase of conference work as follows: "The work of publication has promoted unity in creating a denominational consciousness. It has helped to create theological unity. It has helped to advance missionary enthusiasm and enterprise. It has promoted education, relief and other conference efforts."[1] In the far-flung Mennonite Brethren constituency of North America, church publications were even more important as a "connecting link" than in the more compact settlements of Russia.

As noted in chapter seven, the publishing enterprise among Mennonite Brethren in Russia was late in getting started and was never accepted as a conference responsibility. The conference did sponsor, however, two important publications, the *Confession of Faith* and the monumental work by P. M. Friesen on the history of the M.B. Church (*Die Alt-Evangelische Mennonitische Bruederschaft in Russland*). A. H. Unruh laments the lack of denominational literature among Mennonite Brethren:

It is regrettable that the Mennonite Brethren Church in Russia was so poor in literary works of its own. It had good and competent preachers and evangelists, but few authors. . . . Short devotional pamphlets were imported from foreign countries. In their own midst writers could not be found. Had the Mennonite Brethren Church been willing to make sacrifices for this cause, much would have appeared in print that brethren had in their writing desks at home, and other brethren would have been encouraged to put their ideas into print for the benefit of coming generations.[2]

This observation is certainly also applicable to the Mennonite Brethren Church of North America, even though the restrictions of pioneer life might make this dearth of literary activity and creative writing more

283

excusable during the early period. A survey of the publication efforts in the United States and Canada shows quite clearly, that a relatively small number of brethren in the M.B. Conference through the years have had the deep conviction that "the pen is mightier than the sword" and that the minds of men (also of church members) are molded by what they read. This story with its humble beginnings and a gradually enlarging vision will now be sketched.

I. Pioneering in Publication Efforts
(1884-1906)

It appears that all conference publications in America have been the result of a response to specific church needs. Shortly after the Mennonite Brethren had settled in the United States and began to meet as a conference, they felt the need for information about the work done by their itinerant ministers. At the conference sessions in 1883 Bernhard Pauls of Coffey County, Kansas, was appointed as "editor," to gather reports from the evangelists and have them printed.[3] However, nothing appeared in the minutes the following year concerning this new venture. In response to a question by J. F. Harms, Pauls smilingly replied: "Nothing has been sent to me, consequently I could not publish anything."[4]

An organized effort was initiated in 1884, when the conference elected a committee of three brethren — Abraham Schellenberg, Dietrich Claassen, and J. F. Harms — giving them a three-fold assignment: (1) to work on the preparation of a history of the Mennonite Brethren Church; (2) to publish the annual conference reports, and (3) to publish a conference periodical. It will be recalled that a year later the Mennonite Brethren in Russia commissioned P. M. Friesen to write a history of the M.B. Church. When the brethren in America became aware of these plans, they refrained from this task.

The new committee went actively to work, however, and had the conference report printed in Elkhart, Indiana. The brethren also had numerous meetings, usually in the little hamlet of Canada (Kansas), where Harms was teaching, regarding the establishment of a conference paper. In these meetings the *Zionsbote* was born in the fall of 1884. It appeared as a four-page quarterly and the subscription rate was twenty-five cents per year. After two years as a quarterly, the *Zionsbote* became a monthly periodical; in 1889 it became a weekly paper. Two verses of Scripture were chosen as a motto for the periodical. Elder Schellenberg chose Isaiah 2:3 and Dietrich Claassen Philippians 4:8; these verses appeared on the title page in the upper left-hand corner and upper right-hand corner respectively, until the *Zionsbote* was discontinued at the end of 1964.

The story of the publication efforts of the Mennonite Brethren in America during the first twenty years is inseparably connected with the vision, faith, and perseverance of the man who was selected to be the first editor of the *Zionsbote*, the twenty-nine-year-old John F. Harms (1855-1945).[5] Harms, born and raised in the Molotschna colony of South Russia, had prepared himself for the teaching ministry. From 1873 to 1878 he taught school in the village of Lichtfelde.

In 1878 Harms and his second wife Margaret (nee Isaak)[6] emigrated to America where they made their home at Mountain Lake, Minnesota, for two years. From here he went, in God's providence, to Elkhart, Indiana, where he assisted John F. Funk in his printing establishment. In that year (1880) the *Mennonitische Rundschau* began publication (replacing the *Nebraska Ansiedler* begun in 1877). Harms was the first editor of this paper which in later years became one of the most popular Mennonite weeklies in the German language in North America. In all probability this "apprenticeship" in Christian journalism made Harms such an ardent champion of church publications among the Mennonite Brethren in the years that followed.[7]

The J. F. Harms were not members of the M.B. Church when they came to America. When they moved to Canada, Kansas, however, they joined the M.B. church west of Marion. In the fall of that same year Harms attended the Mennonite Brethren Conference for the first time. His abilities were recognized immediately and he was asked to serve as one of the secretaries. At this conference he was also elected to the "publications committee" and thus became involved in an activity that was to become his major concern in the years ahead. Shortly after he became the editor of the *Zionsbote* Harms established his own printshop in Hillsboro, Kansas.

The life of an editor of a church paper was not easy in those days. (It still is difficult, but perhaps for different reasons.) In 1887 the conference voted to allow Harms fifty dollars for his services as editor. In 1888 the honorarium amounted to only twenty-five dollars. In later years the remuneration for services fluctuated between these two figures. There were also years when he received nothing. If it had not been for other sources of income such as job printing, part-time teaching and even farming, Harms would not have been able to support his family.[8]

From its very beginning the *Zionsbote* found a good reception among the brethren in Russia. Of the subscription monies received in 1889, for instance, $123.41 had come from Russia, and $191.75 from the readers in the United States.[9] Since the Mennonite Brethren in Russia did not have an organ of their own until 1903, when the *Friedensstimme* began to be published, they sent their reports to America to be included in the *Zionsbote*. Thus the *Zionsbote* served as a major link to unite the brotherhood on two continents.

During the winter of 1897-98 Mr. and Mrs. Harms made an extended trip to Europe where they visited many M.B. congregations in Poland and Russia. This ministry also helped to make the *Zionsbote* better known among the Mennonite Brethren of Russia. Upon their return Harms established his home and printing press near Medford, Oklahoma. This was pioneer territory, since the "Cherokee Outlet" had been opened up for settlement only five years earlier. As pointed out in chapter ten, the press was first located on Harms' farm, but later it was moved to Medford. With great dedication the farmer-preacher carried on his work as printer and publisher of the *Zionsbote*.

The year 1904 marks a significant forward step in conference publication. In that year the conference established its own publishing house at Medford with J. F. Harms as editor and manager. With $100.00 advanced by a brother, Harms ordered Bibles from Germany and began the first M.B. conference bookstore. In 1904 the conference also became involved in the production of Sunday school literature by purchasing the *Lektionsblaetter* from P. F. Duerksen who had produced them since 1899.[10]

The missionary concern for the Russian people also found expression in Mennonite Brethren publication efforts. From 1905 to 1912 the *Golos* (Voice) edited by Herman Fast was published by the Mennonite Brethren Conference for the benefit of the Russian brethren in Saskatchewan and North Dakota. This monthly paper, with a circulation of about 1,500 met a real need among the scattered Russian congregations. This mission too found a warm advocate and strong supporter in Harms.

In his ministry through the printed page, J. F. Harms was ably supported by the brethren of the Publications Committee. Among those who rendered valuable services during the early years were Peter Regier, Johann Foth, John Harms, and J. K. Hiebert.[11] When in 1906 J. F. Harms resigned as editor and manager of the Publishing House, an era that might justifiably be described as the "Harms Era" came to an end. With deliberate purpose and unswerving devotion Harms had promoted the work of publications in the brotherhood for more than twenty years. With great reluctance the conference accepted his resignation. Harms felt, however, that because of his wife's poor health he should seek a new place of residence in Canada, at least temporarily. When after approximately fifteen years he returned to Hillsboro in 1921, he again became actively involved in conference publications as assistant editor of the *Zionsbote* (1922-1934) and as contributor to the

Vorwaerts and other periodicals. What A. J. Kroeker was for Mennonite Brethren publications in Russia, J. F. Harms was for M.B. publications in America — its founder and father.

II. CONSOLIDATING PUBLICATION EFFORTS
(1907-1930)

When J. F. Harms resigned at the 1906 conference in Minnesota, the Publications Committee was charged with the responsibility of finding a new editor-manager for the Publishing House. A call was extended to A. L. Schellenberg, oldest son of elder Abraham Schellenberg, to step into the gap. Schellenberg, also a teacher by profession, was reluctant to accept the new assignment. In retrospect he wrote: "With trust in God, and confident of the help of the brethren, I undertook this work though it was quite unfamiliar."[12] Early in 1907 he began the assignment to which he devoted most of his life's energy. The beginnings of his publishing work were not very auspicious. The 1906 conference had decided to relocate the M.B. Publishing House to McPherson, Kansas. This meant that the printing press had to be moved from Medford (Oklahoma) to McPherson where a building to accommodate it had been purchased for $2,500. The press was slow in arriving, for it was snowbound en route fourteen days. Great difficulties were encountered in setting up the plant. Then job work had to be found, for the conference had decided to move the plant to this new location in the hope that such work would make the business financially self-sustaining.

The enterprise was successful almost from the beginning. Schellenberg proved to be a good business manager. The printing of *Der Deutsche Westen*, a weekly newspaper published by H. J. Martens, brought in $1,500 a year. Job work flowed in from the business firms in town. Subscriptions to the *Zionsbote* increased steadily in number. But Schellenberg's concerns went beyond operating the publications business successfully from a financial point of view. At the 1908 convention he made the following observation: "Even though the business has been financially successful, I see the true gain in an increasing readership of the *Zionsbote* and in an improved content of the paper, and I rejoice when brethren and sisters are strengthened and encouraged by it."[13]

Because McPherson was an English-speaking community, the 1909 conference agreed that it was not the most suitable place for the M.B. Publishing House since it offered no German Sunday school or day school for the families of the employees. Consequently the conference authorized a relocation. In 1913 the publishing business was moved to Hillsboro, where a printing plant and the weekly German family paper,

Vorwaerts, had been purchased from Dr. J. J. Entz. The editing of the *Vorwaerts* now also fell to the lot of Schellenberg, "a job which he relished above all others in his publishing career."[14] By 1915 a new two-story building with modern facilities was constructed for the printing business, new equipment was purchased, and the work made steady progress under Schellenberg's able management.

By 1917 the war clouds began to cast their shadows on the M.B. Publishing House. The *Zionsbote* was temporarily prohibited from circulation in Canada.[15] Editor Schellenberg, an outspoken critic of the American entry into the war, was reported as disloyal to a federal investigating agency. An informer charged Schellenberg with "inciting riot" by some of his utterances, submitting two red-penciled copies of the *Zionsbote* in support of these allegations. In the July 11, 1917 issue, a passage was marked in an editorial entitled "Questionable Patriotism" which read: "It is a matter of complete indifference to many a person in our highly praised country that in God's word it is stated: 'We must obey God rather than man.' "[16] The editorial a week later was much more controversial, since Schellenberg described the "Anglophile policy" of the United States government as "a mistake."[17] The ensuing investigation resulted in an order that Editor Schellenberg file with the local postmaster an English as well as a German version of every item in his paper that pertained to public affairs.

Schellenberg weathered the storm from "without," but his editorials as well as his management of the Publishing House caused a minor storm from "within." Schellenberg felt that the criticism of his policies by leading brethren of the conference was unfair, and so he resigned in 1919 as editor and manager of the Publishing House and moved to a farm in Littlefield, Texas. At the time of Schellenberg's resignation the printing establishment had assests in excess of $16,000. The circulation of the papers had increased to 5,500 for the *Vorwaerts*, and to 3,500 for the *Zionsbote*.

When Schellenberg left, the Publications Committee engaged J. D. Fast, who had served as assistant for several years, as editor and manager. In 1921 the Publishing House, with the approval of the conference, purchased the bookstore which professor D. E. Harder had owned and operated for a number of years in Hillsboro. In 1922 P. H. Berg joined the staff of the Publishing House as manager of the expanded book department, and as assistant business manager.

The year 1922 was crucial for Mennonite Brethren publications. Editor J. D. Fast resigned after a service of only three years, and again the committee looked for a man to give leadership to the publishing enterprise. In response to an overwhelming preference of church members whose advice was solicited, and upon petition of the Hillsboro businessmen, the job was again offered to A. L. Schellenberg.[18] Although he had been highly successful as a farmer, Schellenberg returned to the editor's desk and the work which had become so much a part of his life. In the ensuing years he also played a leading role in the Hillsboro community.[19]

In his editorial work Schellenberg was ably assisted by J. F. Harms, the veteran of M.B. publications. Both men were very sensitive to the tragic plight of the Mennonites in Russia in this post-war period; the reports and letters published in the *Zionsbote* and *Vorwaerts* reflected the concern of the editors. The extent of the coverage of the Russian emergency was shown in Schellenberg's summary report early in 1923. Thirty-five of the 197 news reports carried in seven issues came out of Russia.[20]

It was perhaps to be expected that a crusader of Schellenberg's caliber would encounter difficulties as editor of a denominational paper. It was Schellenberg's policy to freely publish controversial material if in his opinion it contributed to the search for truth. A crusading editor of our present day has this to say about Schellenberg: "In news coverage and opinion leadership he was one of the most progressive editors of his time."[21] Eventually, however, Schellenberg's controversial editorial policy as well as increasing tensions in his relationship with the Publications Committee made his resignation inevitable. Schellenberg terminated his work as editor in May, 1930, although he had resigned several months earlier. His article "A last Word from the Editor" published in the May 21 issue of the *Zionsbote*, created considerable resentment in the conference.[22] It is unfortunate that the outstanding achievements of Schellenberg as editor and manager were overshadowed by tensions and misunderstandings during the last few years of his service.

Two books of historical significance were written by Mennonite Brethren in the 1920's. J. F. Harms wrote the *Geschichte der Mennoniten Bruedergemeinde*, which was published by the M.B. Publishing House in 1925. P. C. Hiebert, chairman of MCC, was the main contributor to the book *Feeding the Hungry*, published at Scottdale, Pennsylvania, in 1929.

With the appointment of P. H. Berg as manager of the Publishing House in 1930, M.B. publications entered a more quiet and less controversial period. J. F. Harms continued to serve as assistant editor until 1934. In the meantime, however, the large-scale immigration of Mennonite Brethren into Canada also led to new developments in this phase of conference work.

38. J. F. Harms   39. H. F. Klassen

III. CHANGING PUBLICATION NEEDS
(1930-1963)

1. *Developments in Canada*

In the late twenties the *Mennonitische Rundschau* emerged as one of the most popular Mennonite weeklies among the Mennonite immigrants in Canada, competing with *Der Mennonitische Immigrantenbote*, also a weekly family paper published by D. H. Epp at Rosthern from January, 1924.[23] The *Mennonitische Rundschau*, the oldest Mennonite periodical to appear continuously under one name, made its first appearance in 1880 as the successor to the *Nebraska Ansiedler*. The Mennonite Publishing Company, Elkhart, Indiana, published it until 1908. From 1908 to 1923 it was published in Scottdale, Pennsylvania, by the Mennonite Publishing House.

In 1923 the publication of the two German-language weeklies of the Mennonite Publishing House in Scottdale, *Mennonitische Rundschau* and *Christlicher Jugendfreund*, was transferred to Winnipeg by Hermann H. Neufeld, who at that time established the Rundschau Publishing House. Neufeld, a Mennonite Brethren immigrant from Russia, edited the *Mennonitische Rundschau* for twenty-two years (1923-1945) and helped to preserve its "Russian Mennonite character." Many of the older Mennonite immigrants in Canada remembered the "European edition" of the paper which had been widely circulated among Russian Mennonites prior to World War I, and hence they were eager to subscribe to it again in the new world.

In 1940 the Rundschau Publishing House was reorganized into the Christian Press, Ltd. In 1945 this corporation was purchased by a group of brethren in the Canadian Mennonite Brethren Conference. The Canadian Conference purchased 400 shares of this corporation in 1946, and another 600 in 1956. At the sessions in Virgil, Ontario, in 1960, the conference moved to purchase the remaining 3750 shares and thus become the sole owner of the Christian Press Ltd. This step completed the gradual process of "polarization" in M.B. publications (as noted in chapter thirteen) and resulted in the operation of two publishing centers among Mennonite Brethren in North America — Winnipeg and Hillsboro.

With the acquisition of the Christian Press shares by the Canadian M.B. Conference, the *Mennonitische Rundschau* did not become the organ of the Mennonite Brethren Church, but continued to serve as a Mennonite religious weekly of the larger brotherhood. In 1960 editor H.F. Klassen wrote about the historical significance of the *Rundschau* as follows:

> During the eighty years of its publication this paper has recorded the history of the Russian Mennonites, their trials and tribulations, emigrations and immigrations, drafting of their young men for government forestry service, family life, church life, education and social matters, wars and revolutions, terrible persecutions, refugee problems, pioneering in five countries in South America, language changes and economic struggles — all these happenings and more have been chronicled by the *Mennonitische Rundschau*. [24]

Long before the Christian Press became the publishing house of the Canadian Mennonite Brethren, the conference regarded the *Mennonitische Rundschau* and the *Christlicher Jungendfreund* as semi-official organs of the brotherhood. In response to the report of the Christian Press manager, H. F. Klassen, the delegation in 1949 passed the following resolution: "The Conference appreciates the opportunity, that through certain papers published by the Christian Press it is able to extend its spiritual influence into many homes." [25] The *Zionsbote* was still regarded, however, as the official periodical of the M.B. Church. At the convention held in Herbert (Sask.) in 1951, the conference delegates expressed their sentiments as follows: "We desire that the *Zionsbote* remain the organ of the entire M.B. Church; but we recommend substantial improvements." [26] This "ambivalence" in the publications policy of the Canadian Conference characterizes the attitude of the brotherhood in the post-war period until 1960.

In this earlier period (1945-1960) the growth and expansion of publication efforts in Canada must be attributed to the vision, courage and commitment of a relatively small number of brethren. H. F. Klassen, editor of the *Mennonitische Rundschau* for twenty-two years (1945-1967) and general manager of the Christian Press for the major part of that period, deserves special recognition for his untiring efforts to promote the work of publications in the Canadian Conference. In order not to impose a financial burden upon the fledgling publishing enterprise, Klassen retained his position in a Winnipeg business firm during the first five years, devoting his evenings to the editorial work at the Christian Press. Another man who rendered valuable services in the development of the publishing house, and especially its physical plant, was C. A. DeFehr, who through the years became actively involved in practically every major enterprise of the Canadian Conference. Other brethren who served for shorter or longer terms on the board of directors of the Christian Press during this early period were J. P. Neufeld, F. H. Friesen, C. C. Warkentin and B. B. Janz.

Beginning its operation in 1945 with a substantial deficit, the Christian Press, under the supervision of its competent production manager, J. K. Neufeld, was gradually transformed into a profitable enterprise. In 1950 H. F. Klassen was able to report that in addition to the publication of the two German Mennonite weeklies the Christian Press was printing nine other periodicals in seven different languages as well as four Sunday school manuals. Whereas the financial transactions of the Christian Press in 1944 had amounted to $14,300 (including a deficit of over $4,000) the financial turnover in 1950 amounted to approximately $47,000, yielding a net profit of $4,800.[27]

Encouraged by the prospects of further growth, the shareholders that year decided to relocate the Christian Press. From the small and crowded quarters at 672 Arlington Street, the publishing house in 1951 moved into the spacious, new, two-story building located at 159 Kelvin Street (now called Henderson Highway). The annual conference reports consistently stressed the missionary character of the publishing enterprise. After reporting a profitable financial year at the 1950 convention, the manager added: "Far more important, however, is the main purpose of a Christian publication enterprise: to cultivate Christian attitudes, to proclaim a good message, to report on Divine Providence in the life of the Mennonite brotherhood, to portray a world that moves toward an impending judgment, and to render comfort and aid."[28] At the convention the following year the delegates accepted a part of this mission through the printed page by agreeing to pay for 500 copies of the *Mennonitische Rundschau* out of the conference treasury to make the paper available without charge to needy fellow-believers in South America and Europe.

Another forward step was taken at the convention in 1952 when the Committee of Reference and Counsel recommended the election of a publications committee. This action was motivated by an increasing awareness of the need for appropriate literature in both German and

English in the M.B. constituency. "We have to admit," the recommendation reads, "that in our circles there is a lack of literature that presents the ethical and religious views of our Conference and its Bible exposition."[29] The committee's duties appear to be limited to the production and promotion of appropriate tracts, pamphlets, and books, and did not include the publication of a conference paper. The *Konferenz-Jugendblatt*, as we have seen earlier, was published by the Canadian Conference Youth Committee.

The question of an English family paper was a crucial and sometimes controversial issue in the Canadian Conference during the fifties. When the *Christian Leader* became the official organ of the General Conference in 1951, it appeared that this paper might also meet the needs in the Canadian constituency. At the annual convention that year in Herbert, Saskatchewan, the delegates accepted a recommendation presented by Elmo Warkentin, chairman of the Publications Committee of the General Conference, that the *Christian Leader* be accepted (provisionally) "as the official English language conference paper."[30]

However, official conference action does not always result in the practical realization of any given concern. The *Christian Leader* continued to have only a limited appeal among Mennonite Brethren in Canada. In a report to the constituency, the Publications Committee of the Canadian Conference explains this lack of response as follows: "The *Christian Leader* is an excellent paper. The difficulty has been that Canadian coverage has been lacking and it has failed to become popular in the majority of homes of the members of the Canadian Conference."[31]

The initiative for an English "Mennonite Brethren" family paper was taken by the Board of Directors of the Christian Press. On September 21, 1955, the *Mennonite Observer* made its first appearance with Leslie Stobbe as editor. However, another independent weekly newspaper, *The Canadian Mennonite*, published by D. W. Friesen & Sons Ltd., and edited by Frank H. Epp, was already firmly established by that time. This attractive Mennonite weekly, founded in October, 1953, endeavored to serve all Mennonite groups and communities in Canada. Because of its editorial policy of free discussion of current and even controversial issues, *The Canadian Mennonite* appealed especially to the younger generation, also in M.B. circles. The *Mennonite Observer* thus was faced with the problem of keen competition right from its inception.

In 1957 the conference agreed to terminate the publication of the *Konferenz-Jugendblatt*, and to give its support to the *Mennonite Observer* as a youth paper without making the latter an official organ of the M.B. Conference.[32] The number of subscribers for the *Mennonite Observer* remained relatively small, and the paper had to be subsidized by the Christian Press. After several years, Leslie Stobbe was succeeded by G. D. Huebert as editor of the paper. The last issue of the *Mennonite Observer* was published on December 29, 1961.

For a whole decade (1951-1961) negotiations were carried on between the publications committees and other boards of the Canadian and United States area conferences with the objective of unifying publication efforts. At the convention of the General Conference held in Yarrow, B.C., in 1957, the following recommendation was accepted by the delegates: "We recommend in principle that ways and means be found cooperatively with the Canadian Conference whereby an official English or German organ of our General Conference be gotten into every home of our constituency in the U.S. and Canada, as a unifying link for our entire General Conference."[33] At the Centennial Conference in Reedley three years later the conference reaffirmed its concern for a united voice in publications by passing the following resolution: "That the Board of Reference and Counsel of the General Conference meet with the present Board of Publication and the Canadian Board of Publication and work out suggestive steps leading to a united voice in one conference periodical."[34]

The recommendation prepared by these boards and presented to the area conferences in 1961, however, was not accepted by the Canadian Conference meeting at Coaldale, Alberta, in July of that year. Instead, a recommendation by the Publications Committee of the Canadian Conference was accepted "that we introduce a levy of $1.00 per member for an English family paper, and that every family receive this paper free for one year."[35] In January, 1962, this committee began to publish the *Mennonite Brethren Herald* as the official organ of the Canadian Conference.

Rudy H. Wiebe, a graduate of the Mennonite Brethren Bible College and an English instructor at the University of Alberta, was appointed as first editor of the *Herald*. With vigor and enthusiasm Wiebe applied himself to his new and challenging task. By coincidence, the first issue of the *Mennonite Brethren Herald* also contained an announcement of Wiebe's forthcoming first novel, entitled: *Peace Shall Destroy Many*. The controversy over this novel more than that regarding editorial policies, led to Wiebe's resignation in the summer of 1963.[36] At the termination of Wiebe's services the Publications Committee of the conference addressed Brother Wiebe with these words on the editorial page of the *Herald*: "Through your pioneering effort the *M.B. Herald* has been given direction in the areas of quality and organizational structure. Your thorough and long-range planning has resulted in the high standard of literary achievement which it now enjoys."[37]

During the 1963-64 year, Peter Klassen, music teacher at the Mennonite Brethren Bible College, served as interim-editor of the *Herald*. In July, 1964, Harold Jantz, high school teacher from Virgil, Ontario, assumed the responsibilities as editor of the conference periodical. For almost eight years now Jantz has faithfully and creatively served in this capacity. Since the *Herald* is sent to every Mennonite Brethren home in the Canadian Conference, the paper constitutes the most effective means of keeping members informed and uniting the widely scattered brotherhood in the common faith and task.

It should be added that the *Mennonitische Rundschau* continues to enjoy a widespread popularity after more than ninety years of publication. When H. F. Klassen retired from the editorial office in 1967 (partly because of failing health), Erich Ratzlaff, a high school teacher from British Columbia, succeeded him as editor of this Christian family paper. Under Ratzlaff's able and wise guidance, the *Rundschau* continues its vital role as an inter-Mennonite paper, serving also as a connecting link between Mennonites in North America, South America and Europe.

Through the years several major works were published by the Christian Press in the areas of Mennonite history, church doctrine, and Bible exposition. In 1949 the first volume of *Mennonitische Maertyrer* (written and edited by A. A. Toews) appeared, followed five years later by a second volume. In 1955 the Christian Press printed A. H. Unruh's 847-page volume, *Die Geschichte der Mennoniten Bruedergemeinde*, a book sponsored by the General Conference of the Mennonite Brethren Church. In the same year the Board of General Welfare and Public Relations published the booklet, *True Nonresistance Through Christ* (written by J. A. Toews) which was also printed by the Christian Press. In 1959 the Publications Committee of the Canadian Conference published *Alternative Service in Canada During World War II* by the same author.

Relatively few books in the biblical-theological field have been produced within the Canadian Conference. The expository messages given at the annual Bible conferences in Winnipeg have provided the materials for two books. Messages by A. H. Unruh and H. H. Janzen have been published under the title *Der Ewige Sohn Gottes* (1948) and messages on 1 Corinthians by D. Ewert, F. C. Peters, and J. A. Toews appeared as *Das ernste Ringen um die reine Gemeinde* in 1965. In addition, several pamphlets on Christian ethics and church life have been published from time to time.

The latest development in the history of Mennonite Brethren

publications in Canada is the merger of the Christian Press bookstore with the "Faith and Life" bookstore of the General Conference Mennonites located at Rosthern, Saskatchewan. Initially the combined bookstore is to operate from the present premises of the Christian Press, but the goal of the amalgamation is expansion at a new location.

2. Developments in the United States

As indicated earlier, P. H. Berg became editor-manager of the M.B. Publishing House in 1930. The economic depression of the thirties affected every phase of conference work, including publications. In his report to the General Conference in 1933 Berg stated: "The last three years were in many respects perhaps the most difficult in the history of our country, and our work of publications has felt the impact of the Depression all too keenly."[38] Although the conference saw the need for enlarging the publication business in several directions, including the establishment of a small book bindery, it decided to postpone any expansion until economic conditions would improve. For reasons of economy also the responsibilities of editor and manager were again vested in one person. P. H. Berg must be given credit for his sagacity in keeping the publishing enterprise in operation during this difficult period.

By 1936 there were pressing needs, however, that called for a new venture in publications. Many churches were in the midst of a language transition from German to English. The General Conference meeting in Reedley that year went on record as favoring an English periodical "in order to meet the needs of our English speaking young people."[39] This desire was realized when the *Christian Leader* appeared on March 1, 1937, as the official youth paper of the conference. P. H. Berg served as editor from 1937 through 1939, and J. W. Vogt, pastor of the Hillsboro M.B. Church, from 1940 to 1953. (During the last few years Vogt edited the paper in Corn, Oklahoma.) The Youth Committee was responsible for the publication of the *Christian Leader* until 1951, when it became the official conference organ. The *Leader* was published as a 32-page monthly from 1937 to 1943 when it was changed to a larger format and 16 pages. In 1946 it was changed to a 16-page semi-monthly.

Upon request of the 1939 General Conference the Publishing House began the production of the "Graded Sunday School Lessons" in 1940. Ten years later the English Adult Quarterly replaced the "Graded Sunday School Lessons." Both name and language of the *Vorwaerts* were changed in 1939, when the paper was renamed the *Hillsboro Journal*, and also became bilingual in content. In 1951 the Publications Committee recommended that the conference dispose of the *Hillsboro Journal* since its publication demanded too much staff time to justify continuation. In 1953 this paper was sold and subsequently merged with another local paper.

The election of A. J. Voth as business manager in 1948 was another forward step in the operation of the publishing enterprise.[40] In 1949 the Publishing House undertook an expansion program whereby an $18,000 addition was added to the building, and about $24,000 was spent by 1953 for more adequate equipment.[41] In 1954 P. H. Berg retired from the editorship of the *Zionsbote*. The conference expressed its appreciation by giving him a vote of thanks for his thirty-two years of service in the Publishing House of the brotherhood.

A new chapter in publications was begun in 1954 with the appointment of Orlando Harms to the position of general manager as well as editor for both conference papers — the *Zionsbote* and the *Christian Leader*. Harms brought to his new assignment the experience of teaching in Tabor College (where the author was his student) and also his pastoral experience in the city of Wichita. Under Harms' capable leadership the Publishing House was able to liquidate its indebtedness and the *Leader* was improved in form and content. The bookstore, which had been located in a separate building for a few years, was moved back into the Publishing House in 1955 and its services expanded.

Although negotiations with the brethren in Canada with regard to a united effort in publications continued throughout the fifties, the United States Conference moved forward and initiated a new pattern of meeting the needs of the brotherhood. The first area conference held in Reedley in 1957 voted to accept a plan whereby each congregation would contribute $5.00 per family per year to publications. In return the *Christian Leader* was to be sent to every family of the constituency. Upon ratification by the churches in the United States this plan went into effect in 1958. The response to this new arrangement was gratifying. At the second area conference in Fairview, Oklahoma, Orlando Harms reported:

> It has been very encouraging to receive expressions of enthusiasm regarding the *Leader* plan from many of our ministers. . . . (some) report that, especially young people, as a result of reading the *Leader*, for the first time are beginning to realize what programs in missions, education, relief, and other areas our Conference is carrying on, stating that they "never knew" our Conference was doing all this. No doubt this will also influence their giving, their praying, and their going. [42]

As a result of this plan, the circulation of the *Christian Leader* increased to 6,000 by 1960. The subscriptions to the *Zionsbote*, however, gradually declined and consequently the 1963 General Conference in Winnipeg accepted the motion to "publish the *Zionsbote* until January 1, 1965, at which time all remaining subscriptions be transferred to the *Mennonitische Rundschau*."[43] Thus the eventful pilgrimage of this "Messenger of Zion" in the Mennonite Brethren Church came to an end after eighty years of faithful service.

In addition to the books published by the Christian Press, a goodly number of books and pamphlets have been printed by the M.B. Publishing House in Hillsboro, some on a job basis, and others published by the Publishing House. Among these, according to Orlando Harms are the following: *Jesus kommt wieder* and *Topical Outline Studies in Bible Doctrine* by H. F. Toews; the *Confession of Faith* (both German and English); *Fundamentals of Faith* and *Working by Prayer* by D. Edmond Hiebert; *Kurzgefasste Einleitung ins Alte Testament* by A. H. Unruh; *Der wundervolle Ratschluss Gottes mit der Menschheit* by J. W. Reimer; *The Growth of Foreign Missions in the Mennonite Brethren Church* by G. W. Peters; *The Mennonite Brethren Church* by J. H. Lohrenz; *Sixty Years of M.B. Missions* by Mrs. H. T. Esau; *Your Church and You* by F. C. Peters, and many other books and pamphlets.[44]

In 1946 the Publishing House joined the publication boards of the General Conference Mennonites and the (Old) Mennonites in the production of *The Mennonite Encyclopedia*. The first volume of this invaluable resource for the study of Anabaptist-Mennonite history appeared in 1955, and the fourth and final volume in 1959.

IV. NEW ERA IN PUBLICATIONS
(SINCE 1963)

Some significant developments in Mennonite Brethren publication efforts have occurred during the last decade. In 1963 the Board of Reference and Counsel of the General Conference of Mennonite Brethren recommended to the convention the establishment of a "Christian Literature Commission." The rationale for this recommendation is given as follows:

Inasmuch as there is a great need at home and abroad for the production of appropriate Christian literature in the form of books, pamphlets, etc., and inasmuch as the printed page is of tremendous influence in the world today, and inasmuch as proper literature offers a great opportunity to represent our Mennonite Brethren faith and church and to promote the purpose and program of our Conference, we recommend the appointment of a five-man commission by the Board of Reference and Counsel to study the establishment, organization and function of a Christian Literature Board and to report to the Board of Reference and Counsel before the next General Conference Session.[45]

The conference accepted this recommendation and the Board of Reference and Counsel subsequently appointed the following brethren to the commission: Marvin Hein (chairman), A. J. Klassen, Elmer A. Martens, Werner Kroeker and William Neufeld. Upon receiving the report of the study commission the Board of Reference and Counsel appointed Elmer Martens, A. J. Klassen and William Neufeld to an interim Board of Christian Literature in January, 1965, to serve till the time of the convention in November, 1966. The study commission had outlined the areas of responsibility for the Board of Christian Literature as follows:

a. to coordinate the production of literature in our Conference.
b. to encourage Christian writing and journalism.
c. to disseminate lists of Christian literature of particular value.
d. to produce literature in areas of need.[46]

The interim board did not lose any time in initiating studies and actions to realize the goals it had set for itself. Having received the assignment from the Board of Reference and Counsel to produce a devotional guide for family and personal use, the brethren began publishing *Worship Together* in January, 1966. After several attempts to secure an editor for this bimonthly devotional booklet, A. J. Klassen, board member, was asked to serve as interim editor. The publication of *Worship Together* marked the beginning of a new era in conference publications since it was the first devotional guide prepared by Mennonite Brethren writers and specifically serving Mennonite Brethren interests in missions, education, etc., by related prayer requests. (The latter had also partly been the function of the *Intercessor* published by the Board of Missions prior to 1966.)

The conference meeting for its triennial convention in Corn, Oklahoma, in 1966 was pleased with the detailed report and the ambitious projections of the interim board and elected all three brethren — Martens, Klassen, and Neufeld — by acclamation into the Board of Christian Literature (BCL). The other members on the board were representatives of the Christian education and publication boards of the two area conferences. During the 1966-69 interim the brethren John Unger and H. H. Dueck represented the U.S. and Canadian Christian education boards respectively, and L. J. Franz and Vernon Ratzlaff the publication boards of the two areas. The editors Orlando Harms and Harold Jantz were coopted as ex officio members.

After editing *Worship Together* for eighteen months, A. J. Klassen was succeeded as editor in September, 1967 by George Konrad, professor of Christian education at the Mennonite Brethren Biblical Seminary. Several new features such as hymn of the month suggestions and action plans were introduced under his creative leadership. A survey which the Board of Christian Literature conducted in the spring of 1969, was both disturbing and encouraging. Findings of the survey (to which 1200 families and 130 pastors had responded) were as follows: "Less than half of the families have regular daily devotions (according to reports from pastors). Eighty percent of those who practice family devotions use *Worship Together*."[47]

The devotional guide did not only meet a widely felt need in the

M.B. Conference. At the 1969 convention the board was happy to report an interest in the (Old) Mennonite Conference to investigate the possibility of merging their devotional guide with *Worship Together*. This was the first step in the process that led to the publication of an inter-Mennonite devotional booklet. After prolonged consultations and negotiations among representatives of the (Old) Mennonites, General Conference Mennonites and Mennonite Brethren, the new worship devotional *Rejoice!*, edited by George Konrad, appeared on March 1, 1972. The total printing of the first issue of *Rejoice!* was 26,000, with more than 7,300 of these going into Mennonite Brethren homes.[48]

The Board of Christian Literature rapidly moved into other areas to meet specific needs in the work of the church. In 1968 it published *A Manual for Church Membership Classes* prepared by an editorial commission consisting of Loyal Martin (coordinator), Al Kroeker, I. Tiessen, H. H. Voth, and Katie Funk Wiebe. A work book entitled, *A Study Guide for Church Membership Classes*, written by George Konrad, was also published in 1968. A book of helps for ministers, *The Minister's Manual* was prepared by an editorial commission consisting of Wilmer Kornelson (coordinator), Waldo Hiebert, Orlando Wiebe, and Herbert Brandt.

In 1970 the BCL published an illustrated, colorful forty-eight page booklet entitled *Introducing the Mennonite Brethren Church*, designed to present a basic outline of the historical developments and doctrinal position of the Mennonite Brethren Church. It was prepared in extensive consultation with pastors and conference agencies in order to provide information for young people and new converts who come from a different church background or have perhaps had no contact with any church.

Perhaps the most ambitious undertaking of the young board was the publication of a symposium *The Church in Mission* (1967), edited by A. J. Klassen. This book, dedicated to J. B. Toews as a sixtieth anniversary tribute for his contribution to the brotherhood as an educator, pastor, and missions administrator, contains a series of twenty-one essays, written by as many leaders of the church, on biblical foundations, historical recovery, and newer dimensions of the church's mission.

The vision and personal involvement in the task on the part of the chairman, Elmer Martens, and the secretary-treasurer, A. J. Klassen, have been important factors in the remarkable progress the Board of Christian Literature has made in a relatively short time. Among the present projects of the board is the writing of a history of Mennonite Brethren missions by G. W. Peters, J. B. Toews, and J. J. Toews. Another important projection presently in the early stages of realization is the "Trailblazer Series." This series of pamphlets attempts to recapture the vision, dedication and contribution of former Mennonite Brethren leaders and to make this spiritual heritage available to the present generation.

The motto which appears on the letterhead of the Board of Christian Literature is an appropriate definition of the assignment in publications that the Mennonite Brethren have accepted as their mission to this present age: "Write the vision and make it plain" (Hab. 2:2).

Chapter 18

Serving with Various Gifts: The Ministry in the Church

The role of the ministry became one of the key issues leading to the secession of the original Mennonite Brethren. The new group severely criticized the ministers and leaders in the Mennonite Church. After referring to the ungodly life of church members in the Document of Secession the Brethren pointed out that "even the teachers (preachers) go about and see it, yes even at social festivities sit quietly by; see and hear how people serve the devil. . . . The teachers do not stand in the gap as of old." When in late March, 1860, they were asked to explain the reasons for their withdrawal from the Mennonite Church, the Brethren again focused on the failure of the ministry: "With joy we would even now return to our churches if the ministers (*Lehrer*) would earnestly oppose corruption according to the Word of God and we would assist them with God's help to restore the churches."[1]

From this statement it seems clear that alongside of the criticism of existing church leaders, there emerged among the early Brethren a new concept of the ministry which involved the active participation of church members. As in most church renewal movements, the Brethren returned to the scriptural emphasis of the priesthood of all believers, and considered the "ministry" as a kind of service in which all Christians are engaged, not only a chosen few. It was perhaps providential that among the eighteen "founding fathers" there was not a single ordained preacher or deacon. This compelled the Brethren to rethink and reexamine the question of the ministry in the light of biblical teaching. That this actually happened is evident from their confessional documents. When elder Heinrich Huebert, representing the Molotschna Mennonite Brethren Church, was asked to give an account[2] concerning the practices of his church, he elaborated also on the understanding of the Mennonite Brethren with regard to the ministry. Excerpts from that document reflect this new conception of the Brethren.

In our assemblies and inspirational meetings, we have tried to follow the rule and order given in 1 Corinthians 14, i.e., that one or two, or a maximum of three persons present their lectures, and that in succession. We recognize herein the loving purpose of the apostle: that the church be edified, the gifts stirred up, and the saints prepared for the work of the ministry....

The officiation at the baptismal ceremony is the duty of the elder or deacon (*Diener*). However, as was the case in the house of Cornelius, where Peter "commanded them to be baptized" (Acts 10:48), it may also be performed by another, whom the church has designated.

Likewise, at the communion service, the distributing of the bread and cup is the duty of the elder or deacon.... (but) according to the teaching of the Apostle Paul in 1 Corinthians 11:23-24 it is not absolutely necessary that a teacher (preacher) be present. [3]

This view of the nature of the ministry was not only a return to the teachings of the New Testament, but also to the early Anabaptist conception, in which the ministry is never related to any position or profession, but always is a function of the believer as a member of the Body of Christ. During the more than 100 years of Mennonite Brethren history there have not only been various cultural adaptations of this New Testament ideal, but there has also developed a widening gap between "vision and reality" in the actual practice of congregations and conferences. This chapter will briefly describe changes and developments in several areas of "ministry," and indicate the significance of these trends for the brotherhood.

I. The Ministry of the Word

In order to see the role of the ministry in historical perspective, it is necessary to describe first the practices of the M. B. Church in Russia, before the developments in America are presented.

1. Developments in Russia

The pattern that emerged in early M.B. congregations can be best described as a "multiple lay ministry." The churches elected and subsequently ordained several brethren from their own midst for the preaching of the Word and the spiritual supervision of the congregations. In the Molotschna colony the brethren initially elected were Heinrich Huebert and Jacob Becker.[4] In Chortitza Abraham Unger and Heinrich Neufeld were the first chosen ministers, and when Neufeld withdrew from the fellowship, Aron Lepp was elected to take his place. Soon other brethren were asked to serve as assistants (*Mitarbeiter*) and after a probationary period they were usually ordained to the ministry.

A unique office in the early M.B. Church was that of "administrator" (*Regierer*) for which the scriptural basis was found in 1 Corinthians 12:28. In the summer of 1863 Simon Harms and Jacob Becker (who had withdrawn from the ministry) were elected as administrators.[5] The man who earned special respect and recognition for this office, however, was Philipp Isaak, Elder Huebert's right-hand

man, whose work has been mentioned earlier. The introduction of this
"office" in the M.B. Church is an illustration of the desire of the early
Brethren to see "the gifts stirred up" (to use Elder Huebert's phrase)
and to recover the New Testament concept of the ministry.

Although ministerial candidates in Russia up to World War I
generally did not have any theological or seminary training for the
ministry, they were often chosen from the ranks of the teaching
profession. This, together with the fact that the pulpit ministry was a
shared ministry, provided the intellectual and spiritual resources for a
balanced diet and for adequate nurture of church members. That the
early M.B. Church was well provided with preachers can be seen from
the conference statistics of 1885. The six main churches were served by
four elders and thirty-five ministers.[6]

The office of elder in the early M.B. Church is somewhat of an
enigma. No rationale is given in the available records for introducing
this office some eight years after the founding of the church. Since both
Huebert (in the Molotschna) and Unger (in Chortitza) had experienced
severe opposition and disastrous defeats in their ministry during the
period of storm and stress, it may be that the brethren intended to
strengthen the authority of their leadership by giving these brethren the
status of elders. Of course, they also had the precedent and pattern for
such procedure in the Mennonite Church. As mentioned earlier, Huebert
was ordained as elder in late summer, 1868, and Unger in the fall of 1869.
It will be recalled that Unger was ordained to this office by the Baptist
minister J. G. Oncken — even though the Baptists had no such office in
their church polity.

During the following decade Elder Huebert ordained Abraham
Schellenberg as his successor in the Molotschna, and Daniel Fast in the
Kuban, thus establishing a certain "apostolic succession." The elders in
the early M.B. Church functioned as "superintendents" of parishes or
districts. The 1902 *Confession of Faith*, however, appears to limit the
function of the elder somewhat. It states:

> In the household of the M.B. Church the order obtains, that one elder or a
> substitute for the elder acts as moderator and leader of local churches. The other
> ministers are his co-workers. With the various affairs of the entire denomination
> the suitable elders and other brethren are entrusted.[7]

In the first decade of this century the validity and usefulness of the
office of an elder began to be seriously questioned in the M.B. Church.
In the controversy over "open communion" the elders had emerged as
the defenders of the status quo. David Schellenberg, the only elder in the
Molotschna M.B. Church, was the leader in the conflict with the "open
brethren," especially with J. W. Reimer, conference evangelist.
Moreover, certain aspects in Schellenberg's private life added to the
mounting tensions between the Rueckenau M.B. Church and its elder.[8]

The matter came to a head at Pentecost in 1909, when Schellenberg was deposed from the office of elder and even temporarily forbidden to preach.

This controversy in the Rueckenau church provided the occasion for the reexamination of the scriptural teaching concerning the elder. Many began to agree with the observation of Peter Unruh: "The system is sick, that is why our men get sick."[9] David Schellenberg was the last minister to be ordained elder in the Rueckenau M.B. Church. The view that eventually prevailed in all M.B. churches is summarized by A. H. Unruh as follows:

> From Rueckenau came the interpretation, that according to the Gospel all ministers of the congregation have the status of elders; the council of elders (*Aeltestenrat*) was emphasized, based upon Paul's words in Philippians 1, where he greets the bishops and deacons. Preacher J. W. Reimer coined the expression: "The leader of the church is the man who has the gift of leadership; he is the first among equals."[10]

Generally speaking the multiple lay ministry in the M.B. Church in Russia proved adequate for the time and contributed significantly to the wholesome development of the congregations. In America, however, under the pressures of a changing culture, and exposure to influences from other denominations, a new pattern eventually emerged in Mennonite Brethren congregations.

2. *Developments in the United States*

The pattern of an unsalaried multiple lay ministry was retained by the Mennonite Brethren when they established congregations in the United States. In the list of ministers and deacons of annual conference yearbooks up to World War II (and in some instances later) one finds that all larger congregations had a number of ordained ministers, as well as one or more assistant ministers (*Mitarbeiter*).

The "elder system" was also retained until about 1920, although relatively few ministers were ordained to this office in M.B. churches in America. According to a survey made in the fall of 1971, no elder was ordained in Mennonite Brethren churches after 1919. In one of the former K.M.B. churches the last elder was ordained in 1932.[11] No elder has ever been ordained in the churches of the Pacific District Conference, but John Berg is mentioned as having been elected to this office in the Reedley M.B. Church in 1910. Something similar to the "elder crisis" experienced by the Molotschna M.B. Church in 1909 seems to have occurred in American M.B. churches a few years later. The desire of congregations to eliminate "ranks" among their ministers, and an "apparent struggle for recognition among elders and ministers" are mentioned in the reports as possible for the abandonment of the office of elder.

Transition to Pastoral System

A multiple ministry and congregational stability marked the church-life of the Mennonite Brethren during the first sixty years of their history in the United States. However, in the late 1930's a process of change regarding the nature and role of the minstry began, radically modifying traditional patterns and practices. The shift from an unsalaried multiple lay ministry to a single theologically-trained and paid minister was accelerated by the change from the German to the English language in worship services. The general rise of the educational level among church members also was a contributing factor. Hillsboro, with its college community, for example, introduced the "pastoral system" as early as 1936.[12] Several city churches followed shortly after. In Enid, Oklahoma, (city church) a full-time salaried pastor was engaged in 1937, and in Wichtia, Kansas in 1943. In the Central District the Harvey (city) M.B. Church, and the Mountain Lake M.B. Church led the way in the adoption of the pastoral system in 1940. Sawyer, North Dakota, although a rural congregation, called a full-time pastor in 1938, but this seems to have been an exception to the rule. In the Pacific District at least seven congregations made the transition from an unsalaried lay ministry to a theologically-trained (salaried) pastor between 1940 and 1945. Since the early 1950's practically all Mennonite Brethren churches in the United States have been served by full-time pastors. In several instances congregations who had accepted the "pastoral system" earlier, have returned to a "shared ministry" in recent years. This trend appears to be gaining momentum in both Canada and the United States.

From available church and conference records it appears that the question of the "one pastor system" was never discussed in principle within the context of New Testament teaching nor in the light of the Anabaptist-Mennonite heritage. The arguments for and against the new system are virtually all of a pragmatic nature.

From the responses in a questionnaire, circulated by the author, it seems that few arguments were put forward to retain the lay ministry when the question of changing to a salaried pastor first came up in the churches. (This may be accounted for, at least in part, by the fact that in most cases pastors provided the answers.) In several churches, however, serious discussions apparently took place. Concerns were expressed that the one-pastor-ministry would lead to a neglect of gifted lay brethren and that there would be a lack of variety in preaching. The fear of "outside influences" and added financial obligations were also mentioned. A typical Mennonite argument against the salaried ministry was also Christ's teaching in Matthew 10:8 "Freely ye have received, freely give."

The survey referred to above indicates that a variety of arguments have been advanced for engaging a full-time pastor. These range all the way from the desire to "conform to the American pattern" to a concern for a "more effective ministry." In some instances the transition appears to have been made by default, because it was "an assumed necessity" and there were "no lay ministers available." The deeply felt need for men who would be better trained, who would be able to communicate well in the English language, and who would be able to win and retain the young people for the church — all played an important part in engaging full-time pastors. The larger congregations, especially in an urban setting, tried to meet the need for more visitation and counseling of members by calling a man who could devote himself to these pastoral duties.

Generally, the short-range effects of this transition from a multiple lay ministry to a "professional" ministry appear to be quite positive. Churches report that as a result of this change they enjoy "better preaching," and the "organizational structure of the church has been improved." Others attribute growth in membership and increased church attendance to the work of a full-time pastor. Greater progress in community outreach is also ascribed to the vision and work of the pastor.

Some responses, however, reflect a deep concern with regard to the effects of this change in Mennonite Brethren congregations. It is pointed out, that as a result of the new pattern, "lay participation and interest in church leadership has generally diminished." Others add that less involvement of laymen has resulted in shifting too much responsibility to the pastor. In one instance the general failure of church discipline is ascribed to this change in the spiritual supervision of the congregation. This view seems to be borne out by the responses received to the questions dealing with church practices, which may, however, be a historical coincidence since many other factors are involved in producing this trend.

It is perhaps too early to make a proper assessment of the impact of this change from the multiple ministry to the one-pastor-ministry in the Mennonite Brethren Church. The inadequacy of the "pastoral system" is realized by an increasing number of laymen as well as pastors. Waldo Hiebert, a pastor with many years of experience, shares this view.

"It is hardly possible," he writes, "to see the New Testament church without a multipastoral system. The ministry in the early Christian church was a shared ministry. Paul appointed elders for the new churches, always in the plural. There was a uniqueness in sharing the ministry."[13]

3 Developments in Canada

The pattern of development in church polity and practice of Mennonite Brethren churches in Canada generally conformed to that of their sister congregations in the United States. The process of change, however, has been slowed down and modified by several factors, the most significant being the large scale immigration of Mennonite Brethren in the 1920's, and to a lesser extent the immigration after World War II.

The historical Anabaptist-Mennonite pattern of a multiple lay ministry was perpetuated in early Mennonite Brethren churches in Canada. Congregations elected and ordained brethren from their own midst to serve as preachers and leaders. This practice was enhanced and supplemented by the services of itinerant ministers — usually men of wide experience — who not only enriched the spiritual diet of the local congregation, but also offered wise counsel for the solution of the practical problems many churches faced.

The immigration of the *Russlaender* Mennonite Brethren greatly strengthened the forces of the lay ministry in the churches. As J. H. Lohrenz points out, there were "among them many gifted and devoted ministers, leaders, teachers and men qualified in practical affairs."[14] The Bible schools, although not specifically geared to the training of ministers, nevertheless equipped many brethren for an effective lay ministry in their local congregations. A survey among M.B. ministers in 1963 revealed that 59 percent had enjoyed the privilege of Bible school training.[15] Although the factors just mentioned postponed the change from the multiple ministry to the one-pastor-ministry, they could not prevent it. Cultural pressures and spiritual needs of congregations in an urban environment precipitated many changes, including changes in the role and function of the ministry. Before we describe and analyze these changes, a note on the question of elders in Canadian M.B. churches might be of interest.

According to available information, no brethren were ever ordained as elders in Canada. Several elders, however, came into Canada from the United States and from Russia. Elder David Dyck, who came to Canada from Colorado in 1895, ministered in Winkler and Waldheim (Sask.). Elder Heinrich Voth moved to Canada in 1918, where he served for a short time at Vanderhoof, B.C. From Asiatic Russia (Siberia) two M.B. elders came to Canada in the 1920's. Elder Franz Friesen went to Alberta, where he served at Coaldale and Vauxhall, while elder H. M. Janzen took up residence in Winnipeg. To the writer's knowledge the latter two brethren were never recognized as elders in Canadian M.B. churches. This also applies to elder Wilhelm Dyck (from Millerowo) who resided in Niverville, Manitoba, during the last years of his life. Here too the views of the Molotschna M.B. Church were accepted, according to which the church has not only one, but many elders, even though they are not officially designated as such.

Transition to Pastoral System

As already indicated, the transition from a multiple lay ministry to the one-pastor-ministry came about two decades later in Canada than in the United States. Of seventy-seven churches that responded to the questionnaire only nineteen had engaged a full-time pastor by 1960. From 1961 to 1971 there was a rapid increase in the number of congregations who abandoned the traditional pattern and engaged brethren for special pastoral ministries. Thirty-two churches went through this process in the last decade. A number of congregations reported that they have a minister who receives partial financial support for his work. There are still eleven congregations (mostly rural) who carry on their work under the leadership of unsalaried lay ministers.

That there has been a certain reluctance to make this change can be seen from the fact that twenty-seven congregations had a transitional period of one to ten years between an unpaid lay ministry and a fully salaried pastor. In 1971 there were still at least a dozen congregations who gave only partial financial support to their leading minister.

The arguments advanced for retaining the lay ministry were in many respects similar to those noted earlier in M.B. churches in the United States. Not all objections to the "pastoral system" were on pragmatic grounds. Some stated that they considered the lay ministry more biblical, and others felt that lay ministers were less inclined to aim for popular approval in their preaching.

The reasons given for engaging a full-time pastor are mostly practical. Greater efficiency in the operation of the church program, greater effectiveness in community outreach, and a more systematic visitation ministry are listed as some basic reasons for change.

Since most of the congregations have only recently undergone this change, the assessment of the results of the new form of ministry is quite restricted. Many churches feel that the objectives which motivated them to employ a full-time minister have been realized. Others express concern about the infrequency of lay participation in church work, the lack of variety in preaching, the paucity of money for missions, and the more "formal services" since they have engaged a pastor.

The long-range effects of this new pattern of the ministry remain to be seen. One thing has become increasingly clear during the last few years: it is almost impossible to recruit young men for a lay preaching ministry in Mennonite Brethren churches today. Very few ministerial candidates are elected by congregations from their own midst. More and more churches are looking to the theological schools (and to other churches!) to meet their needs. Although colleges and seminaries can play a major role in the training of ministers and pastors, the calling of men into the ministry remains the responsibility and prerogative of the local congregation. The congregational church polity of Mennonite Brethren implies such a procedure. Hopefully, this practice will not be abandoned, but revived.

4. Brotherhood Concerns About the Ministry

The Board of Reference and Counsel (*Fuersorgekomitee*) of the General Conference of Mennonite Brethren Churches has the constitutional mandate to exercise spiritual watchfulness over doctrine and practice in M.B. congregations. This board has also repeatedly expressed its concerns with regard to the calling and function of ministers. In earlier years this concern was related to ordination procedures. In 1933 the brethren made the following recommendation to the conference:

> The local church which wishes to ordain a brother should make its wish known to the representatives of the neighboring churches for their consideration and endorsement. Having received such endorsement the church will call some experienced brethren who have the confidence of our conference to officiate at the ordination. [16]

In the period following World War II, when many younger men came into the pulpits and pastorates of Mennonite Brethren churches — especially in the United States — the concern for sound doctrine and spiritual unity took on new dimensions and found expression in warnings, cautions and recommendations by the Board of Reference and Counsel. In a statement at the 1948 General Conference the board warns against "the various spiritually disintegrating influences" and counsels the brotherhood to refrain from calling "teachers of the Word" from churches outside the conference fellowship "because they frequently hold teachings which we as a Mennonite Brethren Conference cannot endorse." [17]

After emphasizing the scriptural qualifications for men who are to be called to the ministry, the board recommends the following practice and procedure to safeguard the spiritual unity in the brotherhood:

> The appointed leadership in our churches should consist of brethren who have received their training in our own conference and have proven themselves for a period of several years as true and faithful to the doctrine and policies of the Mennonite Brethren Church. In cases where brethren who do not meet the above qualifications are considered for appointment in our churches, the Committee recommends that such brethren be examined thoroughly as to their testimony of life, their doctrinal beliefs, and policies of church administration. Where the district conference has made no provision for an authorized body to take the responsibility for such an examination it is advised that the Committee of Reference and Counsel of the respective district . . . be charged with the responsibility of the examination. Only with the endorsement of the examining committee should the local church consider the appointment of such a brother. [18]

The conference responded positively to this recommendation and expressed its appreciation for the concern and work of the board by a standing vote. Moreover it reelected the incumbent board members — A. H. Unruh, B. B. Janz, J. B. Toews, H. H. Flaming, and J. W. Vogt — by acclamation.

The pattern for the election and ordination of ministers contained in the above recommendation, was accepted as a guideline by provincial (Canada) and district (U.S.) conferences. However, not all congregations were willing to "walk according to the same rule." The spirit of individualism and the emphasis on local autonomy continued to threaten the scriptural relationship of interdependence and unity in the brotherhood.

In their continued search for a solution to this problem the members of the board prepared a document of historic significance for the triennial convention held in Winkler in 1951. This paper, entitled "A Statement to the Conference," written and submitted in four parts, contains the following:

Part   I. A frank analysis of our spiritual status.

Part   II. An appeal for reaffirmation of the historic principle of the interrelationship of Mennonite Brethren Churches.

Part III. Proposed ways and means to be considered as a possible way to meet the expressed needs.

Part   IV. Suggested efforts toward unification of our doctrinal position. [19]

The main purpose of the statement, it appears, was to provide the scriptural and practical rationale for the establishment of a Board of Elders (*Aeltestenrat*). In the introduction to part three this intent is explicitly stated:

> In view of the rapid changes in our churches of the past two decades where the ministry becomes less the product of the church, the local congregations having in many instances passed through the transition from the "collective ministry" to the pastoral system, it is the judgment of your Committee of Reference and Counsel that it is urgent that we make provisions to safeguard the accepted Biblical principle of a collective leadership as also expressed in No. 35 of our Confession of Faith which in part reads: "All questions relating to doctrine and life in the congregation are decided according to the example of the Apostolic Church as we read in Acts 15:1-28, etc." . . . After much prayer and study of the Scriptures the Committee proposes that the Conference consider the establishment of a Board of Elders to meet more fully the expressed need.[20]

The implications of this document gave rise to a spirited discussion on the conference floor. Although the delegates expressed their appreciation for the concerns presented by the committee, they passed a motion to refer the document to the churches, and district conferences for further study. The request for a larger committee, however, was granted. Only a brief reference to the above document was made at the

1954 General Conference by the Board of Reference and Counsel: "We recommend that in view of the reactions of all the District Conferences . . . the Conference order the revision of said document, transferring the duties assigned to the Board of Elders to the Committee of Reference and Counsel."[21]

For better or worse, the efforts to centralize authority in one body of "collective leadership" had failed. A. H. Unruh, a member of the Committee of Reference and Counsel at that time, analyzes the reactions to the proposal for a Board of Elders. According to Unruh, some brethren looked upon this proposal as a violation of the autonomy of the local church and a liquidation of old traditions in the M.B. Church. Others believed that the early practice of having elders who were responsible for several churches was unscriptural. The fear of falling back into a system which had been abandoned, led to a protest against the establishment of a Board of Elders.[22]

The history of Mennonite Brethren during the last two decades provides ample proof that the concerns of the brethren in the Committee of Reference and Counsel were justified. Unless the brotherhood accepts a greater responsibility for united action in the calling and training of its ministers, denominational disintegration cannot be ruled out.

II. The Ministry of Deacons

Throughout the history of the M.B. Church ministers and deacons have been inseparably linked in the work of the church. The early Brethren accepted the office of the "diaconate" on the basis of scriptural teaching and in keeping with their Anabaptist-Mennonite background. Among the Mennonites of Dutch origin the office had been primarily one of caring for the poor and needy of the congregation and had to do largely with material aid.[23] In the early M.B. Church the function of deacons appears to have been expanded to include other ministries. The *Confession of Faith* of 1902 reflects this enlarged conception:

Concerning the office of the deaconry we believe, that the church shall choose men according to the example of the apostolic church, as such are designated in Acts 6:1-6; and 1 Tim. 3:8-10. These are by virtue of their calling into service placed under duty to supply the poor and suffering in their want with the provisions given by the church, and according to the measure of their gifts to assist in the building up of the church and to serve according to the teaching of Paul . . . (in) Rom. 12:7-11.[24]

The first brother to be elected to this office in the Molotschna was Franz Klassen, one of the signatories of the Document of Secession and the man whom the church had authorized for the "laying on of hands" at the first ordination of ministers.[25] In Chortitza the first deacons in the M.B. Church — Cornelius Unger and Benjamin Nickel — were ordained in October, 1869, by the visiting Baptist minister J.G. Oncken.[26]

In North America the Mennonite Brethren followed the pattern established in Russia. Every congregation elected one or more deacons to serve in the traditional manner. That the validity and relevance of the office was never questioned or became a matter of brotherhood concern can be seen from the fact that no resolutions have ever been passed at General Conference sessions related to the ministry of deacons. There is, however, one reference to the ministry of deaconesses in the conference minutes of 1919. At that convention the question was raised whether the conference should enter into the endeavor of training deaconesses and also recognize that office. In response the conference elected a committee to do some preliminary work,[27] but there is no record of any subsequent conference action in this matter.

In recent years many questions have been raised in Mennonite Brethren churches with regard to the role and relevance of this ministry in the present day. Material affluence and state welfare seem to make the office unnecessary. The motivation for change, however, appears to be rooted in democratic thought rather than in biblical insight. In general Mennonite Brethren still believe that the diaconate is scriptural and relevant, but its role must be redefined in the light of changing cultural and economic conditions. The responses to the previously mentioned questionnaire indicate that Mennonite Brethren are going through a process of change of their views and practices regarding the ministry of deacons.

Trends with Regard to the Term of Service

A question which has often surfaced in the discussion on the diaconate in the last decade or two is whether deacons should be elected and ordained for life, or for a definite time period. Since the work and term of service of the pastor is subject to periodic reviews, the argument runs, the work and tenure of deacons should be treated in the same manner. Moreover, leading brethren in the conference have emphasized the fact that ordination in the New Testament is not for an "office" or position for life, but for a specific function or service. The latter view would make room for a specified term of service, or at least give the congregation the right to review the role and function of deacons.

This new approach is reflected more strongly in the responses from the churches in the United States. All congregations in the Southern District answering this question report that they elect their deacons for a specific time period. Terms of service range from one to five years, with the average being about three years. In the Central District only one church still ordains deacons for life, the rest have also adopted the policy of commissioning deacons for a term of several years. In the Pacific District most churches elect couples for a definite term of service.

Some churches indicated that the older deacons were retained for life. Others stated that deacons elected for a definite period could be reelected. In several instances it is mentioned that this change in policy has only been made in recent years. A few congregations report that they have no deacons.

The Canadian M.B. churches present a somewhat different pattern. Here more than one-half of the congregations responding (thirty-four out of sixty-four) still elect their deacons for life. The survey also reveals that most of the thirty congregations that have changed to the new policy in electing deacons belong either to the younger churches or mission churches, where a historical tradition is less likely to have influenced the decision. Since a number of churches have not answered this question, it can be assumed that the whole issue is in a state of flux. The general trend in the election of deacons is toward a definite term of service.

Trends with Regard to the Role of Deacons

The survey indicates a trend toward widening the role and function of deacons in Mennonite Brethren churches. This trend is most noticeable in community evangelism and in the visitation ministry. In the Southern District ten congregations report a greater involvement of deacons in community outreach, and eighteen report a greater participation in visitation work. In the Central District two congregations indicate a wider role for deacons in evangelism, and six a larger ministry in visitation. In the responses from the Pacific District, thirteen churches state their deacons are becoming more involved in community evangelism, and twenty-four report a larger role in visitation work.

In Canada the trend toward a wider role and function of deacons is also clearly evident. Twenty-one congregations reported that their deacons are involved in community evangelism, and fifty reported increased participation in visitation.

Other functions mentioned (in both Canada and the United States) include teaching and counseling, spiritual oversight of church members, involvement in the exercise of church discipline, and general assistance in the pastoral ministry. In the light of scriptural teaching and also in the light of the historic role of deacons it is rather strange that modern deacons (at least in M.B. churches) play a minor role in the administration of church finances. It appears that this function is assigned more and more to brethren who are businessmen. Whether the limitation of the term of service is related to this phenomenon has not been established.

Whereas the ministry of preachers and pastors can be readily observed and evaluated because it is performed in public, the work done by deacons is largely behind the scenes. According to the statistical report presented at the Centennial Conference, 450 deacons were serving in Mennonite Brethren churches in North America at that time.[28] The spiritual impact of such a large and dedicated "task force" in the life and growth of the church can hardly be overestimated.

III. THE MINISTRY OF EVANGELISM

The prominent part that evangelism has played in the founding and early growth of the Mennonite Brethren Church, both in Russia and in America, has been described in previous chapters. The first organized efforts on a conference level on both continents were related to itinerant evangelism. From the records it would appear, moreover, that every preacher in the early M.B. Church had accepted Paul's charge to Timothy: "do the work of an evangelist" (II Tim. 4:5).

The spiritual burden for spreading the Gospel was not a "delegated responsibility" of the "ministry," but was the personal concern of individual members. The early Brethren were known (and sometimes feared!) for their efforts to win people to Christ through personal work. The present-day emphasis on "visitation evangelism" was also a well-known practice among them.

Since 1909, when the General Conference was divided into "districts," evangelism has been a regional or area concern. Great changes have taken place in both the United States and Canada during the last sixty years in the methods and scope of evangelistic outreach in Mennonite Brethren communities. The developments since 1910 will be set forth briefly, divided into two periods.

1. Era of Multiple Lay Evangelists
(1910-1954)

Most of the work of evangelism during this period, especially in the first three decades, was done by brethren who would devote several weeks or even months every year to this ministry. For the "farmer-evangelist" the late fall was usually the most convenient season for such work; for the "teacher-evangelist" the summer season could be reserved for evangelism in the churches.

According to J. H. Lohrenz, the major portion of the home mission effort in those years was directed toward evangelistic work in the churches.[29] The committee for home missions (*Innere Mission*) of the district conference acted in an advisory and coordinating capacity in making arrangements. The work consisted of holding "protracted evangelistic meetings" in churches and, in the earlier years, often in schoolhouses. This method of conducting prolonged evangelistic services annually became an established pattern in practically all Mennonite Brethren churches of North America. Since Mennonite

Brethren lived mostly in rural areas, this method proved to be a very effective means of community outreach.

The Mennonite Brethren Church was blessed during those years with a large number of brethren who were willing to become involved in evangelism. Among the evangelists who have done more extensive work in the United States in the earlier years are J. S. Regier, J. H. Ewert, Adam Ross, A. J. Harms, H. S. Voth, W. J. Bestvater, H. D. Wiebe, P. E. Penner, J. F. Thiessen, D. F. Strauss, and J. H. Richert.

A little later, in the thirties and forties, other evangelists entered this field of service. Among these one could mention David Hooge, J. N. Willems, J. D. Hofer, G. B. Huebert, J. B. Toews, B. J. Braun, A. P. Koop, R. C. Seibel, G. H. Jantzen, Harry Neufeld, J. J. Toews, and many others whose names appear in conference records and church reports. Of special interest is the fact that many missionaries, either while candidates or when on furlough, would devote themselves to evangelistic work in the churches. Among those well-known in the earlier years were N. N. Hiebert and F. J. Wiens. In later years J. N. C. Hiebert, J. A. Wiebe, P. V. Balzer and J. H. Lohrenz, among others, became well-known for their evangelistic ministry in the churches.

In Canada the pattern of evangelism in M.B. churches was similar to that in the United States. C. N. Hiebert and H. S. Rempel were widely known in the pioneer settlements for their work as evangelists and Bible colporteurs. Several of the brethren mentioned above as being active in evangelistic work in churches in the United States, also served in Canadian churches from time to time. With the coming of the Mennonite Brethren from Russia in the 1920's, the "company of the preachers" was greatly enlarged and strengthened.

In the twenties and thirties, when the German language could still be effectively used for evangelistic outreach in Mennonite communities, several older brethren were extensively used of God in this work. Abraham Nachtigal, H. H. Goossen, C. C. Peters, and others are well remembered by the older generation. In the forties and fifties, the period of bilingualism in Canadian M.B. churches, a younger group of brethren became active in evangelism. Several of these were Bible school or Bible college teachers who devoted their summer months to evangelistic work. Among these were G. W. Peters, F. C. Peters, J. H. Epp, G. D. Huebert, J. A. Toews, A. P. Regier, B. W. Sawatzky, J. F. Redekop, P. R. Toews and others. Among the pastors and ministers active in this field were H. H. Janzen, Abraham Huebert, and D. B. Wiens. The latter three also carried on an effective ministry among the Russian people.

After World War II the number of "volunteers" for this ministry gradually declined. As a result, churches began to invite evangelists

40. C. N. Hiebert   41. H. S. Rempel

from other denominations or interdenominational organizations. A. H. Unruh comments on this change:

> More and more (evangelism) became the work of invited evangelists. Formerly it often took people a longer period of time to find peace through prayer and the searching of the Scriptures. Gradually it appeared, that everything had to happen in one evening. Although this is possible, it must not become a fixed pattern. Our people accepted methods which prevailed in other churches. [30]

The influence of "outside" evangelists on the life of the church became a brotherhood concern which found expression in discussions on the conference floor. At the 1953 convention of the Canadian Conference the question of a conference evangelist was considered.

> In the discussion it is pointed out, that it is a great disadvantage for the Conference if the churches can not have evangelists from our own Conference with our principles of faith. Hence it is highly desirable, that our churches be enabled to invite our brethren for evangelistic work. [31]

Since no brother was found to serve as conference evangelist, the conference recommended a number of brethren for such a ministry, and also agreed to support evangelists through the Canadian Conference treasury. In many churches, especially those with full-time pastors, another method was adopted to meet the need of an evangelistic emphasis: the Sunday evening services were specifically planned to be evangelistic in nature. This arrangement did not achieve the desired results, however, since unchurched families and other non-Christians would rarely attend a Sunday evening service, although many would come to the morning worship service. This called for a change of approach and in some churches the emphasis in the services has been reversed.

2. Era of Conference Evangelists
(1954-1972)

After 1954 both area conferences became actively interested and involved in evangelism.

In the United States

At the 1954 General Conference in Hillsboro the U.S. delegates elected a three-man Board of Evangelism. At the United States Conference in Reedley three years later the board was enlarged to six, with three brethren appointed by district committees on Home Missions and Evangelism. Loyal A. Funk was elected chairman of the board. He served in that capacity until 1971, when he accepted a pastorate in Vancouver, Canada. Also in 1957 Waldo Wiebe accepted the call to serve as conference evangelist.[32] Brother Wiebe was in great demand and served on both sides of the forty-ninth parallel. In 1959 he reported that during the previous two years he had served in thirty-six evangelistic campaigns — twenty-eight in the United States, and eight in Canada.[33] Reports from the churches and the committee indicated that the ministry of Evangelist Wiebe had resulted in many commitments to Christ.

In 1963, after six years of service, Wiebe asked to be released from the ministry, largely because of the serious and prolonged illness of his wife. David J. Wiens, pastor of the Harvey (N.D.) M.B. Church succeeded Wiebe as conference evangelist. Wiens terminated his services in the summer of 1966.

A year earlier, in 1965, the Board of Evangelism and the Board of Christian Education had merged in order to facilitate a more coordinated thrust in community outreach. Under the leadership of Elmo Warkentin, the executive secretary of this board, the program of the "Decade of Enlargement" was aggressively promoted. The program was designed to involve every church member and every church agency in winning the people of the community for Christ and the church.[34] In response to a 1968 questionnaire seventy-seven Mennonite Brethren churches provided the following information regarding evangelism: Up to 1965 only seven churches had conducted evangelistic training programs. By 1967 thirty-one churches had conducted such programs, and forty-one churches reported that they were planning an evangelistic training program in 1968.[35]

The "primacy of proclamation" as a method of evangelism has not been abandoned, however. In 1971 Henry J. Schmidt, a senior at the

Mennonite Brethren Biblical Seminary and a former pastor, was appointed as conference evangelist.

In Canada

On the basis of some preliminary studies on Canadian Conference evangelism by J. J. Toews and I. H. Tiessen, the 1958 convention delegates elected a Committee on Evangelism with J. J. Toews as chairman. The 1959 conference accepted in principle the appointment of an evangelist and with it a complete program for greater congregational participation in evangelism. At the same convention H. H. Epp, pastor of the M.B. church in Blaine, Washington, was accepted as conference evangelist. When Epp terminated his ministry after five years, the conference was without a full-time evangelist for two years.

During this time, when the brethren in the United States were rethinking and reshaping the evangelistic strategy of the local congregations, the Board of Evangelism in Canada was engaged in a similar process. The new approach is reflected in the 1966 appointment of J. J. Toews, a teacher at the Mennonite Brethren Bible College, as Executive Secretary of Evangelism and Church Extension. The chairman of the Board of Evangelism, J. M. Schmidt, made the following comments in support of the board's new plan:

Within our local churches we have spiritually minded laymen who possess a spirited interest in evangelism. This dynamic task force is waiting for leadership, for instruction. . . . It is imperative that we . . . utilize this potential resource as well as train others for evangelism if our brotherhood it to be maintained and its number increased. . . . To accomplish this goal in a greater measure, we trust this conference will react favorably to the recommendations of this Committee. [36]

The ministry of Toews was well received in was released for a "sabbatical" in 1969 to cor Boschman, pastor of the Linden M.B. Church serve in the interim period. Because his evan widely-felt need, especially among the yo subsequently appointed for an indefinite peric return to the work in 1971, both brethren are en, of evangelism throughout the Canadian Conferer

In recent years Lay Institutes for Eval Campus Crusade, have been attended by many members of Mennonite Brethren churches in both Canada and the United States. An inter-Mennonite study conference, Probe '72, held in Minneapolis in April of 1972, had among its more than 2,200 participants, some 125 to 150 Mennonite Brethren. This gathering was of historic significance in that it focused on an "Anabaptist style" of evangelism. After more than one hundred years, Mennonite Brethren are still deeply involved in the church's primary task.

IV. The Radio Ministry

This chapter would be incomplete without at least a brief summary of gospel broadcasting by M.B. churches, institutions, and conferences. In view of their evangelistic and missionary concern, it is somewhat strange that Mennonite Brethren were rather slow in adopting this modern medium of mass communication. Several reasons for this hesitancy could be citied. Initially Mennonite Brethren shared with other Evangelicals the suspicion that radio was an instrument of evil. The programs that were aired by most stations confirmed this suspicion. Rural isolationism and the language barrier were contributing factors. Moreover it was felt that the church-centered strategy of all Mennonite Brethren missionary endeavors could not be observed in a radio ministry. During and after World War II the attitude gradually changed when the congregations realized that radio could be used for the glory of God and the salvation of men as they listened to such broadcasts as the Old-Fashioned Revival Hour and other popular gospel programs.

Local Radio Programs

The earlier period (1940-1960) is marked by a great proliferation of effort. In Canada many local churches and institutions began their own radio programs. The Gospel Tidings, released over a Saskatoon radio station as early as 1940, was perhaps the first radio program produced by Mennonite Brethren in Canada. In 1955 the *Konferenz-Jugendblatt* listed the following radio programs sponsored by Mennonite Brethren across Canada:

Gospel Bells Radio Program (Alberta)
The Gospel Hour (British Columbia)
Sonntagmorgen-Gottesdienst (Yarrow, B.C.)
The Bible School Hour (Abbotsford, B.C.)
The Herbert Bible School Radio Broadcast (Saskatchewan)
Gospel Echoes (Bethany Bible School, Saskatchewan)
The Gospel Light Hour (Released in Manitoba and Ontario)
The Glorious Gospel Program (St. Catharines, Ont.)
Moments of Blessing (Niagara Falls, Ont.)
The Chapel Speaks (Coldwater, Ont.)[37]

A few of these programs have been discontinued since then, but the others are continuing their ministry to the present day. In addition to the programs mentioned above, the Winkler M.B. Church (Manitoba) and the Kitchener M.B. Church (Ontario) have also produced their own radio programs for a number of years.

In the United States gospel radio broadcasts were first initiated by local congregations. Among those mentioned in early reports are the programs of the M.B. churches of Buhler, Kansas, and of Delft, Minnesota. The Mennonite Brethren churches at Shafter and Dinuba have broadcast the morning worship service for many years. Two Mennonite Brethren laymen in California have owned and operated their own private radio stations for years, broadcasting only good musical and religious programs. Egon Hofer established the KRDU radio station at Dinuba, and E. J. Peters founded his own station at Wasco. The conference schools, Tabor College and Pacific Bible Institute, have also sponsored broadcasts.

Conference Radio Programs

In both Canada and the United States the desire for a united voice and a concentrated and coordinated thrust in gospel broadcasting came to fruition in the late sixties.

In Canada the Gospel Light Hour has come to be recognized in several provinces as the voice of the Mennonite Brethren Church. It came into being in 1946 as a venture of faith on the part of three students — Henry Brucks, Henry Poetker, and Bert Loewen — all of the Mennonite Brethren Bible College in Winnipeg. In 1954 the Gospel Light Hour affiliated with the Manitoba Mennonite Brethren Conference which began to subsidize the work.[38] In 1966 the Gospel Light Hour was broadcast over nine stations in Manitoba, Saskatchewan, and British Columbia.

At the Canadian Conference that year the Committee on Evangelism presented the following recommendation:

That we provide a Canada-wide radio program by integrating the English Gospel Light Hour on the basis suggested by the Manitoba Conference. . . . That the program be called the Canadian Gospel Light Hour and be identified with the respective province where aired . . . .[39]

At the 1967 convention in Coaldale, Alberta, the chairman of the Committee on Evangelism was able to report that the provincial conferences of British Columbia, Alberta, Manitoba and Ontario had decided to air the Gospel Light Hour in their constituencies, and to assume financial responsibility. In 1969 the program was also released over a station in Nova Scotia.

It should be noted that the German program *Licht des Evangeliums*, its Low German counterpart, and the Russian Gospel Light Hour were not affected by the above recommendation. The Russian program on which D. B. Wiens, Vancouver, is the speaker has been beamed to the Soviet Union for a number of years now. Subsidized by the Board of Missions, this program penetrates Russia from the Philippines and Korea on the east and from Ecuador, the Dutch Antilles, and Monaco on the west.[40] It may indeed be the most significant witness of the Mennonite Brethren in the present day.

In the United States the Words of the Gospel program, sponsored for a number of years by the Pacific District Conference, was eventually accepted as the radio-voice of the brotherhood. At the 1968 conference the Coordinating Board presented the following recommendation which was accepted by the delegates:

Because of our commission to use every means available to effectively present the Gospel; because of the overwhelming need to meaningfully extend our outreach in this Decade of Enlargement; and because Mennonite Brethren can present Christ through radio in a way not possible through other media.

We recommend to the United States Conference of Mennonite Brethren churches that immediate and positive steps be taken to produce and sponsor a national Mennonite Brethren radio broadcast. We further recommend, that the existing program, "Words of the Gospel" be the basis of the future radio program under supervision of the United States Board of Evangelism and Christian Education. [41]

The Words of the Gospel broadcast has found widespread acceptance in the churches as well as among radio stations. In 1971 the board reported that more than half of the time for the release of the program had been donated by various radio stations.[42] According to the latest radio-log (Fall, 1971) the program is presently being aired over thirty radio stations in sixteen states. In addition, it is also released over station WIVV in Puerto Rico.

The words of Romans 10:18 are applicable to the radio ministries of the Mennonite Brethren: "Their voice has gone out to all the earth, and their words to the end of the world."

Chapter 19

Facing Cultural Change

The relation of Christianity to culture constitutes a problem that has perplexed the true followers of Christ through the centuries.[1] In the Anabaptist-Mennonite tradition the tension between Christian faith and culture has often resulted in serious controversies and conflicts in the sphere of ethics. A changing culture demands a periodic reformulation of the Christian answer as well as periodic reevaluation of the Christian response to various social, economic, and political issues. Through the years, Mennonites in general, and Mennonite Brethren in particular, have not found it easy to be *in* the world, and yet *not of* the world.

Because of migration from country to country with the resultant changes in language, vocation, education and customs, the Mennonite brotherhood possibly has encountered greater cultural changes than many other religious bodies. This in turn has created greater problems in relating an unchanging faith to new cultural patterns.

During the relatively short period of a little more than one hundred years, the Mennonite Brethren have experienced the repeated impacts of tremendous cultural change: they have come from Europe to America, they have changed their language of communication from German to English; they have moved from the country to the city in large numbers; they have largely left agricultural pursuits and entered the various professions; and they have risen economically from lower class to middle class (or even upper middle class!) in society. Only a cursory survey of some of these changes and their influence on the faith and life of the M.B. Church will be attempted. Since the nature and effects of immigration have been described in previous chapters, they will not be treated here.

I. From German to English

That the High German language achieved the status of a "church-Latin" among Mennonites and Mennonite Brethren in the past can be described partly as an accident of history. The Mennonites who fled from the Netherlands in the sixteenth century and settled in the Vistula Delta (East Prussia) remained a pure Dutch community for over two centuries. It was with great reluctance that the Mennonites of Prussia gave up the Dutch language in their worship services in the second half of the eighteenth century.[2]

By the time the Mennonites emigrated to Russia, however, the German language was in general use among them. (Had they emigrated fifty years earlier, their descendants in Russia and later in America in all probability would have continued to speak Dutch.) In Russia, two factors tended to promote the close association, if not identification, of German culture and Mennonite faith: the geographic and social isolation from the Russian people, and the aversion to identify with an inferior Slavic culture. The availability of German devotional and educational literature, moreover, helped to strengthen the link between German and Religion (*Deutsch und Religion*). According to several Mennonite historians, the Mennonites of Russia were linguistically and culturally German, and their literature had strong overtones of German culture and German national life with which the Mennonites had acquired a strong feeling of kinship.[3]

This identity with German culture was threatened by the "russification" policy of the Imperial government which began in 1870. The desire to preserve the German language was, among others, a motivating force that brought the Mennonites, including the Mennonite Brethren, to America in the 1870's. This is sometimes overlooked in the analysis of motivation for emigration. A brief survey of the "language question" in the M.B. churches of the United States and Canada may be helpful in understanding this historic problem in the brotherhood.

The Language Problem in the United States

The preservation of the German language was a matter of deep concern among early Mennonite Brethren in America. At the third convention held in 1881 in Nebraska the brethren passed a resolution that "every congregation elect a man to plan and promote week-day schools (*Wochenschulen*)."[4] Two years later Bernard Pauls urged the delegates to do more to "preserve and promote the German language." Consequently it was recommended that teachers who have a command of both the German and the English languages be appointed for the district schools in order that "one hour every morning and one hour every evening can be devoted to instruction in German. . . ."[5]

In 1884 J. F. Harms began a private school at Canada, Kansas, which provided elementary instruction in German, English and Bible. After two years a school association took over the school and enabled

Harms to continue the educational effort at Lehigh, Kansas, for two more years. Shortly after the discontinuation of the school at Lehigh, a similar *Vereinsschule* (school of the association) was begun at Buhler, Kansas. J. F. Duerksen was the teacher and promoter of this new institution. Similar elementary schools were conducted in the German language in other communities. In 1898 there were forty-two private schools in the Kansas Mennonite settlements alone.[6]

The acceptance by the conference of the German Department of McPherson College (Kansas) in 1899, and the establishment of the Corn Bible Academy (Oklahoma) in 1902, are further indications that the Mennonite Brethren were interested in the preservation of the German language in their churches and schools. The Anglo-Saxon cultural environment of the new world was much more attractive, however, than that of Russia had ever been for the Mennonite immigrants. Hence they did not develop the kind of psychological attachments to German culture and German national life as did their brethren in Russia during the last decades of the nineteenth century and later.

Nevertheless, during the early years of World War I, there was considerable pro-German sentiment in Mennonite Brethren churches in the United States. Editor A. L. Schellenberg[7] in all probability was a spokesman for the brotherhood when in his editorials he criticized American entry into the war, and refuted the charges of German atrocities.[8]

Although the churches were trying to preserve the German language, by 1930 they were fighting a losing battle. On a conference level German was perhaps preserved a little longer than in some local congregations. Until 1939, for instance, all conference minutes, not only those of the General Conference, but also of the district conferences, were recorded and published in German.

Transition from German to English

Although the transition from German to English was begun in most M.B. congregations in the first quarter of this century, it was not completed until much later. The answers in the questionnaire (mentioned in chapter eighteen) indicate a bilingual transition period from ten to thirty years in a number of congregations.[9] Of the ten congregations in the Southern District still using the German in their worship services in 1940, none were left fifteen years later. All the younger congregations in this district — seventeen out of twenty-seven — report that they have always used English in public worship.

In the Central District six churches indicated that they had never gone through a language change. Between 1940 and 1955 all the others (ten) began to conduct their services exclusively in English. In the Pacific District again a large number (nineteen) have never had any language problem. However, the Spanish-American M.B. churches of California also have to face the language issue as did their older German-speaking sister congregations. One congregation in Fresno uses the Spanish language exclusively at present (1972) and another has entered the stage of bilingualism. Of the nine congregations still having German services in 1940, none were using the German language twenty years later.[10]

In general it would appear that the language change in the United States was not nearly as controversial an issue as it was in Canada. There were a few voices that pled for retaining the German language for public worship. A concern for the spiritual nurture of older members is mentioned frequently in the reports as an argument not to change. The apprehension was also expressed that with the introduction of the English language "English customs" would enter the church.

The reasons given for changing from German to English in public meetings are interesting. Along with such weighty arguments as the spiritual needs of the young people (who could no longer understand the German) and the desire for a more effective outreach in an English-speaking community, some secondary causes for change are also mentioned. The inability of the new pastor to understand or speak German, for instance, is given as the reason for change in several congregations. It would appear that the introduction of the "pastoral system" and the language change were parallel phenomena in a number of congregations.

The long-range effects of this transition from German to English are generally positive according to the reports from the churches. The withdrawal of some older members from active involvement in the work and worship of the church has been compensated by improved community relations, and by a greater interest on the part of the young people in the study of the Scriptures and in Christian service. The fear of some older brethren, however, that with the breach of the language barrier unwholesome influences would find their way more easily into the churches, was not completely unfounded. A sense of nonconformity and separation from the world, which was formerly reinforced by a linguistic barrier, can now be maintained only by a greater effort in systematic teaching of biblical principles and by the cultivation of a deeper spiritual life. Not all congregations have risen to the challenge of new opportunities on the one hand, and new dangers on the other, provided by the assimilation to the larger "outside" language group.

The Language Problem in Canada

Although the early Mennonite Brethren in Canada were not as conservative culturally as the Old Colony, *Kleine Gemeinde*, or Sommerfelder Mennonites, they nevertheless were concerned about preserving the German language for their families and churches. At the second annual convention held in Herbert (Saskatchewan) in 1911 the brethren agreed "to appoint a committee which is to explore ways and means to promote a German school in which young people can also receive instruction in Bible."[11] In later years every local congregation was urged to elect a committee that would initiate and supervise a program of instruction in German and religion.

The transition from German to English in the *Kanaedier* M.B. churches began after World War I, but was delayed and the problem was intensified by the arrival of large contingents of *Russlaender* Mennonite Brethren in the twenties. In individual congregations the process of change was slowed down in later years by subsequent immigrant groups coming to Canada after the Second World War.

The Mennonite Brethren from Russia provided a strong impetus for the building of private schools — Saturday schools (for children), high schools and Bible schools — in which the emphasis on German and religion was often closely linked. Although the concern for the preservation of the German language was initially motivated by religious and cultural factors, it took on some political overtones in the thirties, occasioned by the coming to power of Adolf Hitler and the rise of the Third Reich. Many Mennonites, including some Mennonite Brethren, moved from an identification with German culture to an identification with Hitler's Germany. A Berlin newspaper made the following claim in 1934: "The Mennonites are one of the strongest pillars of Germanism in Canada."[12]

There are several reasons for this phenomenon among the *Russlaender* Mennonites of Canada during the 1930's. Hindenburg's Germany had provided substantial aid to the Mennonites who escaped from Soviet Russia in 1929-30. The strong anti-Communism of the Third Reich also met with the approval of the former victims of Communist oppression. Moreover, Hitler's economic achievements were widely acclaimed not only in Mennonite papers, but also in the Canadian press. All this led to an indiscriminate endorsement of Third Reich policies on the part of some Mennonite leaders.

Other Mennonite and Mennonite Brethren leaders warned against the dangers of this "political Germanism." B. B. Janz, eminent Mennonite Brethren leader, wrote an article for the *Lethbridge Herald* in January, 1939, which also appeared in four Mennonite weeklies, "Am I a National Socialist — God Forbid." Janz rejected "the extravagant emphasis on language, which includes a certain contempt for other languages."[13] Janz differentiated between culture and politics. "Preservation of the German language," he said, did not mean "adherence to German politics."[14] The vast majority of Mennonite Brethren agreed with Janz.

Nevertheless, the pro-German attitude of a vocal minority in several Mennonite communities did not go unnoticed by their Canadian neighbors. When war broke out in 1939, opposition groups did not always differentiate between cultural and political pro-German leanings. A hatred for everything German was a basic ingredient in the war hysteria that swept through the country. The Saskatchewan Branch of the Canadian Legion urged the nationwide ban of the German language at public services.[15] To demonstrate this anti-German attitude, several Mennonite churches were burned to the ground by superpatriots. Among these were the M.B. churches at Vauxhall (Alberta) and Newton Siding (Manitoba) — both destroyed in 1940.

The war and its aftermath helped Mennonite Brethren (as well as other Mennonites) to dissociate themselves completely from political Germanism and partly even from cultural Germanism. The new emphasis in the postwar period was on the significance of knowing and understanding German for the home and church, and on the importance of a "second language" for higher education.[16] Occasionally its value for missionary outreach was stressed in urban centers (like Winnipeg), where large German-speaking communities existed.

How widespread this concern for the preservation of the German language was in the Canadian M.B. Conference can be seen by a resolution that was presented to the convention in 1950 by the Board of Reference and Counsel. The first part reads:

> The Conference acknowledges the need for the preservation of the German language, and for that reason requests that churches establish Saturday schools wherever possible, where children may be given the ABC's of the German language and of religious instruction. The Conference further requests that church leaders, Sunday school superintendents, Sunday school teachers, and German-speaking public school teachers cultivate the German language wherever possible and also ask parents to speak German with their children. [17]

It is difficult to conceive of a more comprehensive approach to the solution of the problem than is embodied in the above resolution. But history has a way of bypassing resolutions when the latter no longer conform to the real needs on a congregational level. Although the annual reports of the "Committee for the German Language" appear in the conference minutes until 1962, the language problem ceased to be an issue on the conference floor several years earlier. On the local church level the language issue was often debated loud and long, and much spiritual energy was lost in the process. In the fifties Canadian M.B. churches were in the midst of an inevitable language change.

Transition from German to English

According to the reports received, all Canadian M.B. churches conducted their services in German until 1940. Only twelve of the seventy-seven churches responding had made the transition to the exclusive use of English in public services by 1961. Twenty-two others made the change in the decade from 1961 to 1971. Half of the congregations who had completed their "transition interlude" reported that their bilingual period had lasted from ten to twenty-five years. With one or two exceptions all other congregations (not in the above category) indicate that they carry on bilingual worship services. (In most of these churches, however, the Sunday school for children is conducted in English only.) Several congregations in which a large number of immigrants from Europe and lately from Paraguay have been admitted to membership still carry on their services almost exclusively in German.

The arguments for retaining the German language encompassed a wide range of interest and concern. In some churches it was argued that the language which had been good enough for the "fathers," should be good enough for the younger generation. Others feared the elimination of older preachers from the pulpit ministry. Twenty-nine out of seventy-seven reported that their congregation had retained the German language in order to serve the older people and the recent immigrants attending their services.

Concern for the spiritual welfare of the young people appears to have been a primary motive in bringing about a language change in M.B. congregations in Canada. Thirty-two congregations gave this as the main reason for changing to English. Twenty-four also added the desire for community outreach as another factor. In a few instances the inability of the pastor to speak German precipitated the change. One pastor commends the older members for their "understanding" attitude in this process of change.

The effects resulting from this change are similar to those listed by congregations in the United States. In twenty-three responses the fact that people of non-Mennonite background are attending services now is attributed to this change. Consequently many of these also become church members. According to others (five), there is now a more active participation of youth in the work of the church. Still others (four) refer to the elimination of the "generation gap" as a result of changing to English.

In some congregations the immediate effects have been painful. A number of reports (eight) indicate that older people feel neglected; some of them withdraw from the fellowship; others move away. At least seven churches report that the change of language in public worship has not produced any discernible effects — neither good nor bad.

The long-range effects of this linguistic and cultural transition in the Mennonite Brethren Church of North America cannot be assessed at this point. Some preliminary observations, however, can be recorded. The claim often made in the discussion of this issue — that the removal of the language barrier would immediately result in a more effective evangelistic outreach in the community — is not substantiated by statistics. The obstacles to effective witnessing appear to lie on a deeper level. Another noticeable trend as a result of accepting the language used by most other evangelical groups is the increased number of intermarriages between members of the M.B. Church and those of other denominations. This has a tendency to weaken denominational loyalties. On the positive side of the ledger it should be recorded that Mennonite Brethren have assumed a leadership role in the promotion of evangelism as well as social action in both rural and urban communities as a result of changing to the national tongue in the communication of their message.

II. FROM FARM TO CITY

What Leland Harder writes about the life-style of Mennonites in general at the beginning of the twentieth century is also applicable to Mennonite Brethren. "At the turn of the present century," Harder observes, "to have asked where the typical Mennonite lived or what he did for a living or where he went to church would have elicited simple and straightforward answers: The typical Mennonite lives in a rural community, he farms for a living, and he attends a country church."[18] Mennonite Brethren in North America prior to 1920 had two city missions (Minneapolis and Winnipeg) but no organized, self-supporting urban congregations.

There has been a tendency in Mennonite and Mennonite Brethren circles to characterize the Anabaptist-Mennonite movement as essentially a rural movement. However, a historical study of Anabaptist origins shows the overwhelmingly urban background of the "radical reformers" of the sixteenth century. The cradle of Anabaptism was located in some of the major cultural and commercial centers of Europe — Zurich, Basel, Nuernberg, Augsburg, Strassburg, Cologne, Amsterdam, Emden, and others. Severe persecution resulted in large-scale extermination and in the withdrawal of the remaining groups to rural areas. If persecution drove the Anabaptists from the city to the country, one is inclined to agree with Harder "that the identification of the 'Mennonite way of life' with agriculture was a historical accident."[19] The image of the Mennonites as an agrarian group emerged in Prussia and found its classical expression in Russian and early American Mennonite history.

The close association of the "Bible and the plow" is also a part of the Mennonite Brethren tradition. The depreciation of the city and the elevation of rural life were confirmed for the brethren by their study of the Scriptures. The historical record of cities (from Sodom and Gomorrah in Genesis to Babylon in Revelation) is a gloomy one and for Mennonite Brethren, urban centers were at once the seat and symbol of worldliness and sin. Cities were places for establishing "missions," but not for planting Mennonite Brethren churches. That the last book of the Bible also presents the redeemed community as an urban community (New Jerusalem) was apparently overlooked.

Much more research is needed on the urbanization process in the Mennonite Brethren Church.[20] From the conference records and statistics it is clear that urbanization is a phenomenon of the last thirty years. Revolutionary changes have taken place in the life-style and vocational pattern of Mennonite Brethren families since World War II. The rapid urbanization of Mennonite Brethren has not only resulted in the organization of a relatively large number of city churches, but it has also seriously affected the very existence of many rural congregations. Many of these have reported a decrease in membership in recent years, and a significant number have been dissolved.

Although the history of extinct churches is not directly related to urbanization it might be instructive to briefly consider this sad phase of M.B. history. The following table is based on a recent study.[21]

TABLE VI

Number and General Location
of Extinct M.B. Churches

In the United States

Central District . . .	17
Southern District .	36
Pacific District	. . 11
Total	64

In Canada

Ontario	2
Manitoba	17
Saskatchewan	12
Alberta	4
British Columbia	2
Total	37

Several observations need to be made regarding the figures given above. Of the 101 churches listed as extinct all were located in rural areas with the exception of two in the Pacific District (Portland and Los Angeles). Several "extinct" churches merged with nearby larger congregations when membership dropped to a level where the congregation could not effectively carry on its work and worship. In several areas — Saskatchewan, Manitoba, North Dakota, and Oklahoma — the dissolution of the churches close to metropolitan centers is directly related to the urbanization process. It is also noteworthy that the disintegration of small rural congregations was often triggered by the moving away of the leader or minister of the group.

In the United States the largest number of extinct M.B. churches is found in the state of Oklahoma. This fact seems to be related to the Depression of the thirties and the general migration to California. In Canada the prairie provinces of Manitoba and Saskatchewan show the largest number of extinct congregations. Here too the Depression forced many families to leave the farm and a significant number of these moved to British Columbia or Ontario. Others moved to the cities in their respective province to find employment.

The motivation for movement from farm to city has been alluded to in several earlier chapters. The urbanization of Mennonite Brethren must be viewed in the context of the general trends in the population as a whole. Until 1961 the Mennonites, including the Mennonite Brethren, were the most rural of the twenty largest religious groups in Canada.[22] In the United States, according to Leland Harder's analysis, about 33 percent of the gainfully employed members of the General Conference Mennonites were still farmers in 1960, in comparison to only 4 percent for the nation.[23] This pattern is rapidly changing, however, and Mennonites may be passing through the greatest urbanization process of any religious group in North America at present. Mennonite Brethren appear to be spearheading this movement in both Canada and in the Pacific District of the United States.

The table on the following page shows the increase in the number and membership of city churches in the United States and Canada from 1951 to 1971.[24]

This table shows not only the overall growth of M.B. churches in urban areas, but also the relative increase in certain districts of the constituency. In both Canada and the United States Mennonite Brethren have gravitated toward the West Coast where they have established a number of city churches during the last twenty years. In two regions, Alberta and the Central District, city churches were rather late in making their appearance, but even these most rural areas of the

Mennonite Brethren Conference are now making rapid progress in urbanization. In Alberta, for instance, all four city congregations were established within a period of 12 years (1956-1968).

·TABLE VII
Number and Membership of City M.B. Churches[25] in 1951 and 1971

United States

District	Number	1951 Membership	Number	1971 Membership
Central District			9	490
·Southern District	2	197 ·	9	1,241
Pacific District	7	1,482	18	3,153
Total	9	1,679	36	4,884

Canada

Province	Number	1951 Membership	Number	1971 Membership
Ontario	2	517	7	1,500
Manitoba	3	977	10	2,580
Saskatchewan	3	195	7	877
Alberta			4	522
British Columbia	3	738	12	2,189
Total	11	2,427	39	7,637

In a number of cities Mennonite Brethren have established more than one congregation. A closer study of these metropolitan centers reveals that every one of them has a large Mennonite Brethren rural hinterland which serves as a "feeder" for the city churches. In Canada this is true of Kitchener (with three M.B. churches), of St. Catharines (with two), of Winnipeg (with eight), of Saskatoon (with three), and of Vancouver (with seven). In the United States this would be true of Fresno with six congregations, and of Wichita, which has two M.B. churches. The city of Omaha, which also has three M.B. congregations, appears to be an exception to this rule. Here the missionary strategy of the conference has resulted in establishing several small churches. Studies that have analyzed migration patterns conclude that the majority of rural migrants relocate in urban centers less than one hundred miles from their point of migration. Trends in Mennonite Brethren constituencies would substantiate these findings.

In Canada the urbanization process among Mennonite Brethren has been accelerated by the immigrants from Europe after World Wars I and II. Many of those who arrived in the 1920's took up employment and residence in the cities; and practically all families who arrived after World War II located in the city or moved to the city after a brief stay with relatives on the farm. In the latter group there were many who already had an urban experience in Europe. In Mennonite Brethren churches in such cities as Winnipeg, Calgary, or Vancouver, most members are first or second generation Canadians.[26]

According to the statistical information presented above, more than one-third of all Mennonite Brethren in North America now live in larger cities. The proportion of urban to rural membership varies, naturally, from province to province and from district to district. In Manitoba, for instance, more than 55 percent of Mennonite Brethren are classified as urban, the majority of these living in Winnipeg. In California more than 40 percent of all Mennonite Brethren live in cities. If the congregations in the larger towns (e.g. Reedley, Dinuba, Shafter, etc.) should be added, the percentage could easily be doubled. The trend in all areas of the M.B. constituency is toward greater urbanization. What does this mean for the future of the spiritual heirs of the Anabaptists?[27]

In the urban situation Mennonite Brethren are confronted with new and unprecedented opportunities for growth and expansion. City churches have excellent opportunities for systematic instruction and spiritual nurture of members. Their Sunday services and weekday meetings are not affected by poor roads or inclement weather, which often result in the cancellation of services in isolated and scattered rural churches, especially during the winter months. More significant, perhaps, are the many opportunities for an effective community outreach. There are virtually "doors unlimited" for personal evangelism, tract distribution, visitation work, city mission work, teaching children's classes, etc. Many urban congregations are deeply involved in an intensive program of "evangelism in depth," unknown to rural churches and perhaps beyond their range of possibility.

On the other hand, Mennonite Brethren in city churches are exposed to serious dangers. In his studies Leland Harder found that "the more urban a Mennonite congregation, the less likely a member to register as a war dissenter; but the more urban a Mennonite congregation, the more likely it is to recruit members from the non-Mennonite world."[28] It would thus appear, that as congregations become more "acculturated," they are increasingly tempted to surrender their spiritual heritage and their confessional identity. There is a greater pressure in the urban environment to conform to the

42. The Rueckenau Church in Russia. Built in 1883.

common ethical norms and practices of the community, or of other churches.

There are other moral and spiritual hazards which Mennonite Brethren in an urban setting have to face. Urban life has a tendency to weaken family ties and family solidarity. No longer is the family the closely-knit social and economic unit that it used to be on the farm. In the city, where every member of the family has his or her particular work or vocation (and the problem is intensified where the wife and mother also works outside the home) the feeling of "togetherness" is lost, and with it the blessings of mutual correction and encouragement. A corollary of this disintegration of family life is the increased frequency of divorce in urban Mennonite Brethren churches — the rate being considerably higher than in rural congregations. It would seem that although Mennonite Brethren move in the direction of increased urbanization, the survival and continued influence of a substantial segment of rural churches would be beneficial to the course and development of the brotherhood in the future.

III. From Poverty to Affluence

Another factor which has changed the life-style of Mennonite Brethren, especially after World War II, is a growing affluence and prosperity. Only a few general observations on this aspect can be made at this time.

The early history of the brotherhood in America was marked by a continuous struggle for economic survival. Grain farming on the edge of the agricultural frontier — whether in Kansas, North Dakota, or Saskatchewan — was a hazardous undertaking, conditioned by the unpredictable fluctuations of weather conditions and world markets. The limited financial resources of the M.B. churches during the pioneer

43. The Corn, Oklahoma Mennonite Brethren Church.

44. The Elmwood Mennonite Brethren Church, Winnipeg.

era were reflected in the annual contributions to missions. Total contributions to the conference treasury (*Bundeskasse*) in 1883 amounted to $1,258.21.[29] The situation was not much better ten years later when $971.11 was collected for home missions; in addition, $955.50 had been contributed to foreign missions.[30]

By their proverbial industry and traditional frugality Mennonite Brethren, along with the other Mennonites, had achieved a modest prosperity by the late 1920's. The 1929 stock market crash and the Depression that continued throughout the thirties, forced even the thrifty and hard-working Mennonites down to the poverty level. All aspects of conference work had to be curtailed drastically. In Canada, the economic problems of the Mennonite Brethren were accentuated by the fact that the immigrants from Russia, who constituted more than half of the conference membership, had not yet paid off their transportation debt (*Reiseschuld*) when the Depression set in. Instead of being able to make contributions to missions, many families were forced by circumstances to accept government relief in order to survive.

World War II caused an upswing in the economy in both Canada and the United States. The unemployed went back to work and the farmers received higher prices for their produce. For more than thirty years now North Americans have enjoyed a growing prosperity without any serious economic recession. Mennonite Brethren have shared fully in this material progress. Since World War II, and coinciding with their rapid urbanization, Mennonite Brethren have been climbing steadily upward on the economic ladder, so that today the majority of them have achieved the status of a comfortable middle class society. Although this fact is generally admitted, it has not been properly documented thus far.

One of the indices of material prosperity in the life of a church body is the amount of financial investment in church buildings. The total value of all church properties of the Mennonite Brethren Conference of North America in 1951 was estimated at $2,678,920.[31] Seventeen years later, in 1968, the investments in church properties for that one year alone amounted to $1,304,000. In the fifties and sixties several congregations erected magnificent and spacious church edifices costing from a quarter to half a million dollars.

Fortunately, there was also a substantial increase in the giving for the work of the church. Total contributions for all phases of conference work in 1938 amounted to $195,678. By 1959 this figure had risen to $3,203,904, an increase of over 1600 percent in twenty-one years. Average per-member-giving during the same period increased from $13.41 to $125.50.[32] Although absolute giving has increased sharply, it is doubtful whether relative giving (in proportion to income) is higher today than thirty years ago. Faithfulness in stewardship apparently has not kept pace with growing affluence. Luxurious homes, expensive cars, summer cottages, vacation travel, and a hundred and one other things consume an increasing part of the budget in many Mennonite Brethren homes. A keen analyst of present developments among Mennonite Brethren confirms the "upward trend" alluded to above:

> . . . in the last ten years the M.B.'s really have moved. There are Mennonite Brethren — not Mennonites as such, mind you, but members of *our* church — who are presidents of universities or provincial cabinet members; whose stocks are listed (and going up) on the Toronto Stock Exchange; who must choose between Rhodes Scholarships to Oxford or Woodrow Wilsons to Harvard; who conduct major symphony orchestras or sing in opera productions; who are listed in *The Oxford Companion to Canadian History and Literature.* The list could be multiplied, and, with variations, mirrored in the U.S.A. [33]

Material progress and prosperity in the life of a brotherhood has the potential for either blessing or curse. Money invested in the salvation of man, wealth dedicated to the expansion of Christ's kingdom, material means used for the alleviation of human need and suffering — all this can be a great blessing. But when wealth is used for self-indulgence and self-glory, it constitutes a grave spiritual danger and undermines the effective witness of the church. In Russia, many Mennonite Brethren viewed the Bolshevik Revolution of 1917 and the subsequent confiscation of all property as God's judgment on Mennonite materialism. May history not have to repeat itself in America. [34]

IV. GENERAL OBSERVATIONS

Throughout the history of the M.B. Church faith and culture have often been in conflict. Occasionally serious tensions developed in the brotherhood when adaptation to cultural change was interpreted as ethical compromise. The cultural pattern of a past age has often been accepted as the scriptural pattern and hence as normative for all time. The Mennonite Brethren who came from Russia in the twenties, for instance, found the wedding ceremonies and celebrations of their Canadian brethren "worldly" and "unethical." In the Mennonite constituencies in Prussia and Russia certain stereotyped forms had been generally accepted. In Canada, with its Anglo-Saxon cultural roots, different practices prevailed — not only in society at large but also in the older M.B. churches. Here the wedding ceremony made provision for a number of attendants (bridesmaids and best men) and even for a "ring ceremony." These novel features were at first categorically rejected by ministers coming from a European background even though one could possibly find more scriptural support for the new than for the old practice.

The brotherhood has not always found it easy to differentiate between cultural and ethical values. Several instances may be cited. In

1890 the "wearing of a beard" came up for discussion on the conference floor. The minutes state that "the Conference regrets that in this matter vanity is being served," without specifying in what way.[35] In the 1920's the bobbed-hair style for women was in vogue. At the convention in Henderson in 1927 the conference went on record that "the cutting of hair by our sisters is in direct contradiction with the Word of God as found in 1 Cor. 11:6."[36] It seems paradoxical that a brotherhood which at one time took disciplinary action against clean-shaven brethren and bobbed-hair sisters would in later years look with suspicion on young men with beards and young women with long hair.

Life insurance became an issue in the conference as early as 1897. The farmer-brethren who had established their financial security by investment in land, thought it wrong and unscriptural if someone (mostly professional people) would invest in a life insurance policy. The 1897 conference delegation decided unanimously, "that anyone belonging to the Mennonite Brethren Church is not permitted to carry a life insurance policy."[37] In later conventions the conference reaffirmed its stand on this question. By 1927, however, the brotherhood was no longer united on this issue. Two resolutions were presented to the conference that year — containing a reaffirmation of the previous decision, and one pleading for tolerance in this matter. Eighty-eight delegates voted for the first, and thirty-seven for the second resolution, with a number of abstentions.

Although life insurance was presumably rejected on theological grounds (people who bought insurance were accused of a lack of trust in God) it can be seen in retrospect that this issue was clearly related to cultural change, i.e. to the urbanization and professionalism that affected the life and security of Mennonite Brethren as well as other groups. There is no record that the 1927 motion was ever rescinded, but life insurance is generally accepted today as a necessity of modern life.

Other practices which were long regarded as binding biblical norms — such as the "holy kiss" and the "head-covering" for women — are now interpreted by Mennonite Brethren theologians as being a part of the cultural pattern in the apostolic age. The "brotherly handshake" has replaced the "brotherly kiss" in most M.B. churches during the past few decades.

One of the most controversial issues in the Canadian Conference during the 1950's was the question of television. Serious discussions took place on the conference floor in 1954 and again in 1958. In 1954 the Committee of Reference and Counsel warned the brotherhood against this new threat to the faith and morals of the church by issuing a lengthy declaration. The detrimental effects of television for the home are listed as follows:

(1) It will lead to a deterioration of morals.

(2) It will create a false conception of life in the family, since the motion pictures present a strange, unnatural world.

(3) It will lead to a greater toleration of the use of tobacco and beer which are constantly featured in the commercials.

(4) It will undermine the principles of Christian marriage by its stories and pictures of unfaithfulness in married life.

(5) Women will be negatively influenced by the example of the actress on the screen and will forsake their divinely ordained role in marriage and family.

(6) Children will early be poisoned (in their minds) and will not have any time for school-assignments.

(7) In the light of the above it is clear that living in such an atmosphere will result in a shallow spiritual life and interest in spiritual things will be lost.

The fact that Billy Graham presents a religious program on television does not change the situation. The terrible damage which through this invention is inflicted on the church, cannot be rectified by an occasional religious program. [38]

The above statement has been quoted at length for several reasons. On the one hand it shows the serious concern of Mennonite Brethren leaders (and many members) for the purity and power of the church. On the other hand this spiritual zeal appears to be somewhat misplaced, since the attack is directed not only against objectionable television programs, but against television sets, against the "invention" itself. Although the 1958 resolution had a stronger emphasis on the *use* of television, the constituency remained confused on the specific intent of the statement. This ambiguity was unfortunate since it allowed for two interpretations. The more conservative congregations considered the possession of a television set a violation of the conference resolution and hence excommunicated some members on that basis. The more liberal congregations accepted the resolution as a warning against questionable programs.

This controversy is another illustration of confusing cultural issues (i.e. the invention of television) with ethical concerns (i.e. the watching of objectionable television programs.). In retrospect it would appear, however, that the whole controversy may have been a blessing in disguise, since it alerted the constituency to the dangers that could arise for church and family by an indiscriminate acceptance of the programs that were presented by this new instrument of the mass media.

In concluding this chapter on Mennonite Brethren adjustment to cultural change, the following paragraph from an article on "Cultural Change and Christian Ethics" appears pertinent:

Some cynics would claim — and we hear such voices occasionally in our brotherhood — that the Christian ethic is merely the product of a "cultural lag." They maintain that the secular ethic of today will be the Christian ethic of tomorrow. We reject this claim, although we do not deny that in Christian communities a "cultural lag" can often be observed. This is, however, a good thing. An instant cultural adaptation provides no opportunity for discernment and discrimination. A "cultural lag" makes it possible to reject what is sinful and to accept what is good in a changing culture. Moreover, the Christian ethic of the

New Testament is supra-cultural and supra-national. It is our responsibility, however, to formulate comprehensive Biblical principles, in which cultural changes can be incorporated without sacrificing ethical or spiritual values. [39]

The late B. B. Janz on one occasion offered this practical advice to the brotherhood: Never use the gospel-horse to pull the culture-wagon; but hitch culture to the gospel and let it promote the cause of Christ. May it ever be thus in the Mennonite Brethren Church!

Chapter 20

Giving to Caesar:
Perspectives and Problems
In Church-State Relations

The proper relations between the church and the state have always been among the Christian church's most vexing problems. Ernst Troeltsch is reported to have said that there is no ultimate solution, only a periodic reformulation of the problem. The early Christians, as well as the Anabaptists of the sixteenth century, were not as pessimistic as Troeltsch, but believed that the New Testament provided directives with respect to Christian responsibility to the state.

Church historians generally agree on the course taken by the early Christian church. Roland Bainton states categorically that the "early Church was pacifist to the time of Constantine."[1] He also claims that Christians abstained from politics for three hundred years, and that involvement came later as a result of the union of church and state.[2]

The Anabaptist-Mennonites of the sixteenth century returned to the New Testament and early church pattern as a model for the true church in their day. They were neither anarchists nor revolutionaries (except for the revolutionary fringe at Muenster). They accepted the state as a divine institution and insisted that Christians must be "subject to the powers that be."[3] However, the Anabaptists placed a major limitation on the authority of the state: it had no jurisdiction in the spiritual realm. A government attempting to rule the hearts of men, they declared, was overstepping its functions and tasks.

In spite of their acceptance of the divine origin of the state, the Anabaptists rejected all participation in government (magistracy) or holding of government office. The basic rationale for this attitude is given in the earliest Anabaptist Confession of Faith: "The sword is ordained of God outside of the perfection of Christ."[4] Inside the "perfection of Christ" (Christ's kingdom or the church) the members are governed by the example of Christ and the teachings of the Apostles. A speaker at the Zofingen debate of 1531 said, "Jesus gave us an example as is stated in 1 Peter 2, that we follow His footsteps under the cross."[5]

The Anabaptists believed that the church of Christ is by definition an element in society, not society as such. Their opponents, whether Protestant or Catholic, were unwilling to accept this view and continued to look upon the church as coextensive with society. This was the great theological watershed of the Reformation: "In the one view the Church is the *Corpus Christi* the body of Christ, which consists of believing folk, and of them solely; in the other view the Church is *Corpus Christianum*, the body of a 'christened society'."[6] Their view of the church enabled the Anabaptists to reject participation in government, while at the same time becoming redemptively involved in the life of society. The unwillingness of Mennonites to participate in the political life of the nation, and especially their rejection of military service, has been a major cause of their persecution and migration through the centuries.

The Mennonites of Russia, as spiritual heirs of the early Anabaptists, have in their confessional documents generally adhered to the "Anabaptist Vision." However, at the time of the founding of the M.B. Church in 1860 the historical situation was vastly different from that encountered by the sixteenth-century Anabaptists. In South Russia the Mennonite colonies enjoyed almost complete civil autonomy and thus constituted little "states" within the state. They were not always able to resolve the tension between their confession (i.e. the separation of church and state) and their practice of self-government on a local level. Even worse, some descendants of the victims of state oppression in earlier times themselves employed coercive measures in dealing with religious dissenters in their own midst. Although the early Brethren suffered at the hands of local Mennonite civil authorities, it would appear from the historical records that they did not identify these with the "state," but considered them rather as an extension of the "church." The state (government) for the Mennonite Brethren was represented by the Tsar and other government officials in Petersburg, not by the colony administrator.

A brief survey will be made of the efforts of Mennonite Brethren to give "to Caesar the things that are Caesar's and to God the things that are God's" (Matt. 22:21).

I. MENNONITE BRETHREN AND POLITICAL INVOLVEMENT

The documentary evidence on the attitude of Mennonite Brethren toward the state and participation in the political process is very meager. Several factors in the European experience of the M.B. Church account for this lack of involvement. In the larger Mennonite colonies (Molotschna and Chortitza) the Mennonite Brethren were a small and for a while merely tolerated minority group and thus did not have an active part in local government. On the national level a representative assembly (*Duma*) was set up for the first time only in 1905, and after a brief and stormy history it came to a tragic end in 1917.[7] Whether the Mennonite Brethren would have been able to resist the social and economic pressures against non-involvement had "democratization" in Russia succeeded, is doubtful. One of their leaders, B. H. Unruh, advocated regular political action by Mennonites prior to 1917.

In article IX of the Mennonite Brethren *Confession of Faith* (1902) the views of the church with reference to the state are expressed in typical Anabaptist terminology: "We believe and confess, that God, who is King of all kings and Lord of all lords, has put into all lands rulers and powers for the common good and welfare and the leading of a good, honorable civil life. For there is no power but of God. . . ."[8] The section ends significantly with the second petition of the Lord's Prayer: Thy Kingdom come!

Mennonite Brethren in America

The transfer of citizenship from Russian autocracy to American democracy did not affect the basic attitude of Mennonite Brethren toward the state and political involvement. They continued to maintain their historic position of non-participation in political activities. At the first conference (unofficial), held in Nebraska in 1878, the delegates passed a resolution that "brethren are not to serve in any government offices (*Aemter*)."[9] Bender's statement that Mennonite Brethren never had "any tradition or regulation forbidding participation in governmental functions at any level, except participation in the police function" is based on inadequate information.[10]

The concern of the brotherhood on this matter finds expression at the convention in 1888: "In regard to being a delegate to national political conventions, it is strongly advised that, while we desire a good government, members should be careful so as not to defile their conscience. However, the conference does not want to form a definite resolution in this matter."[11] Two years later, however, a resolution was passed to the effect "that members of the church refrain from participation and involvement in the contentions of political parties, but are permitted to vote quietly at elections, and may also vote for prohibition."[12] Discussions and resolutions of the Mennonite Brethren reflect a strong conservative position on the subject of political involvement.

Until recent years the Mennonite Brethren continued to be "the quiet in the land" (*Die Stillen im Lande*) and their participation in the life of the community was restricted to serving on school boards, town councils, and other activities which could be described as civic rather than political. However, social and economic pressures are gradually effecting a change of attitude. These pressures are reinforced by a popular misconception that there is a basic difference between the modern "welfare state" and the "police state" of earlier times. The modern democratic state, so the argument runs, has become so "christianized" that the church must cooperate with it, even though it formerly separated itself from a non-Christian or semi-Christian state.[13] That such participation in government on "higher levels" historically has led to a loss of vision and to a subservience of the church to state interests is often overlooked in such discussions. The history of the Dutch Mennonites in the nineteenth century and of the German Mennonites in the twentieth century would substantiate this observation.

Mennonite Brethren participation in political activities has to the present been moderate (mostly on lower levels of government), and their expression of patriotism has generally been modest. In many communities where the Mennonites have constituted a large part of the population (e.g. Mountain Lake, Hillsboro, Buhler, Winkler, Steinbach, Hepburn, etc.) they have as a matter of course accepted local office and operated the municipal government. Peter Kroeker, a member of the M.B. Church, served as mayor of Winkler for several years in the early sixties. A relatively large number of Mennonite Brethren have served as aldermen on town and city councils. In Alberta, Raymond Ratzlaff, a member and choir director of the Linden Mennonite Brethren Church, served in the provincial cabinet of the Social Credit government for a number of years. Involvement on this level appears to have been exceptional among Mennonite Brethren, but not among General Conference Mennonites.[14]

It should be noted in passing that the Social Credit Party, founded in 1935 by William Aberhart, the principal of the Calgary Prophetic Bible Institute, had a special attraction for Mennonites and Mennonite Brethren. Aberhart's constant appeal to Scripture for economic and social reform gave to his movement the appearance of a "Christian" political party. In Alberta and British Columbia Mennonite Brethren have been among the staunchest supporters of the Social Credit movement. It would appear that in the United States Mennonite Brethren have through the years displayed a similar attitude toward the Republican Party. The relationship between the profession of a "left wing" Reformation theology and the adherence to a "right wing" political philosophy needs further examination and study.

During the Second World War Mennonite Brethren experienced

severe tensions between the claims of Christ and the church on the one hand, and the demands of the state on the other. In 1943 the conference adopted a resolution which reads:

> . . . We confirm our undivided loyalty to our country and to our government which has graciously provided ways and means affording our young men a chance to serve their country without being compelled to become a part of the military power which would be contrary to our confession of faith and their conscience. [15]

The most comprehensive statement on the problem of political involvement was presented to the 1966 conference by the Board of Reference and Counsel.[16] Following the presentation of historical perspectives and basic scriptural principles for any form of political involvement, a number of practical guidelines are given. Because of their significance and relevance, they are presented here in full:

> 1. We believe that we should pray for those holding political authority that we may live in peace and quietness. 1 Tim. 2:1-2.
> 2. We believe that the chief concern of all Christians should be the extension of the Kingdom of Christ. Political involvement can easily become an "entanglement" which defeats this purpose. Matt. 6:33; 2 Tim. 2:4; Matt. 28:18-20.
> 3. We believe that government is of God, but that the Church should not attempt to ally itself with any specific political ideology or political party, since none is intrinsically Christian. Rom. 13:1-7.
> 4. We believe that the defense of the political order in general or of a specific political system is not the responsibility or duty of the Christian church. John 18:36.
> 5. We believe that the Church and its members individually should be constructively critical of the political order, always seeking to promote justice, respect for human dignity, and conditions of peace. James 5:1-6; 1 Peter 3:13-17.
> 6. We believe that Christians ought to practice good citizenship but that when the claims of the state run counter to the claims of Christ, the latter must prevail. 2 Peter 2:11-17; Acts 5:29.
> 7. We believe that "super-patriotism" and "militant nationalism" are unbecoming to a Christian. We believe that as Christians we are called to a higher calling and that our primary allegiance is to a heavenly Kingdom. Christians ought not to give undivided loyalty to any political unit. Philippians 3:20; Colossians 1:13.
> 8. We believe that it is proper for Christians to vote, to exert influence on governmental officials (provided that neither means nor ends are un-Christian), and also under special conditions to stand for political office, if neither the attempt to gain the position nor the exercising of its functions requires a compromise of Christian ethics. Colossians 3:17.

Although the conference accepted these recommended "guidelines" for political involvement, a small minority of delegates took strong exception to point seven. These brethren believed that patriotism and nationalism were Christian virtues. The influence of nationalism on the thought and practice of the M.B. Church in both Canada and the United States has been increasingly noticeable in the last few years.[17] If present trends continue, Mennonite Brethren may drift into what F. H. Littell has called "Protestant nativism." The argument of most Mennonite Brethren leaders against greater participation in government can be summarized by stating that the church can deal more effectively with the world's problems by giving its independent witness in word and deed "in the Name of Christ."

II. Mennonite Brethren and Government Service

Closely related to the question of political involvement is the question of the Christian's attitude toward war and military service. From the very beginning Mennonite Brethren have shared with the larger Mennonite brotherhood and with an ever-widening circle of other evangelicals the conviction that "Christian nonresistance is a way of life in obedience to the will of God as revealed in Jesus Christ and the holy Scriptures."[18] When the Brethren in 1860 declared that "in the Articles (Confession of Faith) we are according to our convictions from the Holy Scriptures in full accord with our beloved Menno" they did not exclude the doctrine of nonresistance.

Menno's teaching on this point is clear and unequivocal: The regenerated do not go to war nor engage in strife. "They are the children of peace who have beaten their swords into plowshares and their spears into pruning hooks and know war no more. They give to Caesar the things that are Caesar's and to God the things that are God's."[19]

The attitude of Mennonites (including Mennonite Brethren) in Russia toward universal military training after 1870 has been mentioned earlier. The form of alternative service they rendered in peacetime (forestry service) and during World War I Restricted Medical Corps (*Sanitaetsdienst*) has also been described. The imposition of compulsory government service on all citizens by the Imperial Decree of 1870 was no doubt the primary cause of emigration to America. The desire to preserve the principle of nonresistance without compromise also prompted many Mennonite Brethren to leave and to establish congregations in the new world. Since the problems and experiences of the brotherhood in the United States and Canada differed somewhat, the story of Mennonite Brethren involvement in government service in these countries will be treated separately.

Government Service in the United States

The First World War

After more than forty years (1874-1917) of peace and tranquillity the Mennonite Brethren churches were suddenly faced with a situation from which they had endeavored to escape. When a conscription act became law on May 18, 1917, it contained a paragraph exempting members of the historic peace churches (Mennonites, Church of the Brethren, and Quakers) from military service, but added that "no person shall be exempted from service in any capacity which the

President shall declare noncombatant."[20] The churches now were confronted with the problem of noncombatant service.

The committee that was sent to Washington in June, 1917, included representatives of the Mennonite Brethren and Krimmer Mennonite Brethren, as well as from the Western District Conference (GC Mennonites). Their request for complete exemption from any state service did not result in any commitment on the part of the government. According to Gingerich, a considerable number of the men drafted from all branches of the church entered either full military service or noncombatant service. The noncombatants had little difficulty with the military authorities. On the other hand the larger group, who could not conscientiously engage in noncombatant service, were in many instances subjected to almost unbelievable mistreatment and even torture.[21] Only toward the end of the war did a satisfactory policy with regard to alternative service become operative.

An estimate of the number of Mennonites drafted during World War I places the figure at 2,000. The following summary by Hershberger provides an overall view of Mennonite involvement in government service during that time:

> The various Mennonite groups demonstrated varying degrees of loyalty to the principles of nonresistance; but the large majority of Mennonites refused service of any kind under the military. They were genuine nonresistants. A substantial minority accepted non-combatant service, while a few accepted combatant service. Limited records of the Mennonite majority who declined all service under the military indicate that approximately 10 percent were court-martialed and sent to prison, chiefly at Leavenworth; 60 percent accepted alternative service, either farm or reconstruction work; and 30 percent remained in the camps until the close of the war, most of these not having had an opportunity to appear before the Board of Inquiry.[22]

In discussing this phase of M.B. history, J. H. Lohrenz makes a positive evaluation of the stand taken by members of the church. He claims (although without documentation) that members of the M.B. Church "refused combatant service (and that) most of them declined any form of service within the military establishment. . . ."[23]

The experiences during the war shook the churches in their complacency and many brethren began to rethink the teachings of Christ with regard to nonresistance and peace. In spite of the apparently good record of most young men from M.B. churches, the feeling was widespread that the brotherhood had not been adequately prepared for the tests of faith and practice that the war had brought. (It might be mentioned here that up to 1919 the M.B. Conference had not issued a single statement on the subject of nonresistance, and there had also been no committee in charge of peace and nonresistance concerns.)

The 1919 conference constitutes a significant landmark in the history of the brotherhood with regard to this aspect of Christian discipleship. At the convention held in Mountain Lake, Minnesota, that year the delegates accepted a statement which reaffirmed the historic Anabaptist-Mennonite position with regard to war and military service. The statement, written as a supplement to paragraph sixty-six in the *Confession of Faith*, begins thus:

. . . On the matter of war we believe and confess, that the way it is waged by the worldly powers, it is manifestly contrary to the principles of the kingdom of Christ, and therefore our members are forbidden to participate in it. We much more have to wage a spiritual warfare against the powers of darkness . . . (There follow a number of Scripture quotations). [24]

The same conference also created a Committee on Nonresistance to which H. W. Lohrenz, Gerhard Wiens, and John Berg were appointed. This committee was reelected at the 1921 convention.

That the social concerns of the Mennonite Brethren in that immediate post-war period went far beyond the question of the church's relation to government service can be seen in the decision of the conference to send a special "letter of thanksgiving" (*Dankschrift*) to President Warren G. Harding in late 1921. The letter is one of recognition for the President's interest in disarmament and the abolition of war. [25] Three years later, however, the Committee on Nonresistance presented a report which expressed a concern about the ultimate objective of certain "peace conferences" which members had attended. According to the report, the aim of these conferences appears to be the creation of a "warless world" which the brethren found unscriptural. [26]

In 1927 the Southern District Committee on Nonresistance was requested to serve as the General Conference committee. Under the able leadership of P. C. Hiebert, it continued to alert the conference, throughout the thirties, to the growing menace of militarism, and to the need for biblical instruction and spiritual preparedness. In 1936 the concerns for relief and nonresistance were merged under the new constitution. P. C. Hiebert, J. W. Warkentin, D. C. Eitzen, A. E. Janzen and M. A. Kroeker served on this committee for many years.

The Second World War

When Mennonite Brethren met for their triennial convention in 1939 at Corn, Oklahoma, many nations of Europe (as well as Canada) were already in the throes of the Second World War. The attempt to give to Caesar the things that are Caesar's and to God the things that are God's found expression in two resolutions presented to the conference. One was related to the needs of the church and called for the approval of the Mennonite Central Peace Committee, and for the promotion of the peace doctrine through systematic teaching and the distribution of appropriate literature. The other resolution was directed to the government (of both Canada and the United States) and contained an expression of loyalty and appreciation for government policy in "pursuing a program of liberty and justice toward all men."[27]

To allay general suspicion which had been created by the propaganda of certain German newspapers and Nazi agencies the second resolution included the following statement: "The delegates further wish to go on record as having no sympathy or connection with organizations of foreign origin who are carrying on propaganda in these countries."[28]

Just two years later, on December 7, 1941, the Japanese attack on Pearl Harbor also brought the United States into the world conflict. This time the churches were more informed and better prepared than in 1917. Moreover, the MCC Peace Section had made preliminary contacts with Washington, so that the government was also more aware of the presence and position of conscientious objectors.[29] As a result, a plan for Civilian Public Service (CPS) was provided under the United States Selective Service and Training Act of 1940 for conscientious objectors who were unwilling to perform any kind of military service. In the six and one-half years that men were drafted under this law, nearly 12,000 young men were assigned to CPS camps to perform "work of national importance." Of these 4,665 or 38 percent were Mennonites.[30]

The erosive influence of patriotism and militarism on the practice of nonresistance by Mennonite Brethren is evident from the following statistics: According to the Draft Census Study, Mennonite Brethren had 39 percent of their drafted men in CPS, 26 percent in I-A-O (noncombatant service), and 34 percent in the regular military service. The other groups ranged between the Old Order Mennonites, who had 100 percent of their drafted men in alternative service, and the Mennonite Brethren in Christ (now United Missionary Church) who had only 10 percent in CPS.[31]

A summary of the final draft census of all Mennonites broken down according to church groups, giving the number of men and the percentages in each classification, for the entire conscription period 1940-47, is given below.

TABLE VIII

Draft Census of Various Mennonite Church Groups[32]

Name of Group	I-A		I-A-O		IV-E		
	No. of Men	Per-centage	No. of Men	Per-centage	No. of Men	Per-centage	Total
(Old) Mennonite	980	29.9	349	10.6	1943	59.5	3,272
General Conference Mennonite	1799	57.7	486	15.6	828	26.6	3,113
Old Order Amish	23	2.9	27	3.5	722	93.5	772
Mennonite Brethren	225	31.5	228	31.9	260	36.4	713
Mennonite Brethren in Christ	527	78.5	112	16.7	32	4.8	671

Conservative Amish							
Mennonite	34	13.8	24	9.7	187	76.3	245
Brethren in Christ	63	25.9	56	22.2	126	51.8	245
Church of God in Christ							
Mennonite	10	5.0	3	1.5	187	93.5	200
Defenseless Mennonites	91	54.8	58	34.9	17	10.2	166
Krimmer Mennonite							
Brethren	65	48.1	21	15.5	49	36.3	135
Evangelical Mennonite							
Brethren	16	14.6	29	26.6	64	58.8	109
Old Order Mennonite	0	0.0	0	0.0	72	100.0	72
United Zion Children	41	74.6	3	5.5	11	20.0	55
Hutterian Brethren	2	6.2	1	3.1	29	90.6	32
Reformed Amish Christian	0	0.0	0	0.0	6	100.0	6
Church of God							
(Mennonite)	0	0.0	0	0.0	3	100.0	3
Summary	3876	39.5	1397	14.2	4536	46.2	9,809

If only 46 percent of the Mennonite men drafted entered Civilian Public Service (see table above), why did 54 percent choose to enter military service? Although no simple answers are possible, the conclusions arrived at by the Draft Census Study are as follows. "The order of the relative strength of the influences which channeled men into military service is as follows: associates, family, finance, and lack of peace teaching."[33]

The several Mennonite conferences used various methods to help the CPS men at the time of their discharge. The U.S. Mennonite Brethren Church gave each man, CPS and army, a twenty-five dollar love gift when he returned from service. In addition, each CPS man was given five dollars per month up to $150.00 for the time he was in CPS.[34] Not to be overlooked is the fact that the churches contributed a total of over three million dollars in money and goods to the MCC for the operation of CPS camps.

Although the tragic war, which had brought untold suffering as well as loss of life and property to millions, eventually came to an end, the draft for compulsory government service in the United States did not. Except for a seventeen-month break in 1947-48, conscription for service has become a part of the American way of life. The Mennonite Brethren record for the past four years (given below) shows clearly that the brotherhood is deeply divided on the principle of nonresistance.

TABLE IX
Mennonite Brethren Men in Government Service[35]

Form of Service	1968-69	1969-70	1970-71	1971-72
Alternative Service	102	123	108	97
Military Service	135	115	76	71

Several comments need to be made with regard to the above statistics. Since the term of service is two years, the figures are overlapping. It has also not been possible to ascertain the relative number of those who chose a noncombatant service in the military. The assumption is that probably the majority of those listed above were in the I-A-O category. It is encouraging to notice the rising percentage of those entering alternative service.

In a response to questions in a recent survey (1971) sixty-four congregations indicated that they had had one or more members in military service during the last five years. The total number involved was approximately 225 (some churches had not specified the exact number). Only two congregations reported that they had taken disciplinary action against members who had served in the military.

Conference statements on the subject of nonresistance in the postwar period reflect deep concern about the preservation of the principle on the one hand, and a certain amount of uncertainty with regard to its practical expression on the other. In 1948 the Committee of Reference and Counsel presented a comprehensive document to the conference on the doctrine of nonresistance. With regard to alternative service the statement (which was accepted by the delegates) had this to say:

. . . the Conference expects that our men eligible for service, whenever called upon, will render valuable service for our people and country in two channels according to their conscientious convictions:
1. In agriculture and forestry projects, mental hospitals, and other institutions of civilian character, and in the field of rehabilitation and relief.
2. As noncombatants in the medical corps, not bearing arms nor participating in the training with weapons, rendering service to the sick and wounded soldiers, to nursing and the saving of lives, but not participating in any services that would tend toward the destruction of human life, and no service in defense plants. [36]

The last recommendation appears to be partly inspired by the historic precedent of a "restricted medical corps" in Russia, and partly the result of pressures from the constituency. Unfortunately, the recommendation was made without prior investigation whether the government (Washington or Ottawa) would recognize such a restricted medical corps for conscientious objectors. It was only in October, 1954, that J. B. Toews and Orlando Harms (as conference representatives) went to Washington, D.C., to explore the possibilities of such a service with officials in the Pentagon. The response of the Pentagon was negative. Consequently the 1954 conference meeting in Hillsboro rescinded the 1948 motion with reference to noncombatant service. [37]

The temporary uncertainty with regard to conference policy led to confusion in the constituency. Some churches interpreted the 1948 resolution as an acceptance of any form of noncombatant service.

Government officials used the document as a lever to pressure conscientious objectors into accepting noncombatant service with the argument that such service was recommended by their denomination.[38]

A 1951 resolution (one that has not been rescinded) called for disciplinary action against members who entered combatant military service. If after due admonition they would fail to obey the Word of God, they "shall be further dealt with according to the Scriptures and their membership in the church discontinued."[39] Considering this recommendation (which carried with only two dissenting votes) in the light of the statistical evidence presented above, it is obvious that there is a "credibility gap" here between profession and practice that undermines the integrity and testimony of the brotherhood.

Government Serice in Canada

The traditional policy of the Canadian government with respect to conscientious objectors has been very liberal. From 1808 to 1855 members of the historic peace churches were recognized as CO's, and were exempted from military service: but they were required to pay some "tribute to Caesar" in the form of a tax. The statute of 1808 provided for an annual payment of twenty shillings in peacetime and five pounds in wartime by all men between sixteen and sixty years of age.[40] From 1855 to 1867 Mennonites were unconditionally exempted from military service. In 1868 the newly formed Dominion government provided exemption not only for members of the historic peace churches but for "any inhabitant of Canada of any religious denomination . . . upon such conditions and such regulations as the Governor-in-Council may from time to time prescribe."[41]

As noted earlier, the more conservative Russian Mennonite groups who decided to come to Canada in the 1870's were not satisfied with the above provision and requested a clarification of the "conditions" that might be prescribed. In response to their petition the Governor General issued a special Order-in-Council in 1873 which stated clearly that they would be completely exempted from any military service. This Order-in-Council later also applied to members of the early Mennonite Brethren Church in Canada.

The First World War

Although Canada entered the war on the side of Great Britain in 1914, conscription was not introduced until 1917. The Military Service Act of 1917 contained a so-called "conscience clause" which exempted any member of a recognized peace church "who conscientiously objects to the undertaking of combatant service."[42] It will be observed at once, that this Act did not exempt from all military service, but from combatant service only. Consequently, a double standard prevailed

during World War I in the treatment of conscientious objectors: The
descendants of the Russian Mennonites were exempted from all service
by the Order-in-Council of 1873; the Mennonites of Ontario and members of other historic peace churches were subject to the provisions of
the Act of 1917. Since most of the latter lived in rural areas, following
agricultural pursuits, they were often granted exemption because of
their being employed in an essential industry. There were a few,
however, who were ordered by local tribunals to perform noncombatant
service in the army, and upon refusal to comply, were given prison
sentences of varying length.

The Mennonite Brethren in Canada during World War I were all
covered by the Order-in-Council of 1873 and thus were not affected
directly by the world conflict. However, they supported Red Cross and
other relief agencies. The issue of nonresistance apparently never came
up for discussion on the conference floor. With respect to government
war bonds, local congregations permitted their members to purchase
them with the proviso that the government be informed that the funds
thus raised should be used for the purchase of foodstuffs.[43]

In the 1930's the Mennonite Brethren became actively concerned
about the preservation and propagation of the principles of peace and
nonresistance. One could cite two main reasons for this renewed interest
in the subject. The new leadership of the M.B. Church in Canada was
composed largely of brethren who had experienced the horrors of war
and revolution. They also remembered all too well the *Selbstschutz* in
which the principle of nonresistance had been violated — mainly as a
result of inadequate teaching in the churches. The other reason for
renewed concern can be found in the world situation, especially in the
rise of military dictatorships in Europe. The resolution of 1934 (the first
on this issue ever to be presented to the Canadian Conference)
significantly begins thus: "The Conference is cognizant of the serious
situation in the world, which suddenly can be plunged into war — the
greatest misery of mankind."[44]

A Committee on Military Problems was also elected in 1934, to
provide leadership in this area of brotherhood concern. By 1936 the
war-clouds gathering over Europe prompted the leadership of the M.B.
Church to come before the conference with definite proposals for
alternative service in the event of a world conflagration. The resolution
presented that year to the Canadian convention meeting in Waldheim,
Saskatchewan, clearly reflects the views of B. B. Janz, the chairman of
the committee, as well as the Russian experience of many delegates.

The Conference of Mennonite Brethren Churches of Canada bases its
responsibilities toward the state on the word of Scripture: "give to Caesar the
things that are Caesar's and to God the things that are God's." With our firm
resolve for the principle of nonresistance, not to shed man's blood, we recognize

as a Conference our definite obligation as citizens toward our homeland, not only in the form of taxes, but also in any service that is not contrary to our conscience. The word of Jesus in Mark 3:4 and in Luke 6:9 ". . . to save life . . . (not) to destroy it," is our criterion for the acceptance or choice of the form of service. . . . Hence we as disciples of Jesus should not oppose, for instance, the noncombatant medical corps (*Sanitaetsdienst*). [45]

This approach to alternative service is mentioned here because it became a divisive issue at the beginning of World War II. The *Russlaender*-Mennonites, and among them especially the Mennonite Brethren, favored a restricted medical corps; the *Kanaedier*-Mennonites, including Mennonite Brethren, were opposed to a form of service so closely related to the military establishment. Many of the latter also expected another complete exemption from any form of service on the basis of the agreement of 1873. By 1939 some of these irreconcilable differences had to be faced realistically by the Committee on Military Problems, and this realism found expression in the committee's first recommendation to the conference: "(We recommend) that our own members must not be coerced, if they cannot participate with a good conscience in the medical corps." [46]

During the next few months world events moved swiftly to the brink of war. On September 10, 1939, Canada declared war against Germany, and on that day a new chapter in church-state relations began for the Canadian Mennonites.

The Second World War [47]

The peace churches were slow in organizing for alternative service, probably for two reasons: In the first place, there was no conscription in Canada; and secondly, there was a lack of unity among the western Mennonite groups on the question of the nature of alternative service. However, when the Canadian Parliament passed the National Resources Mobilization Act in June, 1940, the matter of an acceptable form of service for CO's became urgent.

The idea of a civilian alternative service had in the meantime been widely accepted among the Ontario Mennonite and Brethren in Christ Churches. In Western Canada, except for a large conservative group in Manitoba, there was also a strong movement to offer to the government a plan for alternative service. Consequently the Military Problems Committee of Western Canada (representing largely the M.B. Church and the General Conference Mennonites) contacted the Military Problems Committee of the Historic Peace Churches of Ontario for possible joint action. In November, 1940, a delegation of eight members, four from the West and four from the East (B. B. Janz and C. F. Klassen representing the Mennonite Brethren) met in Ottawa where they submitted to the authorities a memorandum with concrete proposals for alternative service. [48]

During their first interview with Major General La Fleche, Deputy Minister of War, they were told in no uncertain terms that any form of civilian service of national importance would not be acceptable. This was a great disappointment to the delegates. After a season of prayer and serious consultation in their hotel room, the delegates felt that the Holy Spirit moved them to make an appointment with the Honorable J. G. Gardiner,[49] Minister of War. In an interview that same day, Mr. Gardiner assured them that a civilian alternative service would be provided for conscientious objectors. In May, 1941, the Honorable Mr. Gardiner announced in the House of Commons the first call-up for Alternative Service.

By September 30, 1945 (shortly after the end of the war) there were 10,870 men in Canada classified as conscientious objectors. By provinces their distribution was as follows:

TABLE X

Distribution of Conscientious Objectors According to Provinces[50]

1.	Manitoba	3021
2.	Ontario	2636
3.	Saskatchewan	2304
4.	British Columbia	1665
5.	Alberta	1184
6.	Nova Scotia	29
7.	Quebec	26
8.	Prince Edward Island	3
9.	New Brunswick	2
		10,870

It will be readily observed that the overwhelming majority of conscientious objectors were registered in the five western "Mennonite" provinces. Although no complete record of the religious affiliation of men in Alternative Service is available, the writer found that in four major mobilization districts 4,425 out of 6,158 CO's were Mennonites.[51] This ratio of Mennonites to other conscientious objectors would probably be an accurate reflection of the ratio on a national scale. The exact number of Mennonite Brethren in Alternative Service could also not be established.

From 1941 to 1943 most of the conscientious objectors served in Alternative Service Work camps operated by the Department of Mines and Resources. Although the first call-up was for a four-month period, the time was later extended for the duration of the war. The government provided maintenance and traveling expenses to and from camp, and a remuneration of fifty cents per day. The churches were also allowed to appoint religious advisors or "chaplains."[52]

After 1943, because of a general labor shortage in the country, most of the men were assigned to work of "national importance" in agriculture or industry. Another form of alternative service (initially favored by the *Russlaender*-Mennonites) was provided by Order-in-Council P.C. 7251 in September, 1943, which permitted conscientious objectors to enlist as noncombatants in the Royal Canadian Army Medical Corps or the Canadian Dental Corps. The total number of men who actually served under this arrangement was only 227. Among them were a number of Mennonite Brethren.

Although the war in Europe came to an end in May, 1945, and in the Pacific theatre in August, Alternative Service men were not completely demobilized until August 15, 1946. Contrary to the experience of Mennonite Brethren in the United States, there has been no compulsory government service for CO's in Canada since then, because the draft was terminated at the end of the war.

Throughout the period of Alternative Service (1941-46) the Mennonite Brethren Conference endeavored to give moral and financial support to its members who were engaged in "service for peace." At the 1942 conference the delegation authorized the Committee on Military Problems to appoint a minister to serve in the ASW camps as spiritual adviser and pastor.[53] At the convention a year later the delegates voted to collect fifty cents per member in support of this ministry. A special matter of concern were the wives and dependents of the men in government service. The wage of fifty cents per day was hardly enough to meet the personal expenses of the married men. In 1942 the committee recommended the establishment of regional committees as well as regional treasuries for the purpose of making adequate provision for this need. In determining the amount of financial support in any given case the committee was to be guided by the principle that no dependent was to suffer want.[54]

It is difficult to assess the total impact of the Alternative Service program on church and state. J. F. MacKinnon, Chief Alternative Service Officer during the war, paid the following tribute to the Mennonites:

> The Mennonites cooperated in every way from the beginning of Alternative Service. There was very close cooperation between Mennonite bishops and Alternative Service officials. Perhaps it can be said that this group contributed more than any other group to Alternative Service. [55]

The men who returned home from Alternative Service camps brought with them a new zeal and devotion for work in the church and community. Many found their way to Bible school or Bible college and became leaders in the M.B. Church.

There were also a few members who had entered military service. When they returned at the end of the war, the churches faced a problem in church discipline. At the first convention after the war (1946) the conference agreed on the following procedure as a provisional guideline:

Those returning (from the military) owe the church an explanation concerning their action. If they are willing to acknowledge that they have acted contrary to our Confession of Faith, and if the church is satisfied with their repentance for this deviation from the Confession of Faith, the hand of fellowship may (again) be extended to them. [56]

At the same convention the brethren also agreed to make non-resistance a part of the commitment of an candidate for baptism and church membership. In subsequent years the Canadian Conference carried on an active and extensive program of peace education through special lecture series, appropriate literature and peace conferences.

According to the circulated questionnaire, no members of the M.B. Church in Canada have served in the armed forces during the last five years (1966-71). What the record would have been like, had Canada also had a universal military training program like the United States, is a matter of conjecture.

III. MENNONITE BRETHREN IN VOLUNTARY SERVICE

Compulsory service constitutes the "first mile" in a disciple's life; voluntary service exemplifies the principle of the "second mile." As a specialized concept the term "voluntary service" originated in the latter part of World War II and has been sponsored and administered largely by the MCC and several of the larger Mennonite groups. The idea of Voluntary Service was born out of a deep conviction that the church must give a sustained Christian testimony in various areas of need through a program of practical service "In the Name of Christ." [57]

Voluntary Service was first undertaken as a summer service program. A year-round Voluntary Service was inaugurated in 1947-48. The MCC program developed rapidly and by 1957 had 193 workers in summer service units, and 112 in year-round service.

The 1957 Mennonite Brethren General Conference gave its approval to Voluntary Service in the following resolution:

(a) That we stand in approval of Voluntary Service wherever and whenever it remains in line with the evangelical policies of the church.

(b) That mature young people from our churches who are members in good standing, are well established in faith and who have a missionary motive for service be encouraged to enter voluntary service. [58]

In 1960 the Board of General Welfare and Public Relations reported to the conference that sixty workers from M.B. churches were engaged in MCC service — twenty-five in relief and foreign service, and thirty-seven in Voluntary Service. The latter group constituted only a small part of the total task-force in VS. According to the MCC report on VS in 1970, there were thirty long-term units serving in North America — nineteen in Canada and eleven in the United States. Of the VS units serving in Canada more than one half were located in the economically depressed province of Newfoundland. Services ranged all the way from combating poverty in Appalachia to serving in a school for the mentally retarded in British Columbia; from helping in the Material Aid Center in Kitchener to working in a medical program in Kentucky. This practical expression of a "faith working through love" has provided many opportunities for sharing the Christian faith.

Christian Service

A new form of voluntary service, called "Christian Service," was initiated by the Board of General Welfare in 1960. It was an attempt to utilize the service potential of Mennonite Brethren young people to a greater degree in church-related ministries. The purpose of the new program was stated (in part) as follows:

1. To interpret and encourage the vision of Christian Service among our conference young people.

2. To develop dedication and loyalty to our M.B. Conference program and principles through service.[59]

The response to this new opportunity for service was most gratifying. Dwight Wiebe, the associate secretary of the board responsible for the Christian Service program, reported enthusiastically at the 1966 convention: "Judging by the present rise of interest, it will not be long until each Mennonite Brethren Church in Canada and the United States will have one or more young persons away from home serving the Lord."[60] The 1969 *Yearbook* of the General Conference lists eighty-four workers who were involved in Christian Service programs in North America. Of these twenty-six were serving in Nova Scotia (Canada). With one or two exceptions, the latter were all engaged in teaching.

Mennonite Disaster Service

Another avenue of voluntary service in which Mennonite Brethren have actively participated for a number of years is Mennonite Disaster Service (MDS). The program was organized by Mennonite laymen in the United States and Canada to aid the victims of natural disasters such as floods, tornadoes, storms, earthquakes, and fire by cleanup and reconstruction work, largely in damaged homes. Such work supplements the familiar Red Cross operations which primarily provide emergency relief and medical supplies. Generally MDS operates by assembling groups of men who, at their own expense and with their own tools, proceed to the disaster area and work for a period of several days or weeks doing what they can do to restore damaged homes.

The Canadian M.B. Conference recommended this avenue of service to its congregations in 1958. Most Mennonite Brethren congregations have so-called "contact men" who organize local groups in the event of an emergency call from the regional, national or international MDS committee. In recent years Mennonites and Mennonite Brethren have had many opportunities to serve in disaster areas.

Such services to the community have been an important Christian witness to the state and to the larger society. This ministry of compassion has also been recognized by governmental agencies and officials. In 1970 the Canadian Broadcasting Corporation paid tribute to the constructive peace witness of the Mennonites in a national telecast. In that same year Richard Nixon, the President of the United States, gave expression to his appreciation in a warm personal letter of recognition to the MDS Committee.

The above ministries do not exhaust the nature and scope of involvement of Mennonite Brethren in "voluntary service." Many services are performed on a congregational level in the community. As Christians who give their primary allegiance to Jesus Christ and his kingdom, Mennonite Brethren can make one of their greatest contributions to state and society through intercessory prayer and ministries of compassion.

Chapter 21

Understanding Biblical Revelation: Developments and Distinctives In Mennonite Brethren Theology

The Mennonite Brethren Church, throughout its history, has emphasized biblical authority in all matters of faith and practice. The early Brethren recovered much of the biblical orientation of apostolic Christianity and of the early Anabaptist movement. They became people of the Word. This meant, according to Hugo W. Jantz, that

they allowed God's Word to shine its warm and holy light into their lives within the cultural and social milieu in which their lives had to be lived. Together and alone they asked, openly and honestly: "How does God want us to think about him, and us, and the world? What is God telling us to do?" [1]

That the Bible constituted the final authority in faith and life for the Brethren is evident from the confessional documents. In the Document of Secession the Brethren cite or quote at least seventeen passages of Scripture to support their convictions. The "Brief Statement of the Rules and Outward Regulations of Our Church" submitted to the authorities by elder Heinrich Huebert in 1868, again makes constant reference to Scripture. [2]

The first definitive *Confession of Faith* of the Mennonite Brethren [3] published in 1902 begins with the words: "We believe with the heart and confess with the mouth before all men according to the contents of the Holy Scriptures, the Word of God. . . ." [4] The *Confession* is characterized by the use of biblical terminology and extensive quotations from Scripture.

Like their early Anabaptist-Mennonite forefathers, the Mennonite Brethren were biblicists with a kind of intuitive apprehension about creeds and confessions. Hence they have never attached as much weight to them as many other denominations have. To safeguard the brotherhood against the snares of creedalism which can easily develop

361

into a dead and barren orthodoxy, the brethren appended the following
conclusion to the 1902 *Confession*:

Every confession of faith, as every other teaching and exposition of Scripture, is
subject at all times to examination and estimation under the guidance of the Holy
Spirit, according to the Holy Scriptures . . . the only infallible written preserved
resource of the necessary and sufficient revelation of God to humanity for our
salvation. [5]

The search of the early Brethren for biblical patterns and principles
for the fellowship of believers did not occur in a theological vacuum,
however, but in a definite church-related and historical context. In their
attempts to understand biblical revelation the brethren were influenced
(perhaps much more than they realized) by their spiritual heritage as
well as by the literature and ministries of contemporary evangelicals.

Even a cursory survey of the theological pilgrimage of the
Mennonite Brethren Church through a period of some 112 years shows
that the various theological influences to which the brotherhood has
been exposed have not always been properly integrated into M.B.
theology. In the early years as well as in later times the biblicism of the
Mennonite Brethren has been threatened by various schools of
theological thought.

No definitive study of the nature of Mennonite Brethren theology is
possible within the scope of this chapter.[6] However, a brief survey of
several historical movements, both earlier and later, and their influence
on Mennonite Brethren distinctives, follows.

I. Historical Roots of Mennonite Brethren Theology

The early Brethren emphasized an experiential Christianity, based
on the teachings of the New Testament, but they also had a remarkable
appreciation for the historical dimension of faith. P. M. Friesen, eminent
Mennonite Brethren historian, more than sixty years ago summarized
the ideological roots and formative influences of Mennonite Brethren
theology in these words:

Therefore we as Mennonites, are heirs in spirit and blood, of the Waldenses,
the Bohemian Brethren, the South German and Swiss, and (in blood) overwhelmingly of the Dutch Anabaptists, for the latter were first named
"Mennonites." Herein also lies proof of our indubitable kinship to the "Renewed
(Zinzendorf-Herrnhut) Brethren Church" and to those of the Dutch Anabaptists,
partly the strict Mennonites of Amsterdam, partly the free Anabaptists who
"adhere to Menno's guidelines," the Rhynsburger Brethren, or Collegiants, also
known as Dunkards (that is immersionists), who between 1611 and 1640 gave
rise to the English Baptists. Their members included Milton . . . Bunyan . . .
Carey . . . and C. H. Spurgeon. From Count Zinzendorf's songs, essentially, (and)
from Spurgeon's Sermons and other writings, there have flowed upon us streams
of blessing. And is it necessary to mention Oncken, Koebner and August Liebig?
Menno Simons, courageously and humbly, recovering that "which was from the
beginning" has erected a wonderfully simple and convenient house for us, in
which we dwell "on the foundation of the apostles and prophets, where Jesus
Christ is the cornerstone." Those already named, as well as the evangelical

Pietists: Phil. Hiller, Gerh. Tersteegen, Ludwig Hofacker, Fr. W. Krummacher and many others through their writings, and Pastor Eduard Wuest personally, have brought new light, new warmth, and food into the house of Menno, which, though once good, had become practically desolate, empty and cold.[7]

In this passage Friesen identifies three main streams, or perhaps better, one main stream and two tributaries — in the spiritual heritage of the Mennonite Brethren: Anabaptist, Pietist, and Baptist. For a brief discussion of these influences we turn first to the main historical source of Mennonite Brethren theology: early Anabaptism.

Anabaptist Influences

Throughout this book, and especially in the discussion of the confessional statements of the early M. B. Church, the influence of Menno Simons and other Anabaptist leaders on the theological views of the Mennonite Brethren has been indicated. Confessions of faith have been an important channel for transmitting the Anabaptist heritage to succeeding generations. According to A. J. Klassen "two of the three official Mennonite Brethren confessions of faith draw heavily upon many of these earlier Anabaptist-Mennonite confessions."[8] In fact, the earliest confession accepted by the Mennonite Brethren of the Molotschna was the *Friesisch-Flaemisch* confession of 1660, published by the Rudnerweide Mennonite Church in 1853.

The 1902 *Confession* carefully preserves the distinctives of Anabaptist-Mennonite theology. This is true not only in such articles as "Concerning the Taking of an Oath," "Concerning Revenge, Nonresistance and Love of Enemies" and "Concerning the washing of the feet by the Lord and among believers," but also in articles dealing with the nature of the church and the calling of ministers.[9] In both of these latter areas the brotherhood character of the church is emphasized.

Although perhaps unaware of the continuing Arminian-Calvinist controversy in Western Protestantism, the brethren in good Anabaptist tradition carefully avoided the pitfalls of either extreme position. This is how they formulated their views: "Concerning divine election and man's will we believe, that from eternity it has been the free good-pleasure and gracious purpose of God to redeem sinners to the praise of his glory . . . that all who obey His Gospel and believe on Him should not perish but have everlasting life."[10]

This emphasis on spiritual identity with the views of the Anabaptists, and especially of Menno Simons, is found repeatedly in the correspondence of the Brethren. As early as December 27, 1860, the Brethren make the following claims in a letter addressed to the Supervisory Commission:

We are not a newly-established sect, as the worthy Supervisory Commission likes to call us. On the contrary, we are the seed of the imperishable Word of God, which was preached to us by the Apostles, explained through the Holy Spirit, and have become a fruit of the living faith of our beloved founder (*Stammvater*) Menno Simons, who in all his church regulations and confessions of faith practiced and established them even as we; hence we can rightly call ourselves the genuine descendants of true Mennonitism.[11]

In his studies of the Mennonite Brethren Church C. Krahn arrived at the same conclusion, namely that the new movement constituted a return to the biblical principles and practices of the early Anabaptists:

It would not be correct . . . to say that the *Bruedergemeinde* movement brought a new conception of the Gospel through the Pietistic and Baptist influence which formed it . . . the new movement consciously felt itself related to 16th Century Anabaptism. It did not want to be Pietistic, nor Baptist, but rather Mennonite. It wanted to be and remain historical, consistent Mennonitism, a pure Menno-nitism that was based not upon birth, but rebirth.[12]

Through the years the doctrinal framework of M.B. theology has remained basically Anabaptist-Mennonite. The emphasis on human response to the gracious divine initiative in salvation, the significance of the church as a "company of the committed" in which mutual aid and mutual admonition are exercised, the importance of discipleship as an expression of the new life, in which Christ's love-ethic must govern all human relationships — these and many other biblical truths are deeply rooted in the Anabaptist heritage. Although there has been a weakening of the church's theological foundations in recent times (as will be shown later), the confessional documents of the M.B. Church to the present day strongly maintain this historical connection and orientation.

Pietistic Influences

"No other single religious movement has had such an impact on the Mennonites in all countries, with the exception of the Netherlands, as Pietism."[13] This great influence of Pietism on the spiritual heirs of the early Anabaptists may be due to an inner kinship of the two movements. Max Goebel referred to Pietism as a "grandchild of Anabaptism."[14] Albrecht Ritschl, an outstanding historian of Pietism, described the latter movement as a weakened form of Anabaptism.[15] Whatever the original generic relationship may have been, there is no question with regard to the great impact of Pietism on Mennonitism, and especially Russian Mennonitism in the nineteenth century.

As pointed out in chapter three, Pietistic influence was a major factor in bringing about a new life movement that eventually resulted in the formation of the M.B. Church. As P. M. Friesen so vividly describes the contribution of Pietism: "The evangelical Pietists . . . have brought new light, new warmth, and food into the house of Menno, which, though once good, had become practically desolate, empty, and cold."[16]

As noted earlier, there were several channels by which Pietism brought new light and food into the house of Menno. Pietistic literature, such as Hofacker's sermons and Johann Arndt's *Wahres Christentum* gave its quiet but persistent witness to the divine resource for spiritual renewal. The major channel of this influence was without question "Pfarrer" Eduard Wuest, whom Orlando Wiebe has described as "the chief representative of evangelical Pietism."[17] Of John Wesley it has been said that he did not originate a new theology, but that he did bring new fire into an old theology. This was also the contribution of Wuest to Mennonitism: he brought "new warmth," the warmth of a vital Christian experience, into what was otherwise a sound theological structure.

The special contribution of Pietism to Mennonite Brethren theology is precisely this — it revitalized in many areas the rather dead and traditional Mennonite orthodoxy. According to C. Krahn, "the emphasis on a personally experienced salvation, on the Christian outreach at home and abroad, and the use of newer forms of spreading the Gospel is particularly due to the revitalization which came through Pietism."[18]

P. M. Friesen considered Pietism as a basically wholesome and beneficial movement which served as a necessary corrective and complement to nineteenth century Mennonitism. Friesen described Wuest as the "second reformer" of the Mennonites, Menno Simons being the first.

Along with these positive contributions of Pietism its limitations should also be pointed out. Its emphasis on the "joyous justification doctrine" and a strong emotional aspect in the salvation experience produced some negative effects in the early M.B. Church. The emphasis on the inward experience of God's grace and its outward application to all areas of life was not always kept in proper balance. Pietism also lacked the concept of a believers' church. In Wuest's own congregation at Neuhoffnung believers and unbelievers, all baptized in infancy, remained "side by side" even though Wuest had originally emphasized the need for a separated church of believers only.[19]

Although Anabaptism and Pietism are similar in many ways, there are also some basic differences between the two movements in their conception of the Christian life. Ernst Crous describes these differences as follows:

> In Anabaptism the new birth is sealed in baptism, sending the pilgrim forth on the strenuous way of discipleship and love in action with the kingdom of God as its final goal. Pietism begins with the struggle for personal repentance from sin (*Busskampf*), followed by assurance of salvation and freedom to enjoy the new possession with relatively little concern for the strenuous responsibilities which confront the Anabaptist disciple.[20]

The M.B. Church has been described as "Mennonite in doctrine, Pietistic in spirit."[21] This evaluation is in harmony with Friesen's metaphor that Pietism has brought "new warmth" into the house that Menno built. Pietism's major contribution to M.B. theology must be seen in the "spirit" which it instilled, rather than in the "content" which it provided. However, in some areas this "spirit" has weakened the structure and has led to a lack of emphasis on Christian discipleship, church ordinances and social concerns.

Baptist Influences

In chapter five the influence of the German Baptists during the formative period of the Mennonite Brethren Church received considerable attention. The specific contribution of Baptist teaching to Mennonite Brethren theology, however, needs further clarification and definition.

The influence of the German Baptists on the new life movement in Russia prior to 1860 was practically nonexistent. By 1860 literature advocating baptism by immersion had reached the Mennonite Brethren. Both Jacob Reimer and Johann Claassen were in possession of tracts and pamphlets dealing with the subject of baptism.

In the Einlage (Chortitza) M.B. Church Baptist influence was strong from the very inception of the church. In addition to the active correspondence which Abraham Unger carried on with J. G. Oncken, the father of the German Baptist movement, Baptist preachers such as August Liebig and Karl Benzien ministered to the young M.B. Church for prolonged periods of time. Baptist influence during this earlier period is observable in several areas of Mennonite Brethren doctrine and practice.

Although some of the early Brethren claimed to have discovered baptism by immersion in the writings of Menno Simons,[22] Baptist influence on the mode of baptism in the M.B. Church cannot be denied. "In view of the fact," Bender observes, "that Baptist influence was present at the beginning of the M.B. movement, it is probably correct to assume that immersion came from that source."[23] If it did not originate from that source, it was certainly confirmed by Baptist literature and teaching. The fact that the Chortitza Brethren, who had had direct contacts with the German Baptists, became the proponents of strict immersionism in the M.B. Church, would give added support to that assumption.

The *Einlage Confession of Faith*, prepared in 1873 and published by Abraham Unger in 1876, also bears the stamp of Baptist influence.[24] In order to convince government officials in 1873 that the Mennonite Brethren Church was fully equipped with a confession of faith of its own, certain brethren took a Baptist confession and rewrote it to include Mennonite distinctives (e.g. footwashing, nonresistance). This Baptist-Mennonite confession (as A. H. Unruh calls it) proved to be a deterrent in the development of the young church. Soon protests were heard in the Molotschna Mennonite Brethren Church concerning the strong Baptist views expressed in the confession. Russian officials were no less confused and repeatedly requested information as to which Mennonites belonged to the Baptist Church.[25] This problem was not resolved until the Chortitza Brethren, with the assistance of P. M. Friesen and Johann Wieler (two high school teachers from the Molotschna) prepared a series of documents which clarified their relationship to the Baptists.

It would appear that the Mennonite Brethren have also been influenced by the Baptists in their church polity. The introduction of "parliamentary rules" for conducting church and conference business sessions can be traced to the influence of August Liebig in Chortitza. Liebig also introduced the Sunday school and the public "prayer meeting" as part of the Sunday worship service.[26] A stronger emphasis on congregational church government in Mennonite Brethren churches also appears to be connected with early Baptist influence.

Although the association of the Mennonite Brethren with the Baptists in Russia and in the United States[27] led occasionally to questions of organizational unity, a complete merger of the two groups was never seriously considered. After tracing the historical development of Mennonite Brethren-Baptist relations in Russia and America, and showing from the confessional documents how the Brethren have refuted the allegations that they were "Baptists," F. C. Peters concludes his study of the question with the following observations:

(1) The early Mennonite Brethren were definite in their desire to remain Anabaptist in their confessions. Every attempt was made to declare themselves in harmony with the basic tenets as set forth by Menno Simons.

(2) The radical advances toward affiliation with the Baptists were made by isolated individuals who failed to receive the support of the brotherhood.

(3) It seems rather clear that the Mennonite Brethren revival was meant to be a return to the Anabaptist vision, rather than a deviation from it. The desire to build a community of believers who had personally committed themselves to follow Jesus Christ, and who were willing to live a separated life of holiness, was certainly in keeping with what the Anabaptist forefathers felt was the New Testament pattern for a believers' church.[28]

This cursory survey shows that the formative influences which converged in the Mennonite Brethren Church produced a theology that was true to the Anabaptist vision, was permeated by the spirit of Pietism, and also reflected the polity of the Baptists. The confluence of these streams of evangelical thought in Mennonite Brethren theology has produced certain distinctives which deserve a closer scrutiny.

II. CHARACTERISTIC DISTINCTIVES OF MENNONITE BRETHREN THEOLOGY

With the Christian church through the ages and with contemporary evangelical Christian denominations and groups, Mennonite Brethren share a common faith as expressed in the Apostles' Creed and in the other great doctrines of revelation and redemption as given in the confessions of conservative Protestantism. However, their understanding of the Gospel, and their historic experience have led Mennonite Brethren to certain emphases which account largely for the spiritual dynamic of the group's message and ministry. The following list of distinctives is by no means exhaustive, but has been selected to provide a general theological profile of the M.B. Church.

1. *Practical Biblicism*

The biblicism of the early Mennonite Brethren, like that of their Anabaptist forefathers, was practical, rather than propositional, in nature. They turned to the Scriptures, not to construct systems of theology, but to find the solution to their spiritual problems. They searched the Scriptures daily for spiritual nurture and guidance. Wesley Prieb has aptly described this practical biblicism of the Mennonite Brethren:

"The early members of our church were often recognized by their bulging coat pocket which contained a well-worn Bible. The *Bibelstunden* became the basis of their fellowship and worship. Reading the Word was part of their daily family pattern."[29]

As mentioned in the introduction to this chapter, the Brethren were averse to any rigid dogmatism and creedalism that might displace the authority of the Bible. Seldom, if ever, did they ask: What does our *Confession of Faith* say? But often one could hear the question: What does the Scripture say? In their study of the Bible the Brethren developed an elementary hermeneutic — they discovered the locus of scriptural authority in the teaching of Christ and the Apostles. In the statement prepared by Daniel Fast in the spring of 1865, which contained the first major refutation of the *Froehliche Richtung*, this principle of Scripture interpretation is clearly evident. According to Fast, true godliness does not find expression in dancing, leaping, and shouting as some teach on the basis of certain Old Testament passages. In the teaching of the Apostles the mark of a true faith is not an outward happiness, but a genuine love.[30]

In later years the Mennonite Brethren have endeavored to institutionalize their biblicism. In order to emphasize the centrality of the Scriptures in the curriculum, the Brethren put the word "Bible" into the name of the schools they built: Bible school, Bible academy, Bible institute, Bible college and Biblical seminary. In their somewhat simplistic biblicism, the Brethren have sometimes been guilty of stressing the "letter," rather than the "spirit" of Scripture. A collection of "proof-texts" has occasionally been construed as representing a "biblical approach" or as "Scriptural teaching."

In general, however, even this sort of naive biblicism has served the churches well. It has compelled the brotherhood again and again to turn to the Bible for a reexamination of traditional beliefs and practices. In a continued emphasis of practical biblicism lies the hope for a continued spiritual renewal of the church.

2. *Experiential Faith*

From the beginning and throughout their history Mennonite Brethren have taught that the Christian life begins with a radical inward renewal. This renewal they defined as conversion or the new birth.[31] This spiritual renewal is effected by a personal faith in Christ as Savior and Lord. The early Brethren emphasized the need for an "experiential faith" in contradistinction to a "memorized faith" (*auswendig gelernter Glaube*) which they felt was the condition for membership in the Mennonite Church of that day.

In the *Confession of Faith* this distinctive is set forth as follows:

Concerning *conversion, renewal* or *the new birth* we believe that through the living and powerful Word of God man is awakened from sin. John 1:9. If he is now obedient and does not close his heart against the working of divine grace, he receives repentance unto life, to see his sin, repent of it, confess and forsake it; and in recognition of the holy and just judgment of God through prayer seeks refuge in Christ as the only Savior from the guilt of sin and the lust thereof, and receives through faith in Him forgiveness of sins, justification, and the witness and sealing of the Holy Spirit that he is a child of God and heir of life eternal.[32]

From this description of "conversion" it is obvious that the brethren had a comprehensive concept of man's salvation experience. The brethren apparently were more interested in the new life of the individual than in the experience that had brought it about. In this connection it is perhaps significant, that only one account of a conversion-story of an early church leader has been preserved in the records — that of elder Abraham Schellenberg. The "dated" conversion became a distinctive of Mennonite Brethren in later years.

The need for conversion, for spiritual renewal, received primary emphasis in Mennonite Brethren preaching. David Gerhard Duerksen (1850-1910) was one of the greatest preachers the M.B. Church has produced. His one hundred extant sermons represent a mature expression of second-generation Mennonite Brethren theology. According to a study made by A. J. Klassen, twenty-eight of these sermons are related to the subjects of the new birth, sin and salvation.[33]

For Duerksen the new birth was a complete conversion from the old life to a new life in Christ. He believed that God transformed the total person: his mind, his will, and his emotion. "In Duerksen's theology, regeneration is central. He describes the 'look to Jesus' as the 'most necessary look.'"[34]

The form of this distinctive in M.B. theology has been preserved to the present day. However, something seems to have happened to the content in the experience of third and fourth generation Mennonite

Brethren. As the conversion experience is duplicated at younger and still younger ages, a subtle change takes place in the meaning of the concept.[35] Conversion for a six-year-old obviously does not have the same meaning as for the man of thirty-six. In his provocative study *New Wineskins for Old Wine*, Delbert Wiens calls attention to the dilemma of perpetuating a religious experience under vastly different conditions.[36]

To preserve the integrity of the Mennonite Brethren Confession as well as the validity of the conversion experience, a new and more comprehensive definition of the experience is needed. The relation of Christian nurture to Christian experience needs to be set forth in the context of New Testament teaching.

3. *Personal Witnessing*

Among early Mennonite Brethren witnessing to God's saving grace was not the prerogative of a select group, but the privilege and responsibility of every member. Among the charter members of the M.B. Church there were no ordained church officers, and this fact may have been a blessing in disguise. Lay members began to spread the message of salvation in the framework of their own contacts within their communities. New converts frequently witnessed to their families and friends. This missionary activity of ordinary members was an important factor in the expansion of the M.B. Church.

In the early years Mennonite Brethren were known for their zeal in witnessing. The "joyous assurance" of sins forgiven (a dimension of Christian experience that can be traced to the influence of Pietism) gave them great liberty and boldness in sharing their faith. This is how C. Krahn describes it:

> The new emphasis upon a strong personal experience of the grace of God with its accompanying assurance of salvation produced a very sturdy and active type of Christian, and led to the development of an almost unbelievable zeal for witnessing for the Gospel in home and foreign missions.[37]

Although personal evangelism still constitutes an integral part of the "practical theology" of Mennonite Brethren, it has lost much of its original spontaneity and dynamic in recent years. The emphasis has shifted from a simple sharing of the experience of God's grace to a knowledge of the techniques in personal work. In the new approach method has often been more important than motivation. Courses in personal work and "institutes for evangelism" have emphasized the "know-how" rather than the constraining love of Christ. Without the latter, the most eloquent testimony is but a "noisy gong or a clanging cymbal."

4. *Christian Discipleship*

Like their Anabaptist forefathers, Mennonite Brethren have considered discipleship as belonging to the very essence of the new life.

It is a concept which implies the transformation of the entire way of life of the believer so that it might be fashioned after the teachings and example of Christ. The secession of the Brethren was not primarily related to doctrinal issues, but to ethical concerns. In the document submitted to the elders the Brethren do not take issue with the teaching in the Mennonite Church, but with the life and practice of its members. "We fear the inevitable judgment of God," they wrote, "because the public godlessness and wickedness are crying to God in heaven."[38] In the new movement, therefore, one could find a strong ethical emphasis.

In the social and cultural context of that time, a life of discipleship for Mennonite Brethren was related to specific moral problems. Since drinking of alcoholic beverages had become a grave social problem, the Brethren agreed on a pathway of complete abstinence. Because many of them had been enslaved by the tobacco habit prior to their conversion, the Brethren took a strong stand against the use of tobacco. Outside observers would occasionally refer to them as the church of the "non-smokers." Opposition to dancing, card-playing and the commercial movie theatre have also characterized Mennonite Brethren ethics through the years. The scriptural teaching that the believer's body is a temple of the Holy Spirit (1 Cor. 6:19) was a basic motivation in refraining from such practices.[39] Although separation from the world was no doubt often understood in far too narrow terms, there was nevertheless a genuine desire not to be conformed to the world.

Nonresistance, a particular aspect of discipleship, is a distinctive which Mennonite Brethren have in common with historic peace churches. Mennonite Brethren believe that Christians should not participate in war or violence but exercise Christian love toward all men.

5. *Brotherhood Emphasis*

Even before 1860 the members of the new life movement among the Mennonites in South Russia were known as "Brethren." The official name of the new group, "Mennonite Brethren Church" was consequently not the result of an artificial or arbitrary process of selection, but rather the expression of a new and vital relationship which the Brethren had experienced in their fellowship. In the early M.B. Church there was a real revival of the biblical concept of *koinonia* in which the root idea is "participating in something in which others also participate," that is "a conscious sharing with someone else in a joint possession, usually on a continuing basis."[40]

Like their Anabaptist forefathers, the Mennonite Brethren have conceived of the church as a brotherhood in which there are no classes, no clergy and laity, no artificial distinctions but a fellowship of equals.

The New Testament designation of "brother" and "sister" were revived and given a new and deeper meaning. These terms indicated to them that members of the church were closely bound together by the ties of love and mutual concern, and that they should act toward each other as members of a great family of whom God is the Father.

Menno's high regard for the "church" also finds expression in Mennonite Brethren theology. The Brethren always viewed the Christian life as being lived in the context of the fellowship of believers. In a very real sense one could describe their theology as being church-centered. For them the congregation was a company of committed disciples who had entered into a covenant with their Lord and with each other for holy living and faithful service. This aspect is reflected in the M.B. *Confession of Faith*:

> The characteristics of the true church are: The fruits of conversion and of the right faith of Jesus Christ revealed in a life of sanctification according to the teaching of Christ and His apostles; the diligent searching of the Scriptures and the preaching of the pure gospel in all the world; practice of the holy ordinances of Christ which are baptism and the Lord's Supper; the free confession of God and Jesus Christ before all men; fervent brotherly love, fellowship and submission among themselves and love of their neighbors; diligence to uphold the unity of the spirit through the bond of peace; taking up the cross in following Jesus. . . .[41]

Although the Brethren emphasized personal acceptance of Christ as Savior and Lord, they had a strong consciousness and conviction with regard to the corporate nature of salvation. For them the church was not merely an aggregate of individual believers, but an organism, the body of Christ. "Without this corporate oneness," F. C. Peters wrote some years ago, "there can be no church."[42] It is this consciousness of interdependence which forms both the basis and the motivation for church discipline — a Mennonite Brethren distinctive which seems to be rapidly disappearing.

This "brotherhood-consciousness" saved the brethren from individualism and an overemphasis on the autonomy of the local church. In describing the distinctive characteristics of early Mennonite Brethren theology, A. H. Unruh makes the following observation: "Although the brethren as individuals and as groups lived in widely scattered areas, they constituted only 'one' church. The brethren in the Molotschna, in Chortitza, and on the Kuban considered themselves as one church, which walked according to the same rule."[43]

In recent years the brotherhood-consciousness and church loyalty among Mennonite Brethren has been undermined and weakened by the inroads of American individualism as well as by modern interdenominationalism.

6. *Evangelism and Missions*

"The divine assignment to preach the Gospel to every creature is the privilege and responsibility involving every member of the brotherhood." This statement from a recent report of the Board of Missions and Services indicates the central place that Mennonite Brethren have given to evangelism and missions in their theology. If, as has been claimed, the Mennonite Brethren Church "was born in an atmosphere of missions and missionary endeavor,"[44] then it is not surprising that Mennonite Brethren theology is evangelistic in spirit.

As indicated earlier, no other cause or concern has received such wholehearted and universal support in the M.B. Conference as the work of missions and evangelism. The report on foreign missions to the Centennial Conference in 1960 gives eloquent expression to this conviction:

Missions is an integral part of the Mennonite Brethren Church. It is incorporated in our concept of the Christian life. Missions is a natural expression of a Christian duty and privilege. This was so from the beginning of the movement. . . . This emphasis upon missions has never ceased, and numerous members have volunteered for foreign and home mission services, while others have contributed of their means to make the work possible.[45]

This missionary concern has been a Mennonite Brethren distinctive from the inception of the church. In examining the missionary activities of the Mennonites in Russia, Gerhard Lohrenz found that mission work among the native population was carried on primarily by the Mennonite Brethren. According to Lohrenz, "many of the old church joined the new Mennonite movement because they shared the rising vision for evangelism. . . ."[46]

A survey of conference periodicals, yearbooks and other literature leads one to the conclusion that no other subject has received as much attention among Mennonite Brethren as missions and evangelism. It has been a major factor in maintaining a spirit of unity in the far-flung constituency of the Mennonite Brethren. Moreover, the "foreign missions program of the Mennonite Brethren Church has been used of God to keep the brotherhood spiritually dynamic, evangelical and evangelistic."[47]

In the past (and in some churches in the present) this evangelistic emphasis has not always been properly related to social concerns. Mennonite Brethren have occasionally been charged with being indifferent to the material needs of men. They were interested, critics have said, in saving souls, not in saving people.

Although that indictment may at times have been applicable to some individuals and to certain churches, it cannot be generalized on the basis of available records. Through the years Mennonite Brethren have been involved in ministries of relief and general welfare. Increasingly the view that the church must minister to the total needs of man has won acceptance in the brotherhood as a whole. The merger of the boards of "missions" and "welfare" in 1966 symbolically expressed this integrated approach of the Mennonite Brethren witness. In fact, the simultaneous emphasis on both, evangelism and social concern, has been described as one of the primary distinctives of the Mennonite Brethren Church.[48]

7. Christ-centered Eschatology

With many Christians through the ages Mennonite Brethren hold to the faith of Christ's second coming as the blessed hope of the church. The certainty of Christ's return for the early Brethren was firmly established in the teachings of Scripture. "We believe and confess, that the Lord Jesus, our King, in like manner as He visibly ascended into heaven, shall come down again from heaven." This is the introductory statement in the article treating "last things" in the Confession of Faith. The entire section is presented in terminology taken from the Scriptures with Christ as the central figure throughout.

Historically, Mennonite Brethren have emphasized the glorious fact of Christ's return without special adherence or commitment to a particular "system" of eschatology. A. H. Unruh comments as follows on the eschatological views of the early Brethren: "They exhorted (each other) to watchfulness and to a holy walk. The present views with regard to the rapture and the millennium were apparently foreign to them. However, they joined in the prayer: 'Amen. Come Lord Jesus.' "[49]

Although extreme Dispensationalism (as set forth in Larkin's charts and Scofield's footnotes) has at times obscured the centrality of Christ as the blessed hope of the church, Mennonite Brethren have generally believed that Jesus Christ, who by His first coming has begun a spiritual kingdom which shall not be destroyed, will come again to vindicate His rule and bring His kingdom to a glorious consummation. The practical implications of this great event for sanctification and service have been recurring themes in Mennonite Brethren teaching and preaching.[50]

This brief summary of certain distinctives in Mennonite Brethren theology is far from complete. It reflects, however, the desire of Mennonite Brethren to be "the people of God" in this world — a people who have experienced God's mercy and who have endeavored to obey God's Word as they understood its teaching under the guidance of the Holy Spirit and in the light of their spiritual heritage.

III. Outside Influences on Mennonite Brethren Theology

In their theological pilgrimage of more than one hundred years, Mennonite Brethren have been exposed to various "winds of doctrine" that have modified, and at times seriously threatened, the basic scriptural and historical framework of their theology. Two of these theological movements which have influenced Mennonite Brethren thought and practice will be considered briefly.

1. *Fundamentalism*

Fundamentalism, a movement in conservative American Protestantism in the first half of the twentieth century, was primarily a reaction against the growth of theological liberalism and modernism. The movement derived its name largely from two sources: (1) the publication in 1909 of a series of twelve small volumes in defense of conservative theology called *The Fundamentals* and (2) the World Christian Fundamentals Association, which was organized in Philadelphia in 1919. The movement reached its height in the late 1920's after which it declined rapidly in volume and strength.[51]

The "fundamentals" on which the association generally concentrated its emphasis were the following: the inerrancy of the Bible, the virgin birth of Jesus, the physical resurrection of Jesus Christ, a substitutionary theory of the atonement, and the imminent, bodily second coming of Christ. It can be readily seen why Mennonites, with their historic position of orthodoxy and evangelicalism, would be affected by the Fundamentalist movement. Most Mennonites, according to Bender, sympathized warmly with the struggle against modernism.[52] By and large, however, they did not formally join the Fundamentalist ranks, although they almost without exception held to the fundamentals and considered themselves fundamentalists in a descriptive sense.

It would appear that Mennonite Brethren have been more susceptible to Fundamentalist influences than any other Mennonite group. When the National Association of Evangelicals (NAE) was organized in 1944, the only Mennonite body to join it was the Mennonite Brethren Church. The more conservative Mennonite bodies were aided in their resistance to Fundamentalist influences by their traditional objection to outside contacts, and by their strong emphasis on nonresistance which the Fundamentalists usually sharply rejected.

In commenting on the positive influences of Fundamentalism on the M.B. Church V. Adrian makes the following statement: "Fundamentalism was valuable for a time and to some degree. Its principle was to concentrate its defence and apologetics in that area of Christian faith which was most under attack and which was absolutely essential to Christian faith."[53]

The liabilities of a fundamentalistic attitude have also been evident in the M.B. Church. Fundamentalism, essentially an apologetic movement, built its theology on very narrow premises. The "five points" of Fundamentalism, valuable as they are, do not exhaust the content of the Christian faith and message. The liabilities of such a concentration on certain biblical truths are that other major doctrines are often minimized or neglected since they do not fit into the "system."

Fundamentalism has concentrated on Christian dogmatics, rather than on Christian ethics. It has emphasized man's relationship to God but has failed to give equal emphasis to man's relationship to his neighbor as taught by Christ: "And a second is like it, you shall love your neighbor as yourself" (Matt. 22:39). Fundamentalism has exalted "the work of the cross" but has been strangely silent about "the way of the cross" and the demands of Christian discipleship.[54]

Mennonite Brethren teaching on the ethic of love and nonresistance has fared badly under the influence of Fundamentalism. Since many liberal theologians were pacifists in their attitude toward war, Fundamentalists generally rejected nonresistance as part of a liberal theology, without differentiating between humanistic pacifism and biblical nonresistance.[55] Hyper-Fundamentalists have through the years been known for their support of militarism and nationalism. This spirit of super-patriotism is also noticeable in some sections of the M.B. Church.

Considerable influence has been exerted upon Mennonite Brethren churches through attendance of their young people at Fundamentalist Bible institutes. According to Daniel B. Stevick, the Bible Institute of Los Angeles and the Moody Bible Institute were in the vanguard of the Fundamentalist movement.[56] After World War I (and even earlier) a number of Mennonite Brethren ministers, leaders, and Bible school teachers had received their training in these and other schools of a similar theological position.

Fundamentalist views were also widely disseminated through periodical literature. The *Sunday School Times* had a fair circulation among Mennonite readers. More influential in Mennonite Brethren churches was the *Defender* magazine, published in the twenties, thirties, and forties by Gerald B. Winrod in Wichita, Kansas. Among Canadian evangelicals, including Mennonite Brethren, T. T. Shields, pastor of the Jarvis Street Baptist Church in Toronto, exerted a similar influence through *The Gospel Witness and Protestant Advocate*.

Much research is needed in order to accurately assess the nature and scope of the impact of Fundamentalism on the theology of the M.B. Church. This much, however, can be said from present observations: Fundamentalism has had a restricting influence on the gospel message as portrayed in the New Testament, and has weakened the historic evangelical Anabaptist foundations of Mennonite Brethren faith and practice.

2. *Dispensationalism*[57]

Possibly no other theological system has influenced Mennonite Brethren theology during the past fifty years as much as dispensationalism. In the thinking of many Bible students this form of Scripture interpretation is identified with premillennialism, and even with true biblicism.

Although age schemes are almost as old as the Christian church, modern dispensationalism is of comparatively recent origin. According to Lewis S. Chafer, "scholarly research of the Bible with dispensational distinctions in view was made during the last century in England by J. N. Darby, Charles H. Mackintosh, Wm. Kelly, F. W. Grant and others who developed what is known as the Plymouth Brethren Movement."[58] John Nelson Darby (1800-1882), the outstanding leader of the early Plymouth Brethren, had much to do with systematizing and promoting dispensationalism.

Dispensationalism is a system of thought which conceives of redemptive history (as revealed in Scripture) not in terms of one organically-related *Heilsgeschichte*, but in terms of seven distinct dispensations of time, during each of which "man is tested in respect of obedience to some specific revelation of the will of God" (Scofield). According to the more moderate view of Ryrie, "a dispensation is a distinguishable economy in the outworking of God's purpose."[59] Each dispensation includes the aspects of distinctive revelation, testing, failure and judgment. Such a view of redemptive history and such a system of Scripture interpretation have far-reaching implications for the message and mission of the church.

Through what channels has dispensationalism found its way into the Mennonite Brethren Church? It may be of interest that dispensationalism made its appearance in Mennonite Brethren churches on both sides of the Atlantic almost simultaneously during the first decade of the twentieth century.

In earlier years Darby himself spread the movement by his travels to Germany where the Plymouth Brethren became known as Darbyites (*Darbisten*). In Germany the Blankenburg Alliance Conference (founded in 1885) served as a center for the propagation of dispensationalist teachings. The Mennonite Brethren of Russia appear to have had their first direct contact with the Plymouth Brethren through F. W. Baedeker, who was instrumental in leading Jacob W. Reimer to a vital salvation experience. Reimer, who became one of the leading evangelists and preachers of the M.B. Church, frequently attended the Blankenburg Conference, where he also took an active part in the program.[60]

Through his association with the leaders of the Blankenburg Conference, Reimer became a strong advocate of dispensational teaching, especially in the realm of eschatology. He and other like-minded brethren invited prominent Bible teachers from abroad to lecture at the annual short courses for ministers and church workers, which were usually held on the grounds of one of the large estates at Steinbach, Apanlee or Juschanlee.[61] These "prophetic conferences" were instrumental in introducing millennial teachings on a large scale to the Mennonite constituency in South Russia. According to A. J. Klassen, "Jacob Reimer became the leading advocate of millennialism in the Mennonite Brethren Church."[62]

In America dispensationalism was popularized by several prominent Bible teachers. Probably no other one man has been more influential in spreading dispensational teachings than C. I. Scofield. Through his Bible study course, participation in Bible conferences, numerous pamphlets, and most of all through the *Scofield Reference Bible* he reached the evangelical constituency in the United States and Canada with this doctrine. The *Scofield Bible* found its way into almost every minister's study in the M.B. Church (including the writer's), and many were tempted to regard his "footnotes" as equally inspired with the biblical text. Other men whose writings became very popular in the Mennonite Brethren churches were Lewis S. Chafer and Arno C. Gaebelein. The books of Erich Sauer, teacher at the Wiedenest Bible School in Germany, have also enjoyed great popularity in Canadian M.B. churches in the years following World War II.

There is a reason for this ready and indiscriminate acceptance of dispensationalism in Mennonite Brethren circles. Since the above-named men were known for their positive attitude toward the authority of Scripture and the doctrine of salvation by grace, dispensational teaching was accepted as an integral part of evangelicalism.

In the light of the Mennonite Brethren *Confession of Faith*, which represents the brotherhood's understanding of biblical revelation, the issues which are raised by dispensationalism are crucial for the life and mission of the church. Perhaps the most serious question is raised by the dispensationalist teaching that certain parts of the Bible apply almost exclusively to national Israel and not to Christians. In their attempts to "rightly divide" the Word of truth, dispensationalists have at times reduced the evangelical canon to the Gospel of John and the Pauline Epistles. According to Scofield, the Sermon on the Mount must be viewed as the constitution of a future kingdom, and as such it is "pure law."[63] In such a view of Scripture it is relatively easy to relegate Christ's teaching on discipleship to another age.

Although Mennonite Brethren, like the earlier Anabaptists, have consistently held to the view of a progressive revelation in Scripture and to the finality of the New Testament, they have at the same time accepted the significance and relevance of the whole Bible for the faith and work of the church. The artificial and arbitrary division of Scripture found in dispensationalism is foreign to historic Mennonite Brethren theology.[64]

The doctrine of the "postponement" of Christ's kingdom by dispensationalists has far-reaching implications not only for Christian ethics, but also for the mission of the church. Since the "Great Commission" in the New Testament is inseparably linked to the establishment of Christ's kingdom on earth, dispensationalists have relegated the fulfillment of Christ's command — at least in part — to a future kingdom. In the millennium the Great Commission will be carried out more fully through a converted Israel. The Jews will finish the task begun by the Christians. Such teaching can easily become an alibi for the failure of the church.

The author is inclined to agree with the observation that "the Darbyist eschatology has never captured the whole M.B. Church as though it were an integral part of M.B. theology."[65] It has not found expression in the official confessional documents of the General Conference, although a number of leading brethren have advocated such teaching.

In their *Confession of Faith*, and generally also in their teaching and preaching, Mennonite Brethren have accepted the whole gospel as relevant for the present age. Such a view makes no provision for the "postponement" of the kingdom, nor for a suspension of Christian ethics or Christian missionary responsibility. Mennonite Brethren confess Christ's lordship over all of life, which implies obedience to all Christ's commandments and especially His last command to evangelize the whole world.

Chapter 22

Cooperating with Other Groups: Inter-Church Relations

In response to the accusation of the Mennonite elders that the early Brethren thought of themselves as the "only true Christians," the latter replied: "We do not consider ourselves the only true Christians, and are ready to concede at any time, that there can be other true Christians, known only to the Lord."[1] The last phrase appears somewhat enigmatic, since the Brethren had just found such "true Christians" in elder Johann Harder and other members of the Ohrloff Mennonite Church.

Through the years Mennonite Brethren have moved away from their original exclusiveness and narrowness and have discovered a host of true Christians in the larger Mennonite brotherhood, as well as among other evangelical bodies. Occasionally the Mennonite Brethren have initiated a wider fellowship and cooperation; at other times they have simply responded to invitations extended to them. The sharing of a common faith and task with others who also "call upon the name of the Lord" has been an enriching and stimulating experience for Mennonite Brethren congregations.

As noted earlier, the German Baptists were among the first other "Christians" with whom the Mennonite Brethren in Russia established cordial relations. Somewhat later, in the 1880's, some Mennonite Brethren entered into a working fellowship with the young Russian Baptist movement. (See chapter seven.) Still later, in the 1890's, the M.B. Church began to cooperate with the Baptist Missionary Union of Boston in launching its first missions endeavor in India. This cooperation with the Baptists did not involve any compromise of faith or practice on the part of the M.B. Church.

It took a little longer for the Brethren to enter into fraternal relations with the "true Christians" in the Mennonite churches. As a result of socioeconomic conditions described in Part One, Mennonite Brethren cooperated with the "churchly" Mennonites in public education, general welfare, and alternative service. Associations on a different level were the inter-Mennonite Bible conferences initiated by Elder Schellenberg in the Rueckenau M.B. Church in 1875. At these periodic gatherings, a brotherly dialogue generated a better understanding between the new and the old churches and created an atmosphere of mutual love and respect.

In the decade prior to the Communist Revolution the remaining barriers between the M.B. Church and the Mennonite Church largely disappeared. In 1910 the Mennonite Brethren were invited for the first time to participate as voting delegates to the General Conference (*Allgemeine Konferenz*) of the "churchly" Mennonites.[2] Two years later, when a "Commission for Church Affairs" (KfK) was created, Heinrich Braun was elected to represent the Mennonite Brethren on the three-man commission.

The common experience of incredible hardships during the period of anarchy and civil war (1917-1921) brought the two Mennonite church bodies even closer together. During the "second awakening" among the Russian Mennonites in the 1920's the evangelistic teams that traveled from village to village, and from colony to colony, were usually composed of representatives of both groups.[3] The Evangelical Mennonite Brethren also wholeheartedly participated in this new form of cooperative evangelism.

During their almost one-hundred-year history in North America Mennonite Brethren have entered into fraternal association and cooperation with various Mennonite and non-Mennonite groups for a closer fellowship and for a more efficient execution of their God-given task. Since these inter-church and inter-group relations have been established on various levels, the survey of these associations will move from the local to the inter-continental level.

I. Cooperation on a Local Level

In most Mennonite settlements as well as in many urban communities Mennonite Brethren churches are usually found in close proximity to other Mennonite churches. Moreover, since Mennonite settlements in North America were generally not as compact as those in Russia, other evangelical churches were often established in the same geographical area. This pattern of settlement and development provided a natural setting for increasing contacts and associations between the Mennonite Brethren and other groups. On the local level a working fellowship has often been established in areas of common interest.

In the area of *education* Mennonite Brethren have cooperated with other Mennonite churches in the founding of Christian (private) schools. The Mountain Lake Bible School (formerly known as the Mountain Lake Preparatory School) started in 1886, has been supported through the years by the various churches of this Minnesota community. A leading Mennonite Brethren educator, Cornelius Wall, was a teacher of this school from 1936 to 1946.

The Immanuel Academy at Reedley, California, has been sponsored as a joint-venture of the Reedley and Dinuba Mennonite Brethren Churches, and the Zion Krimmer Mennonite Brethren Church. (The latter joined the M.B. Conference in 1960.) The Lustre Bible Academy (formerly Lustre Bible School) has for many years been an inter-Mennonite institution in which the Mennonite Brethren, the Evangelical Mennonite Brethren, and the General Conference Mennonites have cooperated closely. The Salem College and Academy, opened in 1945 in Salem, Oregon, also operates on an inter-Mennonite basis.

In Canada the Mennonite Educational Institute (MEI) at Clearbrook, British Columbia, has from its beginning been supported not only by six local M.B. churches, but also by the West-Abbotsford Mennonite Church. Before the Mennonite Brethren established their own high school in Winnipeg in 1945, they were actively involved in the support of the Mennonite Collegiate Institute (MCI) located at Gretna, Manitoba.

The Steinbach Bible Institute had its beginning in the fall of 1931 when Jacob W. Reimer, a leading Mennonite Brethren theologian and educator, and Isaac Ediger, a minister of the "Alliance" Mennonite Church, began to conduct both day and evening classes. In 1938 a Bible School Association was organized, composed of members of four Mennonite churches (including the Mennonite Brethren) of the Steinbach area. The "Tabor" Bible School of Dalmeny, Saskatchewan (now extinct) was also a cooperative venture of the M.B. and E.M.B. churches of that community.

Mennonite Brethren have also cooperated with other Mennonite groups in *medical care*. A number of hospitals have been established on an inter-Mennonite basis. In Manitoba, for instance, Mennonite Brethren have cooperated in the founding and maintenance of the following institutions: Concordia at Winnipeg (1930), Bethel at Winkler (1935), and Bethesda at Steinbach (1937).[4]

Another important aspect of Mennonite Brethren involvement in inter-church cooperation on a local level is the work of *evangelism* and community outreach. In the forties and fifties these "community crusades" in the M.B. constituency were largely sponsored by inter-Mennonite organizations. The "tent evangelism" campaigns conducted by George Brunk (OM) in the late fifties at Winkler, Steinbach and Winnipeg (Manitoba) and at Chilliwack, Abbotsford and Vancouver (British Columbia) were sponsored by the various Mennonite churches of those areas.

A few years later, however, when the Janz Brothers Evangelistic Team came to Winnipeg, the base of operations and support had been broadened to include non-Mennonite church groups. Nearly 100 metropolitan area churches cooperated in the Greater Winnipeg Crusade for Christ conducted from April 22 to May 6, 1962. All M.B. churches of the city (five at that time) took an active part in this effort. The same pattern of inter-church cooperation in evangelism was evident in the Greater Fresno Crusade for Christ with Bill Glass (September 26 to October 3, 1971). In Fresno all M.B. churches except one participated in this city-wide evangelistic effort which involved more than 100 churches.

A somewhat new and different pattern of inter-church cooperation in evangelism has emerged in the city of Vancouver (Canada) in recent years. There about fifteen churches in the South-Vancouver area established a more permanent organization in 1969 by joining forces in the Christian Witness Crusade. The four M.B. churches of this area cooperate with three Mennonite churches, four Baptist churches, one Alliance, one Presbyterian, one Free Methodist and one independent congregation. The organization has sought to project and to maintain a sustained interest and a continuing program of community outreach. Periodic "evangelistic crusades" have constituted only a part of this cooperative effort; much emphasis has been placed on the distribution of appropriate literature stressing the "one gospel" which all evangelical churches proclaim. Perhaps the most significant aspect of this inter-church effort has been the visitation program in which teams from all the participating churches reached more than 10,000 homes in South-Vancouver.

Similar patterns of inter-church cooperation have emerged in many other centers of the M.B. constituency in both Canada and the United States. In many instances Mennonite Brethren have provided initiative and leadership in these joint ventures of faith. Although the follow-up program has occasionally caused some tensions, these have in most instances been amicably resolved by the cooperating groups.

In addition Mennonite Brethren pastors and preachers have been actively involved in inter-church ministerial meetings. In some areas these are largely inter-Mennonite in composition. In the Kitchener-Waterloo area inter-Mennonite ministerial meetings have been held annually since 1950. In central Kansas (Hillsboro, Hesston, Newton) such meetings or "seminars" have also been carried on for some time.

Inter-Mennonite pastors-fellowship meetings have been held regularly in such cities as Vancouver, Saskatoon, Winnipeg, and in many other areas. In the Mountain Lake area Mennonite Brethren pastors participate in the local (largely Mennonite) ministerial association, as well as in the county-wide organization which includes a number of other groups.

II. COOPERATION ON A REGIONAL LEVEL

(The "region" may refer to either the state or district in the United States, and to the province in Canada.)

In Canada

In Canada many inter-Mennonite activities and projects have been sponsored through the years by provincial organizations. This pattern of provincial organizational structures dates back to the 1920's when the immigrants from Russia organized immigrant committees (*Immigrant-enkomitees*) in all the western provinces. The Mennonite and Mennonite Brethren immigrants met annually for the discussion and disposition of common problems, such as the liquidation of the transportation debt, material aid to destitute families, assistance in new colonization projects, support for the mentally ill (in order to prevent their deportation to the country of their birth) and other mutual concerns of pioneers in a new country.

The provincial MCC organizations of the present day are an outgrowth of the earlier immigrant meetings. Mennonite Brethren have played a leading role in the establishment and promotion of inter-Mennonite activities on a provincial level. In British Columbia the late A. A. Toews and his successor George Thielman (both M.B. ministers) have headed the provincial MCC for many years. The late B. B. Janz (Alberta), Isaac Block (Saskatchewan) and John Unruh (Manitoba), all Mennonite Brethren, have given leadership in their respective provinces for a number of years.

Apart from the joint efforts in relief, inter-Mennonite cooperation has taken on different forms in the various provinces. In Manitoba, for instance, Mennonite Brethren have actively cooperated with the other Mennonite groups in establishing the Eden Mental Health Center near Winkler in 1967. The center provides services for both inpatients and outpatients.[5]

A special kind of inter-Mennonite fellowship has been carried on by the churches of Alberta for several decades in the form of annual Bible discussions (*Bibelbesprechungen*). These Bible discussion meetings differed from the regular Bible or Deeper Life conferences in that the messages were not delivered by one or two special speakers; instead the truth of the Bible (either a chapter of Scripture or a short epistle) was discussed by a "team" of brethren, who also interacted with the audience in the form of a dialogue. The "team" usually consisted of four or five ministers, representing the various Mennonite conferences, who would conduct a *Bibelbesprechung* in a given area for three or four days and then move on to the next town or settlement. The itinerary was worked out by a committee in such a way that all areas of the province would be served during the winter months.

In British Columbia an important milestone in inter-Mennonite cooperation was reached in 1970, when the Mennonite Brethren and the General Conference Mennonites by an overwhelming vote decided to unite their two Bible schools: the Mennonite Brethren Bible Institute (Clearbrook) and the Bethel Bible Institute (West-Abbotsford).[6] The strong vote in favor of a joint program meant that approximately 9,000 Mennonites began to work together in the support of a single Bible institute program. The new name for the united Bible institutes on the former M.B.B.I. campus is Columbia Bible Institute.

In addition to the inter-Mennonite projects and activities mentioned above, nearly all provinces have "peace conferences," Sunday school conventions, and special "anniversary celebrations"[7] on an inter-church basis.

In the United States

Inter-Mennonite associations and activities of Mennonite Brethren are not as fully developed in the United States as in Canada because of a difference in historical experience. The Mennonite Brethren who came to Canada in the 1920's and later had been deeply involved in inter-Mennonite cooperation prior to their coming to the new world. However, the Mennonite Brethren who came to the United States in the 1870's had left Russia at the time when the scars of secession were barely healed. This difference in experience partly accounts for the difference in attitude toward inter-Mennonite cooperation in the two countries.

Among the older agencies that were organized on an inter-Mennonite basis one could mention the Mennonite Teachers Association (Kansas). In recent years the various Mennonite conferences have cooperated on a regional or state level in Mennonite Disaster Service and in MCC auction sales.

One area of exemplary cooperation of all Mennonite groups in the United States has been the field of mental health. In California Mennonite Brethren have been actively involved in the establishment of Kings View Homes, the second of Mennonite Central Committee mental hospitals to be built after World War II. Kings View Hospital, located two and one half miles southwest of Reedley, was opened February 11, 1951. The large M.B. churches of Reedley and Dinuba have in the past provided many volunteers for the recreational, devotional, and educational program of Kings View Homes. The administrator of the institution from its inception has been Arthur Jost, a member of the Reedley M.B. Church. With its outpatient clinics constantly expanding their services, Kings View Homes perform a vital Christian ministry in the community.[8]

In Kansas Mennonite Brethren have participated in the establishment of Prairie View Hospital. This mental hospital, sponsored by Mennonite Mental Health Services Inc. (a section of MCC), was opened on March 15, 1954. Located on a fifty-acre tract of land east of Newton, Prairie View Hospital has been expanding its services through the years. Several Mennonite Brethren psychologists and psychiatrists have served on its staff.

Mental health centers such as Kings View and Prairie View have in recent years become increasingly community-oriented. Because these centers have joined with public agencies (usually by way of contractual relationships) they are able to serve all persons in the community regardless of their ability to pay. This cooperation with public agencies, however, does not affect the integrity of these mental health centers as private agencies with a Christian perspective in the healing arts.

III. Cooperation on a National Level

In a few areas Mennonite Brethren in the United States and Canada have found it necessary and advantageous to enter into inter-church associations which have been operating largely within national boundaries.

In the United States

World War II gave a great impetus to inter-Mennonite cooperation through the joint effort of all major Mennonite bodies to define a common peace position, and to administer Civilian Public Service. The Mennonite Central Peace Committee organized in 1939 as the official agency of seven Mennonite bodies (including the Mennonite Brethren) to work in this field, turned over its work to the MCC and its Peace Section in January, 1942.[9]

Through P. C. Hiebert, the chairman of the Board of General Welfare and Public Relations, who also served as chairman of MCC, the Mennonite Brethren were kept well-informed on this phase of inter-Mennonite activity. In 1943 they also went on record as approving the expansion of this inter-Mennonite witness against war and for peace in the following statement:

... we approve the management of our Civilian Public Service camps and also the several forms of detached service assignments such as rehabilitation work in mental hospitals, needed dairy farm work, the several health and rehabilitation projects in Florida and Puerto Rico, and also the continued aid lent to our brethren in South America. [10]

In the post-war period Mennonite Brethren have continued to cooperate with the MCC Peace Section and its Washington Office in all questions related to Selective Service. In recent years the MCC Peace Section has served as the Selective Service approval arm for service projects for Mennonite and Brethren in Christ mission boards, and for most church-related health and welfare institutions. On January 1, 1970, there were 1200 men serving under this arrangement, which was the largest total number in church-related programs since the creation of the cooperative Selective Service umbrella by the MCC Peace Section in 1951. [11]

A new chapter in inter-church relations among evangelical churches and groups in the United States began in 1944 with the founding of the National Association of Evangelicals (NAE). This association of conservative evangelical Christians came into being as a counterpart to the National Council of the Churches of Christ in America. Among Mennonite Brethren the initial impulse for affiliation with the NAE came from the Board of Foreign Missions which submitted a request for affiliation to the Committee of Reference and Counsel. At the 1945 convention held in Dinuba, California, this committee recommended:

> that the General Conference make application for association with the National Association of Evangelicals for the following reasons: (1) To support morally the stand against modernism. (2) To have in times of need an adequate representation for our Foreign Mission activities, in case our own institutions are unable to take care of this. (3) To remain in contact with evangelical efforts in the Sunday school work. [12]

In subsequent years the conference reaffirmed the decision of 1945 with regard to affiliation with the NAE and also voted subsidies for debt liquidation on several occasions. As a result of the division of the General Conference into two area conferences after the 1954 convention, the U.S. Conference in 1968 passed a resolution to become an official member of NAE. [13] In 1971 H. H. Dick, General Secretary of the United States Conference, reported on the benefits of affiliation with subsidiary agencies of the NAE, especially for the Board of Missions and Services and the Board of Evangelism and Christian Education. Of significance for future inter-church relations is the following statement in the report: "We feel that NAE has a real respect for the position of the Mennonite Brethren, and that we have not only learned from them but have also been able to contribute." [14] This contribution, it might be noted here, Mennonite Brethren were able to make partly because of their association with MCC. The latter organization was able, for instance, to provide the personnel for NAE for relief work at Hue in South Vietnam. The relationship of Mennonite Brethren with both organizations, MCC and NAE, has from time to time created unique opportunities for a meaningful witness.

In Canada

As mentioned earlier, inter-Mennonite cooperation in Canada received a great impetus as a result of Russian Mennonite immigration. The prospect of immigration of thousands of coreligionists from Soviet Russia was the major motivation in the 1922 organization of the Canadian Mennonite Board of Colonization (CMBC) by the several Mennonite bodies of Saskatchewan and Manitoba. Under the able leadership of "Bishop" David Toews[15] this organization was directly responsible for negotiating immigration arrangements and aiding in the resettlement of the Russian refugees. In the mid-twenties (1923-1927) the immigrants formed an organization of their own, known as the Central Mennonite Immigration Committee (CMIC). Some of the duties of the CMIC were to advise the CMBC in helping the immigrants establish new homes and to build Mennonite communities.[16]

However, as the provincial immigration committees gradually assumed greater responsibilities, the CMIC lost its significance. At a meeting held in Rosthern in 1934, the committee decided to merge completely with the Canadian Mennonite Board of Colonization. Through the years Mennonite Brethren have been active in both organizations. B. B. Janz served as vice-chairman of the CMBC for many years. Other Mennonite Brethren who have served in this inter-Mennonite relief and service agency were C. A. DeFehr (Man.), A. A. Wiens (B.C.), G. Friesen (Ont.), A. A. Toews (Alta.). C. F. Klassen served as "collector" of transportation debts (Reiseschuld) from 1930-1945.

A milestone in inter-Mennonite cooperation was reached in 1963 when a Canada-wide Mennonite organization, MCC (Canada), was born. In order to avoid overlapping of services, promote efficiency, and present a united witness the following organizations merged: The Canadian Mennonite Relief and Immigration Council (earlier known as CMBC), the Nonresistant Relief Organization, Canadian Mennonite Relief Committee, and Conference of Historic Peace Churches of Ontario. The functions of MDS (Mennonite Disaster Service) and of the Historic Peace Church Council were also assumed by the new organization. Thus MCC (Canada) assumed the responsibilities of at least six former inter-Mennonite agencies.[17]

J. M. Klassen, a member of the Steinbach M.B. Church, was appointed to the position of executive secretary of MCC (Canada). Prior to his appointment Klassen had served as MCC director in Korea for three years, and as assistant director of the Foreign Relief and Service department at the MCC office in Akron for two years. Klassen served in this new capacity for seven years (1964-1971) and did much to promote cooperation and goodwill among the various groups who had united for ministries of compassion and for a united voice to government in areas of common concern. In 1971 Klassen returned to teaching and was succeeded by Daniel Zehr from Ontario.

The cooperation of Mennonite Brethren with the other Mennonite groups in the Alternative Service program during World War II has been described in the chapter on church-state relations, and thus need not be discussed here.

In recent years Mennonite Brethren in Canada have tried to relate more meaningfully to other evangelical groups in the country. A new day dawned for inter-evangelical association in 1964 with the organization of the Evangelical Fellowship of Canada (EFC). Begun as the vision of a few Canadians who had participated in the National Association of Evangelicals, the EFC endeavored to unite the scattered evangelicals of Canada and to strengthen a positive Christian witness. Individual Mennonite Brethren leaders, mostly from the province of Ontario, were active in the establishment and development of the EFC from the beginning.

In 1969 the Board of Spiritual and Social Concerns of the Canadian M.B. Conference made a special study of various inter-church relationships. In response to questions from several churches with regard to the attitude of the conference to the EFC, the board sent out the following statement: "Having considered the position and purpose of the Evangelical Fellowship of Canada we would encourage churches and individuals of our Conference to become involved in this united evangelical witness in Canada if they so desire."[18]

Evangelicals in general, and Mennonite Brethren in particular, have been slow in responding to this challenge of pooling their human resources for a stronger evangelical witness in the country. This is especially true of the Mennonite Brethren in Western Canada. Geographical distance may be one reason, since the annual conventions of EFC have been held in Toronto — rather far removed from British Columbia — the province with the strongest concentration of Mennonite Brethren.

In order to strengthen the organizational base of the EFC the 1972 annual assembly decided that membership in the organization should be opened to denominations. However, denominations will be entitled to send a maximum of two representatives only to the General Council of the EFC.[19] At present (1972) the following Mennonite Brethren serve on the Council of EFC: Harold Jantz, John G. Baerg, and F. C. Peters. Victor Adrian is chairman of the EFC Commission on Christian Education.[20]

IV. COOPERATION ON A CONTINENTAL LEVEL

The vision of Mennonite Brethren has been broadened and their mission has been strengthened by their association and cooperation with other groups on a continental (North American) level.

In Ministries of Compassion[21]

Of greatest significance for Mennonite Brethren in all their inter-church relations during the past fifty years has been their involvement in the work of the Mennonite Central Committee. Organized on July 27, 1920, in response to a "Macedonian call" from the starving and suffering Mennonites in Russia, this inter-Mennonite agency has truly been "a Christian resource to meet human need" during a period of unprecedented world upheavals and human suffering. The desire to respond to man's need with a witness of Christian love and peace grew in vision and compulsion as various emergencies were faced both within and without the brotherhood. Through the MCC the M.B. constituency has served and been served in ministries which it could not have carried on alone. As Marion W. Kliewer expressed it in 1960: "Together with other Mennonites we have been able to reach out to help many needy peoples and to witness of our faith to the world."[22] In God's providence, a Mennonite Brethren educator and leader, P. C. Hiebert, was destined to play a key role in the founding and expansion of this relief and service agency. For thirty-three years (1920-53) Hiebert served as chairman of MCC.

The services of MCC have been administered largely through five main sections: Foreign Relief and Services, Voluntary Service, Peace Section, Mennonite Mental Health Services and Mennonite Aid Section.[23] In addition, a number of subsidiary or related organizations have operated under the MCC umbrella: Mennonite Indemnity, Inc., Menno Travel Service (MTS), and Mennonite Economic Development Associates (MEDA).

In reflecting on fifty years of MCC work and witness, long-time executive secretary William T. Snyder made the following observations at the annual meeting in Chicago in January, 1970:

These have been years of terrific upheaval world-wide, but they have also been years of forward movement on the part of Mennonite and Brethren in Christ churches. Slightly over 4500 persons have served under appointment of the Mennonite Central Committee for longer or shorter periods of time during the past fifty years. Our service has been in areas of strife, rapid social change, and outright war. I believe that the Mennonite Central Committee has maintained its service stance during the past fifty years that have also seen the growth in mission and service thrusts for the individual conference programs. Our people have not been on the barricades in the political and social revolution, but there has been a quiet revolution in our churches with greater numbers of people getting involved in the acute problems of our times.[24]

The age of MCC service personnel has averaged around twenty-six

45. MCC executive committee in 1951: H. A. Fast, Orie O. Miller, C. F. Klassen, P. C. Hiebert, H. S. Bender, J. J. Thiessen, C. N. Hostetter, Jr.

years. "We within MCC are greatly challenged and stimulated as we attempt to administer a program in which the preponderant number of participants are young people," Snyder stated. "While these young people are, on the whole, possessed with better training, broader knowledge and a world view that is considerably above that of a generation ago, there is the same deep interest in the church."[25]

The following table shows Mennonite Brethren participation in MCC services over a five-year period in relation to the two largest groups in the MCC constituency.

TABLE XI

Church Affiliation of MCC Workers[26]

	1966	1967	1968	1969	1970
Mennonite Church (Old)	228	250	252	279	294
General Conference Mennonite	186	188	208	212	214
Mennonite Brethren	50	62	61	53	62

The above statistics reveal two things: One, whereas participation in MCC services has gradually increased in the other two Mennonite conferences, this is not the case with Mennonite Brethren; and two, the participation in relation to membership is also far lower than that in the other groups. Representation according to M.B. population would call for an almost 100 percent increase in applicants for MCC service.

Perhaps no single factor would account for this lack of greater involvement. However, one answer may be found in the reservations that many Mennonite Brethren have had in identifying with certain service programs sponsored by MCC. This concern of the brotherhood found expression in a statement submitted to the General Conference in 1954 by the Board of Reference and Counsel. The motivation for outlining some specific guidelines of cooperation were given as follows:

> Because of the constantly expanding program of MCC, with periodical additions of new phases of service, some of them not related to the specific aspect of relief, and because of growing uncertainty in our Conference constituency as to our responsibility towards such projects . . . it is deemed advisable that we as a Conference define our principles which are to govern our future relationship with the Mennonite Central Committee in order to maintain the full confidence and cooperation of our entire constituency in this ministry.[27]

Consequently the conference accepted a resolution which stated that for every MCC activity not related to emergency relief and the rehabilitation of suffering coreligionists, a special statement of objective should be submitted to the district conferences and to the General Conference for consideration and ratification. In the sixties, as a result of closer cooperation of MCC with the various mission boards, many issues with a potential for misunderstanding and tension have been eliminated. In retrospect it appears that all other inter-Mennonite activites that have been initiated during the past fifty years have been inspired directly or indirectly by the exemplary cooperation of the various groups in the Mennonite Central Committee.

In Overseas Missions

An expanding foreign missions program has led the Mennonite Brethren to cooperate with other missionary agencies for a more effective execution of their task. As early as 1919 the Board of Foreign Missions found it necessary to affiliate with the Foreign Missions Conference of North America, not as a "constitutional," but only as an "affiliated" member.[28] The occasion for affiliation was the stipulation of the British government that permission to enter British territories for mission purposes could only be obtained through this organization.

When the Evangelical Foreign Missions Association (EFMA) was born in 1943, the Board of Foreign Missions of the Mennonite Brethren Conference became affiliated with this new organization. The brethren H. W. Lohrenz, A. A. Schroeter, and J. B. Toews attended the organizational meeting of EFMA which was held in Columbus, Ohio. Among the services that might be derived through such an affiliation the following could be mentioned: (1) Representation before the government in matters of passports and visas; (2) assistance in obtaining transportation; and (3) advice in remitting funds to foreign countries.[29] Through the years the relationship of the Mennonite Brethren to the EFMA has been very helpful in resolving many technical and legal difficulties in the operation of a worldwide missions program. As general director of the NAE and executive secretary of the

EFMA, Clyde W. Taylor of Washington, D.C., has given strong leadership to this interdenominational effort.

Of perhaps even greater significance for M.B. missions has been the organization in 1962 of the Council of Mission Board Secretaries (COMBS). It is a consultative group composed of the secretaries of the various North American Mennonite and Brethren in Christ mission boards. In addition to the benefits derived from mutual sharing and fellowship, COMBS has entered into a consultative relationship with MCC.

Already in 1954 the Mennonite Brethren Conference had expressed the desire "that our participation in the important ministry of relief be as closely as possible coordinated with the missionary objectives of our Conference of bringing the Gospel to the people to whom we minister relief."[30] Ten years later this vision became reality when the representatives of the mission boards of the MCC constiuency met with MCC members and staff in Chicago, May 7-8, 1964. According to William T. Snyder this meeting was a milestone in making cooperation and trust more specific. "The consultations we have had since 1964," Snyder reported in January, 1970, "have been of mutual benefit to both MCC and the Boards."[31]

The general secretary of the Board of Missions and Services, Vernon R. Wiebe, who also represents the M.B. Conference in COMBS, had expressed similar sentiments some months earlier in an article, "Does MCC Do Mission Work?" After reporting how several mission boards had done "follow-up work" in places where MCC relief and service ministries had prepared the people for church-planting, Wiebe added: "This transaction is indicative of the good relationship that exists between MCC and COMBS. We are agreed that relief and rehabilitation 'in the Name of Christ' should result in a church being born. . . . Our Japan work began this way."[32]

However, aid is not all one way. While MCC aids the missions in establishing new fields, the missions help MCC in relief distribution. All who follow governmental aid programs know that the key problem in relief aid is distribution. Aid is often in danger of falling into wrong hands because of dishonest persons who distribute it. Here, according to Wiebe, "the missionary force and the national church rise to the occasion. The Congo and Biafra (Nigeria) are prime examples. Missionaries and national church leaders know who the needy are and see that they get the supplies."[33] Inter-Mennonite relations, however, have not been restricted to service activities.

In Faith Conferences

It has been said that historically Mennonites have found it easier to work together than to worship together. This traditional pattern was changed when the first all-Mennonite ministers' meeting was held in Chicago in 1963. A similar meeting was held in 1965 and again in 1968. Mennonite Brethren took an active part in this inter-Mennonite endeavor. Approximately seventy Mennonite ministers from eleven North American Mennonite groups attended the 1968 sessions in Chicago. The theme for that conference was, "Our Resources in Christ," based upon a study of the Epistle to the Colossians.

The inter-Mennonite ministerial meetings gave birth to the concept of a larger fellowship — the All-Mennonite North American Bible Congress. The three-day faith and life convention held in Winnipeg, July 16-19, 1970, was attended by delegates representing at least eight denominations: 107 from the General Conference (Mennonite), 41 from the (Old) Mennonite, 39 from the Mennonite Brethren, 25 from the Brethren in Christ, 28 from the Evangelical Mennonite Church, 10 from the Evangelical Mennonite Brethren, 8 from the Evangelical Mennonite Mission Church, and six from other denominations.

The first inter-Mennonite faith conference on a continent-wide basis was both encouraging and disappointing. An encouraging aspect was the complete lack of consciousness of denominational differences.[34] Discouraging was the weak representation of Mennonite Brethren in a constituency where they have a large membership. Of the 100 delegates Mennonite Brethren were entitled to, only thirty-nine made their appearance. According to one M.B. pastor involved in the planning committee, this lack of participation was due to the suspicion with which many Mennonite Brethren still view an inter-Mennonite fellowship — even though it centered in the study of the Scriptures.

Another inter-Mennonite venture on a much larger scale was Probe 72, the All-Mennonite Congress on Evangelism held in Minneapolis, to which reference has been made earlier. As Mennonite Brethren met with concerned Christians from the other Mennonite groups for prayer, fellowship and consultation, many barriers were broken down. Mennonite Brethren discovered that the M.B. Church has no monopoly on evangelistic concern, and that their vision is shared by many leaders and members in other Mennonite bodies.

In recent years both larger Mennonite conferences (the "Old" Mennonite and the General Conference Mennonite) have made overtures to the Mennonite Brethren inviting them to a closer cooperation and fellowship in order to achieve a more adequate expression of "oneness in Christ."[35] The response to these communications by the Board of Reference and Counsel (which the conference later approved) was cordial but cautious: "It is our studied opinion . . . that the consensus of our brotherhood at the present is not such that we could engage actively in meetings and discussions having to do with merger or other bold steps to achieve church unity organically."[36]

However, the statement does express a deep appreciation for increasing opportunities to share in discussion and fellowship with Mennonite and other related bodies. It also makes specific reference to cooperation in such inter-Mennonite agencies as the MCC, and expresses the hope that such fruitful relationships will continue in the future.

V. COOPERATION ON AN INTER-CONTINENTAL LEVEL

The largest inter-Mennonite fellowship in which Mennonite Brethren have participated for over forty years is the Mennonite World Conference (MWC). This conference, whose scope and concern today encompasses approximately half a million Mennonites around the globe, had its beginning in a vision of a few European Mennonite leaders after World War I. Christian Neff (1863-1946), pastor of the Weierhof (Palatinate) Mennonite congregation and eminent leader of South German Mennonites, may be considered the "father" of the MWC.[37]

Under his initiative, and in cooperation with brethren from Switzerland and the Netherlands, the first MWC was held in Basel in 1925 to observe the 400th anniversary of the birth of the Swiss Anabaptist movement. Attendance at the first conference was small, with only one delegate from North America (H. J. Krehbiel, president of the General Conference Mennonite Church), and only a few from Holland, France, and Germany.

At the second MWC held in Danzig (Germany) in 1930 the program was devoted exclusively to the history of past Mennonite relief efforts and current relief operations. Among the three representatives from Canada was C. F. Klassen, a leading M.B. layman.

The third MWC convened in the Netherlands in 1936 and was especially marked by the observance of the 400th anniversary of Menno Simon's renunciation of the papacy. Although the major addresses were historical in nature, there were also serious discussions on contemporary issues. The attendance was much larger than in the previous conferences, with a goodly number from Germany, a few from France and Switzerland, and about fifteen from North America. Of the Mennonite Brethren who attended, P. C. Hiebert and C. F. Klassen took an active part in the program of the conference.

The delegates assembled at Amsterdam were keenly aware of the deteriorating international situation and the growing menace to world peace by the rise of Adolf Hitler. Their concern found expression in a "Mennonite Peace Manifesto" which was prepared after consultation with Mennonite groups and individuals in Brazil, Paraguay, Canada, the United States, Holland and Switzerland. The document, signed also by M.B. representatives, closed with the following appeal:

> We therefore appeal to all brethren and sisters to witness vigorously to our peace principles in our congregations everywhere, and to witness to the world our desire to render service in the spirit of Christ. Let us labor together, that we may accomplish this service of love, and also that we may give spiritual and material help to our brethren who are convinced that God has called them to refuse military service, or who may be called upon to suffer for their peace conviction. [38]

The anticipated world conflict came three years later, and the Fourth Mennonite World Conference, planned for 1940, had to be postponed indefinitely. In the meantime Christian Neff had died and the MCC then assumed the responsibility of convening the conference in 1948. Harold S. Bender succeeded Neff as president of the MWC in 1947 and gave outstanding leadership to this world-body until his death in 1962. This fourth MWC held in Goshen (Indiana) and Newton (Kansas) was attended by a large number of delegates and visitors. P. C. Hiebert delivered the conference sermon. The following discussion topics indicate the widening interest and concern of MWC: Relief, Faith and Life, Nonconformity to the World, Missions, Youth Work, the Peace Witness, Colonization and Christian Education. Overseas attendance was still quite limited, with twenty-seven delegates representing eight different countries.

In 1951 the M.B. General Conference gave its first official approval to MWC participation. During the conference sessions held in Winkler that year the following resolution was passed: "(a) . . . we favor representation at the Mennonite World Conference to be held in Switzerland in the summer of 1952. (b) That the district conferences send brethren whom they appoint for this purpose." [39]

In 1952 the Mennonite brotherhood from around the world gathered again in Switzerland, this time at St. Crischona near Basel. The main theme for this conference was "The Church of Christ and Her Commission." The following ministers and leaders represented the Mennonite Brethren of North America: C. A. DeFehr (Winnipeg), B. B. Fast (Winnipeg), C. F. Klassen (Abbotsford), H. F. Klassen (Winnipeg), G. Pries (Winkler), J. A. Toews (Winnipeg), J. B. Toews (Reedley), J. W. Vogt (Corn), C. Wall (Mountain Lake.) [40] Four of these brethren presented major addresses and papers.

In 1954 the General Conference of Mennonite Brethren reaffirmed its earlier stand on active participation in the work of the MWC. However, the rationale for continued participation does not seem to reflect a desire for mutual sharing and learning. The resolution reads: "That in view of the opportunities, channels, and challenges of giving a positive Evangelical testimony, we again send representatives to the Mennonite World Conference to be held in Karlsruhe, Germany, in

46. Editors and Publishers groups at the 1952 Mennonite World Conference, Basel, Switzerland.

1957."[41] Although general attendance at the Sixth Mennonite World Conference was higher than at St. Crischona in 1952, Mennonite Brethren participation was down somewhat — perhaps because the MWC was held in the same year that the General Conference met for its triennial sessions.

In 1957 the M.B. General Conference meeting in Yarrow, British Columbia, ratified the constitution and Bylaws of the Mennonite World Conference. The purpose, as given in Article I, clearly reflects the original vision of Christian Neff.

1. The purpose of the Mennonite World Conference is to bring the Mennonites of the world together in regularly recurring meetings of brotherly fellowship. It seeks thereby to strengthen for them the awareness of the world-wide brotherhood in which they stand.

2. By its recurring sessions the Conference seeks, under the leadership of the Holy Spirit, to deepen the faith, hope, and stimulate and aid it in its ministry of the world, that is, in greater obedience to the Lord Jesus Christ, and in the promotion of His kingdom in the world. [42]

The Seventh Mennonite World Conference which convened in Kitchener, Ontario, in August, 1962, made history as the largest representative inter-Mennonite gathering ever held. A total of 12,207 persons were registered for the conference. Thousands of others, driving in for several sessions, attended but did not register. A "roll call of nations" showed that at least twenty-five countries were represented, indicating the truly international nature of the conference. In all, at least 500 non-North Americans participated in the sessions.[43]

The program was planned to meet the needs of the entire Mennonite brotherhood. Beginning with Bible study in the morning, the conference moved through formal lectures to an early afternoon lecture and response presentation to discussion sessions according to special interests, to the inspirational messages of the evening. Each day was concluded with a brief devotional meditation.[44]

Mennonite Brethren were again deeply involved, not only in the program, but also in the planning of this conference. C. J. Rempel, a lay leader from the Kitchener M. B. Church served as secretary of the committee for local arrangements. Approximately one dozen M.B. members (including one sister!) participated in the program by giving lectures, reports, or Bible studies.

The Eighth Mennonite World Conference was again held on European soil, namely in the historic city of Amsterdam. Here the spiritual heirs of Menno Simons gathered for a full week of fellowship and discussions during the last week of July, 1967. Although attendance was not as high as in Kitchener five years earlier, representation was wider than ever before and included many delegates from the Third World with a non-ethnic Mennonite background. From the roll call on opening night it appeared that representatives from the following thirty countries were present: *Asia* — Indonesia, India, Japan, Taiwan, Vietnam; *Africa* — Algeria, Congo, Ethiopia, Ghana, Kenya, Nigeria, Rhodesia, Tanzania; *Latin America* — Argentina, Brazil, Colombia, Mexico, Paraguay, Uruguay; *North America* — Canada, United States; *Europe* — Austria, Belgium, England, France, Germany, Italy, Luxembourg, Netherlands, Switzerland.[45] Greetings were also received from churches in three additional countries — Russia, Somalia, and Puerto Rico.

The international character of this inter-Mennonite gathering was also evidenced by the fact that provision had been made for four official conference languages: French, Dutch, German, and English. Simultaneous translation facilities were available in all meeting rooms except the large hall where the plenary sessions were held. For the plenary sessions all papers presented had previously been translated and mimeographed in the three languages other than the one used by the speaker.

Since 1952 every Mennonite World Conference has also issued a conference statement or message to the Mennonite congregations of the world. In view of the great diversity in historical background and also in theological perspective, it was not easy to arrive at a consensus on the content of such a message. Increasingly, however, the messages have been Christ-centered, emphasizing the central truths of the Gospel. The 1962 statement begins with this paragraph:

Jesus Christ is Lord. He is the Eternal Word, the only Son of God, who entered into history to become man, took upon Himself the form of a servant, identifying Himself with us sinful men in all our need. By His life, His atoning death, and His glorious resurrection He has reconciled us to God, redeemed us from our sin and its consequences, making us, by grace, new creatures and calling us to a life of holiness, discipleship, and service. [46]

The Ninth Mennonite World Conference was held in July, 1972, in Curitiba, Brazil. For the first time in its history, the MWC met in a country of the Third World. The theme for the conference, "Jesus Christ Reconciles," was appropriate in view of the turbulent religious, social and political conditions of the present era.

Since World War II the following brethren have been appointed by the M.B. Conference to serve on the Presidium of the MWC: P. C. Hiebert, C. F. Klassen, H. H. Janzen, J. B. Toews, B. J. Braun, J. A. Toews and Marvin Hein. The last two brethren are currently serving as members of the Presidium.

In recent years "regional" inter-Mennonite conferences have been sponsored by the MWC Presidium on several continents. In 1966 such conferences were held in Paraguay and Brazil. In 1969 a similar conference was held in Kinshasa, the capital of the Congo (Africa) in connection with the meetings of the Presidium. In October, 1971, the representatives of the younger churches of the various Mennonite groups of southeast Asia met for fellowship and consultation in India.

Thus the Mennonite World Conference has not only fostered a spirit of greater understanding and unity among the various Mennonite groups in North America and Europe, but also among the emerging churches in Asia, Africa, and South America. The objective of all MWC activity was aptly expressed in H. S. Bender's parting message to the worldwide brotherhood: "As God shows us the way, even in mutually facing our practical and doctrinal problems, let us work towards unity — not unification."[47] It is the desire of Mennonite Brethren that Christ's high-priestly prayer "that they may all be one" (John 17:21) may find greater realization in all their inter-church relationships — not only with other Mennonite groups, but also with all other Christians who belong to the company of committed followers of Christ.

Chapter 23

Mennonite Brethren
Around the World

This history of the M.B. Church would be incomplete without a glimpse of Mennonite Brethren around the world. From a small German-speaking fellowship-group which met on January 6, 1860, in Elizabethtal, Molotschna, South Russia, to launch a new movement, the church has expanded into a multi-national and multi-lingual worldwide brotherhood of approximately 80,000 members.[2] These are scattered on five continents — North America, South America, Europe, Africa, and Asia; represent four major racial groups; and speak more than a dozen languages. What was said at one time of the British Empire is applicable to the Mennonite Brethren today: The sun never sets on the M.B. Church!

It was the missionary vision and commitment of the M.B. churches in the Old World (Europe) and the New World (North America) that led to the establishment of Mennonite Brethren congregations in the Third World (Asia, Africa, Latin America) during the last eighty years. Through "obedience in partnership" the sending brotherhood, the missionaries, and the national workers have been able, under God, to plant churches in twelve countries and render special services in several others (e.g. radio ministry over HCJB, Quito, Ecuador). A brief summary account of the founding and development of Mennonite Brethren churches in the "regions beyond" follows.

ASIA

In Asia, the continent with the largest land area and with more than one half of the world's population, Mennonite Brethren have established churches in India, China and Japan. (The M.B. churches established in Asiatic Russia have been considered in Part One and will not be treated here.) India constitutes the chronological starting point for this story.

Occupying the Field

Mennonite Brethren mission work in India dates back to 1890, when Abraham and Maria Friesen began their ministry among the Telegus at Nalgonda in the state of Hyderabad. As mentioned in chapter seven, the Friesens were accepted by the Baptist Missionary Union of Boston, but were virtually independent in the administration and operation of the mission, receiving their full financial support from the M.B. churches of Russia. The Mennonite Brethren Church in India was officially organized on January 4, 1891.[3] When the Friesens left for their first furlough in 1897, the church numbered 700 baptized members.

Two years later, in 1899, the M.B. Conference of North America sent out its first missionaries to India. The party, consisting of Mr. and Mrs. N. N. Hiebert and Elizabeth Neufeld, was joined in India by Anna Suderman, who had already been working for a year in a mission in the Bombay Presidency. The composition of this group, according to A. E. Janzen, made it possible for the missionaries to employ the methods of Jesus and thus initiate a most fruitful ministry. Janzen writes:

> The initial group of four M.B. missionaries to India was made up of a preacher and his wife, a teacher, and a nurse. By way of preparation and divine calling this group had embodied within its number the potential of the Lord's method — preach, teach, heal; a preacher, a teacher, a nurse were in the staff.[4]

Because the Baptists felt that their territory south of the city of Hyderabad was too extensive for their staff and resources, they gladly agreed to share the missionary task among the Telegus with the Mennonite Brethren. The American M.B. Mission thus eventually assumed responsibility for an area of 10,000 square miles, with approximately 1,500,000 people.

The young mission experienced severe trials. After only eighteen months of service, the Hieberts had to return to the United States because of poor health. Undaunted by this disappointing experience, the conference sent out Mr. and Mrs. J. H. Pankratz in 1902 to give leadership to the mission. After prayerful investigation, a place for a mission station was purchased at *Mulkapet*, a suburb of Hyderabad. With the assistance of some Telegu evangelists from Nalgonda, evangelistic campaigns were conducted at once in the suburbs of the city as well as in the villages to the south. In March, 1904, the first small M.B. church on this new field was organized. Later the mission center was transferred to *Hughestown*, and from there to *Shamshabad*.[5]

The arrival of additional workers made a gradual expansion possible. In the late fall of 1904 the D. F. Bergtholds arrived. Two months later Mrs. Bergthold died after a short, severe illness. Bergthold found a helpmeet in Anna Epp who had been sent out by the M.B.

Church of Russia to serve on the German Baptist field in India. After some time Bergthold obtained a government permit to begin a work at *Nagarkurnool*, eighty miles south of the city of Hyderabad. Here the Bergtholds shared the joys and hardships of pioneering in a new field on which there was not a single Christian. In due time they established a home, a church, a school, and a hospital.

With the coming of Mr. and Mrs. J. H. Voth in the fall of 1908, further advance was possible. They were directed to *Deverakonda*, a field which the American Baptists transferred to the Mennonite Brethren in 1910. Although this field was in an area frequently visited by drought and famine, the people readily responded to the call of the gospel. Preparatory work had been done in this field by missionaries from Nalgonda and a church was organized. Through the zealous efforts of missionary Voth the Telegu church here was established and grew rapidly.

The mission experienced further growth when the F. A. Janzens arrived in the fall of 1910. They subsequently established a fourth mission station at *Wanaparty*, the center of a tiny independent kingdom. The friendly attitude of the Rajah (king) was an important factor in the establishment of a mission here.

Single ladies comprised a significant part of the missionary force in India from the beginning. Among these Katharina Schellenberg, a medical doctor, deserves special recognition. She arrived in India in the spring of 1907 and began her ministry of healing at Nagarkurnool, where the mission built its first hospital in 1912. Other single ladies who must be numbered among the pioneers were Katharina Lohrenz, who arrived in 1908 and Anna Hanneman, who came in 1915 to take the place of Miss Lohrenz who had died of typhoid in 1913. Both were involved in a teaching ministry at Mulkapet. Mary C. Wall, a trained nurse who also arrived in 1915, was placed in charge of the medical work at Deverakonda.

Among the mission stations transferred by the American Baptists to the Mennonite Brethren in 1910 was the one at *Kalvakurty* as well. Various missionaries served intermittently in Kalvakurty, but due to a shortage of staff it was impossible to have a resident missionary in this field for a number of years. In a miraculous manner God met this need in 1935 by bringing the J. J. Dicks from Russia to India.[6] Escaping from persecution in Communist Russia, the Dicks and their small daughter had followed a tortuous route across the deserts of Central Asia and through dangerous mountain passes into India. Although they had intended to go to relatives in Canada, they decided to stay when they saw the whitened harvest fields of India.

The borders of the field were again substantially enlarged in 1937, when the Mennonite Brethren assumed responsibility for *Gadwal* and *Mahbubnagar*. The American Baptist Mission offered these fields, bordering the M. B. field, because of a shortage of personnel. A good foundation had been laid in both fields by the Baptist missionaries. The J. A. Wiebes provided leadership in Mahbubnagar and the A. A. Unruhs at Gadwal for many years. Church growth in Gadwal has been more rapid than in any other area of the M.B. mission in India.

With the acquisition of the mission at *Naryanpet-Mukthal* in 1954 (again adjacent to the M.B. field) from an independent missionary, Mr. Billington, the M.B. mission had extended its borders to the present limits. These nine stations, plus the *Jadcherla* medical center, now comprise the Mennonite Brethren field in India.

Building the Church

The Lord has used various channels and agencies to build the church in India. Early Mennonite Brethren missionaries emphasized the primacy of evangelism and spent a good part of their time in touring the villages preaching the gospel. As the work progressed and administrative responsibilities increased, a major share of the evangelistic work was assumed by the nationals. According to J. H. Lohrenz, longtime missionary to India, the "native evangelist preacher, who is faithful and true to his Lord, holds the key to successful evangelism in rural India."[7]

In the earlier period all the converts came from the outcaste community, although the claims of the gospel were also presented to the caste people. This fact made it more difficult to find adequate national leadership for the growing congregations. However, in the last few decades a number of high caste Hindus have accepted Christ and taken an active part in evangelism, education, and church administration.

From the beginning missionaries realized the importance of institutional work as an integral part of evangelism and church extension. An indigenous, self-governing and self-propagating church requires a literate membership. Schools were established on all stations. Because of the problems of transportation, children received board and room in "hostels" on the mission compounds. In addition to reading and writing, children learned gardening, housekeeping, sewing and the like, and became part of the church life of the community.

In addition to the elementary schools, other schools were established to meet growing educational needs. By 1950 the primary schools were enrolling 2000 pupils, the middle schools 900, and the high schools 200. These schools proved to be a great asset in building the indigenous church.

To meet the need for trained church workers a Bible school was established in 1920. In the early years the missionaries Pankratz and

Bergthold were in charge of the school. From 1930 to 1945 it was continued at Shamshabad under the able leadership of Mr. and Mrs. J. H. Lohrenz. One proof of the usefulness of the Bethany Bible School (as it is called now) is the fact that by 1950 it had trained some 400 workers for service in the churches and community.

The medical work has kept pace with the schools in meeting urgent needs. India has to cope with leprosy, malaria, bubonic plague, cholera, typhoid, ulcers, parasites and a multitude of skin and eye diseases. Epidemics spread quickly among people already suffering from malnutrition. Hospitals and clinics were established at Wanaparty, Shamshabad, Deverakonda and Gadwal, but the facilities were inadequate to meet growing needs. The founding of the Jadcherla medical center in 1952 by Dr. Jake Friesen was an answer to a long-felt need. The ministry of missionary doctors and nurses to inpatients and outpatients has been an effective avenue of evangelism through the years.[8]

The production and distribution of Christian literature, and the proclamation of the "good news" by means of radio have also been important means in building the church and reaching the multitudes of India. Because of the general poverty of the people (mostly "untouchables" and people of low caste) who composed the membership of the M.B. Church in India, the work had to be heavily subsidized until recently by the Mennonite Brethren of North America.

Attaining Maturity

Great and revolutionary changes have taken place in India since the country achieved independence in 1947. A rising nationalism and opposition to foreign influence have also affected the pattern of M.B. missionary involvement in India. In God's providence these winds of change have aided in the indigenization of the M.B. Church in that country.

The mission station pattern has given way to a church-centered ministry. Mission property has been transferred to the national church as rapidly as possible and advisable. The administration of churches, schools, and hospitals was turned over to national church leaders. Although the new and larger financial responsibilities appeared to be beyond the church's resources, the national Christians have risen to the challenge in a remarkable manner. By 1970 the Andhra Mennonite Brethren Church was prepared not only to support its local program, but also to provide one-fourth of the total conference budget for Bible training, literature, and radio evangelism.[9]

Of utmost importance for the future development of the M.B. Church in India is a strong and positive spiritual leadership. In recent years a number of men have emerged with exceptional ability and

47. Golden Jubilee of the M.B. Church in India, 1968.

vision. Among these, according to Phyllis Martens, are the following: M. B. John, pastor of the large Mahbubnagar church; D. J. Arthur, conference evangelist, now teaching at Yeotmal Union Seminary; N. P. James, principal of Shamshabad Bible school and college; J. Paranjyothi, conference chairman and Bible teacher; and R.R.K. Murthy, former head of literature and radio work, now in high-caste evangelism.[10]

The Mennonite Brethren Church in India is well on its way to become self-supporting, self-governing and self-propagating. However, many of the institutions which have been established and maintained by the Mennonite Brethren of North America, are too elaborate and costly for the national churches to operate independently. Financial assistance will be required for some time lest these institutions become such a burden to the local churches that they cannot carry on the more essential work of direct evangelism. Contact and communication between the M.B. Church of India and the Mennonite Brethren of North America will no doubt increasingly take on the character of a fraternal relationship for mutual encouragement in a common faith and task.

MENNONITE BRETHREN IN CHINA

China, the nation with the largest population in the world, has also been included in the missionary vision and concern of Mennonite Brethren. Although information about the Chinese Christian Church (including the M.B. Church) has suffered an almost total eclipse during the past twenty years of Communist rule, recent developments give rise to the hope that the Bamboo Curtain may be lifting and that an "open door policy" may eventually make it possible to reestablish contacts with the churches in that land.

In North China

The first missionary effort in which Mennonite Brethren became involved was pioneered by K.M.B. missionaries Mr. and Mrs. H. C. Bartel. Arriving in China in 1901, they labored under an independent mission for several years. In 1905 the Bartels began a mission in the Shantung and Honan provinces of North China. The China Mennonite Mission Society, organized in 1906, assumed the responsibility for this field. J. H. Lohrenz comments as follows on the progress of this mission: "The Lord prospered this Mission in a wonderful way, and it was destined to become the largest Mennonite mission in China."[11]

Mennonite Brethren have been closely related to this mission in several ways. Brethren from the M.B. Church have served on the Board of Directors of the mission. Among the missionaries, a fairly large number of M.B. church members have been active on the field, including the P. D. Kiehns, P. P. Baltzers, Bena Bartel, Emma Bartel, Tena Kornelsen, and Paulina Foote. Jonathan Bartel, M.B. missionary in Japan and son of the founder of the mission in North China, gives the following account of the work:

Eventually six city churches and many village churches, all with national pastors and evangelists, were established on this field with a total membership of somewhere around two to three thousand. A Bible school was also operated on the Shantung field with Loyal Bartel as principal. In 1940 some 70 students were enrolled. Bartels also had an orphanage during the first years of the work. Many pastors and evangelists came from these orphans.[12]

Another mission was established in Inner Mongolia by K.M.B. missionaries Mr. and Mrs. F. V. Wiebe in 1923. For some time Mr. and Mrs. J. S. Dick (M.B.) had the supervision of this station. The Communist invasion of this territory in the 1940's made missionary activity virtually impossible.

In South China

The South China Mission was started independently by Mr. and Mrs. F. J. Wiens in 1911 among the Hakkas at Shanghang in Fukien Province.[13] Although the General Conference of Mennonite Brethren had authorized its Board of Missions to begin a work in China, acceptance of the mission among the Hakkas was delayed until 1919. During the following six years eight missionaries were sent to China to reinforce the staff: Mr. and Mrs. J. S. Dick (1920), Mr. and Mrs. B. F. Wiens (1921), Mary and Sophia Richert (1922), Paulina Foote (1924) and Adelgunda Prieb (1925).

In 1921 F. J. Wiens reported an indigenous church of 450 members, eleven outstations supervised by national pastors, and seventeen schools in which thirty teachers were employed. Statistical information for later years is not available, but reports from missionaries indicated a constant growth of the Hakka M.B. Church, a constant increase in attendance at station and village schools, and a remarkable expansion of the medical work.

This period of prosperity and progress only lasted for about eight years. Recurrent political unrest which culminated in the confrontation of the Nationalists and the Communists in 1927, caused the evacuation of the missionaries. On their way to the coast, traveling by river boat, they were overtaken by bandits who robbed them of some of their belongings. The incredible sufferings which the young church endured during the time of civil strife and disorder will perhaps never be fully known.[14]

In 1929 the J. S. Dicks made an attempt to return to the field and resume the work, but after six months of harassment and threats they were forced to leave. In 1935 Mr. and Mrs. F. J. Wiens returned once more to the people who had become so dear to them. They found the buildings of the mission stations demolished, the members of the church scattered and the schools closed. Wiens did not rebuild the stations, but spent several years in itinerant evangelism. World War II and the Japanese invasion of China severed all connections with the Hakka M.B. Church.

In 1947 Roland Wiens, son of the founder of the mission, and his wife returned for a third attempt. In spite of lack of communications and Communist occupation, the couple remained until May 1951, when they left the field for Hong Kong and were transferred to mission work in Japan.

In West China

The West China Mission of the Mennonite Brethren came about through the dissolution of the China Mennonite Mission Society in 1946, at which time the M.B. Board of Missions accepted responsibility for work which the H. C. Bartels had started in the early forties on the Szechuan-Kansu border. The experiences of the Bartels in this backward and dangerous hinterland of China constitute a story of extraordinary courage and faith.

After negotiations were completed in 1946, the M.B. Board of Missions sent out the P. D. Kiehns and the sisters Bena and Emma Bartel to this field. In 1947 the P. P. Baltzers and the Harold Baltzers joined the missionary staff in West China. J. H. Lohrenz wrote in 1950 that "the Lord signally blessed the testimony of his messengers in this difficult field. . . . The organized M.B. Church on the field numbers about 150 members."[15]

In 1951 the last missionaries were forced to leave the field and return home. Loyal Bartel, a son of H. C. Bartel, stayed, however, although his family went to the United States. Through letters he has sent to members of his family it is evident that the Church of Jesus Christ, including the Mennonite Brethren, has survived in spite of persecution, civil war, and cultural revolution, and that the "powers of death" have not prevailed against it.

MENNONITE BRETHREN IN JAPAN

Although Protestant missions in Japan date back more than a hundred years, Mennonite Brethren entered "the Land of the Rising Sun" less than twenty-five years ago. The first Mennonite Brethren workers, Henry and Lydia Thielmann, came to Japan in April, 1949, under the auspices of the Mennonite Central Committee. In a very real sense the MCC ministry of compassion in the immediate post-war period opened the door for Mennonite missions in Japan.[16] The Thielmanns, assisted by other MCC workers, began a relief and rehabilitation work in a devastated section of the city of Osaka, on Honshu Island.

It was in the metropolitan area of this large city that the Mennonite Brethren began their work of evangelism. In 1950 Ruth Wiens was sent out as their first missionary. In densely populated Japan, with its 110 million people (600 per square mile compared to 52 in the United States), housing was a number one problem, especially in the post-war years. With the assistance of the Thielmanns the Board of Missions was able to purchase a twelve-room house in *Ikeda*, a suburb of Osaka. Within two years this house became the dwelling of eight adult missionaries and six children: Ruth Wiens, Rubena Gunther, Mr. and Mrs. Harry Friesen, Mr. and Mrs. Harold Gaede, and Mr. and Mrs. Roland Wiens and family (who had lately escaped from China). As the work expanded, additional properties were acquired in various parts of greater Osaka.

The initial contacts for evangelism were provided by teaching classes in conversational English. The transition from English classes to Bible classes was a natural development. Several students came to know Christ and committed their lives to Him. In family-oriented Japan, however, the planting of churches required a wider outreach which would include family-units. A multiple approach through children's classes, youth work and women's gatherings has proved highly successful. An observation of Jonathan Bartel highlights this approach: "Through laying strong emphasis on the salvation of both husband and

48. The Ishibashi M.B. Church in Osaka, Japan.

wife we believe the Lord has given us some very stable congregations. Often there have been as many or more men than women."[17]

Twenty years of teaching, preaching, and witnessing by some twenty missionaries has resulted in the establishment of sixteen churches and evangelism centers, fourteen of these in the Osaka area. Of these, twelve have full-time Japanese pastors. Eleven churches receive no subsidy from North America and also have full administrative control over local operations and community outreach.

The Japanese M.B. Conference, with a membership of about 1000, was organized in 1967 and is responsible for a radio ministry and camping program. Although the national churches manage their local affairs and ministries very well, they still need assistance in evangelizing Japan's millions. One way to reach the masses is via radio and television. In the projections of the Board of Missions and Services in 1969 this matter was given special emphasis:

"Increased utilization of the mass media must be seriously considered. Over 96 percent of Japanese homes have television; the average person watches television 22 hours per week. . . . Some films will be shown in conjunction with evangelism crusades."[18] Through its daily ten-minute program Morning Light, and through occasional telecasts, the Japanese conference endeavors to confront the masses with the claims of Christ. It is estimated that the Morning Light program has a potential listening audience of thirty-five million.

A highly literate and well-educated church membership calls for advanced theological training for pastors and church leaders. An early Bible institute at Kasugade developed into Osaka Biblical Seminary, a joint project of the Mennonite Brethren and two Baptist groups. Ruth Wiens and Harry Friesen have been teaching in this seminary; all pastors until now have attended this school. Apparently because of some doctrinal differences, the Japanese M.B. Conference recently decided to withdraw from Osaka Biblical Seminary and start its own school. In keeping with missions policy, this decision was made by the national conference independently of the position of the Board of Missions and Services on this matter. The new school began in April, 1971, in the Tshibushi church with one student.

The prospects appear to be bright for a wholesome and scriptural development of the Mennonite Brethren Church in Japan. Administratively and financially the conference is moving rapidly toward complete independence. An enlarged vision and deepened concern for the evangelization of the whole nation is noticeable in the churches. The establishment of a new church in Japan's third largest city, *Nagoya*, provides an opportunity for a practical expression of this wider interest. It is not impossible that the churches of Japan (which has sometimes been called "the rudder of Asia") may yet play a leading role, under God, in the penetration of the Asian continent with the gospel of Christ.

AFRICA

Africa, the world's second largest continent, has in the twentieth century become the continent of emerging nations and of an emerging Christian church. The rapidity of transition from "colony to nation" and from "mission to church" is without precedent in modern history. "The 'darkness' of the huge continent," Robert G. Nelson observes, "may now reflect only our own unwillingness to look again in corrected perspective."[19] In his report on Africa David B. Barrett describes the rapid growth of the Christian Church in the Third World and then adds:

> This trend, which is seen most dramatically in Africa, has far-reaching significance throughout the world. Not only is Christianity becoming a great part of black Africa . . . but also Christianity, which has been for long a religion of predominantly white races, will have started to have more colored than white members. . . .[20]

Mennonite Brethren are happy to be identified with this story of trials and triumphs of the Christian Church in Africa.

Mennonite Brethren interest in missionary activity in Africa dates back to the 1890's. In 1896 P. H. Wedel and H. E. Enns, supported by funds from the M.B. Conference, proceeded to the Cameroons field of the North American Baptist Mission Society.[21] Because of the severe tropical climate, Mrs. Wedel was soon obliged to leave, her health broken. After seven months on the field, Enns died. Wedel, whose health also failed, left for Europe to seek medical help, but he died en route and was buried in the ocean on August 10, 1897. Mrs. Enns, too, succumbed to the climate a few months later.

Although the missionary interest of the conference was diverted to India in subsequent years, in the hearts of many members a deep desire lingered to extend the Mennonite Brethren witness to the Dark Continent.

MENNONITE BRETHREN IN ZAIRE
(Formerly the Belgium Congo)

In 1912 Aaron and Ernestine Janzen left for the Congo under the Congo Inland Mission (CIM) which had been organized the year before. Their financial support came largely from friends within M.B. churches. They served in the Kasai Province in east central Congo for about two terms (1913-1920), opening the Nyanga field and station. Because of a deep conviction that God had called them to open a field for their own conference they asked for a release from the CIM, which was granted with reluctance.

After an exploratory trip that extended into the Kwango Province some 300 miles west of Nyanga, A. A. Janzen selected a field at *Kikandji*, south of the important commercial center of Kikwit. Since Kikandji proved to be unsuitable for a mission center, the Janzens sought and found a more desirable location at *Kafumba* ("nest of the elephants"), thirty-five miles due south of Kikwit. In God's providence Kafumba was destined to become a strategic center for M.B. missions in the Congo.

Meanwhile a second center of M.B. missions emerged at *Bololo*, in the Kasai district, about 450 miles northeast of Kafumba. In 1933 Mr. and Mrs. Henry G. Bartsch,[22] who had been assisting the Jantzens at Kafumba for a year, set out in search of a location for a mission to the Dengese tribe. The site chosen was at Bololo, some fifteen miles north of the Sankuru River. Because of almost insurmountable obstacles of transportation and communication, the mission was transferred to Djongo Sanga in 1946. Between 1933 and 1942 other workers served for short terms on the Bololo field, including the Herman Lenzmanns from Canada and the Karl Kramers of Germany.

The mission at Bololo was severely tested in the early years. Being the first and only Protestant mission in a large area, it experienced strong opposition not only from hostile tribesmen, but also from Roman Catholic priests. Educational efforts and medical services, however, paved the way for evangelism, and in due time a small church was established. World War II had its effect on the Bololo mission: the Bartsches left on furlough in 1942 and war conditions made it virtually impossible to send out new workers; the Kramers, being German citizens, were interned as "enemy aliens." From 1942 to 1946 the Dengese field was without a resident missionary.

Both missions in the Congo (Kafumba and Bololo) had through the years applied for acceptance into the Mennonite Brethren Conference. The A.A. Janzens requested recognition as M.B. missionaries as early as 1919, and the Africa Mission Society made its first application to the Board of Foreign Missions in 1936. The conference at Corn, Oklahoma, in 1939 favored the acceptance of a mission in Africa in principle, but formal arrangements for taking over full responsibility were not completed until 1943. The Bololo (Djongo Sanga) field was later given to the Africa Evangelistic Band because of its distance from the main Kwango field.

Rapid Expansion

The post-war period witnessed a rapid expansion of the missionary staff in the Congo. Between 1944 and 1949 twenty-one workers were commissioned by the M.B. Church to go to Africa — the largest number of missionaries ever to be sent out to one field in so short a time.

Kafumba continued to be the center of M.B. missions in the Congo. The area it served included some 300 villages. A number of institutions were established here, including a primary school, a teacher-training school, a Bible school, a hospital, an orphanage and a printing office. The operation of these institutions required a large staff. Although most of the twenty-five instructors in the primary school (which had an enrollment of about 500 pupils by 1950) were Congolese, missionaries were needed to supervise and staff the other institutions. Among the pioneers at Kafumba (in addition to the A. A. Janzens) were Kathryn Willems, the Frank Buschmans, the Irvin L. Friesens, Mathilda Wall, Mary Toews, and Erna Funk. An indigenous church was established which experienced healthy growth.

Mission and church were extended rapidly into new ares. *Matende*, fifty-six miles southeast of Kikwit, was opened in 1946. Its area is roughly thirty miles square, serving 100 villages with a population of over 50,000. Under the leadership of the A. F. Kroekers, the A. J. Esaus and Margaret Dyck a church came into being here. Institutions included a dispensary and a boys' and girls' boarding school.

Kipungu, located some sixty miles southwest of Kikwit, was opened in 1948. It serves an area including 200 villages and 200 company posts with a population (in 1950) of over 40,000. The John B. Kliewers, Anna Enns, and Anna Goertzen were among the first to serve here. Again, a dispensary and an elementary school played an important auxiliary role in building the national church.

When the Unevangelized Tribes Mission was dissolved, the Mennonite Brethren acquired the mission's stations established at *Kajiji* and *Panzi*. Because of its elevation and excellent climate, Kajiji became an important center for educational and medical work. *Lusemvu* was acquired from an independent missionary and added to the M.B. field.

A summary report to the Centennial Conference in 1960 provided the following picture of the work in the Congo:

> Through the efforts of more than seventy missionaries and a number of fine national co-laborers, seven centers of operations have been opened. Some 6000 believers have been baptized and churches have been organized. A Bible institute, a teacher-training school, a school for missionary children, two hospitals, several dispensaries and a network of lower-level schools have been established. Considerable literature is being published for schools and churches. For all this we praise the Lord. [23]

While this report was in preparation, ominous storm-clouds were already gathering over the Congo, threatening the very existence of the fledgling Mennonite Brethren Church.

1960: Independence

In 1960 the spotlight of the world turned to Africa, with a special focus on events and developments in the Belgian Congo. In that single year many magazines and newspapers printed more articles about Africa than in all their previous history. The crisis in the Congo was the center of attention.

The Belgians had expected to move gradually toward independence during the course of a few years. The explosive nationalism in the Congo made a gradual transition impossible. Many Congolese imagined independence to be a cure-all for their social and economic ills. The Belgian government yielded to the political pressures of the Congo and of world opinion. Elections were held in May, 1960, and on June 30 of that same year the Belgian Congo officially became the Republic of the Congo thus making it the fifteenth African free state.

The change of regime apparently did not pose an immediate threat to North American missionaries, nor to the young churches. Then suddenly came the news: "M.B. Missionaries Leave Congo." According to a report in the *Christian Leader* two cables were received in the Missions Office on July 19. The first indicated that thirty-one missionaries and their children had left for the United States, and the second said that the rest of the staff was to follow. [24]

It was later discovered that the reason for the hurried evacuation was a rebellious army which was dissatisfied with the slow pace of nationalization of government institutions and agencies. Although the mutiny was short-lived, it was especially directed against all foreign (white) domination and influence, including that of the missionaries. "Should a re-entry be possible under more ordered political circumstances," the Board of Missions reported, "it is clear the work would assume an altered character."[25]

After Independence a new epoch began for the Mennonite Brethren Church in the Congo. By 1962 many missionaires had returned. However, the prevailing unrest in the Kwango Province prevented them from returning to the stations, except in Kikwit and Kajiji. Leopoldville (now Kinshasa) temporarily emerged as the center of operations. Of special significance was the development of gospel broadcasting in the trade languages of Kituba and Lingala.

Soon the educational and evangelistic ministries could be resumed in the interior. In Kafumba the small printing press was flooded with requests for Christian literature. At Kajiji hospital services were expanded. *Ecole Belle Vue* ("School of the Beautiful View") was transformed into a theological institute for the Congolese in cooperation with the CIM. In *Pai Congila*, a 220-bed government hospital, plagued by a shortage of medical personnel, asked the Mennonite Brethren to staff and operate it. Thus another center was added in 1962 to the M.B. mission in the Congo — a center which proved to be fruitful for evangelism and church extension.

Shortly before a new storm was unleashed over the Kwango Province, the following statistics were reported: 9 stations, 62 outposts, 11 pastors, 57 church leaders, and 8000 members.[26]

1964: The Jeunesse Rebellion

Two years before the so-called "cultural revolution" swept across China, a similar revolution occurred in the Congo. The Jeunesse (youth) revolution was led by youthful gangs who were dissatisfied with the failure of independence and with the continued influence of foreigners in the Congo. The movement originated in the Matende area with Pierre Mulele, trained behind the Bamboo Curtain, as its leader. Although the primary targets of the Jeunesse were not the mission stations, but government centers, the former also came under attack as part of the "establishment."

By the end of January, 1964, Mennonite Brethren mission stations were threatened. On short notice, taking with them only the most necessary personal belongings, missionaries evacuated the field by plane and truck.[27] A little later, after Missionary Aviation Fellowship (MAF) had run some air checks on mission stations in the area, Bob Kroeker reported: "Most of the village chapels and out-schools in rebel territory have been burned to the ground. Four of our mission stations were destroyed."[28]

49. A pastors' seminar in Zaire.

Among the latter was Kafumba, the pride and joy of the missionary staff. Several decades of sacrificial labor was completely destroyed. Would a new church emerge from the ashes of the old? Many missionaries, deeply convinced of God's overruling providence, believed that even this tragedy could be a blessing in disguise.[29]

The Church Marches On

Slowly the rebels were pushed back by government forces. The national church went through a period of reorientation and repentance since some members had participated in this movement of militant nationalism. The missionaries returned to give counsel and guidance in the restoration — not of the ruined stations, but of the disorganized M.B. churches. The crisis has hastened the process of indigenization in the Congo. The destruction of the mission stations, notably Kafumba, has caused mission personnel to locate in such strategic centers as *Kikwit* and *Kinshasa*. The Bible institute has been moved from Kafumba to Kikwit.

Purged in the fires of persecution and suffering, the young Mennonite Brethren Church in the Congo continues to serve the Lord with sincere dedication. Although the average per capita annual income in the Congo is about eighty-seven dollars, the churches operate with very little foreign subsidy. The entire primary school system has been taken over by the churches. Teachers and administrators through junior high school are Congolese.

The national churches still need help in education (senior high) and theological training. A new school, *L'Ecole de Theologie Evangelique de*

Kinshasa, has been established jointly by ten denominations, including the Mennonite Brethren, to meet the need for trained pastors and church workers. In the radio ministry, literature production, and medical work, continued assistance is also needed.

One of the most pressing problems the church faces at the present time is the fusion of church and mission. Even more problematic appear to be the new measures taken by leading men in the Protestant Congo Council to establish one united "Church of Christ" in Zaire. Under God, the Mennonite Brethren Church in the Congo will also weather these new storms, arising partly out of a strong feeling of nationalism.

According to a 1970 field report, the Mennonite Brethren Church in the Congo has a membership of over 9,000, in sixty local churches and eighty-eight outposts. Nelson concludes his analysis of the Congo crisis with the following optimistic note: "Christianity has enough of a foothold in Congo that it should survive and grow. It does not necessarily follow that it will. The continuing role of Christian missionaries and the churches that support them will play a very decisive part."[30]

LATIN AMERICA

Latin America consists of twenty republics, ten of which are north and ten south of Panama. In most of these countries political colonialism was overthrown 150 years ago. Spanish is the prevailing language in eighteen of these republics. In Brazil the official language is Portuguese and in Haiti it is French. Instability and change are characteristic of the political life in most Latin American countries. Roman Catholicism has been the dominant religion ever since the coming of the Portuguese and Spaniards in the sixteenth century. However, in the last two decades the Protestant church in Latin America has been growing faster than anywhere else in the world. Today there is also a Mennonite Brethren Church in seven of these republics. Only a brief glimpse of the emerging M.B. Church in Latin America will be presented.

Mennonite Brethren in Brazil

Brazil, the fifth largest country in the world and the giant of South America, opened its doors to Mennonites and Mennonite Brethren in 1930. They came from the "Gates of Moscow" via Germany to the state of Santa Catarina in Southern Brazil.[31] Although the larger contingent of refugees had decided to go to Paraguay, some 1200 chose to settle in Brazil. A large German community in Santa Catarina, plus the encouragement from the Hanseatic Colonization Society in Brazil, were important factors in their decision.

The MCC was not favorably disposed toward colonization in Brazil because Brazil refused to grant exemption from military service. The Dutch Mennonites, who collectively did not hold to the principle of nonresistance anymore, gave financial assistance to the settlers in Santa Catarina. A German relief organization, *Brueder in Not*, also rendered substantial aid. According to J. W. Fretz, the Brazilian settlers were probably less concerned about preserving their nonresistant position than were their brethren in North America.[32] Since only those born in Brazil were subject to military service, the issue was not one of immediate concern to the newly arrived immigrants.

In God's providence, colonization was to lead to evangelization and to the establishment of both German and Portuguese-speaking M.B. churches in Brazil. The small group of Mennonite Brethren was thrust into this vast land in order to raise up a gospel witness for the salvation of many.

The Immigrant M.B. Church

The first Mennonite Brethren churches were established in the two original settlements of Mennonites in Santa Catarina: *Witmarsum*, along the banks of the Alto Rio Krauel, and *Auhagen* on the crest of a nearby mountain, commonly referred to as Stoltz-Plateau. Early years were marked by incredible pioneer hardships, but with Dutch and German assistance, the settlers managed to survive.

Among the spiritual leaders of the group were two Mennonite Brethren elders, Jakob Huebert and Heinrich Ekk, and several M.B. ministers. In addition Gerhard Wiens of the Evangelical Mennonite Brethren, and Heinrich Martens of the Mennonite Church, belonged to the spiritual leadership of the two colonies. Martens apparently attempted to organize a united Mennonite Church of Brazil, but the effort failed.[33] Later, other attempts at amalgamation of all Mennonite groups were made by the leader of the settlement, but they also failed, largely because of the opposition of the large M.B. Church.

The M.B. church at Witmarsum was organized under the leadership of elder Jakob Huebert. Although the early years were marked by internal and external tensions, the M.B. church continued to grow as many new converts joined the church through baptism.

In 1934, because of extremely adverse economic conditions, the settlers on the Stoltz-Plateau decided, by a majority vote, to abandon the Auhagen settlement. By 1937 more than half the families had left, and by 1951 the last settler pulled up stakes and moved elsewhere. Some Auhagen settlers joined their friends at Witmarsum, but a majority eventually moved to the Curitiba area in Parana state, where they established the *Bouqueirao* settlement. A number of families from Witmarsum also made the trek to Curitiba. Elder Jakob Huebert joined the group at Curitiba in 1936 and during the next few years several M.B. churches were established in the area.

The Krauel settlement continued to be plagued by economic problems and religious tensions. In 1949 a new resettlement committee discovered land suitable for agricultural purposes in the southernmost state of Brazil, Rio Grande de Sul, about twenty-five miles southeast of the city of Bage, and forty miles north of the Uruguayan border. Under the leadership of Jacob Epp, a leading industrialist of the Witmarsum settlement, the *Bage* colony was founded. By 1951 the settlement had grown to eighty-two families, most of them Mennonite Brethren. Under the leadership of elder Gerhard Rosenfeld, who had weathered all the religious storms on the Krauel, the M.B. Church began a new chapter in its history.[34] During the last twenty years the Bage M.B. Church has carried on an effective church extension program among its Brazilian neighbors, and several churches have been established in the area.

After 1951 the Krauel settlement rapidly disintegrated. Those who did not move to Bage resettled in the state of Parana in a colony called *Neu Witmarsum*, about forty-five miles northwest of Curitiba. Here the larger group belonged to the Mennonite Church, but an M.B. Church was also organized.

Curitiba, however, emerged as the main center of the German-speaking Mennonite Brethren. Through the faithful teaching ministry of such brethren as Gerhard Sukkau, C. C. Peters, and others, the church's missionary vision was enlarged and mission work among Portuguese-speaking people was begun in several places. "There is hardly a church of the German Mennonite Brethren Conference," reported J. J. Toews after a visit to Brazil, "which does not have an extension work among the Brazilians."[35]

The establishment of a Theological Institute in Curitiba by the South American M.B. Conference was an important factor in this church extension program. When the "Convention" (the Portuguese-speaking M.B. Conference) began to assume greater responsibility for the work among Brazilians, the "Association" (the German-speaking M.B. Conference) directed its missionary efforts more to the large German communities in Santa Catarina. In *Blumenau, Joinville*, and other places, local congregations and evangelistic centers have been established. A German-speaking M.B. church has also been organized in the large metropolis of *Sao Paulo*. The membership of the Association in 1971 was 1,021.

The National M.B. Church

The Mennonite Brethren Church among Brazilians had an inconspicuous beginning. An orphanage was opened in 1947 near Curitiba as the first experiment of outreach in Brazil by the Board of

50. Conference of the German-speaking M.B. Church "Association" in Brazil.

Missions of North America. The vision for this work was born in the heart of Jacob Unruh of Shafter, California.

The local M.B. churches gave their wholehearted support to the Unruhs, and later to the Erven Thiessens, in their dedicated and sacrificial ministry to Brazilian orphans. The work done at *Lar das Criancas* (official name of the orphanage) gained the recognition and respect not only of the people in the community, but also of high-ranking government officials. This ministry of love and compassion prepared the way for evangelism and church extension.

One of the first orphans to be received into *Lar das Criancas* was Carmen Pombeiro. Carmen became a Christian and is now the wife of Walter Rempel, a pastor and leader in the Convention. Former members of the orphanage and graduates of the mission school were among the charter members of the first national Mennonite Brethren church in Brazil. This church, located in *Uberaba*, a suburb of Curitiba, had a baptized membership of ninety-six in 1963, and an average attendance of 180.

Due to increasing difficulties with Brazilian legal authorities the Board of Missions in 1966 decided to close the home for orphans and return the children to relatives and guardians. Thus a very fruitful experiment in missions came to an end. The influence of this ministry, however, is still being felt throughout the area. According to Henry Esau, a Mennonite Brethren teacher in Brazil, "Lar das Criancas was the first to make an outreach into the interior and helped to establish the churches."[36]

Of primary significance for the growth and expansion of the Mennonite Brethren Church among the Portuguese-speaking people was the establishment in 1964 of the Parana Bible Institute. Located adjacent to the orphanage, it was designed to train national workers. With John Klassen as first teacher, classes began with eight students. Thus it happened that two Bible institutes were built at Curitiba, only eight miles apart, one offering instruction in Portuguese and one in German, both receiving aid from North America. In the interests of good stewardship and a more coordinated thrust in missionary outreach, the two schools are now being merged.

From Uberaba the light of the gospel penetrated into the interior. In *San Mateus* a church was organized in 1960. Uberaba members had relatives in *Palmas*, 250 miles away, and in due time a church was organized there. A church was also founded at *Clevelandia* where an earlier attempt to establish a Mennonite colony had failed.

Of special interest in this program of church extension is the work of Linda Banman from Winkler, Manitoba — one of the first missionaries to Brazil. After doing pioneer work in San Mateus and Clevelandia, Miss Banman went to *Francisco Beltrao*, where she was able to start a small fellowship.

By 1967 the Convention of Mennonite Brethren Churches in Brazil was ready to register with the government. It now bears full responsibility for evangelism among the Portuguese-speaking people, though the work is still heavily subsidized by the Board of Missions.

The Convention has experienced rapid growth. From one congregation in 1959 it has expanded to twenty-one in 1968. The 1969 conference report shows the rise in membership as follows: 1959-86; 1962 - 160; 1965 - 296; 1968 - 414.[37] The growth rate since 1968 has been around 33 percent per year.

In the last decade churches have also been established in two of the most rapidly growing urban centers of South America: *Sao Paulo* and *Curitiba*. To provide instruction and nurture to these emerging churches constitutes a tremendous challenge, especially since many converts have formerly been enslaved by spiritism as well as various other "isms."

That South America is regarded by Mennonites as "the Continent of Tomorrow" was highlighted in 1972 by the fact that the Ninth Mennonite World Conference was held in Curitiba, Brazil. Whether the Mennonite Brethren Church in Brazil will be able to retain (or recover) an Anabaptist theological orientation will depend on its readiness and ability to integrate its emphasis on evangelism with the New Testament emphasis on discipleship.

MENNONITE BRETHREN IN PARAGUAY

Paraguay, a land-locked country, lies in the central part of South America between Argentina, Brazil, and Bolivia. Slightly larger than California, it is one of the smallest South American countries with a

51. Conference of the Portuguese-speaking M.B. Church "Convention" in Brazil.

population of around two million. The Paraguay River divides the country into unequal and quite different parts: the Gran Chaco, with its subtropical climate, west of the river, and Alto-Paraguay, only half as large, to the east-southeast. Until recently, only five percent of the population live in the Chaco.

The people are largely a mixture of Spanish and Indian, with the Indian (Guarani) predominating. The great majority of the people are Roman Catholic, although the attachment on the part of many is no more than nominal. The number of Protestants in the country is not large, the Mennonites constituting the largest Protestant body. In addition to these groups there are several Indian tribes, which until recently roamed freely through the plains and bush of the Chaco.

After World War I, and again after World War II, Paraguay opened its doors wide for Mennonite immigrants from Europe and North America at a time when virtually all other doors were closed to them. Today Paraguay has the heaviest concentration of Mennonites in South America and also the largest Mennonite Brethren Church. The coming of the Mennonites to the Paraguayan Chaco, was not an "historical accident" (as some have described it) but an act of God's providence, since it was through these immigrant settlers that the gospel was first brought to the Indians, and later to the native Paraguayans. For the sake of convenience, the Mennonite Brethren who came from Russia will be referred to as the "immigrant church" and the M.B. converts among the Indians and Paraguayans as the "national church."

The Immigrant M.B. Church

Between 1928 and 1947 five Mennonite colonies were established in Paraguay: *Menno* in 1928, by Mennonites from Canada (mostly Sommerfelder) who feared the inroads of Canadianism; *Fernheim*, in

1930, by Mennonites who had escaped from the "Gates of Moscow" via Germany; *Friesland*, in 1937, by Mennonites from Fernheim, who were disillusioned by the economic prospects in the Chaco; *Neuland* in 1947, (in territory adjoining the other two Chaco colonies of Menno and Fernheim) by refugees from Russia after World War II; and *Volendam*, in 1947, also by Mennonite war refugees.[38]

Mennonite Brethren churches were established in all colonies immediately after settlement, except in the Menno Colony. The experiences of common sufferings in the past, and of economic necessities in a pioneer settlement, made cooperation with other Mennonite groups not only possible, but also spiritually profitable. Let us briefly trace the growth and development of M.B. churches in the several colonies.

Fernheim

The Fernheim M.B. Church was organized on June 9, 1930, under the leadership of Isaak Braun. It consisted of 50-60 members. Later, when the group was enlarged by new arrivals, the entire Mennonite Brethren Church was divided into two groups, largely because of poor roads and communications: the *Schoenwieser Lokale* and the *Lichtfelder Lokale*. The name in each instance was that of the village in which meetings were being held. Upon the arrival of another group of immigrants from Russia via Harbin, China, in 1932, a third group was formed under the leadership of Johann Schellenberg, called the *Orloffer Lokale*. In 1947 the first two united as the Filadelfia Mennonite Brethren Church with a total membership of 400.

In Filadelfia, the educational, industrial, and business center of Fernheim, the Mennonite Brethren built a brick church in 1945 with a seating capacity of 350. In 1950 another church building was erected with a seating capacity of 1000. Because of difficulties in communication, the *Orloffer Lokale* remained separate and in 1953 had a membership of 440.

The ministers of the congregations for many years received partial financial support from the brotherhood in North America. Sunday schools and young people's work are carried on regularly. While the regular church services are held jointly with the GCM and EMB groups, the first Sunday of each month is set aside for worship and communion of the Mennonite Brethren group alone.

In primary and secondary education all three groups cooperate. Of great significance for church and community has been the *Zentralschule*, which offers a four-year high school course and two years of teacher training. The local Bible school has done much to raise the spiritual life in the congregations and to stimulate missionary interest. Among the brethren from North America who have rendered valuable services in

52. Baptismal candidates at the outdoor baptistry at the Filadelfia M.B. Church in Paraguay.

Fernheim the following might be mentioned: C.C. Peters, G. Sukkau, V. D. Toews and Jacob Franz.

During the early 1940's Fernheim, and to a lesser extent Friesland, were seriously affected by the German Nazi program and philosophy. The Mennonite Brethren Church split over this issue. In 1947, through a prolonged spiritual ministry of B. B. Janz from Canada, the groups were reconciled through repentance and forgiveness.

Friesland

The M.B. church in Friesland was founded on October 3, 1937, under the leadership of Kornelius Voth by members who had left the Fernheim settlement in the Chaco. The original membership of 153 had increased to 234 by 1953. With North American aid, a brick church building with a seating capacity of 400 has been constructed in the village of Grossweide. Church life and services are patterned after those in Fernheim.

Since Friesland is located in the eastern and older section of Paraguay, the Mennonites in this colony are exposed to the inroads of Paraguayan manners and low morals. On the other hand the close proximity of several larger Paraguayan communities provides an opportunity for Mennonite Brethren for a positive Christian witness.

Neuland

The *Gnadental* Mennonite Brethren Church (named after the village in which the church building was located) was officially organized on April 8, 1948, under the leadership of Wilhelm Loewen by members who were mostly recent immigrants from Russia and Poland. By 1955 the membership had risen to 317, less than half of the number of members in the Mennonite Church.

Separated families, as a result of the war, constituted a major moral and social problem for church and community in the early years. The total population of the colony in 1950 was 2,314, composed of 641 family units, of which 253 families were without father or husband.

In the sixties a relatively large number of settlers from Neuland have emigrated to Canada to be reunited with relatives or to find better economic opportunities. In 1956 the total population was 2,162; ten years later it numbered only 1,700, in spite of a high birth rate (53.7). Membership in the M.B. Church has also declined. The Mennonite Brethren of Fernheim give spiritual assistance, since most of the M.B. ministers have also left the colony.

Volendam

The M.B. Church in Volendam was at first affiliated with the Friesland M.B. Church. In November, 1949, it was formally organized as an independent congregation under the leadership of Franz Janzen with a membership of 138. A new brick church with a seating capacity of 400 was built in the village of Mariental in 1950.

The aspirations and hopes expressed in this building program did not materialize. Although MCC and North American Mennonite conferences provided material aid as well as personnel, Volendam's economic progress was very slow. A considerable number of families migrated to Canada. From a population of 1,800 in 1950 the number had dwindled to 650 by 1966. By that time the Mennonite Brethren church had a membership of forty-five and was largely dependent on the church in Friesland for nurture and spiritual supervision.[39]

The National M.B. Church

More encouraging and even exciting has been the growth and development of M.B. churches among Indians and Paraguayans. Soon after their arrival in the Chaco several Mennonite leaders in Fernheim felt a burden for the moral and spiritual welfare of the Lengua Indians who surrounded the colony.

In September, 1935, forty-eight members of the various Mennonite groups in Fernheim organized a missionary association under the name, *Licht den Indianern* (Light to the Indians). The association immediately began to work among the Lengua Indians with Gerhard B. Giesbrecht as its first missionary. Courageously Giesbrecht faced the problem of learning the unwritten language of the Lengua. For eleven years he preached before the first convert was won. From Coaldale, Alberta, Canada, Bernhard Epp arrived to share in the task. A number of coworkers from Fernheim and Neuland joined the missionary staff. Dietrich Lepp put the language into writing and later translated the New Testament. By 1951 the Lengua M.B. Church had become a reality, although it was composed of only twenty-eight baptized members.

Meanwhile the Chulupi Indians had crossed the Pilcomayo River from Argentina into the Paraguayan Chaco, looking for employment and, perhaps even more, for spiritual help. They set up their camp on a vacant plot of land near Filadelfia. J. H. Franz, also from Coaldale, Alberta, was sent out in 1946 to begin a work among the Chulupi. Franz was assisted in this mission by Cornelius Isaak, who later lost his life in an attempt to contact the Moro, and Gerhard Hein, two young brethren from Fernheim. The Chulupi were more open to the gospel than the Lengua, and thus a church was established among the Chulupi in March 1958, when twenty-two were baptized.[40]

Also in 1946, the Board of Missions (Hillsboro) by agreement with the Fernheim missions association, had assumed financial responsibility for the mission work among the Chaco Indians. However, the association has continued in existence, representing the participation of the Chaco Mennonites in this mission among the Indians. A witness has also been established among the Guarani Indians, who in recent years have flocked into the Fernheim colony looking for employment.

At present there are three M.B. churches among the Lengua Indians with a membership of over 700. The main church center is located at *Yalve Sanga*. Four congregations and several preaching centers have also been established among the Chulupi, with approximately 800 members. At a large rally in Filadefia in July, 1966, "Johann Giesbrecht," one of the first Lengua converts, gave this testimony: "The Mennonites have not only brought the gospel to us; they have also shown us a whole new way of life!"[41] That "new way" is everywhere in evidence as one observes the Lengua and Chulupi Christians in their work and worship.

A number of Mennonite Brethren, who resided in Asuncion, the capital of Paraguay, became acquainted with the desperate spiritual needs of Spanish-speaking Paraguayans. Albert Enns, who came to Paraguay as one of the Russian immigrants in 1948, must be regarded as the pioneer in "city missions" in that country.

Coming to Asuncion in 1955, Enns and others began to distribute Christian literature and visit homes. After two years of sowing the seed, there were some positive responses and a small fellowship group was

53. The Chulupi Indian M.B. Church in Paraguay.

formed. Today there are four congregations in Asuncion, and another at San Istanislao, some forty miles from Friesland. Combined membership is close to 200.

With help from the Board of Missions and Services it has become possible to start both an elementary school and a Spanish Bible institute in Asuncion. The staff for both schools comes from the Paraguayan Mennonites. In the young people trained in these and similar institutions rests the hope for the continued progress of the church of Christ in Paraguay.

MENNONITE BRETHREN IN URUGUAY

Uruguay, the smallest of the South American republics, with a predominantly white population, opened its doors to Mennonite immigrants in 1948. The Mennonites who eventually established settlements at El Ombu, Gartental and Colonia in 1950-51 were largely displaced persons from West Prussia and Central Poland. The group from Poland was composed largely of Mennonite Brethren who settled at *El Ombu* in 1950 and organized a congregation under the leadership of Tobias Voth. In the group that arrived in 1951 were a number of M.B. families from Russia who established a small church at *Gartental.*

The El Ombu settlement, located some 180 miles northwest of Montevideo, had a very restricted land area. Thus another Mennonite settlement was established in 1955 at Delta, sixty miles northwest of

Montevideo. A few years later the M.B. group from El Ombu decided to resettle as a body at *Sarandi* not far from Delta. Relocation, inflation and other economic problems have at times threatened the very survival of the small M.B. churches in the interior of Uruguay. The brotherhood from North America has rendered spiritual and material aid from time to time.

From the beginning of Mennonite immigration many young people sought employment in Montevideo, a large metropolis which contains half the population of the country. The Mennonite Brethren established a hostel in the city which also served as a fellowship center. The John Walls from Ontario, the J. P. Neufelds from Manitoba, and other couples have rendered valuable services in Montevideo as well as in the country churches.

Through this witness some Spanish-speaking people were contacted and brought to Christ. This called for a Spanish-speaking worker. The Daniel Wirsches, who had previously labored in Colombia and Mexico, were sent out by the Board of Missions and Services in 1968 to give leadership to the work. Today there is a Spanish M.B. church in Montevideo with Walter Preza, a Uruguayan, as pastor. The Spanish and German M.B. churches are united in one conference.

Mennonite Brethren in Colombia

Mennonite Brethren work in Colombia dates back to the immediate post-war period. In April, 1945, the Daniel Wirsches arrived at Palmira, Valle, as the first M.B. missionaries to this large South American republic with over twenty million people. Shortly thereafter the Board of Missions was able to acquire an independent mission station at *La Cumbre*. Daniel Wirsche's brother David arrived in Colombia in

54. The Uruguay M.B. Conference in session at Gartental.

December. In the two years following, a number of missionaries joined the Wirsche brothers: the John Dycks, Annie E. Dyck, Lillian Schafer, Kathyrn Lentzner and Mary Schroeder in 1946; Lydia Golbeck and the Jacob Loewens in 1947; the Harry Bartels and Ruth Loewen in 1948.

Through the presence of many new workers who were there also for language study, the La Cumbre congregation which had existed for some time was revived and strengthened. Later the church here grew when persecution in other regions forced many Christians to seek refuge in the mountains around La Cumbre. A primary school was started, and somewhat later also a high school. The latter was moved to Cali in 1966.

However, in the early years the interest and concern of the board and of the missionaries centered primarily on the region known as the "Choco," the hot and humid coastal lowlands in the northwestern part of the country. In 1947 the John Dycks with several single ladies established themselves at *Istmina*, while the Jacob Loewens and the David Wirsches moved to *Noanama*, a point from which they could reach the Indians who were their particular concern. It was a difficult pioneer work among primitive, illiterate people.

At both these places churches, schools, and dispensaries were built. Since the native Waunana language was as yet unwritten, the missionaries worked on the production of a grammar, a dictionary and the translation of Bible stories. By Christmas of 1952 Loewen was able to give the Noanama Indians the Christmas story in their own language.[42]

By 1955 storm clouds were gathering over the evangelical Christian churches of Colombia. The work of the Mennonite Brethren was also tested by severe persecution. In 1956 the work in the Choco was forbidden. For the time being, the Waunana were lost to M.B. missions. Persecution spread to all regions in Colombia, including La Cumbre. God, however, protected and preserved the missionaries as well as the young M.B. Church, and no members were killed. Before this storm had subsided, the mission experienced another severe blow: the death of John and Mary Dyck in an airplane crash on March 9, 1957.[43]

In 1958 a new day dawned for evangelical missions in Colombia when the Liberal party came into office in the national elections. The persecution had proved to be a blessing in disguise, purifying the Christian churches and changing the course of national politics. Since 1958 Mennonite Brethren have had a wide-open door for evangelism and church planting in Colombia.

A new missionary strategy, also begun in 1958, has been highly significant for Mennonite Brethren church extension in Colombia. On the last day of that year a vision was born to begin work in *Cali*, a metropolis with a population of over 700,000. The Ernest Friesens, John

Savoias, Ebner Friesens, and others in the course of a few years established a cluster of six or seven congregations in the city and its suburbs. Cali has become the most important Mennonite Brethren center in Colombia.

Meanwhile in the country around La Cumbre a number of outstations have been developing into congregations. The seven rural churches now have their own pastors as well as a supervisor over all country work.

The indigenization of both rural and urban churches is proceeding rapidly. An important factor in this process is the seminary extension program begun in 1968 for the training of national leaders. By means of this arrangement theological training is brought to the students in the towns and villages. The United Biblical Seminary of Colombia, a joint venture of about eight church groups (including the Mennonite Brethren), operates in four centers: Cali, Medellin, Bogota, and Caribe. It is an exciting and innovative approach in training church workers.

The present status of the M.B. Church in Colombia is summarized by Phyllis Martens as follows: "In all, there are some 24 congregations and preaching points in Colombia, including the groups still existing in the Choco. . . . Membership proper is about 650, Sunday school attendance close to 2000. Officers of the Colombia conference are all national brethren."[44]

MENNONITE BRETHREN IN PERU

As a result of the M.B.-K.M.B. merger in 1960, the territory of Mennonite Brethren missions was expanded to include Peru — the center of the ancient Inca Empire. Ten years earlier Sylvester Dirks had come to Peru to begin a new work for the Krimmer Mennonite Brethren. Working in cooperation with the Wycliffe Bible translators, Dirks established a mission center at Atalaya, east of Lima and of the Andes mountain range.

The primary concern of these missionaries was to reach the Campa Indians and give them the Scriptures in their own language. Some ten K.M.B. missionaries came to Peru to work among the Campa Indians, including the Paul Friesens and the Joseph Walters. As a result of their labors there emerged not only a Campa Indian Church at *El Encuentro* ("The Meeting") but also a Spanish-speaking church in nearby *Atalaya*.

Isolation and difficult climatic conditions in the Peruvian jungle have called for a special measure of dedication on the part of the workers among the Campa Indians. In 1963 the Board of Missions, however, was able to report that the language of the Campas had been reduced to writing, and that the Gospels of Mark and John and the book of Acts had been translated into Campa. By 1969 the Evangelical Campa

55. Cali M.B. Church in Colombia.

56. A group of believers in Peru.

57. Radio choir at HCJB in Quito, Ecuador.

Church was organized and well on its way to self-support and independence.[45]

MENNONITE BRETHREN AT HCJB

There are no Mennonite Brethren churches in *Ecuador*, but most German-speaking people in South America have heard of HCJB, the "voice of the Andes" in Quito, which also has a "German voice." For the past nineteen years Mennonite Brethren have been fully responsible for the German department of this worldwide ministry. The David Nightingales (from British Columbia) and Sally Schroeder (from Manitoba) were among the pioneers of this work which was begun in 1953. Mail response indicates growth of influence. Whereas the total number of letters received in 1953 was 57, the letter-response for the month of August alone in 1968 was 2287.[46] The radio ministry of the German department has indirectly contributed to church growth in several South American countries.

MENNONITE BRETHREN IN PANAMA

Until 1903 Panama, the narrow strip of territory at the southern tip of Central America, was a department of the Republic of Colombia. The Waunana Indians, living in northwestern Colombia and southern Panama, continued to cross the border freely, ignoring the new political division after Panama's independence.

An independent mission had begun a work among the Empera tribe of the Choco Indians in 1953. In 1956 anthropologist Jacob Loewen, former missionary in Colombia, made his first visit to this area in the course of his study of all Choco dialects. He was joined by David Wirsche in this work. When the Waunana Indians in Colombia heard that their former missionary friends were now teaching the Panama Indians, many of them migrated there and settled in the *Chitola* area.

The unique method of evangelism to reach the Indian tribes has been a "summer reading course." In the words of Phyllis Martens: "This approach — missions via the teaching of reading — is in fact Panama's unique and highly successful donation to the history of Mennonite Brethren missions."[47] The missionaries continued the summer reading classes until the Indians were able to conduct a year-round literacy program of their own. The report of the Board of Missions and Services to the General Conference in 1969 contains this terse but significant note on the progress of the work in Panama: "The four churches have experienced spiritual growth. The ministry of Glen Prunty, and the visits of David Wirsche, James Harrison and John Goertz have assisted the churches in maturing in the Word of God."[48] By their own choice these churches will be associated with the Mennonite Brethren.

58. A Bible study in **Panama**.

59. **A church group in Mexico.**

MENNONITE BRETHREN IN MEXICO

It seems somewhat strange that Mexico, next-door neighbor of the United States to the south, has received the missionary attention of the Mennonite Brethren only a little more than twenty years ago. Although it is a North American federal republic, Mexico has more in common religiously and politically with the rest of the Latin American countries in Central and South America.

Between 1922-27 several thousand Old Colony and Sommerfelder Mennonites from Manitoba and Saskatchewan moved to Mexico and established large settlements in the states of Chihuahua and Durango.

These groups had left Canada out of protest to the secularization process, chiefly the Canadianization to which they were being subjected in the public schools. The moral and spiritual plight of these Mennonites motivated the Mennonite Brethren to enter Mexico.

Because of government restrictions against foreign "missionaries" the Board of Missions bought a farm at *Nuevo Ideal* with the understanding that Mennonites could be hired to work it. The missionaries soon discovered, however, that whereas the Mennonite colonists were slow to respond, the Mexicans were eager to hear the message. As a result, evangelistic efforts have been directed more toward the Mexican people. This shift in emphasis has also led to a geographical shift — from Nuevo Ideal to *Guadalajara* as the center of M.B. operations in Mexico.

The Spanish-speaking churches are small, scattered over a wide area. The withdrawal of mission funds and personnel in recent years has made it difficult for the struggling fellowship groups to carry on an effective program. The church buildings in *Ciudad Diaz Ordas* and *Piedras Negras,* according to veteran missionary Sylvester Dirks who visited M.B. missions in Mexico in 1970, are out of proportion to the small groups who gather for worship. Dirks shares the view of other informed leaders that "the hope of Mexico is in the training of national leaders."[49]

EUROPE

After four centuries, Mennonites from America — spiritual heirs of the sixteenth century Anabaptists — returned to Europe in the wake of the most disastrous war in history. They came to Germany, Austria and other countries of Western Europe as ministers of relief and messengers of reconciliation under the auspices of the Mennonite Central Committee. This ministry of compassion opened the door (as it did in Japan) for evangelism and church-planting by Mennonite Brethren. Trailblazers in this ministry were H. H. Janzen and Cornelius Wall, who preached in the refugee camps (established for Mennonites who had fled from Russia and West Prussia) in the years immediately following World War II.

MENNONITE BRETHREN IN GERMANY

Could Germany, the land of the Reformation of the sixteenth century, and the birthplace of modern missions in the eighteenth century, be a mission field in the twentieth century? The Mennonite Brethren, and many other Evangelicals who studied the religious scene in post-war Germany, answered the question in the affirmative. The fact that many Mennonite Brethren in America still spoke the German fluently, made it easier to respond to the spiritual needs of Germany.

Neuwied on the Rhine became the first center for a ministry of church extension and evangelism. The C. N. Hieberts carried on an extensive program of visitation-evangelism in the early fifties. A congregation originally composed of Russian and Polish Mennonites was organized and began to grow under the spiritual ministry of the J. W. Vogts, and the Hugo Jantzes.

Radio and literature work was developed under the leadership of Mr. and Mrs. Cornelius Balzer. The radio program *Quelle des Lebens*, aired over Radio Luxembourg, supported and strengthened the Mennonite Brethren witness in West Germany. The growth of this radio ministry prompted the transfer of "headquarters" first to *Griesheim* and later to *Kaiserslautern*. Roland Marsch has been the pastor of the Neuwied congregation since 1967. Present membership is close to 100, and includes a number of converts from Lutheranism and Catholicism.

Neustadt (an der Weinstrasse) became the second city for M.B. evangelistic activity. (Both Neuwied and Neustadt were early Anabaptist centers, where several Mennonite churches have survived to the present.) From 1946 to 1950 the MCC maintained its relief headquarters for the French zone of Germany here. Also under MCC auspices, a religious program for children was begun in 1948 by Elizabeth Wiebe.

When the MCC left, Miss Wiebe continued her work and in 1957 a general evangelistic program was started. The group was organized formally in 1958 under the guidance of G. H. Jantzen. Church growth here has been slow.

The *Lage* M.B. Church (relocated here from nearby Muessen) in northern Germany, is largely composed of members who have returned from South America or have lately come out of Russia. Under the faithful ministry of the J. W. Vogts these scattered families were gathered and organized into a church in 1966. Since 1968 the John N. Klassens have been in charge of the work at Lage.

The youngest M.B. church in Germany is located in the city of *Traunreut*, about thirty miles from the Austrian border. This "outpost" of the Wels (Austria) M.B. Church has developed into a small congregation during the past few years under the spiritual ministry of the Lawrence Warkentins.

MENNONITE BRETHREN IN AUSTRIA

It is difficult to imagine that in Austria, which in the sixteenth century had many flourishing Anabaptist churches, 95 percent of the people today profess to be Roman Catholics. The influx of refugees from East-European countries after World War II, and the desperate need for

60. Congregation at the M.B. Church in Lage, Germany.

61. Following the baptism of 18 believers, the Tulpengasse Church in Vienna, Austria, met for fellowship on the banks of the river.

relief, rehabilitation and reconstruction in general, opened the door for the MCC and for the Mennonite Brethren in Austria.

In 1953 the J. W. Vogts and the John Gossens began work among the refugees in the camps around *Linz*, the capital of Upper Austria. When the A. J. Neufelds arrived in 1955, these believers were organized into a congregation, a church was built, and the witness expanded to

Austrian nationals. Although actual church membership by 1960 was only 25, weekly attendance averaged 220.[50] For more than ten years Gerhard Jantz has given effective leadership to the local congregation and several preaching centers.

From Linz the A. J. Neufelds brought the message to the city of *Steyr*, where the H. K. Warkentins from California had prepared the way by showing religious films and witnessing. Eventually, a small church was established in Steyr.

The outreach from Linz was extended to the city of *Wels*, some thirty miles west. Here the Lawrence Warkentins established the believers, and before they left for Traunreut, transferred leadership responsibility to Georg Emrich, the first national pastor in the M.B. churches of Europe.

The work in *Vienna* dates back to 1949, when MCC began a ministry of material aid and spiritual nurture here. In 1968 the Vienna group with Helmut Funck as pastor, was accepted into the European M.B. Conference. Meanwhile a second group has been formed in Vienna as a result of the A. J. Neufelds' work. A small fellowship group is also meeting in *Salzburg*. Hence there is now a Mennonite Brethren witness in five strategic cities of Austria — the only Anabaptist-Mennonite group in the country.

Two training schools for Christian workers play a key role in the M.B. church extension program in Europe: *Bienenberg* (Switzerland) and *Brake* (North Germany). In both schools Mennonite Brethren teachers have been on the staff through the years. Bienenberg is a Mennonite institution; Brake operates on a nondenominational level. Senior students and graduates of these schools assist in the work of Mennonite Brethren churches.

These scattered congregations in Germany and Austria are united in one conference, which they call *Bund der Mennoniten Brueder Gemeinden*. This *Bund* (covenant or union) of "earnest Christians," which numbers slightly more than Gideon's army, is committed to Christ and His Great Commission, as are their brethren in many nations around the world.

Compared with the large Protestant bodies of America and of the world, the Mennonite Brethren are but a small and insignificant group. However, to the extent that this worldwide M.B. brotherhood remains faithful to its calling and to Christ's teaching, it will continue to hear the words of the Lord in Revelation 3:8 ". . . Behold, I have set before you an open door, which no one is able to shut; I know that you have but little power, and yet you have kept my word and have not denied my name."

TABLE XII

CHURCH GROWTH

Statistical Report of Mennonite Brethren Churches

YEARS 1969 — 1971

I. MEMBERSHIP REPORT

Membership Beginning	Year	Canada	U.S.	Tot.	Net Incr.
	1963	15,221	13,319	28,540	
	1964	15,288	13,510	28,789	258
	1965	15,462	13,764	29,226	428
	1966	15,807	14,081	29,888	662
	1967	15,916	14,245	30,161	273
	1968	16,218	14,422	30,640	479
	1969	16,660	14,645	31,305	665
	1970	17,056	14,796	31,852	547
	1971	17,396	14,934	32,330	478
	1972	17,982	14,767	32,749	419

Additions:				
Following Baptism	1969	673	390	1,063
	1970	651	432	1,083
	1971	789	452	1,241
3 Year Totals		2,113	1,274	3,387
Certificate of Transfer or Testimony	1969	773	338	1,111
	1970	873	288	1,161
	1971	764	436	1,200
3 Year Totals		2,410	1,062	3,472

Decreased:				
By Death	1969	(143)	(122)	(265)
	1970	(118)	(129)	(247)
	1971	(118)	(138)	(256)
3 Year Totals		(389)	(379)	(768)
Other	1969	(907)	(455)	(1,362)
	1970	(1,066)	(453)	(1,519)
	1971	(849)	(917)	(1,766)
3 Year Totals		(2,822)	(1,825)	(4,649)

II. CHURCH GROWTH

Year	Membership			Rate of Grow.	No. of Chur.	Ave. Mbr.	No. of Min.	Ratio to Mem.	No. of Deac.	Ratio to Mem.
	Can.	U.S.	Tot.							
1938	6,111	8,103	14,214		115	124	385	1 / 37	240	1 / 59
1942	8,075	8,903	16,978	16%	131	130	386	44	196	87
1944	8,754	9,047	17,801	5%	131	136	399	45	240	74
1947	9,579	9,590	19,169	7%	141	136	462	41	262	73
1950	11,167	10,262	21,429	11%	142	151	533	40	329	65
1953	12,206	10,611	22,817	6%	146	156	520	44	349	65
1956	13,172	11,212	24,384	6%	149	164	509	48	378	65
1959	13,946	11,582	25,528	4%	161	159	582	44	450	57
1962	14,578	13,221	27,799	8%	172	162	601	46	501	55
1965	15,807	14,081	29,888	7%	220	136	532	56	585	51
1968	16,660	14,645	31,305	5%	219	143	527	59	639	49
1971	17,982	14,767	32,749	5%	222	148	466	70	679	48

Footnotes

PREFACE

1. See J. F. Harms, *Die Geschichte der Mennoniten Bruedergemeinde* (*1860-1924*) (Hillsboro, Kan.: Mennonite Brethren Publishing House, 1924); J. H. Lohrenz, *The Mennonite Brethren Church* (Hillsboro: M.B. Publishing House, 1950); A. H. Unruh, *Die Geschichte der Mennoniten-Bruedergemeinde* (Winnipeg: Christian Press, 1955); and the most comprehensive source, the *Mennonite Encyclopedia* (hereafter *ME*), edited by H. S. Bender and C. H. Smith (4 vols., Scottdale, Pa.: Mennonite Publishing House, 1955-59).

CHAPTER I

1. Richard Niebuhr, *The Kingdom of God in America* (Chicago: Willett, Clark, and Co., 1937), p. 1.
2. P. M. Friesen, *Die Alt-Evangelische Mennonitische Bruederschaft in Russland* (*1789-1910*) (Halbstadt: Raduga, 1911), p. 191.
3. Cf. J. A. Toews, "Die Ersten Mennoniten Brueder und Menno Simons," *The Voice*, VI (Nov.-Dec., 1957), 1-3.
4. Friesen, *op. cit.*, p. 174.
5. C. Henry Smith, *The Story of the Mennonites* (Fourth Edition Revised and Enlarged by Cornelius Krahn, Newton, Kansas: Mennonite Publication Office, 1957), pp. 1-2.
6. Cf. George H. Williams, *The Radical Reformation* (Philadelphia: Westminster Press, 1962).
7. For a study of the various "types" of Anabaptists see Friedmann, *ME*, I, 114-116.
8. The story of the early beginnings is told more fully by Fritz Blanke in *Brothers in Christ* (Scottdale, Pa.: Herald Press, 1961).
9. Quoted by John Howard Yoder in *Introduction to Mennonite History*, edited by C. J. Dyck (Scottdale, Pa.: Herald Press, 1967), p. 29.
10. H. S. Bender, *Conrad Grebel, c1498-1526* (Goshen, Indiana: Mennonite Historical Society, 1950), p. 137.
11. W. R. Estep, *The Anabaptist Story* (Nashville: Broadman Press, 1963), p. 10.
12. Smith, *op. cit.*, p. 64.
13. *The Complete Writings of Menno Simons* (hereafter *CW*), translated from the Dutch by Leonard Verduin and edited by John C. Wenger (Scottdale, Pa.: Herald Press, 1956), p. 668.
14. *Ibid.*, p. 669.
15. *Ibid.*, p. 671.
16. See Wm. Keeney, *Introduction to Mennonite History*, p. 94.
17. *CW*, pp. 739-44.
18. *Ibid.*, p. 740.
19. *Ibid.*
20. *Ibid.*, p. 741.
21. Guy F. Hershberger, (ed.), *The Recovery of the Anabaptist Vision* (Scottdale, Pa.: Herald Press, 1957), p. 47.

CHAPTER II

1. Cf. Smith, *op. cit.*, p. 271. Smith describes the Prussian Mennonites in the Vistula Delta as a "pure Dutch community."

2. See Frank H. Epp, *Introduction to Mennonite History*, p. 127.

3. Gerhard Lohrenz in *A Legacy of Faith*, edited by Cornelius J. Dyck (Newton, Kansas: Faith and Life Press, 1962), p. 174.

4. *Ibid.*

5. Robert Kreider, "The Anabaptist Conception of the Church in the Russian Mennonite Environment," *MQR*, XXV (January, 1951), 22.

6. See article "Chortitza Mennonite Settlement," *ME*, I, 569-74.

7. See article "Molotschna," *ME*, III, 732-37.

8. Frank H. Epp, *Introduction to Mennonite History*, p. 133.

9. Kreider, *op. cit.*, p. 18.

10. G. Lohrenz, *op. cit.*, p. 173.

11. Smith, *op. cit.*, p. 421.

12. Harms, *op. cit.*, p. 1.

13. Friesen, *op. cit.*, pp. 211-12. (Free translation by author.)

14. Cf. Letter of explanation quoted by P. M. Friesen, *ibid.*, p. 199.

15. *CW*, p. 734.

16. *Ibid.*, p. 283.

17. Kreider, *op. cit.*, p. 22.

18. See C. H. Wedel, *Abriss der Geschichte der Mennoniten* (Newton, Kansas: Bethel College, 1901), III, 168.

19. *Ibid.*, p. 171.

20. *Ibid.*, p. 170.

21. Quoted by Harms, *op. cit.*, p. 2.

22. Smith, *op. cit.*, p. 426. Among the innovations to which objections were raised was also Fast's ordination by a Frisian elder, rather than by one of his own wing of the church, and the founding of the Ohrloff secondary school (*Vereinsschule*).

23. Friesen, *op. cit.*, p. 119.

24. Wiens had banned three members who had administered corporal punishment to a Hutterite youth in compliance with an order of the village mayor. Details are given by Franz Isaac, *Die Molotschnaer Mennoniten* (Halbstadt, Taurien, 1908), pp. 115-22.

25. Friesen, *op. cit.*, p. 123. The entire farewell address is given by Friesen, pp. 120-28.

26. J. H. Lohrenz, *The Mennonite Brethren Church*, p. 23.

27. Quoted by Franz Isaac, *op. cit.*, p. 55.

28. Cf. *ibid.*, p. 63.

29. Kreider, *op. cit.*, p. 25.

30. A. Braun, quoted by Kreider, *ibid.*, p. 27.

31. Jacob P. Becker, Unpublished "Memoirs," translated by D. E. Pauls and A. E. Janzen (Copy in Archives of Pacific College), pp. 23-25. Revised and published as *Origin of the Mennonite Brethren Church* (Hillsboro, Kan.: Mennonite Brethren Historical Society of the Midwest). References indicate pagination in the earlier manuscript.

32. Heinrich Balzer, "Faith and Reason," translated and edited by Robert Friedmann, *MQR*, XXII (1948), 90.

33. See Wedel, *op. cit.*, III, 154; Smith, *op. cit.*, p. 421; also John Horsch, *Mennonites in Europe* (Scottdale, Pa.: Mennonite Publishing House, 1942), p. 275.

CHAPTER III

1. A designation used by A. J. Klassen to describe this spiritual revival among the Mennonites. "The Roots and Development of Mennonite Brethren Theology to 1914" (Unpub. M.A. thesis, Wheaton College Graduate School, 1966), p. 33.

2. There is no satisfactory equivalent of *Kleine Gemeinde* in English. The terms, the "small church" or the "little church" do not convey the full meaning which the term *Kleine Gemeinde* has acquired in Mennonite history. Originally it was called *Kleine Gemeinde* because it was a minority group. In 1952 the church adopted a new name: Evangelical Mennonite Church.

3. J. H. Lohrenz, *op. cit.*, p. 24.

4. Bender, in "Kleine Gemeinde," *ME*, III, 197.

5. Cf. chapter two

6. Balzer, "Faith and Reasons," *MQR*, XXII (1948), 87.

7. The *Vereinsschule* was a secondary school established primarily for the training of teachers.

8. Even the "great" Cornies is reported to have participated in audible prayers. Friesen, *op. cit.*, p. 78 (footnote).

9. *Ibid.*

10. *Ibid.*, p. 79.

11. According to Robert Friedmann, *Mennonite Piety through the Centuries*, (Goshen, Ind.: Mennonite Historical Society, 1949), p. 68, and Kreider, *op. cit.*, p. 28, this congregation was composed principally of Lutherans who had united with the Mennonites. Among them were such prominent families as the Langes, the Lenzmanns, the Klatts and others.

12. Becker, "Memoirs," p. 26.

13. Cf. A. J. Klassen, *op. cit.*, pp. 34-35.

14. The name "Brethren" was applied to believing church members long before 1860. It was often used in derision by those who did not share their views.

15. See P. M. Friesen, *op. cit.*, p. 86, for a comprehensive list of such men.

16. *Ibid.*, p. 80.

17. The "Templers" had originated in Wuerttemberg, Germany, as followers of a theologian by the name of Christoph Hoffmann. The latter sponsored a kind of Zionist movement, the chief objective of which was to build a new temple in Jerusalem. The ideas of the "Jerusalem Friends" were brought to the Molotschna by Johannes Lange, a teacher at the *Bruderschule*.

18. Friesen, *op. cit.*, p. 168. Friesen thinks that Wuest tends to exaggerate his profligacy in his memoirs.

19. *Ibid.*

20. *Ibid.*, p. 181.

21. *Ibid.*, p. 169.

22. Becker, *op. cit.*, p. 30.

23. See article by Victor Adrian, "Born of Anabaptism and Pietism," *Mennonite Brethren Herald*, (March 26, 1965). For a more comprehensive study of the relationship of Pietism to Anabaptism or Mennonitism the following references might be helpful: Robert Friedmann, *Mennonite Piety through the Centuries*; C. Krahn, "Pietism," *ME*, IV, 176-79; A. J. Klassen, "The Roots and Development of Mennonite Brethren Theology to 1914."

24. Friesen, *op. cit.*, p. 187.

25. Quoted by Friesen, *op. cit.*, p. 188. According to Jacob Becker, communion had been observed by the brethren "several times in all quietness and peace" even before they made this request. Becker, *op. cit.*, p. 44.

26. *Ibid.*

27. *Ibid.*

28. *Ibid.*

29. *Ibid.*, p. 46.

30. *Ibid.*, p. 47.

31. The original German Document of Secession is reproduced in full by the following authors. Friesen, *op. cit.*, pp. 189-92; Isaac, *op. cit.*, pp. 174-76; Peter Regier, *Kurzgefasste Geschichte der Mennoniten Brueder-Gemeinde* (Berne, Indiana: Light & Hope Publishing Co., 1901), pp. 15-20. It is given in translation by A. J. Klassen, "Mennonite Brethren Confessions of Faith: Historic Roots and Comparative Analysis," (Unpub. S.T.M. thesis, Union College of B.C., 1965), pp. 133-35.

32. C. Krahn, "Some Social Attitudes of the Mennonites of Russia," *MQR*, IX (1935), 173.

33. Friesen, *op. cit.*, p. 238. According to the testimony of elder Heinrich Huebert and others, the sermons of Ludwig Hofacker (a German Pietist) were a very effective means for the conversion of many individuals in the Molotschna as well. *Ibid.*

34. The baptism was performed by Gerhard Wieler, a converted schoolteacher, in the little Tokmak river. *Ibid.*, p. 246.

CHAPTER IV

1. So Horsch, *op. cit.*, p. 279; Smith, *op. cit.*, p. 433; Kreider, *op. cit.*, p. 29; so also Wedel, an earlier historian, *op. cit.*, p. 178.

2. Adolf Ehrt, *Das Mennonitentum in Russland von seiner Einwanderung bis zur Gegenwart* (Berlin: Verlag von Julius Beltz, 1932), p.58.

3. Friesen, *op. cit.*, p. 192.

4. Becker, *op. cit.*, p. 52.

5. Friesen, *op. cit.*, p. 192. The statement was not signed by Bernhard Fast, who disagreed with it, nor by Johann Friesen, elder of the *Kleine Gemeinde*, who was absent. All subsequent statements bear the signatures of these five elders.

6. *Ibid.*, p. 196.

7. Isaac, *op. cit.*, p. 180. Isaac contends that the statement was not composed by the elders. They only signed a document prepared by the Colony Administrative Office.

8. Friesen, *op. cit.*, p. 193.

9. Quoted by Friesen, *ibid.*

10. See Becker, *op. cit.*, pp. 57-59.

11. See Friesen, *op. cit.*, p. 195 (footnote).

12. Harms, *op. cit.*, p. 13.

13. Isaac, *op. cit.*, p. 178.

14. See Isaac, *op. cit.*, pp. 179-180 for complete text.

15. A. H. Unruh, *Die Geschichte der Mennoniten-Bruedergemeinde*, p. 55.

16. Friesen, *op. cit.*, p. 197.

17. Cf. Becker, *op. cit.*, pp. 67-69.

18. Friesen, *op. cit.*, p. 198.

19. *Ibid.*, p. 200.

20. According to Franz Isaac, the "minority report" of Elder Harder was withheld from the Supervisory Commission by the Colony Administrative Office. Hence the latter body was under the impression that the elders were all united in their stand against the Brethren. Pastor Dobbert discovered this irregularity (if not deception) in 1864, when he was commissioned by the government to investigate the entire controversy and the charges made against the Brethren. See Isaac, *op. cit.*, pp. 184-85.

21. Cited by Christian Neff, *ME*, I, 613.

22. Friesen, *op. cit.*, p. 200.

23. J. H. Lohrenz, *op. cit.*, p. 31.

24. Becker, *op. cit.*, p. 80.

25. *Ibid.*, p. 84.

26. According to Friesen, Abram Braun, resident of Grossweide, "saved him (Cornelsen) and his family from fever and death, because he dared to take these refugees into his home." Friesen, *op. cit.*, p. 206.

27. Harms, *op. cit.*, p. 29. Huebert knew the baptizer, but refused to divulge his name.

28. The "ultimatum" of October 11 was repeated on October 30, 1860, with the provision of a two-month period of grace, in which the Brethren were to return to their former churches. Friesen, *op. cit.*, p. 296.

29. Claassen describes this experience in Petersburg as a test of patience (*Geduldsprobe*) for him. *Ibid.*, p. 297.

30. *Ibid.*, p. 207. Since no Suez Canal, nor Trans-Siberian Railway existed at the time the trip would have meant a voyage by boat around the Cape of Good Hope, South Africa.

31. J. H. Lohrenz, *op. cit.*, p. 33. For a fuller account of Janzen's treatment see Friesen, *op. cit.*, pp. 268-69.

32. Friesen, *op. cit.*, pp. 311-12.

33. *Ibid.*, p. 297.

34. The document is given in full by Friesen, *ibid.*, pp. 297-98.

35. *Ibid.*, pp. 273-74.

36. *Ibid.*, p. 213 (English translation by F. C. Peters, as given in *An Introduction to Mennonite History*, p. 213.)

37. Friesen, *op. cit.*, p. 212. Friesen suggests that Ohrloff's reputation in Petersburg as the intellectual and cultural center since the days of Johann Cornies may have influenced government officials.

38. *Ibid.*, p. 217.

39. *Yearbook* (General Conference, 1960), p. 38.

CHAPTER V

1. Krahn, "Social Attitudes . . ." *op. cit.*, p. 173; see also Smith, *op. cit.*, p. 435.

2. Regier, *op. cit.*, p. 43.

3. Friesen, *op. cit.*, pp. 312, 313 (footnote).

4. *Ibid.*, p. 281.

5. *Ibid.*, p. 299.

6. Harms, *op. cit.*, p. 45.

7. *Ibid.*, p. 61.

8. Friesen, *op. cit.*, p. 295.

9. *Ibid.*, p. 296.

10. Harms, *op. cit.*, p. 23.

11. Friesen, *op. cit.*, p. 292.

12. Isaac, *op. cit.*, p. 175, *et al.*

13. Becker, *op. cit.*, p. 78.

14. As quoted by Becker, *ibid.*, p. 80. "Uninhibited water" the Brethren interpreted to mean "running water," which would imply baptism by immersion.

15. *Ibid.* The "three others" were apparently young women who had not been baptized before. According to P. Regier, the mode was trine immersion. *Op. cit.*, p. 45.

16. Becker, *op. cit.*, p. 90.

17. Friesen, *op. cit.*, p. 242.

18. *Ibid.*, p. 246. An old brother was admitted to communion by Jacob Reimer in Rudnerweide.

19. *Ibid.*, p. 247.

20. *Yearbook* (General Conference, 1963), p. 38.

21. Krahn, "Social Attitudes . . ." *op. cit.*, p. 173.

22. The full text of all these reports is given by Becker, *op. cit.*, pp. 97-103.

23. *Ibid.*, p. 98.

24. There appears to be no acceptable English equivalent to the term *Froehliche Richtung*. It has been variously translated as the "emotional movement," the "false freedom movement," the "movement of enthusiasts," etc.

25. Friedmann, *Mennonite Piety*, p. 69. Friedmann discusses this "awakening" in relation to Pietism.

26. See Friesen, *op. cit.*, pp. 221-236; Unruh, *op. cit.*, pp. 108-134; and Harms, *op. cit.*, pp. 25-32 for further study of the movement.

27. Friesen, *op. cit.*, p. 183.

28. Friesen quotes extensively from the correspondence of Bartel with Johann Claassen and with other brethren. These letters provide a valuable insight into the nature of the *Froehliche Richtung*. See Friesen, *op. cit.*, pp. 222-224.

29. Smith, *op. cit.*, p. 75.

30. From memoirs of H. Epp, quoted by Friesen, *op. cit.*, p. 280.

31. *Ibid.* p. 224. In a letter to Claassen (in Petersburg) Becker describes a meeting that became so noisy that several members could not "endure" it any longer and went to another home. Yet Becker justifies such behavior as proper and scriptural.

32. Unruh, *op. cit.*, p. 111.

33. Galatians 3:28.

34. Through members of the latter group, this issue was transplanted to Kansas in 1876 where it caused serious concern and considerable confusion in some congregations. Harms, *op. cit.*, pp. 74-75.

35. Friesen, *op. cit.*, p. 232.

36. Gerhard Wieler, who had imposed this restriction on the members had himself photographed in Petersburg a few months later. This shows the hypocrisy of these spiritual despots. See Friesen, *op. cit.*, p. 279.

37. The correspondence on this issue is found in Friesen, *op. cit.*, pp. 222-232, and in Unruh, *op. cit.*, pp. 115-116.

38. Cf. Harms, *op. cit.*, p. 30.

39. Friesen, *op. cit.*, pp. 357-360 contains the entire document.

40. *Ibid.*, p. 359.

41. The meetings were held on June 1 and 2, 12 and 13, and 26 and 27 in the villages of Blumstein and Gnadenheim. The minutes of the meetings are known as the *Juniprotokoll*.

42. See Friesen, *op. cit.*, pp. 362-365 for complete record of these minutes. It is interesting to note, that in the refutation of the movement the brethren stress the finality of the New Testament.

43. *Ibid.*, p. 235.

44. *Ibid.*, p. 371.

45. *Ibid.*, pp. 371-374.

46. 1 Corinthians 10:11.

47. Unruh, *op. cit.*, pp. 130-134. Unruh discusses thirteen specific lessons we have learned from the errors of the *Froehliche Richtung*.

48. *Ibid.*, p. 131.

CHAPTER VI

1. Friesen, *op. cit.*, p. 387.

2. *Ibid.*, p. 236. Although at first strongly opposed to emigration to America, as Friesen points out, Smith reports that they did come to the United States later (Smith, *op. cit.*, p. 438). The pressures of militarism in the United States during World War I again prompted them to move — this time to Canada. The author learned to know a number of "Breadbreaker" families in Alberta during the 1940's, where some of them joined the Mennonite Brethren Church.

3. Friesen, *op. cit.*, p. 388 (footnote).

4. *Ibid.*

5. The place of assembly in Mennonite Brethren circles was always called *Versammlungshaus* (meeting place) or *Bethaus* (House of Prayer) in contradistinction to *Kirche* (church), a common usage in the Mennonite Church.

6. See Friesen, *op. cit.*, p. 412.

7. J. H. Lohrenz, *op. cit.*, p. 37.

8. Unruh, *op. cit.*, p. 141.

9. Oncken even preached to several large audiences in Mennonite churches — proof that both church and state officials had changed their attitude since Liebig's visit in 1866.

10. Harms, *op. cit.*, pp. 38-39, speaks of Oncken's "inferior help" for the congregations. Friesen, *op. cit.*, p. 383 (footnote) expresses a similar sentiment.

11. *Yearbook* (General Conference, 1969), pp. 18-20.

12. Friesen, *op. cit.*, p. 384.

13. *Ibid.*, p. 385.

14. Klassen, "Roots and Development . . ." *op. cit.*, p. 143.

15. As reported by Klassen, *ibid.*, pp. 143-144.

16. Friesen, *op. cit.*, p. 398.

17. *Ibid.*, p. 419. In a letter to a friend Friesen analyzes the nature of true greatness in the Church of Christ, with special reference to the Mennonite brotherhood.

18. Friesen, *op. cit.*, p. 455.

19. See Heinrich Sawatzky, *Templer Mennonitischer Herkunft* (Winnipeg: Echo Verlag, 1955) for an interesting account of this movement.

20. Friesen, *op. cit.*, p. 394.

21. *Ibid.*, p. 395.

22. See A. A. Toews, *Mennonitische Maertyrer* (Winnipeg: Christian Press, 1949), I, 29-30.

23. Cf. *ME*, IV, 390.

24. *ME*, II, 400. Some of these families had just recently joined the Krimmer Mennonite Brethren.

25. *ME*, IV, 1015-16.

26. Friesen, *op. cit.*, pp. 427-429.

27. *Ibid.*, pp. 416-417.

28. *Ibid.*, pp. 403-407.

29. Smith, *op. cit.*, p. 440.

30. Jansen not only contacted British and United States government officials, but also began to correspond with leading American Mennonites, especially John F. Funk. See Smith, *ibid.*, pp. 444-447.

31. Quoted by Friesen, *op. cit.*, p. 413. J. H. Lohrenz estimates that about 400 members left Russia, *op. cit.*, p. 42.

32. *Ibid.* In less than fifty years, Schellenberg's intuition became a stark and tragic reality.

33. *Ibid.*, p. 414.

34. *Ibid.*, p. 409.

35. *Ibid.*

36. *Ibid.*, p. 410.

37. *Ibid.*, p. 416.

38. Kreider, "Anabaptist Conception of the Church," *op. cit.*, p. 31.

39. See Wedel, *op. cit.*, III, 185.

40. Krahn, "Social Attitudes . . .," *op. cit.*, pp. 173-174.

41. It may be of interest to note that Johann J. Harder, a son of elder Johann Harder, joined the Krimmer Mennonite Brethren in 1869 through rebaptism, and became a pioneer minister of that body.

42. Friesen, *op. cit.*, "Introduction," p. III.

CHAPTER VII

1. Smith, *op. cit.*, p. 384.

2. See Sidney Harcave, *Russia, A History* (Chicago: T. B. Lippincott, 1959), pp. 360-379 for a detailed account of Russian expansion into Asia.

3. Frank H. Epp, *Mennonite Exodus* (Altona, Manitoba: D. W. Friesen & Sons, 1962), p. 19.

4. See monograph by Heinrich Goerz, *Die Mennonitischen Siedlungen der Krim* (Winnipeg: Echo Verlag, 1957) for a description of economic, cultural and religious developments in the Mennonite settlements of the Crimea.

5. The "Kroeker Brothers" may be regarded as the "fathers of Christian publications" in the Mennonite Brethren Church of Russia. Their contributions will be discussed later.

6. Cited by A. J. Klassen in "Research Note: Sermons of David Duerksen," *Journal of Church and Society*, I:2 (1965), 64. It should be added here that the Mennonite Brethren Historical Library at Pacific College has a set of Duerksen's sermons on microfilm.

7. "Memrik," *ME*, III, 571.

8. Friesen, *op. cit.*, pp. 470-73.

9. He once confided to his colleagues, including the author, that it was this method of preaching which had saved him from bankruptcy as a preacher, a bankruptcy which he felt was often the fate of preachers who used the topical method.

10. Unruh, *op. cit.*, pp. 258-63, gives G. P. Froese's account of this experience in full.

11. *Ibid.*, pp. 201-203. See J. H. Lohrenz, *op. cit.*, pp. 311-12 for brief biographical sketch of H. Neufeld.

12. "Terek," *ME*, IV, 696. See also C. P. Toews, *Die Tereker Ansiedlung* (Rosthern: Echo Verlag, 1945).

13. Unruh, *op. cit.*, p. 203. See also J. H. Brucks and H. Hooge, *Neu-Samara* (Clearbrook, B.C.: Fraser Valley Printers, 1964) and Peter P. Dyck, *Orenburg am Ural* (Yarrow, B.C.: Columbia Press, 1951).

14. See Epp, *Mennonite Exodus*, p. 19.

15. C. Krahn in *ME*, IV, 520. Since P. M. Friesen completed his work in 1911, there is very little in his book on the Mennonites of Siberia.

16. H. M. Janzen, cited by Unruh, *op. cit.*, p. 209.

17. Friesen, *op. cit.*, p. 479. See also the book *Im Weichselbogen* (Winnipeg: Christian Press, 1971) by Erich L. Ratzlaff for comprehensive account of the Mennonite Brethren Church in Central Poland.

18. Unruh, *op. cit.*, p. 239.

19. As given by Epp in *Mennonite Exodus*, p. 21.

20. See "Forestry Service," *ME*, II, 353.

21. J. J. Toews, "Cultural Background of the Mennonite Brethren Church" (Unpublished Master's Thesis, University of Toronto, 1951), p. 235.

22. Friesen, *op. cit.*, p. 669.

23. *ME*, I, 8.

24. D. H. Epp, a nimister of the Mennonite Church, began publishing the *Botschafter* two years later, in 1905.

25. Neff in *ME*, III, 246.

26. Klassen, "Roots and Development . . .," p. 169.

27. G. Lohrenz, *A Legacy of Faith*, p. 178.

28. Quoted by G. Lohrenz, *ibid.*

29. G. W. Peters, *The Growth of Foreign Missions of the Mennonite Brethren Church* (Hillsboro, Kansas: M.B. Publishing House, 1952), pp. 53-54.

30. Stundism comes from the German *Stunde*, meaning "hour" (for worship and fellowship). This religious movement was caused by the Pietistic revival among Russians and Germans in the nineteenth century. See *ME*, IV, 649.

31. Quoted by G. Lohrenz, in *A Legacy of Faith*, p. 178.

32. As a member of a Baptist-Mennonite delegation to the U.S.S.R. in March, 1970, the author attended a meeting in Moscow in which Karev gave a historical survey of the Evangelical Christian-Baptist movement in which he stressed this influence. A mimeographed copy of Karev's history, "The Russian Evangelical Baptist Movement" (English translation by Frederick P. Loman) is now available in the Archives of Pacific College, Fresno. Karev's account of the origin of the M.B. Church is based on inadequate and sometimes false information.

33. J. J. Toews, "The Missionary Spirit of the M.B. Church in Russia," in *The Church in Mission*, edited by A. J. Klassen (Fresno, Ca.: Board of Christian Literature, 1967), p. 147.

34. Friesen, *op. cit.*, p. 560.

35. Although young Abraham Friesen was then the right-hand man of his father in the latter's large and prosperous business concerns, he had the approval and blessing of his parents for this venture. G. W. Peters *op. cit.*, p. 55.

36. J. J. Toews, in *Church in Mission*, p. 150.

37. *Ibid.*, p. 151.

38. *Ibid.*, p. 152.

39. Quoted by Friesen, *op. cit.*, p. 377.

40. *Ibid.*, p. 378.

41. *Ibid.*

42. *Ibid.*, p. 379.

43. Steinbach was the center of "Mennonite aristocracy," the home of wealthy estate-owners (*Gutsbesitzer*) such as the Schmidt family. Here more liberal views with regard to communion had prevailed for some time.

44. As reported by Unruh, *op. cit.*, p. 231. It seems strange that the question of communion, which originally had led to separation from the old church, now almost resulted in a schism within the M.B. Church.

45. Friesen, *op. cit.*, p. 379.

46. *Ibid.*, p. 440.

47. In 1930 the General Conference accepted a ruling permitting marriage with non-immersed believers. This ruling was rejected by the 1939 General Conference which returned to the earlier position. In 1948, finally, the conference made provision for the intermarriage of M.B. members with non-immersed believers. See *Resolutions of the General Conference of the Mennonite Brethren Church, 1878-1963* (Board of Reference and Counsel, 1964), p. 57.

48. Friesen, *op. cit.*, p. 259.

49. See Klassen, "Roots and Development . . .," pp. 161-163. The Darbyite Ernst Stroeter introduced pre-millennialism among the Mennonites of South Russia through these conferences.

50. Friesen, *op. cit.*, p. 540.

51. Unruh, *op. cit.*, p. 233; also Klassen "Roots and Development . . .," p. 164.

52. The Mennonites of Brazil and Paraguay continued the practice of having and inter-Mennonite K.f.K. to take care of all common religious problems of the settlements. On his first trip to the Paraguayan Chaco in 1951, the author was welcomed by the members of the K.f.K. of the Fernheim colony.

53. *ME*, III, 218.

54. Not to be confused with the "Christian and Missionary Alliance" of North America.

55. The author's father, A. A. Toews, was leading minister of this church in Lichtfelde from 1924-26. He always referred to the church as the E.M.B. Church, also in his first volume of *Mennonitische Maertyrer* (e.g. pp. 186, 198, *et al*).

56. J. C. Wenger, *Glimpses of Mennonite History and Doctrine* (Scottdale, Pa.: Herald Press, 1947), p. 98. Friesen conducted "alliance" fellowship meetings, however, in his home during the years of his residence in the city of Sevastopol.

57. The main center of the new church was in the village of Lichtfelde, where their meetinghouse was also located.

58. Friesen, *op. cit.*, p. 724. When Jakob Kroeker went to Germany, Jacob G. Thiessen (late of Vancouver, B.C.) was elected in his place.

59. The Evangelical Mennonite Brethren, however, practiced only baptism by immersion.

60. Friesen, *op. cit.*, p. 723 (footnote).

61. *Ibid.*, pp. 724-727.

62. The author was baptized and received into membership of the E.M.B. Church at Namaka, Alberta, in 1929.

CHAPTER VIII

1. Friesen, *op. cit.*, p. 413. Cf. Also "Expansion to American Continent," Chapter 6.

2. Epp, *Mennonite Exodus*, p. 29. The property liquidation laws applied only to persons with German citizenship.

3. *Ibid.*, p. 28.

4. Among them A. H. Unruh, J. A. Toews, Sr., and others.

5. Peters, *Mennonite Life*, X:1 (January, 1955), 31-35. Peters contends that the Russian experience cannot be used as a decisive precedent in defense of the 1-A-O position — the noncombatant service in the United States army.

6. John B. Toews, in *Lost Fatherland* (Scottdale, Pa.: Herald Press, 1967), p. 24, gives an excellent description of the experiences of the Mennonites during the war and after.

7. See "Allgemeiner Mennonitischer Kongress," *ME*, I, 60-61.

8. John B. Toews (*op. cit.*, p. 26) indicates that some units of the *Selbstschutz* seem to have existed prior to the German occupation.

9. *Ibid.*, p. 28.

10. *Ibid.*, p. 29.

11. Epp, *Mennonite Exodus*, p. 36.

12. See A. A. Toews, *Mennonitische Maertyrer* (2 vols., 1949 and 1954) for a comprehensive list of martyrs of faith and victims of terror.

13. The author vividly remembers this period, when as a young boy he spent days on end in the basement of the house with other members of the family, listening to the artillery bombardment and fighting on the village street.

14. Epp, *Mennonite Exodus*, p. 37.

15. Toews, *Lost Fatherland*, p. 38.

16. Hiebert, author-editor, *Feeding the Hungry* (Scottdale, Pa.: Mennonite Central Committee, 1929). See especially chapter six.

17. The author and other members of his family were also among those who benefited from the AMR feeding kitchens established in the villages.

18. Matthew 4:4.

19. Luke 12:15.

20. Cf. Epp, *Mennonite Exodus*, p. 221.

21. See H. P. Toews, *A. H. Unruh, D.D., Lebensgeschichte* (Winnipeg: Christian Press, 1961), pp. 24-30.

22. H. P. Toews, *op. cit.*, p. 27.

23. A. A. Toews, *Mennonitische Maertyrer*, I. 291.

24. Quoted by Unruh, *op. cit.*, p. 335, from *Unser Blatt*, January, 1926.

25. In his memoirs (unpublished) my father describes his personal experience during this period. He was one of the teachers who lost his position.

26. Information given by J. B. Toews, son of the late J. A. Toews, Sr., in personal interview.

27. The author belongs to the large number in the latter category. In many ways the movement could be described as "lay evangelism."

28. N. L. Saloff-Astakhoff, *Christianity in Russia* (New York: Loizeaux Brothers, 1941), p. 72.

29. G. Lohrenz, in *A Legacy of Faith*, p. 183.

30. A. A. Toews, *Mennonitische Maertyrer*, I, 68.

31. Quoted in *ibid.*, p. 69.

32. *Ibid.*, p. 70.

33. *Ibid.*, p. 71.

34. *Ibid.*, p. 133. This optimism was shared by many other Mennonites at the time, since the "liberals" in the provisional government favored such a policy.

35. *Ibid.*

36. *Ibid.*, p. 131. This village had the reputation of being strongly in favor of the *Selbstschutz*. Because the Mennonites of this village had violated their historic principle of nonresistance, Dyck and his co-workers had to pay with their lives.

37. Article reprinted from *Unser Blatt* (October, 1925), in A. H. Unruh, *op. cit.*, pp. 351-365.

38. *Ibid.*, p. 361.

39. It should be noted here that, at first, some Mennonite Brethren churches were very reluctant to cooperate in this venture. Cf. Epp, *Mennonite Exodus*, p. 72, also pp. 126-130.

40. *Ibid.*, pp. 101-105. Epp gives an excellent account of the negotiations that led to the repeal of the Order-in-Council.

41. The government in Kharkov, the capital of the Ukraine, objected to the name "Mennonite" because it was a religious designation. Hence the name *VBHH* was chosen in order to obtain a charter. Details are given by J. B. Toews in *Lost Fatherland*, pp. 74-76.

42. *Ibid.*, p. 55. The author of *Lost Fatherland* is a nephew of the late B. B. Janz.

43. *Ibid.*, pp. 102-103.

44. *Ibid.*, p. 82.

45. Quoted by Epp, *Mennonite Exodus*, p. 48.

46. "Kulak" (literally "fist") was the name given to well-to-do farmers by the Communists. As a class they opposed Soviet policies, especially the collectivization of the land.

47. The entire address is reprinted in Unruh, *op. cit.*, pp. 335-349.

48. A vivid account of the experiences of this "suffering servant" is given in A. A. Toews, *Mennonitische Maertyer*, I, 47-56. His letters and poems bear an eloquent testimony to the depth of his faith and commitment to Christ.

49. Quoted by Smith, *op. cit.*, p. 508.

50. Aron D. Rempel, *et al.*, *At the Gates of Moscow* (Yarrow, B.C.: Columbia Press, 1964).

51. Epp, in *An Introduction to Mennonite History*, p. 143.

CHAPTER IX

1. Originally a larger delegation had been planned, but only Bender and Wiens were able to obtain visas in time for the trip. Cf. Epp, *Mennonite Exodus*, pp. 459-461.

2. The author had the opportunity to meet with Mennonite Brethren leaders in March, 1970, in Taschkent as well as in Moscow. These interviews gave a general impression of faith and worship of M.B. churches.

3. Epp, *Mennonite Exodus*, pp. 462-463.

4. *Ibid.*

5. The Evangelical Christians and Baptists (actually two branches of Russian Baptists) united on October 21, 1944, to form the All-Union Council of Evangelical Christian-Baptists. Cf. Serge Bolshakoff, *Russia Nonconformity* (Philadelphia: Westminster Press, 1950), p. 121.

6. See article, "Mennonites in the U.S.S.R." by N. Teodorovich, in *Bulletin, Institute for the Study of the U.S.S.R.*, XV: 10 (October, 1968), 31.

7. V.F. Krestyaninov, *Mennonity* (Moscow, 1967), 224 pp. Copy in private library of the author.

8. *Ibid.*, p. 80.

9. Teodorovich, *op. cit.*, p. 34.

10. Krestyaninov, *op. cit.*, p. 138.

11. *Ibid.*, pp. 176-177. According to a table on p. 177, the proportion of older members in cities is still smaller. In Tomsk, for instance, almost ninety percent were under fifty.

12. In personal interviews with several M.B. ministers in 1970 I was impressed again and again with the fact of constant church growth through baptisms, mostly from the ranks of the young people.

13. Krestyaninov, *op. cit.*, pp. 110-112. The Soviet Constitution of 1936 makes no provision for conscientious objectors. In article 133 it simply states, "The defense of the Fatherland is the sacred duty of every citizen of the U.S.S.R." Quoted by Smith, *op. cit.*, p. 508.

14. See article by G. H., "The Mennonites in Soviet Russia," *Mennonite Life*, XIV: 3 (July, 1969), 108.

15. The discriminatory decrees against settlers with a German background were rescinded under N. Krushchev in 1955. See documents re: "Religious and Ethnic Groups" in *ibid.*, pp. 122-124.

16. Krestyaninov, *op. cit.*, p. 79.

17. The Mennonite Brethren in Russia deny the existence of an "underground church" in their country; they readily admit that the unregistered groups suffer from harassment and many restrictions because of their lack of legal recognition.

18. Krestyaninov, *op. cit.*, p. 159. (Translated and quoted by G. H. in "The Mennonites in the U.S.S.R.," *op. cit.*, p. 112.

CHAPTER X

1. The contributions of Funk and Krehbiel are duly acknowledged in the seventy-fifth anniversary publication, *From the Steppes to the Prairies*, edited by C. Krahn (Newton, Kansas: Mennonite Publication Office, 1949).

2. Quoted by K. Schnell, in *ibid.*, p. 72. In the years to come, Funk's own home often served as a hostel to the immigrants in transit to Kansas or Nebraska.

3. Christian Krehbiel was chosen president, David Goerz, a recently arrived immigrant as secretary, and John F. Funk as treasurer. *Ibid.*, p. 78.

4. Leland Harder, in a chapter entitled, "The Russian Mennonites and American Democracy under Grant" (*From the Steppes to the Prairies*, pp. 54-67) presents a very interesting account of this debate in the U.S. Congress.

5. Krahn, *From the Steppes to the Prairies*, p. 8.

6. From *ME*, IV, 777 (with slight revisions).

7. C. Henry Smith reports that of the 1275 families that arrived in 1874, 200 families went to Dakota, 230 to Manitoba, 15 to Minnesota, 80 to Nebraska, and 600 to Kansas. The rest, 150 families, remained in the East. *The Coming of the Russian Mennonites* (Berne, Indiana: Mennonite Book Concern, 1927), p. 107.

8. The KMB Church practiced "forward immersion." According to J. F. Harms (*op. cit.*, p. 72) the Krimmer Mennonite Brethren were reluctant to unite with the Mennonite Brethren because the latter had communion-fellowship with the Baptists and also because of their teaching on the millennium.

9. The interested student is advised to consult such sources as A. H. Unruh, *op. cit.*, J. H. Lohrenz, *op. cit.*, J. F. Harms, *op. cit.*, and especially the *Mennonite Encyclopedia*, vols. I-IV. *The Mennonite Brethren Churches of North America* (Hillsboro, Kansas: M.B. Publishing House, 1954) by Henry J. Wiens, contains a popular, although very sketchy account of local histories.

10. J. H. Lohrenz, *op. cit.*, p. 60.

11. See chapter six for a brief account of his work and influence as an "itinerating preacher" (*Reiseprediger*).

12. Harms, *op. cit.*, p. 75.

13. Two important conference leaders of the twentieth century had their spiritual roots in this congregation: H. W. Lohrenz, President of Tabor College for many years, and P. C. Hiebert, chairman of MCC from 1920-1953. Both men were ordained by elder Johann Foth in 1907.

* To assist the reader in locating churches, the first occurrence of the name of each church has been italicized.

14. J. H. Lohrenz, *op. cit.*, p. 322. In addition to church and conference responsibilities, Elder Schellenberg provided for a large family: there were seven children in his first marriage with Katharine Lohrenz and twelve children in his second marriage with Suzanna Flaming.

15. See *Konferenzberichte nebst Konstitution* (1883-1919) (Hillsboro: M.B. Publishing House, 1920), Minutes for 1894, p. 168; Minutes for 1895, p. 176; and Minutes for 1897, p. 198.

16. Harms, *op. cit.*, p. 108.

17. See booklet, *Seventy-Five Years of God's Grace* (1881-1956), p. 9.

18. *Ibid.*, p. 16.

19. *Ibid.*, p. 20.

20. *ME*, II, 538.

21. *ME*, III, 313. See also J. H. Lohrenz, *op. cit.*, p. 68.

22. The "urbanization" of Mennonite Brethren will be dealt with in a later chapter in connection with a study of Mennonite Brethren and cultural change.

23. Smith, *The Coming of the Russian Mennonites*, p. 175. To overcome this objection, the Burlington Railroad Company finally agreed to provide a deep well for a number of one quarter section farms.

24. Wiens, *ME*, II, 698.

25. *ME*, I, 389.

26. The membership had dropped to eighteen in 1954. The 1960 *Yearbook* of the General Conference does not list it under the congregations of Nebraska.

27. The development of conference organization among Mennonite Brethren will receive special consideration in a later chapter.

28. See Harms, *op. cit.*, pp. 81-84.

29. This concession to the Volga brethren was one of the main reasons for not recognizing the 1878 conference by the churches in Dakota and Minnesota. *Ibid.*, p. 84.

30. The story of the Delft and Mountain Lake M.B. Churches is told in the illustrated booklet, *80th Anniversary 1877-1957* (Mountain Lake, Minn., 1957).

31. Elder Voth's contributions in conference organization and church extension will be treated in chapter thirteen.

32. *Ibid.*, p. 26. Among them such pioneers as the N. N. Hieberts, the John H. Voths, and the A. A. Janzens.

33. See Harms, *op. cit.*, p. 86. The underlying causes of this loss of membership to the Seventh-Day Adventists in many M.B. churches of this period merits special research.

34. The present Silver Lake Church is the only M.B. congregation in South Dakota that has survived from the early settlement period.

35. Contrary to the pattern developed in Russia, few new settlements in the United States were promoted and supported by the "mother churches."

36. The Sawyer M.B. Church was largely a fruit of Reimche's efforts, See Unruh, *op. cit.*, p. 445.

37. The membership of the Harvey church in 1954 was two hundred and ten; the combined membership of the Harvey city and country churches in 1971 was only one hundred and ninety-two.

38. Harms, *op. cit.*, pp. 210-211.

39. It will be recalled that the M.B. congregation in Woodson County was dissolved in 1892.

40. See Harms, *op. cit.*, p. 95.

41. This whole episode — the long trek from Kansas to Colorado and from there to Texas and finally to Oklahoma — could be entitled: In Search of Utopia. This experience shows that many moves of Mennonite Brethren have been made on the basis of inadequate information and little investigation.

42. See article by Marvin Kroeker, "Mennonites in the Oklahoma 'Runs'," *Mennonite Life*, X (July, 1955), 114.

43. The church and town were named after a nearby post office which had received the name because of the large amount of corn raised in the immediate vicinity. The town carried the German name "Korn" until 1918, when it was changed to its present spelling. Cf. *ibid.*, p. 116.

44. Other M.B. churches established in 1890's at Gotebo, and Caddo County became extinct between 1910-1920 and members joined the Corn congregation. Members of the extinct K.M.B. congregation in Weatherford joined in the late 1930's. See *ME*, I, 711.

45. M. Kroeker, "Mennonites in the Okla. 'Runs'," *op. cit.*, p. 117.

46. See article by P. C. Grunau, "North Enid Mennonite Brethren Church," *Mennonite Life*, IX (October, 1954), 176-177.

47. A local land agency donated $2,500 toward this project! See Harms, *op. cit.*, p. 204.

48. *Yearbook* (General Conference, 1969), pp. 144-145. Total membership of these congregations in 1969 was somewhat over 300.

49. According to J. H. Lohrenz, Oregon was represented at the General Conference as early as 1892. *Op. cit.*, p. 80.

50. At present comprised by the congregations in the states of Arizona, California, Oregon and Washington.

51. This number includes six mission stations — the result of church extension work.

52. See *50th Jubilee, 1905-1955* (Reedley M.B. Church), p. 5. According to Unruh, (*op. cit.*, p. 474) one hundred and thirty members withdrew. He also mentions an "extreme holiness" teaching as a contributing factor in the schism.

53. This is a decline of more than 100 from 1954 when membership reached 595. Here we notice the same trend as in the congregations of towns in the prairie states: young people gravitate toward the larger metropolitan centers to find professional employment. The membership in the Reedley church also declined from 1436 in 1957 to 1335 in 1971.

54. See *50th Jubilee, 1905-1955*, p. 57. The founding and development of educational institutions will receive further treatment in chapter sixteen.

55. P.F. Wall, in *ME*, III, 396.

56. Gary B. Nachtigall's unpublished M.A. thesis entitled: "A Study of the Migration and Settlements of the Mennonites in Fresno and Tulare Counties of California," (Fresno State College, 1971), pp. 30-39, contains this epic story.

57. Harms, *op. cit.*, p. 170.

58. *Ibid.*, p. 172.

CHAPTER XI

1. In German the names "Canada" and "Canaan" have a similar ring. The writer recalls how older members among the immigrants would often refer to their new homeland by the latter term.

2. Up to 1867, Canada was a crown colony of Great Britain, with limited powers of self-government.

3. See J. A. Toews, *Alternative Service in Canada During World War II* (Winnipeg: Christian Press, 1959), pp. 14-19 for an account of government policy and legislative provisions for conscientious objectors.

4. These names are used to identify the two original Mennonite settlements in southern Manitoba. The East Reserve was identical with the land grant of seven townships offered to the deputies of 1873, and coextensive with the present municipality of Hanover. The boundaries of the West Reserve corresponded roughly with those of the present municipality of Rhineland and portions of adjoining municipalities, particularly Stanley.

5. "Minutes of Meeting of M.B. Church of North America" (1879-1882), p. 16.

6. See Frank Brown in his account of the 75th anniversary of the *Mennonite Brethren Church, Winkler, Manitoba* (1888-1963), p. 3. Brown mentions representatives of Swedenborg, Holdemann and of the Mormons.

7. *Konferenzberichte (1883-1919)* (Hillsboro, Kansas: M.B. Publishing House, 1920), p. 25.

8. As reported by Frank Brown, *op. cit.*, p. 4.

9. *Ibid.*, p. 8.

10. *Ibid.*, p. 42.

11. An interesting account of the religious, cultural, educational and industrial development of this Mennonite town is given by Frank Brown in an article, "Winkler, Manitoba," *Mennonite Life*, XI (July, 1956), 120-125.

12. Unruh, *op. cit.*, p. 499. The "Sommerfeld Mennonites" originated as a separate group in 1890 when the Bergthal Mennonite Church divided into a minority progressive wing and a majority conservative wing (Sommerfelder). "Old Colony Mennonites" is a socio-religious group in Manitoba which originally came from the Chortitza and Fuerstenland colonies in Russia. See *ME*, IV, 38-42.

13. See the comprehensive account of this mission by Miss Anna Thiessen, *Die Stadtmission in Winnipeg* (Winnipeg: Regehr's Printing, 1955).

14. *Ibid.*, p. 7.

15. See Anna Thiessen's account, *ibid.*, pp. 48-78, on the history of the girls' home.

16. Unruh, *op. cit.*, p. 492.

17. See article on "Saskatchewan," *ME*, IV, 424-426.

18. Harms, *op. cit.*, p. 218.

19. Quoted in "Short History of Laird Mennonite Brethren Church," (Unpublished manuscript), p. 1.

20. This congregation is now (1971) extinct.

21. As given by Harms, *op. cit.*, pp. 212-228 and Unruh, *op. cit.*, pp. 512-515, *et al.*

22. Sources with regard to date of founding and number of charter members do not always agree.

23. The writer remembers this "patriarch" of the M.B. Church as one who would encourage young brethren in the work of the ministry.

24. Again Unruh, *op. cit.*, and Harms, *op. cit.*, provide most of the data. Much information can also be obtained from the brief acounts on local congregations in the *Mennonite Encyclopedia*.

25. See Harms, *op. cit.*, p. 222.

26. *Ibid.*, p. 229. Brother Hiebert also served as a Bible colporteur in both North and South Saskatchewan, and thus met a great need in providing Christian literature.

27. The full "Bible School Story" will be told in chapter sixteen.

28. These terms are employed by E. K. Francis in his book *In Search of Utopia* (Glencoe, Illinois: The Free Press, 1955) to describe the Mennonites who arrived in the 1920's and in the 1870's, respectively. For more than two decades these designations were widely used, especially in Manitoba and Saskatchewan, to describe basic cultural differences between the two groups.

29. J. H. Lohrenz, *op. cit.*, p. 193.

30. *Ibid.*, p. 208.

31. Information on local congregations in Manitoba can be found in Unruh, *op. cit.*, and in the *Mennonite Encyclopedia*.

32. This constitutes more than one half of the total membership in the province which today (1971) stands at 4,500.

33. J. H. Lohrenz, *op. cit.*, p. 193.

34. Information found in Unruh, *op. cit.*, J. H. Lohrenz, *op. cit.*, and conference yearbooks.

35. Francis, *op. cit.*, p. 212.

36. Except for a small group organized by the elder H. Voth in 1918 at Vanderhoof, B.C., which soon disbanded.

37. *Yearbook* (Candian Conference, 1936), pp. 101-102.

38. See article by Peter F. Bargen, "The Coming of the Mennonites to Alberta," *Mennonite Life*, XI (April, 1956), 83-87. Also J. H. Lohrenz, *op. cit.*, and Unruh, *op. cit.*

39. See report of J. B. Janz as given by Unruh, *op. cit.*, p. 527.

40. Bargen, *op. cit.*, p. 86.

41. The writer was baptized and ordained to the ministry in this church.

42. See pamphlet by G. G. Baerg, *A Brief History of Mennonites in British Columbia* (Yarrow, B.C.: Columbia Press, 1967), pp. 3-4.

43. Peter D. Loewen in article, "Entstehung und Entwickelung der M.B.G. zu Yarrow, B.C.," in *Mennonitische Rundschau*, Vol. 94 (July 7, 1971), 2.

44. The ethical implications of working in the hopyards apparently did not come up for consideration in the early years.

45. For detailed account of the origin of the Abbotsford settlement see booklet by H. J. Willms, *Die Sued-Abbotsford Ansiedlung* (Yarrow, B.C.: Columbia Press, 1955).

46. This congregation was known as the McCallum Road M.B. Church for a number of years.

47. A comprehensive account of this church extension program is found in the book by Peter Penner, *Reaching the Otherwise Unreached* (Winnipeg: Christian Press, 1959).

48. See Penner, *op. cit.*, pp. 32-43, *et al.*

49. See article by Robert Giesbrecht, "Entwickelung der Vancouver M.B. Gemeinden," *Mennonitische Rundschau*, Vol. 94 (July 9, 1971), 1, 5.

50. A comprehensive account of Mennonite Brethren history in Ontario can be found in the booklet *Er fuehret . . . Geschichte der Ontario M.B. Gemeinden* (n.p., 1957) by Isaac H. Tiessen *et al.*

51. See F. C. Peters and H. Regehr (compilers and editors), *Beschluesse und Empfehlungen der Kanadischen Konferenz der Mennoniten-Bruedergemeinde, 1910-1960* (Winnipeg: Christian Press, 1961), p. 13. The Ontario Conference had joined the General Conference in 1939.

52. Tiessen, *op. cit.*, p. 9.

53. See *ibid.*, pp. 67-75 for history of New Hamburg and Hespeler M.B. churches.

54. *Ibid.*, p. 85.

55. Huebert, in *ibid.*, pp. 85-86.

56. The settlement took its name from Twenty Mile Creek, about twenty miles from Niagara Falls.

57. An attractive booklet entitled *Mennonite Brethren Church of St. Catharines*, published for the twenty-fifth anniversary in 1968 (no publisher given) contains a vivid account of the many activities of the church.

58. See Tiessen, *op. cit.*, pp. 23-26, for an account of church extension work in Ontario.

59. Information given by Ernest Dyck in "The History of the Mennonite Brethren Church in Quebec," (Unpublished manuscript, 1971).

60. *Yearbook* (Canadian Conference, 1971), p. 21.

CHAPTER XII

1. This administrator was the *Oberschulze* David Friesen, the man who was so strongly opposed to the formation of the Mennonite Brethren Church from 1860-65. Could this have been an influence which prevented Wiebe from joining the Mennonite Brethren?

2. See chapter on "A Damascus Road Experience" by David V. Wiebe in *Grace Meadow* (Hillsboro: M.B. Publishing House, 1967), pp. 20-23.

3. *Ibid.*, p. 25.

4. Quoted by David V. Wiebe, *ibid.*, p. 27.

5. So Wiebe, *ibid.* Wiebe denies that the group ever practiced "trine immersion," as reported, for instance, by H. S. Bender in the *ME*, III, 243.

6. Wiebe also denies the charge that "forward immersion" was chosen in order to avoid becoming a part of the Mennonite Brethren group. *Grace Meadow*, p. 27.

7. Bender, *ME*, III, 243.

8. Wiebe, *Grace Meadow*, p. 28. Cf. controversy on this issue in the early M.B. Church.

9. As given in *Ausgabe des Fuefzigsten Jubilaeum-Jahres* (Chicago: K.M.B. Publishing House, 1919), p. 4. Free translation from the German by the author.

10. This is the figure given by Wiebe in *Grace Meadow*, p. 28. Bender reports that the group numbered forty baptized members in 1874. *ME*, III, 243.

11. Johann Harder was the son of the well-known elder Johann Harder of the Ohrloff Mennonite Church. An autobiographical sketch of his life and spiritual pilgrimage is given in *Ausgabe des Fuenfzigsten Jubilaeum-Jahres*, pp. 5-8.

12. Wiebe, *Grace Meadow*, p. 36. Wiebe states that only three families of their church group remained in the Crimea.

13. *Ibid.*, p. 38.

14. A fascinating account of "the great Mennonite invasion" of Kansas is found in David V. Wiebe's other book, *They Seek a Country* (Hillsboro: M.B. Publishing House, 1959), pp. 66-72.

15. Wiebe, *Grace Meadow*, p. 36.

16. *Ibid.*, pp. 53-54.

17. *Yearbook* (K.M.B. Conference, 1954), p. 14.

18. *Konferenzbeschluesse der K.M.B. Gemeinde, 1882-1940* (Inman, Kansas: Salem Publishing House, 1940), p. 2.

19. *ME*, IV, 1034.

20. The church is listed for the last time in the *Yearbook* (United States Conference, 1960), p. 63. The membership at that time stood at sixty-three, and the pastor was W. W. Harms. Many joined the Lehigh-Gnadenau merger whiled other joined the Hillsboro M.B. Church.

21. *ME*, II, 203.

22. *ME*, IV, 404.

23. *Konferenzbeschluesse der K.M.B. Gemeinde*, p. 5.

24. Many families in the South Dakota congregations have their historic roots in another Anabaptist movement dating back to the sixteenth century — the Hutterian Brethren. Their ethnic background is Austrian or Tyrolese.

25. *ME*, II, 203.

26. Two sons and one son-in-law have been active M.B. conference workers through the years: Jacob as principal of the Bethany Bible Institute, Hepburn, Sask., and as associate secretary of the Board of Missions and Services; Henry as evangelist of the Canadian Conference; and Sylvester Dirks (son-in-law) as missionary to Peru.

27. Because the majority of the group belonged to the "Kleinsasser clan" (all related to the leader Rev. John Z. Kleinsasser) the tract of land came to be known as the "Kleinsasser Colony." See Gary Nachtigall, *op. cit.*, p. 31.

28. See *50th Anniversary*, Zion Mennonite Brethren Church (Dinuba, 1961), pp. 5-8.

29. C. F. Plett in *ME*, I, 310.

30. Bender in *ME*, III, 244.

31. *Ibid.*

32. *Konferenzbeschluesse der K.M.B. Gemeinde*, p. 15.

33. Smith, *The Story of the Mennonites*, pp. 658-659.

34. Wiebe, *Grace Meadow*, pp. 58-59.

35. Cf. Wiebe, *ibid.*, p. 57. The writer was impressed with the exemplary conduct of K.M.B. students attending Tabor College when he was studying there from 1937 to 1940.

36. *Ausgabe des Fuenfzigsten Jubilaeum-Jahres*, p. 21.

37. C. F. Plett, in *Missionaries Home and Abroad, 1869-1960* (Freeman, S.D.: Pine Hill Printery, 1960), pp. 93-94.

38. *ME*, III, 244.

39. In their report to the K.M.B. Conference in 1919, Hofer and Tschetter presented a comprehensive picture of their activities in city mission work. As in most early Mennonite city mission programs, children and social outcasts were the main target groups. *Ausgabe . . . , op. cit.*, pp. 23-26.

40. All issues of the 1961 *Christian Leader* carry the double imprint on the front cover.

41. *ME*, III, 245.

42. *Yearbook* (K.M.B. Conference, 1954), pp. 21-22.

43. *ME*, III, 244.

44. Plett, *Missionaries . . .*, p. 85.

45. See *Yearbook* (K.M.B. Conference, 1954), pp. 25-30.

46. Plett, *Missionaries . . .*, p. 3, *et al.*

47. *Yearbook* (K.M.B. Conference, 1960), p. 86.

48. See D. V. Wiebe, "The Gnadenau Schools" in *Grace Meadow*, pp. 68-72.
49. *Konferenzbeschluesse der K.M.B. Gemeinde*, p. 31.
50. *Ibid.*, p. 36. From some references it would appear that support for Tabor College began in 1911.
51. *Yearbook* (K.M.B. Conference, 1957), p. 45.
52. Wiebe, *Grace Meadow*, p. 67.
53. See *Grace Meadow*, p. 64. According to D. V. Wiebe, the Eckert group questioned Wiebe's status as elder, since he had been ordained in the *Kleine Gemeinde*.
54. Quoted from a brief biography of J. A. Wiebe in *ibid.*, p. 66.
55. Quoted in Yearbook (K.M.B. Conference, 1960), p. 86.
56. *Yearbook* (K.M.B. Conference, 1954), p. 14.
57. *Yearbook* (K.M.B. Conference, 1960), p. 87.
58. *Yearbook* (General Conference, 1960), p. 28.

CHAPTER XIII

1. The first joint conference was held in 1910. The significance of this event is discussed by Friesen, *op. cit.*, pp. 540-547.
2. Cf. J. H. Lohrenz, *op. cit.*, p. 72.
3. *Ibid.*
4. See Janzen, *Resolutions*, p. 113.
5. *Konferenzberichte (1883-1919)*, pp. 90-91.
6. J. H. Lohrenz, *op. cit.*, p. 329. In 1895 Wedel and his wife left for the mission field in Cameroon, Africa. After two years of successful service his health broke down. He died on his way home and was buried at sea.
7. See *Konferenzberichte*, (1904), pp. 298-308.
8. *Ibid.*, (1908), p. 393.
9. *Ibid.*, (1909), p. 419. For an interpretive analysis of Home Missions in the M.B. Conference see chapter "Facing the Mission of the Church at Home," in *The Church in Mission*, pp. 178-204.
10. *Konferenzbeschluesse* (1879-1882), p. 3.
11. *Ibid.*, p. 17. The brethren were acquainted with this mission through the articles in *Der Sendbote*, periodical of the German Baptists.
12. Janzen, *Church in Mission*, p. 158.
13. *Konferenzberichte* (1898), p. 208.
14. Janzen, *Resolutions*, p. 135.
15. *Konferenzberichte* (1909), p. 416. An interesting discussion took place on the conference floor with regard to the qualification of the Smiths for such work.
16. *Ibid.*, (1908), p. 396.
17. *Ibid.*, (1889), p. 89.
18. *Ibid.*, (1898), p. 209.
19. *Ibid.*, (1899), p. 217.
20. *Ibid.*, (1890), p. 107.
21. The late J. F. Harms, the conference secretary for many years and associated with Schellenberg in the Executive, has shared with the writer some of his observations about the rivalry that would manifest itself from time to time between leading elders on the conference floor.
22. Friesen, *op. cit.*, II, pp. 36-37.
23. *Konferenzberichte* (1902), pp. 268-269.
24. Janzen, *Resolutions*, p. 11.
25. *Ibid.*, p. 12.
26. In 1963 the name of the conference was changed. The words "of North America" were deleted, and the word "church" (singular) was changed to "churches." The latter change implied a re-orientation in the concept of the church. See *Yearbook* (General Conference, 1963), pp. 43-45.
27. J. H. Lohrenz, *op. cit.*, p. 81.
28. Janzen, *Resolutions*, p. 13.
29. The early ties of the Winkler M.B. Church with the Minnesota churches, initiated through the ministry of elder H. Voth, appear to have been the motivation for joining the Central District for a time.
30. Although membership in the Northern District on January 1, 1948 was approximately one-half of the total conference membership, there were only two

brethren from Canada on the seven-man Committee of Reference and Counsel, two out of nine on the Board of Trustees, and two out of five on the Board of Foreign Missions. See *Yearbook* (General Conference, 1948), pp. 43, 155.

31. *Yearbook* (General Conference, 1924), p. 19.

32. *Ibid.*

33. Janzen, *Resolutions*, p. 108.

34. The expression, "fuer bedraengte Kinder Gottes," occurs in the yearbooks of 1900, 1901, 1902, 1903 and 1904. See *ibid.*, p. 41.

35. *Konferenzberichte*, pp. 224, 225.

36. Reported by Clarence Hiebert in *Church in Mission*, p. 348.

37. At the conference in Reedley in 1921 Wilhelm Neufeld reported on the famine and destitute conditions of the brethren in Russia. The conference then agreed to put forth every effort ($1.00 per member every month is suggested) to alleviate suffering and channel these funds through MCC. *Yearbook* (General Conference, 1921), p. 50.

38. *Yearbook* (General Conference, 1924), p. 60.

39. *Konferenzberichte*, pp. 502-503.

40. See "Statistical Report," *Yearbook* (General Conference, 1954), p. 130.

41. See Thiessen, *Die Stadtmission in Winnipeg*, pp. 47ff.

42. *Beschluesse und Empfehlungen*, pp. 141-145.

43. *Yearbook* (Canadian Conference, 1944), p. 15.

44. *Yearbook* (Canadian Conference, 1950), p. 90.

45. *Yearbook* (General Conference, 1943), pp. 25, 27.

46. *Yearbook* (Canadian Conference, 1944), p. 19.

47. *Yearbook* (Canadian Conference, 1946), pp. 73, 77.

48. See J. H. Lohrenz, *op. cit.*, for an account of the home missions work of the Southern District Conference, pp. 140-144; the Central District Conference, pp. 155-158; and the Pacific District Conference, pp. 168-172.

49. *Yearbook* (Pacific District Conference, 1942), p. 23.

50. *Yearbook* (General Conference, 1945), p. 57.

51. *Yearbook* (General Conference, 1951), p. 120.

52. *Yearbook* (Pacific District Conference, 1951), p. 55.

53. *Yearbook* (General Conference, 1954), pp. 59, 61.

54. *Yearbook* (General Conference, 1954), pp. 17-19.

55. Both practices have become quite general throughout the M.B. Church in North America, especially after 1963.

56. *Yearbook* (General Conference, 1936), p. 68.

57. Janzen, *Resolutions*, p. 1.

58. It should be mentioned here that as a result of the Nazi movement, the M.B. churches in Paraguay had been divided into two camps. A prolonged ministry of B. B. Janz in the colonies of Fernheim and Friesland resulted in reconciliation and renewal. Hence the reference to the "reorientated church."

59. *Yearbook* (General Conference, 1948), p. 3.

60. Janzen in *Church in Mission*, p. 164.

61. *Ibid.*, p. 165.

62. *Ibid.*, p. 166.

63. *Yearbook* (General Conference, 1963), p. 121.

CHAPTER XIV

1. Friesen, *op. cit.*, p. 388.

2. Institutional education will be dealt with in chapter sixteen.

3. Cf. Unruh, *op. cit.*, p. 241.

4. *Ibid.*

5. *Ibid.*

6. See article, "Sunday School," in *A Century of Grace and Witness 1860-1960* (Hillsboro: M.B. Publishing House, 1960), p. 50.

7. Walter Quiring, a Mennonite historian, in private correspondence with A. H. Unruh, lists the Sunday school as one of the innovations brought into the larger Mennonite brotherhood by the Mennonite Brethren.

8. *Konferenzberichte*, p. 15.

9. Janzen, *Resolutions*, p. 162.

10. *Ibid.*

11. *Ibid.*

12. *Konferenzberichte*, p. 268.

13. Redekopp in *A Century of Grace and Witness*, p. 50.

14. *Yearbook* (General Conference, 1924), pp. 46-47.

15. *Yearbook* (General Conference, 1939), p. 20.

16. According to our survey in the fall of 1971, several Sunday school classes in the Reedley M.B. Church were still conducted in German.

17. *Yearbook* (General Conference, 1951), p. 76.

18. In *A Century of Grace and Witness*, p. 51.

19. *Yearbook* (United States Conference, 1958), p. 19.

20. *Yearbook* (United States Conference, 1960), p. 47.

21. *Yearbook* (United States Conference, 1961), p. 25.

22. In 1951 the name of the Sunday School Committee of the General Conference was officially changed to "Church School Committee." (*Yearbook*, General Conference, 1951, p. 75). This change of name reflects the enlarged vision of the brethren in this field with regard to the nature and scope of Christian education in the local church.

23. See *Yearbook* (United States Conference, 1959), p. 18.

24. Explained more fully in chapter eighteen.

25. Cited by Unruh, *op. cit.*, p. 654.

26. See report in *Yearbook* (Canadian Conference, 1943), pp. 32-35.

27. *Yearbook* (Canadian Conference, 1957), pp. 57-58.

28. *Yearbook* (Canadian Conference, 1961), p. 109.

29. *Yearbook* (Canadian Conference, 1962), p. 216.

30. *Yearbook* (Canadian Conference, 1964), p. 51.

31. *Yearbook* (Canadian Conference, 1965), pp. 53-54.

32. *Yearbook* (Canadian Conference, 1964), p. 50.

33. *Yearbook* (General Conference, 1969), p. 110.

34. *Yearbook* (Canadian Conference, 1969), p. 105.

35. Mission Sunday schools have been subjected to severe criticism because they served as a means of segregating the children of the community from the children of church members. It should be remembered, however, that in the 1950's most M.B. Sunday schools in Canada were still conducted in German, and thus this "mission Sunday school" appeared to be the best solution.

36. H. F. Toews, cited by Unruh, *op. cit.*, p. 652.

37. Quoted by Ruth Wiens in "A Study of the Present Task of the Sunday School in the Light of Its Historical Background and Today's Changing World" (Unpublished M.R.E. thesis, M.B. Biblical Seminary, 1965), p. 2.

38. Cf. Peters, "A Study of Youth Work in the Mennonite Brethren Church" (Unpublished B.D. thesis, M.B. Biblical Seminary, 1965), p. 5.

39. Friesen, *op. cit.*, pp. 569-653.

40. As given by Unruh, *op. cit.*, p. 164.

41. *Ibid.*, p. 241. The writer was a member of a Christian "boys' club" (*Knabenverein*) in the 1920's. The club would meet on Sunday afternoons, and had as a primary objective the conversion of unsaved friends.

42. In "Our Youth," *A Century of Grace and Witness*, p. 63.

43. Wiebe translates *Jugendvereine* with the more modern designation of "Christian Endeavors." *Ibid.*

44. *Ibid.*

45. The complete draft of the constitution of the *Jugendverein* of the Winkler M.B. Church is reproduced by Unruh, *op. cit.*, pp. 641-645.

46. Alan Peters, *op. cit.*, pp. 10-11.

47. *Yearbook* (General Conference, 1945), p. 66.

48. *Yearbook* (General Conference, 1933), p. 62.

49. *Yearbook* (General Conference, 1951), p. 19 (with slight revisions).

50. Cf. *Yearbook* (General Conference, 1943), p. 58.

51. See Alan Peters, *op. cit.*, p. 11.

52. *Ibid.*, p. 25.

53. *Yearbook* (Canadian Conference, 1944), p. 85.

54. *Yearbook* (Canadian Conference, 1945), p. 104.

55. *Ibid.*, p. 106. In accepting this recommendation the delegates also went on record that *The Christian Leader*, the youth paper of the M.B. General Conference, should be more widely recommended and read by Canadian young people.

56. *Yearbook* (Canadian Conference, 1957), p. 103.

57. *Yearbook* (Canadian Conference, 1962), p. 231.
58. Wiebe, in *A Century of Grace and Witness*, p. 66.
59. *Ibid.*, p. 67.
60. Harold Jantz, in *Mennonite Brethren Herald* (January 14, 1972), p. 12.
61. *Yearbook* (Southern District Conference, 1969), p. 15. The present director (1972) is Victor Timnick, returned missionary from Austria.
62. The K.M.B. churches had been cooperating with other Mennonites at Camp Byron prior to 1960. See *Yearbook* (Central District Conference, 1961), p. 48.
63. See Peter Penner, "A Historical Survey of the Home Mission Work of the Mennonite Brethren Conference of Canada" (Unpublished Th.B. thesis, Mennonite Brethren Bible College, 1957), p. 81.
64. *Konferenz-Jugendblatt* (May-June, 1952), p. 7.
65. See *Konferenz-Jugendblatt* (February-April, 1949), pp. 12-14.
66. Peter Penner, *Reaching the Otherwise Unreached*, p. 101.
67. *Yearbook* (Ontario Conference, 1971), pp. 30-31.

CHAPTER XV

1. Becker, *op. cit.*, p. 98.
2. *Ibid.*, p. 102.
3. *Ibid.*, p. 101.
4. *Ibid.*, p. 92.
5. Esther Horch, "Music in the Mennonite Brethren Church," (Unpublished manuscript), p. 2.
6. Herbert C. Richert, "Music History: Mennonite Brethren, U.S.A." (Unpub. manuscript), p. 1.
7. "Hymnology of the Mennonites of West and East Prussia, Danzig, and Russia," *ME*, II, 879.
8. *ME*, II, 878.
9. *ME*, II, 878.
10. Other commonly used German hymnals of non-Mennonite Brethren origin were *Glaubens-Harfe* (German Baptist, 1885); *Pilgerklaenge* (1907); *Wahrheits-Kluenge* (1920); *Frohe Botschaft* (1896); *Die Kleine Palme* (1895), *No. 2*, and *No. 3*; *Lieder fuer Kinder Gottes* (1899); *Liederperlen; Jubel Klaenge; Evangeliums Saenger; Silber Klaenge; Gebet und Danklieder; Kleiner Liederschatz; Lobe den Herrn* (1905) and many others.
11. *Yearbook* (Canadian Conference, 1952), p. 89.
12. *Yearbook* (General Conference, 1945), p. 73.
13. *Ibid.*
14. *Yearbook* (General Conference, 1948), p. 96.
15. *Yearbook* (General Conference, 1951), pp. 96-98.
16. Paul William Wohlgemuth, "Mennonite Hymnals Published in the English Language," (Unpub. doctoral diss., University of Southern California, 1956), p. 336.
17. Herbert C. Richert, Music Editor, *Mennonite Brethren Church Hymnal* (Hillsboro, Kan.: Mennonite Brethren Publishing House, 1953), p. iii.
18. *The Hymn Book* (Winnipeg: Canadian Conference of the Mennonite Brethren Church of North America, 1960), p. iv. Cf. *Yearbook* (Canadian Conference, 1955), p. 101.
19. *The Hymn Book*, p. iv.
20. *Yearbook* (Canadian Conference, 1963), p. 12.
21. *Yearbook* (General Conference, 1963), p. 121.
22. *Yearbook* (General Conference, 1966), p. 128.
23. *Worship Hymnal* (General Conference of Mennonite Brethren Churches, 1971), p. iii.
24. *The Hymn*, XXIII (January, 1972), 30.
25. Unruh, *op. cit.*, p. 744.
26. *Konferenzberichte* (1919), pp. 498-501.
27. Eva Janzen, "Story of My Life," (Unpublished manuscript, 1970), p. 10.
28. Richert, *op. cit.*, pp. 3-4.
29. *Ibid.*
30. *Konferenzberichte* (1893), p. 155.
31. *Konferenzberichte* (1919), pp. 498-501.
32. *Yearbook* (General Conference, 1921), pp. 48-49, 76.
33. *Yearbook* (General Conference, 1924), p. 48.
34. *Yearbook* (General Conference, 1927), pp. 66, 72.

35. *Yearbook* (General Conference, 1945), p. 73.
36. *Yearbook* (United States Conference, 1959), p. 42.
37. Horch, *op. cit.*, pp. 3-4.

CHAPTER XVI

1. This is true, for instance, of the connection made between "German and religion" in the Bible academies (high schools) as well as in the Bible institutes in their earlier history.
2. In *Church in Mission*, p. 208.
3. *The Voice*, VII:5 (Sept.-Oct., 1958), 8.
4. S. A. Witmer, *The Bible College Story: Education with Dimension* (Manhasset, N.Y.: Channel Press, 1962), p. 39.
5. J. H. Lohrenz, *op. cit.*, p. 76.
6. Cited by F. C. Peters in "The Coming of the Mennonite Brethren to the United States and Their Efforts in Education" (Unpublished Th.D. dissertation, Central Baptist Theological Seminary, 1957), p. 105.
7. Cf. J. W. Vogt in *ME*, I, 710.
8. Cf. the sixtieth anniversary booklet *Hitherto the Lord Has Helped Us* of the Mennonite Brethren Church, North Enid, Oklahoma (1957), pp. 31-33.
9. Cited by F. C. Peters, "Coming of the Mennonite Brethren," p. 170.
10. *Ibid.*, p. 171.
11. It will be recalled that this was the period of tensions in the Reedley M.B. Church which led to the withdrawal of some 150 members and the establishment of an independent congregation in Dinuba. Cf. chapter ten.
12. *A Century of Grace and Witness*, p. 39.
13. Inter-Mennonite schools such as the Mountain Lake Bible School and the Lustre Bible Academy will be considered in the chapter dealing with inter-church relations (chapter twenty-two).
14. "M.B. Bible Schools in Canada" in *Konferenz-Jugendblatt*, Vol. eleven, No. 62 (Nov.-Dec., 1955) gives a historical survey of the M.B. Bible schools operating at that time. See also *The Bible School Story: Fifty Years of Mennonite Brethren Bible Schools in Canada 1913-1963*, edited by A. J. Klassen.
15. Both Bestvater and Harms (the latter through John F. Funk, Elkhart) appear to have been inspired to establish Bible schools in their own brotherhood by the pattern and program at the Moody Bible Institute.
16. As given in the *Konferenz-Jugendblatt* (Nov.-Dec., 1955), p. 9.
17. Cf. John G. Doerksen, "History of Education of Mennonite Brethren in Canada" (Unpublished M.Ed. thesis, Winnipeg, 1963), p. 50.
18. *Ibid.*
19. Harms had been a student of the Bible Institute of Los Angeles and was a graduate of Moody Bible Institute of Chicago. See report in *Konferenz-Jugendblatt* (Nov.-Dec., 1955), p. 12.
20. *Ibid.*, p. 13.
21. Doerksen, *op. cit.*, p. 84.
22. Cf. *ibid.*, p. 68. Schierling had attended the Tschongraw Bible School (Crimea) for four years.
23. *The Torchbearer: the Coaldale Bible School Jubilee Yearbook, 1929-1954*, pp. 26-30.
24. Doerksen, *op. cit.*, p. 70.
25. See Doerksen *op. cit.*, pp. 77-81; 85-87.
26. H. Warkentin in *ME*, IV, 1000.
27. As reported in the *Mennonite Brethren Herald*, IV:12 (March 26, 1965), 5.
28. Cf. Doerksen, *op. cit.*, p. 132.
29. *Ibid.*, p. 125. The "rivalry" was not between the schools, but between the supporters of these schools.
30. See *ibid.*, pp. 107-114, for an historical account of the development of Eden Christian College.
31. Quoted by H. P. Peters, *History and Development of Education Among the Mennonites in Kansas* (Hillsboro, 1925), p. 164.
32. *Konferenzberichte* (1898), p. 208.
33. Quoted by H. P. Peters, *op. cit.*, p. 165.
34. *Konferenzberichte* (1899), p. 216.
35. According to F. C. Peters (*op. cit.*, p. 124) there were more basic reasons for

terminating the relationship with McPherson College. One reason was the desire of many brethren to build a conference school. Another reason suggested is that the nature of the educational pattern in the German Department (instruction in German and Bible) was not found to be feasible in the United States.

36. Cf. A. E. Janzen, *A History of Tabor College*, Part One (Hillsboro: M.B. Publishing House, 1958), p. 11. P. C. Hiebert was minister of the M.B. church at Dallas, Oregon during 1907-1908.

37. *Ibid.*, p. 17. Other names suggested were "Mennonite Brethren Academy" and "Mennonite Brethren College."

38. Prieb in article, "Tabor College," *ME*, IV, 679.

39. Janzen, *History of Tabor*, p. 27. Lohrenz served as president from 1908 to 1931.

40. Franz in *A Century of Grace and Witness*, p. 32.

41. The erection of the dormitory was made possible by an annuity gift of $15,000 by Miss Mary J. Regier, one of Tabor's former students. See H. P. Peters, *op. cit.*, p. 176.

42. Prieb, *ME*, IV, 680.

43. *Yearbook* (General Conference, 1933), pp. 41-42.

44. Cf. Wesley Prieb in *ME*, IV, 681.

45. Among the teachers at the M.B. Bible College in Winnipeg prior to 1965 there were seven who had received part of their training in Tabor — including three presidents.

46. G. W. Peters in *ME*, IV, 103.

47. *Annual Catalogue* (1953-1954), pp. 41-43.

48. In his thesis "A Follow-Up Study of the Graduates of Pacific Bible Institute-Junior College from 1946 to 1959" Harold E. Gaede has explored various aspects of the further education, vocation, and life of the graduates of the school in the earlier period. (Unpublished M.A. thesis, Fresno State College, 1960).

49. *Pacific College Catalog* (1971-1972), pp. 11-12.

50. Witmer, *op. cit.*, p. 26.

51. *Yearbook* (Canadian Conference, 1939), p. 25.

52. Provision was made for an "advanced class" to be taught during the 1943-44 school year at the Winkler Bible School.

53. Witmer, *op. cit.*, p. 82.

54. Cf. *Yearbook* (Canadian Conference, 1965), p. 117.

55. Doerksen, *op. cit.*, p. 166.

56. *Proceedings of the Seventh Mennonite World Conference* (1962), p. 175.

57. *Yearbook* (General Conference, 1948), p. 76. The Commission was composed of the following brethren: Northern District: H. H. Nickel, A. A. Kroeker; Central District: H. E. Wiens, D. E. Friesen; Southern District: J. W. Vogt, P. C. Hiebert; Pacific District: H. R. Wiens, Waldo Wiebe.

58. See *Yearbook* (General Conference, 1951), pp. 118-120. The Commission also reported that M.B. ministers up to that time had received their theological training in fifteen different schools or seminaries.

59. It should be mentioned that the Canadian delegation abstained from discussions and voting on the "unification issue." A major reason for abstention was the view of the majority of the Canadian delegates that their churches were not as yet ready to commit themselves to support a seminary program.

60. Although the early catalogs of the seminary contain a Confession of Faith, there is no reference to the school's basic theological stance as an Anabaptist-Mennonite institution.

61. See *Catalog* 1965-1966, pp. 17-18.

62. *Yearbook* (General Conference, 1969), p. 33. The responses of the two area conferences are also given in the *Yearbook*, pp. 33-38.

63. Friesen, *op. cit.*, pp. 637-638.

CHAPTER XVII

1. In *A Century of Grace and Witness*, p. 45.

2. Unruh, *op. cit.*, p. 254. The "Kroeker Brothers" did much to remedy this situation prior to World War I as noted in a earlier chapter.

3. *Konferenzberichte*, p. 14.

4. Harms, *op. cit.*, p. 264.

5. In his brief autobiography, *Meine Lebensreise* (Hillsboro, Kansas, 1943) Harms gives an interesting account of the early period of his life up to the time of his emigration to the United States.

6. Harms' first wife, Marie Isaac, died in childbirth in 1876.

7. It was during these years also that Harms attended the Evangelical College, Naperville, Ill., for two years.

8. See Harms, *op. cit.*, pp. 263-274, for an account of the financial arrangements the conference made with him from year to year.

9. *Ibid.*, p. 266.

10. Cf. Orlando Harms, *A Century of Grace and Witness*, p. 45.

11. See J. H. Lohrenz, *op. cit.*, p. 90.

12. See article, "Ein letztes Wort vom Editor," *Zionsbote* (May 21, 1930), p. 15.

13. *Konferenzberichte* (1908), p. 395.

14. This view is expressed by T. R. Schellenberg in an article entitled "Editor Abraham L. Schellenberg," *Mennonite Life*, IX (Jan., 1954), 22.

15. *Konferenzberichte* (1919), p. 497.

16. Quoted by T. R. Schellenberg, *op. cit.*, p. 26.

17. *Ibid.*

18. *Ibid.*

19. He served as mayor of the town for several terms, and sat on the Board of Directors of Tabor College. *Ibid.*, p. 27.

20. As cited by F. H. Epp in *Mennonite Exodus*, p. 126.

21. *Ibid.*

22. See "Eine Erklaerung," *Yearbook* (General Conference, 1930), p. 44. This "explanation" was in response to Schellenberg's "last word" (*Zionsbote*, May 21, 1930) in which he charged the Hillsboro church leadership as well as certain brethren of the Publications Committee with continued "hostility and molestations."

23. The paper's name was changed to *Der Bote* in 1935. In 1947 it merged with the *Christlicher Bundesbote* and thus became an organ of the General Conference Mennonite Church (*ME* I, 395).

24. In *A Century of Grace and Witness*, p. 49.

25. *Yearbook* (Canadian Conference, 1949), p. 19.

26. *Yearbook* (Canadian Conference, 1951), p. 8.

27. *Yearbook* (Canadian Conference, 1950), p. 34.

28. *Ibid.*, p. 36.

29. *Yearbook* (Canadian Conference, 1952), p. 137.

30. *Yearbook* (Canadian Conference, 1951), p. 8.

31. In the *Mennonite Observer*, VII:52 (December 29, 1961), 10.

32. *Yearbook* (Canadian Conference, 1957), p. 95.

33. *Yearbook* (General Conference, 1957), p. 62.

34. *Yearbook* (General Conference, 1960), p. 115.

35. *Yearbook* (Canadian Conference, 1961), p. 229.

36. The novel, written about Mennonites from Russia living in Western Canada during World War II (1944), was considered far too "critical" by many readers, although it was given a positive review by such well-known Christian magazines as *Christianity Today*.

37. *The Mennonite Brethren Herald*, II:26 (June 28, 1963), 3.

38. *Yearbook* (General Conference, 1933), p. 47.

39. *Yearbook* (General Conference, 1936), p. 39.

40. It should be noted that until 1951 the manager and editors were not appointed by the Board of Publications (which is the present practice) but were elected by the conference.

41. See *A Century of Grace and Witness*, p. 46.

42. *Yearbook* (United States Conference, 1958), p. 22.

43. *Yearbook* (General Conference, 1963), p. 138.

44. Harms, *A Century of Grace and Witness*, p. 47. For a comprehensive though not exhaustive guide to literature by and about Mennonite Brethren the reader should consult *A Bibliographic Guide to Information* (Winnipeg: Christian Press, 1971), compiled by Herbert Giesbrecht.

45. *Yearbook* (General Conference, 1963), p. 41.

46. Report, *Yearbook* (General Conference, 1966), p. 108.

47. *Yearbook* (General Conference, 1969), p. 88.

48. *Newsletter* (Board of Christian Literature, Number 11, April, 1972), p. 1. This subscription number was almost the same as that for *Worship Together*.

CHAPTER XVIII

1. Franz Isaac, *op. cit.*, p. 182.

2. The occasion for this "brief explanation" (*Kurzgefasste Erklaerung*) was the charge of local authorities that a young man had been baptized by an "unauthorized" (unordained) person. See Friesen, *op. cit.*, p. 388.

3. Translation by A. J. Klassen, "Brief Statement of the Rules and Outward Regulations of Our Church," *Journal of Church and Society*, I:2 (Fall, 1965), 62, 63.

4. The list of four candidates as well as all voters (and how they voted!) is found in Friesen, *op. cit.*, p. 295.

5. On the advice of the brethren Becker resigned from the ministry because of his involvement with the *Froehliche Richtung* (*Ibid.*, p. 201).

6. *Ibid.*, p. 438. In addition twenty deacons and twenty candidates are mentioned.

7. *Confession of Faith* (American Edition), p. 27.

8. See account of this whole affair by A. P. Willms as given by Unruh, *op. cit.*, pp. 233-235.

9. Quoted by Unruh, *ibid.*, p. 235.

10. *Ibid.*

11. According to the reports sent in by the churches and other information gathered by the writer, the following elders have been ordained in Mennonite Brethren and former Krimmer Mennonite Brethren churches in the United States with year and place of ordination in parenthesis: Heinrich Adrian (1881, Parker, S.D.), Johann Foth (1884, Ebenfeld), Heinrich Voth (1885, Bingham Lake), David Dyck (1890, Lehigh), Jacob Friesen (1895, Joes, Co.), P. P. Regier (1902, Enid), John J. Kliewer (1908, Henderson), P. P. Rempel (1910, Hillsboro), B. B. Fadenrecht (1912, Munich, N.D.), H. H. Flaming (1914, Corn), John J. Friesen (1915, Gnadenau), Jacob M. Tschetter (1917, Yale, S.D.), Jacob Reimer (1919, Bessie, Okla.), David W. Tschetter (1925, Bridgewater, S.D.), and K. K. Willms (1932, Zoar). No date is given for the ordination of Gerhard P. Regehr in the Mountain Lake M.B. Church.

12. The Buhler M.B. Church had a salaried pastor six years earlier (1930), but the Buhler situation was unique in several respects.

13. See article, "The Ministry a Shared Task," *The Christian Leader* (July 14, 1970), p. 3.

14. J. H. Lohrenz, *op. cit.*, p. 193.

15. Cf. *The Bible School Story (1913-1963)*, p. 17.

16. *Yearbook* (General Conference, 1933), p. 65.

17. *Yearbook* (General Conference, 1948), p. 106.

18. *Ibid.*, pp. 106-107.

19. Cf. *Yearbook* (General Conference, 1951), pp. 124-144.

20. *Ibid.*, p. 131.

21. *Yearbook* (General Conference, 1954), p. 20.

22. Unruh, *op. cit.*, p. 591.

23. They were designated as "minister to the poor" (*Armendiener*), or "keeper of the alms" (*Almosenpfleger*).

24. *Confession of Faith* (American Edition), p. 24.

25. Friesen, *op. cit.*, p. 201.

26. *Ibid.*, p. 382.

27. *Konferenzberichte*, p. 504.

28. *Yearbook* (General Conference, 1960), p. 103.

29. J. H. Lohrenz, *op. cit.*, p. 141.

30. Unruh, *op. cit.*, p. 832.

31. *Yearbook* (Canadian Conference, 1953), p. 38.

32. *Yearbook* (United States Conference, 1957), p. 29.

33. *Yearbook* (United States Conference, 1959), p. 14.

34. See *Yearbook* (United States Conference, 1965), pp. 20-26, for an analysis and assessment of the program.

35. *Yearbook* (United States Conference, 1968), p. 21.

36. *Yearbook* (Canadian Conference, 1966), p. 91.

37. See the March-April, 1955 issue of this periodical for a brief historical sketch of these radio ministries. See also Peter Penner, "A Historical Survey of the Home Mission Work of the Mennonite Brethren Conference of Canada" for brief notes on M.B. radio ministries.

38. John M. Schmidt was the radio-evangelist of the Gospel Light Hour for thirteen years (1950-1963).

39. *Yearbook* (Canadian Conference, 1966), p. 94.

40. During his brief visit to the Soviet Union in March, 1970, the author discovered that the Russian Gospel Light program is well known in various parts of that vast country.

41. *Yearbook* (United States Conference, 1968), p. 12.

42. Cf. *Yearbook* (United States Conference, 1971), p. 42.

CHAPTER XIX

1. An excellent historical survey of the various positions taken by the church through the centuries is found in the book by H. Richard Niebuhr, *Christ and Culture* (Harper: 1951).

2. See Smith, *The Story of the Mennonites*, p. 279.

3. *Ibid.*, p. 703. See also F. H. Epp, *op. cit.*, p. 317, and C. Krahn in *ME*, III, 371.

4. *Konferenzbeschluesse* (1879-1882), p. 12.

5. *Konferenzberichte* (1883-1919), p. 14.

6. Cf. Wiebe, *Grace Meadow*, p. 69.

7. See account of his work in chapter on publication.

8. See T. R. Schellenberg in *Mennonite Life*, IX:1 (January, 1954), 25.

9. The importance of a gradual transition from the use of one language to another for the preservation of spiritual values can hardly be overestimated. The author was involved in a church situation at one time where a congregation made a complete language change within one year. This lack of continuity caused hardship in communication for both young and old.

10. In Reedley some Sunday school classes for older people were still held in German in 1971.

11. *Yearbook* (Canadian Conference, 1911), p. 14.

12. Quoted by F. H. Epp in paper "National Socialism Among Canadian Mennonites in the 1930's" prepared for the fifteenth Conference on Mennonite Educational and Cultural Problems (Bluffton, 1965), p. 1.

13. Quoted by Epp in *Mennonite Exodus*, p. 325.

14. Quoted by Epp, *ibid.*

15. Cited by Epp, *ibid.*, p. 324.

16. See report in *Yearbook* (Canadian Conference, 1962), pp. 143, 149.

17. *Yearbook* (Canadian Conference, 1950), p. 90.

18. Leland Harder, "Mennonite Mobility and Christian Calling," *Mennonite Life*, XIX:1 (January, 1964), 7.

19. *Ibid.*, p. 11.

20. On urbanization of Mennonites in Canada see the October, 1968, issue of *Mennonite Life*. On the urbanization of Mennonites in general, and especially of the General Conference Mennonites, see the January, 1964, issue of the same periodical.

21. The survey was made by students of the Mennonite Brethren Biblical Seminary during the winter quarter, 1972. It may not be accurate in all details, but indicates the dimension of this problem.

22. See Leo Driedger in "A Perspective on Canadian Mennonite Urbanization," *Mennonite Life*, XXIII:4 (October, 1968), 149.

23. Harder, *op. cit.*, p. 9.

24. The division between urban and rural churches is somewhat arbitrary. Churches located in cities with a population of 10,000 or more have been classified as urban.

25. Information gathered from *Yearbook* (General Conference, 1951), pp. 222-242, and the *Calendar of Activities* (1971), pp. 30-42.

26. See study by Peter Letkemann, "Mennonites in Vancouver — A Survey," *Mennonite Life*, XXIII:4 (October, 1968), 161.

27. "Die Stadtgemeinde in der Mennonitischen Bruderschaft," *The Voice*, V:4 (1956) by J. A. Toews, attempts to answer this question.

28. Quoted by J. Richard Burkholder in a review entitled, "From Farm to City," in *Mennonite Life*, XIX:1 (January, 1964), 46.

29. *Konferenzberichte* (1883), p. 9.

30. *Ibid.*, p. 153. Of some significance is the fact that specially designated gifts for foreign missions were almost twice as high that same year.

31. *Yearbook* (General Conference, 1951), p. 20.

32. *Yearbook* (General Conference, 1960), p. 104.

33. Rudy Wiebe in "The Meaning of Being Mennonite Brethren," *Mennonite Brethren Herald*, IX:8 (April 17, 1970), 4. According to some estimates there are today more than a dozen millionaires within the M.B. Church of North America.

34. See "Der Materielle Wohlstand — Eine Geistliche Gefahr," by J. A. Toews in *The Voice*, XIV:4 (1965), 10-13.

35. *Konferenzberichte* (1890), p. 109.

36. *Yearbook* (General Conference, 1927), p. 69.

37. *Konferenzberichte* (1897), p. 198.

38. See *Yearbook* (Canadian Conference, 1954), p. 85. This "declaration" was accepted by the conference and reaffirmed at the 1958 convention with slight changes. See *Yearbook* (1958), pp. 154-155.

39. J. A. Toews in *The Voice*, XV:6 (1966), 3.

CHAPTER XX

1. Roland Bainton, *Christian Attitudes Toward War and Peace* (New York: Abingdon Press, 1960), p. 14. Even Walter Bienert, who finds some justification for the Christian's participation in war in the New Testament admits that Christians in the second century could not reconcile their Christian vocation with military service. Cited by J. A. Toews, *True Nonresistance Through Christ* (Winnipeg: Christian Press, 1955), p. 54.

2. Bainton, *op. cit.*

3. Cf. Menno Simons, *CW*, p. 922.

4. See "The Schleitheim Confession of Faith" (1527) as reprinted in Wenger, *Glimpses of Mennonite History and Doctrine*, p. 210.

5. Quoted by Bender in *ME*, IV, 613.

6. Leonard Verduin, *The Reformers and Their Stepchildren* (Grand Rapids: Wm. B. Eerdmans, 1964), p. 17. This well-documented book contains one of the most penetrating analyses of the basic issues that divided the Anabaptists and the Reformers.

7. The two Mennonites, H. Bergmann and P. Schroeder, who served as elected members of the *Duma* for some time, were not members of the M.B. Church. Cf. *ME*, II, 108.

8. *Confession, op. cit.*, p. 39.

9. Harms, *op. cit.*, p. 83.

10. See Bender in *ME*, IV, 615.

11. *Konferenzberichte* (1888), p. 70.

12. *Ibid.* (1890), p. 107. An 1893 resolution forbids members to hold the office of justice of the peace or constable. A member may be a notary public. Cf. *ibid.*, p. 156.

13. See J. A. Toews, "Can a Christian Participate in Government?" in *The Voice*, VII:1 (1958), 4-7 for an attempt to answer this question.

14. Cf. *ME*, IV, 615, 616.

15. *Yearbook* (General Conference, 1943), p. 67.

16. *Yearbook* (General Conference, 1966), pp. 24-25.

17. The national flag displayed in many American M.B. churches is a symbolic expression of this feeling.

18. Guy F. Hershberger, *War, Peace and Nonresistance* (Scottdale: Herald Press, 1953), p. 15.

19. Menno Simons, *CW*, p. 94.

20. Quoted by Melvin Gingerich in *Service for Peace* (Akron, Pa.: Mennonite Central Committee, 1949), p. 7.

21. See *ibid.*, p. 10, for account of mistreatment.

22. Hershberger, *op. cit.*, p. 111.

23. J. H. Lohrenz, *op. cit.*, p. 105.

24. *Konferenzberichte* (1919), p. 502.

25. *Yearbook* (General Conference, 1921), p. 52.

26. *Yearbook* (General Conference, 1924), pp. 62-64.

27. *Yearbook* (General Conference, 1939), p. 51.

28. *Ibid.*

29. Although the origin of the term "conscientious objector" (CO) remains obscure, it was used during World War I to designate persons whose conscience forbade them to perform military service.

30. See "Civilian Public Service," *ME*, I, 604. A complete list of CPS camps and units (151) is also given in *ME*, I, 607-609.

31. As given by Gingerich, *op. cit.*, p. 91.

32. As given by Hershberger in *The Mennonite Church in the Second World War* (Scottdale: Mennonite Publishing House, 1951), p. 39.

33. Gingerich, *op. cit.*, p. 92.

34. *Ibid.*, p. 354.

35. Information supplied by Lynn Roth, United States, M.B. Conference Office.

36. *Yearbook* (General Conference, 1948), p. 104.

37. *Yearbook* (General Conference, 1954), p. 121. The full report of the "mission to Washington" is found on pp. 114-121.

38. See report, *ibid.*, p. 120.

39. *Yearbook* (General Conference, 1951), p. 124.

40. Cf. J. A. Toews, *Alternative Service . . .* , p. 15.

41. *Ibid.*, p. 16.

42. Cited in *ibid.*, p. 41.

43. See *The Winkler Mennonite Brethren Church*, p. 7.

44. *Yearbook* (Canadian Conference, 1934), p. 77.

45. *Yearbook* (Canadian Conference, 1936), p. 80.

46. *Yearbook* (Canadian Conference, 1939), p. 62. See Toews, *Alternative Service . . .* , pp. 32-33 for an account of the debate at an inter-Mennonite conference in Winkler.

47. A comprehensive account of the service of conscientious objectors is given in *Alternative Service . . . .*

48. See *Alternative Service . . .* , pp. 35-36.

49. See Gingerich, *op. cit.*, p. 414. The favorable response by "Jimmy" Gardiner to their petition was considered by the delegates as a definite answer to prayer.

50. *Alternative Service . . .* , p. 49.

51. *Ibid.*, p. 99.

52. The author served in this capacity in the ASW camps of B.C. for almost six months in 1943, and for shorter periods in Alberta in the years following.

53. *Yearbook* (Canadian Conference, 1942), p. 30.

54. *Ibid.*

55. *Alternative Service . . .* , p. 111.

56. *Yearbook* (Canadian Conference, 1946), p. 159.

57. Related to VS, but not identical to it, is "Pax Service," actually an alternative to I-W Service, a program of overseas service by young men serving as conscientious objectors under the United States Selective Service Act, who volunteer for service abroad under MCC.

58. *Yearbook* (General Conference, 1957), p. 102.

59. *Yearbook* (General Conference, 1960), p. 131.

60. *Yearbook* (General Conference, 1966), p. 45.

CHAPTER XXI

1. Jantz in *Mennonite Brethren Herald*, IX:3 (Feb. 1, 1970), 2.

2. Cf. Franz Isaac, *op. cit.*, pp. 193-195.

3. The 1902 *Confession of Faith* is the first confession written by Mennonite Brethren and officially adopted by the whole conference.

4. *Confession of Faith* (American Edition), p. 5.

5. *Ibid.*, pp. 46-47.

6. For the earlier period of M.B. history such a study has been made by A. J. Klassen in "Roots and Development of Mennonite Brethren Theology to 1914" (Unpublished M.A. thesis).

7. Friesen, as given in translation by A. J. Klassen "Roots and Development . . .," pp. 59-60. (With slight changes in translation.)

8. *Ibid.*, p. 61.

9. Cf. *Confession of Faith* (American Edition), pp. 18-27.

10. Translated from original *Glaubensbekenntnis der Vereinigten Christlichen Taufgesinnten Mennonitischen Bruedergemeinde in Russland* (Halbstadt: Raduga, 1902), pp. 17-18.

11. Friesen, *op. cit.*, p. 204.

12. Krahn, *MQR*, IX (1935), 173.

13. C. Krahn, in "Pietism," *ME*, IV, 176.

14. Cited by Friedmann, *Mennonite Piety . . .* , p. 4.

15. Cited by Friedmann, *ibid.*

16. Friesen, *op. cit.*, p. 41.

17. Wiebe in *Church in Mission*, p. 132. Wiebe made a special study of Johann Arndt's book, *Wahres Christentum*, which was so popular among the Russian Mennonites in the nineteenth century in his thesis: "Johann Arndt: Precursor of Pietism" (Unpublished dissertation, University of Iowa, 1965).

18. In *ME*, IV, 178.

19. Cf. "Antrittspredigt," Friesen, *op. cit.*, p. 181.

20. Crous in *The Recovery of the Anabaptist Vision*, p. 241.

21. G. W. Peters, *op. cit.*, p. 33.

22. See Becker, *op. cit.*, p. 80.

23. *ME*, I, 227.

24. A mimeographed English translation of this confession is available in the Archives of Pacific College, Fresno.

25. Cf. F. C. Peters' article, "The Early Mennonite Brethren Church: Baptist or Anabaptist?" *Mennonite Life*, XXV:2 (October, 1959), 176ff.

26. J. H. Lohrenz, *op. cit.*, p. 38.

27. Cf. *Konferenzberichte* (1892), pp. 141-145.

28. F. C. Peters, in *Mennonite Life* (Oct., 1959), 178.

29. Prieb in *A Century of Grace and Witness*, p. 78.

30. Cf. Friesen, *op. cit.*, p. 359.

31. A. E. Janzen's statement, "conversion leads to the miracle of regeneration," in *Mennonite Brethren Distinctives* (p. 6), should not leave the impression of a cause-effect relationship. For Mennonite Brethren conversion and regeneration have always been two aspects of our salvation experience.

32. *Confession of Faith* (American Edition), p. 13-14.

33. Klassen in *Journal of Church & Society* (Fall, 1965), p. 64.

34. A. J. Klassen, "Roots and Development . . .", p. 191.

35. See Vernon E. Janzen, "An Evaluation of Current Concepts of Conversion held by Mennonite Brethren in the United States" (Unpublished B.D. thesis, Mennonite Brethren Biblical Seminary, 1966), chapter five, for an analysis of present trends in the M.B. Church.

36. D. Wiens, *New Wineskins for Old Wine* (Hillsboro: M.B. Publishing House, 1965), p. 5.

37. Krahn, "Some Social Attitudes of the Mennonites in Russia," *MQR*, IX:4 (Oct., 1935), 173.

38. Friesen, *op. cit.*, p. 189.

39. Cf. Clarence R. Hiebert, "Ethical Emphases of the Mennonite Brethren Church in North America" (Unpublished M.A. thesis, Phillips Univ., 1959). Hiebert's comprehensive study of M.B. ethics shows that the spiritual concerns, as expressed in conference resolutions, were often related to local problems and not to the broader social and moral issues of society at large.

40. Cf. H. S. Bender, *These Are My People* (Scottdale: Herald Press, 1962), p. 44.

41. *Confession of Faith* (American Edition), p. 20. The reference to "following Jesus" (*Nachfolge*) as a mark of the "true church" is probably unique and to our knowledge is not found in other confessions of faith in this context.

42. F. C. Peters, "Group Consensus in Mennonite Brethren Ethics" (Study Paper in private files of the writer), p. 2.

43. "Die Grundzuege der Theologie der Vaeter der M.B. Gemeinde" (Paper presented at Study Conference in Winnipeg, 1956), p. 32.

44. J. H. Lohrenz, quoted by Unruh, *op. cit.*, p. 327.

45. *A Century of Grace and Witness*, p. 13.

46. G. Lohrenz, in *A Legacy of Faith*, p. 183.

47. A. E. Janzen, *Mennonite Brethren Distinctives*, p. 18.

48. Marvin Hein, moderator of the M.B. General Conference, in private interview with the author expressed the view that this blending of evangelistic and social concerns was possibly the "genius" of the M.B. Church.

49. Unruh, "Die Grundzuege der Theologie . . ." *op. cit.*, p. 39.

50. Cf. A. J. Klassen's analysis of David Duerksen's sermons, "Roots and Development . . .," pp. 194-195.

51. See article on "Fundamentalism" by H. S. Bender, in *ME*, II, 418-419.

52. *Ibid.*, p. 419.

53. V. Adrian, "Born of Anabaptism and Pietism," *op. cit.*, p. 8.

54. The book by Carl F. Henry, *The Uneasy Conscience of Modern Fundamentalism* is an attempt to correct this one-sided emphasis.

55. L. E. Maxwell, long-time principal of Prairie Bible Institute, in his earlier years identified nonresistance with theological liberalism.

56. Daniel B. Stevick, *Beyond Fundamentalism* (Richmond, Va.: John Knox Press, 1964), p. 19.

57. Two more recent books on the subject are: *Dispensationalism in America* (Richmond, Va.: John Knox Press, 1958) by C. Norman Kraus, who takes a more critical approach, and *Dispensationalism Today* (Chicago: Moody Press, 1965), by C. C. Ryrie, who makes an able apology for modern (revised) dispensationalism.

58. Quoted by Kraus, *op. cit.*, p. 19.

59. Ryrie, *op. cit.*, p. 29.

60. See J. H. Lohrenz, *op. cit.*, p. 319.

61. A list of these speakers is given by A. A. Toews, *Mennonitische Maertyrer*, I, 370-371.

62. Klassen, "Roots and Development . . .," p. 162.

63. Cf. *The New Scofield Reference Bible*, p. 997 (footnote).

64. The one-sided emphasis on the "eternal security" of the believer (as found in both Fundamentalism and Dispensationalism) is also based on an arbitrary selection of Scripture passages, where the promises are appropriated and the warnings rejected.

65. Adrian, "Born of Anabaptism and Pietism," *op. cit.*, p. 7.

CHAPTER XXII

1. Cf. Isaac, *op. cit.*, p. 182.

2. Cf. Unruh, *op. cit.*, p. 280.

3. See section on "Spiritual Revival and Missionary Outreach" in chapter eight for an account of this "second awakening."

4. Cf. *ME*, III, 47.

5. See *MCC Workbook* (1967), D-2.

6. The Conference of United Mennonite Churches in B.C. meeting on May 30, 1970, endorsed cooperation by a vote of nearly 90 percent. The Mennonite Brethren delegates expressed themselves in favor of this working fellowship by a vote of 93 percent a week later. See *Mennonite Brethren Herald* (June 26, 1970), p. 10.

7. Those who have escaped from the Soviet Union after World War II, for instance, meet from time to time for a Thanksgiving festival (*Dankfest*).

8. Students of the M.B. Biblical Seminary (Fresno) receive part of their "field education" through clinical involvement at Kings View Homes.

9. Cf. *ME*, III, 46.

10. *Yearbook* (General Conference, 1943), p. 68.

11. See *MCC Workbook* (1970), B-5.

12. *Yearbook* (General Conference, 1945), p. 74. Although a General Conference board made the recommendation, the resolution affected primarily the M.B. churches in the U.S.

13. *Yearbook* (U.S. Conference, 1968), p. 11.

14. *Yearbook* (U.S. Conference, 1971), p. 22. That the contribution of Mennonite Brethren is desired and appreciated was experienced by the author when in 1960 he was asked to present a paper on "The Christian and Armed Combat" at the meeting of the Social Action Commission of NAE in Chicago.

15. In government circles and in English communities in general, Toews was referred to as "bishop," not "elder."

16. See *ME*, I, 543, for other functions of *Das Zentrale Mennonitische Immigrantenkomitee*.

17. See *Yearbook* (Canadian Conference, 1964), pp. 110-113 for complete constitution of MCC (Canada).

18. *Yearbook* (Canadian Conference, 1969), pp. 342-343.

19. See editorial by Harold Jantz in the *Mennonite Brethren Herald*, XI:7 (April 7, 1972), 11. The apprehension that the representatives of smaller denominations (who would join EFC) would dominate the organization, motivated the restriction of denominational representation.

20. The M.B. Conference is not as yet a member of the EFC. These men represent either their local churches or have joined as individuals.

21. The most comprehensive account of the history of MCC for the first thirty years of its existence is found in J. D. Unruh's account, *In the Name of Christ* (Scottdale, Pa.: Herald Press, 1952).

22. In *A Century of Grace and Witness*, p. 25.

23. See *Handbook* of the Mennonite Central Committee (Fourth Edition, 1954), pp. 12-22. In recent years the Mennonite Aid Section has become a subsidiary agency.

24. *MCC Workbook* (1969), K-1.

25. Quoted by Harold Janz, *Mennonite Brethren Herald*, IX:4. (February 20, 1970), 10.

26. Information taken from *MCC Workbook* (1969). G-7, G-8.

27. *Yearbook* (General Conference, 1954), p. 21.

28. Cf. *Yearbook* (General Conference, 1943), p. 23.

29. *Ibid.*, p. 24.

30. *Yearbook* (General Conference, 1954), p. 21.

31. *MCC Workbook* (1969), K-1.

32. *Mennonite Brethren Herald*, VIII:15 (July 25, 1969), 19.

33. *Ibid.*

34. One Bible school teacher (M.B.) made the comment that the opinions expressed in group discussions had not varied as much as the views of a group of Mennonite Brethren at a denominational faith conference. See *M.B. Herald*, VIII:14 (August 7, 1970), 12.

35. These communications have been reprinted in the *Yearbook* (General Conference, 1966), pp. 30-33.

36. *Ibid.*, p. 33.

37. See article on Christian Neff in *ME*, III, 820, which presents an interesting account of the contribution of this devoted churchman.

38. Quoted by J. A. Toews in *Alternative Service . . .*, pp. 28-29.

39. *Yearbook* (General Conference, 1951), p. 72.

40. See *Die Gemeinde Christi und Ihr Auftrag* (Karlsruhe: H. Schneider, 1953), p. 407.

41. *Yearbook* (General Conference, 1954), p. 20.

42. *Yearbook* (General Conference, 1957), p. 114.

43. Statistical information from C. J. Dyck, (ed.), *Proceedings of the Seventh Mennonite World Conference* (Elkhart: Mennonite World Conference, 1962), pp. 8, 9.

44. *Ibid.*, p. 9.

45. Information by C. J. Dyck, (ed.), *Proceedings of the Eighth Mennonite World Conference* (Elkhart: Mennonite World Conference, 1967), p. VIII.

46. *Proceedings of the Seventh Mennonite World Conference*, p. 675.

47. Quoted by Rudy Wiebe in *Mennonite Brethren Herald*, I:29 (August 10, 1962), 3.

CHAPTER XXIII

1. Manuscripts are presently in preparation for a three-volume history of the M.B. Church in Asia, Africa, Latin America, and Western Europe. Hence only a brief and cursory survey will be attempted in this chapter. A popular account of the story of the Mennonite Brethren missions, *The Mustard Tree*, by Phyllis Martens, has just been published by the Boards of Christian Education in cooperation with the Board of Missions and Services. (Winnipeg: Christian Press, 1971).

2. This number includes some 20,000 Mennonite Brethren in the Soviet Union, but not an undetermined number in China.

3. J. J. Toews in *The Church in Mission*, p. 150.

4. A. E. Janzen, *The American Mennonite Brethren Mission in India, 1898-1948* (Hillsboro: Board of Foreign Missions, 1948), p. 3.

5. *Ibid.*, pp. 30-32.

6. J. J. Dick has given an interesting account of this experience in the booklet: *From Exile in Russia into Mission Work in India* (Hillsboro: M.B. Missions Office, 1940).

7. Quoted by Phyllis Martens, *op. cit.*, p. 12.

8. *Ibid.*, p. 15.

9. Cf. *ibid.*, pp. 27-28.

10. *Ibid.*, p. 25.

11. J. H. Lohrenz, *op. cit.*, p. 250.

12. Quoted by Phyllis Martens, *op. cit.*, p. 50.

13. See F. J. Wiens, *Fifteen Years Among the Hakkas of South China* (n.p., n.d.) for an interesting account of this pioneer effort.

14. Cf. *ibid.*, p. 168.

15. J. H. Lohrenz, *op. cit.*, p. 258.

16. Not only the Mennonite Brethren, but also the Mennonite Church (OM), the General Conference Mennonites, and the Brethren in Christ, established missions in Japan between 1949 and 1953.

17. Quoted by Phyllis Martens, *op. cit.*, p. 108.

18. *Yearbook* (General Conference, 1969), p. 56.

19. Robert G. Nelson, *Congo Crisis and Christian Mission* (St. Louis: Bethany Press, 1961), p. 19.

20. Quoted in *Mennonite Brethren Herald*, IX:1 (January 9, 1970), 18.

21. Both men had studied in the Rochester Baptist Seminary and made their commitment to the Baptist Mission Society. This was a great disappointment to the M.B. Conference who had hoped that these brethren would open an M.B. field in Africa. Cf. J. H. Lohrenz, *op. cit.*, p. 261.

22. The financial support for the Bartsch family was provided by the newly organized *Afrika Missionsverein*, composed mostly of M.B. members.

23. *A Century of Grace and Witness*, p. 16.

24. *The Christian Leader* (July 26, 1960), p. 6.

25. *A Century of Grace and Witness*, p. 17.

26. As given by Phyllis Martens, *op. cit.*, p. 86.

27. See "Mission News," *The Christian Leader* (February 4, 1964), p. 8.

38. As quoted by Phyllis Martens, *op. cit.*, p. 88.

29. When the author stood amidst the ruins of Kafumba in 1969, several senior missionaries expressed this view: the catastrophe had resulted in the employment of new methods of missionary outreach.

30. Nelson, *op. cit.*, p. 104.

31. See chapter eight for an account of this emigration.

32. J. W. Fretz, *Pilgrims in Paraguay* (Scottdale: Herald Press, 1953), p. 170.

33. See A. H. Unruh, *op. cit.*, p. 807.

34. When the writer ministered in the Bage settlement in 1951, the economic as well as religious prospects appeared very bright for a wholesome development.

35. Quoted by Phyllis Martens, *op. cit.*, p. 144.

36. Quoted by Phyllis Martens, *ibid.*, p. 146.

37. *Yearbook* (General Conference, 1969), p. 111.

38. For a detailed study of the early history of these settlements see Fretz, *Pilgrims in Paraguay*, and Willard and Verna Smith, *Paraguayan Interlude* (Scottdale: Herald Press, 1950).

39. Information from personal notes of the writer who ministered in Volendam in 1966.

40. Contacts were also established with the Moro tribe. K. Isaak became the first missionary martyr. See booklet by A. E. Janzen, *The Moro's Spear* (Hillsboro; Board of Missions, 1962).

41. The writer, with other members of the presidium of the MWC was present in the meeting when this testimony was given.

42. Cf. Phyllis Martens, *op. cit.*, p. 177.

43. The fascinating story of their life and work is found in the book written by Margaret Epp, *But God Hath Chosen* (North Newton, Kansas: Mennonite Press, 1963).

44. Martens, *op. cit.*, p. 182.

45. Cf. *Yearbook* (General Conference, 1969), p. 59.

46. See article, "Mennonite Brethren Mark 15 Years at HCJB," *Christian Leader* (October 8, 1968), p. 6.

47. Martens, *op. cit., p. 192.*

48. *Yearbook* (General Conference, 1969), p. 58.

49. See "Mexico Revisited," *Christian Leader* (July 14, 1970), p. 8.

50. *Yearbook* (General Conference, 1960), p. 54.

Appendixes

APPENDIX 1. FINANCIAL RESPONSE TO MENNONITE BRETHREN MISSIONS, 1881-1973 — TABLE XIII

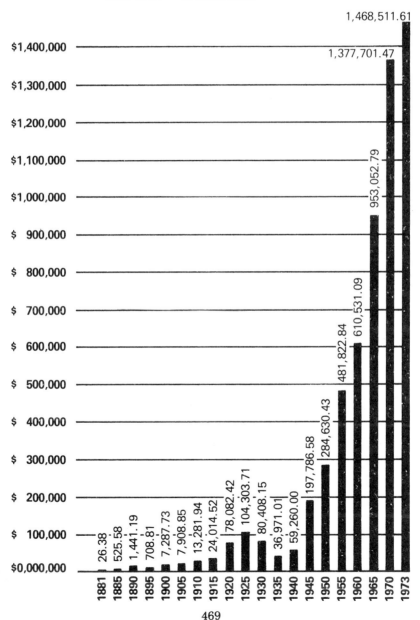

APPENDIX 2. CHRONOLOGICAL LISTING OF EVENTS

CANADA	UNITED STATES	OVERSEAS
		1517 Luther begins Reformation in Germany
		1519 Zwingli begins Swiss Reformation
		1525 Grebel & Blaurock begin Anabaptist fellowship in Switzerland
		1536 Menno Simons leaves Catholic fold, joins Dutch Anabaptists
		1540 Anabaptists migrate to Vistula Delta
	1683 Swiss Mennonite immigrants found Germantown	
		1763 Catherine II of Russia invites Mennonite settlers
	1786 OMs migrate from Pennsylvania to Ontario, Canada	
		1788 Russian Mennonite privileges chartered
		1789 Chortitza Russian Mennonite colony founded
		1800 Paul I reaffirms Menn. privileges
		1804 Molotschna Menn. colony founded
		1812-19 Kleine Gemeinde founded to protest liberalism in larger Mennonite church
		1817 Cornies becomes president of Agriculture Improvement Society

1820 Cornies founds Ohrloff sec. school
    Kulturkampf between progressive
    and conservative elements begins

1835 Gnadenfeld Church migrates from
    Prussia to Russia

1845 Wuest pastors Separatists neigh-
    boring Mennonites

1850 Spritual awakening begins in Rus-
    sian Mennonite colonies

1857 *Bruderschule* founded

1859 Wuest dies
    Brethren observe private com-
    munion

Jan. 6, 1860 Molotschna MB Church
    founded

June 1860 First MB immersion baptism

1861-62 Chortitza MB Church founded
    Struggle for recognition

1863 MBs settle in Kuban area

1864 Gov't recognizes MBs as Menno-
    nites

1865 Excessive emotionalism stabilized

1866 Liebig aids MBs in church polity

1867 First MB missions festival

1868 Huebert ordained first MB elder

1869 Oncken ordains MBs in Chortitza
    Jacob A. Wiebe founds KMB
    Church

1865-85 MBs expand in Russia

1870 Russian govt. terminates Mennonite military exemption

1872 First MB conference in Russia

1874 Emigration of Russian Mennonites to America

1876 Unger publishes adapted Baptist Confession

1880 Russian Menn. cooperate in Alternative Service — Forestry

1873 GCs & OMs form Bd. of Guardians to aid Russian Menn. immigrants Mennonites file for military exemption under Ulysses Grant

1874 First MBs settle and organize at Ebenfeld, Ks.
KMBs settle at Gnadenau, Kansas

1876 MBs organize at Henderson, Neb.; Group meets at Turner City, S.D.

1877 Mountain Lake, Minn. baptism & church organization
Organization at Woodson County, Ks.

1878 Ebenezer MB Ch. org. at Buhler, Ks.
Informal conference of Neb. & Ks. MBs

1879 Neb. MBs organize at Boone County & Culbertson
Elder Schellenberg comes to Kansas
First official U.S. MB conference
2nd KMB church org., Inman, Ks.

1880 Johannestal MB church org. near Hillsboro
Menn. Rundschau begins publication
Alexanderwohl Ks. MB church begins

1874 Conservative Russian Mennonites settle in Manitoba

1884-5 Mass revivals among Russian Mennonites

1885 Russian MBs participate in Blankenburg (Germany) Alliance Conference

1890 MBs send 1st missionaries, Abr. Friesens, to India

1881 Salem KMBs org. at Jansen, Neb. 1st American MB mission offering

1884 Lehigh Ks. MBs organize J. F. Harms begins 1st U.S. MB school at Canada, Ks. *Zionsbote* published

1885 Bingham Lk. Minn. MBs build church

1886 Salem KMB est., Bridgewater, S.D. Bethel KMB at Yale, S.D. KMB mission, Elk Park, N.C. Mtn. Lk. inter-Menn. Bible School begins

1887 Mtn. Lk. MBs hold July 4 missions festival

1888 US MB Sunday school established

1889 1st MB Sunday sch. convention

1890 KMBs establish orphanage in Ks.

1891 MBs try organization at Dallas, Ore.

1893 Corn & Cooper Okla. MBs established

1894 MB mission to Comanche Indians established

1894-9 9 MB churches est. in Cherokee Strip

1897 Bethel KMB at Weatherford, Okla.

1886 First Can. MB baptism at Burwalde, Manitoba

1888 First Can. MB church org. at Burwalde (Winkler), Manitoba

1889 Sun. school est. at Winkler

1890 OMs, UMCs, etc. move to Alberta

1896 Winkler MBs estab. Grossweide affiliate

1902 MB *Confession of Faith* published

1903 A.J. Kroeker publishes *Friedensstimme*

1904 Menn. estab. *Raduga* Publishing Co.

1905 Progressive MBs form *Allianz-Gemeinde* in Molotschna

1908 MB Committee for Evan. among Russians supports 9 workers

1910 MBs celebrate 50th anniversary

1911 P. M. Friesen's *Alt Ev. Menn. Bruedershaft* published

1912 All-Menn. KfK organized

1897-1900 3 MB churches est. in N.D.

1900 1st MB SS periodical published

1901 1st KMB missionaries, H. C. Bartels, go to China

1902 Okeene, Okla. MBs organize Springfield, Ks. KMBs organize 1st US MB Bible Sch. est. at Corn

1904 MB Publishing House established

1905 MB churches est. in Reedley & Escondido, Ca.; Dallas, Ore.; Balko, Okla.

1906 MBs organize at Hooker, Okla.; Loveland, Col.

1907 Bessie, Okla. MBs organize Bethel KMBs est. at Hooker, Okla.

1908 Tabor College established

1909 Rosedale, Ca. MBs established Conference divides into districts

1910 MBs organize at Bakersfield, Ca.; South Side Mission in Minneapolis MBs begin giving for relief

1911 Zion (Dinuba, Ca.) KMBs established Inola, Okla. MBs organize

1912 Lodi, Ca. MBs organize Immanuel Academy established at Reedley, Ca.

1898 1st Sask. MBs org. at Laird
1899 KMBs est. at Laird, Sask.

1901 KMBs est. at Langham, Sask.
1901-18 6 N. Sask. MB churches establ.

1904-14 8 S. Sask. MB churches organize

1907 MBs meet in Winnipeg, Manitoba

1913 Wpg. city mission begins
1st Can. MB Bible School establ. by J. F. Harms at Herbert, Sask.

1913 Dorrance, Ks. & Collinsville, Okla. MBs organize

1915 KMBs est. Zoar (Ks.) Academy
D.M. Hofer begins Lincoln Ave. Mission, Chicago
KMBs publ. *Der Wahrheitsfreund*

1916 MBs org. at Littlefield, Texas

1917 Lustre, Mont. MB church organized
Universal conscription prompts Mennonite petition for exemption

1918 KMBs est. Garden City, Ks. church & Salem Hospital, Hillboro, Ks.
MBs organize at Shafter, Ca.

1919 MB conference accepts S. China mission
Madera, Ca. MBs organize
KMBs 50th anniversary, Bridgewater, S.D.
KMB church est. at Doland, S.D.
Last MB elder ordained in Okla.
US MBs endorse non-resistance
World Christian Fundamentals Assn. organizes; MB sympathizers

1914 WWI begins; German prohibited for public assembly or press

1915 Russ. property liquidation begins; Menn. org. noncombatant medical corps

1917 Tsarist regime overthrown
All-Menn. Congress discusses alternative service, etc.

1917-20 Bolshevik Revolution & reign of terror
Menn. youth organize self-defense corps

1918 MBs establish Tschongraw Bible School in Ukraine

1920 Famine follows civil war Russ. Menn. study commission investigates emig. to N.A.

1922 Feeding kitchens est. in Ukraine by American Menn. Relief

1923 Ministers & teachers of religion barred from public schools

1923-26/27 Mass Menn. emigration to Canada

1924 Govt. closes Tschongraw Bible School

1924-25 Major revivals in Menn. colonies

1920 Hooker, Okla. Bible Sch. begins Emmanuel KMBs org., Onida, S.D. MCC organized to send aid to USSR

1921 Emmanuel KMBs organized near Chasely, N.D. Enid, Okla. MB Bible School organized

1922 Winton, Ca. MBs organize

1923 Ingalls, Ks.; Orland. Ca. MBs org.

1924 Los Angeles, Ca. MBs established

1925 S. Reedley (Dinuba) MBs organize

1926 Fairview, Okla. Bible Sch. begins City Terrace MB mission est. in Los Angeles, Ca.

1922 Can. Menn. Bd. of Coloniz. organized to aid Russ. Menn. immigrants

1923 *M. Rundschau & Chr. Jugendfr.* move from Scottdale to Rundschau Publ. House (Christian Press), Winnipeg

1925 Kitchener, Ont. MBs established Winkler Bible School organized Girls' Home est. in Winnipeg

1925-33 15 churches org. in Manitoba by Russlaender MBs

1926 Coaldale, Alta. MBs organize

1926-28 6 Sask. churches organized by Russlaender MBs

1927 New Hamburg & Pt. Rowan, Ont. MBs org. Hepburn, Sask. Bible School establ.

1927-33 8 Alta. MB churches organized by Russlaender

1928 Collectivization of USSR farms

1929 Last emigration of Mennonites from USSR

1930-40 Dissolution of Menn. congregations
Cessation of overt religious activity

1928 Lustre Bible Academy established

1930 Harbin Menn. settle in Reedley, Ca.

1931 ETTA established; Can. & US MBs become members

1935 Tabor College becomes General Conference school

1936 Gen. Conf. appoints Youth Committee
1st salaried MB pastor, Hillsboro

1937 Blaine, Wash. MB church est.
Christian Leader published

1928 Tabor (Dalmeny, Sask.) Bible Sch. org.

1929 Coaldale, Alta. Bible Sch. established

1930 Yarrow B.C. MB church organized Inter-Menn. Concordia Hospital begins in Winnipeg

1931 Steinbach, Man. Inter-Menn. Bible School begins
Greendale & Agassiz, BC MBs establ.

1932 MBs organize in S. Abbotsford, B.C.; Hespeler, Leamington & Vineland, Ont.
Ontario MB conference established
Canad. MBs org. Africa Mission Society

1933 Swift Current, Sask. MBs organize Gem & LaGlace, Alta. Bible Sch. establ.

1934 Arnold, B.C. MB church established

1935 N. Abbotsford & Black Creek, B.C. MBs organize
Winkler Inter-Menn. Hospital est.

1936 South End Wpg. MB church establ. Abbotsford (Columbia) Bible Sch. est.

1937 Virgil, Ont. MB church established 1st Vancouver, B.C. MB church est. Steinbach, Man. Inter-Menn. Hospital established

1938 Ontario and Greendale, B.C. Bible Schools established

1939 Ontario MBs form conference

1940 Canad. peace churches submit Alt. Service proposals to govt cf. National Resources Mobiliz. Act

1941 Regina, Sask. MBs organize

1942 Black Creek, B.C. Bible Sch. org.

1943 St. Catharines, Ont. MB church est.

1944 S. Sask. West Bank Bible Camp organized
MBBC founded in Winnipeg
MEI High Sch. est., Clearbrook, B.C.
Strawberry Hill, B.C. MBs organize

1945 Konferenz-Jugendblatt published
Menn. High schools est. in Yarrow, Winnipeg, Virgil
E. Chwk., Matsqui, B.C. MB churches est.

1946 Ont. MBs join Canadian conference
Conference becomes Chr. Press shareholder
Gospel Light Hour begins (Winnipeg)
Pincher Creek, Alta. MBs organize
Alta. MB High sch. begins, Coaldale

1939 Last all-German Conference minutes published
Outbreak of World War II

1940 CPS organized cf. US Selective Service & Training Act
San Jose, Ca. & Kingwood Bible (Salem, Ore.) MBs organize

1941 Central & Southern Districts appoint youth committees

1942 Bethany (Fresno, Ca.) MBs org.
Menn. Central Peace Comm. becomes MCC Peace Section

1943 Wichita, Ks. 1st MB church org.

1944 Pacific Bible Institute established in Fresno, Ca.

1945 Hartland Christian Assn. begins
MBs affiliate with NAE

1941-43 Relative religious freedom in USSR under Nazi occupation; then trek & forced repatriation

1943 Belgian Congo becomes MB mission

1945 MB missions begin in Colombia, Brazil, Paraguay, W. China

1947 Chilliwack, E. Aldergrove, Kelowna MB churches established
E. Chwk Bible sch. organized
Eden (Ont.) Christian College est.

1948 Camp Arnes organized at Lake Wpg.

1949 Camp begins at Winkler, Manitoba

1950 Abbotsford, B.C. MB church establ.

1952 *Youth Worker* published

1953 N. Sask. establ. Redberry Bible Camp

1954 Canadian area conference established

1955 2nd Vancouver MB church established
Unruh's MB *Geschichte* published
Menn. Observer published

1956 Calgary, Alta. MB church established

1957 *Konf. Jugendblatt* absorbed by *Menn. Observer*
MB church est. in Saskatoon, Sask.

1947 Bethesda KMBs org. at Huron, S.D.
The Christian Witness replaces KMB *Wahrheitsfreund*

1948 Pacific Dist. organizes youth committee

1951 MBs approve MWC participation
MCC establishes Kings View Hospital, Reedley, Ca.

1954 Gnadenau KMB church joins MB conference
KMBs org. at Hutchinson, Ks.
MCC opens Prairie View Hospital, Newton, Kansas
U.S. area conference established

1955 Biblical Seminary est. in Fresno
U.S. German-English transition complete

1955-59 *ME* published jointly with OMs & GCs

1957 Gen. Conf. approves Voluntary Service

1948 Japan MB mission established
Immigrant churches in Brazil & Paraguay form conference

1950 Mexico MB mission begins

1951 MB mission begins in Europe

1953 MBs staff HCJB German Dept. Quito, Ecuador

1956 1st N.A. Menn. deputation visits USSR

1958 Columbia (B.C.) Bible Camp begins
MBs endorse MDS
Inter-Menn. Brunk revivals in Manitoba & B.C.
Transition to pastoral system begins
Late 1950s Niagara Christ. Fwship established
1960 Canadian Conf. becomes owner of Christian Press
Early 1960s 3 MB churches est. in Vancouver area
5 MB churches est. in Winnipeg
Camp Evergreen est. in Alta.
2 Ont. mission churches join conf.
1961-66 8 new MB mission churches in B.C.
1961-67 4 new MB mission churches in Ont.
1962 Edmonton, Alta. MB church established
MB Herald replaces Menn. Observer
MBs join Wpg. Crusade for Christ
1963 MBs organize 2nd Saskatoon church MCC (Canada) organized
1964 1st MB church org. in Quebec MBs participate in EFC
1965 MB churches est. in Lethbridge, Alta.; Clearbrook (Bakerview) & Vancouver (Pacific Grace), B.C.

1960 MB Centennial celebration Reedley
KMB-MB merger
Bd. of Welfare initiates Chr. Service
Eugene, Ore. MB church organized
1963 MBs attend first all-Menn. Minister's Mtg. in Chicago
1964 Zionsbote ceases publication
1965-75 U.S. MB Decade of Enlargement

1960 Congo Independence: missionary evacuation
1962 MB missionaries return to Congo
1964 Jeunesse Rebellion: 2nd miss. evac.
1965 Spiritual awakening among USSR Mennonites

1966 U.S. MBs begin STP
General Conference appoints BCL

1968 U.S. conf. becomes NAE member

1971 *Worship Hymnal* published

1972 Probe '72 All-Menn. Congress on Evangelism in Minneapolis

Late 60s Saanich & King Rd. (Abbotsford), BC churches established

1968 Culloden (Vancouver) church establ.

1969 Vancouver churches join Christian Witness Crusade
Mt. Edward Bible Fwship begins in Dartmouth, Nova Scotia

1970 All-Menn. N.A. Bible Congress, Wpg.
St. Laurent (Montreal, Que.) MBs est.
GC & MB Bible schools merge at Columbia (CBI), Clearbrook, B.C.

1971 Richmond, B.C. MB church establ. Orchard Pk. church est. in Ont.

1973 Canadian MBs vote in favor of joint seminary

APPENDIX 3. MENNONITE SETTLEMENTS IN EUROPEAN RUSSIA

4. Mennonite settlements in European Russia

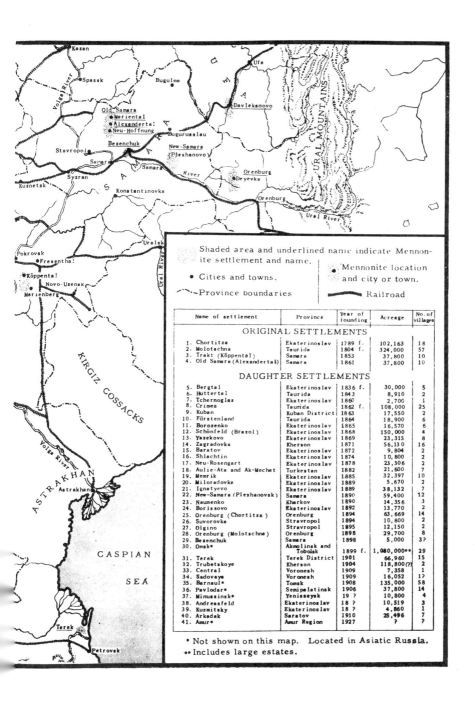

Shaded area and underlined name indicate Mennonite settlement and name.

● Cities and towns.

—Province boundaries

'Mennonite location
and city or town.

Railroad

Name of settlement	Province	Year of founding	Acreage	No. of villages
ORIGINAL SETTLEMENTS				
1. Chortitza	Ekaterinoslav	1789 f.	102,163	18
2. Molotschna	Taurida	1804 f.	324,000	57
3. Trakt (Köppental)	Samara	1853	37,800	10
4. Old Samara (Alexandertal)	Samara	1861	37,800	10
DAUGHTER SETTLEMENTS				
5. Bergtal	Ekaterinoslav	1836 f.	30,000	5
6. Huttertal	Taurida	1843	8,910	2
7. Tchernoglas	Ekaterinoslav	1860	2,700	1
8. Crimea	Taurida	1862 f.	108,000	25
9. Kuban	Kuban District	1863	17,550	2
10. Fürstenland	Taurida	1864	18,900	6
11. Borozenko	Ekaterinoslav	1865	16,570	6
12. Schönfeld (Brazol)	Ekaterinoslav	1868	150,000	4
13. Yasekovo	Ekaterinoslav	1869	23,315	8
14. Zagradovka	Kherson	1871	56,130	16
15. Baratov	Ekaterinoslav	1872	9,804	2
16. Shlachtin	Ekaterinoslav	1874	10,800	2
17. Neu-Rosengart	Ekaterinoslav	1878	23,306	2
18. Aulie-Ata and Ak-Mechet	Turkestan	1882	21,600	7
19. Memrik	Ekaterinoslav	1885	32,397	10
20. Miloradovka	Ekaterinoslav	1889	5,670	2
21. Ignatyevo	Ekaterinoslav	1889	38,132	7
22. New-Samara (Pleshanovsk)	Samara	1890	59,400	12
23. Naumenko	Kharkov	1890	14,356	3
24. Borissovo	Ekaterinoslav	1892	13,770	2
25. Orenburg (Chortitza)	Orenburg	1894	63,669	14
26. Suvorovka	Ekaterinoslav	1894	10,800	2
27. Olgino	Stavropol	1895	12,150	2
28. Orenburg (Molotschna)	Orenburg	1898	29,700	8
29. Bezenchuk	Samara	1898	5,000	3?
30. Omsk*	Akmolinsk and Tobolsk	1899 f.	1,080,000**	29
31. Terek	Terek District	1901	66,960	15
32. Trubetskoye	Kherson	1904	118,800(?)	2
33. Central	Voronesh	1909	7,358	1
34. Sadovaya	Voronesh	1909	16,052	1?
35. Barnaul*	Tomsk	1908	135,000	58
36. Pavlodar*	Semipalatinsk	1906	37,800	14
37. Minussinsk*	Yenisseysk	19 ?	10,800	4
38. Andreasfeld	Ekaterinoslav	18 ?	10,519	3
39. Kuzmitsky	Ekaterinoslav	18 ?	4,860	1
40. Arkadak	Saratov	1910	25,496	7
41. Amur*	Amur Region	1927	?	?

● Not shown on this map. Located in Asiatic Russia.

●● Includes large estates.

Bibliography

PRIMARY SOURCES

Becker, Jacob P. "Memoirs," unpublished manuscript in Pacific College Library, Revised and published as *Origin of the Mennonite Brethren Church.* Trans. by D. E. Pauls and A. E. Janzen, Hillsboro, Kan.: Mennonite Brethren Publishing House, 1973.

Friesen, P. M. *Die Alt-Evangelische Mennonitische Bruederschaft in Russland (1789-1910).* Halbstadt: Raduga, 1911.

Glaubensbekenntnis der Vereinigten Christlichen Taufgesinnten Mennonitischen Bruedergemeinde in Russland. Halbstadt: Raduga, 1902.

Harms, J. F. *Die Geschichte der Mennoniten Bruedergemeinde.* Hillsboro, Kan.: Mennonite Brethren Publishing House, 1924.

Isaac, Franz. *Die Molotschnaer Mennoniten.* Halbstadt: H. J. Braun, 1908.

Lohrenz, J. H. *The Mennonite Brethren Church.* Hillsboro, Kan.: Mennonite Brethren Publishing House, 1950.

Regier, Peter. *Kurzgefasste Geschichte der Mennoniten Brueder-Gemeinde.* Berne, Ind.: Light & Hope Publishing Co., 1901.

Simons, Menno. *The Complete Writings of Menno Simons.* Translated from the Dutch by Leonard Verduin and edited by John C. Wenger. Scottdale: Herald Press, 1956.

Unruh, A. H. *Die Geschichte der Mennoniten-Bruedergemeinde.* Winnipeg: Christian Press, 1955.

BOOKS AND PAMPHLETS

Ausgabe des Fuenfzigsten Jubilaeum-Jahres. Chicago: K.M.B. Publishing House, 1919.

Baerg, G. G. *A Brief History of Mennonites in British Columbia.* Yarrow, B.C.: Columbia Press, 1967.

Bainton, Roland. *Christian Attitudes Toward War and Peace.* New York: Abingdon Press, 1960.

Bender, Harold S. *Conrad Grebel, c 1498-1526.* Goshen, Ind.: Mennonite Historical Society, 1950.

_____. *These Are My People.* Scottdale: Herald Press, 1962.

Blanke, Fritz. *Brothers in Christ.* Scottdale: Herald Press, 1961.

Bolshakoff, Serge. *Russian Nonconformity.* Philadelphia: Westminster Press, 1950.

Brown, Frank, *Mennonite Brethren Church, Winkler, Manitoba* (1888-1963). Altona, Man.: D. W. Friesen, & Sons, 1963.

Brucks, J. H., and Hooge, H. H. *Neu-Samara am Tock.* Clearbrook, B.C.: Fraser Valley Printers, 1964.

A Century of Grace and Witness 1860-1960. Hillsboro: Mennonite Brethren Publishing House, 1960.

Confession of Faith. American ed. Hillsboro: Mennonite Brethren Publishing House, n.d.

Dick, J. J. *From Exile in Russia into Mission Work in India.* Hillsboro: Mennonite Brethren Missions Office, 1940.

Dyck, Cornelius J., ed. *Introduction to Mennonite History.* Scottdale: Herald Press, 1967.

_____., ed. *A Legacy of Faith.* Newton, Kan.: Faith and Life Press, 1962.

Dyck, Peter P. *Orenburg am Ural.* Yarrow, B.C.: Columbia Press, 1951.

Ehrt, Adolf. *Das Mennonitentum in Russland von seiner Einwanderung bis zur Gegenwart.* Berlin: Verlag von Julius Beltz, 1932.

80th Anniversary 1877-1957. Mountain Lake, Minn.: (M.B. Church), 1957.

Epp, Frank H. *Mennonite Exodus.* Altona, Manitoba: D. W. Friesen & Sons, 1962.

Epp, Margaret. *But God Hath Chosen*. North Newton, Kan.: Mennonite Press, 1963.

Estep, W. R. *The Anabaptist Story*. Nashville: Broadman Press, 1963.

50th Anniversary, Zion Mennonite Brethren Church. Dinuba, Calif., 1961.

50th Jubilee, 1905-1955. Reedley, Calif.: Reedley Mennonite Brethren Church, 1955.

Francis, E. K. *In Search of Utopia*. Glencoe, Ill.: The Free Press, 1955.

Fretz, J. W. *Pilgrims in Paraguay*. Scottdale: Herald Press, 1953.

Friedmann, Robert. *Mennonite Piety Through the Centuries*. Goshen, Ind.: Mennonite Historical Society, 1949.

Giesbrecht, Herbert, comp. *A Bibliographic Guide to Information*. Winnipeg: Christian Press, 1971.

Gingerich, Melvin. *Service for Peace*. Akron, Pa.: Mennonite Central Committee, 1949.

Goerz, Heinrich. *Die Mennonitischen Siedlungen der Krim*. Winnipeg: Echo Verlag, 1957.

Harcave, Sidney. *Russia, A History*. Chicago: T. B. Lippincott, 1959.

Harms, John F. *Meine Lebensreise*. Hillsboro, Kansas, 1943.

Henry, Carl F. *The Uneasy Conscience of Modern Fundamentalism*. Grand Rapids: Eerdmans, 1947.

Hershberger, Guy F. *The Mennonite Church in the Second World War*. Scottdale: Mennonite Publishing House, 1951.

————., ed. *The Recovery of the Anabaptist Vision*. Scottdale: Herald Press, 1957.

————. *War, Peace and Nonresistance*. Scottdale: Herald Press, 1953.

Hiebert, P. C., ed. *Feeding the Hungry*. Scottdale: Mennonite Central Committee, 1929.

Hitherto the Lord Has Helped Us. North Enid, Okla.: M.B. Church, 1957.

Horsch, John. *Mennonites in Europe*. Scottdale: Mennonite Publishing House, 1942.

The Hymn Book. Winnipeg: Canadian Conference of the Mennonite Brethren Church of North America, 1960. Translation of *Gesangbuch*, 1952.

Janzen, A. E. *The American Mennonite Brethren Mission in India, 1898-1948*. Hillsboro: Board of Foreign Missions, 1948.

————. *A History of Tabor College, Part One*. Hillsboro: Mennonite Brethren Publishing House, 1958.

————. *Mennonite Brethren Distinctives*. Hillsboro: Mennonite Brethren Publishing House, 1966.

Klassen, A. J., ed. *The Bible School Story (1913-1963)*. Clearbrook, B.C.: Canadian Board of Education, 1963.

————., ed. *The Church in Mission*. Fresno: Board of Christian Literature, 1967.

Krahn, C., ed. *From the Steppes to the Prairies*. Newton, Kan.: Mennonite Publication Office, 1949.

Kraus, C. Norman. *Dispensationalism in America*. Richmond, Va: John Knox Press, 1958.

Krestyaninov, V. F. *Mennonity*. Moscow, 1967.

Martens, Phyllis. *The Mustard Tree*. Winnipeg: Christian Press, 1971.

Mennonite Brethren Church Hymnal. Hillsboro: Mennonite Brethren Publishing House, 1953.

Mennonite Brethren Church of St. Catharines (25th Anniversary). n.p., 1968.

Missionaries Home and Abroad, 1869-1960. Freeman, S.D.: Pine Hill Printery, 1960.

Nelson, Robert, G. *Congo Crisis and Christian Mission*. St. Louis: Bethany Press, 1961.

Niebuhr, H. Richard. *Christ and Culture*. New York: Harper, 1951.

Niebuhr, Richard. *The Kingdom of God in America*. Chicago: Willett, Clark & Co., 1937.

Penner, Peter. *Reaching the Otherwise Unreached*. Winnipeg: Christian Press, 1959.

Peters, G. W. *The Growth of Foreign Missions of the Mennonite Brethren Church*. Hillsboro: Mennonite Brethren Publishing House, 1952.

Peters, H. P. *History and Development of Education Among the Mennonites in Kansas*. Hillsboro, 1925.

Ratzlaff, Erich L. *Im Weichselbogen*. Winnipeg: Christian Press, 1971.

Rempel, Aron D., *et al. At the Gates of Moscow*. Yarrow, B.C.: Columbia Press, 1964.

Ryrie, C. C. *Dispensationalism Today*. Chicago: Moody Press, 1965.

Saloff-Astakhoff, N. L. *Christianity in Russia*. New York: Loizeaux Brothers, 1941.

Sawatzky, Heinrich. *Templer Mennonitischer Herkunft*. Winnipeg: Echo Verlag, 1955.

Seventy-Five Years of God's Grace (1881-1956). Hillsboro: (Hillsboro M.B. Church).

Smith, C. Henry. *The Coming of the Russian Mennonites*. Berne, Ind.: Mennonite Book Concern, 1927.

————. *The Story of the Mennonites*. 4th ed., rev. and enl. by Cornelius Krahn. Newton, Kan.: Mennonite Publication Office, 1957.

Smith, Willard and Verna, *Paraguayan Interlude*. Scottdale: Herald Press, 1950.
Stevick, Daniel B., *Beyond Fundamentalism*. Richmond,Va.: John Knox Press. 1964.
Thiessen, Anna. *Die Stadtmission in Winnipeg*. Winnipeg: Regehr's Printing, 1955.
Tiessen, Isaac H., *et al. Er Fuehret . . . Geschichte der Ontario MB Gemeinden*. n.p., 1957.
Toews, A. A. *Mennonitische Maertyer*. 2 vols. Winnipeg: Christian Press, 1949-1954.
Toews, C. P. *Die Tereker Ansiedlung*. Rosthern: Echo Verlag, 1945.
Toews, H. P. *A. H. Unruh, D.D., Lebensgeschichte*. Winnipeg: Christian Press, 1961.
Toews, J. A. *Alternative Service in Canada During World War II*. Winnipeg: Christian
        Press, 1959.
_____. *True Nonresistance Through Christ*. Winnipeg: Christian Press, 1955.
Toews, John B. *Lost Fatherland*. Scottdale: Herald Press, 1967.
The Torchbearer: The Coaldale Bible School Jubilee Yearbook, 1929-1954. n.p., 1954.
Unruh, J. D. *In the Name of Christ*. Scottdale: Herald Press, 1952.
Verduin, Leonard. *The Reformers and Their Stepchildren*. Grand Rapids: Eerdmans, 1964.
Wedel, C. H. *Abriss der Geschichte der Mennoniten*. Newton, Kan.: Bethel College, 1901.
Wenger, J. C. *Glimpses of Mennonite History and Doctrine*. Scottdale: Herald Press, 1947.
Wiebe, David V. *Grace Meadow*. Hillsboro: Mennonite Brethren Publishing House. 1967.
_____. *They Seek a Country*. Hillsboro: Mennonite Brethren Publishing House, 1959.
Wiens, F. J. *Fifteen Years Among the Hakkas of South China*. n.p., n.d.
Wiens, Henry J. *The Mennonite Brethren Churches of North America*. Hillsboro:
        Mennonite Brethren Publishing House, 1954.
Williams, George H. *The Radical Reformation*. Philadelphia: Westminster Press, 1962.
Willms, H. J. *Die Sued-Abbotsford Ansiedlung*. Yarrow, B.C.: Columbia Press, 1955.
Witmer, S. A. *The Bible College Story: Education with Dimension*. Manhasset, N.Y.:
        Channel Press, 1962.
Worship Hymnal. Fresno: General Conference of Mennonite Brethren Churches, 1971.

PERIODICAL ARTICLES

Adrian, Victor. "Born of Anabaptism and Pietism." *MB Herald*, IV (March 26, 1965),
        Insert.
Balzer, Heinrich, "Faith and Reason," Trans. and ed. by Robert Friedmann. *MQR*, XXII
        (April, 1948), 75-93.
Bargen, Peter F. "The Coming of the Mennonites to Alberta." *Mennonite Life*, XI (April,
        1956), 83-87.
Barrett, David B. quoted in "Church not dying out: Center of Gravity Shifting South-
        ward," reprinted from *Christianity Today, MB Herald*, IX (January 9, 1970), 18.
Bender, H. S. Mennonite World Conference message quoted by Rudy H. Wiebe. *MB
        Herald*, I (August 10, 1962), 3.
Boldt, John. "Winkler Bible Camp." *Konferenz-Jugendblatt*, May-June, 1952, p. 7.
Brown, Frank, "Winkler, Manitoba" *Mennonite Life*, XI (July, 1956), 120-125.
Burkholder, J. Richard. "From Farm to City." *Mennonite Life*, XIX (January, 1964), 46.
Dirks, Sylvester. "Mexico Revisited." *Christian Leader*, Vol. 33 (July 14, 1970), 8.
Driedger, Leo. "A Perspective on Canadian Mennonite Urbanization." *Mennonite Life*,
        XXIII (October, 1968), 149.
Friesen, F. H. and Schellenberg, A. W. "Readers, Please Note!" *Mennonite Observer*, VII
        (December 29, 1961), 1, 10.
G. H. "The Mennonites in Soviet Russia." *Mennonite Life*, XIV (July, 1969), 108.
Giesbrecht, Robert. "Entwickelung der Vancouver MB Gemeinden." *Mennonitische
        Rundschau*, July 9, 1971, pp. 1, 5.
Grunau, P. C. "North Enid Mennonite Brethren Church." *Mennonite Life*, IX (October,
        1954), 176-177.
Harder, Leland. "Mennonite Mobility and Christian Calling." *Mennonite Life*, XIX
        (January, 1964), 7.
Hiebert, Waldo. "The Ministry a Shared Task." *Christian Leader*, Vol. 33 (July 14, 1970), 3.
Jantz, Harold. "Banff School of Fine Arts Becomes Meeting Place with God." *MB Herald*,
        XI (January 14, 1972), 12.
_____. "Editorial." *MB Herald*, XI (April 7, 1972), 11.
_____. "Snyder Lauds Vitality of Inter-Mennonite Efforts." *MB Herald*, IX (Feb. 20,
        1970), 10.
Jantz, Hugo W. "The Bible: Almost Nobody Reads the Bible Anymore." *MB Herald*, IX
        (Feb. 1, 1970), 2-3.

_____. "Mennonites Reach Historic Decision in B.C." *MB Herald*, IX (June 26, 1970), 10.

Klassen, A. J. "Two Significant Early Mennonite Brethren Documents." *Journal of Church and Society*, I (Fall, 1965), 58-63.

_____. "Sermons of David Duerksen." *Journal of Church and Society*, I (Fall, 1965), 64.

Krahn, C. "Some Social Attitudes of the Mennonites of Russia." *MQR*, IX (October, 1935), 165-177.

Kreider, Robert. "The Anabaptist Conception of the Church in the Russian Mennonite Environment, 1789-1870." *MQR*, XXV (January, 1951), 17-33.

Kroeker, Marvin, "Mennonites in the Oklahoma 'Runs'." *Mennonite Life*, X (July, 1955), 114-120.

Letkemann, Peter. "Mennonites in Vancouver — A Survey." *Mennonite Life*, XXIII (October, 1968), 161.

Loewen, Peter D. "Entstehung and Entwickelung der MBG zu Yarrow, B.C. *Mennonitische Rundschau*, July 7, 1971, pp. 2-3.

"MB Bible Schools in Canada." *Konferenz-Jugendblatt*, Vol. 11, No. 62 (November-December, 1955).

"Mennonite Brethren Mark 15 Years at HCJB." *Christian Leader*, Vol. 31 (October 8, 1968), p. 6.

"MB Missionaries Leave Congo." *Christian Leader*, Vol. 23 (July 26, 1960), 6.

"Mission News," *Christian Leader*, Vol. 27 (February 4, 1964), 8.

Neufeld, Alma, and Schultz, Marie. "West Bank Bible Camp: 1948 Retrospect." *Konferenz-Jugendblatt*, V (February-April, 1949), 12-14.

"Objectives of a Christian High School." *MB Herald*, IV (March 26, 1965), 4-5.

Peters, F. C. "Education Among the Mennonites in Russia." *The Voice*, VII:3-5(May/June-September/October, 1958).

_____. "Noncombatant Service Then and Now." *Mennonite Life*, X (January, 1955), 31-35.

_____. "The Early Mennonite Brethren Church: Baptist or Anabaptist?" *Mennonite Life*, XXV (October, 1959), 176-178.

Publications Committee of the MB Conference. "A Note of Appreciation." *MB Herald*, II (June 28, 1963), 3.

"Rejoice — A Reality." *Newsletter*, No. 11 (April, 1972), 1.

"Review." *The Hymn*, XXIII (January, 1972), 30.

Schellenberg, A. L. "Ein letztes Wort vom Editor." *Zionsbote*, May 21, 1930, p. 15.

Schellenberg, T. R. "Editor Abraham L. Schellenberg." *Mennonite Life*, IX (January, 1954), 19-28.

Teodorovich, N. "Mennonites in the U.S.S.R." *Bulletin*, Institute for the Study of the U.S.S.R., XV (October, 1968), 31.

Toews, J. A. "Can a Christian Participate in Government?" *The Voice*, VII:1 (1958), 4-7.

_____. "Cultural Change and Christian Ethics." *The Voice*, XV:6 (1966), 1-3.

_____. "Die Ersten Mennoniten Brueder u. Menno Simons." *The Voice*, VI (November-December, 1957), 1-3.

_____. "Der Materielle Wohlstand — Eine Geistliche Gefahr." *The Voice*, XIV:4 (1965), 10-13.

_____. "Die Stadtgemeinde in der Mennonitischen Bruderschaft." *The Voice*, V:4 (1956).

"Urbanization of Mennonites in Canada." *Mennonite Life*, XXIII (October, 1968).

Wiebe, Rudy, "The Meaning of Being Mennonite Brethren." *MB Herald*, IX (April 17, 1970), 4.

Wiebe, Vernon R. "Does MCC do Mission Work?" *MB Herald*, VIII (July 25, 1969), 19.

Wiens, Delbert, "New Wineskins for Old Wine." *Christian Leader*, Special Insert, Vol. 28: 21 (October 21, 1965).

"Winnipeg Bible Congress Unites the Generations." *MB Herald*, IX (August 7, 1970), 12-13.

ENCYCLOPEDIA ARTICLES

Bender, H. S. "Abreisskalender, Christlicher." *Mennonite Encyclopedia*. Edited by H. S. Bender and C. H. Smith. 4 vols. Scottdale: Mennonite Publishing House, 1955-59. Hereafter *ME*. I, 8.

_____. "Baptism." *ME*, I, 224-228.

_____. "Fundamentalism." *ME*, II, 418-419.

————. "Inter-Mennonite Relations." *ME*, III, 44-48.
————. "Kleine Gemeinde." *ME*, III, 197-199.
————. "Krimmer Mennonite Brethren." *ME*, III, 242-245.
————. "Neff, Christian." *ME*, III, 820.
————. "State, Anabaptist-Mennonite Attitude Toward." *ME*, IV, 611-618.
————. "United States of America: Immigration." *ME*, IV, 776-777.
Bergmann, Cornelius, and Krahn, Cornelius. "Chortitza Mennonite Settlement." *ME*, I, 569-574.
Block, Th. "Forestry Service," *ME*, II, 353-354.
Braun, A. "Friedensfeld." *ME*, II, 400.
Dahlenberg, Paul. "Cordell." *ME*, I, 711.
Epp, D. H., and Krahn, C. "Kommission fuer Kirchenangelegenheiten." *ME*, III, 218.
Friedmann, Robert. "Anabaptist: Modern Interpretations." *ME*, I, 114-116.
Gingerich, Melvin. "Civilian Public Service." *ME*, I, 604-611.
Hiebert, J. D. "Goessel MB Church." *ME*, II, 538.
Hiebert, P. C. "Lehigh MB Church." *ME*, III, 313.
Krahn, C. "Allgemeiner Mennonitischer Kongress." *ME*, I, 60-61.
————. "Central Mennonite Immigration Committee." *ME*, I, 542-543.
————. "Hymnology of the Mennonites of West and East Prussia, Danzig, and Russia." *ME*, II, 875-879.
————. "Literature, Mennonites in: IV. Russia and Russo-German Emigres." *ME*, III, 369-371.
————. "Memrik Mennonite Settlement." *ME*, III, 571-572.
————. "Molotschna Mennonite Settlement." *ME*, III, 732-737.
————. "Old Colony Mennonites." *ME*, IV, 38-42.
————. "Pietism." *ME*, IV, 176-179.
————. "Russia." *ME*, IV, 381-393.
————. "Siberia." *ME*, IV, 517-521.
————. "Terek Mennonite Settlement." *ME*, IV, 695-696.
Lohrenz, Gerhard. "Zagradovka." *ME*, IV, 1015-1016.
Neff, Christian. "Claassen, Johannes." *ME*, I, 612-613.
————, and Krahn, C. "Kroeker, Jakob." *ME*, III, 246.
Neufeld, I. G. "Boone County." *ME*, I, 389.
Pauls, D. C. "Zoar Academy and Bible School." *ME*, IV, 1034.
Peters, G. W. "Pacific Bible Institute." *ME*, IV, 103.
Plett, C. F. "Bethel KMB Church." *ME*, I, 310.
————. "Emmanuel KMB Church." *ME*, II, 203.
————. "Salem KMB Church." *ME*, IV, 404.
Prieb, Wesley. "Tabor College." *ME*, IV, 679-681.
Rempel, J. G. "Saskatchewan." *ME*, IV, 424-426.
Unruh, B. H. "Duma." *ME*, II, 108.
Vogt, J. W. "Corn Bible Academy. *ME*, I, 710-711.
Wall, P. F. "Los Angeles MB Church." *ME*, III, 396.
Warkentin, H. "Yarrow Bible School." *ME*, IV, 1000.
Wiens, H. E. "Henderson MB Church." *ME*, II, 698.

CATALOGS, HANDBOOKS, PROCEEDINGS, YEARBOOKS

Bethany Bible Institute, *Catalogue*. 1953/54.
Calendar of Activities: Mennonite Brethren Churches. 8th ed. Fresno: Evangelism and Christian Education Office, 1971.
Epp, F. H. "National Socialism Among Canadian Mennonites in the 1930's." *Fifteenth Conference on Mennonite Educational and Cultural Problems*. Bluffton, 1965.
Janzen, A. E., comp. Resolutions of the General Conference of the Mennonite Brethren Church, 1878-1963. Hillsboro: Board of Reference and Counsel, 1964. Mimeographed.
Konferenzberichte der Mennoniten Bruedergemeinde von Nord Amerika 1883-1919 nebst Konstitution der Mennoniten Bruedergemeinde von Nord Amerika. Hillsboro: Mennonite Brethren Publishing House, 1920.
Konferenzbeschluesse der K.M.B. Gemeinde, 1882-1940. Inman, Kan.: Salem Publishing House, 1940.
Konferenzbeschluesse der Mennoniten Bruedergemeinde von Nord Amerika 1879-1882. Hillsboro, 1949. Mimeographed.

Krimmer Mennonite Brethren Conference. *Yearbook*. 1954-1960.
Mennonite Brethren Biblical Seminary. *Catalog*. 1965-66.
Mennonite Brethren Churches. *Yearbook*.
    Canadian Conference, 1911-1971.
    Central District Conference, 1961.
    General Conference, 1921-1969.
    Ontario Conference, 1971.
    Pacific District Conference, 1942-1951.
    Southern District Conference, 1969.
    U.S. Conference, 1957-1971.
Mennonite Central Committee. *Handbook*. Fourth ed. Akron, Pa.: MCC, 1954.
_____. *Workbook*. 1967-1970.
Mennonite World Conference. *Die Gemeinde Christi und Ihr Auftrag*. Karlsruhe: H. Schneider, 1953.
_____. *The Lordship of Christ: Proceedings of the Seventh Mennonite World Conference*. Edited by C. J. Dyck. Elkhart: MWC, 1962.
_____. *The Witness of the Holy Spirit: Proceedings of the Eighth Mennonite World Conference*. Edited by C. J. Dyck. Elkhart: MWC. 1967.
Minutes of the Meeting of the Mennonite Brethren Church of North America. 1879-1882. Typewritten.
Pacific College. *Catalog*. 1971-72.
Peters, F. C., and Regehr, H., comp. & ed. *Beschluesse und Empfehlungen der Kanadischen Konferenz der Mennoniten-Bruedergemeinde, 1910-1960*. Winnipeg: Christian Press, 1961.

THESES AND DISSERTATIONS

Doerksen, John G. "History of Education of the Mennonite Brethren in Canada." Unpublished M.Ed. thesis, Winnipeg, 1963.
Gaede, Harold E. "A Follow-Up Study of the Graduates of Pacific Bible Institute — Junior College from 1946-1949." Unpublished M.A. thesis, Fresno State College, 1960.
Hiebert, Clarence R. "Ethical Emphases of the Mennonite Brethren Church in North America." Unpublished M.A. thesis, Phillips University, 1959.
Klassen, A. J. "Mennonite Brethren Confessions of Faith: Historic Roots and Comparative Analysis." Unpublished S.T.M. thesis, Union College of B.C., 1965.
_____. "The Roots and Development of Mennonite Brethren Theology to 1914." Unpublished M.A. thesis, Wheaton College, 1966.
Nachtigall, Gary B.. "A Study of the Migration and Settlements of the Mennonites in Fresno and Tulare Counties of California." Unpublished M.A. thesis, Fresno State College, 1971.
Penner, Peter. "A Historical Survey of the Home Mission Work of the Mennonite Brethren Conference of Canada." Unpublished B.D. thesis, Mennonite Brethren Bible College, 1957.
Peters, Alan. "A Study of Youth Work in the Mennonite Brethren Church." Unpublished B.D. thesis, Mennonite Brethren Biblical Seminary, 1965.
Peters, F. C. "The Coming of the Mennonite Brethren to the United States and Their Efforts in Education." Unpublished Th.D. dissertation, Central Baptist Theological Seminary, 1957.
Toews, J. J. "Cultural Background of the Mennonite Brethren Church." Unpublished M.A. thesis, University of Toronto, 1951.
Wiebe, Orlando. "Johann Arndt: Precursor of Pietism." Unpublished Ph.D. dissertation, University of Iowa, 1965.
Wiens, Ruth. "A Study of the Present Task of the Sunday School in the Light of Its Historical Background and Today's Changing World." Unpublished M.R.E. thesis, Mennonite Brethren Biblical Seminary, 1965.
Wohlgemuth, Paul W. "Mennonite Hymnals Published in the English Language." Unpublished doctoral dissertation, University of Southern California, 1956.

UNPUBLISHED MANUSCRIPTS

Dyck, Ernest. "The History of the Mennonite Brethren Church in Quebec." 1971.
Horch, Esther. "Music in the Mennonite Brethren Church." 1972.
Janzen, Eva. "Story of My Life." 1970.

Karev, A.V. "The Russian Evangelical Baptist Movement, or Under His Cross in Soviet Russia." English translation by Frederick P. Loman. Evansville, Ind.; n.d. Typescript.
Peters, F. C. "Group Consensus in Mennonite Brethren Ethics." Study Paper.
Richert, Herbert C. "Music History: Mennonite Brethren, U.S.A." 1971.
"Short History of Laird Mennonite Brethren Church."
Unruh, A. H. "Die Grundzuege der Theologie der Vaeter der MB Gemeinde." Winnipeg: Study Conference Paper, 1956.

Index